Introduction to Private Security

John S. Dempsey
Suffolk County Community College

THOMSON

WADSWORTH

Australia • Brazil • Canada • Mexico • Singapore • Spain • United Kingdom • United States

THOMSON

WADSWORTH

Introduction to Private Security
John S. Dempsey
With Production Contributions by Michael Pittaro

Senior Acquisitions Editor, Criminal Justice:
Carolyn Henderson Meier

Assistant Editor: Meaghan Banks

Editorial Assistant: Beth McMurray

Marketing Manager: Terra Schultz

Marketing Assistant: Emily Elrod

Marketing Communications Manager: Tami Strang

Project Manager, Editorial Production: Jennie Redwitz

Creative Director: Rob Hugel

Art Director: Vernon Boes

Print Buyer: Linda Hsu

Permissions Editor: Bob Kauser

Production Service: Sara Dovre Wudali, Buuji

Text Designer: Carolyn Deacy

Photo Researcher: Billie Porter

Copy Editor: Kristin Rose McComas

Cover Designer: Yvo Riezebos Design

Cover Image: Top left and right: © Bill Varie/Corbis.
Middle left: © David Hoffman Photo Library/Alamy.
Bottom: © Sarah Lean/National Geographic

Compositor: Interactive Composition Corporation

Text and Cover Printer: West Group

Printed in the United States of America
1 2 3 4 5 6 7 11 10 09 08 07

Library of Congress Control Number: 2007925560

ISBN-13: 978-0-534-55873-4
ISBN-10: 0-534-55873-9

Thomson Higher Education
10 Davis Drive
Belmont, CA 94002-3098
USA

For more information about our products, contact us at:
Thomson Learning Academic Resource Center
1-800-423-0563

For permission to use material from this text or product,
submit a request online at **http://www.thomsonrights.com.**
Any additional questions about permissions can be
submitted by e-mail to **thomsonrights@thomson.com.**

Dedication

To my family—Marianne, my love and best friend; my children, John, Donna, and Cathy, and my daughter-in-law Diane; and in memory of Anne Marie, my special hero—your love and patience have sustained me over the years. Finally, to Danny and Nikki Dempsey and Erin and John Gleeson, my grandchildren: Who loves you more than the Grand Dude?

About the Author

John S. Dempsey was a member of the New York City Police Department (NYPD) from 1964 to 1988. He served in the ranks of police officer, detective, sergeant, lieutenant, and captain. His primary assignments were patrol and investigations. He received seven citations from the department for meritorious and excellent police duty. After retiring from the NYPD, Mr. Dempsey served until 2003 as Professor of Criminal Justice at Suffolk County Community College on Eastern Long Island where he won the college's prestigious "Who Made a Difference Award" for his teaching and work with students. In 2005, he was designated Professor Emeritus by the college. Mr. Dempsey also serves as a mentor at the State University of New York–Empire College where he teaches criminal justice and public administration courses and mentors ranking members of law enforcement and criminal justice agencies.

In addition to this book, Mr. Dempsey is the author of *Policing: An Introduction to Law Enforcement* (West, 1994); *An Introduction to Public and Private Investigations* (West, 1996); *Introduction to Investigations,* Second Edition (Thomson Wadsworth, 2003); and *An Introduction to Policing,* Fourth Edition with Linda S. Forst (Thomson Wadsworth, 2008).

Mr. Dempsey holds AA and BA degrees in behavioral science from the City University of New York, John Jay College of Criminal Justice; a master's degree in criminal justice from Long Island University; and a master's of public administration degree from Harvard University, the John F. Kennedy School of Government.

He lectures widely around the country on policing and criminal justice issues and is a member of the Academy of Criminal Justice Sciences (ACJS), the International Association of Chiefs of Police, ASIS International, the Northeastern Association of Criminal Justice Sciences (NEACJS), the Criminal Justice Educators Association of New York State, the Pennsylvania Association of Criminal Justice Educators, and the Midwestern Criminal Justice Association. His latest academic distinctions were the Outstanding Contributor Award from the ACJS Community College Section in 2004 and the Fellows Award from the NEACJS in 2005.

Mr. Dempsey is married and has four children and four grandchildren.

Brief Contents

Contents

PART I

Private Security History, Business, and Concepts

PART II

Private Security Categories

Jobs in Security Features

Procedural Security Features

Preface

To the Student

Introduction to Private Security is a basic introductory text for college students who are interested in learning about the U.S. private security industry, what it does, and how it is done. The private security profession is a noble one. I sincerely hope this text teaches you how to continue the great tradition of private security.

Introduction to Private Security is designed to give you a general overview of private security in our society so that you can understand why and how it is performed. It will show you the jobs available in security and how you can go about getting them, what skills you will need, and what you will do if and when you get these jobs. In addition, I try to give you an idea, a sense, and a flavor of security. I want you to get a clear look at the private security industry, not only for your academic interest but more importantly, also to help you determine if private security employment is what you want to do with the rest of your life. After all, is that not what much of college should be about—making an intelligent, well-informed career choice, as well as learning about life?

This is not a "how-to-do-it" book. There are numerous books and courses on how to perform the duties inherent in private security that you will be able to research later, when and if you decide to seek a position in the private security industry and qualify for one. You will receive "how-to" information from your future employers, associates and colleagues, and the many professionals and professional organizations active in the field that shape it. The endnotes, bibliography, and information about professional organizations in the field are an essential part of this book. Use these sources to do further research in the particular areas of your interest.

Introduction to Private Security explores these issues from the perspective of a law enforcement professional, student, and teacher of private security. I wrote this text in part out of a desire to combine the practical experience gained from a lifetime in law enforcement with the equally valuable insights gained from my years of formal education and teaching. It is designed to make you aware of what the private security industry is, what it does, and how it is done, while also sensitizing you to the complexities and ambiguities of modern private security. A special emphasis is placed on ethics and professionalism in the industry and the need for public law enforcement and private security to work together to solve common problems.

To the Instructor

My overall philosophy to focus on the needs of students who wish to learn about private security in our society permeates this text. This is, above all, a text for students. In response to reviewer feedback, this edition provides the latest in academic and practitioner research, as well as the latest statistical information, court cases, careers, and technological advances that are shaping the future of the private security industry.

A text-specific website is available with tutorial quizzing, online glossary, flash cards, games, Internet links, InfoTrac® College Edition activities, Internet activities, and course resources and updates.

Pedagogical Features

Within each chapter, I have included the following pedagogical elements:

- *Key Terms* emphasize key concepts to be learned in the chapter, the *Running Glossary* defines these terms immediately next to where each term is introduced, and an end-of-book *Glossary* collects all of the terms into one group for reference.

- *Chapter Goals* serve as chapter "road maps" to orient students to the main learning objectives of each chapter.

- Each *Chapter Introduction* previews the material to be covered in the chapter.

- The *Chapter Summary* reinforces the major topics discussed in the chapter and helps students check their learning.
- *Learning Checks* are questions that test the student's knowledge of the material presented in the chapter.
- *Application Exercises* are projects that require students to apply their knowledge to hypothetical situations much like those they might encounter in actual private security positions. They can be assigned as final written or oral exercises or serve as the basis of lively class debates.
- *Web Exercises* ask the student to research private security topics on the Internet.

Boxed Features

In an effort to increase student interest, I have included several types of boxed features in each chapter to supplement the main text:

- *You Are There*! features take the student back to the past to review the fact pattern in a particular court case or to learn the details about a significant event or series of events in history. They are intended to give the students a sense of actually being at the scene of a significant event.
- *Jobs in Security* boxes include samples of actual employment positions in the private security industry.
- *Private Security Connections* give examples of professional organizations, associations, and resources that offer students the opportunity to do further research and gain employment.
- *Exhibits* include statistics, helpful hints, facts, and other key information necessary to understand the subject.

Supplements

The following supplements are provided to assist instructors in the preparation and execution of their courses and to assist students in absorbing the material. Supplements are available to qualified adopters. Please consult your local sales representative for details.

- *Instructor's Resource Manual with Test Bank* The extensive *Instructor's Resource Manual* is available in both print and electronic formats.

The instructor's resources include learning objectives, detailed chapter outlines, key terms and definitions, class exercises, and discussion questions for each chapter of the text. The *Instructor's Resource Manual* also features a full test bank containing multiple-choice, true-false, fill-in-the-blank, and essay questions for each chapter, accompanied by a full answer key with page number rejoinders. This resource will save instructors hours of preparation.

- *eBank Microsoft PowerPoint Slides* Instructors may enhance lecture presentations with these handy slides, which allow students to review the current edition while providing a solid visual backup to lessons. Their ready-to-use format prepares instructors to teach at a moment's notice, while giving the option to customize according to specific presentation needs and style.
- *Companion Website* The new companion website provides many chapter-specific resources, including chapter outlines, learning objectives, glossary, flash cards, crossword puzzles, and tutorial quizzing.

Acknowledgments

I would like to sincerely thank outstanding senior acquisitions editor Carolyn Henderson Meier for her faith, patience, and constant assistance in this project. Also, I applaud the intelligent and excellent copyediting of Kristina Rose McComas and the super production efforts of Jennie Redwitz and Sara Dovre Wudali, and photo editor Billie Porter.

I also thank the reviewers of this text who provided outstanding and detailed feedback, including: John O. Ballard, Rochester Institute of Technology; Curtis R. Blakely, University of South Alabama; Timothy A. Capron, California State University–Sacramento; Russ Cheatham, Cumberland University; Timothy G. Collins, ICM School of Business and Medical Careers; George R. Franks Jr., Stephen F. Austin State University; David A. Gordon, Katharine Gibbs School; Tad Hughes, University of Louisville; Michael L. Hummel, California University of Pennsylvania; Paul H. Johnson, Weber State University; William E. Kelly, Auburn University; Robert Meadows, California Lutheran University; John T. Krimmel, The College of New Jersey; Benn Prybutok, Montgomery County Community College; William Ruefle, University of

South Carolina; and Dean Van Bibber, Fairmont State Community and Technical College.

A special note of appreciation to Michael Pittaro of Lehigh Valley College for his gracious assistance in the final stages of manuscript review and production. I will be forever indebted to Michael and Wadsworth's exemplary editorial and production team for their graciousness and help. Without their support and enthusiasm, this book would not have been completed.

Jack Dempsey

The History and Professionalization of Private Security

©Bettmann/Corbis

GOALS

- To acquaint you with the rich, colorful history of private security in Rome and England
- To explore the history of private security in the United States
- To familiarize you with the relatively recent movement to achieve professionalism in the private security industry
- To explore college programs in private security
- To acquaint you with current ethical standards in the private security industry

Introduction

The swiftness, scale, sophistication, and coordination of the terrorist operations on September 11, 2001, coupled with the extraordinary planning required, made most people realize that terrorism and mass murder had come to the United States. Many law enforcement officers, emergency response personnel, private security employees, and ordinary citizens will never be the same; 9/11 had indeed changed their world. These terrorist attacks jolted Americans out of their sense of complacency, and perhaps lethargy, and made them realize that their sense of security was lost forever.

The word *security* comes from the Latin word *securus* (a compound adjective formed from the prefix *se-* [without] and *cura* [care] and came into English as "without care," "free from care," "free from danger," or "safe").[1] The events of 9/11 have prompted Americans to turn to security professionals to help them remain safe and deal with our changed world. The security industry in the United States consists of publicly funded local, state, and federal law enforcement agencies, as well as private security organizations. This book is about one of those organizations: the private security industry.

The federal government–sponsored task force on private security defined the **private security industry** as

> Those self-employed individuals and privately funded business entities and organizations providing security-related services to specific clientele for a fee, for the individual or entity that retains or employs them, or for themselves, in order to protect their persons, private property, or interests from various hazards.[2]

In other words, private security services are provided by private, not public, funds. The private security field is much different from the public security field. Today,

when a citizen needs help, he or she can generally call 911 and receive some type of official police response. It could be a city, village, town, county, state, or even tribal police officer. Moreover, in some communities, police response may even be a function of a private security agency operating under the auspices of the local government. Formal, organized, public police departments are relatively new in history. What happened when a citizen needed help in the times before the formation of public police departments? To whom did he or she turn? How did our ancestors protect themselves and their property from the criminals within their midst?

Most of what has been written about the history of law enforcement and the measures society has taken to protect itself from crime and disorder has centered on the public police. However, long before the establishment of formal police departments, private citizens established methods to protect themselves against crime and disorder. Over the centuries, these methods have progressed from such primitive activities as hiding in caves or walling off entire towns and cities for protection to contemporary activities, which employ sophisticated operational methods that frequently include division of labor, tools of management, and state-of-the-art technology.

This chapter will discuss the history of private security from early times to today, concentrating on the early development of private security; ancient Rome, early England, and the United States in colonial times; the eighteenth, nineteenth, and twentieth centuries; and the new millennium. It will also discuss the emergence of professionalism in the private security industry, including the role of college education in that professionalization. Additionally, it will include a discussion of current ethical standards and dilemmas common to the industry and discuss the role of history in today's emphasis on homeland security.

private security industry The industry that provides private and corporate security programs to the United States.

Early Development of Private Security

We do not know much about the early history of policing—maintaining order and dealing with lawbreakers—except that it had always been a private matter. Citizens were deemed responsible for protecting themselves and maintaining an orderly society. Despite numerous efforts to organize security and safety, modern-style police departments, as we know them today, did not appear until the fourteenth century in France and the nineteenth century in England.

As far back as prerecorded history, nomadic tribes banded together and used guards and security methods to protect themselves and their families and the livestock that they relied on from wild beasts and raiding enemies. As Milton Lipson tells us, the first security guard may have been the nomadic shepherd:

> Private security originated in that clouded time when man began to domesticate animals and graze his herds. To safeguard these from both human and animal marauders and to keep them from wandering, one or more of the clan would act as a guardian, a security guard—a shepherd. In time, he was joined by a dog who acted as his valued assistant. The march of the centuries has not materially changed one of the earliest methods of security.[3]

Researchers also point to other early forms of maintaining peace and security:

> The history of humankind can be seen as a series of attempts to provide for safety, security, and freedom from fear and danger. Humans have developed weapons, built barriers around dwellings, and devised codes of conduct to protect property and welfare.[4]

Also, as security writer Harvey Burstein has written,

> The idea that people have a right to protect their property, whether real or personal, has existed since time immemorial. The exercise of this right long predates the notion that government help for that purpose might be forthcoming in the form of a public police or law enforcement agency.[5]

Private Security in Ancient Rome

We know very little about policing, public or private, in the ancient world. However, we do know that public law enforcement was largely ineffective

JOBS IN SECURITY

Reference Book for Jobs in Security

Note: "Jobs in Security" boxes are a special feature of this textbook and will be found throughout the book. They contain examples of a diverse selection of jobs or job-seeking information, pertaining to the chapter subject, advertised prior to the publication of the book. Students can use their computers to access similar types of jobs.

A good reference book for jobs in private security, as well as other jobs in criminal justice areas, is *Careers in Criminal Justice and Related Fields: From Internship to Promotion*, 5th ed., by Scott Harr and Kären Hess (Belmont, CA: Wadsworth, 2006).

There are also many resources available via the Internet.

and limited formal governmental mechanisms for law enforcement. For the most part, security and protection were confined to military forces and the individual citizen. Ancient Rome, perhaps, can give us the best example of early security initiatives in the ancient world.

Scholars often compare the crime problem in ancient Rome to the crime problem on the American frontier where there was no formal criminal justice system in place and therefore, no effective law enforcement. Violence was common in Roman life, much of it inspired by politics. (Consider, for example, the assassination of Julius Caesar by Republican nobles on March 15 [the Ides of March], 44 BCE). Courts and assemblies were frequently disrupted by rogue mobs. Wealthy people hired bands of retainers—slaves and gladiators—to defend themselves and their property. The famous orator, Cicero, for example, is reported to have had three hundred thugs under hire in 61 BCE, mostly to intimidate his political opponents.[6] The Roman satirist Juvenal (40 CE–120 CE) offers the following vivid description of what it was like to walk the streets of Rome in his time: "Only a fool would go out to dinner without having made his will."[7]

Throughout their history, the Romans and Greeks created some formal organized groups that served as early attempts at maintaining safety and security. Around the sixth century BCE in Athens and the third century BCE in Rome, citizens took the law into their own hands by arresting offenders and punishing them, but unpaid magistrates (judges) appointed by the citizens were responsible for presiding over cases. In most societies, people in towns would group together and form a watch, particularly at night, at the town borders or gates to ensure that strangers, particularly those deemed to be enemies, did not attack the town.[8] In the fifth century BCE, Rome created the first specialized investigative unit, called **questors**, or "trackers of murder."[9]

How did Roman citizens, with no viable and effective urban police patrol, protect their lives and property against criminals? Martin A. Kelly tells us,

> Roman civilians accepted the roles of quasi-policemen. Rough and ready and with a sense of civic responsibility, they often made citizen arrests when a crime was committed. In addition, they served in local civilian patrols and joined fraternal protective associations. The Romans also assigned their slaves to a variety of security and body-guarding tasks, and they enlisted animals, particularly dogs and geese, as protectors.[10]

Historians, scholars, and other researchers have discovered that the Romans may have been responsible for creating the prototypes of some of our modern physical security devices to protect homes and businesses. These ancient Roman prototypes led to the development of modern-day secure entrance doors, the Bard locking device, and the padlock.

The Romans also used humans, primarily slaves, to protect their buildings. For instance, the security guard at the entrance to a Roman building was known as the "janitor," or servant of the Roman god Janus, who protected entrances. The janitor was usually a eunuch–slave (castrated male slave) who was chained to the building's doorway. He controlled access to the entrance with the aid of a large watchdog. The Romans also used geese as watch animals, a primitive forerunner of our current security alarm systems. The geese, with their acute sense of smell, aggressiveness, and loud honking noise, were effective in keeping intruders away and alerting residents to the presence of

EXHIBIT 1.1   Ancient Roman Security Guards

- Buildings

Janitor	Security guard at entrance to buildings

- Stores

Peritates	Security guard at stores

- Homes

Cancellarius	Security guard at gate to master's quarters
Cubicolarius	Security guard in front of master's bedroom while he slept

- On the street

Satellites	Inner protective group surrounding guarded person
Nomenclator	Walked next to guarded person and announced those who approached
Stipatores	Walked alongside *satellites*, running interference
Vanguards	Preceded *satellites* (also known as *ante ambulones*)
Pedisequire	Walked behind and followed the *satellites*
Lanternari	Carried torches at night to light the way through the streets

Source: Martin A. Kelly, "Citizen Survival in Ancient Rome," *Police Studies*, Winter 1988, pp. 77–82, 175–180.

intruders. Wealthy and influential Romans used a large group of personal guards when they were traveling on the streets, similar to the large protective groups used today in presidential or other dignitary protective details. (Exhibit 1.1 provides the Latin names for some of these guards and the duties they engaged in.)

Given the political chaos and corruption in Rome, many citizens feared the government and their representatives. For example, mere criticism of the government was a punishable offense. Individuals caught criticizing the government would likely be punished by the confiscation of their estate and banishment from Rome. Upon conviction of a defendant, the informer could collect one quarter of the confiscated estate. To reinforce the need to communicate in silence and to be watchful of informers, many Roman householders hung baskets of roses, the classical symbol of silence, from their ceilings as reminders. The expression *"sub rosa"* (beneath the roses) in our modern language usage means "what is said here, remains here."

questors Investigative units created in fifth-century Rome.

Private Security in England

The American system of law and security was borrowed from the English. This section will discuss security in early English history, thief-takers, the Bow Street Runners, and Peel's police—the Metropolitan Police for London.

The European Feudal System provided a high level of security for individuals and society. Under the feudal contract, the lord provided for the safety of individuals and property and supplied arms and treasures to vassals who governed the work of the serfs bound to the land.[11]

In early England, law enforcement was perceived to be the duty of all citizens, even though some officials were charged with enforcing the law and keeping the peace. Before formal police departments, individuals called **thief-takers** served as a type of private police force in sixteenth-, seventeenth-, and eighteenth-century France and England. These thief-takers were private citizens with no official status who were paid by the king for every criminal they arrested—similar to the bounty hunters of the American West.

The major role of the thief-takers was to combat highway robbery committed by highwaymen, such as the legendary outlaws Robin Hood and Little John. By the seventeenth century, highwaymen made traveling through the English countryside so dangerous that no coach or traveler was safe. In 1693, an Act of Parliament established a monetary reward for the capture of any highwayman. A thief-taker was paid upon the conviction of the highwayman and also received the highwayman's horse, arms, money, and property.

The thief-taker system was later extended to cover offenses other than highway robbery, and soon a sliding scale of rewards was established. Arresting a burglar or a footpad (street robber), for example, was worth the same as catching a highwayman, but catching a sheep stealer or a deserter from the army brought a much smaller reward. In some areas, homeowners joined together and offered supplementary rewards for the apprehension of a highwayman or footpad in their area. In addition, whenever there was a serious crime wave, Parliament awarded special rewards for thief-takers to arrest particular felons.

In many instances, a criminal would agree to become a thief-taker in order to receive a pardon from the king for his or her own crimes. Thus, many thief-takers were themselves criminals. Thief-taking was not always rewarding because the thief-taker would not be paid unless the criminal was convicted. The job also could be dangerous because the thief-taker had to fear retaliation from the criminal and his or her relatives and associates. Many thief-takers would entice young people into committing crimes and then have another thief-taker arrest the youths during or soon after committing the crime. The two thief-takers would then split the financial reward. Some thief-takers were known to frame innocent parties by planting stolen goods on their persons or in their homes. Although some real criminals were apprehended by the professional thief-takers, the system generally created more crime than it suppressed.

One of the most notorious of the thief-takers of the early 1700s in England was Jonathan Wild. Wild was well-known among the criminal element in London as a brothel operator and the first great English criminal mastermind. He conceived the idea of charging a fee for locating and returning stolen property to its lawful owners. As his private thief-taker business prospered, he also began to apprehend criminals wanted by the government. Wild was totally unscrupulous. Upon learning of a theft, he would attempt to persuade the thieves to give him the stolen goods in exchange for a portion of the money paid by the victim for the return of the property. Wild was incredibly successful at detecting criminals and was personally responsible for the arrest and subsequent execution of hundreds of felons. In the end, he was found guilty of stealing the very property he returned to the grateful owners, crimes that brought about his own execution. On May 24, 1725, as he was being taken to the execution site, thousands of people jeered, showering him with stones and dirt. He was hanged before a cheering throng of spectators, which were estimated at more than 5,000. However, after his death, Wild became a folk hero. His body was disinterred and his skull and skeleton exhibited publicly as late as 1860.

Henry Fielding, the eighteenth-century novelist best known for writing *Tom Jones*, is also credited with laying the foundation for the first modern private investigative agency. In 1748, during the heyday of English highwaymen, Fielding

thief-takers Individuals who served as a form of private police in sixteenth-, seventeenth-, and eighteenth-century France and England.

was appointed magistrate in Westminster, a city near central London. He moved into a house on Bow Street, which subsequently became his office. Fielding, in an attempt to decrease the high number of burglaries, street and highway robberies, and other thefts, established relationships with local pawnbrokers. He provided them with lists and descriptions of recently stolen property and asked them to notify him should such property be brought into their pawnshops. He then placed the following ad in the London and Westminster newspapers:

> All persons who shall for the future suffer by robber, burglars, etc., are desired immediately to bring or send the best description they can of such robbers, etc., with the time and place and circumstances of the fact, to Henry Fielding Esq., at his house in Bow Street.[12]

Fielding's actions brought about what we can refer to as the first official crime reports. Fielding was able to gain the cooperation of the high constable of Holborn and several other public-spirited constables. Together they formed a small investigative unit, which they named the **Bow Street Runners**. These were private citizens who were not paid by public funds but rather, permitted to accept thief-taker rewards.

Eventually, Fielding's efforts were rewarded by the government, and his Bow Street Runners were publicly financed. In 1763, Fielding was asked to establish, with public funds, a civilian horse patrol of eight men to combat robbers and footpads on the London streets. The patrol proved a success but was disbanded after only nine months due to a lack of government support.

During the Industrial Revolution, businesses and industries in England were already actively involved in private policing. One business, Crowley's Iron Works, prepared the *Law Book of Crowley's Iron Works*, which resembled an entire civil and penal code, to govern and regulate their employees. Moreover, in rural eighteenth-century England, wealthy landowners paid gamekeepers to protect their property, while middle-class tradesmen formed voluntary protection societies to assist each other with crime control.[13]

At this point, due to the dissolution of the social patterns in the Middle Ages and the ever-increasing urbanization and industrialization of London, crime was rampant on the streets, and there was considerable debate over whether to form a professional police department. Although there was certainly enough crime to justify forming a civil police force, most people did not want a formal, professional police department for two major reasons. For one, many citizens felt a police force would threaten their tradition of freedom. Additionally, the English had considerable faith in the merits of private enterprise, and they disliked spending public money. Individual merchants hired men to guard their property; merchant associations also created the merchant police to guard shops and warehouses. Night watchmen were employed to make rounds, and agents were hired to recover stolen property. Residents of the various parishes into which the major cities of England were divided hired parochial police. In addition, it was common practice for private citizens to carry arms for protection.

In 1828, after much public debate, Sir Robert Peel, England's Home Secretary, drafted the first police bill, the Act for Improving the Police in and near the Metropolis (*The Metropolitan Police Act*). Parliament passed it in 1829. This act established the first large-scale, uniformed, organized, paid, civil police force in London. Over 1,000 men were hired. Although a civil force, as opposed to a military force, it was structured along military lines, with officers wearing distinctive uniforms.

The Economist paints a vivid picture of this historic change from relying on private security to relying on publicly provided law enforcement in an attempt to deal with rising crime and disorder:

> [The new law] swept away the assorted gangs of parish constables, inquiry agents, soldiers, and roughnecks who gave the streets of London what little order they then enjoyed and set up the Metropolitan Police. Since then, London's "Bobbies" . . . have provided a model—in theory if not always in practice— of how to maintain public order. The British police form a blue-uniformed professional body created by the government, paid for from taxes and responsible to elected bodies. They are public servants.[14]

However, it must be mentioned that despite the creation of publicly funded police, private guards and private police continued to be used to recover stolen property and to provide protection for private persons and businesses.

Bow Street Runners Private investigative unit formed by Henry Fielding in mid 1700s in England.

Private Security in the United States

The U.S. system of policing, both public and private, was patterned after the English system. This section will cover the history of attempts in the United States to control crime and disorder. It will discuss the colonial experience, the eighteenth and nineteenth centuries, the twentieth century, and the first few years of the new millennium.

Colonial Experience

The American colonists did not have an easy life. They were constantly at risk from foreign enemies, their brother and sister colonists, and Native Americans. Their only protection was their own selves and, at times, the military or militia. By the seventeenth century, the colonies started to institute a civil law enforcement system that closely replicated the English model. At the time, the county sheriff was the most important law enforcement official in the county. However, in addition to enforcing the law, he collected taxes, supervised elections, and had much to do with the legal process. Sheriffs were not paid a salary but, much like the English thief-taker, were paid fees for each arrest they made. Sheriffs did not patrol but stayed in their offices.

In cities, the town marshal was the chief law enforcement official, aided by constables (called *schouts* in the Dutch settlements) and night watchmen. The night-watch routine was sometimes performed by the military. The city of Boston created the first colonial night watch in 1631 and three years later created the position of constable. In 1658, eight paid watchmen replaced a patrol of citizen volunteers in the Dutch city of Nieuw Amsterdam. This police system was inherited by the British in 1664 when they took over the city and renamed it New York. By the mid-1700s, the New York night watch was described as "a parcel of idle, drinking, vigilant snorers, who never quell'd any nocturnal tumult in their lives; but would perhaps, be as ready to joining in a burglary as any thief in Christendom."[15]

When serious breaches of the peace occurred, including riots or slave revolts, the governors called on the colonial militia or the British army. Many cities, including Port Pontchartrain (Detroit), New Orleans, and Fort Washington (Cincinnati), were under martial law for much of their early existence.

Despite the presence of law enforcement officials in the colonies, law enforcement was still mainly the responsibility of the individual citizen, as it had been in early England. There was little law and order on the colonial frontier. When immediate action was needed, the frontier people took matters into their own hands. This led to an American tradition of vigilantism. In the rural southern colonies, law enforcement primarily consisted of slave patrols, armed civilians who worked with the local county courts and the militia to enforce slave laws.

The Eighteenth and Nineteenth Centuries

Historically, American policing attempted to control crime and disorder in both urban and frontier environments. Although the urban and frontier experience differed in many ways, both could be classified as brutal and corrupt.[16] It was during this period of American history that organized and professional private security organizations began to have a positive impact on crime and disorder.

In America's urban experience, the first organized, paid, public police department was created in Boston in 1838, followed by New York City in 1845 and Philadelphia in 1854. By the outbreak of the Civil War, Chicago, New Orleans, Cincinnati, Baltimore, Newark, and a number of other large cities had their own police departments. As a result, constables and sheriffs were relieved of much of their patrol and investigative duties.

Despite the creation of these public police departments, policing in the United States in the nineteenth century did not approach the professionalism of Peel's London police. In his 1991 book, *Low Life: Lures and Snares of Old New York*, Luc Sante says,

> The history of the New York police is not a particularly illustrious one, at least in the nineteenth and early twentieth centuries, as throughout the period the law enforcement agents of the city continually and recurrently demonstrated corruption, complacency, confusion, sloth and brutality.[17]

Local urban police were overwhelmed and could not provide important services, such as the detection and recovery of stolen goods. In Chicago, business owners created the private Merchant's Police, which protected stores that subscribed to its services by paying a fee of fifty cents a week.

Although life in America's cities was difficult, life on the frontier was grueling. Early settlers faced tremendous problems from the weather, the terrain, Native Americans, and the criminals within their own ranks. Formal law enforcement on the frontier

©Private Collection/Peter Newark American Pictures/The Bridgeman Art Library Nationality/copyright status: American/out of copyright

At the outbreak of the Civil War in 1861, Pinkerton (left) offered his services to the federal government and was assigned the task of protecting President Abraham Lincoln (center). This was no easy task because the newspapers printed Lincoln's travel plans. Pinkerton is credited with detecting and preventing at least one assassination plot.

The modern U.S. private security industry owes much of its origins to Allan Pinkerton. Pinkerton was born in Glasgow, Scotland, in 1819, and immigrated to the United States. He worked for a short time as a deputy sheriff in Cook County, Illinois, and was then appointed the first detective of the Chicago Police Department in 1849. In 1850, he was appointed as a special U.S. mail agent in Chicago investigating mail thefts. In the early 1850s, he opened his own private detective agency, the North-Western Police Agency, in partnership with Chicago attorney Edward Rucker, who left the partnership after a year. The agency was then renamed the **Pinkerton National Detective Agency**. Its trademark was an open eye, with the slogan, "The Eye That Never Sleeps"; this led to the common use of the expression "private eye" as a reference to private investigators. The agency was an immediate success.

In addition to working with the local police, the Pinkertons were hired by railroad corporations to patrol their trains and set up security systems. Pinkerton pioneered numerous investigative techniques, such as shadowing or suspect surveillance and undercover operations. Among Allan Pinkerton's other major accomplishments were establishing the practice of handwriting examination in U.S. courts and proposing a plan to centralize criminal identification records. Pinkerton built a comprehensive file of pictures and facts on criminals that was a major source of criminal information prior to the twentieth century. He also advanced the cause of international police cooperation by sharing information with Scotland Yard and the French Sûreté.

His agency was the first to hire a female detective, Kate Warne, in 1856. He established a code of ethics for his employees and made sure they kept it. He prohibited his employees from accepting gratuities or rewards and removed politics from his operations. In 1857, Pinkerton formed the **Pinkerton Protective Patrol** to provide watchmen services for businesses and private individuals.

was rare. What little law enforcement existed in the Old West consisted mainly of the locally elected county sheriff and the appointed town marshal, and also sometimes the U.S. marshal, the U.S. Army, or the state militia. On the frontier, private police were much more effective than public law enforcement. Although they often acted in the same manner as the English thief-takers, taking a percentage of the stolen property they recovered, America's private police were much more professional and honest than those found in early England.

Pinkerton National Detective Agency Private detective agency established by Allan Pinkerton in the 1850s.

Pinkerton Protective Patrol Agency established by Allan Pinkerton in 1857 to provide watchman services for businesses and private individuals.

You Are There!

Allan Pinkerton Saves President-Elect Abraham Lincoln

Note: "You Are There" boxes are special features of this textbook that take the reader back to the past to learn the details about a significant event or series of events in history. They are intended to give readers a sense of actually being present at the event or events.

Allan Pinkerton, the founder of the Pinkerton Detective Agency, is credited with saving the life of Abraham Lincoln, president-elect of the United States.

As Pinkerton was investigating threats against a railroad, he uncovered information regarding a conspiracy to assassinate Lincoln as he traveled through Maryland during his procession to Washington to take his presidential oath. Pinkerton foiled the plot by arranging for Lincoln to travel through Baltimore in disguise—as an invalid in a shawl. Pinkerton's operatives cut telegraph wires on the route and detained reporters until the president-elect reached Washington. Lincoln arrived safely in Washington, DC, and took the oath of office, becoming president of the United States.

Pinkerton had an earlier relationship with Lincoln. When he founded his detective agency, he provided security services to the Illinois Central Railroad. Together with the railroad's vice president, George McClellan, he consulted with the railroad's lawyer, Abraham Lincoln. Later, McClellan, one of Lincoln's Union generals and eventually chief of all Union forces, hired Pinkerton to head his intelligence branch. Operating under the pseudonym E. J. Allen, Pinkerton's operatives provided valuable information from behind enemy lines. Pinkerton himself conducted intelligence missions behind enemy lines.

SOURCES: Edwin C. Fishel, *The Secret War for the Union: The Untold Story of Military Intelligence in the Civil War*, New York: Houghton Mifflin, 1996; and J. Anthony Lukas, *Big Trouble: A Murder in a Small Western Town Sets Off a Struggle for the Soul of America*, New York: Simon & Schuster, 1997.

At the outbreak of the Civil War in 1861, Pinkerton offered his services to the federal government and was assigned the task of protecting President Abraham Lincoln. He is credited with detecting and preventing at least one assassination plot. In addition to protecting Lincoln, he operated a secret espionage unit that gathered military intelligence for the Army of the Potomac. Pinkerton and his men, who included fugitive slaves, gathered information on Southern spies and slipped behind Confederate lines to learn their military plans. He personally made several undercover missions under the alias of Major E. J. Allen. On one occasion, he posed as a Confederate supporter and was given a personal tour of enemy lines by a top-ranking officer.

After the war, the agency again concentrated on railroad robberies and security and "rode shotgun" on stagecoaches in the West. By the 1880's, Pinkerton's firm had offices in nearly two-dozen cities. In the West, Pinkerton's customers included the United States Department of Justice, various railroad companies, wealthy Eastern bankers, and major land speculators. Some people considered the Pinkerton Detective Agency an official arm of the federal government. It is interesting to note that the government still uses private security agencies for protection; see Chapter 2 of this text.

In 1884, Allan Pinkerton died, and the management of the agency was taken over by his sons, Robert and William. The agency continued its success in arresting train robbers and notorious gangsters, like members of the James Gang and Robert Leroy Parker (Butch Cassidy) and Harry Longbaugh (the Sundance Kid) of the Wild Bunch gang. They also arrested John and Simeon Reno, who organized the nation's first band of professional bank robbers. The Pinkertons, as they were called, were also hired in the East by mining and manufacturing companies to suppress labor organizations such as the Molly Maguires in 1874 and 1875. The Molly Maguires were a secret society of Irish coal miners credited with massive violence against coal companies in eastern Pennsylvania. The Pinkertons infiltrated the organization and had many of the Mollies arrested and some hanged. Between 1866 and 1892, the Pinkerton Protective Patrol participated in seventy labor disputes and opposed over 125,000 strikers. The Pinkertons were despised by labor leaders. They employed informants throughout the United States and its territories, and offered cash rewards for information.

In competition with the Pinkerton agency during the latter part of the nineteenth century was the Rocky Mountain Detective Association, which pursued and

Cole
Younger

Bob
Younger
(rear)

Jesse
James

Frank
James

©Corbis

The James Boys and the Younger Brothers

The infamous outlaw Jesse James (left), along with his brothers, Frank and Cole, and Bob Younger, committed a remarkable string of bank, stagecoach, and train robberies throughout the 1870s from Iowa to Texas and from Kansas to West Virginia. In 1874, Allan Pinkerton of the Pinkerton National Detective Agency joined the crusade to bring down the James–Younger gang. Jesse James was killed on April 3, 1882, by someone simply looking to collect the $10,000 bounty that would be awarded to the individual who captured him. By the 1880s, Pinkerton's firm had offices in nearly two dozen cities.

apprehended bank and train robbers, cattle thieves, murderers, and the road agents who plundered highways and mining communities throughout the Southwest and the Rocky Mountains.

Another competitor was Wells, Fargo & Co. In 1850, Henry Wells and William Fargo formed the American Express Company, which transported bank documents from Buffalo, New York, to New York City. In 1852, they expanded into California to

transport valuables, including gold, under the name of Wells, Fargo & Company. By the end of the 1850s, the company was using the railroads to transport valuables, and it operated as a mail-carrying service and stagecoach line out of more than a hundred offices in the Western mining districts. Because they carried millions of dollars in gold and other valuable cargo, they found it necessary to create their own guard company to protect their shipments. The Wells-Fargo private security employees were effective in preventing robberies and thefts. Moreover, criminals, who were able to hold up their banks and carriers, were relentlessly hunted down by specially trained and equipped agents.

In 1865, **Railway Police Acts** were established in many states to give the railroad industry the right to establish a proprietary security force. The new railway police were given full police powers to protect company equipment, including rolling stock and property, and to protect railways against attacks by Native Americans and organized bands of train robbers. The Railroad Special Agent also protected against rail-station robbers, pickpockets, and con men. Thousands of patrol officers and detectives were hired by the railroads. By the early 1900s, some 14,000 railroad police were employed as investigators and patrol officers.

As industrialization continued, companies began to use in-house and contractual private security forces to protect company assets and to perform strikebreaking activities. The use of private security agents as strikebreakers led to bloody confrontations between labor and management. Generally, the private security forces were successful in breaking strikes, but in 1892 the tide changed. Three-hundred heavily armed agents from the Pinkerton Protective Patrol were defeated by strikers they tried to evict from the Carnegie Steelworks in Homestead, Pennsylvania. During these tumultuous times, Congress began investigations of private security firms, and many states throughout America passed laws prohibiting armed mercenaries from entering their borders. In addition, many large companies in the shipping, iron, and steel industries established private security forces to protect property and maintain order in their company towns and factories. As most official law enforcement consisted of local police departments who had limited geographical jurisdiction, the major private investigations firms, such as Pinkerton, provided effective law enforcement and investigations beyond these local political boundaries.

During these post–Civil War years and the westward expansion, there was tremendous

Railway Police Acts Laws established in many states in the nineteenth century giving the railroad industry the right to establish a proprietary security force.

You Are There!

The Strike at the Carnegie Steelworks of Homestead, Pennsylvania

The Pinkerton Detective Agency provided its Protective Patrol's "watchmen" to protect management's interests in labor unrest and strikes at plants, mines, and railroads. The patrol members were dressed in military uniforms and trained in military discipline and weaponry. During the late 1890s, the Pinkertons intervened in approximately seventy strikes, often with violent consequences. An event in 1892, however, changed the Pinkerton policy of intervening in industry strikes.

In July 1892, at the Carnegie Steelworks in Homestead, Pennsylvania, a labor dispute between management and the workers union, the Amalgamated Association of Iron and Steel Workers, led the company to close the plant and lock out 3,800 workers. The strikers then seized and occupied the plant, and management hired three hundred Pinkerton watchmen to take it back. On July 6th, the watchmen arrived at the plant on two barges on the Monongahela River and were confronted by thousands of strikers and their supporters on the bank of the river. The battle waged for twelve hours as the Pinkertons and the workers engaged. A rifle and artillery battle ensued, leaving seven strikers and three Pinkertons dead and dozens injured. The Pinkertons were forced to surrender, and many of them were badly beaten by the workers.

In the wake of the defeat of the Pinkertons, the Pennsylvania governor dispatched 8,500 troops from the State National Guard to Homestead. The guardsmen secured the plant, and Homestead was placed under martial law. By mid-August it was back in full operation, employing 1,700 replacement workers (scabs). By mid-November, the union conceded and three hundred of the locked-out workers were rehired with slashed wages.

The negative publicity that followed the Homestead action led to U.S. Congressional hearings and many state laws prohibiting armed mercenaries from entering their state boundaries. In response, the Pinkerton agency discontinued its practice of supplying men for intervention in labor disputes.

SOURCE: J. Anthony Lukas, *Big Trouble: A Murder in a Small Western Town Sets Off a Struggle for the Soul of America,* New York: Simon & Schuster, 1997, pp. 82–83.

---

lawlessness associated with the gold-mining industry and cattle theft. Citizens formed vigilante groups to rid their territories of undesirables and criminals, and struggles ensued between these vigilantes and outlaw gangs. In the 1880s, the Wyoming Cattle Growers Association created a private detective organization, the Association Detectives, to fight cattle rustling. In New Mexico, groups of armed men formed to protect individual cattle herds. In Texas, cattlemen hired the Home Rangers, who were paid by local ranchers and had official status granted by the governor to shoot on sight any unauthorized stranger on ranch property. In addition, in urban areas in the East, merchants began to form associations to help themselves deal with common problems. One of the first of these common assistance alliances was the Jewelers' Security Alliance, created in New York in 1883 to alert jewelers and law enforcement about jewelry-related crime.

The middle of the nineteenth century saw the advances of modern technology and business improvements in the private security industry. In the early 1850s, Edwin Holmes invented the first electric burglar-alarm system using a bell that rang if a door or window were opened. He began to sell this alarm system to wealthy New Yorkers. In 1858, he established the first central-station burglar-alarm company, the Holmes Protection Company. Holmes' electronic burglar alarm predated the electric light and telephone by about twenty-five years. By 1880, he had offices in Boston, New York, and Philadelphia.

In 1859, Washington Perry Brink formed Brink's Inc., a freight-and-package delivery service in Chicago. In 1891, Brink's carried its first payroll for the Western Electric Company, and by 1900, it had a fleet of eighty-five wagons transporting materials, including payrolls and valuable goods. In 1917, after two of its employees were killed in a robbery holdup, Brink's introduced the armored car to carry money and valuables. By 1956, Brink's had become the world's largest armored-car company. In 1983, it began making high-quality monitored alarm systems for homeowners. During its long history, Brink's has been called on to protect some of the world's most valued treasures, including the baseball bat with which Hank Aaron broke Babe Ruth's lifetime home-run record, the first rock samples brought home from the moon by the astronauts, the diamond ring that Richard Burton gave to

Elizabeth Taylor, the U.S. Declaration of Independence, and the world's largest uncut diamond.[18]

In the late 1800s, the telegraph, invented by Samuel F. B. Morse, became a dominant medium of communication. In 1874, fifty-seven diverse telegraph-delivery companies merged to create the American District Telegraph Company (ADT), the forerunner of one of today's leading alarm companies—ADI. In the 1890s, with the advent of call boxes and multisignal electric protection systems, ADT became a preeminent security protection company. The multisignal call boxes allowed watchmen at businesses to do more than just signal for police or fire department assistance—they could now send a specific signal to the ADT office at designated times to let the central monitoring office know that all was well. If a watchman did not transmit his scheduled signal, help was dispatched. In the first quarter of the twentieth century, ADT became synonymous with emergency call systems and burglar, holdup, and fire alarm systems.

Studying the rise of private security during the nineteenth century, the National Advisory Committee on Criminal Justice Standards and Goals, in its *Private Security Task Force Report*, attributed the rise to three main factors: (1) ineffective public police protection; (2) increased crimes against the expanding railroads; and (3) increased industrialization, which was accompanied by mounting conflict between factory owners and their workers.

See Exhibit 1.2 for highlights of nineteenth-century developments in private security.

The Twentieth Century and the New Millennium

The beginning of the twentieth century saw the continuation of the growing need for security services due to the rapidly increasing industrialization of America and the need to address labor and management problems. Plants and factories continued to create in-house, proprietary security forces and to hire outside contract security firms to protect company goods and property and to deal with union disturbances.[19]

The business and technological advances of the nineteenth century continued into the twentieth century. In 1909, William J. Burns, a former U.S. Secret Service investigator and the former director of the Bureau of Investigation (the forerunner of the FBI), started the William J. Burns Detective Agency. It has been said that no other detective in

EXHIBIT 1.2 Nineteenth-Century Highlights in U.S. Private Security

- 1850—Henry Wells and William Fargo form the American Express Company to transport goods east of the Missouri River. In 1852, they expand west as Wells, Fargo and Company.
- 1855—Allan Pinkerton starts the Pinkerton Detective Agency to provide contract protection services for the railroads as they expand westward.
- 1857—Pinkerton starts the Pinkerton Protection Patrol to provide contract watchmen for businesses.
- 1858—Edwin Holmes establishes the first burglar alarm company—the Holmes Protection Company.
- 1859—Washington Perry Brink forms Brink's Inc. as a freight and package delivery service in Chicago. In 1891, Brink's carries its first payroll for Western Electric Company and by 1900 has a fleet of eighty-five wagons transporting materials, including payrolls and valuable goods.
- 1865—Railway Police Acts were established in many states.
- 1874—The American District Telegraph Company (ADT) offers central burglar-alarm services.
- 1883—Jewelers formed the Jewelers Security Alliance for protection against burglary.

American history was more successful or better known than Burns, who was called "the greatest detective the U.S. has ever produced" and "America's Sherlock Holmes."[20] After years of bringing counterfeiters to justice, Burns gained extensive national renown by his work in the prosecution of public land frauds in California and Oregon, and investigating corrupt civic leaders in San Francisco. His agency became the major investigating agency for the American Banker's Association and grew to become the second-largest (after Pinkerton) contract guard and investigative service in the United States. Burns was a public hero for many years, except among labor union leaders who disliked his efforts for management in strike-breaking and the infiltration of unions.

During the 1930s, in the face of growing crime, U.S. industries continued to emphasize factory and plant security to prevent crime. They also continued to use private security firms to combat labor unrest and strikers, and to infiltrate unions. As the result of a 1937 Congressional inquiry into labor–management unrest, Pinkerton's eliminated the use of undercover work involving labor unions.

Actions by contract security services during strikes in the automobile industry in the middle 1930s also proved controversial.

A vast expansion of private security began in the years prior to and during World War II, as U.S. businesses became the principal supplier of material and goods to Britain and France in support of their war efforts. In 1941, as the United States entered World War II, President Roosevelt issued an executive order giving the Secretary of War the authority to establish military guards, patrols, and other appropriate measures to protect national defense–related industries and premises from sabotage. In addition, federal guidelines enacted by government agencies, including those contained in the Department of Defense's *Industrial Security Manual*, were put into contracts given to private-sector contractors for manufacturing and producing goods. Because these requirements were mandatory, those who wanted to be awarded government contracts were obligated to institute security programs and to designate a security officer who would be responsible for the programs' implementation and maintenance. These programs were the impetus behind the large proprietary, or in-house, security departments that we see in industry today. These new regulations required contractors to employ comprehensive security measures to protect materials necessary for the war effort from sabotage and espionage.

This wartime concern for the prevention and detection of espionage and sabotage brought about a government decision to bring plant watchmen and security personnel into the U.S. Army as an auxiliary unit of the military police. Before the end of the war, more than 200,000 industrial security personnel were sworn into the U.S. Armed Forces by the Internal Security Division of the War Department and were required to sign an agreement placing them under the Articles of War. These guards were responsible for protecting material at approximately 10,000 factories. Later, the increased need for security in defense-related industries during the Korean War and the Cold War led to the establishment of the **Industrial Defense Program** in 1952. This program, now known as the **National Industrial Security Program**, oversees, advises, and assists approximately 11,000 defense-related facilities. This great growth in private security as the result of the war continued on into the Vietnam War era and beyond.

In the post–World War II period, improved and professionalized methods of private security developed. In 1955, the American Society for Industrial Security (ASIS) was created as the first professional association for private security professionals. It is now known as ASIS International, and its influence on the development of professionalism is discussed in the next section. At this time, businesses, such as retail establishments, hotels, restaurants, theaters, warehouses, trucking companies, industrial companies, hospitals, and other institutional and service industries, began to expand their security interest beyond the mere concept of having security guards and started to develop comprehensive security programs. Increased and more sophisticated crime led companies and industries to focus on security programs to address this crime and to enhance security methods to protect their property and personnel.

Also at this time, security consulting firms and private investigating firms were multiplying and concentrating on methods to handle such crimes as fraud, arson, burglary, white-collar crime, and the like. In 1954, George R. Wackenhut and three other former FBI agents formed the Wackenhut Corporation as a private investigative and contract security firm. Companies also began to band together to create and share industry-specific intelligence. These business alliances or bureaus began to provide valuable information and services and shared this information in the form of "hot lists" and newsletters to alert each other to common criminal threats. Today, of course, most of this information is computerized. (Recall that earlier in this chapter a prototype of this form of common-assistance alliance was discussed—the Jewelers' Security Alliance, created in 1883, to alert jewelers and law enforcement about jewelry-related crime). Among the first of these twentieth-century cooperative central repositories of criminal information was the National Automobile Theft Bureau (NATB), which was created in the early twentieth century. NATB developed vehicle-theft databases and managed vehicle-theft investigations for the insurance industry. Another was the Insurance Crime Prevention Institute (ICPI), which was created in the

Industrial Defense Program Federal program established in 1952 to oversee, advise, and assist defense-related facilities; now known as the National Industrial Security Program.

National Industrial Security Program Federal program established in 1952 to oversee, advise, and assist defense-related facilities; formerly known as the National Industrial Defense Program.

1970s to investigate insurance fraud. In 1992, the NATB and the ICPI merged to create the National Insurance Crime Bureau, which today is the nation's premier not-for-profit organization dedicated exclusively to fighting insurance fraud and vehicle theft—crime estimated to cost the American public $30 billion annually. The increased use of credit cards at this time also led to the creation of numerous information bureaus to perform credit checks and background investigations.

Due to rapidly increasing crime and growing social disorder in the United States, increased interest in private security continued into the 1960s and 1970s, and the responsibility for preventing crime, which had formerly been the monopoly of the public police, began to change. The first official report on private security in the nation, commissioned by the U.S. Department of Justice's National Institute of Justice (NIJ), *Private Police in the United States: Findings and Recommendations*,[21] was published in 1971 by the RAND Corporation think tank This was followed in 1976 with *Private Security: Report of the Task Force on Private Security* for the National Advisory Committee on Criminal Justice Standards and Goals.[22]

In comparing the growing emphasis in the United States on private police to the English emphasis on the need for public police in the nineteenth century, *The Economist* noted,

> Peel's Metropolitan Police was a response to the failure of the pre-modern system of policing to cope with the upsurge of crime that industrialization produced. To some people the growth in the private sector now has been a reaction to the failure of an "outmoded" public police to cope with rising crime in post-industrial countries. The police clear up only a fifth of the crimes reported to them in America; in Britain, a quarter; in Canada, one sixth. . . . The private sector has rushed into a vacuum of demand for law and order left unfulfilled by the State.[23]

In addition, during the late 1960s and early 1970s, attention began to focus on crime on our nation's airlines. From 1968 to 1972, there were 134 aircraft-hijacking attempts. Also, a tremendous number of bomb threats were made against U.S. airlines.

In response, the Federal Aviation Administration began compulsory point-of-departure screening of airline passengers in 1972. This screening was made the responsibility of the airlines and was carried out primarily by contract security firms. Similar procedures were established in other countries. The performance by selected firms in this area was extremely poor, and many feel that the success of the 9/11 al-Qaeda hijackers was caused by the inadequate performance of these firms.

The rise and influence of U.S. multinational corporations also produced new security threats, such as terrorist threats and the kidnappings of corporate executives and their families, and further spurred the growth of corporate security. It was estimated that businesses paid more than $250 million in ransoms to kidnappers during the 1970s alone. As early as 1978, General Motors alone had a private police force of 4,200 employees—more than the public police in all but five American cities.

1n 1980, the National Institute of Justice hired Hallcrest Systems Inc., a group of highly experienced security consultants to national law enforcement agencies, to conduct a three-year national study of the roles and resources of the private security industry in the United States, including its nature, extent, and growth. The results of Hallcrest's study were published in 1985 as *The Hallcrest Report: Private Security and Police in the United States*. The government also contracted Hallcrest Systems to conduct further research, which was published in 1990 as *Private Security Trends 1970–2000: The Hallcrest Report II*. These first comprehensive studies of the U.S. private security industry, known collectively as the **Hallcrest Reports**, demonstrated the growing and superior role of private security as compared to public law enforcement.[24]

The following are some of Hallcrest's key findings:

■ U.S. businesses lose approximately $114 billion or more a year to crime.

■ Governments, at all levels, pay for private-sector services through the increasing privatization of services. In 1975, state and local government spending for private-sector services was $27 billion; in 1982, it rose to $81 billion. Additionally, federal expenditures for private-sector services in 1987 were $197 billion.

■ In 1990, private businesses and individuals spent $52 billion for private security. (In 1985, this expense was $22 billion).

Hallcrest Reports Two comprehensive reports commissioned by the U. S. National Institute of Justice concerning the private security industry in the United States.

- In 1990, 1.5 million people were employed annually by private security agencies. (In 1985, this number was 1.1 million.) By contrast, only 600,000 persons were employed as sworn public law enforcement officers in 1990.

- Private security expenditures will rise to $104 billion by the year 2000, and the private security industry will employ almost 1.9 million persons.

- The average annual rate of growth in private security employment is forecast to be 2.3 percent from 1990 to 2000, higher than the annual 1.2 percent rate of growth for the entire U.S. workforce as projected by the Bureau of Labor Statistics.

Hallcrest believed that four interrelated factors largely explained the greater employment and expenditure shift from public to private protection and the increasing growth of private security compared to the public police during the 1980s and 1990s. These factors were (1) an increase in crimes in the workplace; (2) an increase in fear (real or perceived) of crime; (3) the limitations on public protection imposed by the "fiscal crisis of the state"; and (4) an increased public and business awareness and use of the more cost-effective private security products and services. Private security spending continued to overtake public law enforcement spending in the 1990s. According to Dean J. Champion, the following are reasons for the growth of private security forces in the United States in the 1990s:

- Increasing public awareness and fear of crime
- The trend toward specialization of all services
- More sophisticated electronic surveillance devices and monitoring systems
- Lowering of business insurance rates for companies employing private police
- A lack of confidence in the ability of regular police officers to protect business interests[25]

Despite lower crime rates in the 1990s and 2000s, private security expenditures and hiring have kept increasing significantly. A study of crime rates in the United States shows that crime increased greatly each year in the 1960s, 1970s, and early 1980s, then dipped somewhat in the mid-1980s, climbed a bit in the early 1990s, and then dropped significantly from 1993 until the present time. The Department of Justice, in their *National Crime Victimization Survey* (NCVS), reports that rates of violent crime and property crime have steadily declined from 1993 until today. It reports that the latest criminal statistics show that the total amount of crime today is at its lowest level since 1973, when the NCVS began to study crime. Homicides, in particular, were at their lowest levels since the 1960s.[26]

Criminologists have differed consistently over the reasons for the recent drop in crime, but the most common reasons expressed have been (1) demographic changes in the ages of the highest crime-committing age groups, (2) the increased incarceration of very high-rate offenders, and (3) more aggressive and productive policing caused by new sophisticated record systems that enable police to predict and target criminal activities and offenders. Perhaps, although it has not been reported, the increased crime-deterrent effects of so many private security officers in businesses and neighborhoods have also contributed to this crime reduction.

The terrorist bombings of 9/11, as indicated in the introduction to this chapter, shocked America and the world and caused renewed attention to the need for improved methods of security and a renewed commitment to ensuring public and private safety. The effects of 9/11 will be addressed later in this chapter and throughout this text.

See Exhibit 1.3 for highlights of twentieth-century developments in private security.

Professionalization of Private Security

Traditionally, there had been a lack of professionalism in the private security industry in terms of certification, training, employment standards, and ethics. In an effort to improve the industry's image and increase its effectiveness, many forward-thinking professionals have risen to the forefront of an effort to professionalize the private security industry. This section will discuss the efforts to achieve professionalism that started in the 1950s and continues today.

In the early 1950s, five private security professionals began meeting regularly to discuss issues affecting their new business specialty—industrial security. Led by Paul Hansen, director of the Industrial Security Division of Reynolds Metals, the men agreed to form a national association of security directors and recruit from companies working

EXHIBIT 1.3	Twentieth-Century Highlights in U.S. Private Security

- 1909—William J. Burns starts the William J. Burns' Detective Agency.
- 1917—Brinks introduces the armored car to carry money and valuables.
- 1954—George R. Wackenhut and three other former FBI agents form the Wackenhut Corporation as a private investigative and contract security firm.
- 1955—The American Society for Industrial Security (ASIS), now known as ASIS International, is founded.
- 1957—ASIS writes its Code of Ethics.
- 1971—The RAND Corporation publishes *Private Police in the United States: Findings and Recommendations.*
- 1976—The National Advisory Committee on Criminal Justice Standards and Goals publishes the *Report of the Task Force on Private Security.*
- 1977—The first ASIS Certified Protection Professional (CPP) certification is issued.
- 1977—Private security spending begins to surpass public law enforcement spending.
- 1980—Private security employment is 1 million persons and expenditures are $20 billion; law enforcement employment is 0.6 million persons and expenditures are $14 billion.
- 1985—Hallcrest I (*The Hallcrest Report: Private Security and Police in America*) is published.
- 1990—Hallcrest II (*The Hallcrest Report II: Private Security Trends: 1970–2000*) is published.
- 1990—Private security employment is 1.5 million persons and expenditures are $52 billion; law enforcement employment is 0.6 million persons and expenditures are $30 billion.
- 2000—Private security employment reaches 1.9 million persons and expenditures are $103 billion; law enforcement employment is 0.7 million and expenditures are $44 billion.

on manufacturing contracts for the U.S. Department of Defense. These corporate relationships with national defense had been forged during World War II, when U.S. manufacturing was part of the war effort. The industrial security industry at this time had been moving from concentration

ASIS International Professional organization of private security professionals.

Certified Protection Professional (CPP) Professional certification awarded to security professionals by ASIS International.

on guards, fences, locks, and manual alarms to improvements such as central stations for alarm monitoring in major cities, monitoring of perimeters and entrances, and employee background investigations for security clearances, both corporate and governmental.[27]

By 1955, this group of security professionals had recruited 254 charter members to the inaugural meeting of the American Society for Industrial Security (ASIS), now known as **ASIS International**. The new association elected Hansen as its first president. The new association's primary goals were developing a corporate structure for the organization; increasing membership; compiling a directory of members; and developing an annual conference, a code of ethics, a monthly publication, certification, research, and public relations. In a short time, ASIS began to improve the image of private security.

In 1980, when ASIS celebrated its twenty-fifth anniversary, membership had risen to 13,000 and there were 122 local chapters around the world. The organization was also publishing its magazine, *Security Management*, and it had already begun a certification process, with the **Certified Protection Professional** (CPP) designation awarded to nearly 1,700 security professionals. It also had developed the research-oriented, tax-exempt ASIS Foundation in 1966, which pioneered research, education, and scholarships in private security. By the early 1990s, ASIS membership had risen to 25,000 and by the end of the decade to 30,000.

In the aftermath of 9/11, government officials turned to ASIS International to help formulate new strategies to combat terrorist threats and to help safeguard the nation's crucial infrastructure. In the post-9/11 environment, ASIS became an educational organization with an advocacy mission that began to affect government decisions in homeland security. Additionally, ASIS established a Commission on Guidelines to create minimum guidelines or standards for the private security industry.

In June 2004, the Department of Homeland Security (DHS) Secretary announced that ASIS International had been named a private-sector partner in the new national terrorism information-sharing and alert-notification program, the Homeland Security Information Network–Critical Infrastructure (HSIN-CI) Pilot Program. This operational, cross-agency, cross-sector, cross-discipline program that uses readily available technology, including telephones, computers, faxes, and the Internet, will allow ASIS International to participate in information exchange with federal authorities regarding terror alerts and other terrorism-related incidents and issues.[28]

As of 2006, ASIS International has more than 34,000 members and is the preeminent international organization for professionals responsible for security, including managers and directors of security. In addition, corporate executives; other management personnel; consultants; architects; attorneys; and federal, state, and local law enforcement become involved with ASIS International to better understand the constant changes in security issues and solutions. ASIS International is dedicated to increasing the effectiveness and productivity of security professionals by developing educational programs and materials that focus on both the fundamentals and the most recent advancements in security management. It is headquartered in Alexandria, Virginia, and publishes a monthly magazine and an academic journal.[29]

It offers three certification programs:

■ Certified Protection Professional (CPP): This certification designates individuals who have demonstrated competency in all areas constituting security management. Nearly 10,000 individuals have received the CPP certification since its inception in 1977.[30]

■ Professional Certified Investigator (PCI): Holders of the PCI certification have demonstrated education and/or experience in the fields of case management, evidence collection, and case presentation.

■ Physical Security Professional (PSP): The PSP certification is for those whose primary responsibility is to conduct threat surveys; design integrated security systems that include equipment, procedures, and people; or install, operate, and maintain those systems.

These certifications are offered to individuals meeting specific criteria of professional knowledge and recognizes them for having shown a high level of competence by improving the practices of security management. Candidates must meet certain basic standards of experience and formal education and must pass stringent comprehensive written examinations. These certifications are highly coveted by members of the security industry. Exhibit 1.4 lists the eligibility requirements and exam structure and content for the CPP certification. Boxes in other chapters of this text will cover the education and experience criteria for the PSP and the PCI certifications.

ASIS International offers professional development programs in numerous cities throughout the country each year and also offers a variety of online courses. (Exhibit 1.5 lists some of these professional development programs.) It also operates an annual seminar and exhibits in a major city each year that is attended by security directors and managers, security consultants, law enforcement professionals, homeland security officials, high-level executives of critical infrastructure businesses, government and military personnel with security responsibilites, and other professionals responsible for security operations. ASIS International also sponsors the annual International European Security Conference, the Emerging Trends in Security Conference, and the annual Goverment Industry Conference on Global Terrorism.

Membership costs $150 yearly, for which members receive the organization's monthly trade magazine, *Security Management*; admission to all ASIS International regional meetings; access to ASIS-NET, a subscription-based network for security professionals; a yearly subscription to *ASIS-Dynamics*, the organization's newsletter; and a yearly subscription to the organization's academic journal, *Security Journal* which is copublished with Perpetuity Press of Leicester, England. Members also receive discounts at all ASIS learning workshops.

The ASIS International websites, ASIS Online and Security Management Online, first inaugurated in the mid-1990s, have become the repositories of the wealth of knowledge available in the industry. Today, the society continues to use the web as a major conduit for information-sharing and offers its members increasing access to online educational programs, including a wide array of virtual seminars. See Exhibit 1.6 for a list of a ASIS International online training resources.

In addition to its own programs, ASIS International and the prestigious Wharton School of Business at the University of Pennsylvania, one of the nation's premier business schools, have partnered to offer a two-week Wharton/ASIS Program for Security Executives designed for chief security officers and high-level security managers and taught by senior faculty from the Wharton School.[31]

In addition, professors and educators at colleges and universities around the world research, develop course material, and teach future security professionals. These academics are essential to the development of professional security education.

Other professional organizations have entered into joint cooperative ventures with ASIS

EXHIBIT 1.4   **The Certified Protection Professional (CPP) Examination**

ELIGIBILITY
Candidates wishing to take the CPP examination must first satisfy the following requirements:

Experience and Education
Nine (9) years of security experience, at least three (3) years of which shall have been in responsible charge of a security function;
Or
An earned Bachelor's Degree or higher from an accredited institution of higher education and seven (7) years of security experience, at least three (3) years of which shall have been in responsible charge of a security function.

EXAM STRUCTURE AND CONTENT
The CPP examination is a 200-question, multiple-choice test covering tasks, knowledge, and skills in seven broad subjects identified by CPPs as the major areas involved in security management. All exam questions come from the official reference books. No questions on the exam are taken from any other source. The subject areas are:

Security Management
- Countermeasures Selection
- Financial Management
- Management Systems
- Personnel Management
- Planning, Organization, Leading, and Communications Management
- Vulnerability Assessment
- Risk Assessment
- Countermeasures
- Policies
- Internal Relations
- External Relations
- Identification and Disposition of Abusers
- Prevention Programs
- Types of Solutions
- Loss Prevention
- Liaison
- Substance Abuse

Investigations
- Investigative Resources
- Methods of Investigation

- Results and Reports of Investigation
- Types of Investigation

Legal Aspects
- Administrative and Regulatory Agency Requirements
- Civil Liability Torts
- Civil Rights and Fair Employment
- Contract Considerations
- Crimes, Criminal Procedures, and the Criminal Justice System
- Due Process and Constitutional Immunities

Personnel Security
- Employment Selection and Retention Standards
- Evaluation of Information
- Screening Techniques
- Security Awareness Programs
- Disciplinary Action

Physical Security
- Employee and Visitor Control
- Alarms
- Barriers
- Facility Planning
- Guard Patrol and Weapons
- Materials Control
- Mechanical, Electrical and Electronic Devices, and Equipment
- Perimeter Boundaries, Gates, and Lobbies
- Protective Lighting
- Security Surveys
- Parking, Traffic Control, Communications, and Security Transportation

Protection of Sensitive Information
- Control
- Identification
- Sensitivity

Emergency Management
- Implementation
- Plan Development
- Types of Emergency

SOURCE: ASIS International, *CPP Examination Eligibility, Structure, and Content*. Retrieved September 24, 2006, from http://www.asisonline.org.

International. In the 1980s, the International Association of Chiefs of Police (IACP), the National Sheriffs' Association (NSA), and ASIS International began joint meetings in order to foster better cooperation between the public and private sector. In 1986, these organizations, with funding from the NIJ, established the Joint Council of Law Enforcement and Private Security Associations.[32]

The IACP Private Sector Liaison Committee, composed of representative members from all facets of the private security and law enforcement sectors, with the assistance of the NSA, the National

EXHIBIT 1.5 **Some ASIS International Professional Development Programs**

Physical Security: Introductory Applications and Technology
Physical Security: Advanced Applications and Technology
Introduction to Crisis Management
Advanced Crisis Management
Assets Protection Course: Concepts and Methods
Emerging Trends in Security
Managing Physical Security
Functional Management
Enhanced Violence Assessment and Management
Executive Protection
Security Business Practices
Interview and Interrogation Techniques
Liability for Investigators
Security Force Management
Transportation Security

SOURCE: ASIS International. Retrieved September 24, 2006, from http://www.asisonline.org.

EXHIBIT 1.6 **Some ASIS International Virtual Forums and Online Training Programs**

Biometric Technology
FDA Bioterrorism Security Awareness
General Security Awareness for Port Facility Personnel
General Security Awareness for Shipboard Personnel
General Security Awareness for Vessel Personnel
U.S. Customs–Trade Partnership against Terrorism (C-TPAT)
Digital Video and Networking Training
Practical Crisis Management
HIPAA Basic Information Security Training
Homeland Security
Safe Hiring Audit: Implementing and Measuring Due Diligence
Identity Theft
Strategic Marketing of Security: A Low-Cost and High-Return Method
Effective Facility Security
Anti-Terrorism Considerations for Protecting Facilities
How to Do a Vulnerability Assessment
Effective Assessment and Response for Workplace Threats of Violence
Advanced Violence Assessment

SOURCE: ASIS International. Retrieved September 24, 2006, from http://www.asisonline.org.

Association of Security Companies, the National Association of Security and Investigator Regulators, and ASIS International, has developed private security officer selection, training, and licensing guidelines.[33]

Numerous other associations and organizations are trying to move private security toward a new professionalism that includes codes of ethics and value statements, education and training, minimum standards, and membership in a professional organization. The following are examples of these organizations.

▪ The International Foundation for Protection Officers (IFPO) was established as a nonprofit organization in 1988 for the purpose of facilitating the training and certification needs of protection officers and security supervisors from both the commercial and proprietary sectors. IFPO offers several certification and training programs: Entry Level Protection Officer, Basic Protection Officer, Certified Protection Officer, Certified Protection Officer Instructor, Security Supervisor, and Certified Security Supervisor. These courses have training manuals and are available online and in CD-ROM format.[34]

▪ The Academy of Security Educators and Trainers was founded in 1980 as a nonprofit professional society, and its current membership consists of academics, trainers, law enforcement, and government officials from national, state, and local agencies; self-employed professionals; and security officers, supervisors, and directors from major international corporations in the banking, transportation, security service, communications, energy, retail, chemical, insurance, petroleum, and utility industries. The Academy assists in the proper growth and development of security education and training by meeting to design and develop courses and seminars and by hosting an annual international security roundtable conference.[35]

▪ The International Association for Healthcare Security and Safety works to improve and professionalize security and safety in healthcare facilities through educational programs designed to meet the challenges and complexities of protecting modern medical facilities. It offers certification in numerous security positions specific to the hospital security industry, particularly the Certified Health Care Protection Administrator designation.[36]

■ The National Association of School Safety and Law Enforcement Officers, organized in 1969, is a professional organization for security executives and professionals that works to improve safely and security in America's schools by providing a forum for those in the executive and professional ranks of education and law enforcement.[37]

■ The Association of Certified Fraud Examiners (ACFE), established in 1996, is a professional organization for fraud examiners that offers its own CFE certification program.[38]

■ The Security Industry Association provides its members with a full-service international trade association promoting growth and professionalism within the security industry by providing education, research, technical standards, and representation.[39]

Although private security has professionalized greatly in the past fifty years, considerable work remains. One of the leading problems in the industry today is the quality of selection, training, and performance of security personnel. Generally, proprietary guards—those hired directly by a company—are better trained and qualified than contract guards who are employed by a contract guard agency and hired out to individual employers. Although police departments are required to have significant educational and training standards for their officers, the average security officer receives less than eight hours of pre-employment training. In the 1990s, several bills were introduced in Congress recommending minimum training for all security personnel (the 1991 Gore Bill, the 1993 Sundquist Bill, and the 1993 Martinez Bill); however, the federal government has yet to pass legislation mandating standards or minimum training for private security employment.[40] However, as Chapter 2 will show, many individual states in the United States have made tremendous progress in establishing mandatory licensing,

regulating, hiring and training standards. Also, many industries and companies have adopted voluntary measures.

In December 2004, President Bush signed Senate Bill 2845, popularly known as the Intelligence Reform Bill and the 9-11 Implementation Bill. The bill included the **Private Security Officer Employment Authorization Act of 2004**, giving employers the ability to request criminal background checks from the FBI's database for applicants and holders of security positions. It covers both contract and propriety security personnel. It gives employers the opportunity, if the applicant or employee consents, to send fingerprints or other positive identification to the FBI for a criminal background check. The employer will not have direct access to the results of the FBI check but will be given enough information to make an informed decision. For example, if the state has standards for qualification to be a private security officer, it will notify the employer as to whether the applicant or employee meets the state standards. If the state does not have standards, it will notify the employer as to whether the applicant or employee has been convicted of "a felony; an offense involving dishonesty or a false statement if the conviction occurred during the previous ten years; or an offense involving the use or attempted use of physical force against the person of another if the conviction occurred during the previous ten years." It will also notify the employer if the applicant or employee has been "charged with a criminal felony for which there has been no resolution during the preceding 365 days." The act also provides for criminal penalties for knowingly and intentionally misusing information obtained pursuant to it.[41]

The provisions of the new law had been introduced into many sessions of Congress over the years but had never been passed. Among the supporters of the new law were the major contract guard companies, acting through NASCO and ASIS International, which recognized that improved screening of contract guards was a powerful step toward making workplaces safer. This bill was prompted by the failure of privately employed contract security screeners at U.S. airports to properly do their jobs, resulting in al-Qaeda terrorists boarding airplanes that led to the disastrous events of 9/11. Chapter 2 will discuss in depth the issues of security-guard hiring and training standards.

Another major issue facing private security is the imposition of industry **minimum standards or guidelines** to ensure the enhanced effectiveness

Private Security Officer Employment Authorization Act of 2004 Law passed in 2004 giving employers the ability to request criminal background checks from the FBI to process criminal history records checks for candidates for security job positions.

minimum standards or guidelines Efforts to increase the professionalization of private security employees by requiring them to meet specific standards prior to employment.

and professionalism of the industry. ASIS International established its Commission on Guidelines in early 2001 to create minimum standards or guidelines for the security industry. It felt that minimum standards or guidelines addressing specific concerns and issues would increase the professionalism, effectiveness, and productivity of the industry. It develops its guidelines in cooperation with other industries, the Security Industry Standards Council, and the American National Standards Institute (ANSI).

As of 2006, ASIS International has established and published guidelines on general security risk assessment, chief security officers, business continuity, private security selection and training, threat advisory system response, and workplace violence prevention and response. It is also is in the process of designing guidelines regarding pre-employment background screening, physical security measures, and information asset protection.[42]

Other industries that impact security have also started to provide minimum standards for their own industries. Much of this effort has been spurred on by 9/11. The American Chemistry Council, the U.S. Department of Agriculture, the International Standards Organization, the Environmental Safety and Health Training Association, and the Biometric Consortium have recently proposed or issued standards or minimum guidelines affecting the security operations and training of their members.[43] Also, ASTM International, formerly known as the American Society for Testing and Materials, one of the largest standards development organizations in the world, recently announced that it would develop standards for high-rise evacuation equipment to be used when primary routes to a safe zone are cut off in disaster situations. ASTM is also working more broadly to develop standards and guidance on homeland security applications, such as antiterrorism, physical security measures for buildings, and hospital preparedness. The National Fire Protection Association is working on premise security guidelines and equipment installation guidelines. ANSI also has recently assembled a Homeland Security Standards Panel to catalog existing voluntary standards and identify gaps in coverage. Most of this panel's work is centered on biometrics, emergency management, and chemical and biological threats.[44]

College Education and Private Security

In 1976, only five colleges in the United States offered a bachelor's degree in private security, and no master's programs were available. By 1990, forty-six colleges offered a bachelor's degree and fourteen offered a master's degree.[45] Today these numbers have changed drastically, and college education is becoming vastly more important in private security.

Many professional and educational institutions and associations have assisted progressive-thinking leaders in the private security industry in creating college-level courses and programs specific to the industry. ASIS International is one of the associations at the forefront of academic research and interest in private security. Through its efforts, New York University's Management Institute began a two-year certificate course in industrial security management as early as 1963. In 1978, ASIS International created a Standing Committee on Academic Programs in Colleges and Universities, which has served as a liaison between the organization and academics throughout the nation to foster and promote high-quality security education. The committee sponsors a writing competition to encourage research and scholarly writing among college students. It also solicits fully researched papers on security topics from undergraduate and graduate students, which are judged by a panel of security academics and practitioners.[46]

The Academy of Criminal Justice Sciences, the largest professional organization in the field of criminal justice education, research, and policy analysis, has a membership subsection devoted to security and crime prevention. The security/crime prevention section, established in 1993, promotes scholarship and academic offerings, and its goal is to further the partnership between the public and private sectors. It is affiliated with the *Journal of Security Administration*, an innovative and scholarly semiannual journal. The American Society of Criminology also works closely with students who are considering career paths in criminal justice.

In 1997, ASIS International began a series of annual academic practitioner symposiums to address the future of security education in which academics and practitioners have engaged in discussions to develop courses to introduce business students to the subject of security. These symposiums provide a forum for academics and security practitioners to meet, share ideas, and discuss potential improvements in security education. At these symposiums, participants have created a model introductory security course for business students and follow-up courses on risk assessment and legal issues. Attendees have also examined how security, loss prevention, asset protection, risk management, and resource protection relate to one another and have examined functional areas such as fire science and protection, disaster recovery, antiterrorism, and emergency management.[47]

They have also analyzed the relationship between security, law enforcement, and justice administration. The participants agreed that the main difference between security and related criminal justice degrees is that security programs focus on problem identification and prevention, rather than on reacting to incidents—the main thrust of enforcement and criminal justice programs. They also discussed why security is generally not accepted as an academic discipline, why employers should hire job candidates with a security degree rather than those without one, and why relatively few employers stipulate a security degree as a requirement for security management positions.[48]

Joseph W. Koletar, director of forensic and investigative services for Deloitte and Touche LLP, proposed that only through the development of a researched body of knowledge would security gain its place in academia and be properly prepared to equip the security practitioners of the future. Koletar proposed that the following elements be part of a security degree, in addition to the normal coursework associated with a liberal arts undergraduate degree: oral and written communication, criminal justice operations, criminal and civil law and procedure, statistics and quantitative methods, business operations and risk management, business economics, marketing, and technical courses such as access-control systems or fire and safety.

Today, PhD programs in security are increasing, and academic and professional certifications are more prevalent and more attainable, particularly using online options. As examples, North Dakota State University in Fargo and George Washington University in Washington DC have introduced doctoral programs. The American Military University (AMU) has partnered with ASIS International to deliver an abundance of online degree programs. AMU offers certificates and degrees at the undergraduate and graduate levels focusing on such topics as homeland security, intelligence, information technology, and counterterrorism.[49]

Enrollment in academic security programs and internships is on the rise, both at the undergraduate and graduate level, says Robert McCrie, professor of security management at John Jay College of Criminal Justice. "Those going into security see a correlation between the private sector and serving the country as a whole. They see private security as a part of homeland security."[50] According to Professor McCrie, "The statistics paint a bright future for private security and those students looking to enter the market. It also looks bright for those looking to make a career change."[51]

The increased demand for quality security education since 9/11 has altered course content and stimulated the development of many new degree programs. Since then, over one-hundred private and state colleges and universities have rushed to create counterterrorism, disaster management, and homeland security courses, and thousands of students are pursuing degrees in these areas, including emergency and disaster management, making them some of the fastest-growing fields in academia. These new programs include certificate programs, as well as bachelor's, master's, and doctoral programs. They use an interdisciplinary approach, teaching students about various social sciences and practical theories and techniques. They are directed at local officials, first-responders, and corporate managers who have the major responsibility of dealing with problems connected with disasters and terrorism. Many new professional certifications have also been developed, some centered around a homeland security theme, such as the one offered by the American College of Forensic Examiners, and others focusing on specific technical subjects, such as the PCI and PSP certifications offered by ASIS International.

In 2004, the Federal Office of Emergency Management reported that there were 115 colleges offering these programs and 100 more colleges considering adding these types of courses.[52] The Department of Homeland Security, in 2004 alone, gave $70 million in grant money to colleges and universities to assist in developing new courses.[53] In 2004, the American Association of Community Colleges announced it would appoint a 21-member task force on homeland security training for first responders.

The study of terrorism and emergency management has grown out of traditional disaster studies, which were once the domain of community colleges and focused on managing "first-responders"—the police, fire, and paramedic departments that respond to hurricanes and riots. These new courses seek to educate local officials and corporate managers who have the major duty of mitigating disasters.

This continuing attention paid to college education is starting to affect salaries. Security executives responding to the *ASIS International Employment Survey* reported that they earned 26 percent more on average if they held a four-year college degree, and those with a master's degree earn an additional 15 percent more.[54]

Ethics and Private Security

Ethics are extremely important in the private security profession, as in all professions, industries, businesses, and indeed in all endeavors and behaviors in life. **Ethics** can be defined as the practical normative study of the rightness and wrongness of human conduct. All human conduct can be viewed in the context of basic and applied ethical considerations. Basic ethics is the rather broad moral principles that govern all conduct, while applied ethics focuses these broad principles on specific applications. For example, a basic ethical tenet assumes that lying or stealing is wrong. Applied ethics would examine and govern under what conditions such a wrong would indeed take place and deal with constructing resultant personal conduct, for the subject matter of ethics is human conduct.[55]

The Greek philosopher Aristotle, in his classic *Nicomachean Ethics*, stated that "every art and every inquiry and similarly every action and choice is thought to aim at some good."[56] Is Aristotle's "good" what we mean as ethics? This author thinks so. Could Aristotle's definition of good or ethics be the same as our modern saying, "Do the right thing?" Yes! If one is ethical, he or she does the right thing, and similarly, if one does the right thing, he or she is ethical.

This section will discuss the ethical concerns of security firms and their employees, as well as several issues endemic to the concept, business, and operations of the private security industry.

Ethical Conduct of Security Firms and Their Employees

Many private security organizations and associations have issued their own **ethics codes or values statements** to guide members of their organizations. ASIS International, for example, has promulgated its own ethical standards and has devoted an entire section of their comprehensive

---

ethics The practical, normative study of the rightness and wrongness of human conduct.

ethics codes or values statements Formal statements of businesses or organizations representing their ethical and values standards.

| EXHIBIT 1.7 | ASIS International Code of Ethics |

PREAMBLE

Aware that the quality of professional security activity ultimately depends upon the willingness of practitioners to observe special standards of conduct and to manifest good faith in professional relationships, ASIS International adopts the following *Code of Ethics* and mandates its conscientious observance as a binding condition of membership in or affiliation with the Society.

CODE OF ETHICS

I.   A member shall perform professional duties in accordance with the law and the highest moral principles.

II. A member shall observe the precepts of truthfulness, honesty and integrity.

III. A member shall be faithful and diligent in discharging professional responsibilities.

IV. A member shall be competent in discharging professional responsibilities.

V.   A member shall safeguard confidential information and exercise due care to prevent its improper disclosure.

VI. A member shall not maliciously injure the professional reputation or practice of colleagues, clients, or employers.

ARTICLE I

A member shall perform professional duties in accordance with the law and the highest moral principles.

Ethical Considerations

I–1 A member shall abide by the law of the land in which the services are rendered and perform all duties in an honorable manner.

I–2 A member shall not knowingly become associated in responsibility for work with colleagues who do not conform to the law and these ethical standards.

I–3 A member shall be just and respect the rights of others in performing professional responsibilities.

ARTICLE II

A member shall observe the precepts of truthfulness, honesty, and integrity

Ethical Considerations

II–1 A member shall disclose all relevant information to those having a right to know.

II–2 A right to know is a legally enforceable claim or demand by a person for disclosure of information by a member. Such a right does not depend upon prior knowledge by the person of the existence of the information to be disclosed.

II–3 A member shall not knowingly release misleading information, nor encourage or otherwise participate in the release of such information.

ARTICLE III

A member shall be faithful and diligent in discharging professional responsibilities.

Ethical Considerations

III–1 A member is faithful when fair and steadfast in adherence to promises and commitments.

III–2 A member is diligent when employing best efforts in an assignment.

---

assets protections course to this crucial area. In this section, students engage in dialogue on the ethical implications of situations faced in the security profession and confront real world and theoretical problems. This subject is also covered in depth in the *Protection of Assets Manual,* which serves as the text for the course. Additionally, ASIS International has produced a one-and-a-half-hour videotape entitled *Ethics in the Security Profession.* The tape is narrated by Jack Ford, NBC television's chief legal commentator, who leads a panel of security experts in a Socratic dialogue on ethics in the security profession. Practical applications of the principles of the ASIS International Code of Ethics frame three scenarios: an anonymous letter regarding

employee theft, a vendor/contractor ethical issue; and an executive kidnapping. Exhibits 1.7 and 1.8 are samples of codes of ethics and values statements issued and enforced by ASIS International and Securitas (one of the largest private security firms in the world).

When we discuss ethical violations in the conduct of security firms or their employees, we are generally discussing breaches of conduct that are either wrong in themselves or wrong in the context of the job or responsibility the organization or employee is undertaking; we are also discussing violations of the organizations' ethical or value statements. For example, if a member of ASIS International fails to safeguard confidential information or to

III–3 A member shall not act in matters involving conflicts of interest without appropriate disclosure and approval.

III–4 A member shall represent services or products fairly and truthfully.

ARTICLE IV

A member shall be competent in discharging professional responsibilities.

Ethical Considerations

IV–1 A member is competent who possesses and applies the skills and knowledge required for the task.

IV–2 A member shall not accept a task beyond the member's competence nor shall competence be claimed when not possessed.

ARTICLE V

A member shall safeguard confidential information and exercise due care to prevent its improper disclosure.

Ethical Considerations

V–1 Confidential information is nonpublic information, the disclosure of which is restricted.

V–2 Due care requires that the professional must not knowingly reveal confidential information, or use a confidence to the disadvantage of the principal or to the advantage of the member or a third person, unless the principal consents after full disclosure of all the facts. The confidentiality continues after the business relationship between the member and his principal has terminated.

V–3 A member who receives information and has not agreed to be bound by confidentiality is not bound from disclosing it. A member is not bound by confidential disclosures made of acts or omissions which constitute a violation of the law.

V–4 Confidential disclosures made by a principal to a member are not recognized by law as privileged in a legal proceeding. The member may be required to testify in a legal proceeding to information received in confidence from his principal over the objection of his principal's counsel.

V–5 A member shall not disclose confidential information for personal gain without appropriate authorization.

ARTICLE VI

A member shall not maliciously injure the professional reputation or practice of colleagues, clients, or employers.

Ethical Considerations

VI–1 A member shall not comment falsely and with malice concerning a colleague's competence, performance, or professional capabilities.

VI–2 A member who knows, or has reasonable grounds to believe, that another member has failed to conform to the Society's Code of Ethics shall present such information to the Ethical Standards Committee in accordance with Article VIII of the Society's bylaws.

SOURCE: ASIS International, *Code of Ethics*. Retrieved September 24, 2006, from http://www.asisonline.org. Reprinted by permission.

exercise due care to prevent its improper disclosure, or accepts a task beyond her or his competence or claims competence when in fact she or he does not possess it, that person is unethical; he or she is not doing the right thing. As another example, if a member of the Securitas organization steals or violates the responsibilities imposed by the organization's value statement, such as not reporting improprieties, he or she is engaging in unethical behavior; he or she is not doing the right thing.

Violations of ethics can be criminal if a criminal statute is violated and the person committing them can be prosecuted within the criminal justice system. If the violation is noncriminal but in violation of ethical or value standards, the person committing the violation can be subject to administrative sanctions and lose her or his job. These are usually the easiest ethical problems, and they can be corrected by removing the offender from the organization.

Of course, not all ethical violations may be as obvious as these examples. Consider, for example, the Rebecca Schaeffer case presented in the You Are There! feature of this chapter. The private investigator's action was not illegal at that time as these records were accessible to the public. But should the private investigator have determined the reason Bardo wanted the information before providing it to him? Think of the options the investigator had. Ethics is not always an easy subject.

| **EXHIBIT 1.8** | **Securitas Values Statement** |

Our job is to safeguard the things that our customers value most—at home, at work and in the community. For people to entrust us with the responsibility of protecting their property and handling their money, they have to have confidence in our values as a company, which is why we place such high demands on our staff: We require that each of our employees respect and protect our ethical philosophy, a philosophy that unites us as a company and builds trust for our customers.

OUR VALUES

Integrity, Vigilance, Helpfulness
Our philosophy is based on our three core values: Integrity, Vigilance, and Helpfulness

Integrity—To be trusted to work unsupervised on a customer's premises and with valuables. Securitas employees must be honest. We are uncompromising in our truthfulness, which means that we openly express our opinions, we do not withhold information and we always report improprieties.

Vigilance—To be good at what we do requires constant observing, listening and assessing. Securitas guards are always attentive and have developed a professional intuition that helps them notice things that others don't. That's why they are always aware of potential risks or incidents that take place on a customer's premises.

Helpfulness—Our job is about more than protecting property or cash; it's about making people feel safe. Securitas employees always lend assistance and intervene during incidents, even when they are not directly related to their jobs.

***Ethics*—An Everyday Concern**
Our business is based on trust. To make sure that our customers trust us, we have to trust that each and every Securitas employee shares our values and follows our ethical philosophy. We've taken great strides to instill a collective set of values within our organization, in terms of recruitment and day-to-day operations.

SOURCE: Securitas, *Our Values, 2004.* Retrieved September 24, 2006, from http://www.pinkertons.com.

Ethical Issues Endemic to the Security Industry

Generally, ethical issues that may be endemic to the concept, business, and operations of the private security industry itself, as opposed to ethical violations by individual firms or employees, are the most difficult to deal with. Many feel that private security has a number of inherent elements that may be unethical in themselves or inconsistent with the concepts of democratic policing that we cherish in the United States.

According to the Law Commission of Canada, four core principles ought to support democratic policing (both public and private): justice, equality, accountability, and efficiency. *Justice* means that all individuals should be treated fairly and their rights respected. *Equality* means that all people should receive policing services sufficient to feel safe in their community and that there should be representation and participation from all members of society in the delivery of policing services. *Accountability* requires that the actions of a person are subject to review and that there are formal channels that individuals can use to lodge a complaint. *Efficiency* means that the services are provided in a cost-effective manner.[57]

Obviously, the ideals of democratic policing as espoused by the Law Commission, when applied to private security, by their very nature present a problem because private security is different from policing. There are clear differences in the objectives of policing and private security. The police are charged with protecting the public at large while the private security industry operates for profit and is accountable only to its clients. In addition, the police generally apprehend criminals after they have committed a crime, whereas private security seeks to prevent crimes. The police are fundamentally reactive—they respond after they are called—whereas private security is proactive—they seek to prevent crimes and incidents so they are *not* called.[58]

Thus, private security would have difficulty in conforming to one of the Law Commission's stated core principles—equality. Regarding the principle of equality, private security officers or private security firms cannot ensure that all persons receive services sufficient to feel safe in their community because they work for certain people—their clients—and not for all of the people in the community. However, they should conform to the other principles— justice, accountability, and efficiency: justice, in that private security officers should treat all persons

You Are There!

The Rebecca Schaeffer Case

Rebecca Schaeffer was a beautiful young actress with a great future in acting. In the mid-1980s, she had a top-rated television show, *My Sister Sam.* In 1989 she starred in a movie—a scene in that movie and the actions of a private investigator cost the actress her life when a demented 19-year-old fan and stalker fired one shot into her chest from a .357 Magnum pistol on the doorstep of her Los Angeles home. The murderer, after being turned away by security personnel at the Burbank studio where Schaeffer filmed her TV series, paid a private investigator $250 to obtain Schaeffer's home address.

Robert Bardo was a straight-A student who dropped out of high school in 1985. In school he had been a loner and social outcast, never talking to other students, preferring instead to stand alone, nodding, on the school sidewalks. After dropping out of school, he became a janitor at a local fast-food chain, slept 15 hours a day, and watched television. He had never had a date and never lost his virginity. In August of 1986, Bardo began to idolize Schaeffer after seeing her in *My Sister Sam.* He was infatuated by her beauty, intelligence, and innocence. She became Bardo's imaginary goddess.

Bardo began writing Schaeffer, and in June 1987, he traveled to her Burbank studio, carrying a large teddy bear and a letter to her. Security guards rebuffed him. He returned a month later, this time with a knife, but again he was unable to see her and returned to his home in Arizona. In 1989, Schaeffer appeared in a bedroom scene with an actor in the film *Scenes from the Class Struggle in Beverly Hills.* This incensed Bardo.

Bardo read an article in *People* magazine describing how another demented stalker had obtained the address of another actress, Theresa Saldana, and had stabbed her numerous times. Bardo then paid $250 to a private detective who obtained Schaeffer's home address from California's Motor Vehicle Department records.

On the day of Schaeffer's murder, Bardo took an overnight bus from Arizona to Los Angeles Union Station and a local bus to the Fairfax district where Schaeffer lived. After walking aimlessly for 90 minutes, he went to her apartment and pushed her buzzer; after a one-minute conversation with her, he handed her a note. He then went to a nearby diner and ordered onion rings and cheesecake for breakfast. An hour later, as Schaeffer opened her door for the second time that morning, Bardo fired one shot into her chest, killing her.

In December 1991, Bardo was sentenced to life in prison without parole. Since then, California has toughened its laws regarding access to certain Motor Vehicle Department information.

Source: National News Media, 1989, 1990, 1991.

---

fairly and respect their rights; accountability, in that the actions of each private security officer and the firm itself are subject to review and that there are formal channels that individuals can use to lodge a complaint; and efficiency, in that the services should be provided in a cost-effective manner.

Regarding the equality issue, some are concerned with basic equity problems in the process of buying one's own private protection. As Samuel Walker of the University of Nebraska at Omaha has written, "There are equity problems. Wealthy neighborhoods are able to purchase additional protection, whereas poor neighborhoods receive less protection because financially strapped city governments are unable to hire more police."[59]

Similarly, while the practice of using regular police officers to supplement private security has generally been permitted by state law, the use of private money to pay for police has raised questions. In 1998, for example, then-Mayor Rudolph Giuliani of New York City was sharply criticized for approving a plan by a business improvement district to pay $5 million for a police substation in the Wall Street area. Community groups complained that officers would be pulled from more dangerous precincts to patrol one of the safest areas in the city.[60]

Some argue that the use of public police at private shopping malls is also an equity issue. However, some police officials say that having public officers at private malls is just an extension of the community-policing concept and insist that this practice does not raise questions of equity because everyone benefits. For example, Dean Esserman, former chief of the Stamford, Connecticut, Police Department, whose five district offices are all provided free by merchants who also routinely contract for uniformed police on overtime to patrol the Stamford Center Mall and other private businesses, says, "Our

A significant percentage of public police officers moonlight as private security officers during their off-duty hours, often to supplement their income. Some say this practice can create conflicts of interest; for example, an off-duty officer moonlighting for a private security firm may be caught between the duty to enforce the law and the interest of his or her temporary employer. What do you think?

©Fat Chance Productions/Getty Images

responsibility is to provide safety and security for the city of Stamford, period."[61] Another official also says it makes sense to send officers to malls, "This is where the people are," says Philip J. Dinicola, deputy police chief of Woodbridge, New Jersey.[62]

Regarding two of the other values espoused by the Law Commission of Canada for democratic policing, justice and accountability, some say that private security itself violates these values because it is not generally under the control of the government, as the police are. For example, Marcia Chaiken and Jan Chaiken, in a NIJ report, warn that private security officers are not accountable because they are not bound by the decisions of the U.S. Supreme Court regarding civil liberties issues, such as *Miranda*.[63] Samuel Walker also refers to this issue: "Supreme Court decisions such as *Miranda* apply to public police. . . . private security officers are not bound by these decisions."[64]

These are valid issues. The significant diversification or pluralization of policing, with more emphasis being placed on the use of private security in the past two decades, raises important questions about the best forms of accountability for private security. Current themes in this important area of policy development focus on private security powers and on accountability through government regulation, civil law, criminal law, industry self-regulation, market forces, and industry standards and third parties.[65]

Today, many challenge the view that private police are not held accountable to the same degree as public police. In most jurisdictions in North America and Europe, there is now formal state regulation of at least some private security employees and organizations. The primary type of regulation is industry self-regulation, which typically seeks to achieve similar objectives to those of formal state regulation, often through similar means. Some countries, such as England, have officially encouraged industry self-regulation as an alternative to formal state regulation of private policing.

Like the police, private security organizations and personnel are subject to the criminal laws of the jurisdictions in which they operate and may be held accountable for violations of these laws. Furthermore, civil suits against private policing personnel and organizations have been plentiful and often successful. In addition, mechanisms for collective bargaining, grievance processing, and arbitration in the workplace, along with broader labor legislation regarding such matters as procedures for union certification, strikes, and lockouts, provide vehicles by which private policing activities can be held accountable to management, workers, and unions. In addition, the marketplace itself provides opportunities for private policing to be held accountable to the public as consumers. Companies that engage in inappropriate, overly aggressive, or ineffective services will find their customers shifting their patronage to other companies.[66]

Another ethical issue for many is the practice of public police officers **moonlighting** as private security officers. Some say that this practice can create conflicts of interest; for example, an off-duty officer moonlighting for a private security firm may be caught between the duty to enforce the law and the interest of his or her temporary employer.

As a recent example, in the wealthy towns of Southampton and Easthampton on Long Island, New York, off-duty police officers face few restrictions on working for private security firms.

moonlighting Term for police officers working in private security jobs during their off-duty hours.

For decades, this region has been a popular site for high-priced fund-raisers, invitation-only movie premiers, extravagant corporate promotions, and fashion shoots. Some residents point a finger at the local police officers, who, when in uniform, are responsible for maintaining law and order but, when moonlighting as security guards, are protecting the people creating chaos. Many think the officers and departments allowing these officers to work as private guards are involved in a conflict of interest—who do they work for, the public or the private hosts? In 2004, at hip-hop promoter Sean (P. Diddy) Combs' riotous July 4th extravaganza in Bridgehampton, New York, neighbors were infuriated by the pounding music, the rowdiness of the 1,500 guests, and the estimated 400 illegally parked cars clogging their streets. Combs had hired a security firm owned by a town police officer and his wife. There was a delay in shutting down the party by on-duty officers responding to complaints by the neighbors. Police were first called at 5 P.M. but did not start towing cars or writing parking tickets until 8 P.M. and did not shut down the party until 10:30 P.M., when security guards were forced to link arms to hold back a horde of party crashers. The town board had only issued a permit for 400 guests to attend a 45-minute musical performance, cocktail party, and movie premiere. Town officials say they were sandbagged by Mr. Combs.[67]

In East Hampton Village, Police Chief Gerald Larsen has attempted to address this ethical issue by ending the policy of allowing off-duty officers to work armed and in uniform for private hosts. "I decided it was better to avoid the appearance of bending the rules for anyone," Larsen said. Now the hosts pay the village for a police presence, and Chief Larsen pays these officers overtime. "That way, there's no confusion about who they work for: the village," he said.[68]

Homeland Security and the Professionalization of Private Security

In response to the tragic events of 9/11, the federal government significantly restructured the law enforcement functions of the federal government. In the immediate aftermath of the attacks, it created the **Transportation Security Administration** (TSA) as a federal agency to replace the poor-performing private screeners at all of the nation's airports. Later, it merged twenty-two previously disparate domestic agencies into one large department, the **Department of Homeland Security** (DHS), to protect against threats to the homeland. This new agency consists of more than 170,000 employees and includes the duties of many former agencies, including the Coast Guard, the U.S. Customs Service, the Secret Service, and the Immigration and Naturalization Service, along with numerous federal communications, science, and technology agencies. State and local law enforcement agencies and the private security industry joined in the post-9/11 efforts to protect the nation's borders and infrastructure from attack.[69]

As we have seen earlier in this chapter, the private security industry in the United States has always attempted to address the issues of security in the workplace; however, the events of 9/11 intensified the importance of such security. According to the Business Roundtable, an association of chief executive officers of leading American corporations, "Security is now a rising star in the corporate firmament. The people responsible for security have become much more visible to the top of the business and much more important to the business itself."[70] Also, market research on the security industry reported that the global security industry has moved from a peripheral activity to center stage.[71]

Today, members of corporate executive protection departments and others concerned with personal protection pay constant attention to terrorist threats and develop plans to deal with these eventualities in this country and abroad.[72] Most multinational corporations have detailed executive protection plans, crisis management teams, and threat assessment strategies.[73]

Companies without security departments or those with smaller security departments often hire large contract security companies to provide

Transportation Security Administration (TSA) Federal agency established in the aftermath of the 9/11 terrorist attacks to protect the nation's transportations systems and ensure freedom of movement for people and commerce.

Department of Homeland Security (DHS) Federal cabinet department established in the aftermath of the 9/11 terrorist attacks to protect the nation from terrorism.

corporate, executive, and homeland security services. These companies emphasize strategic prevention and conduct a threat assessment before establishing a prevention plan.

The following are examples of post-9/11 increased security:[74]

■ The Empire State Building in New York City is more controlled now, and the building's managers say they have added $6 million per year worth of security measures. At Yankee Stadium, there are more police officers and private security guards during games. Bags and backpacks are forbidden, trash cans and parking have been eliminated along the perimeter wall, and there are more security cameras.

■ In New Jersey, state officals developed a list of the 110 privately owned sites they considered most likely to become targets, from office buildings to chemical plants, and allocated $46 million to help pay for security.

Hospitals have made a big investment in security and emergency preparedness, particularly in New York City, which took the brunt of the 9/11 attacks. Bellevue Hospital Center's former portable decontamination shower, hooked up to a hose, has been replaced by an enclosed, permanent, $500,000 structure with air filters, fifty-six high-speed water nozzles, and the ability to decontaminate as many as five hundred people an hour. At St. Vincent's Manhattan Hospital, the pharmacy has a stockpile of 350 injection kits loaded with atropine, an antidote for some nerve gases, and more than 100 with a cyanide antidote. St. Vincent's ambulances have all been equipped with gas masks and bodysuits to protect the paradmedics and with antidotes to chemical agents. Hospitals across New York State have spent more than $200 million on security and emergency reponse measures that were not contemplated before 9/11. They have built negative–air pressure rooms that germs cannot escape, bought bodysuits and respirators, and installed backup computer systems. New York City's Health and Hospitals Corporation bought a radio system linking its eleven hospitals, in case the hospital's phone system fails.[75]

Immediately after the 2001 terrorist attacks, ASIS International's board of directors realized that private security possesses such an incredible body of knowledge and is already involved in protecting so much of the nation's critical infrastructure and ensuring homeland security that they needed to bring together representatives of security-related organizations to express the views of the security industry to the government. In late 2002, ASIS International sponsored a security policy summit in Washington, DC, involving representatives from the Office of Homeland Security and many attendees from security-related organizations. Panelists led discussions about the Homeland Security Act, privacy, and security officer standards. Frank Cilluffo, a director of policy for the Office of Homeland Security, stated, " . . . the private sector is on the front lines in this war [terrorism]."[76]

Each subsequent chapter of this text will contain the latest information relative to the chapter's subject, regarding the private security industry's efforts to improve security in our homeland.

Summary

■ The word *security* comes from the Latin word *securus*—*se* (without) and *cura* (care)—and came into English as "without care," "free from care," "free from danger," or "safe."

■ The private security industry has been defined as "those self-employed individuals and privately funded business entities and organizations providing security-related services to specific clientele for a fee, for the individual or entity that retains or employs them, or for themselves, in order to protect their persons, private property, or interests from various hazards."

■ The beginnings of private security date back to prerecorded history when groups of people banded together to protect themselves and their families from wild beasts and raiding enemies.

■ In Ancient Rome, security consisted of the military, slaves, and persons privately hired to protect people.

■ In early England, private security consisted of private individuals who grouped together to protect themselves and others, private investigators, and early rudimentary forms of public law enforcement.

- In 1819, the first large-scale, uniformed, organized, paid, civil police force was created in London, England.

- Colonial America adopted the early English model of public policing and used the military and militia. In the mid-nineteenth century, Eastern cities created formal police departments and the frontier used sheriffs and the military.

- The modern U.S. private security industry owes much of its origins to Allan Pinkerton, who created the Pinkerton National Detective Agency in the early 1950s.

- In the mid-nineteenth century, the advances of modern technology began to improve the private security industry, including burglar alarm systems, armored cars, the telegraph, and multisignal electronic protection systems.

- In the early part of the twentieth century, rapid industrialization and union–management unrest caused industries to emphasize corporate and plant security and develop proprietary security forces and/or hire outside contract security forms.

- During the years prior to and during World War II, the government established military guards, patrols, and other appropriate measures to protect national defense–related industries from sabotage. Before the end of the war, more than 200,000 industrial security personnel were under the supervision of the U.S. Armed Forces.

- The Industrial Defense Program was developed in 1952 and led to an intense emphasis on private security to protect industries and businesses.

- In 1955, ASIS (the American Society of Industrial Security), now known as ASIS International, was developed to professionalize private security.

- In 1976, there were only five colleges offering degrees in private security; today there are hundreds of such programs, and they are increasing every year.

- During the 1960s and 1970s, rising crime and social disorder drastically increased the need for private security, and in the 1960s and 1970s, a rash of airplane hijackings led to the development of security and passenger screening at the nation's airports.

- By the 1980s and 1990s, private security personnel began to outnumber and outspend public policing.

- The tragic events of 9/11, the terrorist attacks on the United States of America, brought about the creation of the Department of Homeland Security and a dramatic increase in homeland security measures by federal, state, and local law enforcement agencies and private security agencies.

- Ethical conduct is extremely important in the operations of private security.

Learning Check

1. Discuss the contributions of the early Romans to the history of private security.

2. Discuss the contributions of the early English to the history of private security.

3. Name and discuss a major contributor to the development of private security in England.

4. Identify and discuss the contributions of Allan Pinkerton to the development of private security in the United States.

5. Name and discuss two other major contributors to the development of private security in the United States.

6. Name and discuss three technological innovations that improved the private security industry in the nineteenth century.

7. List and discuss several ways the private security industry has increased its professionalization in the twentieth century.

8. Discuss the effect of World War II on the development of private security in the United States.

9. Discuss the recent increase in college programs in private security and cite three specific examples.

10. Discuss the ethical issues that may be endemic to the security industry's concept, business, and operations.

Application Exercise

Your professor in this course is attending the annual national convention of the Academy of Criminal Justice Sciences and has invited you and your fellow students to accompany her. She has indicated that you may present a paper at the convention on any issue regarding the professionalization of private security in the United States in the second half of the twentieth century. The paper must be five to six pages long, double-spaced. In addition to preparing the paper, you will be required to present it to an assembled panel of other students from all over the United States in a ten-minute oral report.

Web Exercise

You are about to graduate with a bachelor's degree in private security from your college and have already received a job offer with the security department of a major firm in your area. You want to work hard at this job and eventually work yourself up to a management-level position in the firm. You are familiar with the Certified Protection Professional (CPP) designation and have heard from people in the company that this designation will help you advance your career. You want to begin the process to obtain this designation. Access the ASIS International website and obtain the following:

- Information regarding when you can take the examination
- CPP eligibility requirements
- A list of subject areas that will be tested in the examination

- A list of reference materials to help you prepare for the examination
- The application form to take the examination

Key Terms

ASIS International, p. 16
Bow Street Runners, p. 6
Certified Protection Professional (CPP), p. 16
Department of Homeland Security (DHS), p. 29
ethics, p. 23
ethics codes or values statements, p. 23
Hallcrest Reports, p. 14
Industrial Defense Program, p. 13
minimum standards or guidelines, p. 20
moonlighting, p. 28
National Industrial Security Program, p. 13
Pinkerton National Detective Agency, p. 8
Pinkerton Protective Patrol, p. 8
private security industry, p. 2
Private Security Officer Employment
    Authorization Act of 2004, p. 20
questors, p. 4
Railway Police Acts, p. 10
thief-takers, p. 5
Transportation Security Administration
    (TSA), p. 29

2

The Business of the Private Security Industry

©Michael Newman/PhotoEdit

GOALS

- To introduce the private security industry in the United States and to show how it differs from public policing
- To describe the enormous size and scope of the private security industry today
- To examine traditional problems in the private security industry in terms of licensing, regulating, hiring, and training standards
- To explore the current licensing, regulating, hiring, and training standards in the private security industry
- To explore the recent movement for reform in private security standards

Introduction

As indicated in Chapter 1, the tragic events of 9/11—the terrorist attacks against New York City's World Trade Center and the U.S. Pentagon—brought the issues of safety and security to the forefront of the minds of most people in the United States and the world.

The public and private security industry—those institutions and people who attempt to maintain law and order and enforce the law in the United States—is enormous. We can almost say that it is a growth industry, expanding every year. In the wake of 9/11, this industry is expanding even more.

The U.S. security industry spends an immense amount of money and provides jobs for millions of people. The industry operates on all governmental levels: the local level (villages, towns, counties, and cities), the state level, and the federal level. The public agencies are funded by income taxes, sales taxes, real estate taxes, and other miscellaneous taxes. Additionally, the security industry is served by the private sector, which hires more people and spends more money than all the public agencies combined. Students interested in seeking a career in private security will find a vast number and many different types of jobs from which to choose.

When we speak of crime and physical and personal security, we generally think of the police, those men and women in uniform patrolling our streets and arresting persons who break the law. As we saw in Chapter 1, ever since the development of organized police departments in the nineteenth century, the police have controlled the market in crime prevention and security. The Civil War era began to see the emergence of private forces. By the 1940s and 1950s, the nation saw the growing use of private security firms in corporate and industrial America. Since the 1960s, these private agencies have competed actively with the police for the crime prevention and security needs of the nation. Today, private security forces have taken prominence over public police.

This chapter will introduce and discuss the diverse private security industry in the United States, explain the need for it, and explain how it differs from policing. It will also explore the size and scope of this industry today. Additionally, it will discuss some of the problems encountered in the private security industry regarding licensing, regulating, hiring, and training standards and will discuss the regulations some states have established to control hiring and training in the industry and efforts being made to improve standards. Finally, the chapter will discuss homeland security and the business of the private security industry.

What Is the Private Security Industry?

Consider the following description of a visit to England from the noted weekly business and public affairs magazine, *The Economist:*

> If you fly into Heathrow airport, employees of a private-security firm empowered by law to open your luggage will screen you. If you sail into certain British ports, you may find them guarded by private firms, possibly providing a level of security once described by the International Maritime Bureau as "utterly appalling." Having survived that, if you make your way into London by train, you will be watched over by the British Transport Police, a hybrid body neither public nor private. Only when you emerge onto the streets do you at last enter the jurisdiction of what you think of as the real police.

> Then, when you go into an office or a factory, or if, perhaps you do some shopping in a mall, you will find public order protected not by the police but by employees of a private firm paid for (and responsible to) the shopkeepers or managers. Surprising as it may seem, if your itinerary takes you to, say, a nuclear-power station, or a military garrison, or a government office, these too you will find guarded by private firms. Finally, if you break the law and find yourself in the hands of the occasional ordinary constable, you will discover, as you enter the police station, that the first person you meet at the desk is likely to be not a police officer but a civilian. The station itself will be guarded, likely as not, by a private firm, as are many courts and . . . some prisons.[1]

As you can see from this vivid description, the private security industry today regulates much

JOBS IN SECURITY

Securitas Security Services USA Inc.

MANAGEMENT

Securitas Security Services USA Inc. is one of the largest private security providers in the United States with over six hundred offices. It constantly advertises security jobs on its website. The following are some examples of its management offerings:

Area Vice President
Global Loss Prevention Vice President
Regional Loss Prevention Manager
Director, Audit and Compliance

These management positions require a minimum of a bachelor's degree in criminal justice, business administration, or a related discipline; professional certification as a Certified Protection Professional (CPP) or Certified Fraud Examiner (CFE); strong knowledge, skills, and experience in the industry; fluent language skills (speaking, reading and writing); and numerous other qualifications.

SECURITY OFFICERS

Securitas Security Services USA Inc. constantly advertises security jobs on their website. The following are the responsibilities and necessary education/experience standards required for the Security Officer position.

Responsibilities

■ Assist in protecting personnel and physical property from injury, damage, or destruction, resulting from acts of negligence, carelessness, theft, fire, explosion, sabotage, and related matters.

■ Conduct foot patrols throughout client's leased spaces verifying that pre-designated doors, locks, rooms, property, and areas are secure.

■ Maintain vigilance at entrances to client's areas while enforcing regulations relating to admission of personnel and materials.

■ Provide assistance and direction to employees, guests, and service people visiting or conducting business with the client.

■ Assist and cooperate with authorities under emergency conditions.

■ Respond to calls for assistance in preventing interference or disruption of operations.

■ Make preliminary reports and assist in the investigation of activities as assigned by security management.

■ Monitor the CCTV system for any unusual or suspicious activity in or around the area.

■ Complete special assignments, projects, and/or orders directed by management.

■ Operate security control and access control devices; prevent unapproved or unlawful entry; monitor premises and remote entrances using closed circuit television; and monitor and activate life/safety alarms and systems.

Education/Experience

■ Must be able to meet and continue to meet any applicable state, county, and municipal licensing requirements for security officers

■ High school diploma

■ Some college, military with an honorable discharge, or law enforcement experience preferred

■ Knowledge of security operations and procedures, preferably three to five years experience in the security industry or a related field

■ Computer skills; Casi access control systems, digital video recorders, Microsoft Windows, e-mail, and the ability to learn new systems quickly

■ Ability to communicate effectively both in writing and verbally. Strong report writing skills

■ Good organizational skills

■ Good interpersonal and customer service skills

■ Ability to maintain professional composure when dealing with unusual and stressful circumstances

■ CPR/AED certified

■ Ability to pass a background check

■ Ability to pass physical standards tests that are reasonably related to the essential duties of the job, as well as to the health and safety of the employee and to the health and safety of others

Source: Securitas Security Services USA Inc., *Career Opportunities*. Retrieved October 1, 2004, from http://198.66.210/employment/security/misc.asp.

of life and business in England, just as it does throughout the world. You can also see how varied the industry is. In this section, we will describe the private security industry by using definitions and descriptions of it given by researchers and experts in the field. These descriptions will give you a sense of the diverse nature of the industry and will answer three questions: What is the private security industry? What does it do? How does it do it?

As early as 1974, the National Advisory Commission on Criminal Justice Standards and Goals, in its *Report of the Task Force on Private Security,* defined the industry as follows:

> Those self-employed individuals and privately funded business entities and organizations providing security-related services to specific clientele for a fee, for the individual or entity that retains or employs them, or for themselves, in order to protect their persons, private property, or interests from various hazards.[2]

Robert J. Fischer and Gion Green, authors of *Introduction to Security*, 7th ed., describe security as "a stable, relatively predictable environment in which an individual or group may pursue its ends without disruption or harm, and without fear of disturbance or injury."[3] Author George E. Rush of California State University defines a private security agency as "an independent or proprietary commercial organization whose activities include employee screening, investigations, maintaining the security of persons or property, and/or performing the functions of detection and investigation of crime and criminals and apprehension of offenders."[4] Another pair of authors in 2003 described private security as "the vast industry that provides security to much of corporate America and increasingly, to much of public America."[5]

Perhaps the best way to describe the differences between public and private law enforcement or policing is to say that both are concerned with the prevention of crime and the apprehension of criminals, but police personnel are generally paid by public (tax) funds, whereas private security personnel are generally paid by the private sector, either private corporations or private persons.

There are many ways to categorize or define the major segments of the private security industry. William C. Cunningham and Todd H. Taylor, two of the authors of the *Hallcrest Reports* discussed in Chapter 1, divided the private security

industry into three broad conceptual areas or basic components:

- Physical security: Protecting people and property. Typical activities of physical security include guarding building entrances, preventing shoplifting, patrolling buildings and other premises, and maintaining order.

- Information security: Protecting information. Typical activities of information security include protecting against the unauthorized use of computer programs and preventing the theft of corporate research and development plans.

- Personnel security: Protecting people. Typical activities of personnel security include executive or celebrity protection and background investigations of prospective employees.[6]

ASIS International (recall from Chapter 1 that ASIS International is the leading professional association for private security personnel in the world) has divided the security industry into four major conceptual disciplines that cut across almost all security occupational areas mentioned later in this section:

- Physical security: Physical security focuses on the protection of people, property, and facilities through the use of security forces, security systems, and security procedures. Physical security personnel oversee proprietary or contract uniformed security operations; identify security system requirements; access internal and external threats to assets; and develop policies, plans, procedures, and physical safeguards to counter those threats. Physical security can include the use of barriers, alarms, locks, access control systems, protective lighting, closed-circuit televisions, and other state-of-the-art security technology.

- Information security: Information security involves safeguarding sensitive information, including U.S. government-classified information, privacy data, proprietary information, contractual information, and intellectual property. Information security deals with issues such as who should access the data and how the data is stored, controlled, disseminated, and disposed of.

- Personnel security: Personnel security deals with ensuring the integrity and reliability of an organization's workforce. Personnel security encompasses background investigations, drug testing, and other pre-employment screening techniques, in addition to granting security clearances and other information-access privileges.

- Information systems security: Information systems security involves maintaining the confidentiality, reliability, and availability of data created, stored, processed, and/or transmitted via automated information systems. Information systems security personnel develop procedures and safeguards to protect against hackers and other unauthorized efforts to access data, in addition to protecting against viruses and other threats to information systems.[7]

Another facet of security is operational security, which focuses on the daily operations and patterns of behavior of a corporation or organization. Using the previous model dividing the security industry into four major conceptual disciplines, ASIS International has further divided it into the following major security occupational areas:

- Educational institution security: The primary objective of an educational institution security program is to educate the campus community on the potential for crime, both on and off campus. The central themes of a campus crime prevention program are awareness, self-protection, and prevention. The level of violence on and around educational institutions has brought about a need for security at public and private educational institutions at the elementary and secondary school levels, as well as on college and university campuses. Educational institutions may operate a commissioned police department or contract out this responsibility to a security provider.

- Financial services security: This area deals with banking, stock brokerages, insurance companies, and other financial institutions. This area is regulated by various government agencies. Professionals in this area deal with concerns that can result in losses for their organizations.

- Gaming/wagering security: In this area, security personnel are employed to secure and protect the facilities of the gaming and wagering industry and the customers utilizing these facilities.

- Government industrial security: This area is concerned with the classification, declassification, and protection of national security information in the custody of industry. Government industrial security professionals protect special

categories of classified information, including restricted data, formerly restricted data, intelligence sources, and related data.

- Healthcare security: This area deals with premise and personal protection in hospitals, long-term care facilities, clinics, and nursing homes.

- Information systems security: In this area, security employees engage in administrative and organizational measures designed to ensure the loyalty and reliability of personnel and information. It includes securing hardware, software, and communication networks, as well as the security specialties of computer security, telecommunications security, and Internet security.

- Lodging security: This area is concerned with safeguarding the visitors and possessions of hotels, motels, resorts, and other similar facilities.

- Manufacturing security: In this area, security personnel protect the plants, products, and interests of those participating in this industry.

- Retail security; This area is concerned with preventing the loss of inventory and ensuring the integrity of employees. It is also involved in the investigation of all types of fraud, including credit card and check fraud.

- Security sales, equipment, and services: Persons in this area are involved in the selling, equipping, and servicing of products used to enhance premise and personal security for industry and society.

- Transportation security: This security specialty includes all security efforts in airports, airplane hangers, trucking, and land or sea transportation operations.

- Utilities security: Utility security employees are involved in the protection of personnel, property, equipment, and other corporate resources of public and private utility companies and providers.[8]

Another attempt to classify the private security industry was provided by *Hallcrest II,* which identified nine distinct categories of the private security industry:

- **Proprietary** (in-house) **security:** A particular company has its own security department

---

proprietary security In-house corporate or business security.

| EXHIBIT 2.1 | Private Security Industry Categories |

Major Conceptual Disciplines
Physical security
Information security
Personnel security
Information systems security

Major Security Occupational Areas
Educational institutions
Financial services
Gaming/wagering
Government industrial
Health care
Information systems
Lodging
Manufacturing
Retail
Security sales, equipment, services
Transportation
Utilities

SOURCE: ASIS International, *Professional Development: Security Disciplines*. Retrieved April 18, 2000, from http://www.asisonline.org/careerdisc.html; and *Professional Development: Security Specialty Areas*. Retrieved April 18, 2000, from http://www.asisonline.org/careerspecialty.html.

■ Contract guard and patrol services: **Contract security** services are services leased or rented to another company

■ Alarm services

■ Private investigations

■ Armored car services

■ Manufacturers of security equipment

■ Locksmiths

■ Security consultants and engineers

■ Other—including categories such as guard dogs, drug testing, forensic analysis, and honesty testing[9]

The Economist divides private security into four broad categories:

■ Guarding: This includes armed and unarmed security guards, alarms and electronic surveillance equipment, and executive protection.

contract security External companies hired to provide security.

■ Risk management: This includes firms advising other companies on methods to protect them from crime.

■ Investigation and detection: This involves investigating crimes, employee backgrounds, and the like.

■ Control in the criminal justice system: This includes the criminal justice system employing private security companies to perform such duties as running prisons and guarding courts.[10]

As you can see, no matter which model or category one follows, the duties and responsibilities of the private security industry are numerous and diverse. Exhibit 2.1 provides a list of private security industry categories.

Size and Scope of the Private Security Industry

David H. Bayley and Clifford D. Shearing, in their study, *The New Structure of Policing: Description, Conceptualization and Research Agenda*, reported that policing is being restructured and transformed in the modern world by the development of private protective services as important adjuncts to public law enforcement. They report that a host of nongovernmental agencies have begun to provide security services and, in most countries, private security personnel outnumber police.[11]

It is difficult to estimate the total size and scope of the private security industry and to compare it to the public security industry. As researcher Samuel Walker reports, "The size of the private security industry is difficult to determine because it involves many small, private agencies, part-time employees, and security personnel that are employed by private businesses."[12] In addition, according to *The Economist*, "The most visible and fastest-growing parts of the private security business are in areas that were once the preserve of the public police. Since the functions of private security firms are much wider than those of the public, the equivalent numbers of private security guards and public police are not strictly comparable."[13]

You Are There!

Akal Security

Akal Security, based in New Mexico and owned by the Sikh Dharma nonprofit religious community, was reported in 2004 to be among the fastest-growing security companies in the United States. It has 12,000 employees and over $1 billion in federal contracts protecting vital and sensitive government sites, from military installations to federal courts, from airports to water supply systems.

It is the nation's largest provider of security officers for federal courthouses and judges, with contracts worth $854 million for four hundred buildings in forty-four states. In 2004, it won a $250 million dollar contract to provide security guards at five Army bases, including Fort Lewis, Fort Hood, Fort Riley, Fort Campbell, and Fort Stewart, and three weapons depots in Sunny Point, North Carolina; Blue Grass, Kentucky; and Anniston, Alabama. It also has a $100 million contract to provide protection for 150 federal buildings and offices in Minnesota, Wisconsin, Illinois, and Indiana, as well as the Ronald Reagan Building and the International Trade Center in Washington, DC. It handles security at the Baltimore–Washington International Airport and the major airports in Honolulu and Albuquerque, as well as at four new detention centers run by the Homeland Security Department where foreigners await deportation. It also serves as the provider of security for Los Angeles's city buildings and transportation and protects the municipal water systems in Phoenix and Tucson.

Although the owners of Akal are members of the Sikh religion and must wear turbans and facial hair according to their religion, it hires mostly former police and military officers, almost none of them Sikhs. Akal's contract with the guards prohibits them from wearing turbans or having facial hair.

SOURCE: Leslie Wayne, "Sikh Group Finds Calling in Homeland Security," *New York Times,* September 28, 2004, pp. A-1, C-4.

Researcher and Business Estimates

As we were leaving the twentieth century and moving into the new millennium, it was estimated that the private security industry had three times more employees than the police, with approximately 1.8 million private security personnel and specialists in the United States; private security responds to 50 percent of all crimes committed on private property; there are 60,000 private security firms in the United States, and Americans spend $90 billion a year on private security.[14]

Generally we can say that the size of the U.S. private security industry is enormous, and it has grown exponentially over the past several decades. It is one of the fastest-growing industries in the United States and has tripled the public law enforcement industry in terms of money spent and persons employed. A tremendous number of jobs are available in the industry.

Currently, there is no government, business, or academic clearinghouse that can give us one accurate statistical picture of the private security industry; however, there have been several attempts to do this by certain researchers, businesses, and the United States Department of Labor. Perhaps the following observations and studies by researchers and experts in this area will give you a sense of the breadth and scope of this large business. This section will cover researcher and business estimates over the past two decades, the latest information from the United States Department of Labor's Bureau of Labor Statistics, and a recent study by a major professional association in the security business, the *ASIS International Employment Survey.*

During the last two decades of the twentieth century, most major corporations in the United States had developed private security forces to perform **overt** and **covert** functions. Overtly, they perform visible patrols designed to provide protection and loss prevention. Covertly, private security forces engage in surveillance or countersurveillance regarding trade secrets. The covert functions of private security have been increasing steadily. According to the Society of Competitive Intelligence Professionals, a membership organization for people involved in creating and managing business knowledge, over 80 percent of the Fortune 1000 companies have regular in-house "snoops" on the payroll. Corporate spying has reached

overt Conducted openly.

covert Undercover; secret.

the point where companies everywhere are now concerned with finding and eliminating spies and securing their files and corporate secrets.[15]

The following are some other examples of the size and scope of the private security industry today:

- The installation of security systems in single-family homes has more than doubled in five years.[16]

- In the past few decades, about 25,000 new gated communities (perhaps the modern American version of the medieval moat) have been developed.[17]

- Sixty-seven percent of all new buyers of cellular phones reported that they purchased the phones for safety reasons.[18]

- It is reported that private security agencies service a larger proportion of the central burglar alarm market than do police departments.[19]

Some examples of the increasing use of private security at large scale events follow:

- Thirty thousand private security personnel were employed to protect the 1996 Olympic Games in Atlanta, Georgia. That number translates into three security officers for every athlete that participated in the games.[20]

- During the 2002 Olympic Winter Games in Salt Lake City, Utah, almost $213 million was spent for security arrangements, and more than 40,000 private security personnel were employed.[21]

- For the 2004 Olympic Summer Games in Athens, Greece, the Greek government spent more than $1.2 billion for security and bought a $325 million security package from a California company that is a major provider of security systems for the U.S. military. This system collected and managed the data from the hundreds of surveillance cameras, underwater sensors, vehicle-tracking devices, motion detectors, and other security tools around the many Olympic venues.

- In 2004, as the U.S. military shipped thousands of military police to Iraq for Operation Iraqi Freedom, it needed to replace those who were doing security duty at important military installations around the country, including Fort Bragg, North Carolina; West Point, New York; and over forty other military installations. The 4,100 soldiers who were shipped overseas were replaced by 4,385 private security guards who were contracted from two large private security firms, Wackenhut Services and Vance International, for $194 million.[22]

It is believed that the cost of private security is paid for by corporate America, but it must be noted that the consumer also pays for it. The cost of the private guard standing in front of, or inside the corner jewelry store will necessarily be reflected in the price we pay for a bracelet in that store. The cost of the undercover security agent who tries to apprehend shoplifters in Sears, Kmart, Wal-Mart, or Target is reflected in the cost of everything we purchase in those stores.

Many of the major private security firms, as well as many small ones, have a presence on the Internet. Students are urged to access these sites to find the many jobs and career opportunities in this area. In addition, several professional organizations in this industry have a presence on the Internet.

The dominance of private security over the police affects not only the United States. A 2002 report by the Law Commission of Canada discussed the movement in Canada to rely more and more on private security firms to provide for economic and physical security.[23] The private security industry in South Africa is one of the fastest-growing sectors of its economy. About 6,000 active security firms are registered in South Africa, with about 150,000 active officers, compared to 120,000 police officers employed by the government. In terms of functional crime control, private security officers outnumber the police by two to one. This ratio rises to three to one if in-house private security officers are included.[24] In the United Kingdom, it is estimated that between 300,000 and 500,000 people work in the security business, and that number is set to grow as demand for reliable security increases.[25]

Department of Labor, Bureau of Labor Statistics Study

Every year, the U.S. Department of Labor's Bureau of Labor Statistics publishes its *Occupational Outlook Handbook*. This service contains a wealth of information regarding the major industries and occupations in the United States. For each major occupation, it discusses several categories of

Occupational Outlook Handbook Published yearly by the U.S. Department of Labor's Bureau of Labor Statistics. Contains extensive information regarding the major industries and occupations in the United States, including nature of the work, working conditions, training, job qualifications, advancement, job outlook, earnings, and related occupations.

Profiles of Some Major Private Security Companies

ALLIED-BARTON

Allied-Barton is the largest American-owned security services company in the United States. It has sixty offices, with over 37,000 employees serving over 2,100 companies nationwide. It has forty-eight years of experience and serves more than 100 of the Fortune 500 companies.

BRINK'S COMPANY

Brink's Company is based in Richmond, Virginia, and has almost 50,000 employees. It operates in more than 120 countries and has annual revenues of $4 billion. It has three operating units: Brink's Inc., the world's largest provider of secure transportation and cash management systems; Brink's Home Security, a home security monitoring service for more than 850,000 customers in over two hundred markets in the United States and Canada; and BAX Global, an industry leader in global supply chain management and transportation solutions.

GUARDSMARK

Guardsmark provides security services, including uniformed officers and individualized protection of client assets; investigations, including undercover agents; consulting, such as safety and in-depth security program surveys; background screening; facility design, including technical and physical security

infrastructure; and worldwide executive protection, emergency operations, white-collar crime programs, and computer programs.

SECURITAS

Securitas is one of the world's largest security services companies and is headquartered in Sweden. It has over six hundred offices in the United States under the name Securitas Security Services USA, Inc. In 2003, Securitas merged the offices and functions of the former Pinkerton, Wells Fargo, Burns, American Protective Services, and First Security private security organizations under the Securitas name.

WACKENHUT

Wackenhut Corporation is the U.S.-based division of Group 4-Falck A/S, the world's second-largest provider of security services, based in Copenhagen, Denmark, with activities in more than eighty-five countries. Wackenhut is headquartered in Palm Beach Gardens, Florida, and provides contract services to the business, commercial, and government markets. Its security-related services include uniformed security officers, investigations, background checks, emergency protection, and security audits and assessments. Its services also include facility operations and management, fire suppression prevention, and airport crash–fire–rescue.

information: the nature of the work; working conditions; employment; training, other qualifications, and advancement; job outlook; earnings; related occupations; and sources of additional information. The latest *Occupational Outlook Handbook* contains information on several occupational categories related to the private security industry: security guards and gaming surveillance officers; private detectives and investigators; insurance claim investigators; and security and fire-alarm system installers. It also contains information about all the other law enforcement–type jobs within the criminal justice system, including police officers and detectives, correction officers, court personnel, and the like, that are generally considered part of the public security industry, as opposed to the private industry. (Exhibit 2.2 provides statistics pertaining to private security employment.) The following is a synopsis of the current employment statistics, job outlook, and yearly earnings for the major occupations in the private security industry.

It will give the reader a thorough understanding of the size, scope, and breadth of the industry.[26]

Security Guards and Gaming Surveillance Officers
Security guards and gaming surveillance officers held more than 1 million jobs in the United States. More than half the jobs for security guards were in investigations and security services, including contract security guards and armored car agencies. These agencies provide security services on a contract basis, assigning their guards to buildings and other sites as needed. The other half of the security officers were employed directly by proprietary organizations in the following industries: educational services, hospitals, food services and drinking establishments, traveler accommodations (hotels), department stores, manufacturing firms, owners of real estate (residential and nonresidential buildings), and government. Guard jobs are found throughout the country, most commonly in metropolitan areas.[27]

EXHIBIT 2.2	U.S. Department of Labor Statistics Regarding Private Security Employment, 2006

Category	Number Employed	Projected Employment Growth Rate
Private guards and gaming surveillance officers	1 million	As fast as average
Private detectives and investigators	43,000	Faster than average
Insurance investigators	263,000	As fast as average
Security and fire alarm systems installers	47,000	Faster than average

SOURCE: Bureau of Labor Statistics, U.S. Department of Labor, *Occupational Outlook Handbook, 2006*. Retrieved September 29, 2006, from http://www.bls.gov/oco.

Gaming surveillance officers worked primarily in gambling industries and traveler accommodations, which include casino hotels. Gaming surveillance officers were employed only in those states and Native American reservations where gambling has been legalized.

Industries employing the largest number of security guards were as follows: elementary and secondary schools, general medical and surgical hospitals, local government, traveler accommodation, and investigation and security services.

The Department of Labor reports that opportunities for security guards and gaming surveillance officers should remain favorable in the future. Numerous job openings will stem from employment growth attributable to the desire for increased security and from the need to replace those who leave this large occupation each year. In addition to full-time job opportunities, the limited training requirements and flexible hours attract many persons seeking part-time or second jobs. However, competition is expected for higher-paying positions that require longer periods of training; these positions usually are found at facilities that require a high level of security, such as nuclear power plants and weapons installations.

Employment of security guards and gaming surveillance officers is expected to grow at the average rate for all occupations through 2014 as concerns about crime, vandalism, and terrorism

continue to increase the need for security. Demand for guards also will grow as private security firms increasingly perform duties—such as monitoring crowds at airports and providing security in courts—that were formerly handled by government police officers. Job growth is expected to be concentrated among contract security guard agencies because enlisting the services of a security guard firm is easier and less costly than assuming direct responsibility for hiring, training, and managing a proprietary security guard force. Casinos will continue to hire more surveillance officers as more states legalize gambling and as the number of casinos increases in states where gambling is already legal. Additionally, casino security forces will employ more technically trained personnel as technology becomes increasingly important in thwarting casino cheating and theft.

The average security guard earned a median annual salary of $20,300 for the latest reporting year, and the average gaming surveillance officer and gaming investigator earned a median salary of $25,840.

Private Detectives and Investigators Private detectives and investigators held about 43,000 jobs. About a third of these were self-employed, including many who held a secondary job as a self-employed private detective. Almost a fifth of the jobs were found in investigations and security services, including private detective agencies, while another fifth were in department stores or other general merchandise stores. The rest of the jobs were primarily in state and local government; legal services firms; employment services; insurance carriers; and credit intermediation and related activities, including banks and other depository institutions.[28]

Keen competition is expected for these positions because they attract many qualified people, including relatively young retirees from law enforcement and military careers. Opportunities will be best for entry-level jobs with detective agencies or as store detectives on a part-time basis. Those who seek store detective jobs have the best prospects with large chains and discount stores.

The Department of Labor projects that employment in this field is expected to grow faster than the average for all occupations through 2014. In addition to growth, replacement of those who retire or leave the occupation for other reasons should create many job openings. Increased demand for private detectives and investigations will result from fear of crime, increased litigation, and the need to protect confidential information and property of all kinds. More private investigators also will be needed to assist attorneys working on criminal defense and civil litigation. Furthermore, growing financial activity worldwide will increase the demand for investigations to control internal and external financial losses and to monitor competitors and prevent industrial spying.

The median annual salary for private detectives and investigators was $32,000 for the latest reporting period. Earnings of private detectives and investigators vary greatly depending on their employer, their specialty, the geographic area in which they work, and the position they hold.[29] According to a study by Abbott, Langer & Associates, security/loss prevention directors and vice presidents had a median income of $78,000 per year in 2002; investigators, $40,000; and store detectives, $25,000. In addition to typical benefits, most corporate investigators received profit-sharing plans.[30]

Insurance Claims Investigators These employees are part of the larger Department of Labor's category of claims adjusters, appraisers, examiners, and investigators. Insurance claims investigators generally work for property, auto, and casualty insurance companies and deal with claims where there is a question of liability or when fraud or other criminal activity is suspected. Their main role is to investigate claims, negotiate settlements, and authorize payments to claimants. Generally, when insurance adjusters or examiners suspect fraud, they refer the claim to an investigator. The deceptive acts usually involve fraudulent or criminal activity, such as arson cases, false worker's disability claims, staged accidents, or unnecessary medical treatments. Some of the investigations can involve complicated fraud rings responsible for many claimants supported by dishonest doctors, lawyers, and even insurance personnel.[31]

Investigators generally start with a database search to obtain background information on claimants and witnesses; then they may visit claimants and witnesses to obtain a recorded statement, take photographs, and inspect facilities. Investigators may also perform surveillance work by covertly observing claimants for several days or even weeks and may take video or still photographs. They often consult with legal counsel and can be expert witnesses in court cases.

Insurance investigators, along with adjusters, appraisers, and examiners, held about 263,000 jobs. Many insurance companies require that investigators have a college degree, and many prefer to hire former law enforcement officers, military personnel, private investigators, or experienced claims adjusters or examiners. The Department of Labor reports that this occupation is expected to grow at the average rate for all occupations up to 2014. It reports that competition for these jobs will remain keen because it attracts many qualified people. The average earnings of insurance investigators vary significantly, and the median annual earnings for the latest reporting year were $44,000.

Security and Fire Alarm Installers These employees install, program, maintain, and repair security and fire alarm wiring and equipment and ensure that work is in accordance with relevant codes. This category excludes electricians who do a broad range of electrical wiring. For the latest reporting period, employment was 47,000. Projected employment change is faster than average through 2014. Earnings per employee were not reported.

In addition to the occupations just discussed, the Department of Labor Statistics reports that 16,000 of the nation's 476,000 corrections officers are considered members of the private security industry because they work in privately owned and managed prisons. Additionally, the U.S. Armed Forces has almost 72,000 military personnel assigned to protective service occupations similar to those just discussed.

Exhibit 2.3 provides Department of Labor Statistics findings regarding earnings of private security employees for 2006.

EXHIBIT 2.3 U.S. Department of Labor Statistics Regarding Earnings of Private Security Employees, 2006

Category	Median Annual Earnings
Private guards and gaming surveillance officers	$20,030
Private detectives and investigators	$32,110
Insurance investigators	$44,220
Security and fire alarm systems installers	Not reported

Source: Bureau of Labor Statistics, U.S. Department of Labor, *Occupational Outlook Handbook, 2006*. Retrieved September 29, 2006, from http://www.bls.gov/oco

Professional Association Study: ASIS International Employment Survey

The latest **ASIS International Employment Survey** (2006) questioned managers and professionals in the private security industry about the salaries they paid to in-house (proprietary) and contract security workers (see Exhibit 2.4 for a summary of these findings). Respondents were asked about the wages of security officers, investigators, and console operators. According to the survey, unarmed proprietary security officers earned between $13 and $17 per hour. Armed proprietary officers earned $15 to $21 per hour. Unarmed contract security officers were paid $10 to $14 hourly, and armed contract officers earned $17 to $19 per hour. Proprietary investigators earned between $24 and $31 per hour, and contract investigators earned between $31 and $56 per hour. Console operators, both proprietary and contract, earned between $12 and $15 per hour.[32]

The 2006 ASIS International Employment Survey also reported on the salaries of professional and management employees in the private security industry. These employees tended to be much better paid than lower-ranked employees in the industry. The survey included managers, security chiefs, and professionals in the following industries: security services, government security, manufacturing, retail, banking, financial services, health care, education, entertainment, hospitality, gaming, information technology (IT), utilities and energy, transportation, museums, libraries, and cultural properties. It revealed several items of note:

■ Security managers and professionals earned an average of $90,000 a year.

■ Those with international security responsibilities and those who report directly to the CEO received compensation well above the average.

■ Veterans from the military received greater compensation than those without military experience.

ASIS International Employment Survey Yearly survey of managers and professionals in the private security industry regarding salaries paid to proprietary and contract security employees.

EXHIBIT 2.4   ASIS International Employment Survey, 2006: Hourly Wages for Security Officers, Investigators, and Console Operators

Position	Hourly Wages
Unarmed proprietary security guards	$13–$17
Armed proprietary security guards	$15–$21
Unarmed contract security guards	$10–$14
Armed proprietary security guards	$17–$19
Proprietary investigators	$24–$31
Contract investigators	$31–$56
Console operators	$12–$15

SOURCE: Teresa Anderson, "The Key to Earnings," *Security Management*, January 2004, pp. 43–51

■ Professional development and education affected salaries. Those holding the CPP certification earned 18 percent more than those not certified. Professionals with certifications in IT security and finance were among the most rewarded professionals. Those with a master's degree earned much more than those with only a bachelor's degree.

■ Most security professionals received comprehensive benefits from their employees, including health care, dental insurance, and disability insurance.[33]

Why Do We Have Private Security?

The size of U.S. public law enforcement is enormous. Ensuring the safety of U.S. citizens by providing public law enforcement services is an extremely complex and expensive undertaking. The U.S. approach to law enforcement is unique when compared to the rest of the world. Japan and some western European countries, for example, Denmark, Finland, Greece, and Sweden, have single national police forces.[34] The United States does not have a national police force, although many people think of the Federal Bureau of Investigation (FBI) as one. It is not; it is an investigative agency, not a police agency.

In 2006, the Bureau of Justice Statistics of the U.S. Department of Justice reported that, for the latest reporting year, local, state, and federal agencies spent approximately $185 billion for criminal justice agencies, including police, corrections, and judicial services—an increase of 418 percent from twenty years ago. Local, state, and federal criminal justice agencies employed about 2.4 million people, 58 percent at the local level, 31 percent at the state level, and 11 percent at the federal level. Police protection spending amounted to about $83.1 billion of the total national criminal justice budget, up 240 percent from twenty years ago; and local policing expenditures accounted for about 45 percent of the nation's entire criminal justice budget.[35]

Due to the fact that law enforcement is primarily the responsibility of local governments, 77 percent of the nation's police employees worked at the local municipal level. Fourteen percent of police employees worked for the federal government, while state governments employed the remaining 10 percent.[36]

U.S. law enforcement has developed over the years based on a philosophy of local control, the formal and informal use of local neighborhood forms of control to deter abhorrent behaviors. To understand why, remember that the United States was built on the fear of a large central government, as had existed in England when the colonists came here. The primary responsibility for police protection still falls to local governments (cities, towns, tribes, and counties). Although we have state and federal law enforcement agencies, they are minuscule in size and importance when compared with the law enforcement agencies of local government.

Because of the tremendous number of law enforcement agencies and their employees in the United States and the lack of a unified system for the reporting of police personnel, it is difficult to get a perfect picture of the U.S. law enforcement industry. Every few years the BJS attempts to do this as part of its **Law Enforcement Management and Administrative Statistics (LEMAS) Program**.

For the latest reporting year, state and local governments in the United States operated almost 15,766 full-time law enforcement agencies. These include 12,656 general-purpose local police departments (mostly municipal and county departments), almost 3,061 sheriff's offices, and 49 primary state police departments. There are also approximately 1,400 special district police departments, including park police, transit police, constable offices, and other specialized state and local departments not included in the numbers reported here.[37]

In addition to state and local law enforcement agencies and personnel, the latest statistics regarding employment for federal law enforcement agencies indicate that the federal government employed about 156,600 persons dedicated to police protection.[38]

These publicly funded officers make approximately 14 million arrests a year for violations of local, state, and federal laws and perform a multitude of duties involving crime fighting and order maintenance.[39]

Considering the size and activity of the police, why do we also have an enormous private security industry that is actually triple the size of the police in terms of personnel and money spent? Let us consider some of the many reasons.

Limited Jurisdiction of the Police

Although the police have legal police power and jurisdiction throughout the entire nation, they generally only exercise this power on public streets and thoroughfares and in public places. They generally do not enter private premises unless citizens call them for an emergency or for some other police service.

Police patrol public places and try to create a sense of omnipresence (giving the public a belief that the police are always there or if not there, just around the corner—this is the theory behind routine preventive patrols on streets and in public places).[40] We cannot expect the police to perform their basic patrol throughout all the private places in society. This is beyond the scope of society's desire for the police.

In addition, many of the duties of the private security industry are beyond the legal scope of the public police. For example, the police cannot conduct a background check on a new employee in a private job; the private employer must do this. The police cannot escort every business owner to the bank when he or she has a large amount of money to deposit. These are duties for private security personnel. The police jurisdiction is the welfare of all citizens, not the welfare of just a few citizens.

Furthermore, when we think of private investigators, we realize we need them because police power and jurisdiction are limited. There are areas of criminal and noncriminal activity where

Law Enforcement Management and Administrative Statistics (LEMAS) Program Statistical reports on law enforcement personnel data issued by the National Institute of Justice.

conventional law enforcement is either ill equipped or otherwise prohibited from getting involved. In cases of suspected insurance fraud, for example, most public police agencies have neither the personnel nor the expertise or financial resources to undertake intensive investigations. The search for runaway children is also far too large a problem for public agencies, and the surveillance of unfaithful spouses is beyond the authority and jurisdiction of any public service agency.

Reactive Role of the Police

Generally, the role of the police is reactive. They concentrate on arrests and investigations of past crimes. They also perform general patrol of public places and respond to emergencies. Overall, the role of private security is more proactive than that of the public police. Private security is more concerned with maintaining a sense of security by preventing crime and ensuring a feeling of safety rather than responding to past crimes and invoking the sanctions of the criminal law against offenders.

Private security is different from law enforcement. Law enforcement focuses on reaction to past crime and the enforcement of public laws and ordinances, while security professionals are more proactive and focus on identifying and preventing crimes and problems before they occur. In addition, security personnel are more likely to be involved in protecting assets and carrying out a private organization's policies and procedures than in enforcing criminal statutes.[41]

According to Fischer and Green, public law enforcement functions are society or community oriented, while private security functions are essentially client oriented.[42] In other words, public law enforcement's primary obligation is to society, that is, who pays them. On the other hand, private security's obligation is to the client who has hired them and who pays their salary.

Philosophical Differences between the Police and Private Security

There may be two distinct systems of criminal justice in the United States. One is the formal public system involving the police, courts, and correctional agencies. The other system is a private system where situations are handled without the participation of the formal public system.

As early as 1976, the Task Force on Private Security of the National Advisory Commission on Criminal Justice Standards and Goals observed:

> It would appear that a large percentage of criminal violators known to private security personnel are not referred to the criminal justice system. A logical conclusion would be that there is a "private criminal justice system" where employee reprimands, restrictions, suspensions, demotions, job transfers, or employment terminations take the place of censure by the public system.[43]

In other words, most members of society police themselves through informal means and sanctions and do not utilize the formal system of criminal justice.

Workload and Duties of the Police

The police are too busy responding to emergencies, arresting offenders, and providing all the duties we, as a society, ask them to do. We cannot expect them to provide services to every business or person requiring them.

Because of the heavy workload and duties of the public police, many in the business community believe that the police are not doing the proper job for them. A survey by the United States Chamber of Commerce revealed that half of 446 business executives interviewed believed that law enforcement and the criminal justice system do a poor job of fighting crimes against business.[44]

As we saw in Chapter 1, the creation of the London Metropolitan Police in the nineteenth century was caused by the failure of private security measures to cope with the rising crime rates of that time. Conversely, in the later part of the twentieth century, the emphasis on private police was caused by the failure of the public police to deal with crime. Regarding this, Albanese wrote:

> In an interesting reversal of history, public policing, which arose because of the inefficiencies of private security measures, is now faced with a movement back toward privatization. Private security has been assuming law enforcement tasks because of the inability of public police to adapt quickly to major social or technological changes. These changes have

resulted in new manifestations of crime, spurring private entrepreneurs to offer protective services to those who can afford them. This response has played a significant role in the continuing growth of private security.[45]

Licensing, Regulating, Hiring, and Training Standards in the Private Security Industry

Historically, the private security industry, primarily at the entry and nonmanagerial levels, has suffered from a lack of professional standards. Lately, through the efforts of professional associations, members of academia, and government regulating agencies, we have seen significant improvement in this important area, but much more remains to be done. This section will cover the traditional problems with standards in the private security industry; current licensing, regulating, and hiring standards; training standards; and the recent movement for reform.

Traditional Problems with Standards in the Private Security Industry

Traditionally, there has been a lack of personnel standards for the private security industry and their employees in terms of licensing, regulating, hiring, and training. In 1971, a study by the RAND Corporation found that fewer than half of the private security guards in the United States were high school graduates; they averaged 52 years of age; and most were untrained and poorly paid. Rand provided the following stereotype of the "typical security guard":

> . . . an aging white male who is poorly educated and poorly paid . . . between 40 and 55; he has little education beyond the ninth grade; he has had a few years of experience in private security; he earns a marginal wage . . . some have retired from a low-level civil service or military career. [46]

Researchers such as Samuel Walker and others have reported that requirements for employment for private security guards are minimal and, in many cases, training is nonexistent. They say that private security is often a last resort for people unable to find other jobs.[47] Additionally, police officers generally perceive private security officers to be deficient in professional training.[48] *Hallcrest II* argued that there should be better standards and state regulations regarding private security personnel. It also called for more effective licensing and regulation for the industry, as well as industry-imposed standards, an accreditation program, and more research into the operations of private security.[49]

In 1992, a major national magazine featured an article entitled "Thugs in Uniform," describing some serious problems involving private security employees. Some of the reported incidents, which all occurred within a one-week period, included:

- A 41-year-old security guard, mentally disabled since the Vietnam War, set a fire that caused $25 million worth of damage to Hollywood's Universal Studios. He reported that he had set the fire and then reported it hoping to earn praise from his employer, a major national contract security provider.

- A college security guard murdered his former girlfriend with a shotgun.

- A security guard shot his wife to death following an argument.

- A security guard firebombed an apartment at a housing complex his firm was hired to protect.

- A security guard from a major national security firm masterminded a bank holdup.

- A security guard raped two women and sexually assaulted three more after forcing them into abandoned buildings.

- A former armed guard was found guilty of attempted murder and assault with a firearm in connection with an attempted robbery of an armored car whose route he had once driven.

- A school security guard, with an unlicensed firearm, shot and killed two men loitering in the vicinity of the school.[50]

Even before the tragic events of 9/11, there were numerous reports of extremely poor performance by the privately employed airport screeners who were eventually replaced by the federal TSA after 9/11. In 2000, it was reported that the largest provider of airport security personnel had been

You Are There!

Security Company Lies about Its Background Investigations and Training; Airport Screeners Were Felons

In 2000, it was reported that fourteen screeners, hired in the past few years by Argenbright Security Inc., the largest provider of airport security personnel in the United States, to search carry-on bags at Philadelphia International Airport, had been convicted of felonies, including aggravated assault, robbery, theft, and firearms violations prior to being hired. Argenbright Security pleaded guilty to two felonies and agreed to pay $1.2 million in fines and costs.

Two-dozen screeners hired by Argenbright either never took the written test for their jobs or passed the test because the company falsified their results or provided them with the answers. Instead of the company's required 12-hour training course, managers routinely showed screeners a 45-minute videotape. Six of these screeners lacked high school diplomas, but the managers falsified their records to show they had high school equivalency degrees. In other cases, the company altered potential employee histories to account for undocumented gaps in their work histories that might have indicated unlawful employment or time spent in prison or jail.

One employee had been arrested twenty-three times between 1990 and 1993. Another had eight arrests and three convictions, including drug violations, criminal conspiracy, receiving stolen property, and illegal firearms possession.

At the time, Argenbright had 24,000 airport employees, mostly screeners, and also had skycaps with access to sensitive areas. It had 1,300 employees at the Philadelphia airport alone. At that time, prior to 9/11, airline companies were responsible for security at the airports but generally contracted out the job to companies like Argenbright.

SOURCE: Adapted from "U.S. Charges Impropriety in Security at Airport," *New York Times*, April 18, 2000, p. A-18.

convicted of falsifying the background investigations and training of numerous employees at Philadelphia National Airport.[51]

As of 1987, it was reported that only eleven states required training for armed security guards, and some states only required an application and a licensing fee.[52] A 1990 survey of state regulations regarding security guard licensing and training revealed some improvement, reporting that thirty-nine of the states had imposed some licensing regulations. However, it also revealed that seventeen of the states had no training requirements at all.[53]

The lack of standards was not limited to the United States. In the United Kingdom, experts acknowledge that in the past, a small criminal element opting in and out of the security industry had given it a poor reputation and, despite its large size, the industry has never been properly regulated under the law.[54]

Licensing, Regulating, and Hiring Standards

The U.S. Department of Labor's Bureau of Labor Statistics reports that most states require security guards to be licensed. To be licensed as a guard, individuals must usually be at least 18 years old, pass a criminal background check, and complete classroom training in such subjects as property rights, emergency procedures, and detention of suspected criminals. Drug testing often is required, and security personnel may be randomly tested.[55] Many employers of unarmed guards do not have any specific educational requirements.

For armed guards, employers usually prefer individuals who are high school graduates or who hold a high school equivalency certification. For positions as armed guards, employers often seek people who have had responsible experience in other occupations. Generally, armed guards must be licensed by an appropriate government authority, and some receive further certification as special police officers that allows them to make limited types of arrests on duty. Armed guard positions have more stringent criminal background checks and entry requirements than those of unarmed guards because of greater insurance liability risks associated with carrying a firearm. Compared to unarmed guards, armed guards and special police typically enjoy higher earnings and benefits, greater job security, and more advancement potential, and they usually are given more training and responsibility.[56]

Recently, rigorous hiring and screening programs consisting of background, criminal record, and fingerprint checks are becoming the norm in the occupation. In most states, applicants are expected to have good character references and no serious police records and be in good health. They should be mentally alert, emotionally stable, and physically fit in order to cope with emergencies. Guards who have frequent contact with the public are expected to communicate well. Some states, however, such as Colorado, Idaho, South Dakota, Mississippi, and Missouri, have no state licensing requirements for security guards.[57]

Regarding private detective and investigator jobs, most require no formal education, although many private detectives have college degrees. Private detectives and investigators typically have previous experience in other occupations. Some work initially for insurance or collections companies or in the private security industry. Many investigators enter the field after serving in law enforcement, the military, government auditing and investigative positions, or federal intelligence jobs.[58]

Former law enforcement officers, military investigators, and government agents often become private detectives or investigators as a second career because they are frequently able to retire from their first career after twenty years of service. Others enter from such diverse fields as finance, accounting, commercial credit, investigative reporting, insurance, and law. These individuals often can apply their prior work experience in a related investigative specialty. A few enter the occupation directly after graduation from college, generally with associate or bachelor's degrees in criminal justice or police science.

The majority of the states and the District of Columbia require private detectives and investigators to be licensed. Licensing requirements vary widely, but convicted felons cannot receive a license in most states, and a growing number of states are enacting mandatory training programs for private detectives and investigators. Some states have few requirements, and six states—Alabama, Alaska, Colorado, Idaho, Mississippi, and South Dakota—have no statewide licensing requirements for private detectives and investigators, while others have stringent regulations. For example, the Bureau of Security and Investigative Services of the California Department of Consumer Affairs requires private investigators to be 18 years of age or older; have a combination of education in police science, criminal law, or justice, and experience equaling three years (6,000) hours of investigative experience; pass an evaluation by the DOJ and a criminal history background check; and receive a qualifying score on a two-hour written examination covering laws and regulations. There are additional requirements for a firearms permit.

Training in subjects such as criminal justice is helpful for aspiring private detectives and investigators. Most corporate investigators must have a bachelor's degree, preferably in a business-related field. Some corporate investigators have master's degrees in business administration or law, while others are certified public accountants. Corporate investigators hired by large companies may receive formal training from their employers on business practices, management structure, and various finance-related topics. The screening process for potential employees typically includes a background check or criminal history.

Some investigators receive certification from a professional organization to demonstrate competency in a field. For example, the National Association of Legal Investigators (NALI) confers the Certified Legal Investigator designation to licensed investigators who devote a majority of their practice to negligence or criminal defense investigations. To receive the designation, applicants must satisfy experience, educational, and continuing training requirements and must pass written and oral exams administered by NALI.[59]

In 1992, New York State, in the wake of much negative publicity regarding the murder of two persons by a school security guard using an unlicensed handgun, imposed a strict law regulating the licensing and training of security guards. This law went into effect in 1994 and mandates a state licensing procedure for all security guards, including a fingerprint check and a background investigation. It also requires an eight-hour training course and a passing grade on a one-hour examination for each applicant before he or she can apply for a license. (If the guard is to be issued a firearm, he or she must receive an additional forty-seven hours of training.) Once employed, the guard must be given an additional sixteen hours of instruction by the hiring firm and must receive an additional eight-hour training course during each year of employment. It also established an enforcement unit under the New York State Department of State to regulate the entire process.[60]

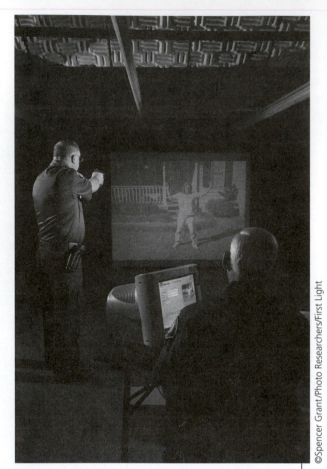

©Spencer Grant/Photo Researchers/First Light

Training requirements are higher for armed guards because their employers are legally responsible for any use of force. This officer is using a laser "gun" for training purposes; when he shoots, the laser registers on the part of the image at which he is aiming. The technology is so sophisticated that the computer-generated scenario changes based on the officer's response to the situation. The results of this lifelike encounter are automatically scored at the end of the session.

Training Standards

The amount of training security guards receive varies. Training requirements are higher for armed guards because their employers are legally responsible for any use of force. Armed guards receive formal training in areas such as weapons retention and laws covering the use of force.[61]

More employers give newly hired guards instruction before they start the job and provide on-the-job training. An increasing number of states are making ongoing training a legal requirement for retention of certification. Guards may receive training in protection, public relations, report writing, crisis deterrence, and first aid, as well as specialized training relevant to their particular assignment.

Guards employed at establishments placing a heavy emphasis on security usually receive extensive formal training. For example, guards at nuclear power plants undergo several months of training before being placed on duty under close supervision. They are taught to use firearms, administer first aid, operate alarm systems and electronic security equipment, and spot and deal with security problems. Guards authorized to carry firearms may be periodically tested in their use of such firearms.

Some large private investigating agencies, such as the Wackenhut Corporation and Securitas, operate their own training schools. The Wackenhut Training Institute in Palm Beach Gardens, Florida, serves as a corporate university offering training services and support to their own employees and other companies, and Wackenhut also conducts training at other sites in the nation, including South Carolina and New Mexico.[62] Securitas Security Services USA, Inc. maintains the Securitas Center for Professional Development, containing libraries with training programs, books, and videos on virtually every security subject. It also creates its own specialized courses for training security teams and professionals. Courses are available as self-study books, instructor-led classes, and online or on CD-ROM as interactive e-learning courses. It offers courses in safety training, emergency response, supervisor and management development, and advanced certification training.[63]

There is substantial controversy regarding standards for private security employee training. Some say that trying to establish uniform and universal training standards for all types of security guards is difficult because various security occupations require certain specific training and not all security guards need the same general training. Some states, such as Arizona, North Carolina, and California, have recognized the differences between various types of security guards and the training required. Many feel that the design of all training courses should begin with an examination of specific job tasks required and then should be developed based on those particular tasks.[64]

For example, the armored car industry experiences about seventy armed robberies a year, which result in an average of five armored car personnel being killed. The risk of violence associated with an armored car robbery is about 54 percent as opposed to just 5 percent for a bank robbery. Due to the high probability of violence, prevention is the major focus of its security efforts. The mission of the armored car transportation industry is limited, and its tasks are specific. It transports cash and valuables to and from establishments such as the Bureau of Engraving, the Federal Reserve, banks and financial institutions, commercial establishments, airports, and ATM machines.[65] According to Mike Gambril of Dunbar Armored Inc.,

> Our goal is to safely and securely deliver our cargo by limiting our exposure. We do this by getting in and out of our customer locations as quickly and efficiently as possible. Therefore, our training is consistent with our tasks. However, because our guards wear uniforms, carry guns and radios, and use other protective security devices, legislators and regulatory authorities often assume that our personnel are security guards with broad law enforcement–type responsibility. This confusion—if it results in unrelated legally mandated training requirements for our industry—can be disastrous.[66]

Gambrill says that, for example, armored car personnel carry guns solely as defensive weapons to protect themselves and the valuables they carry, and the typical armored car guard uses a weapon for self-defense only at distances less than 10 yards. Thus, he argues, laws and regulations requiring armored car personnel to qualify in law enforcement–based firearms training, which typically requires shooting at targets 25 to 50 yards away, does not enhance their abilities; in fact, shooting at these ranges increases the risk of injury to the public at large. Further, he argues that most police-type training includes making arrests and subduing unruly people, and these are tasks that conflict with the armored guard's true responsibilities. Gambrill states, "Any training of armored car personnel that is not focused on the actual work tasks for which they are responsible could result in them being distracted or diverted from their mission."[67]

The concept of minimum training hours is the most basic regulatory standard for training in the United States and Canada and is among the most controversial and contested areas in training standards. **Minimum training hours** mean that employees must undergo at least a certain fixed amount of instructor-based classroom hours of training for skills needed for the job the employee is being hired for. Brian Robertson of the Justice Institute of British Columbia questions the value of minimum training hours in order to be eligible for licensing. Robertson makes the following three arguments regarding reexamining current thinking and developing alternatives to minimum training hours:

1. Regulatory enforcement agencies realistically do not have enough personnel to observe and validate training by all companies engaged in it. Therefore, they cannot meaningfully enforce any control over what happens during those hours of training.

2. Most current theories on adult learning reveal that different learners learn in different ways and at different speeds. Having an instructor teach in a classroom for a fixed number of hours makes no sense in light of this data.

3. The computer-based training concept is the training concept of the future. This type of training does not include instructor-based classroom training for a specific number of hours.[68]

Recent Movement for Reform

Although the professionalization of private security has improved somewhat since the 1970s, a recent report advises that security services need to devote extensive time and resources to hiring the right people, developing them, and striving to ensure they are the right people for the clients' needs.[69] Also, although we have seen significant progress over the past few years in licensing, regulating, hiring, and training standards, a 2004 report indicated that FBI criminal history checks for applicants for security guard licenses in Illinois eliminated four times more applicants than did a state police check. State checks elsewhere are equally deficient.[70]

Despite the rather low licensing, regulating, hiring, and training standards mandated by many states, some security firms, however, have had excellent standards. For example, as a more positive reflection on private security standards, Guardsmark of Memphis, Tennessee, has stringent standards for testing applicants for jobs with their firm. All applicants for jobs as security officers must complete a twenty-four-page application form regarding their personal history, including all prior jobs held, and ten years of residential history. Neighbors and former employers are interviewed. Any thirty-day gaps in the employment background require a notarized explanation. Many

minimum training hours Certain required amount of classroom instruction on skills needed for a job.

applicants are polygraphed, and all are drug screened. Guardsmark claims that only two out of every one hundred applicants survive this process, making it more rigorous than many police departments. Once hired, employees take the Minnesota Multiphasic Personality Inventory (MMPI) assessment. If the results disclose emotional problems, the guard is dismissed.[71]

A professional organization, the **International Association of Security and Investigative Regulators (IASIR)**, attempts to enhance public safety by promoting professionalism in the private security industry through effective regulation. Its membership spans North America and is made up of state and provincial government regulators, private industry and law enforcement officials, and other interested individuals. It meets regularly to discuss such issues as regulatory reform, licensing, reciprocity, and training and education. As an association, it has developed model statutes and training standards and consults with other organizations that have similar interests. It began in 1993 as the National Association of Security and Investigative Regulators (NASIR); however, the organization changed its name in 2001 to the International Association of Security and Investigative Regulators (IASIR) when state licensing regulators met and united for the purpose of sharing information and enhancing their ability to regulate and assist in promoting the professionalism of the private security industry. It monitors national legislation in an effort to ensure the continued growth and professionalism of the private security and private investigative industries. IASIR contends that, from a public policy perspective, in order for standards of security screening and training to be meaningful, there should be a prerequisite of government licensing and that licensure should be a prerequisite to employment. It does not support the employment of a person as a security officer in any form or for any period of time without that person being properly screened and trained.[72]

IASIR's website offers a comprehensive listing of all states' and Canadian provinces' licensing authorities and links to each specific authority's website listing its licensing, regulating, hiring, and training requirements. By clicking on the link to the licensing page of the IASIR website, you reach a map of North America. By clicking on any of the states or provinces, you will link to that state's licensing contact information and links to the jurisdiction's licensing regulations and requirements.

Another professional association, the **Council on Licensure, Enforcement and Regulation (CLEAR)**, is the premier international resource for professional regulation stakeholders. It began in 1980 as a resource for any entity or individual involved in the licensure, nonvoluntary certification, or registration of the hundreds of regulated occupations and professions. It includes representatives of all governmental sectors, the private sector, and many others with an interest in the field of consumer protection. It provides an interactive forum for the exploration of these issues and the collecting and disseminating of relevant information on them. Its venues are professional discipline, credentialing/examination issues, and policy and administration. It holds conferences and training sessions and does not lobby or adopt positions on debatable matters but rather offers neutral ground to those holding diverse viewpoints.[73]

In 2004, ASIS International established a guideline for the selection and training of private security officers, the **Private Security Officer Selection and Training Guideline** (see Exhibit 2.5). This guideline calls for the establishment of national criteria for the selecting and training of all private security employees, including those in proprietary and contract companies.[74]

Licensing, regulation, hiring, and training standards are also an important issue in the United Kingdom. In 2001, in order to improve the security industry's image so that the general public—and the wider business world—has a much clearer understanding of how the industry is regulated and who is entitled to work in it, the United Kingdom passed the **Private Security Act of 2001**, which established the **Security Industry Authority (SIA)**.

International Association of Security and Investigative Regulators (IASIR) Professional organization involved in security industry regulatory reform, licensing, training, and education.

Council on Licensure, Enforcement and Regulation (CLEAR) Professional organization involved in licensing and regulatory reform in the private security industry.

Private Security Officer Selection and Training Guideline ASIS International suggested criteria for improving selection of and training for security officers.

Private Security Act of 2001 Legislation passed in the United Kingdom to professionalize the private security industry.

Security Industry Authority (SIA) Government agency in the United Kingdom that regulates the private security industry.

| **EXHIBIT 2.5** | **ASIS International Private Security Officer Selection and Training Guidelines** |

STATE REGULATION OF PRIVATE SECURITY

- Establish a regulatory body, operating under the direction and within the framework of a state agency.
- Establish fees commensurate with the effort necessary to process applications for registration/licensure/renewal to be used by the regulating body to manage the department and enforce the regulations. Enforcement should include inspection, administrative fines for violation of the state statute, and the implementation of regulations, sanctions, and criminal violations in certain instances.
- Require licenses for licensees/agencies/in-charge/qualifying agents (e.g., education, experience, written exam).
- Establish minimum requirements for agency/licensee-in-charge liability insurance (e.g., minimum of $1,000,000 per occurrence).
- Require regulating bodies to issue private security officer registration/licenses, which should include a photograph and other relevant identification information.
- Require registration/licensure of all private security officers.
- Require all candidates to pass a background investigation before assignment as a security officer.
- Require private security officer training (e.g., orientation/pre-assignment; on-the-job; ongoing/refresher/annual courses).
- Establish additional training requirements for armed security officer training (e.g., classroom, range safety, course-of-fire, re-certification policy, instructor qualifications, etc.).

SELECTION: EMPLOYMENT SCREENING CRITERIA

- At least 18 years of age for unarmed; and 21 years of age for armed, with provisions that the candidate must be able to perform the duties required of the position.
- Must be a citizen or national of the United States, a lawful permanent resident, or an alien authorized to work.
- Candidate must submit current and previous addresses and phone numbers for the last seven years.
- Verify applicant's name, address history, criminal record checks, and social security number.
- Must possess high school diploma or GED or equivalent. Also, the applicant should demonstrate an ability to read, write, and speak English and the language/s most appropriate to his or her assigned duties. Additionally, consideration may be given to the administration of a validated aptitude test for security officer applicants.

- Must not have been convicted of or pled guilty or *nole contendere* to a felony or job-related crime immediately preceding a minimum seven-year period. Any felony conviction discovered in the course of conducting the search should also be considered relevant to the candidate's qualifications for the position. Armed security candidates must not have been convicted of a state or federal misdemeanor involving the use or attempted use of physical force, or the threatened use of a deadly weapon.
- Verify candidate's current and previous employers' addresses and phone numbers for at least the last seven years.
- Verify the candidate-provided license, registration, credential, or certification information against the appropriate agency. Compare given information with that given by the agency. Note any negative license actions or sanctions.
- Must submit fingerprint card or electronic fingerprint for criminal record check.
- Pre-employment—Undergo a drug screen test.
- Post-employment—random drug testing, where permitted by state law and employer policy. It should be conducted by using a valid random testing methodology.
- Submit two current photos for identification and licensing.

TRAINING CRITERIA

- Forty-eight hours of training not to exceed the first one hundred days of employment.
- Pass a written and/or performance examination to demonstrate knowledge of subject matter and qualification to perform basic duties of a private security officer. Training should include the following core training topics.

Training Topics

- Nature and role of private security officers
- Security awareness of private security officers and the criminal justice system, information sharing, crime and loss prevention
- Legal aspects of private security, including evidence and evidence handling; use of force and force continuum; court testimony; incident scene preservation; equal employment opportunity (EEO) and diversity; state and local laws
- Security officer conduct, including ethics, honesty, professional image
- Observation and incident reporting, including observation techniques, note taking, report writing; patrol techniques

- Principles of communication, including interpersonal skills, verbal communication skills, customer service, and public relations
- Principles of access control, including ingress and egress control procedures and electronic security systems
- Principles of safeguarding information, including proprietary and confidential
- Emergency response procedures, including critical incident response and evacuation processes
- Life safety awareness, including safety hazards in the workplace/surroundings, emergency equipment placement, fire preventions skills, hazardous materials, and occupational safety and health requirements
- Job assignment and post orders

Additional Training Topics Depending on the Assignment, Including:

- Employer orientation and policies, including substance abuse and communication modes
- Workplace violence
- Conflict resolution awareness
- Traffic control and parking lot safety
- Crowd control
- First aid, CPR, and AEDs
- Crisis management
- Labor relations

Annual training: This training may consist of on-the-job training, classroom training, computer-based training, or other forms of electronic medium–based training. The type of training should be determined by such factors as the type of facility where the security officer is assigned; the duties of the security officer; the value of the assets being protected; and the level of security risks, threats, vulnerabilities, and criticality of the assignment.

Pre-assignment firearms training: Minimum range and classroom course, taught and administered by a state certified firearms instructor or approved current law enforcement or military firearms certified instructor. Applicants should be required to provide any prior information regarding the suspension or revocation of any firearms certification or license they may have held.

Post-assignment firearms training: Security officers and security agencies should notify the appropriate regulatory body of any discharge of a firearm in the course of the officer's duties. The incident report should contain an explanation describing the nature of the incident, the necessity for using the firearms, and a copy of any report prepared by a law enforcement office. Additional firearms training may be required by the state agency.

Annual firearms training: Follow state-mandated annual firearms training.

Source: ASIS International, *Private Security Officer Selection and Training Guidelines*. Retrieved September 29, 2006, from http://www.asisonline.org/guidelines/guidelines.htm.

Its functions are to license individuals in specific security sectors and to approve security companies; to continue to review the private security industry and monitor and conduct inspections of those in the industry; to set and approve standards of conduct, training, and supervision; and to make recommendations to improve the standards. The SIA works under the auspices of the U.K. Secretary of State. It is the only authority in England and Wales dealing with these private security issues and reports directly to the Secretary of State. It works in partnership with the industry and its customers, the police service, and the public. The following private security sectors are controlled under the SIA: security guarding, door supervisors, vehicle immobilizing, private investigations, security consultants, and key-holders.[75]

Homeland Security and the Business of the Private Security Industry

The status and size of the private security industry has increased exponentially since the terrorist attacks of 9/11. Private security employees perform the majority of the homeland security jobs in our nation, and the private security industry is responsible for the vast majority of the protection provided to our nation's people, businesses, and critical infrastructure. A significant percentage of the billions of dollars in taxpayer monies spent by the federal Department of Homeland Security and local, state, and federal agencies to ensure homeland security goes to the private security industry. As we have seen in this chapter, the role of the police is primarily reactive. They concentrate on arrests and investigations of past crimes and responding to emergencies. The role of private security is more proactive than that of the police. Private security is more concerned with maintaining a sense of security by preventing crime and other incidents and ensuring a feeling of safety rather than responding to past crimes and invoking the sanctions of the criminal law against offenders. Security professionals focus on identifying and preventing crimes and problems before they occur. Prevention of incidents is critical to the mission of homeland security.

Private security personnel are defending power plants, oil refineries, financial centers, computer systems, dams, malls, railroad lines and other prospective terrorism targets. According to a former deputy director of the FBI, "The great majority of critical infrastructure in the United States is not protected by sworn officers. You name any industry and you're going to find private security is protecting it."[76]

According to a senior manager at Columbia University's National Center for Disaster Preparedness,

security firms today are consolidating, specializing, and becoming more professional, and their employees are better screened and equipped to combat homeland security attacks. The demand for increased homeland security has spawned increased efforts to improved standards and training for private security employees. As some examples: Phoenix-based AT Systems Security Inc. formed an aviation branch with guards who get extra training in skyjacking tactics, the terrorist mentality, airport design, aviation law, and incident response. Also, the Arizona Counter-Terrorism Intelligence Center created a training and information-sharing program for about 19,000 security officers who are employed by 201 private security companies in the state.[77]

Many of the improvements in the professionalization of private security have come about due to its increased importance in homeland security, and much of the improvement in our nation's homeland security preparedness since 9/11 is due to the efforts of the private security industry. Lately, through the efforts of professional associations, members of academia, and government regulating agencies, we have seen significant improvement in this important area.

Summary

- The major difference between private security and the police is that the police are generally paid by public (tax) funds, whereas private security personnel are generally paid by the private sector, either private corporations or private persons.

- We need private security to augment the police because the police have limited jurisdiction, are generally reactive as opposed to proactive, and have a tremendous and diverse workload.

- Private security has three times more employees than the police and outspends the police. Private security reports to 50 percent of all crimes committed on private property.

- The major security disciplines are physical security, information security, personnel security, and information systems security. The major security occupational areas are educational institutions, financing services, gaming or wagering, government, industrial, healthcare, information systems, lodging, manufacturing,

retail, security sales/equipment/services, transportation, utilities, and homeland security.

- The *Hallcrest Reports* identified the following categories of private security: proprietary (in-house) security; contract guard and patrol services (leased or rented); alarm services; private investigations; armored car services; manufacturers of security equipment; locksmiths; security consultants and engineers; and others, such as guard dogs, drug testing, forensic analysis, and honesty testing.

- Private security performs overt (uniform) and covert (undercover) functions.

- The U.S. Department of Labor reports that the private security industry employs well over a million security guards and gaming officers; private detectives and investigators; insurance claims investigators; security and fire alarm installers; and executives, managers, and supervisors, and these jobs are increasing daily.

▪ Private security salaries range from $10 an hour to $100,000 a year depending on job function, job title, specific industry, experience, and education.

▪ There have been numerous problems in terms of licensing, regulating, hiring, and training standards for private security employees. However, many states have made tremendous progress in establishing these standards, although there are still no mandatory federal standards.

Learning Check

1. Define the private security industry.

2. Identify and explain three reasons why we have a private security industry in addition to police in our society.

3. Discuss the size and scope of the private security industry in the United States.

4. Give some recent examples of the growth of the private security industry in the United States.

5. Discuss some of the traditional problems in the security industry in terms of licensing, regulating, hiring, and training standards.

6. Discuss the findings of the United States Department of Labor's Bureau of Labor Statistics regarding the employment of security guards and gaming surveillance officers.

7. Discuss the findings of the United States Department of Labor's Bureau of Labor Statistics regarding the employment of private detectives and investigators.

8. Describe the typical hiring standards and training for private security guards.

9. Describe the typical hiring standards and training for private detectives and investigators.

10. Discuss the roles of professional organizations, such as the International Association of Security and Investigative Regulators (IASIR) and others, in improving standards in the private security industry.

Application Exercise

Research the private security licensing agency for your state. Prepare a five- to six-page report discussing it.

Web Exercise

Access the website for the U.S. Department of Labor's Bureau of Labor Statistics, then access the latest edition of its *Occupational Outlook Handbook*. Obtain the latest "job outlook" for private security officers and for police officers. Compare and contrast this information.

Key Terms

ASIS International Employment Survey, p. 44

contract security, p. 38

Council on Licensure, Enforcement and Regulation (CLEAR), p. 52

covert, p. 39

International Association of Security and Investigative Regulators (IASIR), p. 52

Law Enforcement Management and Administrative Statistics (LEMAS) Program, p. 45

minimum training hours, p. 51

Occupational Outlook Handbook, p. 40

overt, p. 39

Private Security Act of 2001 (UK), p. 52

Private Security Officer Selection and Training Guidelines, p. 52

proprietary security, p. 37

Security Industry Authority (SIA) (UK), p. 52

3

Private Security Concepts, Tools, and Systems Integration

©ER Productions/Brand X/Corbis

GOALS

- To introduce you to the major concepts the private security industry uses to organize and run its operations
- To acquaint you with the tools used by the private security industry to achieve its mission
- To introduce you to the latest uses of technology in the security industry
- To evaluate the effectiveness of the various concepts and tools of the private security industry
- To alert you to the importance of systems integration or convergence in private security

Introduction

Security is certainly a major concern of citizens around the world. In 2005, in Misakicho, Osaka Prefecture, in Japan, one of the main selling points for a new planned community overlooking Osaka Bay is its security system:

> Security guards stationed on the premises patrol the housing complex around the clock and accompany children on their way to school to protect them from abduction or attack. There are three body-heat sensors located around each home. If there is a break-in, an alarm sounds and the security guards arrive in about three minutes. Three cameras keep a watchful eye on the community's park and surrounding areas. All the cameras can be accessed by the personal computers included as standard in each home, allowing anyone to check what is happening outside.[1]

Chapter 1 of this text covered the history and professionalization of private security, and Chapter 2 covered the business of the private security industry. This chapter will discuss private security operations— how the security industry does what it does. It will cover the major concepts the private security industry uses to organize and run its operations, including risk management, risk analysis or risk assessment, the security survey, proprietary and contract security, overt and covert security, the command or control center and crisis management teams. It will also discuss the tools used by the industry to achieve its mission, including security guards, canine security, access control systems, alarm systems, and electronic video surveillance, and will discuss the latest technology in electronic access control systems, biometric identification, facial recognition systems, and "smart cards." It also discusses the growing use and importance of systems integration or convergence in private security and the latest homeland security efforts in private security concepts, tools, and systems integration due to the 9/11 terrorist attacks against the United States. This chapter will cover the most important introductory material on these subjects, and more detailed information regarding each topic will be covered in subsequent chapters.

Private Security Concepts

Several essential concepts underlie the private security industry. Among the most important of these are risk management, risk analysis or risk assessment, the security survey, proprietary and contract security, overt and covert security, the command or control center, and crisis management teams.

Risk Management

Rae Archibald, retired vice president of the RAND Thinktank for Public Policy Issues, has stated:

> There is little that a building owner or local government can do to shield high-rise buildings from the kind of catastrophic attacks that occurred on September 11, 2001. Mitigating the effects of an attack, therefore, is of paramount concern. Much can be done in this regard.[2]

Archibald is discussing the concept of risk management. Criminal events and natural disasters are often impossible to predict or to prevent. Even the best security systems, operations, personnel, and planning cannot foresee or prevent these tragic events from occurring. However, businesses and organizations must do their very best to prevent them from occurring, if possible, and deal with them if they occur. Risk management is essential in private security operations.

We have learned a great deal from the tragic events of 9/11. The events that day killed nearly 3,000 persons and caused the loss of billions of dollars worth of capital investment. The government and private industry, through their unprecedented actions, have embarked on a continuous program of risk management and established numerous programs and safeguards to prevent a recurrence of these events and to be prepared to deal with them and mitigate their effects should they occur again.

To further emphasize the importance of risk management, many businesses were severely impacted as a result of 9/11, and some have ceased to exist; however, many businesses were able to continue their operations because they were prepared. They were able to resume their operations because they had engaged in a continuous process of risk management and had backup systems and data in locations not affected by the disaster.

In security operations, **risk management** is the process of balancing the cost of security with the overall corporate goal of producing goods, services, and profits. The essential tools of risk management are risk analysis or risk assessment and the security survey. Once the risk analysis and security survey are completed, management must make decisions on what security measures to use. These decisions are generally based on a careful cost-benefit analysis to ensure that they are economically sound and support the organization's bottom line.

Risk management can also be defined as the "process involved in the anticipation, recognition, and appraisal of a risk and the initiation of action to eliminate the risk entirely or reduce the treat of harm to an acceptable level."[3]

A good risk management program involves four basic steps: identification of risks or specific vulnerabilities; analysis and study of these risks, which includes the likelihood and degree of danger in an event; optimization of risk-management alternatives; and the ongoing study of security programs.[4] Risk management is a continual process. A company does not go through this process just once but rather constantly repeats it, using additional risk analyses and security surveys to study and improve their security and operations and to meet any new problems.

George E. Curtis and R. Bruce Mc Bride define risk management as a comprehensive review of assets that could be damaged, stolen, or lost; presenting countermeasures to reduce such losses; and predicting long-term consequences.[5] They suggest the following questions that can be posed in a risk assessment:

- What are our assets? Assets can be defined as people, equipment, property, business information, and professional reputation.
- How are these assets vulnerable? How can our assets be destroyed, damaged, or altered?
- What are the threats to the assets? Risk managers create scenarios and ask what would happen and what the likelihood is that each might

occur. They use national and international crime and emergency event trends and industry trends to create these likelihoods.

- What is the probability that these scenarios will occur? Risk managers determine this probability based on empirical data and hunches and include local and national data and comparisons with similar institutions.
- What is our liability if such events occur? Risk managers include legal and fiscal liability in this analysis, including criminal and civil actions and insurance rates.
- What do we do to get back to business or restore services if an event occurs? Risk managers include replacement costs, downtime, borrowing cash on a temporary basis, and having backup sites in which to resume business.
- What is the effect on our business and leadership reputation? Risk management considers the effects of what would happen if the business is not able to recover after an incident, including complete business failure, bankruptcy, layoffs, leadership turnover, and other possibilities.[6]

Curtis and McBride report that once major risks have been identified, security professionals must rank each risk in terms of the probability that it could occur and identify countermeasures to deal with them. Then, they identify the costs for personnel, implementing the operational change, buying a piece of equipment, training personnel, or taking no action at all.

Risk Analysis (or Risk Assessment) The major tool in the risk management process is **risk analysis (or risk assessment),** which is the process of identifying potential areas of security problems and loss, and the development and

---

risk management The process used to weigh the costs inherent in protecting a business or corporation from possible crime and natural disasters in light of the benefits received; involves the process of risk analysis or risk assessment.

risk analysis (or risk assessment) The process of identifying potential areas of security problems and loss and the development and implementation of effective measures or countermeasures to deal with these problems.

JOBS IN SECURITY

Wackenhut Security Positions

Wackenhut is one of the nation's largest employers of security personnel. It has three levels of security protection positions:

■ Custom Protection Officers (CPOs): Wackenhut's Custom Protection Officer Division was established in 1989 and seeks out and recruits men and women with criminal justice degrees or background and experience in law enforcement and/or elite military units. They are subjected to a rigorous background check prior to employment and given training that goes well beyond industry standards. They provide many professional services for their employers. Compensation for CPOs exceeds that for other security protection positions.

■ Property Resource Officers: Wackenhut's Property Resource Officers protect commercial office buildings, and provide tenant customer service, access control, and alarm monitoring and response.

■ Security Officers: Wackenhut's Security Officers are trained in a wide range of general subjects, as well as the site-specific security requirements of each assignment, and are assigned to numerous security duties.

OBTAINING JOBS AT WACKENHUT

Wackenhut has job openings for security positions throughout the nation. In order to obtain information about their positions, one can access their website and review job postings for current opportunities by the state in which he or she is interested and then submit a resume to Wackenhut listing the specific position or job title. The applicant should also indicate geographical preference.

As a recent example, its website included the following job postings for particular locations in California, including San Francisco, Sacramento, Concord, Richmond, San Fernando Valley, Madera, Riverside County, San Ramon, and Santa Clara. (Note: One can search for positions in any state in the United States or overseas.) These postings included the following positions: security officer armed, security officer, custom protection officer, sales representative,

area manager, branch manager, flex officer, project manager, receptionist, and control room operator. The following are the responsibilities, requirements, and compensation and benefits for three of these positions:

Security Officer Armed

Job responsibilities—Provide a high-profile image at various client locations

Job requirements—High school diploma; pass a comprehensive background check and drug test; clean DMV report; and current California guard card and gun card

Compensation/benefits—$14 an hour and comprehensive benefits package

Custom Protection Officer Armed

Job responsibilities—Provide high-profile physical security

Job requirements—Former police officer, police academy trained, former military police, former elite military forces, former federal agency officer, former correctional officer, former military career, criminal justice degree

Compensation/benefits—$12 per hour, including comprehensive benefits package

Control Room Operators

Job responsibilities—High level of customer service and telecommunications activity; use of multiple-line phone system, computer system; visitor employee access/egress control

Job requirements—High school diploma; pass pre-employment background investigation to include a clean criminal and driving history and drug-screening

Compensation/benefits—$13 an hour with comprehensive benefits package and opportunities for advancement

SOURCES: Wackenhut Corporation, "Wackenhut Recruitment Center." Retrieved October 11, 2005, from http://www.wackenhut.com/object. php?obj=3c000c; and Wackenhut Corporation, "California Job Postings, Updated: 09/15/05." Retrieved October 11, 2005, from http://www.wackenhut.com/e00029.

implementation of effective measures or countermeasures to deal with these problems. These problems may involve the loss of goods, services, information, or other assets of a business; potential of injury, harm, or emergency; and other similar problems.

According to Clifford E. Simonsen, an effective risk assessment involves the following four elements:

■ Risk: What are the assets that can be subject to risks?

■ Vulnerability: How difficult is it to get to the high-risk assets?

■ Probability: What are the chances that such a risk may occur?

■ Countermeasures: What can security do, given the resources available?[7]

Simonsen says that risk analysis allows management to design countermeasures that are effective but do not interfere with the operations of the business. The risk analysis allows management to make decisions that balance the cost versus the level of protection desired.

Pinkerton Consulting and Investigations offers its risk assessment services to corporations without the ability to prepare their own. It provides its clients with a written report identifying the threats and vulnerabilities, review of security policies and procedures, reinforcement of existing protocols, recommendation of security measures, and implementation of definitive solutions. Pinkerton's assessment team works with these companies to establish performance measurements, standards, and tracking and reporting methods. Their assessment also provides budget estimates for recommended actions.[8]

A recent example of the risk assessment process involved work done by the RAND Corporation in 2005 to assess the risk of chemical terrorism in Los Angeles. Its report discusses how emergency responders should plan for such an event and considers low-cost options in equipment, training, organization, and doctrine that could improve the response to a chemical terrorist event.[9]

Despite the importance of risk management, it is important to note, however, that often managers cannot always make decisions based solely on a cost-benefit analysis. A good example of this is the emergence of school shootings in the 1990s. The possibility of these school shootings occurring was seen as so serious that school districts across the country began installing metal detectors and electronic video systems and employing security guards despite their lack of cost effectiveness. Some problems and issues in life are so important that one cannot put a price on them.

The Security Survey The **security survey** is a comprehensive physical examination of a premise and a thorough inspection of all security systems and procedures. It is an effective tool for helping corporate security professionals reduce crime at their facilities. The survey can point out vulnerabilities and provide security managers with ideas for reducing the company's risks.[10]

Robert J. Fischer and Gion Green write that the object of the security survey is the analysis of a facility to determine the existing state of security, to locate weaknesses in its defenses, to determine the degree of protection needed, and to lead to recommendations for establishing a total security program.[11]

The security survey can be conducted by an in-house security department or contracted out to a security consulting firm. The security survey includes not only a physical inspection of the facilities but also the examination of all police and internal reports and the interview of all personnel familiar with any aspects of the organization.

Specific preformatted forms can be used to conduct the physical assessment of the survey. A comprehensive report is then prepared to assist company managers in making their decisions. Most surveys include employee interviews, examination of crime statistics, and physical assessment. Exhibit 3.1 reviews the areas covered in a security survey.

Proprietary and Contract Security

Proprietary security services are in-house services performed by people employed directly by the organization for which they provide these services. Many of the Fortune 1000 corporations have their own proprietary security departments that

---

security survey A comprehensive physical examination of a premise and a thorough inspection of all security systems and procedures.

proprietary security In-house corporate or business security.

You Are There!

Four Examples of Risk Analysis

The following are some examples of considerations that must be made when conducting a risk analysis for four types of facilities.

PARKING GARAGES

When considering a risk analysis at parking facilities underneath buildings and the opportunities they present for terrorists, such as the 1993 explosion at New York City's World Trade Center where a terrorist bomb exploded when the bomb was brought into the building in a vehicle, security personnel must conduct a risk assessment that considers the following:

■ Threats to persons, such as assault, robbery, or carjacking

■ Threats to vehicles, such as vehicle theft or vandalism

■ Threats to personal property in the vehicles, such as packages

■ Threats to the parking structure from, for example, a terrorist act

Once a security survey and threat assessment have been completed, security should consider a multi-pronged approach to protection, including architecture, lighting, fencing, call stations, panic devices, electronic video surveillance, access control, patrols, and awareness training.

Architecture must be considered in the design of a new facility. An emphasis should be put on clear lines of sight throughout the facility to encourage witness potential. Blind spots (hiding places for criminals) should be eliminated, and open or glassed-in stairwells and glass-enclosed elevators should be used. The roofs of underground or multilevel garages should be high enough to allow electronic video surveillance to function effectively. Underground garages should be constructed with bomb resistance in mind.

BANKS

Banks make extensive use of risk analysis to prevent robberies. By studying past robberies and using statistical analysis, bank security departments identify trends and potential problem areas in need of improvement. In addition to gathering historical information on past robberies, security managers conduct risk assessments at each branch by using the statistical

data and information from bank robbery studies to create a branch risk assessment form to survey and rate the bank's facilities. Security develops a scoring system and rating factor process that allows it to assign a risk assessment score to each facility. This information is then used to determine how to reduce the rating to an acceptable level, such as implementation of additional equipment, increased training, and procedural controls. Security continually monitors robbery statistics with local law enforcement, the FBI, and other banks.

CONVENIENCE STORES

Convenience stores have historically used risk analysis to improve their safety and the safety of their companies. The Southland Corporation of Dallas has 2,100 company-owned and 2,900 franchised 7-Eleven stores. Their security operations are based on several studies conducted since the mid-1970s by Southland, the Western Behavioral Sciences Institute, the National Institute of Justice, the National Association of Convenience Stores, and the Athena Research Corporation. Using these studies, the company gained insight into how robbers think and what deters them from committing crime. The company then developed a crime deterrence program centered on three components: cash control, visibility, and training. The company has also found that using electronic video surveillance and alarms, minimizing the number of escape routes, and building a strong relationship with local police can help reduce crime at its stores.

PURCHASING AN ARMORED VEHICLE FOR EXECUTIVE PROTECTION

Threat assessment is also used in purchasing an armored vehicle. This involves three assessments: the threat, the technology, and the manufacturers. A threat assessment will determine what kind of attackers might pursue the individual in the armored car and what types of weapons they are likely to use. Technology assessment involves considering what type of armor is required (for example, transparent, fibrous, alloy, ceramic, compost); how heavily the vehicle should be armored; and what other protective equipment is needed, such as air scrubbers, self-sealing nonexplosive fuel tanks, remote starters with bomb scans, ram bumpers, deadbolt locks, fire-suppression systems, and special tires. When evaluating vehicle manufacturers, perhaps the most important question is whether the company's vehicles and armoring systems have been independently tested to validate quality and integrity. Also, it must be determined whether they can provide timely worldwide service.

Sources: Dan M. Bowers, "Assigning a Place for Parking Security," *Security Management*, December 1999, pp. 63–67; Terry Mann, "Policies That Pay Off: Although Robberies Are Down, They Are Becoming More Costly and Violent," *Security Management*, February 2000, pp. 42–46; Scott Lins and Rosemary J. Erickson, "Stores Learn to Inconvenience Robbers: 7-Eleven Shares Many of Its Robbery Deterrence Strategies," *Security Management*, November 1998, pp. 49–53; and D. M. Zima, "This Is Not Your Father's Oldsmobile," *Security Management*, April 1997, pp. 47–50.

EXHIBIT 3.1   **Areas Covered in a Security Survey**

A security survey is an exhaustive physical examination of a business or premise and a thorough inspection of all operational systems and procedures. Its object is the analysis of a facility to determine the existing state of security, to locate weaknesses in its defenses, and to determine the degree of protection needed in order to make recommendations for establishing a total security program.

The following describe the areas that must be considered in a security survey:

- **The facility:** Includes the perimeter, the parking lot, all adjacent building windows and rooftops, all doors and windows, the roof, the issuance of entrance keys to all tenants, shared occupancy, areas containing valuables, off hours and nighttime hours, control and supervision of entry, keys and key control, fire risks, computer access, electronic video surveillance, and computer systems.
- **General departmental evaluation:** Includes cash, negotiable instruments, confidential documents on hand, equipment, tools, supplies, merchandise, external or internal traffic, and target items such as drugs, jewelry, or furs. Also includes special fire hazards.
- **Human resources department:** Security of personnel files is extremely important, and all files are confidential. Includes the security of personnel files, including access to the offices and computer systems and background checks on employees.

- **Fiscal departments, including accounting, cashier, accounts receivable, accounts payable, payroll, purchasing, and company bank accounts:** Includes fiscal accountability and security of all money and financial records; controls on cashier embezzlement and collusion with other employees; background checks on employees; controls on cash on hand; audit and control systems; personal protection; holdup alarms; holdup procedures and instructions; theft; and integrity of billing records, invoices, and computer records.
- **Data processing:** Includes auditing procedures, confidentiality of information, off-site storage procedures, program access, monitoring of computer use, access control, offsite backup hardware, and audits of downloads to laptop computers.
- **Shipping and receiving:** Includes inspections of employees entering or leaving area, access control, security of storage areas, and collusion between truck drivers and employees.

Source: Robert J. Fischer and Gion Green, *Introduction to Security*, 7th ed., Boston: Elsevier/Butterworth-Heinemann, 2004, pp. 131–138.

---

provide security services and investigations. Proprietary security personnel are regular employees of the firm and are paid by the firm.

Agencies and private practitioners for a fee provide **contract security** services. For example, a public shopping mall may contract out all security services to a guard service or private security company, such as Securitas or Wackenhut. These contract security services lease or rent their services to the mall, which pays them for these services. The guards and other

security personnel are paid by the contract agency. States and other localities often require contract personnel to be licensed and bonded.

The U.S. Department of Labor's Bureau of Labor Statistics reports that half of the over 1 million security guards in the United States are employed

contract security External companies hired to provide security.

by industrial security firms and guard agencies (contract security). The others are employed by the organization they are responsible for guarding (proprietary security).[12]

Many feel that proprietary guards are more trustworthy than contract guards. The director of corporate security for a major brokerage firm in New York City, who uses a mixture of proprietary and contract guards, believes that his firm must have a certain number of proprietary guards because they receive benefits from the organization and are "company people." He also says there is much less turnover with these employees. He uses the proprietary guards at special posts, such as in the lobby area and on executive floors, and also as supervisors for the contract guards. He uses the contract guards in areas that have limited contact with the public. Security management at New York University Medical Center, on the other hand, only uses proprietary guards, despite their higher cost, because it feels they have a much closer affiliation with the company, are more caring, and present a better appearance.[13]

Often, a business with its own proprietary security may also hire contract security to supplement its regular security. For example, many sports arenas will also hire public police officers as contract security for major games and other events. Many shopping malls hire contract guards to supplement their own proprietary force during very busy shopping periods, such as during the Christmas and New Year's holidays. Local police also often assign additional police services during these busy times.[14]

Some experts say that whether a guard force is contract or proprietary is not as important as whether the program focuses on the company's needs. A security manager must address numerous issues when setting up a guard force program, including technology needs, staffing needs, compensation, training, and oversight. Few security programs

can afford to deploy technology solely because it is cutting edge; it must address the company's bottom line.[15]

One of the major issues regarding contract guards is the liability issue that must be realized and managed by the contracting company. The inappropriate and/or unlawful actions of a contract guard can be a liability for the contracting company, but that liability can be mitigated somewhat by keeping a clear separation between contract guards and the company they are contracted by.

One of the latest trends in retaining a contract security force is **online** or **reverse auctions**. In these, security managers use an Internet auction to search for a contract security force. Providers then place bids. If not properly managed, these reverse auctions can quickly undermine the success of the security department. If a provider is paid too little, that provider is unlikely to be able to fulfill management's expectations. One way to ensure quality in this process is to include in the proposal for bids a breakdown of the pay structure, including a detailed breakdown of the hourly billing rate, and establish minimum standards for officer benefits, hourly wages, uniform costs, training requirements, and vacation and overtime costs.[16]

Overt and Covert Security

Most major corporations in the United States have private security forces performing overt and covert functions. While performing **overt security**, they perform visible patrols designed to provide protective and loss prevention functions. While performing **covert security**, private security forces engage in undercover surveillance to detect lawbreakers and to serve other corporate needs, such as preventing corporate or industrial espionage and the promulgation of trade secrets. The covert functions of private security are increasing. According to the Society of Competitor Intelligence Professions, over 80 percent of the Fortune 1000 companies have regular in-house "snoops" on the payroll.[17]

The Command or Control Center

Many large organizations establish a formal **command center (or control center)** as a management

---

online or reverse auctions Process of hiring a contract security force by using the Internet.

overt security Security using observable methods.

covert security Undercover security operations.

command center (or control center) A management and control unit that monitors all security functions, including alarms, electronic video surveillance, and security guard operations.

and control unit to monitor all security operations, including alarms, electronic video surveillance, and security guard operations. Managers at the control center can direct security operations in routine manners and emergency incidents. The command center personnel are responsible for response and coordination of all activities in accidents, crimes, fires, intrusions, and many other incidents and emergencies. Automated systems can reduce personnel costs, improve response times, and improve operations from the command center.[18]

At Prudential Securities headquarters in New York City, supervisors check in with the control center four times during each tour and are accessible by phone, radio, and pager. At the Stamford Government Center in Stamford, Connecticut, security personnel in the control center can monitor every crucial location in the building twenty-four hours a day, seven days a week.[19]

Another example is the Staples Center in Los Angeles, home to the Los Angeles Lakers basketball team, where security coordinates all access control equipment, including electronic video surveillance, alarms, and sensors, at its command center. In Staples, security staff monitor ninety closed-circuit cameras for the seating area alone from its command center.[20]

Crisis Management Teams

Many large, well-managed organizations have policies and procedures in place for dealing with any crisis or disaster that might arise from crimes or environmental disasters, such as floods, storms, or hurricanes. These plans include a **crisis management team (CMT)** to coordinate all activities with organizational, emergency, and government personnel. A good example is the crisis management teams at corporate and government headquarters during the dawning of the year 2000 and the Y2K emergency awareness. These crisis management teams are generally centered in a command or control center. Managers continually monitor and review their crisis management policies, often relying on internal assessments or benchmarking with other firms to establish these measures. They also respond to homeland security alert levels. To aid companies, the Federal Emergency Management Agency (FEMA) of the Department of Homeland Security (DHS) has issued a list of recommended measures for each of the homeland security alert levels.[21]

Private Security Tools

This section will cover the major tools used by the private security industry to achieve its goals, including security guards, canine security, access control systems, alarm systems, and electronic video surveillance.

Security Guards

We can possibly trace the first **security guard** back to the early history of humankind. It may be that the first guards came on duty when humans began to domesticate animals and graze herds. To safeguard their herds from both human and animal attackers, early people used one or more members of their clan as a guardian or shepherd for the herd.[22] Perhaps one of the earliest forms of contract guard service was the use of the Swiss Guards at the Vatican, which predate the painting of the Sistine Chapel by Michelangelo. Michelangelo designed the uniforms they still wear today.[23] Chapters 1 and 2 discussed the security guard industry and the important issues of standards for these guards.

As indicated in earlier chapters, there are over 1 million security guard positions in the United States, and the business is constantly growing. Some report that there are an estimated 13,000 guarding firms in the United States, including large national firms and very small firms serving local markets. In 2004, the magazine *Security* conducted a survey of all U.S. guarding companies and asked their top executives to describe their companies, the number of officers they employ, their revenue, and their diversification, as well as other company specifics.[24] See Exhibits 3.2 and 3.3 for information about the security guard industry.

The concept of managing security guards is called **guard force management**. Effective guard force management supports all the technical

crisis management team (CMT) Team of corporate executives and specialists prepared to immediately deal with threats or actual emergencies.

security guard A privately and formally employed person who is paid to protect property, and/or assets, and/or people.

guard force management The concept of managing security guards by effectively supporting all the technical security that a company uses in its security operations.

EXHIBIT 3.2 Top Five Guarding Firms by Revenue	
Securitas Security Services	$3.1 billion
Wackenhut Corporation	$1.3 billion
Allied Security	$515 million
Barton Protective Services	$340 million
Initial Security	$268.2 million

SOURCE: "Top Guarding Companies Survey," *Security*, January 2004

EXHIBIT 3.3 Latest Security Guard Company Information

■ The top six security guard firms employed about 19 percent of all security guards in the United States.

■ The six biggest firms employ 189,000 full- and part-time officers.

■ The top contract security guard firm had guarding revenue of $3.1 billion.

■ Guarding firms reported a revenue increase of over 13 percent compared to the previous year.

■ Most contracted security officers work in corporate and office buildings, and retail environments.

■ A majority of guarding companies provide both armed and unarmed officers, usually for static and vehicle patrols.

■ Beyond guards, firms offer investigation services, bodyguards, and security system design and installation.

■ Nearly two in ten guarding firms say they purchased another firm in the previous year.

■ Ninety-five percent of guarding companies say that the impact of the 2001 terrorist attacks led to more business but that much of that additional business was made up of temporary or part-time guards.

SOURCE: "Security's Top Guarding Companies," *Security*. Retrieved January 11, 2005, from http://securitymagazine.com.

security that a company uses in its security operations. Security guards can be assigned to fixed posts, such as the security booth or desk at the entrance to a building, or can be assigned to general patrol around a facility. For example, SAS Institute, a software company, has a state-of-the-art security control center involving closed-circuit television cameras, burglar alarms, an access control system, and a life safety system. Its security department is divided into three groups: uniformed officers, security receptionists, and administration. Uniformed officers patrol the property and respond to incidents on a 24-hour basis. They are not armed but may carry a defensive baton and chemical spray. The company requires all new hires to have at least one year of security work experience in a corporate environment and some college-level security courses. Uniformed officers are trained in conflict resolution techniques, self-defense tactics, and customer service skills. Security receptionists control access into each building from their stations in front lobbies. When using lobby entrances, employees and authorized contractors must display a company-issued photo identification badge before they are permitted to pass the reception desk and enter the facility. Security receptionists receive training from the security department, covering basic access control procedures, the company's security policies, and customer service skills. The administration group manages the security department and provides specialized services, such as security awareness training, pre-employment screening, and executive protection.[25]

Radio City Music Hall, in New York City, maintains a security department that includes a director, three supervisors, three managers, and an in-house staff of forty-one officers who provide 24-hour coverage in three shifts. In addition, a minimum of two emergency medical technicians and a special response team consisting of a supervisor and four security officers are present at each performance.

Pre-employment screening for all personnel includes a background investigation and a credit and criminal record check. The officers' training program is based on a 200-page manual of goals and procedures, on which personnel are periodically tested and retested.[26]

On the negative side, a 2003 article in *USA Today* reported that most of the nation's 1 million-plus security guards are unlicensed, untrained, and not subject to background checks and that this $12 billion-a-year industry is marked by high turnover, low pay, few benefits, and scant oversight. The article reports that according to government officials and industry experts, little has changed since 9/11. It reports that some experts say many security guard companies are "fly-by-night operations" that invest little or nothing in training and do not do sufficient background investigations on its guards. According to one expert, "The security guard industry is a very competitive industry, and their contracts are won and lost based on pennies per hour. It's all about the money."[27]

Armed or Unarmed Guards Some security guards carry firearms and some do not. There are many arguments for and against the arming of guards. The most important is whether or not the protective value of guns is greater than the dangers they can pose to innocent parties and whether firearms intimidate customers and employees. Some situations clearly call for armed protection, such as nuclear power plants and financial institutions. One insurance company executive comments that arming security officers is appropriate around money and not appropriate around people. Insurance companies also discourage firms from arming guards because of liability concerns. Security managers believe that armed guards must be more carefully screened, rigorously trained, and better paid than unarmed guards.[28]

Guardsmark Inc., a major national contract guard service, based in Nashville, Tennessee, disarmed nearly all of its guards in the 1980s in the wake of a fatal shooting by one of its guards during a scuffle in a restaurant.[29]

The National Association of Convenience Stores (NACS), a major professional and trade organization for retail managers and others interested in the retail business, recommends that convenience-store employees not be armed. This is consistent with their research that the presence of defensive weapons creates a greater risk of violence. It is also consistent with their position that guards do not create a safer store. It believes the most effective means of reducing violence is to eliminate resistance of all kinds. It believes that the presence of a security guard, particularly an armed guard, represents a primary form of resistance and has the potential to exacerbate the likelihood that violence will occur during a robbery. It offers the following rationale for this recommendation:

■ Armed security guards represent a resistance force within the convenience store. In an instance where a robber is committed to his crime, combined with the fact that most robbers are armed with handguns, the likelihood of gunfire is increased whenever firearms are present in both offensive and defensive capacities.

■ Not all convenience stores are at risk for robbery. Definitive research exists that shows that for any given calendar year, nearly 80 percent of all convenience stores are robbery-free; 13 percent experience one robbery; and only 7 percent experience two or more. In an environment like this, arming guards in all locations is premature. Even in locations where robberies do occur, the presence of a guard increases the likelihood of violence and injury.[30]

There is also widespread debate within the banking industry about the effectiveness of uniformed security officers, both armed and unarmed. While they may have some deterrent value in thwarting the amateur robber, there is little evidence they deter the professional or experienced robber, and sometimes a robbery can occur without a guard being aware of it. One advantage of uniformed security officers, even unarmed ones, is they offer an appearance of safety for customers. In addition, guards are generally credible witnesses for the police in the event of a robbery.[31]

Some believe that guards should be armed. Security union officials at Elmhurst Hospital Center in New York, where a man abducted his wife and shot her coworker in September 2004, claim that the incident could have been prevented if the hospital security officers were allowed to carry guns. Prior to the incident, security officers had been warned that the suspect might try to confront his wife, an admissions clerk, in the emergency room. When the suspect appeared at the hospital at 8 A.M. on a Saturday morning, an officer began walking toward him, intending to make him leave. However, the suspect pulled a loaded pistol from his jeans and began waving it in the air and pointing it at the doctors, nurses, and patients, who were ducking for cover. He then fired two shots, one hitting a clerk in the jaw, before grabbing his wife and fleeing the hospital with her. Security officers said that if they were allowed to have weapons, the violence might have been prevented. A spokesperson for the hospital, however, said that guns had no place in a facility "where we strive to maintain a caring environment for our patients and staff."[32]

Turnover A major issue regarding security guards is **turnover**. Turnover occurs when an employee resigns, is involuntarily terminated, or retires. It has been estimated that turnover rates among security guards range between 100 and 400 percent a year. As a recent example, in 2006 it was determined that the turnover rate among security guards in downtown Los Angeles was more than 100 percent.[33] In a 2004 article in *Security*, Steven

---

turnover The process of losing employees when they resign, are involuntarily terminated, or retire; a major problem in the security guard industry.

EXHIBIT 3.4   Reasons for High Turnover of Security Guards

There are numerous reasons to explain why employees voluntarily terminate their employment; examples include:

Compensation
Competition
Lack of teamwork
Incompatible management style
Quality-of-life issues
Stress
Pay versus effort
Poor recruiting
Lack of orientation
Lack of training
Ineffective supervision
Lack of leadership
Boredom
Lack of job security
No opportunities for advancement
Not enough hours
Lack of benefits
Lack of standards
Lack of respect
Lack of feedback
Personal reasons

SOURCE: Steven W. McNally, "Turn Away Turnover," *Security*, September 2004. Retrieved January 9, 2005, from http://www.securitymagazine.com.

EXHIBIT 3.5   Strategies to Improve Retention of Security Guards

- Ensure a competitive salary and benefits package by reviewing salaries and benefits to ensure market competition
- Provide new employee orientation and ongoing training
- Recognize and praise employees
- Help employees grow and encourage their professional growth to improve their skills
- Ask and reward employees for ideas and suggestions—often they are in the best position to know what works best, and they need to know employers are listening
- Get employees involved with the company—the better they understand, the more they can offer
- Invest in screening profiles and spend more time in the selection process
- Evaluate the effectiveness of supervisors and managers
- Conduct employee opinion surveys and exit interviews to determine reasons for high turnover

SOURCE: Steven W. McNally, "Turn Away Turnover," *Security*, September 2004. Retrieved January 9, 2005, from http://www.securitymagazine.com.

W. McNally, a CPP and director of security with twenty-nine years of combined professional experience in security management, law enforcement, corrections, military service and consulting, argues that it is incumbent on security professionals and managers to understand the reasons for turnover and have strategies to counter it. The cost of employee turnover can be measured in financial and operational terms. Financial cost estimates vary by industry and compensation level, but reports of turnover costs generally range from 25 to 200 percent of the employee's salary. For example, using a 30 percent estimate for an employee who earns $22,000 a year, turnover costs would amount to $6,600. These costs include advertising, interviewing, background checks, new-employee processing, and training for new personnel. There is also the related cost of covering the lost employee's hours, sometimes at overtime rates, and the problem of the loss of employee productivity, as newly hired guards are not as knowledgeable and productive as experienced ones.[34]

McNally advises that managers should determine and monitor their turnover rates and then conduct a written, anonymous survey to gather officers' opinions on issues that they believe contribute to their retention or their voluntary separation. These surveys can help to develop effective retention strategies.

Although there are many reasons for security guard turnover, most research has revealed that the top reason for turnover is unsatisfactory compensation. Although there is not much that managers can do to correct this situation, as compensation is usually market driven, they can do many other things to assist employees and increase retention. (See Exhibits 3.4 and 3.5 for more information about turnover and retention.)

One communications corporation in Research Triangle Park, North Carolina, reports that its seventeen contract security officers have lasted more than three years, and its director of environmental health, safety, and security attributes this to the diversity of duties assigned to the guards. The reasoning behind this is that when officers are fulfilled and challenged, benefits multiply.[35]

Computerized Guard Tour Systems In use since the late 1970s, **computerized guard tour**

computerized guard tour systems Record the patrol activities of guards and the time and location of each visit they make.

systems, which record the patrol activities of guards and the time and location of each visit they make. They help track officer performance and ensure accurate records. These records can be especially important if the company is sued for lack of security.[36]

In some systems, security officers touch a device (a wand, for example) to a fixed device (such as a bar code or touch button), generating a record of the security officer's presence at each point along her or his route. The data is stored in a handheld device and later downloaded into a computer. A typical software program sorts information, such as the number of times the officer was late making rounds, and generates reports, such as an analysis of guard performance over time.

As an example, at NYU Medical Center in New York City, the guards use a Silent Watchman tour reporting system. Night security officers must make rounds every two hours between 10 P.M. and 6 A.M. The system clocks each check and ensures that each guard makes his or her appointed security rounds. At the end of the tour, information from the Silent Watchman unit is downloaded into a computer and printed out, giving the security manager the time and location of every site visited by the officer. At the Stamford Government Center in Stamford, Connecticut, tour reporting is handled by a Borg Warner system and consists of station stops such as the boiler area, the mechanical room, and the basement, where submersible pumps are located. The guard passes a wand over a unit at each of the stops, and at the end of the tour the information is fed into a computer and printed out.[37]

The latest in computerized guard tour systems are real-time systems that immediately transmit the guards' touching each device along his or her tour to the command or control center. These systems alleviate the safety issues of guard tours, for example, if a guard is injured and cannot communicate, the command or control center will know where she or he was at last report.

Traditionally, supervising security guards required roving supervisors to oversee guard patrols at their work locations to ensure they were performing their assigned duties properly. Recently, a security firm, Journey Security Services, which employs guards using patrolling vehicles in a radius of two hundred miles, adopted a new program to address this problem. It installed an Internet-based, location-based, mobile workforce management global positioning tracking system (GPS) in each guard's cell phone and in the patrolling vehicles. The system allows the supervisors to obtain the current location of each guard on a laptop computer. The system also maintains a permanent chronological log of all the activities engaged in by the guard. Journey Security guards are each given a precise amount of time to patrol an assigned location, and if the guard deviates from the route, an e-mail and pager notify the supervisor immediately. The system also allows supervisors to monitor the exact speed at which the vehicles are traveling.[38]

Recently, Journey Security was providing executive protection services to a client on a shopping trip. The guards knew the client would try to evade them and, before entering the shopping mall, gave the subject a phone and asked him to call them if they got separated. The subject did not know the phone had the GPS tracking system, and the guards were able to maintain surveillance on the subject despite his best efforts to evade them.[39]

Unionization and Security Guards Some security guards belong to labor unions. Approximately 50,000 security guards, 20,000 who work for private security companies and 30,000 who work in the public sector, are members of the Service Employees International Union (SEIU) of the AFL/CIO. SEIU also represents workers in health systems, long-term care systems, building services, and public services. It attempts to obtain better wages, benefits, and more respect on the job for its workers. SEIU has promulgated principles for the security industry.[40] (See Exhibit 3.6.)

Professional Association for Contract Security Guard Companies The National Association of Security Companies (NASCO), founded in 1972, is a professional association for some of the nation's largest contract security guard companies that employ more than a quarter of the nation's security personnel. Member companies include Allied Security, American Security Programs, Barton Protective Services, Command Security Corporation, Day and Zimmermann Security Services, Guardsmark, Initial Security, Securitas, Special Response Corporation, U.S. Security Associates, Vance International, the Wackenhut Corporation, and Walden Security. It promotes professionalism, safety, and education in the industry; supports meaningful standards for the industry; and monitors proposed state and federal legislation and regulations that might affect private security services. NASCO has promulgated ethical standards

EXHIBIT 3.6   Service Employee International Union's (SEIU's) Principles for a Professional Security Industry

The first SEIU security summit established the following principles to make workplaces, neighborhoods, and public institutions safe and secure:

1. Attract and retain officers who are proud, have integrity, are fair, and who will provide the best service possible by ensuring they are provided with living wages, family health insurance, opportunities for advancement, and a strong independent voice in decision making.

2. Establish entry requirements and rigorous training standards that inspire trust and confidence, including:
   ■ Thorough background checks completed before starting a job
   ■ Training in evacuation, emergency response, conflict resolution, and public relations
   ■ Yearly recertification and frequent review of standards so that officers can meet new challenges and/or threats.

3. Improve coordination with firefighters, police officers, and other emergency response workers to ensure the most effective response to crisis situations.

4. Establish whistleblower protections so that officers won't fear speaking out when security isn't what it should be.

5. Ensure that security officers have the same right other workers enjoy—to form strong democratic unions that will raise industry standards.

SOURCE: Service Employees International Union, "Principles for a Professional Security Industry." Retrieved December 28, 2004, from http://www.seiu.org/building/security/our_principles/index.cfm?printer=O.

for its companies and their security guards.[41] (See Exhibits 3.7 and 3.8 of this chapter.)

Canine Security

A dog's nose is more perceptive than the human nose and sophisticated electronic bomb-detecting devices and thus is very effective in detecting bomb odor or bomb vapor. Many different breeds of dogs are trained to become bomb dogs, including German Shepherds, English Setters, and Belgian Malinois, but the most common are Labrador Retrievers, who are strong, hardy, and task oriented.[42]

Bomb-sniffing dogs are passive-response dogs—as opposed to aggressive-response dogs, such as drug, arson, tracking, and cadaver dogs that bark and scratch to signal an alert or positive response.

EXHIBIT 3.7   National Association of Security Companies' Security Company Code of Ethics

As a private business dedicated to supplying security services to the open market, we pledge:
■ To conduct our affairs honestly, fairly and in accordance with the highest of business ethics
■ To respect the sanctity of contract between parties
■ To promote public respect and confidence by rendering efficient and dependable service
■ To conduct our business in full compliance with all applicable laws
■ To honor the confidentiality of our clients' business
■ To be a positive factor in fostering the image of our industry
■ To respect the dignity of our personnel and encourage them to grow in their chosen field
■ To provide competent and professional service to our clients with regard to the safety of our employees, clients, personnel, and the public.

SOURCE: National Association of Security Companies, "Security Company Code of Ethics." Retrieved December 28, 2004, from http://www.nasco.org/nasco/codeofethics.asp. Reprinted with permission.

EXHIBIT 3.8   National Association of Security Companies' Security Officer Code of Ethics

As a private security officer, I fulfill a vital function, the preservation and well-being of those whom I service. In so doing, I pledge:
■ To serve my employer and clients with loyalty and faithfulness, respecting the confidentiality of my job
■ To fulfill my duties in full compliance with the laws of the land
■ To conduct myself professionally at all times, and to perform my duties in a manner that reflects credit upon myself, my employer, and private security
■ To be fair and impartial in discharging my duties without prejudice or favoritism
■ To render reports that are complete, accurate, and honest
■ To remain alert to the interests of the client and the safety of those whom I serve
■ To earn the respect of my employer, clients, and fellow officers through my personal integrity and professionalism
■ To strive continually to improve my performance through training and education, which will better prepare me for my private security duties
■ To recognize my role as that of a private security officer

SOURCE: National Association of Security Companies, "Security Officer Code of Ethics." Retrieved December 28, 2004, from http://www.nasco.org/nasco/officercodeofethics.asp. Reprinted with permission.

©Jim West/The Image Works

Many sporting arenas and other entertainment facilities use bomb-sniffing dogs to create an added sense of security. Here Alcohol, Tobacco, Firearms, and Explosives Division special agents search for explosives before the Major League All-Star baseball game in Detroit. Bomb-sniffing dogs are passive-response dogs—they are taught to back away from an identified substance and sit and look at their handler. These dogs require months of training, and some can recognize twenty or more scents.

Bomb dogs instead are taught to back away from an identified substance and sit and look at their handler. These dogs require months of training, and some can recognize twenty or more scents, from plain forms of gunpowder in pipe bombs to trace amounts of manufactured plastic explosives, like C-4, a plastic explosive.

Since 9/11, government agencies, corporations, cruise ships, and some private persons, who can afford the price, have been willing to pay up to $125 an hour for bomb-sniffing dogs. An annual contract for one dog and handler can exceed $200,000. At the end of July 2004, when the federal government announced a new terror threat, the small group of companies nationwide that supply such dogs reported a surge of interest. One of the largest bomb-sniffing canine operations in the industry has fifty-five dogs today, up from eleven in 2001.

The Transportation Security Administration (TSA) has about 330 bomb dogs, used mainly at airports. A fully trained dog can cost as much as $8,500 to buy. This may seem expensive but, as the director of an agency that provides dogs for New Year's Eve in Times Square said, "If a dog finds an explosive one time, how much is that worth?"[43]

Many sporting arenas and other entertainment facilities, such as Shea Stadium in New York, use bomb dogs to create an added sense of security. According to the vice president of security for Shea Stadium, "It's a message to our fans, players, umpires and coaches that we are doing everything to ensure their safety."[44] In March 2005, bomb threats delayed a National Basketball Association game, and dogs were called in and used to help verify that the calls were a hoax. Dogs and their handlers are also being used to search apartment buildings, public storage facilities, and multilevel parking garages.[45]

The fast-growing industry of bomb-sniffing dogs, or bomb dogs, has no government regulation. A Maryland bomb-dog supplier was convicted of defrauding the federal government in 2003 when he told federal agencies, including the State Department, that his dogs could detect bombs; however, they failed to find fifty pounds of dynamite hidden in a Washington, DC, parking garage. The director of canine operations for the TSA urges the development of standards for private-industry dogs that would be similar to the strict standards of law enforcement and the federal government but feels that some in the field would not achieve or meet these standards.[46]

Access Control Systems

According to the Security Industry Association (SIA), **access control** is the use of qualifying devices or identification methods at various points to control the passage of people and vehicles into or out of an area or structure. Access control limits access to people who have authorization to enter through selected points. In short, it can control *who* goes *where* and *when*.[47] It assures that only authorized persons are allowed into a premise and unauthorized persons are kept out. Access control systems are most effective when designed to limit access starting with the perimeter of the property and working inward.

The most basic access control may be to have a security officer standing at the entrance to a building or a facility and checking the employee identification cards of every person entering, one by one. However, this can be time consuming and leads to backups at peak entrance times, such as the beginning of the workday or the return from lunch. Mechanical locks and keys, and turnstiles, ranging from those with no type of barricade to those with full floor-to-ceiling barricades, are other basic forms of access control. However, high-tech access control solutions, in the form of electronic access control, are increasingly becoming common in both commercial and residential premises.

Electronic access control is the use of electronic card readers, keypads, biometric devices, or a combination of technologies that restrict the passage of persons or vehicles from one point to another. Digital memory can keep track of which doors are used, how frequently, and by whom. Electronic access control is standard in many companies today.

An example of an electronic access control system in a large facility may consist of identification (ID) devices, access control readers, door controllers, and computer administration. The ID device is carried by the user to access the controlled premise; it can consist of an electronic key or tag, a flat card suitable for photo-ID lamination, and a personal identification number (PIN) assigned to the user. Access control readers are devices that allow access only to a preprogrammed set of identifiers, such as a numerical code or a magnetically encoded set of data or biometrics. Readers such as PIN, proximity, magnetic stripe, and biometric readers, are designed to meet access control needs in a variety of environments. Access control readers may be stand-alone units controlling one door each or, in larger systems, may be connected to a door controller. A door controller is the backbone of a multidoor access control system. It decides whether to allow or deny entry based on the information received by the reader. In addition to doors, access control may be used at elevators, parking gates, or other entry points. The most common way to manage an access control system is through central administration with a personal computer. Remote sites can be linked to the central network by modem, fiber optic, microwave, or radio link.

Optical turnstiles (ID-card readers) are often used to regulate access at building entrances to speed staff to work without compromising security. An optical turnstile has two pedestals that control access via a series of electronic beams. In many systems, the entire entry process takes about one second per person. This system frees security officers to patrol and go where they are needed rather than sit at an entry gate. When an authorized card is presented, a person can pass through the lane without triggering an alarm. Attempting to **tailgate**, use an unauthorized card, or otherwise get through the lane without an appropriate card sets off an alarm. Some systems also activate a barrier to prevent an unauthorized person from passing through the turnstiles or lock a door to which the turnstiles lead. If an alarm is triggered in the lobby, an on-site officer can handle the situation; if an alarm occurs at an unmanned door in the facility, the security command center can send an officer to respond.

In electronic access control systems, generally the ID database is tied into the human resources database. Through this interface, the security department is notified of any terminations or other changes that would affect employee access privileges, and ID cards or badges can be deprogrammed instantly.

Systems must be adequately and properly designed. If too many alarms are in the facility and must be monitored by one person at an alarm workstation, they may be ignored as a nuisance, or the alarms may be merely "cleared" by pushing a button on the

---

access control The use of qualifying devices or identification methods at various points to control the passage of people and vehicles into or out of an area or structure; limits access to people who have authorization to enter through selected points.

electronic access control The use of electronic card readers, keypads, biometric devices, or a combination of technologies that restrict the passage of persons or vehicles from one point to another.

tailgating Unauthorized persons closely following authorized employees into restricted areas; also known as piggybacking.

computer by the overworked security member. An overworked security guard might think, "When the machine beeps, I hit this button to make it stop."[48]

One of the most crucial pieces of hardware in an access control system is the lock. Locks must not only withstand forcible entry but they must also release when necessary in an emergency.[49] Also, a major consideration in access control is the coordination of security with fire safety. Everyone must have access to stairwells in a fire emergency; thus, an access-controlled door in the path of a fire exit must feature a fail-safe locking mechanism that automatically unlocks the door in a fire-alarm situation. Also, doors must allow exit from a stairwell at regular intervals.[50]

A recent example of the latest in access control system technology is at One Liberty Plaza in the Wall Street area of New York City. The building is the home of more than forty tenant office spaces, including major international banks and insurance companies. More than 10,000 employees are housed in these offices, and about 15,000 visitors and contractors enter the building every month. In the aftermath of 9/11, the building owners upgraded security and prioritized access control. Prior to 9/11, security consisted of a few security personnel and outdated closed-circuit television (CCTV) cameras. There was no access control. The new system is web-based, and users can access it from any Internet-enabled computer by typing in a username and password. The building has turnstiles in the lobby entryway adjacent to the guard desk.[51]

To obtain access to the building, employees must use their ID-badge/access cards to enter the turnstiles; also, each tenant's facilities are locked and require access via a card reader at each office door. Employees enter or exit the building by touching their cards to the turnstile reader. If the card is recognized, the employee's name, time of entry, and date will be saved to the database and the turnstile will operate. Also, to enter their offices, employees must touch their card to a reader outside of the office. The system is administered by one building administrator, and each tenant has its own administrator to run the system internally for their offices; these administrators do not have access to other tenants' systems. Each tenant facility manager maintains its own employee database and removes past employees and adds new hires and visitors. The building administrator has access to each tenant's database. Tenants can add visitors to its database and designate the duration of the visit. When a visitor arrives, a guard at the security desk requests a photo ID, checks to see that the guest is registered, takes the visitor's photo, and prints a temporary photo-ID badge/card. If the guest has not been preregistered, the visitor center phones the hosting company for authorization. No visitors are allowed access to the building without a temporary, self-expiring, photo guest badge/card.

As a good example of the ease and capability of this system, laptops recently began disappearing from one of the tenant offices. The approximate time of the theft was known, thereby narrowing the list of suspects. Building management ran a report from the computerized access logs of all persons entering and leaving the building during nonbusiness hours. The thief, who was an employee with access to the office from which the laptops were taken, was questioned about his reentry into the business in the middle of the night. He admitted to committing the crime.

At ballparks and sports arenas, security must concern itself with access control of patrons and employees. The traditional access control to a stadium involved handing a ticket to a stadium ticket-taker and getting a torn stub back. This is not efficient, and some stadiums are now using technologies that can speed entry and improve security, such as bar-coded tickets that can be read by electronic ticket readers or optical scanners. In these systems, a fan enters the stadium by scanning a ticket under a reader or inserting a ticket into a machine that reads the bar code and records the seat number, time of entry, and other information. The devices are being used to detect counterfeit tickets, to prevent people from passing stubs to friends outside, and to aid management in monitoring patron flow and deploying stadium staff. If a ticket is counterfeit or already used, the turnstiles lock and security personnel intervene.[52]

Stadiums have always had a problem with the access of stadium workers, such as concessionaires and custodial staff. Some stadiums have representatives from each contracting firm on hand at the employee entrance to make sure that only scheduled workers enter. Some stadiums are now using special day-of-game credentials generated by computer to ensure that only appropriate workers are allowed entrance. These credentials may be ID tags that indicate where in the stadium the particular employee has access. At Staples Center in Los Angeles, all workers (fulltime, parttime, hourly, and contract) are funneled through a single entrance and exit. The security command center approves each arriving employee, and a camera outside of the loading dock records the license plates of all approaching vehicles. Lost entry cards can be deactivated with only a few clicks on a keyboard. If a person is terminated, management can have security deactivate the card without the employee having to turn it in.

As an access control strategy to prevent robberies, some banks are using metal-detection portals. These units, located in the foyer of the bank, are designed to replace the entrance foyer of the branch and are constructed of bullet-resistant material. If a weapon is detected, an alarm goes off, and the inner doors to the bank lock. A person cannot enter unless buzzed in. If no weapon is detected, the inner doors open. Security managers must adjust the metal-detection sensors, so they will activate for weapons but not for objects such as keys and cellular phones. If not adjusted properly, the alarms will become a nuisance, and employees may eventually open the door for anyone who does not initially appear suspicious.[53]

When surveillance cameras are integrated with access control systems in common areas, it is possible for a landlord or condominium or co-op board to not only know who is in the building and where, at any particular time, but also allows them to have access to records of every time someone enters or leaves the building or an apartment. This led Donna Lieberman, the executive director of the New York Civil Liberty Union, to state, "We are in desperate need of legal protections that regulate the use and potential abuse of private information; unfortunately, this is an example of where law is way behind technology."[54]

Few laws and hardly any court cases address how much information about residents a property owner can accumulate, and it is legal to place cameras in public places like hallways, lobbies, and laundry rooms. With surveillance cameras integrated with computer-aided access control systems, it is possible to identify whose card is being used to open a door and then back that information up with a video image of the person actually using a card. Photos and times of persons entering the building and each apartment are recorded. Some fear that landlords could use the information they collect to show that tenants are subletting without permission or doing other things in violation of their leases or contract agreements.

In an interesting recent case in 2005, residents of the 2,480-unit, 7,000-resident, rent-stabilized Peter Cooper Village complex in New York City went to court to stop their landlord from requiring that they be photographed for electronic card keys to their apartment buildings, claiming violation of privacy rights. The residents had been informed that the external locks on their buildings would be changed and that their metal keys would no longer work. The tenants' lawyer said he thought the landlord was trying to empty many of the apartments in order to double or triple the rents, saying that people who are illegally subleasing will not ask for a card key.[55] At the court appearance, the judge set a hearing date to hear the tenants' argument but did not bar the landlord from replacing the external locks with the electronic access control system.[56]

Biometric Access Control Systems Biometric identification systems are increasingly being used in access control systems. **Biometric identification systems** automatically recognize individuals by physiological characteristics. The first biometric system, and the one most widely used, is fingerprint identification. Fingerprints have been accepted in the courtroom as undeniable evidence of subject identification for over a century. Other biometric identification systems being developed for an added layer of security or as a different means of verification and recognition include palm prints, handprints, retinal scans, voice recognition, facial recognition, and signature analysis.[57]

In a biometric access control system, records are stored, retrieved, and compared to real-life readings before a person is identified and approval or access is granted. Overall, biometric systems are easy to use, nonthreatening, and relatively accurate. The simplest equipment configuration includes a reader, cable, and controller box on the secure side of the door. The host computer usually contains controller intelligence. Users key in a PIN, so the biometric unit can retrieve the stored coding that represents the person's characteristics for comparison. If there are sufficient similarities, access is allowed. Some units output to an alarm system if access is denied. Most equipment can operate in a stand-alone mode or be networked. In addition to providing access control, biometric monitoring systems can perform other tasks, such as time and performance monitoring and transaction verification.[58] The reliability of biometric systems is measured by the numbers of false rejects and false accepts and by the system's throughput (transaction) time.[59] A major drawback to all biometrics systems is their high cost.[60] Also, there are the problems of purchasing low-bid biometric equipment.

According to the consulting firm, the Freedonia Group, biometric systems will spur the market for

biometric identification systems Computerized systems that capture physical characteristics and convert them into data for identification purposes.

electronic access controls by 10 percent per year through 2007. It reports that facial recognition, voice recognition, and iris scanning hold favorable prospects to break out of niche use and join fingerprint and hand-geometry systems as more widely deployed biometrics.[61]

Face-recognition technology, often touted as a promising tool in the fight against terrorism, earned a bad reputation after it failed miserably in some well-publicized tests for picking faces out of crowds. Yet, on simpler challenges, its performance is improving. Major casinos now use facial recognition to spot card-counters at blackjack tables. Several states are using face-recognition systems to check for persons who have obtained multiple driver's licenses by lying about their identity.[62]

Facial-recognition systems use cameras and computers to map someone's facial features and collect the data for storage in databases or on a microchip on documents. Making the technology work has required nearly perfect lighting and cooperative subjects, conditions that are not present when trying to spot suspected terrorists and criminals in a crowd. The most damaging publicity for facial recognition came from tests of the face-recognition software and video-surveillance cameras used to spot criminal suspects on the streets of Tampa, Florida, and Virginia Beach, Virginia. The programs did not lead to a single arrest and angered privacy advocates. Another facial-recognition system that scanned 100,000 football fans entering the 2001 Super Bowl in Tampa picked out 19 people with criminal records, but none was among those being sought by the authorities.

Analysts and many industry officials say that too much is being expected from the technology, which is still one of the newest methods in biometrics. Advocates of facial recognition have long promoted it as one of the least-intrusive biometrics and potentially the most powerful because it can make use of a huge amount of existing data, such as the 1.2 billion digitized photographs of people in databases around the world.

Performance in facial recognition plummets in poor lighting, when subjects move past control points without staring directly into the cameras, and when eyeglasses or other objects cover part of the face. Success rates also declined as the databases of potential matches grew and as the photos used got older.

In 2005, the DHS announced its first biometric standard for facial recognition. It provides technical criteria vendors can use to design equipment such as cameras and software for facial recognition. The standard is designed to be consistent with international biometric standards for travel documents and other applications.[63]

Biometric identification systems are not limited to the United States. In 2005, 56 percent of companies in Saudi Arabia reported they were planning to introduce iris scanning and fingerprint recognition systems. However, 31 percent of companies reported that they feared that this technology would be misused by their government agencies.[64]

The latest biometrics being tested for their feasibility are dynamic signature analysis, keystroke dynamics, skin spectroscopy, vein patterns, body salinity, and facial thermography.[65]

Smart Cards **Smart cards** are computerized identification cards with barcodes that enable the card to be used for numerous purposes, including photo ID, access entry, and charging purchases. Since the early 1990s, Princeton University has been equipping all dormitories and other buildings with automatic locks and a system for unlocking the doors using a slim plastic card called a "proximity card," which is issued to each student. The "prox card," similar to a smart card, also serves as a photo ID for the student, a library card, a charge card for all purchases on campus, and a meal card. To get into a dormitory, a student places the card near a black plastic box by the dormitory entrance (thus the name *proximity card*) encasing a transmitter that sends all information regarding the student's entry to the school's main computer. This information is stored for three weeks. Since 1998, Yale University has used a similar system.[66]

Problems at the U.S. State Department headquarters building in Washington, DC, regarding constant thefts of official documents, have been attributed to deep lapses in security. One example of these security problems is that employees and regular visitors are issued photo-ID cards that open turnstiles at the building's entrance when swiped through a slot. However, no one checks to make sure that the card is being used by the right person. Therefore, an unauthorized person can use a stolen or borrowed card to gain entry into the building.[67]

The term *smart card* describes different types of cards, from cards that simply carry data in memory to those that can carry out sophisticated data processing. Security-related uses of these cards include banking applications, identification, and physical access. The latest in smart card technology

smart cards Cards using computer technology for banking applications, identification, and physical access control.

is the microprocessor card. An international smart card association reported that more than 1 billion microprocessor cards were shipped globally in 2004, up from some 815 million the year before. The **microprocessor card** includes chips that are actually microcontrollers built into them. These cards are similar to the motherboard of a computer. Currently they have 64 kilobytes of memory, and it has been predicted that they will soon have as much as 512 kilobytes. These cards originated in the late 1990s with the introduction of the Java card that allows multiple functions, protected by firewalls, to coexist on a single card. Java cards also allow new functions to be added. The card allows all functions to be conducted within the card itself, meaning that data can be stored and modified safely within the card itself. Keeping the data on the card adds additional security. These cards can also store biometric information on them. They work through **applets**—tiny programs that carry out individual applications. This is the fundamental difference between the smart Java card and the traditional prox card that is read-only and thus can hold and store but never change any information. Smart cards have not caught on in the United States as quickly as they have in Europe. Credit card issuers have been slow to transition because of economics. The traditional credit card can be produced for about 26 cents, while microprocessor cards can run between $1 and $3 each. Additionally, they require new readers.[68]

Several government antiterrorism initiatives have driven smart-card technology, including the Patriot Act, the Gramm–Leach–Bliley Act, the Health Insurance Portability and Accountability Act (HIPAA), and the Homeland Security Presidential Directive-12 (HSPD-12). HSPD-12, signed in 2004, establishes a government-wide standard for future forms of identification that are strongly resistant to identity fraud, tampering, counterfeiting, and terrorist exploitation and that can be rapidly authenticated electronically.

Chapter 5 of this text, "Premise Security," also covers specific access control systems on particular premises.

microprocessor card Smart cards with memory chips that are actually microcontrollers built into them. These cards are similar to the motherboard of a computer.

applets Computerized micro programs that carry out individual applications; used in smart card technology.

alarm systems Electronic warning and intruder alert systems.

Alarm Systems

Billions of dollars of property are protected by **alarm systems**, also known as intruder alert systems. Ninety percent of today's alarm systems rely on telephone lines as their method of signal transmission. Sensors, such as motion detectors, at fences, doors, windows, or other entry locations, detect movement or intrusion and send a silent alarm signal over telephone lines to a central monitoring station miles away. The central monitoring station notifies the police. A big problem with these systems is that they can fail if the signal to the central monitoring station is interrupted by nature or human tampering with the telephone lines.[69]

According to the National Burglar and Fire Alarm Association, in the latest reporting year, Americans spent an estimated $23.2 billion on professionally installed electronic security products and services. About 10,000 businesses nationwide were classified as "alarm installing entities." About one-half of the businesses installing alarm systems have annual revenues of less than $250,000 per year and employ four or fewer employees.[70] The Freedonia Group reports that the demand for alarm monitoring services grows by 3.2 percent yearly.[71]

When an electronic security system alarm is triggered, it sends a signal to a centralized monitoring center. Alarm company employees monitoring center operators attempt to verify that the alarm is an actual emergency through a phone call to the premises. If they are not able to confirm the alarm was triggered inadvertently, operators then notify the appropriate responding agency of an alarm at the address. The responding agency, typically police or firefighters, then dispatch authorities to the scene.[72]

These systems can be backed up by a wireless transmission system that kicks in whenever the telephone lines (landlines) are down. Wireless alarm communication has evolved significantly since the 1990s and falls into three general categories: long-range radio networks, cellular alarm transmission systems, and satellite uplinks. Long-range radio networks route the alarm signal from a transmitter at the protected premises through a network of one or more "repeaters" to a receiver unit located at the central station. Cellular alarm transmission systems use the same nationwide cellular infrastructure that cell phones use. Satellite uplinks send a signal skyward to a satellite that beams the signal down to the central monitoring station.[73]

This technology, using a new generation of hardware, can monitor businesses to report break-ins, protect stores against armed robberies, or protect hazardous materials dumping sites or other locations where the posting of a security officer simply is not cost effective.

Alarms are now being used to address the problem of abduction of babies from hospital maternity wards. An average of four to five infants were abducted from hospitals each year between 1992 and 1998, according to the National Center for Missing and Exploited Children. Many hospitals have instituted special procedures to prevent abductions. In addition to uniformed security officers, maternity wards are protected by a combination of alarms, electronic video surveillance, electronic access controls, automatic closing and locking door systems, and ID bracelets worn by the babies. Parents must wear identification wristbands with a number that matches the bracelet on the child. Many hospitals have an infant abduction response plan. Abduction is immediately reported to operators at the hospital's switchboard/central monitoring station who, as a matter of protocol, notify the police, hospital security, and top administrators. The abduction is announced in code over the hospital public address system, and employees immediately respond to prevent the suspicious individual from leaving the building.[74] The latest technology also allows hospital maternity personnel to attach an alarm device to the umbilical cords of newborns that activates an alarm whenever a baby is brought near the doors of the maternity ward. Immediately afterward, the doors automatically lock, the alarm sounds, and the security command center and guards at the hospital entrances and exits are notified.[75]

The National Burglar and Fire Alarm Association (NBFAA) is a professional association dedicated to representing, promoting, and supporting the electronic life safety, security, and systems industry, including traditional burglar and fire alarm installations, closed-circuit television, access control, home automation, structured cabling, and home theater and sound. It represents more than 2,400 business memberships throughout the United States to promote the industry and provide information and training to its members.[76]

The NBFAA founded its national training school to meet the need for standardized training within the industry. Its programs assure minimum levels of competence for those who sell, monitor, install, and service electronic systems. It offers certification for alarm technicians, fire alarm technicians, and advanced alarm technicians. These certification programs require ongoing professional education to maintain professional certification. The school also offers traditional educational courses and on-line training.[77] The NBFAA also has established a foundation, the Alarm Industry Research and Educational Foundation, that performs research and education for the industry.[78]

Another professional organization in this field is the Security Industry Alarm Coalition (SIAC). SIAC's mission is to create a structure for all parties involved in security alarms to reduce the number of false-alarm dispatches and promote alarm management and false-dispatch reduction. It maintains a national liaison with law enforcement leadership and alarm companies. It has created a series of false-alarm standards to assist in alarm dispatch management.[79]

According to the NBFAA, a major problem and issue regarding alarms is the false alarm. A false-alarm dispatch occurs when authorities are notified of a potential emergency in progress at a home or business and after a timely investigation, the investigating officer finds no evidence that warranted an emergency response. Too many false dispatches place an unnecessary drain on police resources. A study by the International Association of Chiefs of Police (IACP) showed that the majority (80 percent) of false-alarm dispatches are triggered by a small portion (20 percent) of alarm users. The same study shows that 80 percent of all false dispatches are related to user error.[80]

As an example, police in Decatur, Alabama, have reported that only 198 out of 2,212 alarm calls received by its police department in 2004 were legitimately related to crime, including bank robberies, burglaries, or other evidence of crime, such as open doors or broken windows. Since 2000, police often fine repeat false-alarm offenders $250 for eleven or more false alarms in a one-year period, with a business's alarm system permit revoked after the twelfth false alarm. One bank ignored police warnings and was fined $1,150.[81]

In order to better manage alarm signal dispatches, the alarm industry has engaged in numerous activities, such as the establishment and enforcement of industry standards through the American National Standards Institute; the promotion and training of best practices; and the creation of a Model Cities Alarm Ordinance for communities that establish a permit, fee structure, and guidelines for service and alarm user education.

The False Alarm Reduction Association (FARA) is a professional association for persons employed by government and public safety agencies in charge of or working in false-alarm reduction. Its goal is to assist in reducing false alarms in their jurisdictions. It does this by facilitating the exchange of information, influencing legislation, and establishing relationships and partnerships with other groups interested in false-alarm reduction. It provides a forum for local government alarm ordinance managers to exchange information on successful false-alarm programs; serves as a clearing house for agencies seeking to reduce false alarms; and fosters an environment of cooperation among law enforcement, the alarm industry, and the alarm user.[82]

FARA has developed several model ordinances, some in conjunction with the NBFAA, designed to be implemented in a cooperative effort with the alarm industry, public safety officials, and the alarm user. These include the Model Burglar Alarm Ordinance, the Model Fire Alarm Ordinance, the Mobile Security Devices Ordinance, and the Smoke-Emitting Devices Ordinance. It also has produced white papers and position papers.[83]

In 2005, the Fremont Police Department, which polices the fourteenth-largest city in California, became the twenty-third jurisdiction in the nation to switch to verified response. **Verified response** requires alarm companies to confirm break-ins or security breaches before officers will be deployed to the scene of a ringing alarm. The Fremont police have reported that they will continue to treat manually activated panic, duress, or robbery alarms as a high priority. It reports that verified response will save the department $600,000 a year in staff time and equipment usage. The Fremont police chief

reported that the 1998 Model States Plan (which established a fine structure for false alarms and a permit that would make it easier for police to know whom to contact at the scene) had resulted in only a modest reduction in false alarms and that of the forty local alarm companies that were supposed to provide the department with a customer list and advise customers that a permit was required, only three had done so in the past four years. In 2004, the Fremont police had responded to 7,000 alarms, of which 6,900 were false. Las Vegas and Milwaukee have also switched to verified response.[84]

In a **central station monitoring** system, remote detection devices installed in houses and businesses automatically transmit alarm signals to a central office. There, trained operators monitor the system twenty-four hours a day, record signals, and take appropriate action, such as referring signals to police or fire authorities.

The Central Station Alarm Association (CSAA), created in 1950, is a trade organization based in Vienna, Virginia, representing central station operators and users of central station protection services. Its website provides users with current news and information on the industry, and it also has a disaster management section and an operations management section. Anyone looking to find a particular alarm monitoring company anywhere in the United States can find information on the site.[85] The CSAA has taken a strong position on false alarms.[86] (See Exhibit 3.9 for the CSAA's position paper.)

Electronic Video Surveillance

The use of **electronic video surveillance** (surveillance and security cameras and **closed-circuit television [CCTV]** systems) has increased rapidly in both the private security industry and law enforcement. Electronic video surveillance systems can passively record and play back video at certain intervals, be actively monitored by security personnel, or be used in a combination of these methods. Some evidence suggests that video surveillance is successful in reducing and preventing crimes and is helpful in prosecuting criminals. Electronic video surveillance and CCTV will be covered extensively in Chapter 6. Also, Chapter 5 contains information about electronic video surveillance at particular premises.

Electronic video surveillance has several objectives, including a reduction in crime and disorder,

verified response Requires burglar alarm companies to confirm break-ins or security breaches before police officers will be deployed to the scene of a ringing alarm.

central station monitoring Remote alarms or detection devices installed in houses and businesses that automatically transmit alarm signals to a central office that is monitored twenty-four hours a day.

electronic video surveillance Systems that allow recording of events, including surveillance and security cameras and closed circuit television (CCTV) systems; can passively record or play back video at certain intervals, be actively monitored, or be used in a combination of these methods.

closed-circuit television (CCTV) A private video system for security monitoring in a building, store, or geographic area.

EXHIBIT 3.9   **Central Station Alarm Association (CSAA) Position Paper on False Alarms Background**

Burglar alarm systems provide a public safety benefit by deterring crime through detection and the resulting dispatch of help. Studies have demonstrated the ability of alarm systems to reduce burglaries. But, along with this benefit have come false alarms that have stretched police resources since the invention of alarms in the 1800s.

However, in recent years innovative technology and increased product reliability have reduced false alarms caused by faulty equipment. Nevertheless, false alarms continue to be a concern primarily because of user-caused false alarms and a dramatic increase in the total number of alarm systems.

THE ISSUE

The concern for the impact of false alarms has drawn elements of the public and private sector together to study the problem to uncover the cause of false alarms and recommend solutions. Various alternatives have been considered, including some [that] would restrict the availability of alarm response through charging for dispatches, suspending response, or requiring private response. The public good requires a solution that keeps this vital public safety tool of alarms and response available and affordable.

THE CURRENT SOLUTION TO THE FALSE ALARM ISSUE

Working together, leaders of the public and private sector have devised a joint response to the false alarm issue with a coordinated effort between government agencies and the alarm industry to reduce false alarms. This joint effort has been a program called Model States. It was conceived and tested by the public and private sector through a program funded by AIREF, a coalition of alarm service companies and alarm equipment manufacturers.

The program gets results by combining a good municipal alarm ordinance, good enforcement of the ordinance, good false alarm data on problem alarm users, and data on alarm company false alarm performance. Results are further ensured by overall management of the project through regional false alarm coordinators hired in cooperation with the police community and funded by the industry's false alarm coalition.

Based on the success in the five model states, the program is being expanded across North America. The alarm industry estimates that joint efforts of this program will have a significant impact with a reduction in false alarms anticipated to be greater than 50 percent. The impact of the remaining false alarms plus the addition of newly installed alarm systems dictates that additional solutions beyond this North American program must also be sought to continue the reduction in false alarms.

ADDITIONAL EFFORTS BY THE INDUSTRY ARE REQUIRED

The responsibility for the next steps in false alarm reduction falls on the shoulders of the alarm industry that has gathered its best people to look for ways to reduce false alarms further, including those ways that could fundamentally change our business. New equipment standards are being formulated to change the operating characteristics and customer interfaces of alarm systems to dramatically reduce customer-caused false alarms. Installation and alarm monitoring operating procedures are also being modified. The manufacturers and alarm service providers together realize these fundamental changes are required to keep alarm services available to all.

SUMMARY

The alarm industry sees evidence that the false alarm problem is solvable. It believes the problem is best addressed with the joint public/private-sector initiative that was initially demonstrated by the Model States program that is now being expanded across North America. In addition, the industry's drive to change equipment and operating standards and its business practices will produce additional reductions.

We firmly believe that the citizen users of alarm systems expect and deserve nothing less than timely and appropriate response to their emergencies with an absolute minimum of false dispatches. All elements of the alarm industry are committed to deliver no less.

making people feel safer, and providing evidence for police investigations.[87] Prior to using such surveillance, a basic security audit is generally conducted to determine whether the electronic video surveillance is needed and how it should

be designed. The two basic recording processes in electronic video surveillance are videocassette recorders and digital recorders. A switcher allows switching between multiple cameras and multiplexes, allowing recording and displaying images of several cameras simultaneously.[88] Surveillance cameras can operate in low-light and nighttime situations by using infrared (light that cannot be seen by the human eye) technology located at the camera head to provide "invisible" lighting for the camera's use.[89]

VCR recorders had been standard in electronic video surveillance; however, this technology has had drawbacks, and tapes become damaged each time they are run through the VCR, resulting in an absence of detail. Digital video systems provide advantages to standard VCR recording in image quality and ease of use.[90] The latest in CCTV technology is the **digital video recorder (DVR)**. A DVR records images directly to a conventional computer hard drive as bits of data, instead of recording analog images to a moving medium like VHS tape. This is fundamentally similar to the technology used in consumer products like TiVo and Ultimate TV. Digital recording is a relatively new technology and in a state of constant flux and evolution. DVRs are sensitive electronic components that are vulnerable to power strikes and electrical interruptions and that need to be carefully handled. Digitally stored images can be preserved indefinitely and can be replicated without loss of quality. DVRs also allow for simultaneous recording and playback, better picture quality than tape, and quick searches of stored data using a wide variety of parameters. Digital closed-circuit television is one of the fastest-growing segments of the security industry.[91]

There is debate in the electronics industry about the value and best use of DVRs; however, most experts believe that they make credible and effective event-based recording a reality. The management of CCTV footage is simplified and the effectiveness is enhanced. Many DVRs have network compatibility and can be programmed to connect to a remote site, over either a network or a dial-up connection. A copy of the video clip can then be transmitted, allowing security to quickly assess the site status. Digital recording also results in reductions in maintenance costs and wasted personnel hours spent searching for video clips.[92]

The state-of-the-art digital system is a **dynamic video surveillance system (DVSS)**. With DVSS, almost anyone with a computer network connection can view video live, "tune into" a surveillance system, or retrieve archived video. DVSS eliminates the problems of videotape storage, video recorder breakdowns, and operators forgetting to change a tape or press the record button.[93] As a sign of future progress, in 2005 a Japanese image software developer announced plans to develop a digital recorder that monitors camera use and can record more than six months of data with 24-hour continuous operation.[94]

Some buildings or premises use fake video cameras as a cheap way to give the illusion of providing detection and deterrence, but this, some say, risks a lawsuit by persons who may be victimized in areas purported to be monitored by the dummy cameras.[95]

British police began using electronic video surveillance technology in the late 1950s to assist in the one-person operation of traffic lights. In the 1960s, the police began discussing the use of CCTV to prevent crime, and by 1969, fourteen different police forces were using it, with sixty-seven cameras in use nationwide. Only four of the departments were using video surveillance at that time.[96] Since then, use of surveillance cameras has increased exponentially in Great Britain.

Research results in Britain have been somewhat incomplete, confusing, and inconsistent. Instead of discussing each conflicting study in this chapter, a reader seriously interested in studying this research can access the reports cited in the endnotes of this chapter.[97] The most recent information from the British Home Office in 2005 is that academic studies of the effectiveness of electronic video surveillance are still inconclusive.[98] However, a 2005 survey of British police officers revealed that most viewed it as a cost-effective tool that can facilitate the speed of investigations and encourage offenders captured on it to plead guilty, thus saving police and court time; and a 2005 survey of the British public revealed that 80 percent of respondents believed electronic video surveillance would reduce crimes in their areas.[99]

Testimony before Congress in 2002 revealed that there were over a million video surveillance cameras in use in the United States. (However, a video security firm cited later in this chapter estimated that there were 26 million surveillance cameras in the United States in 2005). Testimony revealed that the reasons for using video surveillance included

digital video recorder (DVR) Directly records images to a conventional computer hard drive as bits of data, instead of recording analog images to a moving medium like VHS tape.

dynamic video surveillance system (DVSS) The latest state-of-the-art digital video recording system used in electronic video surveillance systems.

preventing and detecting crime, reducing citizens' fear of crime, aiding criminal investigations through post-event analysis of surveillance tapes, and countering terrorism.[100]

Some experts feel there is little evidence to date that electronic video surveillance has had a great impact on crime; however, its symbolic impact as a deterrent is believed by police forces to be significant. Furthermore, police favor it because it expands the visual surveillance of the police without having to increase the number of officers.[101]

Eighty percent of the two-hundred U.S. law enforcement agencies who responded to a survey by the International Association of Chiefs of Police reported that they have used CCTV technology, and the other 20 percent anticipate using it in the future. Sixty-three percent of those using it found it was useful for investigative assistance, 54 percent found it useful for gathering evidence, and 20 percent found it useful in crime reduction. Ninety-six percent of the agencies did not have a way to measure its crime reduction ability, but of the eight agencies that did, three said it had a great effect in reducing crime.[102]

Electronic video surveillance systems make some law-abiding citizens feel safer, while they make others very nervous. In 2005, the police commissioner of the Redlands Police Department in California, which already uses twenty cameras at three sites, reported that the department was planning to install more surveillance cameras throughout the city and anticipates having hundreds of them within a decade. Many citizens reported pleasure at the announcement; however, Mayor Pro Tem (temporary) Gilberto Gil said he does not think more cameras are necessary, "This is absolutely crazy. In my opinion, it's Big Brother coming in," and the associate director of the American Civil Liberties Union (ACLU) of Southern California said she had "grave concerns about the proliferation of cameras and the whole Big Brother aspect of every person's movement being captured throughout the day in many locations."[103]

The installation in Washington, DC, of a network of more than fourteen high-tech video cameras caused privacy concerns over the possible misuse of the videotapes by the government. In addition, critics maintain that the cost of installing them can be equal to half of the annual salary of a new police recruit, raising the question of whether it would be more important to hire more police. However, surveillance cameras have been reported as giving tourists a feeling of confidence.[104]

In 2005, city officials in Chelsea, Massachusetts, planned to install thirty-four round-the-clock surveillance cameras to cover the entire 1.8 square-mile city as an innovative anticrime and antiterror strategy. Officers watching in real time will be able to see crimes unfolding, zoom in on suspects, pan out for a wider view, and review incidents frame by frame. Police will have the ability to call up images on their laptops in their police vehicles, and the cameras can be moved from one problem area to another.[105]

In 2005, it was reported that the New York City Police Department (NYPD) monitors 80 surveillance cameras in public places, as well as 3,000 cameras in the city's Housing Authority's fifteen public housing developments. The cameras in the housing developments were credited by the NYPD with cutting crime by 36 percent, mostly quality-of-life crimes like graffiti and public urination. Other large cities aggressively stepping up surveillance systems include Chicago and Baltimore, financed in part with federal funds.[106]

Grant Fredericks, forensic video analyst with the nonprofit Law Enforcement and Emergency Services Video Association, says that fingerprints used to be the best evidence from crime scenes, but that role is now filled by electronic video surveillance systems. "There's more visual evidence at crime scenes today than any other evidence," he says.[107] Surveillance cameras have been useful in solving many types of cases, including robberies, kidnappings, murders, thefts, fraud, burglaries, and the 2005 terrorist bombings of the London transit system.

One video security firm reports that there are more than 26 million surveillance cameras around the country, including in banks, stores, train stations, and schools, and on highways and rooftops.[108] The increasing use of video monitoring by law enforcement agencies, public agencies, private businesses, and citizens is providing law enforcement agencies with an unprecedented amount of visual information to aid in investigations. When police are investigating crimes, it is a common practice to view any videotapes that have been captured by businesses or public buildings near the crime scene to retrieve any evidence that may show a suspect committing the crime or fleeing the area. In many cases, the video may reveal important leads, such as escape vehicles or accomplices acting as lookouts. Police use evidence and chain-of-custody procedures in these cases and consult with prosecutors.[109]

The proliferation of private surveillance cameras around the nation is transforming police work by providing key tools in investigations. "One of the things we do at the scene of any crime is look for cameras, private-sector cameras," said New York City Police Commissioner Raymond W. Kelly. "It was not standard procedure ten or fifteen years ago."[110]

The tapes can prove more reliable than human witnesses' fuzzy recollections. The improved quality of cameras, recording systems, and digital enhancement means that evidence like a license plate number or face can be easily singled out and enhanced. The objective nature of cameras has been critical in obtaining confessions and gaining convictions. In the 2005 perjury trial of rap performer Lil' Kim, a video shows her standing within a few feet of rap producer Damien Butler, also known as D-Roc, before a shootout, even though she claimed in her grand jury testimony that she did not recall his presence. She was convicted on perjury charges based on her testimony.[111]

Experts say criminals are more likely to make confessions when they realize they have been caught on video. A surveillance video expert from the University of Indianapolis, Thomas C. Christenberry, says, "In the absence of any human witness, the video might be your only witness."[112]

The use of electronic video surveillance has been consistently held by the courts to be constitutional and not a violation of citizens' privacy rights. Although privacy advocates are uneasy about the use of electronic video surveillance to monitor public meetings and demonstrations, courts have generally ruled that people do not have a reasonable expectation of privacy when in public because their actions are readily observable by others.[113] Also, the use of video surveillance on private property is not a violation of the U.S. Constitution.

Despite the complaints of privacy advocates, video evidence can also exonerate a wrongly accused suspect. As an example, a homeless man arrested in New York City in 2000 for a brutal brick attack on a young woman was released after a week in jail, despite having been picked out of a lineup by three witnesses and making a confession of guilt. A review of security tapes at a Virgin Megastore about twenty blocks from the scene revealed that he was in that store at the time of the assault and thus could not have been the attacker. Police reviewed fifteen hours of tapes from thirty-one surveillance cameras inside the store to obtain this exculpatory evidence.[114]

Norman Siegel, former executive director of the New York Civil Liberties Union, wants public hearings on the pros and cons of surveillance cameras: "You are talking about fundamental freedoms: the right to freely travel, the right of anonymity." An NYPD spokesperson, however, claims, "There is no privacy issue here at all. They [the cameras] would only be placed in areas where there is absolutely no expectation of privacy."[115]

Private Security Systems Integration

Integrated security systems are a $1 billion sector of the $60 billion security industry, according to the Professional Security Alliance, a national organization of security integrators.[116] **Systems integration (or convergence)** refers to the process of bringing together corporate subsystems, such as electronic video surveillance, access control, time and attendance, and intrusion detection, in a way so that data is captured only once and is stored in a central repository accessible to all the subsystems. Changes to the database also become immediately available to all subsystems. By contrast, in an interfaced system, each subsystem maintains its own database and must query other subsystems to obtain access to their data.[117] The ultimate goal in systems integration is the merging of various systems with others, such as IT, physical security, access control, electronic video surveillance, building management, human resources, fire safety, and other systems. Integration aims at having only one system that addresses access control and other functions, from the building's front door to the employee's

systems integration (or convergence) The computerized process of bringing together corporate subsystems, such as electronic video surveillance, access control, time and attendance, and intrusion detection, in such a way that data is captured only once and is stored in a central repository accessible to all the subsystems.

workstation. A major benefit of networking is that it allows companies to leverage human resources through remote assistance. For example, one company has networked its access control x-ray stations so that supervisors can remotely oversee operations without going on site. It also teams up with another system to offer users of its x-ray machines a way to remotely contact an expert bomb technician, show that technician the same image that the screeners see live, and consult on interpreting suspicious images on the spot.[118] Internet protocol–enabled equipment helps integrate all systems with other security systems and facilitates remote monitoring.[119]

One of the leading negative issues in networking is bandwidth. Networked cameras that send data-rich images consume a lot of bandwidth. Today, fiber optics technology is being considered for industries that need high-resolution images, such as casinos, airports, and highway/traffic control monitors because it can send more data over a single wire and over a longer distance than can be sent over copper. Fiber optics also does not require amplifiers or surge protectors because it does not conduct electricity. However, most IT networks are on copper. In those cases, technological solutions revolve around finding ways to limit the data to be sent.[120]

A state-of-the-art integrated system begins at new-employee processing when a new employee is entered into a company's human resources and payroll database and the employee receives a photo-ID card. Employees can then open doors, log on to computers, dispense fuel, make long-distance calls, and buy supplies, depending on their level of access. The cards issued to a cleaning crew, for example, will open doors only during specific hours and in specific areas. If an impostor uses a valid card to enter a building, a camera system linked to the human resources database can compare an image of the person entering with the real employee's face and set off an alarm if the faces do not match. Computer access is controlled in similar ways. The networked computer systems can identify people in a variety of ways, including PINs; identification card keys; and biometric readings of the face, hands, retina, and voice. Cameras create a physical record of all activity, and alarms can be sent in a variety of ways, including video images attached to e-mail. Everything is linked to the security side, where systems have the ability to send an alarm across multiple platforms. All this happens across the network, and networks are worldwide. An

integrated system even allows for an e-mail sent with a video clip attached that shows a person coming into the building or leaving with contraband, or coming in and making a legitimate delivery. Systems integration is continually improving security operations.[121]

Homeland Security and Private Security Concepts, Tools, and Systems Integration

Localities and private security professionals have responded in an admirable fashion in numerous ways to the tragic events of 9/11. The increased need for homeland security has spurred unprecedented innovation, growth, and improvement in risk-management techniques and planning, security technology, access control systems, alarm systems, and electronic video surveillance.

Since 9/11, security concerns and businesses' increasing vigilance over their customers and employees have led to a dramatic growth in the video surveillance industry. It is growing about 15 to 20 percent a year, about double the rate before 9/11, according to Joe Freeman, chief executive of JP Freeman, a security consulting company.[122] In May 2005, when two handmade grenades exploded outside a busy New York City office building, detectives immediately began a search for video surveillance cameras in the area. They came up with more than forty video recordings from more than twenty locations, including one directly across the street that showed the explosions. Using the videos, police were able to identify several potential witnesses.[123]

One of the most important improvements is the increased training of security guards in homeland security. The following are just two examples of some of this training:

- California has mandated that its 200,000 licensed security guards receive four hours of counterterrorism training to help the state protect its infrastructure from terrorist attacks. The private sector controls upward of 80 percent of the state's vital structures, including buildings and power plants. This training includes such topics as weapons of mass destruction, responding to terrorist attacks, and potential weapons used by terrorists.[124]

- New York City, in cooperation with the Realty Advisory Board, a building owners' association, and the building service workers' union, started a new program giving forty hours of antiterrorism training to private security guards in the city to help them better protect the city's commercial buildings. The training includes how to spot suspicious packages, how to detect fake documents and IDs, how to help police and firefighters perform evacuations, identification of several types of explosives, and advice on what to do when first responders are called into the building.[125]

Summary

- Risk management is one of the most important tools used by private security professionals. Risk management is the process of balancing the cost of security with the overall corporate goal of producing goods, services, and profits.

- A good risk-management program involves four basic steps: identification of risks or specific vulnerabilities; analysis and study of these risks, which includes the likelihood and degree of danger in an event; optimization of risk-management alternatives; and the ongoing study of security programs.

- Risk analysis or risk assessment is a major tool in the risk-management process and is the process of identifying potential areas of security problems and loss and developing and implementing effective measures or countermeasures to deal with these problems.

- The security survey is a major tool for private security professionals. It is a comprehensive physical examination of a premise and a thorough inspection of all security systems and procedures.

- There are two major types of security services: proprietary services and contract services. Proprietary services are performed by the people who actually are employed by the organization for which they are providing the services. Contract security services are provided by outside firms.

- Many security departments of major organizations and corporations use a command center or control center as a management and control unit to monitor all security operations, including alarms, electronic video surveillance, and security guard operations.

- A major issue regarding security guards is turnover. It has been estimated that turnover rates among security guards range between 100 and 400 percent each year. Another significant issue in this field is whether guards should be armed or unarmed.

- Access control is an important tool for private security and involves the use of qualifying devices or identification methods at various points to control the passage of people or vehicles into or out of an area or structure.

- The most recent form of access control is electronic access control, which involves the use of electronic card readers, keypads, biometric devices, or a combination of these technologies. Biometric systems automatically recognize individuals by physiological characteristics.

- The use of electronic video surveillance (surveillance and security cameras and closed-circuit television [CCTV] systems) has increased rapidly in both public law enforcement and private security.

■ Systems integration or convergence is the process of bringing together all subsystems, such as CCTV, access control, time and attendance, and intrusion detection, in a way in which data is captured only once and is stored in a central repository accessible to all the subsystems.

Learning Check

1. Define *risk management.* Give an example.
2. Identify and discuss the four basic steps in a risk-management program.
3. What is risk analysis or risk assessment? Give three examples.
4. Define the concepts of proprietary security and contract security, and give an example of each.
5. Define the concepts of overt and covert security and give an example of each.
6. What is access control? Name and discuss the four major components of an electronic access control system.
7. Describe how response to a burglar alarm is dispatched.
8. Define electronic video surveillance and identify its major components.
9. How extensive is the use of surveillance cameras and closed-circuit television?
10. What is systems integration? Give an example.

Application Exercise

Identify a large business in your community and arrange for an interview with the security manager. Discuss with the manager the concepts and tools contained in this chapter and ask him or her to compare and contrast them with the actual concepts and tools used in running the company's security operation. Prepare a five- to six-page report detailing and analyzing the information you received in the interview.

Web Exercise

Your professor has asked you to prepare a twenty-minute presentation to your class on the problems of false-alarm dispatch and efforts being made to correct these problems. Access the Internet and find sites discussing this problem. Use these sites to obtain information to prepare your presentation.

Key Terms

access control, p. 72
alarm systems, p. 76
applets, p. 76
biometric identification systems, p. 74
central station monitoring, p. 78
closed-circuit television (CCTV), p. 78
command center (or control center), p. 64
computerized guard tour systems, p. 68
contract security, p. 63
covert security, p. 64
crisis management team, p. 65
digital video recorder (DVR), p. 80
dynamic video surveillance system (DVSS), p. 80
electronic access control, p. 72
electronic video surveillance, p. 78
guard force management, p. 65
microprocessor card, p. 76
online or reverse auctions, p. 64
overt security, p. 64
proprietary security, p. 61
risk analysis (or risk assessment), p. 59
risk management, p. 59
security guard, p. 65
security survey, p. 61
smart cards, p. 75
systems integration (or convergence), p. 82
tailgating, p. 72
turnover, p. 67
verified response, p. 78

Private Security Law

©SW Productions/Royalty Free

GOALS

- To familiarize you with the history and types of law in society, as well as the U.S. legal system, including the criminal-civil law process.
- To introduce you to what many refer to as the private justice system in the United States.
- To familiarize you with the legal powers of private security officers in arrest, search and seizure, and use-of-force situations.
- To alert you to the differences between the public and private police in relation to restrictions imposed by the U.S. Constitution.
- To alert you to the civil and criminal liability problems faced by the private security industry.
- To explain the court testimony process for private security officers.
- To alert you to the importance of law in our efforts for homeland security.

Introduction

As we have seen throughout this textbook, private security personnel outnumber public law enforcement personnel by three to one, and the private security industry spends twice as much as public security does. The same common-law principles apply to private security officers as apply to public police regarding arrest and search and seizure; however, statutory legal principles differ. Also, the constitutional restrictions that govern the public police, particularly regarding the Fourth, Fifth, and Sixth Amendments, do not generally apply to private security employees. Additionally, the issues of civil and criminal liability play a major role in regulating private security operations and procedures.

On October 27, 2005, a jury in New York State's Supreme Court rendered an important decision on the civil liability of private enterprises and private security in terrorism cases. The jury decided that the Port Authority of New York and New Jersey (the owner and operator of the former World Trade Center [WTC] in New York City) was negligent in safeguarding the WTC before the first terrorist attack on the Twin Towers in 1993 that killed six people and injured one thousand. This decision cleared the way for the more than four hundred plaintiffs in the case, including people hurt in the attack, families of the deceased, and businesses, to go forward with claims for lost wages, damage to businesses, and pain and suffering for as much as $1.8 billion. Surely, this decision will impact many other liability claims in terrorist attacks, including the 9/11 terrorist attack that brought down the Twin Towers and killed nearly 3,000 people.[1] Of course, this decision is subject to appeal. This ruling will be discussed later in this chapter.

This chapter will introduce you to the general concepts of law, including the history of law and types of law; the U.S. legal system, including the criminal-civil law process; and evidence. It will then discuss what many call the private justice system in the United States; the legal power of private security officers regarding arrest, search and seizure, and use of force; and civil and criminal liability issues regarding private security. This discussion will include the landmark U.S. Supreme Court decision in *Burdeau v. McDowell* that set the constitutional standards for private security. The chapter will also include the latest U.S. court decisions regarding false arrests and private security and the issues of private security and civil liability, including negligence. It will explain the concepts of the shopkeeper's or merchant's privilege and civil recovery statutes. It will also discuss the courtroom testimony process and private security officers, including preparation for court, appearance and demeanor, and testimony, and the importance of law in our efforts toward homeland security.

Law

Law can generally be defined as a system of standards and rules of human conduct that impose obligations and grant corresponding rights, as well as a system of institutional rules on the creation, modification, and enforcement of these standards. Law, in brief, governs our relationships with each other: our marriages and divorces, the running of our businesses and the relationships with our local merchants, the purchase or lease of property, and all the obligations we have to each other as fellow human beings. In private security, law regulates the conduct of owners, business people, and merchants, as well as the conduct of employees and consumers or shoppers.

Law defines for society behavior that is *proscribed* (forbidden) and *prescribed* (mandated). In this section we present a brief history of the development of law and some of the major types of law in our society.

History of Law

Most societies throughout history have developed methods of governing relationships among their members and resolving conflicts. Some of these methods have been extremely complex, and some have been extremely primitive. The concept of evidence has been essential in all these systems.

The primary heritage of the United States legal system is England's common law. **Common law**

law A system of standards and rules of human conduct that imposes obligations and grants corresponding rights as well as a system of institutional rules on the creation, modification, and enforcement of these standards.

common law Unwritten legal precedents created through everyday practice and supported by court decision.

JOBS IN SECURITY

Job Networking for Legal Investigators— National Association of Legal Investigators

The National Association of Legal Investigators (NALI) was formed in 1967, and its primary focus is investigations relative to litigation. This association may be of interest to persons interested in job networking for legal investigators. Membership in NALI is open to all professional legal investigators who are actively engaged in negligence investigations for the plaintiff and/or criminal defense and who are employed by investigative firms or public defender agencies. Membership in NALI currently exceeds 650 professional legal investigators located throughout the United States and in several other countries. The common bond of these legal investigators is the arena of litigation and the ability to work with attorneys to prepare a case for trial.

SOURCE: National Association of Legal Investigators, "NALI Online." Retrieved October 27, 2005, from http://www.nalionline.org.

refers to a traditional body of unwritten legal precedents created through everyday practice and supported by court decisions during the Middle Ages in English society. As new situations or problems developed in English society, they were addressed by English judges. The decisions of these judges became the law of the land. These decisions generally incorporated the customs of society as it operated at the time. Common law is frequently referred to as *judge-made law.* Because of the paucity of written legal statutes in England, the English judges formalized the customs and mores of the times into court decisions and applied the same rules throughout the entire country. These

shopkeeper's privilege/merchant's privilege
Common-law doctrine that holds that a merchant or shopkeeper can reasonably detain and question a person if she or he has a justified suspicion that the person is committing an illegal act.

decisions were facilitated by written reports of the judicial rulings, which were kept by the courts and served as authority or precedent for subsequent judges. Common law became the basis for the legal systems of most of the English-speaking nations of the world.

A good example of the use of the common-law tradition in private security is shoplifting or theft enforcement. Persons stealing from businesses or employers are prosecuted using the statutory law of theft, but the power to use these laws and retailer rights in this area are based on the common-law tradition of the **shopkeeper's or merchants' privilege**. Department stores, shopping malls, and other retail venues sometimes allow security personnel to detain suspected criminals. This legal concept derives from common law. Under this theory, a shopkeeper can reasonably detain and question an individual if the shopkeeper has a justified suspicion that an illegal act—such as theft—has taken place on the property. The suspect does not ultimately have to be convicted of committing a crime for the detention to be judged proper. Some states, such as New York, have codified shopkeeper's privilege into law, allowing judges to rule on the facts of a case without a trial (through summary judgment) and to throw out lawsuits that do not meet the legal standards of the doctrine. Other states are putting the test of the reasonableness of the detention and the manner in which it occurred to a jury. In Georgia, for example, case law dictates that a jury must decide such issues, removing all possibility of summary judgment motions in false-arrest matters. Retailers in those jurisdictions sometimes find that a jury's assessment may tend to be less dispassionate than a judge's ruling would be. The shopkeeper's or merchant's privilege is fully discussed in Chapter 6 of this text.

Types of Law

Very simply, law has been traditionally divided into *public law* and *private law.* Public and private laws that establish the rules of behavior that govern our relationships with each other (proscribed and prescribed rights and obligations) are generally called *substantive law.* The criminal codes, often called *penal laws,* of the various U.S. states and the federal government are an example of substantive law—these laws define crimes.

Public and private laws that specify the methods to be followed in adjudicating substantive law cases to ensure they are conducted in a way that protects the rights and duties of the participants are called *procedural law.* The various state and federal criminal procedure laws, often referred to as *codes of criminal procedure,* are examples of procedural law—these laws define the rules and methods that must be applied when adjudicating legal cases. Evidence plays a major role in both public and private law. As you study private security law, you will see many examples of public and private law, as well as substantive and procedural law.

Public Law Public law concerns the structures, powers, and operations of a government, the rights and duties of citizens in relation to the government, and the relationships of nations. Public law can be divided into *constitutional law, administrative law, criminal law,* and *international law.* For our purposes we will limit our discussion of public law to criminal law.

Criminal law consists of laws that impose obligations to do or forbear from doing certain acts, the infraction of which is considered to be an offense not merely against the immediate victim but also against society. Criminal laws are backed up by sanctions or punishments, which are applied in the event of conviction. Major breaches of the criminal law, usually defined as those punishable by imprisonment for more than one year, are termed *felonies.* Less serious crimes, called *misdemeanors,* are punishable by imprisonment for a shorter period or by fines or both.

Private Law Unlike public law, private law does not involve government directly but rather indirectly as an adjudicator between disputing parties. Private law provides rules to be applied when one person claims that another has injured his or her person, property, or reputation or has failed to carry out a valid legal obligation. In this chapter we will refer to private law as civil law. **Civil law** governs the relationships between individuals in the course of their private affairs. It deals with such matters as contracts, property, wills, and torts. When two or more persons have a dispute, it is in the best interest of society as a whole to ensure that the dispute is resolved peacefully in a court of law. Unlike criminal law, the government is not an active participant in the case. The government's main interest in civil cases is to provide a forum—a court of law—in which to resolve the dispute. The government's main role in civil cases is to ensure that the case is resolved peacefully according to law.

JOBS IN SECURITY

ASIS International's Employment Resource Service

ASIS International maintains an Employment Resource Service (ERS) for its members. The ERS is a comprehensive employment bank that strives to satisfy the professional security management needs of businesses, government, educational organizations, and private individuals by directing their search to the most qualified, competent base of security experts in the world. Employment listings submitted by potential employers must be management-level positions with specific responsibility for security-related functions. All job listings have been screened by the ASIS International Employment Resource Service to ensure the highest quality of suitability and professionalism. Individual job listings are arranged by both geographic region and salary level.

SOURCE: ASIS International, "ASIS Career Center: Employers and Job Seekers." Retrieved October 27, 2005, from http://www.asisonline.org/careercenter/index.xml.

Based on the types of legal rights and obligations involved, civil law is conventionally subdivided into six major categories: *tort law* (a tort is a legal injury one person has caused another—for example, when a traffic accident involves personal injury or property damage), *property law, contract and business law, corporation law, inheritance law,* and *family law.*

It should be noted that both a criminal law action and a civil law action can arise out of the same set of facts or the same incident. For example, if one person assaults another and causes an injury, the injured person can call the police and cause the assaulter to be arrested. That person may then be processed in the criminal court. But in addition, the injured person may instigate a civil action and sue the assaulter in civil court in order to make the assaulter pay for medical bills.

civil law Law that governs the relationships between individuals in the course of their private affairs, including such matters as contracts, property, wills, and torts.

The U.S. Legal System

The system of law used in the United States is known as the **adversarial system** or adversarial procedure. This is the form of trial procedure that is also used in England and other common-law countries. The defense and prosecution both offer evidence, examine witnesses, and present their respective sides of the case as persuasively as possible. The judge or jury must then rule in favor of or against the defendant in the case.

The adversarial system is different from the *inquisitorial system,* which is used in countries with civil law systems. In the inquisitorial system, the court, together with the prosecution and the defense, investigate the case before it. The court staff and the judge gather evidence and conduct investigations, and the judge's decision of guilt or innocence is based on the investigation.

The adversarial system is clearly distinguishable by its sharply defined roles for litigants and judges. Our system of judicial decision making involves two contestants (generally, attorneys representing their clients) arguing their case before a neutral and mostly passive judge.

The underlying assumption of the adversarial process is that the truth is most likely to emerge as a byproduct of the vigorous conflict between intensely partisan advocates, generally attorneys, each of whose goal is to win. The duty of advocates or attorneys in the adversarial system is to present their side's position in the best possible light and to challenge the other side's position as vigorously as possible. The adversarial system is similar to a sporting event with two teams competing against each other.

The *criminal law process* refers to criminal laws and crimes, whereas the *civil law process* refers to the civil law and concepts, such as torts (personal wrongs), rather than crimes (public wrongs).

A criminal law process generally begins when a person notifies the police that a crime has been committed against him or her or when the police observe a person committing a crime. Generally, the police make a *summary arrest* (without a warrant) or secure an arrest warrant from a criminal court and arrest the person—the *defendant*—believed to have committed the crime on the authority of the

warrant. The case is then processed in a criminal court. The *complainant,* or the person against whom the crime was committed, is represented by a public prosecutor, generally termed a *district attorney.* The defendant has a constitutional right to an attorney in the criminal trial.

A civil law process generally begins when a person (the *plaintiff*) files a complaint or lawsuit *(sues)* against another person (the defendant) in order to obtain legal redress for an alleged wrong committed against him or her. The case is then processed in a civil court. Generally, both parties are represented by attorneys.

Criminal and civil law processes are very similar. The main difference between the two procedures is that defendants who lose a civil suit may be forced to pay damages to the plaintiff and perhaps have their property confiscated in the process, whereas in the criminal law process, defendants may be deprived of their liberty by being sent to prison or jail.

In the criminal and civil law processes, the burden of proof, or standard of proof, is also different. *Burden of proof* can be defined as the requirement of a litigant to persuade the trier of the facts (the jury or judge) that the allegations made against the other party to an action are true.

The burden of proof in civil law is *the preponderance of the evidence* standard; in other words, a preponderance, or majority, of the evidence must support the plaintiff's allegations against the defendant. If the plaintiff fails to meet this standard, the defendant will win the case.

The standard of proof in criminal law is *beyond a reasonable doubt.* Note that there is a difference between factual guilt—that the person really committed the crime for which he or she is accused—and legal guilt. Unless the determination of legal guilt is accompanied by strict adherence to the rules of criminal procedure, there is denial of due process of law. No matter how firmly we may be convinced that the accused actually committed the crime, the full coercive power of the state cannot be imposed until legal guilt has been proven beyond a reasonable doubt. Our belief that a person is innocent until proven guilty reflects the difference between factual and legal guilt.

A good example of the combined use of the criminal law process and the civil law process in private security is the concept of civil recovery laws. Forty-nine of our fifty states have some form of civil recovery law. Civil recovery laws allow businesses to recoup losses they have suffered from theft by recovering the value of damaged or unrecovered

adversarial system   The defense and prosecution in a legal case present their respective sides as vigorously as possible.

merchandise; time and money spent in pursuing the return of the property, including employee, security, investigative, and any other related expenses. The procedure consists of three stages: the inquiry, the letter of demand, and the lawsuit. Most civil recovery proceedings are pursued at the same time as criminal hearings. State laws differ in some regards but tend to have similar provisions regarding penalties, damages, and fees.[2] Civil recovery laws are fully discussed in Chapter 6 of this text.

Evidence

The word *evidence* includes all the means by which an alleged fact, the truth of which is submitted to scrutiny, is established or disproved. The purpose of evidence is to lead to the truth of a charge. The laws or rules of evidence are the rules governing its admissibility. These rules have as their primary purpose the screening out or elimination of all evidence that is irrelevant (not applicable to the issue at hand) or that confuses the issues rather than assisting in the discovery of the truth.

The judge in a case determines the admissibility of the evidence, and the jury determines its weight, or credibility. Either side in a criminal or civil proceeding may introduce evidence. Evidence is presented through the testimony of witnesses. Generally, one of the first orders of business in a trial is to segregate the witnesses from the courtroom proceedings in order to prevent them from tailoring their testimony to fit the evidence that has already been presented. This procedure is not followed for defendants, who have a right to be present throughout the proceeding.

Information is elicited from the witness through a series of questions and answers. The attorney calling the witness first questions that person in direct examination, and then the opposing attorney cross-examines the same witness. The process continues until one or the other attorney informs the judge that she has no more questions for this witness.

The Private Justice System

The **private justice system** is a concept that holds that businesses and corporations might prefer to deal with crime using their own internal systems and controls instead of having crime dealt with through the cumbersome and lengthy formal criminal justice system. The formal criminal justice system involves the participation and cooperation of the police and the court and corrections systems. This system involves strict adherence to formal legal and procedural safeguards provided by statutory law and case law. For example, a business firm might choose to fire an employee found stealing from the firm instead of calling the police and going through the complex procedures of the criminal justice system. Many favor the private justice system as a simple process in which an employee is fired and thus cannot commit any more internal crimes against the business, and they believe that this action also sends a message to other employees that if they are caught stealing, they will also be summarily fired.

Mark Lipman, the founder and owner of Guardsmark Inc., and W. R. McGraw tell us that there are a number of reasons a business firm might prefer to deal with criminals, both internal and external, in its own way. One reason is that private corporations and the private security industry focus on loss prevention to prevent crime. Private security is employed to prevent crime, not to act as an extension of public law enforcement agencies. Often, many firms are satisfied if they can discover the thief's M.O. (*modus operandi*—method of committing the crime) and alter their security operations or procedures to prevent similar thefts in the future. Another major reason for preferring the private justice system is that pursuing prosecution of an offender through the criminal justice system results in time-consuming and protracted complications, including consulting legal staff, gathering evidence, collecting depositions, loss of employee time to testify, and so on. The most efficient solution for a firm, according to Lipman and McGraw, in many cases is a confession, an agreement for restitution, and enhanced security procedures.[3]

The private justice system coexists with the more formal and public criminal justice system, but more and more businesses are tending to avoid using the criminal justice system and are resorting

---

evidence All the means by which an alleged fact is established or disproved.

private justice system A concept that holds that businesses and corporations might prefer to deal with crime using their own internal systems and controls instead of through the cumbersome and lengthy formal criminal justice system.

to their own private methods. In a survey of businesses asking them their reasons for not involving the criminal justice system in cases of employee theft, most of the businesses reported that they did not report them because the loss was considered minimal or they felt they had incomplete evidence of the crime. Some reported they wanted to avoid publicity, trouble, and expense and that they had problems with the criminal justice system.[4] As we will see later in this chapter, most cases of shoplifters detained by private security officers are not reported to the police and are not processed in the criminal justice system.

The financial and world affairs publication, *The Economist,* in an article on the private justice system, reports that the private police carry out their responsibility for maintaining order in a very different way from that of the public police. Public policing, it says, is involved with "bandit catching," whereas private police are concerned with deterrence. The public police react to crime after it has happened, while private police, who often have no greater enforcement powers than ordinary citizens, have to prevent crime from happening in the first place. To keep the peace, they must head off trouble by conducting proactive preventive techniques, such as checkpoints and metal detectors, or simply by being around to keep an eye on things. It suggested that the growth of private police may not only be a response to rising crime but may also be a product of wider changes in society in regard to "mass private property," such as shopping malls.[5] The article says:

> For years, private property was locked away behind people's front doors, or behind the chain-mail fences and stone-and-glass walls of corporate factories and offices. Everything else was public—out in the open and freely accessible. The distinction between public and private space is basic to most countries' law. When Michael Howard, Britain's home secretary, argued that "the purpose of the police is to keep the Queen's Peace," he was referring to an ancient legal distinction between the "royal peace," which existed in public places (the sphere of the police), and "private peace," which prevailed in places subject to private ownership (and where the police have powers of arrest but not surveillance).
>
> This clear distinction has been muddied by the growth of "mass private property," places like shopping malls and gated communities.

Malls look like public spaces. Anyone can go here freely. Crowds mill around as they would in a high street. But malls are private. They are patrolled by security guards. Similarly, with gated communities, they look like ordinary towns or suburbs (though there is no free public access). They too have their own police.[6]

■ ────────────────────────

Legal Powers of Private Security

Courts have generally held that private security personnel obtain their legal authority from the same basic authority that an employer would have in protecting his or her own property. This authority is extended to security guards and other employees hired by an employer by virtue of their employment. In addition, the authority of private security personnel is an extension of private or citizen rights in the United States.

The power of a citizen to arrest, which is the power of private security personnel to arrest, is much different from police power. In most states, a citizen can only make an arrest for a crime committed in her or his presence and the crime must actually have occurred, meaning that if the actions for which the citizen made the arrest were not a crime, then the arrest was illegal and the citizen may be sued for false arrest. A good rule for a security officer to adhere to when working to detect shoplifters is "If I didn't see it, it didn't happen."[7]

In addition to different statutory procedural laws regarding arrests, searches and seizures, and use of force, private security employees are not held to the same constitutional restrictions as the public police. The U.S. Constitution and the Bill of Rights were adopted to protect the people against government actions. In the landmark U.S. Supreme Court case *Burdeau v. McDowell* in 1921, the Court held that the provisions of the Fourth Amendment did not apply to subjects who were arrested or searched by private parties or nongovernmental employees.[8] In this case, J. C. McDowell was fired by his employer for committing alleged unlawful and fraudulent actions in the course of his business duties. After his firing, representatives of his former employer, together with private detectives in their employ, entered McDowell's former private office in a company-rented suite of offices in Pittsburgh and broke into his private desk drawer and safes and removed all the papers therein, including his personal papers and documents. Later, representatives of his former employer notified the U.S. Department of Justice that they were in possession of incriminating evidence against McDowell showing that he had violated the laws of the United States in the use of the mail, and they turned over one such document to them. With this information, Special Assistant Attorney General Burdeau of the U.S. Department of Justice indicated that he was going to present this evidence to a grand jury in the Western District of Pennsylvania in order to seek an indictment against McDowell for violation of Section 215 of the U.S. Criminal Code—fraudulent use of the U.S. mail. In an effort to prevent the government action, McDowell filed a petition in the U.S. District Court for the Western District of Pennsylvania asking for an order for the return of all his private papers. He alleged that his Fourth and Fifth Amendment rights were violated as a result of the seizure of his private papers. The District Judge, though admitting that the federal government had played no part in the seizure of the private papers, ordered that all McDowell's papers be returned to him. The government appealed this decision to the United States Supreme Court, which reversed the decision of the District Judge and ruled that since the government had not participated in the actions removing McDowell's papers, there was no violation of the Fourth and Fifth Amendments.

Justice Day delivered the opinion of the Court:

> The Fourth Amendment gives protection against unlawful searches and seizures, . . . its protection applies to government action. Its origin and history clearly show that it was intended as a restraint upon the activities of sovereign authority, and was not intended to be a limitation upon other than governmental agencies.[9]

The decision in *Burdeau v. McDowell*, although rendered in 1921, still applies today, passing the test of time, and has been upheld in a long series of cases. It enforces the general rule that the Fourth Amendment applies only to arrests and searches and seizures conducted by government officials.

Arrest

Private security officers have the same common-law rights as any citizen. They do not derive their authority from constitutional or governmental rules or actions. Private security personnel have the same rights as any private citizen in effecting an arrest. In addition, because the private security officer acts on behalf of the person, business, or corporation that hires her or him, the basic right to protect those persons and property is transferred to the private security person.

The basic requirements for citizen arrests are generally contained in a state's statutory criminal procedure laws. These "citizen arrest" statutes apply to citizens as well as private security officers. Public police or peace officers generally have broader arrest powers and can make an arrest based on probable cause that a crime was committed, whether in their presence or not.

For citizen or private security arrests to be legal and proper, they must be found to have been warranted by probable cause, reasonable and consistent. According to common law, detention can consist of physical restraint, but it may also arrive out of words, conduct, gestures, or even threats, as long as the detainee believes he or she is not free to leave the premise, and the detention must be reasonable.[10]

In order to explain the legal obligations of private security personnel, we will use as an example the shoplifting arrest by store detectives or loss prevention specialists. As stated earlier, the legal justification for the use of store detectives is the common-law doctrine of the shopkeeper's privilege, or merchant's privilege. Under this theory, a storekeeper or shopkeeper can reasonably detain and question a person if the shopkeeper has a justified suspicion that an illegal act, such as theft, has taken place on the shop's premises. This doctrine holds that even if it is later found that no crime took place, the detention is proper if based on the following conditions:

- Detention: Detention does not need to be physical restraint—it may arise out of words, conduct, gestures, or threats as long as the detainee believes that he or she is not free to leave the premises.

- Probable cause: The detention of the subject must be based on probable cause, significant facts that would cause a reasonable person to believe that an offense has occurred and that the subject committed it.

- Reasonableness: The detention of the subject must be reasonable, considering the factors of physical surroundings, physical contact, and the type and level of any threats.

You Are There!

Burdeau v. McDowell

In this case, J. C. McDowell was an employee of Henry L. Doherty & Co. of New York, serving as director and head of the natural gas division of its Cities Service Company and Quapaw Gas Company, a subsidiary company. Doherty & Co. were the operating managers of the Cities Service Company, a holding company having control of various oil and gas companies and the Quapaw Gas Company. McDowell used one room of a group of rooms leased to the Quapaw Gas Company in a building owned by the Farmers' Bank of Pittsburgh in Pittsburgh as his private office.

In the spring of 1920, Doherty & Co. discharged McDowell for alleged unlawful and fraudulent conduct in the course of his business duties. An official of Doherty & Co. and the Cities Service Company went to Pittsburgh in March 1920, with authority of the president of the Quapaw Gas Company, to take possession of the company's offices. The corporate officer took possession of Room 1320, the room formerly used by McDowell, which had his name on the door, and used its own private detectives to secure the room. At various times subsequent to this, papers were taken from the safes and desk in McDowell's former office. The safes were blown and the locks were broken. A large quantity of papers were taken and shipped to the auditor of the Cities Service Company at 60 Wall Street in New York City. McDowell's former secretary later reported that there were two safes in Room 1320 and that the Doherty & Co. representative and their detectives forcibly broke open the safes and desk drawers and took all the papers in them.

In June 1920, Doherty & Co. representatives turned over a letter, found in McDowell's desk, to a representative of the U.S. Department of Justice. Doherty & Co. claimed that McDowell had violated the laws of the United States in the use of the mails to conduct fraudulent and illegal business and that the letter was part of the evidence of the crime. It also reported that it also had in its possession portions of McDowell's diary in which he had entered data and other documents that were evidence of the crime, and they were prepared to turn them over to the government.

In 1921, McDowell filed a petition in the U.S. District Court for the Western District of Pennsylvania asking for an order for the return of all his papers in the possession of the government. In this petition, McDowell stated that the government (Special Assistant Attorney General Burdeau [U.S. Department of Justice]) intended to present a case against him in a grand jury for an alleged violation of Section 215 of the U.S. Criminal Code, charging him with the fraudulent use of the mails and was prepared to use the seized private papers against him as evidence. He argued that the use of his seized private papers would be a violation of his legal and constitutional rights, and the use of these papers and any secondary or other evidence secured through or by them would deprive him of his rights under the Fourth and Fifth Amendments to the Constitution of the United States. After a hearing, the District Judge ordered all the papers sealed and impounded for a period of ten days, at which time they should be delivered to McDowell unless an appeal was filed by the government, and prohibited their use in any case against McDowell.

In his decision, the judge reported that the papers were stolen from McDowell and that he was entitled to their return. The judge indicated that he did not believe that the government had any role in taking

---

■ Consistency: Retailers must have policies that are applied evenhandedly without regard to the subject's race or other personal factors.[11]

The International Association of Professional Security Consultants (IAPSC) recommends that a retail security officer's best practice for establishing the probable cause standard in shoplifting cases is that the security person meets all of the following six steps:

1. Observe the customer approach the merchandise.

2. Observe the customer select the merchandise.

3. Observe the customer conceal (or otherwise carry away) the merchandise.

4. Keep the customer under constant and uninterrupted observation.

5. See the customer fail to pay for the merchandise.

6. Detain the customer outside the store.[12]

The IAPSC also states that detention should be for limited purposes, such as ascertaining that stolen merchandise is possessed by the suspect, identifying the suspect, investigating the alleged theft, recovering stolen merchandise, and notifying the police of the offense. Many company or store

the papers but should not be allowed to use them after McDowell demanded their return. The judge expressed his view that there had been a gross violation of McDowell's Fourth and Fifth Amendment rights although the government had not been a party to any illegal actions. He stated that these amendments forbade the use of these papers because they were illegally and wrongfully taken from McDowell and were now in the hands of the government.

On appeal to the U.S. Supreme Court, the Court rejected the decision of the District Court and reversed its order to have the papers returned to McDowell. In its decision, Justice Day, writing for the Court, held:

> The Fourth Amendment gives protection against unlawful searches and seizures, . . . its protection applies to governmental action. Its origin and history clearly show that it was intended as a restraint upon the activities of sovereign authority, and was not intended to be a limitation upon other than governmental agencies.
>
> In the present case the record clearly shows that no official of the federal government had anything to do with the wrongful seizure of the petitioner's [McDowell's] property, or any knowledge thereof until several months after the property had been taken from him and was in the possession of the Cities Service Company. It is manifest that there was no invasion of the security afforded by the Fourth Amendment against unreasonable search and seizure, as whatever wrong was done was the act of individuals in taking the property of another. . . .
>
> The Fifth Amendment, as its terms import, is intended to secure the citizen from compulsory testimony against himself. It protects from extorted confessions, or examinations in court proceedings by compulsory methods. The exact question to be decided here is: May the government retain incriminating papers, coming to it in the manner described, with a view to their use in a subsequent investigation by a grand jury where such papers will be part of the evidence against the accused, and may be used against him upon trial should an indictment be returned? We know of no constitutional principle which requires the government to surrender the papers under such circumstances. Had it learned that such incriminatory papers, tending to show a violation of federal law, were in the hands of a person other than the accused, it having had no part in wrongfully obtaining them, we know of no reason why a subpoena might not issue for the production of the papers as evidence. Such production would require no unreasonable search or seizure, nor would it amount to compelling the accused to testify against himself.
>
> The papers having come into the possession of the government without a violation of petitioner's rights by governmental authority, we see no reason why the fact that individuals, unconnected with the government, may have wrongfully taken them, should prevent them from being held for use in prosecuting an offense where the documents are of an incriminatory character.

SOURCE: *Burdeau v. McDowell*, 256 U.S. 465 (1921).

policies further restrict permissible actions in dealing with shoplifting suspects, such as prohibiting pursuing suspects beyond company property.

The courts generally have held that security employers must have arrest policies that are applied evenhandedly without regard to the customer's race or other personal factors. Generally, corporate security departments have formal detention policies to protect the company in the event of a lawsuit. Among the most critical elements of any policy are training and the security department's willingness to assist law enforcement in building a case against the suspect. Generally, management ensures that anyone with authority to detain or arrest someone on the premises is generally trained in arrest procedures, including how to avoid actions likely to result in false-arrest charges. Such training often consists of role-plays involving officers, some playing the role of the shopper and others the role of the security officer. Local prosecutors lecture at such training sessions and explain the court system and the steps in a criminal case, from arrest to conviction. Officers are also trained in maintaining good records regarding each incident, including all information leading to a detention.

Security personnel also generally assist the district attorney's office in all steps of a prosecution. Security directors generally have forwarding information, such as phone numbers and addresses, for any security staff in case they are needed in court after they leave the company.[13]

In some cases, retail stores use **civil recovery** or **civil demand programs** against shoplifters. Most of these programs began in the 1980s. Using these programs, the store instigates civil court proceedings against thieves to recover monetary damages. In civil recovery remedies, the store is a direct party to the action (as opposed to its role in the criminal justice process, where the public prosecutor is not required to consult the store in any plea-bargaining processes) and thus can gain some control of the process to recover lost revenues and deter future theft. Forty-nine states have some version of civil recovery law. Civil recovery generally entitles the merchant to recover the value of damaged or unrecovered merchandise; the time and money spent in pursuing the property, including employee, security, and investigative costs; and any related expenses.[14]

Although we often think that most shoplifting cases involve calling the police and putting a suspect before the criminal justice system, in reality only a small fraction of all shoplifters are turned over to law enforcement officers, and an even smaller proportion are formally booked.[15] Two researchers reported in 2002 that retailers participating in a national survey indicated that they only prosecute 24 percent of all shoplifters they apprehend.[16]

Search and Seizure

Private citizens are also permitted to search persons they have arrested or detained for safety purposes and to retrieve stolen property. As we saw earlier,

the Supreme Court in their landmark decision in *Burdeau v. McDowell* refused to extend the **exclusionary rule** to private sector searches.

As indicated earlier in this chapter, private security officers are not required by the U.S. Constitution to give suspects *Miranda* warnings before questioning, and the exclusionary rule does not apply to the evidence they seize. However, they must be very careful in their operations, as they and their employers can be sued and suffer monetary losses.

The *Miranda* **ruling** and the use of *Miranda* **warnings** apply only to government agencies and not to private employers; thus, in a private investigation, suspects do not have to be warned that what they say may be used against them.

Traditionally, most courts have agreed that private persons are not generally required to use *Miranda* warnings because they are not public law enforcement officers. A few states, however, require citizens to use a modified form of the *Miranda* warnings before questioning, and some states prohibit questioning altogether.

As an example, in 1987 an appellate court in the case of *State of West Virginia v. William H. Muegge* expanded the *Miranda* concept to include private citizens.[17] William Muegge was detained by a store security guard who saw Muegge place several items of merchandise into his pockets and proceed through the checkout aisle without paying for them. The security guard approached Muegge, identified herself, and asked him to return to the store's office with her. The officer ordered Muegge to empty his pockets, which contained several unpaid-for items valued at a total of $10.95. The security officer next read Muegge his "constitutional rights" and asked him to sign a waiver of rights. Muegge refused and asked for a lawyer. The officer refused the request and indicated that she would call the state police. At some time, either prior to the arrival or after the arrival of the state trooper, the defendant signed the waiver and completed a questionnaire that contained various incriminating statements. At the trial, the unpaid-for items were admitted, and the questionnaire was read aloud over the defendant's objection. Although the court felt that the specific *Miranda* warnings were not necessary, it ruled that whenever a person is in custodial control mandated by state statutes, the safeguards protecting constitutional rights apply, and one should not be compelled to be a witness against oneself in a criminal case.

civil recovery/civil demand programs Programs in which retail stores instigate civil court proceedings against shoplifters to recover monetary damages.

exclusionary rule An interpretation of the U.S. Constitution by the U.S. Supreme Court that holds that evidence seized in violation of the U.S. Constitution cannot be used in court against a defendant.

Miranda **ruling/***Miranda* **warning** Court ruling that police must read this warning that advises the person in custody of his or her rights prior to any interrogation.

You Are There!

Some Court Cases on False Arrest and Private Security

CARCONE v. SENPIKE MALL CO. (1993)

Three 12-year-old boys were lingering near a shopping center's fence at the rear of the property. This location had been prone to vandalism in the past. While attempting to detain one of the youths, a mall employee put his hand on one of the boys. All three boys were put into a security vehicle and taken to the security office where they were questioned, photographed, and released to their parents. The parents of the boys sued the mall for false arrest and battery. During the trial, the judge noted that the boys had not done any harm and had merely been in an area the mall considered off limits. No signs were posted. The court found that the touching of the boy was battery, although the contact was minimal, and that placing the youths in the truck, transporting them to the mall, and photographing and detaining them were unreasonable. The court concluded that the youths did not commit any crime, making the detention improper.

GORTANEZ v. SMITTY'S SUPER VALU (1984)

Two youths were accused of stealing a 59-cent air freshener after paying for other merchandise in the store. An off-duty police officer working as a security officer apprehended the youths outside the store. The officer frisked and yelled at one of the suspects but never told the youth what merchandise he was suspected of taking. The other youth intervened and was placed in a chokehold by the officer, resulting in the youth receiving medical treatment. The Arizona Supreme Court determined that, even if the detention was justified, the manner of the detention was not reasonable; there was no verbal request that the youths remain at the scene; no inquiry was made as to whether the youth had the air freshener, and no evidence existed that the youths had tried to flee. The court further noted that the possible theft of a 59-cent item did not warrant such aggressive action by the officer.

BROWN v. WAL-MART (1998)

Calvin Brown and his wife were shopping in a Wal-Mart store in New York State. Brown purchased a ring for his wife and later stated that because he did not want his wife to know about the gift, he placed the ring and the receipt in his pocket. An undercover security officer saw this action and told the assistant manager to detain the man at the store's exit. At the exit, the assistant manager stopped Brown and asked to look in his bag. She checked the items against his receipt and found the ring and its receipt in the bag where Brown had placed it after paying for his other purchases. She apologized for the delay and told Brown that he was free to leave. The detention took approximately ninety seconds. During the detention, however, another customer made derisive remarks to Brown and accused him of being a thief. Brown claimed he was humiliated and sued the store for false imprisonment and infliction of emotional distress. The court ruled that the store's detention was conducted in a reasonable manner and that security had reasonable grounds to believe that the person detained was committing or attempting to commit larceny.

MITCHELL v. WAL-MART STORES (1988)

In this case, Edith Mitchell and her 13-year-old daughter purchased several items from Wal-Mart. When Mitchell left the store, the antitheft alarm sounded. Robert Canady, the store's security guard, forcibly stopped her at the exit, grabbed her bag, and told her to return to the store. Ms. Mitchell described the guard's conduct as "gruff, loud, rude behavior."

The guard ran each item she had purchased through the security gate, and it was discovered that one of the items still had a security tag on it. A Wal-Mart employee admitted that she forgot to remove it at the time of purchase. The examination of Mitchell's bag and its contents took approximately fifteen minutes.

Mitchell brought legal action against Wal-Mart, claiming intentional and negligent infliction of emotional distress, assault, battery, and false imprisonment. The trial court granted Wal-Mart's motion for summary judgment, and an appeal followed.

The Georgia Court of Appeals held that under Georgia's merchant immunity statute, the activation of an antishoplifting or inventory control device constitutes reasonable cause for detaining a person. The court ruled that even if it is assumed that the actions of the guard were gruff and rude, his actions in response to the security alarm gave Wal-Mart probable cause for the forcible stop.

The court also held that the detention of fifteen minutes was of reasonable length to check each item and that the guard never touched Mitchell or accused her of theft. The Court stated that although Mitchell was mortified by the occurrence, "causing embarrassment is not the same as unlawful imprisonment."

SOURCES: Teresa Anderson, "Legal Reporter," *Security Management*, November 1998, pp. 87–88; and Alan Kaminsky, "An Arresting Policy," *Security Management*, May 1999, pp. 59–61.

©Jeff Greenburg/PhotoEdit

The authority of private security personnel is in part an extension of private or citizen rights in the United States. Private citizens are permitted to search persons they have arrested or detained for safety purposes and to retrieve stolen property. Private security officers are not required by the U.S. Constitution to give suspects Miranda warnings before questioning, and the exclusionary rule does not apply to the evidence they seize. However, they must be very careful in their operations, as they and their employers can be sued and suffer monetary losses.

Use of Force

State statutory laws generally specify the type of physical force that citizens can use to detain or arrest a person. Private security employees are bound by these "citizen use of force" statutes. The public police, on the other hand, are generally allowed more discretion in the use of force than are private citizens or private security officers.

Many company or store security policies further restrict permissible actions in dealing with

shoplifting suspects, such as prohibiting pursuing suspects beyond company property and forbidding the use of certain types of physical force or the use of weapons by security officers.

Legal Liability of Private Security

The issue of legal liability, whether criminal or civil, is an increasing concern of the private security industry. This section will discuss civil liability, criminal liability, and liability problems relating to using police officers to work as private security officers.

Civil Liability

Security writer Charles Nemeth writes that there are three main classes of **civil liability**, including intentional tort, negligence, and strict liability, and includes the following actions as specific causes of civil liability action against corporations:

- Assault
- Battery
- False imprisonment
- Infliction of emotional or mental distress
- Malicious prosecution
- Defamation
- Invasion of privacy
- Negligence
- Negligence and security management
- Strict liability torts[18]

The Hallcrest Report II: Private Security Trends 1970 to 2000 reported in 1990 that one of the largest indirect costs of economic crime between 1970 and 1990 was the increase in civil litigation and damage awards involving claims of inadequate or improperly used security to protect customers, employees, tenants, and the public from crimes and injuries. These cases usually involve inadequate security at apartments and condominiums; shopping malls and convenience and other retail stores; hotels, motels and restaurants; healthcare and educational institutions; and office buildings and other business premises. It reported that frequently, private security companies are named as

civil liability Legal responsibility for conduct; includes intentional tort, negligence, and strict liability.

defendants in such cases because they incur two basic types of liability—negligence by the security company or its employees, and criminal acts committed by the security company or its employees.[19] This has not changed in the fifteen years since *Hallcrest II.* Since companies are responsible and accountable for actions occurring in their businesses and on their premises, they can be held legally liable for these actions.

Civil liability generally involves civil wrongs that cause personal harm. In these cases, the injured party initiates the claim of liability. Liability claims can involve intentional **torts** (acts that people intend to do that are not the result of pure carelessness, accident, or mistake—similar to the criminal law concept of intent); **negligence** (behavior that inflicts individual harm or injury from mistake or accident); and **strict liability** torts (similar to intentional torts, but no intention is required). The issue of **vicarious liability** increases the problems for employers because it means that they will also be held legally accountable for their employees' actions or forms of behavior. Vicarious liability generally involves employers, supervisors, or managers who control or are responsible for employees.[20]

Although no intent is required, the law presumes that people who are negligent are acting without due care. In order to prove a case of negligence, the claimant must demonstrate that the following are present: a duty, a breach of duty, and proximate causation (the negligence caused the harm or injury). Companies and employers can also be subject to claims of negligence for negligent hiring, negligent retention, negligent assignment and entrustment, negligent supervision, and negligent training.

False-arrest lawsuits are a common problem for security operators. In a study of 235 state-level lawsuits against retailers for false arrest in the United States between 1960 and 2004, Patricia A. Patrick, a certified fraud examiner and doctoral student at the School of Public Affairs at Pennsylvania State University, and Dr. Shaun L. Gabbidon, a professor with the criminal justice program at the university, found that nearly all the suits were filed for justifiable reasons. Sixty-three percent of the cases were brought by shoppers who had been arrested for shoplifting but were not caught in the act or found to be in the possession of stolen merchandise; proof of actual shoplifting existed in 34 percent of the cases; and in the remaining 3 percent, it was not determined whether shoplifting had occurred.

All of the lawsuits involved shoppers who alleged false arrest while some also cited other charges, including assault, battery, false imprisonment, malicious prosecution, and unlawful detention. Approximately one-third of the lawsuits resulted in damage awards to the shoppers.[21]

In this study, it was determined that the shoppers most frequently brought suits immediately after they were acquitted at trial or after the charges against them were dropped. Most of the cases involved some charges of mistreatment during the investigation. The authors concluded that if retailers have weak cases or lack hard evidence, it is best not to have the shoppers arrested. The study also revealed that many of the adverse court decisions resulted from violation of store policies by managers and security officers, and the authors concluded that stores must ensure that their personnel follow corporate policies.

As an example of civil liability, in a 2004 article on civil liability and hotels, Richard H. de Treville, a security consultant for the Florida Hotel and Motel Association and director of Security Services for Safemark Systems Inc. of Orlando, and Ann Longmore-Etheridge, associate editor of Security Management, report that courts hold hotels to strict current security and safety standards and best practices in liability suits. No claim of ignorance of local standards or any amount of retrofitting will absolve the company from a charge of negligence. The authors propose regular internal security audits, proper records, and the correct use of CCTV to reduce their negligence liability. They suggest internal security audit should involve extensive self-analysis.[22]

Anthony G. Marshall, president of the Educational Institute of the American Hotel and Lodging Association, explains that by common law, hotels are required to exercise reasonable care for the safety and security of their guests, and hotels must face constantly evolving standards by inspecting for hazards. He advises that hotels have two choices: Either report and remove the hazard or

---

torts Personal wrongs, as opposed to criminal wrongs.

negligence Behavior that inflicts individual harm or injury by mistake or accident.

strict liability Civil liability for an action although no intent is present.

vicarious liability Responsibility of employers, managers, or supervisors for the legal actions of their employees.

You Are There!

Some Court Cases on Civil Liability and Private Security

JOHNSON v. LARABIDA CHILDREN'S HOSPITAL (INJURY CAUSED BY SECURITY GUARD)

A federal appeals court ruled in 2004 that a hospital could not be held liable for injuries caused when a security officer struck an irate visitor. In this case, a security officer in a Chicago hospital struck an irate visitor once on the head with a two-way radio he was holding in his hand. The visitor was kicking and punching the officer prior to him hitting her. She received thirteen stitches to close her head wound and was arrested for assault, battery, and disorderly conduct. She pled guilty to a reduced charge. The woman then sued the hospital and the guard for violating her civil rights when the guard used excessive force. In its written opinion, that court noted, "It was only after Stephens [the security guard] had been physically assaulted by Johnson [the visitor] and legitimately feared for his safety and the safety of others present, that he used force to subdue Johnson, striking her once in the head."

ELLIOTT v. TITAN SECURITY SERVICE ET AL. (NEGLIGENT HIRING)

In 2004, an Illinois appeals court ruled that a contract security guard company and the company that hired it could be held responsible for an assault carried out by a guard. The court ruled that the plaintiff could pursue the case because her trust of her assailant stemmed from his position as a security officer. In this case, a woman was staying at an apartment complex, and after returning to the apartment with her hands full of packages, a security guard employed by a contract security services company for the apartment complex opened the door for her and a friendly conversation ensued. Later, the guard returned to the apartment, knocked on the door, and when the woman opened it, he asked her to go out and have a drink with him.

The woman declined. Later that evening, the guard called the woman and asked if he could come up and visit. At first she refused, but then when he asked again, she acquiesced. Another security officer opened the main door for the guard who was now off duty and admitted him into the building. After entering the woman's apartment, the guard sexually assaulted her. He was arrested and eventually convicted of the assault. The woman sued the security company and the building management for hiring the guard, who had a violent criminal background, without conducting a background check.

FRANCISKI v. UNIVERSITY OF CHICAGO HOSPITALS (EMOTIONAL DISTRESS)

The U.S. Court of Appeals for the Seventh Circuit recently ruled that a hospital could not be held liable for intentional infliction of emotional distress for refusing entry to hostile patrons. In this case, the parents of a severely ill child showed hostile, aggressive, and sometimes violent behavior toward staff and other patrons when visiting their child. The parents were refused entry for much of their child's stay and were readmitted shortly after the child died. They sued the hospital for emotional distress. The court ruled that the hospital had the right to prevent violent behavior on its premises.

GAMBLE v. DOLLAR GENERAL STORE (NEGLIGENT TRAINING)

In 2003, the Mississippi Supreme Court ruled that a retail store could be held liable for the acts of an untrained employee. In this case, a store manager pursued and assaulted a person she suspected was a shoplifter. A 19-year-old college student stopped at a store to purchase a new shirt. Not seeing anything she liked, she returned to her car. As she was driving

---

adequately warn guests about it so that the guests can avoid it. The failure to do either can result in a finding of negligence. Marshall recommends that hotels create an in-house security and safety committee composed of representatives from each hotel department, that the committee convene monthly to consider ways to improve security and safety, and that it meet with the general manager to discuss its concerns and possible solutions.[23] Jim Stover, hospitality service director for Wausau

Insurance, reports that hotels must take a reasonable and prudent approach to security.[24]

Lawsuits have also arisen where injured parties allege that because corporations and private security providers are regulated by state agencies, the state should also be held liable for civil and legal liability. Also, when private citizens, community groups, the police, and private security employees jointly participate in crime-combating activities, all these groups should be held jointly responsible

away, she noticed a store employee running up behind her car and writing something down. When the student arrived at another store, she noticed that the employee from the former store had followed her and parked directly behind her. The woman from the store asked the student what she had in her pants and patted her pockets but could find nothing. Then she grabbed her underwear from the back and pulled them up. The student realized at this time that she was being accused of shoplifting and denied it. The store employee then left.

The student went to the police station and reported the incident, saying she had been assaulted and humiliated. She then sued the store for assault, negligent training, intentional infliction of emotional distress, and punitive damages. A lower court found in favor of the student and awarded her actual and punitive damages.

The case was appealed to the Mississippi Supreme Court, and the store argued it had a written shoplifting policy that stated no employee should leave a store to pursue a shoplifter and that no employee should ever touch a suspected shoplifter. The store employee had read the policy and had signed a release saying she understood the policy. However, the court found that the employee, a regional manager who was responsible to go to other stores to train employees on shoplifting prevention, had never been trained herself. The court ruled that the previous jury verdict was reasonable based on the store never training the employee beyond handing her a store policy.

FREEMAN v. BUSCH (NEGLIGENCE)

In 2003, the U.S. Court of Appeals for the Eighth Circuit ruled that a college cannot be held responsible for an assault against a visitor on college grounds. The court also ruled that the person accused of committing the assault, an off-duty campus security officer, was not acting as a college employee when the incident occurred.

In this case, a female high school student attended a party at the invitation of her then-boyfriend, Scott Busch, at his dorm room at Simpson College. The woman became inebriated, passed out, and was allegedly sexually assaulted by Busch and several of his friends. The woman sued Simpson College and Busch, claiming that the college owed her a duty of protection and that Busch, who was a student campus security officer, was acting as an employee of the college when he assaulted her. The U.S. Court of Appeals ruled that the woman had no legal basis in asking the court to recognize a special relationship between a college and the guest of the student. In fact, the court noted that since the late 1970s, the courts have consistently ruled that there is no special relationship between a college and its students because a college is not an insurer of the safety of the students. In addressing the argument that Busch should be held liable as an employee of the college, the court ruled that Busch was not on duty as a security officer that night. As a result, ruled the court, Busch did not owe her a legal duty as a university employee. Nor could the college be held responsible for negligent acts performed by employees while off duty.

Sources: *Johnson v. LaRabida Children's Hospital*, U.S. Court of Appeals for the Seventh District, No. 03-2339; 2004, *Security Management*, September 2004; *Elliott v. Titan Security Service et al.*, Illinois Court of Appeals, No. 1-01-4226, 2004, *Security Management*, June 2004; *Franciski v. University of Chicago Hospitals*, U.S. Court of Appeals for the Seventh Circuit, No. 02-4358, 2003, *Security Management*, January 2004; *Gamble v. Dollar General Store*, Mississippi Supreme Court, No. 2000-CA-01545-SCT, 2003; and *Freeman v. Busch*, U.S. Court of Appeals for the Eighth Circuit, No. 02-2650, 2003, *Security Management*, February 2004.

for liability. This possibility often limits the willingness of police departments to cooperate with community groups, private citizens, and security agencies because if these police–private sector crime-fighting relationships do constitute state action and violate suspects' rights, then both the police and private actors may be liable under the "state-action" doctrine. Some courts have held that prearranged plans and joint activity between the public and private sector can lead to a finding that the entire activity is regulated by constitutional norms, such as the Fourth Amendment's prohibition of unreasonable searches and seizures.

Criminal Liability

The majority of liability problems for security professionals are civil; however, criminal charges can be lodged against security personnel, agencies, businesses, and industrial concerns for certain conduct. In addition, the regulatory processes imposed at federal, state, and local levels can result in criminal penalties and other penalties, such as the revocation and suspension of licenses and permits. Finally, the security industry, as well as its individual personnel, can be subject to **criminal liability** under the Federal Civil Rights Acts, including 42 U.S.C. 1983.

Liability Problems Involving Use of Police Officers as Security Officers

Many police officers throughout the U.S. moonlight (work on their off-duty hours) for private security agencies as private security guards. As was discussed in Chapter 1, the use of public police as private security guards can lead to ethical and equity problems. To whom is the officer responsible—the primary employer (the police department) or the private company? Who is responsible for the officer's liability in the event he or she makes a mistake? Should a police department continue to pay an officer who is out on sick report due to injuries sustained while working for a private firm? If an officer is guarding a local business and he or she observes a crime on the street, which obligation comes first—the obligation to the private business for security or the obligation to his or her oath of duty?[25]

In addition, the use of public police working for private security agencies can lead to legal problems for the firms hiring these officers. According to David H. Peck, an attorney, a former retail loss prevention manager, and a member of ASIS International,

> Employing off-duty police officers in a security capacity raises unique legal issues. While an employer may benefit from an officer's training, experience, and the privileges associated with holding police powers, the employer also exposes itself to additional liability. Being aware of these legal issues will help both the officer and the employer avoid the potential pitfalls of their employment relationship.[26]

The legal issues Peck discusses are Section 1983 violations, assault and battery, negligent hiring, *Miranda* violations, and searches and seizures.

Section 1983 Violations   When private companies hire police officers as private security officers, the company risks legal action in the form of Section 1983 of Title 42 of the U.S. Code (U.S.C.) (Civil Action for Deprivation of Civil Rights) violations. A Section 1983 violation means that a state official or other person acting under the authority granted to them by the state (*under the color of state law*) can be sued for violating a person's constitutional rights. Generally, private corporations or businesses cannot be sued under Section 1983 because they are not state agencies and their employees do not operate under the color of state law; however, by employing off-duty police officers to act as security officers, the courts have ruled that businesses expose themselves to liability under Section 1983. In *Groom v. Safeway* (1997), the U.S. District Court for the Western District of Washington ruled that a store that had hired an off-duty police officer to work as a security guard, who then violated a woman's constitutional rights, was liable for the officer's Section 1983 violation. The court held that the store had hired the security guard to act in his capacity as a police officer in its store and on its behalf, thus cloaking itself with the authority of the state.[27]

Section 1983 reads:

> Every person, who under color of any statute, ordinance, regulation, custom, or usage, of any State or Territory, subjects or causes to be subjected, any citizens of the United States or other persons within the jurisdiction thereof to the deprivation of any rights, privileges or immunities secured by the Constitution and laws, shall be liable to the party injured in an action at law, suit in equity, or other proceeding for redress.[28]

This law was passed in 1871 by Congress to ensure the civil rights of individuals. It requires due process of law before any person can be deprived of life, liberty, or property and provides redress for the denial of these constitutional rights by officials acting under color of state law (under the authority of their power as public officials).

Assault and Battery   Police officers have a qualified legal privilege protecting themselves against unlawful assault and battery charges while conducting lawful arrests; however, the privilege is negated when the officer uses excessive force. A corporation that hires a police officer who uses excessive force is liable for an assault and battery

---

criminal liability Responsibility for criminal action.

You Are There!

Some Court Cases on Premise Liability and Private Security

FEINSTEIN v. BEERS

In 2004, a Massachusetts appeals court ruled that the trustees of a condominium complex could not be held responsible for the assault of a resident when the resident's actions created the risk of such an assault. The resident had left her sliding glass door open a few inches to get more air by placing a small wooden dowel in the track of the door, trying to prevent it from being opened further from the outside. As the resident slept, an intruder entered the house and assaulted her. He used a coat hanger to remove the dowel from the door. The resident had sued the condominium complex for negligence. In the court's ruling against the resident, it wrote that the risk inherent in her actions was obvious to persons of average intelligence. There is no evidence that the complex created the situation that caused the damage.

MAHESHWARI v. CITY OF NEW YORK

The New York Court of Appeals ruled in 2004 that a violent attack on a concertgoer could not have been foreseen by those who planned and carried out security operations. In this case, Ram Krishna Maheshwari attended, in 1996, the Lollapalooza music festival at Downing Stadium in New York, which is owned by the city. The festival was hosted by several metal and rap groups. The sponsor of the festival had agreed to provide supervision of the parking lot during the event and to hire as many trained security personnel as necessary to patrol the parking areas to search for illegal vendors, alcohol, open fires, and littering. While Maheshwari was in one of the parking areas to distribute pamphlets for the International Society for Krishna Consciousness, four men assaulted and beat him, causing serious injury. The attackers were never identified or arrested. Maheshwari sued the sponsor and the city for inadequate security and argued that the city and sponsors should have known of criminal activity at previous Lollapalooza festivals and that it neglected to provide adequate security.

The Court of Appeals ruled against Maheshwari and noted that the attack was not a foreseeable result of lax security nor could the violence have been inferred from past concerts, where criminal conduct was minor. In its written opinion, the court noted, "The record reveals no failure by the organizers of the event to provide adequate control or security. The concert was host to thousands of people over a large area. Security officers cannot be everywhere at once."

MAE BELLE LANE v. ST. JOSEPH'S REGIONAL MEDICAL CENTER

In 2004, the Indiana Court of Appeals ruled that a hospital is not liable for the attack of one patient by another. The court ruled that while a hospital must provide adequate security, it cannot be held responsible for the unforeseen attacks of third parties.

In this case, Mae Belle Lane was waiting with her son-in-law in St. Joseph's Regional Medical Center's emergency room. While she waited, a teenaged boy arrived with his mother. Without warning, the teenager approached Lane and began punching her. Lane's son-in-law then hit the teen, knocking him to the floor and causing the attack on Lane to stop. Lane sued the hospital for negligence, claiming that hospital staff should have protected her from the attack. The Court of Appeals denied the claim based on the fact that the attack was unforeseeable, even to the victim, who testified that she was surprised when the teen assaulted her.

However, the court noted that under Indiana law, businesses such as hospitals owe their patrons a duty to exercise reasonable care in keeping their premises safe. The court also stated that emergency rooms can be a particular concern. "There can be little dispute that a hospital's emergency room can be the scene of violent and criminal behavior. In some cases, the violence spills into the emergency room itself and measures must be taken to control the situation." The security situation at the hospital was not addressed by the court because the basis of the case was not whether security was adequate but whether the attack on Lane was foreseeable.

SOURCES: *Feinstein v. Beers*, Massachusetts Court of Appeals, No. 01-P-1635, 2004, *Security Management*, June 2004; *Maheshwari v. City of New York*, New York Court of Appeals, No. 54, 2004, *Security Management*, November 2004; and *Mae Belle Lane v. St. Joseph's Regional Medical Center*, Indiana Court of Appeals, No.71A05-0310-CV-525, 2004), *Security Management*, January 2005.

claim through the legal concept of vicarious liability (holds a company liable for any actions committed by its employees while acting within the scope of their employment).

Negligent Hiring A business can be held liable for negligent hiring if it knew of any unfitness or dangerous attributes of an employee that it could have reasonably foreseen if it had exercised due diligence. If a business hires an off-duty officer who has had previous problems as a police officer in terms of criminal or improper acts, the company can be sued for negligent hiring.

Miranda **Warnings** As a general rule, security officers are not required to issue *Miranda* warnings, but the courts take a different position when the security officers is also an off-duty police officer. If a security officer is also an off-duty police officer, she or he must advise any person in custody of his or her constitutional rights prior to any interrogation.[29]

Searches and Seizures A search conducted by a private person does not violate the Fourth Amendment freedom against unreasonable search and seizure because it only applies to government agents. If, however, a private party acts as an instrument or agent of the state when conducting a search or seizure, then the Fourth Amendment is applicable (a private party is considered an agent of government if the government knew of and acquiesced in his or her action and the party performing the search intended to assist law enforcement). This applies to off-duty police officers acting as security officers.

Courtroom Testimony and Private Security Officers

Private security officers are often called into court or before other official bodies to present testimony, and juries are often influenced by their appearance and demeanor on the witness stand. It is imperative that officers have a working knowledge of courtroom procedures and the proper way to appear and testify in court. This section discusses the preparation, appearance, and demeanor necessary for courtroom testimony, as well as the testimony itself.

Preparation

Upon being notified of an impending court appearance, the officer ensures that the case is complete and a final report is prepared and then prepares for a pretrial conference with the attorney who is calling her or him into court. At this conference, the officer organizes the facts and evidence and presents a summary of the case for the attorney. He or she must provide the attorney with all reports and other relevant documents or exhibits in the case. At the pretrial conference, the officer and prosecutor review the evidence, discuss the strengths and weaknesses of the case, and discuss the probable line of questioning to be used by both attorneys in the case.

Just before the trial, the officer again reviews the cases, his or her notes, the evidence, and the final report. The investigator also ensures that all evidence is available for presentation to the court.

Appearance and Demeanor

The officers's appearance in court is extremely important. How the jury will perceive his or her credibility will in part be determined by the officer's appearance, demeanor, and professionalism. The officer should be well groomed and dressed in uniform or professional business attire. For a man, professional business attire is a conservative suit; for a woman, it is a conservative suit or dress.

Christopher Vail, a retired investigator for the Inspector General of the U.S. Department of Health and Human Services, offers the following advice on preparation, appearance, and demeanor in court:

■ Know which courtroom you'll be testifying in. If you are unfamiliar with the particular courthouse or courtroom, check it out before the trial so you will know your way around.

■ Do not discuss anything about the case in public or where your conversation may be overheard. Anyone could turn out to be a juror or defense witness!

■ Treat people with respect, as if they were the judge or a juror going to trial. Your professionalism, politeness, and courtesy will be noted and remembered—especially by those who do see you in court in an official capacity.

■ Do not discuss your personal life, official business, biases, prejudices, likes and dislikes, or controversial subjects in public, for the same

©Michael Newman/PhotoEdit

Private security officers are often called into court or before other official bodies to present testimony. The officer's appearance in court is extremely important: How the jury will perceive his or her credibility will in part be determined by the officer's appearance, demeanor, and professionalism. At trial, officers are subject to direct examination by the attorney presenting the evidence and normally to cross-examination by the opposing attorney as well.

reasons. You might impress a judge, juror, defense counsel, or witness the wrong way.

- Judges and attorneys have little patience with officers appearing in court late, so be on time. Know when you will be expected to be called to testify.

- Dress appropriately. Look businesslike and official. If in uniform, it should be clean, neat, and complete. If not in uniform, a sports coat and slacks are as appropriate as a business suit (male and female officers alike).

- Avoid contact with the defense counsel and any defense witnesses before the trial. Assume that they will try to get you to say something about the case that is to their advantage.[30]

Testimony

At trial, officers are subject to direct examination by the attorney presenting the evidence and normally are subject to cross-examination by the opposing attorney as well. Direct examination is the initial questioning of a witness or defendant by the attorney who is using the person's testimony to further her case. **Cross-examination** is questioning

by the opposing attorney for the purpose of assessing the validity of the testimony. After direct examination and cross-examination, each attorney may "redirect" or "recross" the witness.

Before testifying, officers are called to the witness stand and asked to take an oath to tell the truth. They answer "here" when their name is called and move directly to the front of the witness stand, walking behind the tables occupied by the attorneys. They bring any notes or reports to the witness stand in a clean manila file folder. When asked to take the oath, they face the court clerk, hold up the palm of their right hand, and answer in a firm, clear voice, "I do," to the question, "Do you promise to tell the truth, the whole truth, and nothing but the truth, so help you God?" They then proceed to the witness stand and sit down.

The attorney presenting a security officer as a witness in direct examination will ask the individual to state his or her name and profession. Officers should reply slowly, deliberately, and loudly enough to be heard by everyone in the courtroom.

cross examination Questioning by the opposing attorney in a judicial proceeding for the purpose of assessing the validity of the testimony.

Attorneys use the question-and-answer technique for examining witnesses. Generally, they ask a single, pointed question requiring the witness to respond. The answer should be "yes" or "no" unless the attorney asks for elaboration. The officer should hesitate momentarily before answering in order to fully digest the question and also to allow an attorney to raise an objection if appropriate. If the officer does not understand the question, she or he should ask the attorney to repeat it. Officers should realize that certain types of statements are inadmissible in court, including opinions, hearsay, privileged communications, and statements about the defendant's character and reputation. They should answer questions directly and not volunteer information. They should refer to their notes to recall exact details but not rely exclusively on the notes. They should admit calmly when they do not know an answer to a question; should admit any mistakes made in testifying; and should avoid jargon, sarcasm, and humor.

They should state only facts and not try to color or exaggerate their significance, realizing that even the slightest fabrication of testimony is perjury and likely to be discovered during the course of the trial. *Perjury,* which is a criminal offense, occurs when a person makes a false statement while under oath or affirmation.

The questioning by the opposing attorney in the case—the cross-examination—is usually the most difficult part of testifying. The opposing attorney will attempt to cast doubt on the witness's **direct testimony** in an effort to make her or his case more credible. This practice is known as *impeachment*—the process of discrediting or contradicting the testimony of a witness to show that the witness is unworthy of belief and to destroy the credibility of the witness in the eyes of the jury or judge.

Several methods are used to impeach or attack the testimony and credibility of a witness:

■ Showing that the witness's previous statements, personal conduct, or the conduct of the investigation or arrest are inconsistent with the witness's testimony in court

■ Showing that the witness is biased or prejudiced for or against the defendant because of a close relationship, personal interest in the outcome of the case, hostility toward the opposing party, or similar biases

■ Attacking the character of the witness by revealing prior criminal convictions or other irrefutable characteristics that would render testimony unworthy of belief

■ Showing the witness's incapacity to observe, recollect, or recount due to mental weakness, a physical defect, influence of drugs or alcohol, or the like

■ Showing that the witness is in error or that the facts are other than as testified[31]

If the opposing attorney asks the officer whether he or she has refreshed his or her memory before testifying, the officer should admit to this fact. To do otherwise would be inconsistent with the proper preparation for court testimony. Similarly, discussions with attorneys, other investigators, and witnesses about a case are proper because they assist in the proper preparation for court testimony; the officer should answer in the affirmative if asked about these prior discussions.

Regardless of how an officer's testimony is attacked or challenged by the opposing attorney, he or she should treat the opposing attorney with respect. Officers should not regard the opposing attorney as an enemy but as a necessary player in the legal process. They should convey no personal prejudice or animosity through their testimony and should not allow themselves to become provoked or excited. The best testimony is accurate, truthful, and in accordance with the facts. Once again, it is a good idea to pause briefly before answering questions. This short pause will allow the prosecutor or other attorney to raise an objection to the question, if appropriate.

When both attorneys have concluded their questioning, officers should remain seated until instructed to leave. They should then immediately leave the courtroom or return to their seat if appropriate. Exhibit 4.1 covers the "Ten Commandments" of courtroom testimony for security officers.

Homeland Security and Private Security Law

Law is extremely important in our nation's efforts for homeland security. In the aftermath of 9/11, Congress passed the Homeland Security Act of 2002 (H.R.5005-8) that established the federal

direct testimony Statements made under oath by a witness. After a witness testifies, the other party has the right to ask questions on cross-examination.

©John Neubauer/PhotoEdit

An immigration officer carefully inspects the faces of two al-Qaeda suspects on his computer screen as he scrutinizes a passenger's documents. Following the 9/11 terrorist attacks, the United States, like many other countries, has increased security efforts and initiatives due to heightened terrorist activities within the United States and abroad. Passengers and their personal belongings are subject to search. Those suspected of wrongdoing may be questioned, searched, and subsequently arrested if there is probable cause to believe that the person has engaged in or may engage in a criminal activity.

cabinet-level Department of Homeland Security as an executive department of the United States.[32] Also in the aftermath of 9/11, the Congress passed Public Law 107-56, the USA Patriot Act of 2001, that drastically affected government, businesses, and

EXHIBIT 4.1   The Ten Commandments of Courtroom Testimony

  I. Relax and be yourself.

  II. Answer only questions that are before you.

  III. Refer to your report only when allowed.

  IV. Paint the crime scene just as it was.

  V. Be ready to explain why you are remembering details in court if they are not in your report.

  VI. Avoid jargon or unduly difficult language.

  VII. Avoid sarcasm.

  VIII. Maintain your detachment.

  IX. You don't need to explain the law.

  X. Explanation of what you said is possible on rebuttal.

SOURCE: George Hope, "Ten Commandments of Courtroom Testimony," *Minnesota Police Journal*, April 1992, pp. 55–60.

the general public.[33] Both of these laws will be discussed extensively in Chapter 13 of this textbook, *Terrorism and Private Security*.

In addition, court decisions, particularly those involving civil liability, particularly negligence, dramatically influence our society and private businesses and private security professionals. The October 2005 jury verdict in New York State Supreme Court, discussed in the introduction to this chapter, that the owners and operators of New York City's former World Trade Center (the Twin Towers), the Port Authority of New York and New Jersey, were negligent in their security measures and that they were responsible for the deaths, injuries, and damage that resulted from the 1993 bombing of the World Trade Center, no doubt will become an important precedent in future terrorism cases, particularly the 9/11 terrorist attacks. The deaths, injuries, and damages in the 1993 bombing resulted from the detonation of a van packed with explosives by terrorists in the underground parking garage of the complex on February 26, 1993. This verdict came after four weeks of testimony from security experts and three former directors of the Port Authority. The jury took just over a day to reach its decision.[34]

In this case, it was proven that the Port Authority disregarded the advice of its own experts and other experts and was motivated by money, rather than human lives. The trial focused on a report by the Office of Special Planning, an antiterrorist task force convened by a former executive director of the Port Authority, Peter Goldmark. The former director had been concerned that, given terrorist activities in other parts of the world, the World Trade Center, as a symbol of American capitalism and strength, could be a target. The report concluded,

> A time-bomb–laden vehicle could be driven into the WTC and parked in the public parking areas. The driver would then exit via elevator into the WTC and proceed with his business unnoticed. At a predetermined time, the bomb could be exploded in the basement.

The amount of explosives used will determine the severity of damage to that area.[35]

This report was truly prophetic because this is exactly what happened on February 26, 1993.

Among Goldmark's recommendations was the elimination of public parking in the World Trade Center or the adoption of a series of compromise steps, including guarding entrances to the parking lots, random searches of vehicles, and restrictions on pedestrian access. After Goldmark left the Port Authority, his successors decided to ignore his recommendations, citing the potential loss of revenue and inconvenience to tenants. They also decided against most of the compromise measures.

Hopefully, the effect of this decision and the powers of our legal system will cause property owners and operators to give more attention to the security of their premises to ensure the protection of human lives and our homeland security.

Summary

- Law can generally be defined as a system of standards and rules of human conduct that impose obligations and grant corresponding rights, as well as a system of institutional rules on the creation, modification, and enforcement of these standards. Law, in brief, governs our relationships with each other.

- The primary heritage of the U.S. legal system is England's common law. Common law refers to a traditional body of unwritten legal precedents created through everyday practice and supported by court decisions during the Middle Ages in English society.

- Much of private security law is governed by civil law, which governs the relationships between individuals in the course of their private affairs. Civil law is generally subdivided into six major categories: tort law, property law, contract and business law, corporation law, inheritance law, and family law.

- Civil recovery laws allow businesses to recoup losses they have suffered from theft by recovering the value of damaged or unrecovered merchandise, time and money spent in pursuing the return of the property, and other related expenses.

- Evidence includes all the means by which an alleged fact, the truth of which is submitted to scrutiny, is established or disproved. The rules of evidence are a set of regulations that act as guidelines for judges, attorneys, and law enforcement personnel who are involved in the trials of cases.

- The private justice system is a concept that holds that businesses and corporations might prefer to deal with crime using their own internal systems and controls instead of having crime dealt with through the cumbersome and lengthy formal criminal justice system.

- Courts have generally held that private security personnel obtain their legal authority from the same basic authority that an employer would have in protecting his or her own property. This authority is extended to security guards and other employees hired by an employer by virtue of their employment. Private security enforcement rights in dealing with shoplifting or theft enforcement are also based on the common-law concept of the shopkeeper's or merchant's privilege.

- In the landmark U.S. Supreme Court case *Burdeau v. McDowell*, the Court held that the provisions of the Fourth Amendment did not apply to subjects who were arrested or searched by private parties or nongovernmental employees.

■ The issue of legal liability is a significant concern for the private security industry. Civil liability claims include torts, negligence, strict liability torts, and vicarious liability.

Learning Check

1. Define *law*.
2. What is common law?
3. What is statutory law?
4. Explain the differences between the criminal law process and the civil law process.
5. Explain the differences between the arrest powers of private security officers and the public police.
6. Do the same constitutional restrictions apply to private security officers as apply to public police officers? Explain.
7. Are private security employees required to issue *Miranda* warnings to those people they arrest? Explain your answer.
8. Name and explain three issues that corporations may be held civilly liable for regarding security matters.
9. Identify and explain several liability issues a private security firm may face when using police officers as private security officers.
10. Identify five principles of appearance and demeanor a security officer should adhere to when testifying in court.

Application Exercise

You have been hired as the security director for a residential complex in your community. Formerly, the complex used a contractual security firm to patrol and safeguard the complex. Management has decided not to renew their contract due to many complaints of improper security methods used by their guards. Management has asked you to create a small proprietary security staff to patrol the complex and ensure safety for its occupants and visitors. It asks you to prepare a set of written instructions to all security officers, detailing the legal behavior they should adhere to regarding arrests and searches and seizures.

Web Exercise

Use the web to find the statutory law in your jurisdiction regarding the arrest powers of private citizens and police or peace officers. Compare and contrast these laws.

Key Terms

adversarial system, p. 90
civil law, p. 89
civil liability, p. 98
civil recovery/civil demand programs, p. 96
common law, p. 87
criminal liability, p. 102
cross-examination, p. 105
direct testimony, p. 106
evidence, p. 91
exclusionary rule, p. 96
law, p. 87
Miranda ruling/*Miranda* warning, p. 96
negligence, p. 99
private justice system, p. 91
shopkeeper's (merchant's) privilege, p. 88
strict liability, p. 99
torts, p. 99
vicarious liability, p. 99

Premise Security

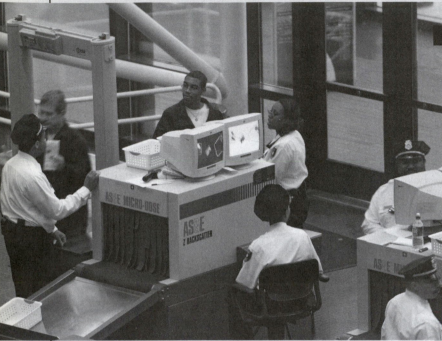

©Dennis Mac Donald/PhotoEdit

GOALS

- To give you a sense of the premise crime situation in the United States.
- To acquaint you with the many types of premises protected by the private security industry.
- To familiarize you with the many security problems that may exist in various premises.
- To introduce you to the methods used by private security to protect various types of premises.
- To show you how the police and private security agencies work together to protect premises.
- To introduce you to academic studies regarding the effectiveness of various security methods for premises.

Introduction

Security is essential to our way of life in the United States. Lawrence W. Sherman, in his *Preventing Crime: What Works, What Doesn't, What's Promising: A Report to the United States Congress*, wrote in 1998:

> Security guards, cameras, alarm systems, safes, and fences have all proliferated in the latter twentieth century, making private expenditures on crime prevention rival public spending. Whether these practices succeed in preventing crime is generally impossible to determine from the available research, given its limitations. Even where they do succeed at preventing crime in target places, it is unclear whether the total number of criminal events in society is reduced or merely displaced to other locations.[1]

Although, as we see in Sherman's quote, in many cases we cannot positively document which security measures work or which do not work in protecting premises in our society, there is no doubt that security measures are necessary. If there were any doubt that premise security is extremely necessary, one only has to think back to the tragic events of 9/11.

People have always been worried about crime and have taken measures to isolate or protect themselves against it. Peace and security in one's neighborhood and home is one of humankind's most treasured values. As Professor George L. Kelling has written, "Citizens have armed themselves, restricted their activities, rejected cities, built fortress houses and housing complexes both inside and outside the cities, and panicked about particular groups and classes of citizens."[2]

This chapter will discuss security problems at various premises in our society and measures used to deal with these problems and keep our premises secure. It will discuss property and premise crime, the police and property crime, and private security and property crime. It will also discuss security in residential places, businesses, educational facilities, public places, transportation facilities, and entertainment facilities. Security in residential places will include neighborhoods, private residences, and public housing developments. Business place security will include security in retail stores, convenience stores, fast-food restaurants, shopping centers and malls, industrial facilities, factories and warehouses, office buildings, public and private utilities, hospitals and healthcare facilities, hotels and motels, and banks. Government buildings and facilities and houses of worship and cemeteries will also be discussed. Educational facility security will include schools, and museums, libraries, and archives. Transportation facilities' security will include airports, bus and train stations, ports, cargo depots, trucks, parking lots and garages. Entertainment place security will include sporting arenas and ballparks, movies, theatres and clubs, pools and beaches, amusement parks, cruise ships, and casinos. The chapter will conclude with a discussion of homeland security efforts on premise security.

It must be remembered that this text is a general introductory text for students interested in obtaining a general knowledge of private security. If students are interested in a more in-depth and sophisticated knowledge of particular areas of premise security, it is suggested that they research the numerous books and websites of professional associations for each particular area of premise security mentioned in this chapter.

Property and Premise Crime

The most recent *Uniform Crime Reports* (*UCR*) published by the FBI indicated that there were approximately 10.2 million serious property crimes, including 2.15 million burglaries, 6.8 million larcenies/thefts, and 1.23 million motor vehicle thefts, reported to the police in the latest reporting year.[3] The *UCR*'s *Crime Clock* indicates that, on average, there is one serious property crime every 3.1 seconds, including one burglary every 14.6 seconds, one larceny/theft every 4.7 seconds, and one motor vehicle theft every 25.5 seconds.[4] Additionally, for the latest reporting year, police arrested about 299,000 persons for burglary; 1.15 million persons for larceny or theft; about 16,000 persons for arson; 280,000 for vandalism; and 134,000 for receiving, buying, or possessing stolen property.[5] Property and premise crime is certainly an important and serious problem in our society.

The economic loss to victims of property crimes, such as household burglaries, motor vehicle thefts and personal thefts, is over $14 million a year.[6] The monetary losses involved in these property crimes are only the tip of the iceberg.

JOBS IN SECURITY

Healthcare Industry

The following are examples of security positions in the healthcare industry.

■ Manager of Safety and Security: For this position, the Salem Hospital of Salem, Oregon, requires a bachelor's degree in law enforcement, safety management, or a related field, as well as previous healthcare management experience.

■ Security Field Supervisor: This position at the InterCon Healthcare Security Services Group of Denver, Colorado, helps manage its twenty-nine sites. The minimum qualifications include a college degree, previous security management, and CPP or CHPA designation.

Source: International Association for Healthcare Security & Safety, *Career Opportunities Job Bank*. Retrieved December 10, 2004, from, http://www.iahss.org/jobbank.html.

There are also tremendous personal, business, and social costs involved. Some of the personal costs are the physical and emotional injuries victims suffer as a result of being a crime victim. Among the business costs of property crime are bankruptcies, business failures, the cost of increased insurance, loss of profit, reduced productivity, higher overhead, and much more. Among the social costs are the cost of investigating, prosecuting, and incarcerating offenders and the emotional effect of crime on our society. Also, consider the enormous personal cost of crime to the victim. Imagine that you come home from a hard day at work or school and you discover there has been a burglary in your home—all of your property and belongings are gone. This experience seriously affects your life and sense of security.

The Police, Private Security, and Property Crime

In response to crime, the police routinely patrol residential and commercial areas looking for suspicious persons and other conditions that may indicate that a crime is in progress. They also respond to calls of these crimes in progress, as well as calls about suspicious persons or circumstances. The police, by their routine patrols, attempt to provide a sense of omnipresence (they are always around or at least always *seem* to be around) in the hope of making citizens and business people feel safe and secure in their neighborhoods. Most of the arrests that the police make are the result of their attempts to provide this sense of omnipresence and their attempts to respond to and investigate the calls made to them. In addition to their omnipresence and response to crime, the police also investigate past property crimes in an attempt to clear (police term for "solve") these crimes and bring those responsible for them to justice.

However, as we saw in Chapters 1 and 2, the public police are limited in personnel and jurisdiction to provide these services to all of society. The private security industry has attempted to fill this gap. Private security efforts are extremely important in investigating and preventing property crime. Businesses and other private concerns make special concentrated efforts to detect and apprehend persons committing these crimes. The private security industry uses numerous methods to prevent and detect premise crime. Some of these methods were detailed in Chapter 3, including crime prevention and deterrence concepts, such as risk management, risk analysis, security surveys and the private security tools of access control, proprietary security departments, propriety or contract security guards, alarm systems, and electronic video surveillance. In addition, each chapter of the text covers particular security methods and tools relating to the subject matter of the chapter.

Furthermore, residents have sought the assistance of private security to help the police protect their community. The following is a good example of the modern philosophy of involving citizens, private security, and the police in anticrime efforts:

> If a resident of a building on 77th Street, between 2nd and 3rd Avenues, in New York City, senses suspicious activity on the block, the resident can press a button in the middle of a key chain transmitter that sends a radio frequency signal to a receiver. Immediately a device mounted on a building on the block receives the signal and a loud siren is triggered with an alert message that screams incessantly,

JOBS IN SECURITY

Hotel Security

The following are examples of available jobs in hotel security.

- Security Manager: At the Waldorf Astoria Hotel in New York City, the individual in this position assists the Director and Assistant Director of Security and Safety. He or she investigates and monitors all initial security reports and develops and maintains programs. A minimum of three years of hotel security supervisory/management experience are required, as well as a college degree.

- Director of Security/Loss Prevention: The Sheraton Atlanta Hotel employs a director of security and loss prevention who designs, implements, and enforces policies and procedures that protect life and property of guests and employees, and directs a staff of several supervisors and security officers on three shifts.

- Loss Prevention Officer: At the Sheraton Studio City Hotel, the loss prevention officer provides security services to both hotel guests and associates, including but not limited to traffic control, guest services, prevention patrol, report writing, first aid, fire safety and all other duties as required. The position requires a state security license, and the company recommends at least two years of security employment with hotel security experience and a Certified Hotel Lodging Security Officer Certification for all applicants.

SOURCE: American Hotel and Lodging Association, *Job Details*. Retrieved December 10, 2004, from http://www.ahla.new-jobs.com.

EXHIBIT 5.1 ASIS International Professional Development Program: Assets Protection Course

ASIS International offers a four-day assets protection course for professionals involved in security management. Topics include:

- Introduction to assets protection
- Security vulnerability
- Locking concepts
- Systems security
- Security lighting
- Emergency planning
- General security management
- Investigations
- CPTED—Crime Prevention through Environmental Design
- Access control

SOURCE: ASIS International, "Training Offerings for ASIS International." Retrieved October 13, 2005, from http://www.asisonline.org.

Residential Places

This section will cover security at residential places in the United States, including neighborhoods, private residences, and public housing developments.

Neighborhoods

Citizens are worried about crime and have taken measures to isolate or protect themselves against it in their neighborhoods. In order to deter crime and attempt to create a sense of safety, the police patrol residential areas and look for suspicious persons and other conditions that may indicate that a crime is in progress. They also respond to any requests for assistance called in to them. The police, by their routine patrols, attempt to provide a sense of omnipresence with the hope of making citizens feel safe and secure.

In their seminal 1982 article in the *Atlantic Monthly*, "'Broken Windows': The Police and Neighborhood Safety," scholars James Q. Wilson and George Kelling expounded on the **"broken windows" theory**

"Intruder on the block, call the police." Also, a police siren and a series of strobe lights go off. The alarm company's central office identifies the caller based on the personal ID code embedded in the alarm signal and calls 911. This is an experimental system being used by the 77th Street Block Association designed to protect their block.[7]

Exhibits 5.1 and 5.2 provide information regarding ASIS International's professional development and physical security professional (PSP) certifications programs available to security professionals.

"broken windows" theory Theory that unrepaired broken windows or disrepair indicate that members of a community do not care about the quality of life in their neighborhood; consequently, disorder and crime will thrive.

EXHIBIT 5.2   ASIS International's Physical Security Professional (PSP) Certification

---

ELIGIBILITY

Candidates wishing to take the PSP examination must first satisfy the following requirements:

Experience and Education

Five years of experience in the physical security field

High school diploma or GED equivalent

The applicant must not have been convicted of any criminal offense that would reflect negatively on the security profession, ASIS International, or the certification program.

Examination Structure and Content

The PSP examination consists of multiple-choice questions covering tasks, knowledge, and skills in subjects identified by physical security professionals as the major areas involved in this field. All exam questions come from the official reference books. No questions on the exam are taken from any other source.

The subjects are:

Physical Security Assessment

A. Identifying assets to determine their value and criticality
   - Nature and types of assets (e.g., property, personnel, and information)
   - Valuing various types of assets
   - Definitions and terminology
   - Risk management principles
   - Core functions of the facility
   - Types of security programs and security processes
   - Qualitative vs. quantitative risk assessments

B. Assessing the nature of the threats so that the scope of the problem can be determined
   - Nature, categories, and types of threats (e.g., natural, manmade)
   - Nature of different types of environments
   - Crime demographics
   - Critical business operations of various types of facilities
   - External organizations and their potential impact on facility's security program

C. Conducting a physical security survey in order to identify the vulnerabilities of the organization
   - Security survey techniques
   - Security technologies and equipment applications
   - Interpretation of building plans, drawings, and schematics
   - Nature and types of data to be collected
   - Methods of collecting relevant data
   - Analysis and interpretation of relevant data
   - Different levels of vulnerability and effects on assets

D. Performing a risk analysis so that appropriate countermeasures can be developed
   - Types of risk analyses
   - Cost and loss analyses
   - Methods of evaluating criticality and probability
   - Appropriate countermeasures related to specific threats
   - Legal issues related to various countermeasures/security applications

---

of policing and neighborhood safety. The article made the following crucial points:

- Disorder in neighborhoods creates fear. Urban streets that are often occupied by homeless people, prostitutes, drug addicts, youth gangs, and the mentally disturbed are more likely than other areas to have high crime rates.

- Certain neighborhoods send out "signals" that encourage crime. A community in which housing has deteriorated, broken windows are left unrepaired, and disorderly behavior is ignored may actually promote crime. Honest and good citizens live in fear in these areas, and predatory criminals are attracted.[8]

Wilson and Kelling believe that the police, by working closely with communities, can ameliorate these situations.

Another scholar, Wesley G. Skogan, surveyed numerous neighborhoods and identified two major categories of disorder that affect the quality of life in the community: human and physical disorder. The human behaviors found to be extremely disruptive to the community were public drinking, corner gangs, street harassment, drugs, noisy neighbors, and commercial sex. The physical disorders that Skogan found extremely destructive to the community were vandalism, dilapidation and abandonment, and rubbish.[9]

Since the 1980s, in an effort to deal with crime and disorder in neighborhoods, the police have

Selection of Integrated Physical Security Measures

A. Identifying measures/components to match the requirement of the appropriate solution/ recommendation
- Relevant terminology
- Types of security measures and their various applications (people and technology)
- Applicable codes and standards
- Appropriate hardware and software
- Ancillary measures
- Materials, equipment and system compatibility

B. Performing cost analysis of the proposed integrated measures to ensure efficiency of implementation/ operation
- Types of security measures/equipment
- Cost estimates and cost-benefit analysis
- Integration of components/measures
- Scheduling

C. Outlining/documenting recommendations with relevant reasons for presentation to facility so the appropriate choices can be made
- Major elements of reports/proposals
- Methods of setting priorities
- Advantages and disadvantages of various security measures and management process
- Drawings and plans

Implementation of Physical Security Measures

A. Outlining criteria for pre-bid meetings to ensure comprehensiveness and appropriateness of implementations
- Bid package components
- Criteria for evaluation of bids
- Technical compliance criteria

B. Procuring systems and implementing recommended solutions to solve identified problems
- Project management functions and processes
- System integration
- Qualifying vendor factors
- Change order reviews
- Procurement process
- Passive and active designs

C. Conducting final acceptance testing and implementing/providing procedures for ongoing monitoring and evaluation of the measures
- Installation/maintenance inspection techniques
- Establishing test criteria
- End-user training requirements
- Maintenance needs of design
- Loss prevention techniques
- System programming techniques
- Asset tracking technologies
- Passive and active designs

SOURCE: ASIS International, "Physical Security Professional (PSP)." Retrieved October 13, 2005, from http://www.asisonline.org.

---

introduced the concept of **community policing.** Community policing is defined as police efforts at maintaining order and delivering services in a proactive relationship with the community, instead of just reacting and responding to each incident that they are summoned to by a 911 call.[10] Using community policing, the police have turned to the public and the business communities for their support and active participation in programs to make the streets safer and the quality of life better. Some **community crime-prevention programs** coordinated with the police include Neighborhood Watch, Crime Watch, Block Watch, Community Alert, citizen patrols, and citizen marches. Residents engage in these programs to watch over their own neighborhoods, look for suspicious people, and lobby for neighborhood improvements, such as increased lighting and other improved city services. Residents report to the police and work with them to make their neighborhoods safer and to motivate criminals and drug users to leave the neighborhoods.[11] Community crime-prevention programs are covered fully in Chapter 12 of this textbook.

community policing Philosophy of empowering citizens and developing a partnership between the police and the community to work together to solve problems.

community crime-prevention programs Anticrime programs in which citizens participate in crime-prevention programs in their own neighborhoods; some examples are neighborhood watch, crime watch, block watch, community alert, citizen patrols and citizen marches.

These police and citizen patrols have not always been successful; however, one particular, relatively recent, effort of the business community to prevent crime and to improve conditions in the communities in which they do business does seem to work. The **business improvement district (BID)** concept involves the combined efforts of the business community and the private security industry with the cooperation of the police. BIDs are private organizations that oversee critical services, such as sanitation and security, for businesses in a defined geographical area or district. BIDs are also fully discussed in Chapter 12.

Some residential or business communities without a BID hire a private contract security company to patrol their streets and check their homes to augment the efforts of the police. These security officers generally patrol in uniform on foot or in distinctively marked police-type vehicles.

Private Residences

The concept that "one's home is one's castle" is very important to Americans. People build perimeter protection such as fences, walls, and shrubbery around their homes to protect them and maintain their privacy. They also spend fortunes on outdoor security lighting, locks, and burglary and anti-intrusion alarm systems.

Citizens worry about burglary. A government-sponsored report indicates that approximately 60 percent of household burglaries occur during daytime hours when houses are most often unoccupied, and burglars select targets based on many factors, including familiarity with the target, convenience of the location, occupancy, accessibility, and potential rewards. Approximately 87 percent of burglars were male, and 63 percent were under 25 years of age. The report recommends installing alarm systems, implementing neighborhood watch programs, and improving the visibility of houses as ways to decrease burglaries.[12]

Homeowners can take numerous proactive security measures to prevent burglary, including alarm systems, security surveys, and private security and self-protection methods.[13] Alarm systems were covered at length in Chapter 3.

Many homes today are built in private, gated communities, which offer owners a sense of security because the entire community is enclosed in perimeter fencing or walls and has one means of entrance and exit to the community. At the entrance–exit, there is generally a conspicuous guard booth manned by a security guard who checks all persons entering the community. Some communities have installed electronic turnstiles at their entrances that require residents to enter an identification card in order for the gates to rise to permit entry. People without identification cards are questioned by the security guard, who checks with the homeowners to see if the person should be admitted.

In multiple dwellings, such as apartment houses, security is often a major concern. Some dwellings employ security guards or doormen to regulate entry into the building and to patrol the building. Others have sophisticated access-controlled entrances that require visitors to be allowed into the building by a particular tenant. Condominium and co-op complexes have similar security concerns and countermeasures. Some condominium and co-op complexes use security guards and electronic video surveillance. The electronic video systems are put into laundry and recreation rooms, parking lots, equipment storage and maintenance rooms, hallways, and entrances.

As an example of condominium security, the Capri Gardens Condominium, a 500-resident complex in North Miami, Florida, which has three four-story residential buildings and a one-story recreation center, uses two uniformed security officers on duty between 8 P.M. and 8 A.M., seven days a week. Their duties include patrolling the grounds, calling police if an incident occurs, and acting as a witness for the police in the event of any crime or incident. The complex also uses electronic video surveillance.[14]

Crime is also a significant issue at building sites for private residences. For example, in 2004, arsonists set fires that destroyed or damaged twenty-six new houses in Indian Head, a semirural southern Maryland community, and tried unsuccessfully to set another eleven homes ablaze. The arson caused $10 million in damage. At the time, officials thought the motives behind these crimes were ecoterrorism or racial animosity toward the houses' new owners, many of whom are African American. A week after the fires, police arrested four men for the crime, one a 21-year-old security guard who worked at the site protecting it. Police suspected the motives of the arsonists were revenge and racial animosity.[15]

business improvement districts (BIDS) Private organizations that oversee critical services, such as security and sanitation, for businesses in a defined geographical area or district.

Public Housing Developments

The following selection from an article in the *Journal of Security Administration,* regarding problems in public housing, paints a sad picture for residents of this housing:

> Crime in properties controlled by public housing authorities presents a different problem for security professionals and the criminal justice system. This problem results from a combination of high-density population, poverty and lack of adequate resources to combat criminal activity. This has been coupled with the increase in illegal drug use to create virtual war-zones in many public housing communities. Drug sales and usage are extensive, leading to prostitution, burglary, and assorted crimes against public housing residents and their property. In this setting it is virtually impossible for tenants and their children to lead a normal life.[16]

Considering the conditions noted in this quote, it is obvious that there are numerous security problems in public housing. These major security problems range from extreme crimes of violence, like murder, rape, felonious assault, and robbery, to property crimes such as burglary, vandalism, and theft. There are also enormous other problems, such as order maintenance, crowd control, alcohol and drug abuse, and drug dealing. The police patrol public housing; however, their resources are limited, and they cannot maintain a continued presence at the housing units because they are often called away to perform other police duties and services.

Large metropolitan areas have housing authorities to support and service public, low-income housing. Many of the housing authorities are governmental or quasigovernmental agencies and have a proprietary security force with police powers. Housing under the control of the U.S. Department of Housing and Urban Development (HUD) employs contract security firms in some of its developments.

Numerous housing authorities across the nation employ contract private security to police their developments. In some public housing developments, residents form tenant patrols in which they patrol throughout their own buildings and establish security desks at the entrance to each building, where they check on persons entering.

Businesses

This section will discuss security operations in major businesses in the United States, including retail stores, convenience stores, fast-food restaurants, shopping centers and malls, industrial facilities, factories, warehouses, office buildings, public and private utilities, hospitals and healthcare facilities, hotels and motels, and banks. Chapter 7 of this text discusses two other important crime concerns to businesses: workplace violence and domestic violence in the workplace.

The police patrol business and industrial areas and look for possible crimes in progress, suspicious persons, and other conditions that may generate crime and disorder. They also respond to any requests for assistance called in to them. However, they generally do not have the jurisdiction and personnel to adequately prevent crime in businesses. The private security industry attempts to bridge this gap.

Retail Stores

Retail stores include large supermarkets, small grocery stores, drug stores, department stores, auto-part stores, appliance stores, furniture stores, clothing stores, and many other types of retail shops throughout the United States. They are generally called point-of-sale retail businesses. These stores can be and often are the targets of crime from inside and outside the business itself. Crimes and security problems in stores run the gamut from all the crimes of violence to property crimes, such as burglary, vandalism, theft, and internal theft. They are also subject to an enormous amount of so-called "white collar" crime, such as computer crime, bad checks, credit card crimes, forgery, embezzlement, and other similar crimes. Stores may also have security problems in terms of order maintenance and parking.

Loss prevention is one of the major concerns of the retail business in the United States. Retail security and loss prevention will be discussed in Chapter 6. Shoplifting and employee theft are major security problems with most retail businesses. Most large retail businesses have a propriety security department, which performs numerous duties regarding loss prevention, safety, and internal auditing. Other smaller businesses and stores may have a proprietary security employee on duty or hire security guards from a contract guard service.

Solid metal security gates are common sights in many downtown business areas and low-income,

©Michael Newman/PhotoEdit

The convenience-store industry has conducted some of the most sophisticated crime-prevention experiments. This is a recommended convenience-store layout with security mirrors mounted close to the ceiling. The mirrors are intended to give retail owners and employees the ability to see most of the store's interior, thereby eliminating or minimizing blind spots where potential shoplifters can easily conceal their stolen merchandise.

crime-ridden areas. However, many feel that these gates are aesthetically unappealing, may actually invite crime by giving a block a disheveled, uncared-for appearance, and attract graffiti.[17]

Convenience Stores

When the average person thinks of a scary situation, he or she may think about being employed as a clerk in a convenience store at 3 A.M. in an inner-city neighborhood or an isolated rural area.

Sherman reports that the convenience store industry has conducted some of the most sophisticated crime-prevention experiments available. These studies suggest there are two types of stores: those with few or no robberies where crime-prevention efforts are unlikely to influence future robberies, and a fewer number of stores with several robberies where prevention efforts may be more productive.[18]

The National Association of Convenience Stores (NACS) is a professional trade association for employees, owners, and others that have an interest in convenience store operations.[19] NACS has published numerous reports and has issued a tremen-

dous amount of advice to its members regarding security at their establishments. Based on official studies, the following are major methods it recommends to maintain security and reduce crime:

- Cash control
- Visibility, including clear sight lines into stores, prominent position of cash registers in the front of the stores, and balanced exterior and interior lighting
- Eliminating escape routes
- Employee training[20]

NACS also recommends electronic video surveillance and alarms. **Cash control** includes keeping as little cash as possible in the cash register and putting all other cash in a secure "drop safe" that employees cannot access. Visibility entails good lighting on the inside and outside of the store and clear views of all areas of the store from the clerk's position in the front of the store and from the outside. Electronic video surveillance is recommended as a deterrent to would-be criminals and as an aid in investigating past crimes. Robbery deterrence training includes ensuring that clerks and other employees remain calm during crimes and other incidents and do not resist robberies.[21]

NACS has also issued reports on using multiple clerks as safety strategies, concealed weapons,

cash control Methods used to safeguard cash in commercial businesses and institutions.

Some Professional Associations Affecting Premise Security

National Association of Convenience Stores (NACS)
International Association of Healthcare Security and Safety (IAHSS)
American Hotel and Lodging Association (AH&LA)
AH&LA Educational Institute (EI-AH&LA)
International Hotel and Restaurant Association (IH&RA)
American Library Association (ALA)
Association of College and Research Libraries (ACRL)

bullet-resistant barriers, robbery awareness and deterrence steps for safer stores, security guards, and loss frequency in the convenience store industry. Contrary to what some believe may be deterrent factors, NACS does not recommend concealed weapons, bullet-resistant barriers, multiple clerks, or security guards as effective deterrents to crime at their stores.[22]

Fast-Food Restaurants

The major security problems at fast-food restaurants include robbery and theft, internal theft, and order maintenance. Corporate fast-food headquarters generally have a proprietary security department that provides training and advice on security. Most of their security practices are similar to those of convenience stores. Some fast-food restaurants in crime-ridden areas may hire contract security guards to maintain order and project a sense of safety and security. Most fast-food restaurants use electronic video surveillance technology. As an example, the Minneapolis-area Subway sandwich stores use three or four cameras in each store.[23]

Video surveillance systems with text insertion are very useful to prevent insider or employee theft. Text insertion is a feature that displays cash register activity on corresponding surveillance footage. For example, if an employee entered a "no sale" on the register, the tape would show that such an activity had occurred by superimposing that information on the corresponding segment of the videotape. This allows restaurant managers to investigate cash shortages or other cases of suspected employee theft. Many systems have remote surveillance capability that allows an owner or security director to view all activity in the store from a remote location.

Shopping Centers and Malls

There are many security problems at large shopping centers and malls. They include vandalism, loss prevention, order maintenance, crowd control, parking security, thefts of automobiles, thefts from autos, terrorism, and the safety of people walking to and from their vehicles.

Security researchers and experts have found that security, both the perception and the reality of it, is a critical factor in determining when and where consumers spend their money. Properly crafted security programs can make a significant contribution to a company's bottom line. Mall owners and managers track information about crime and disorder at their malls and tailor their security programs to those findings. Research has indicated that there is evidence of a correlation between crime at malls and the presence of "problematic" persons, such as gangs and loitering groups of youth. Most malls create a code of conduct for the mall and develop partnerships with law enforcement to ensure a safe shopping environment. Codes of conduct play a valuable role in spelling out what types of behavior by visitors will not be condoned in a retail environment. The public posting of these codes at the entrance and throughout the malls helps reassure shoppers that the shopping center is a controlled environment where their shopping experience will not be disturbed by aggressive, illegal, or offensive behavior.[24]

A study of retail establishments in the United Kingdom revealed that security was given a higher priority by the managers of enclosed malls than by the managers of traditional downtown shopping areas, called town centers. Shoppers also regarded malls as safer than town centers. Town-center shoppers were at least three times more likely than mall shoppers to cite crime as a serious problem. The findings perhaps explain why malls are winning in the fight for retail business. Shopping-mall managers generally prefer an approach to security that combines security guards, radios, and electronic video surveillance. Many malls allow security guards to be proactive in excluding, ejecting, or moving people who create an unacceptable nuisance, even though their behavior might fall short of criminal activity. Malls have found that security means safety, safety means shoppers, and shoppers mean profits for retail businesses.[25] "Every study ever done about how people choose where to shop has 'security' and 'safety' at the top of the list," said the vice president and general manager of a major shopping center.[26]

Many malls hire a contract security service to patrol the inside of the mall and its perimeter parking

You Are There!

How 7-Eleven Protects Its Stores

The Southland Corporation of Dallas has 2,100 company-owned and 2,900 franchised 7-Eleven stores across the United States. Their security operations are based on several studies conducted since the mid-1970s by Southland, the Western Behavioral Sciences Institute (WBSI), the National Institute of Justice (NIJ), the National Association of Convenience Stores, and the Athena Research Corporation. Based on this research, the company gained insight into how robbers think and what deters them from committing crime. It has led to the development of security strategies by 7-Eleven that have reduced robberies by 70 percent in the past twenty years. The average monetary loss to robberies at 7-Eleven is $37. This crime-deterrence program, which has helped the company reduce robberies and made customers and employees feel safer, is based on several major components.

- *Cash control.* The smallest amount of cash possible is kept at the store. 7-Eleven uses a five-hundred-pound cash control unit that serves as a drop safe and can only be opened by authorized personnel (generally the manager), who must enter his or her PIN. There is a ten-minute time delay before the cash unit opens.
- *Visibility.* Stores are brightly lit inside and outside. The cash register and clerks are clearly visible from outside the store, as are all places inside the store.
- *Training.* Employees are trained to handle robberies as calmly and quickly as they would any other transaction. All new employees receive two-day training involving robbery deterrence, violence avoidance, loitering, physical assault, gang activity, and recommended general security procedures to be followed in the event of an emergency situation. The training stresses that the safety of store personnel and customers is far more important

than protecting the company's money or property during a robbery. Store techniques include cooperating with the robber by giving up the money and never resisting, staring, talking unnecessarily, or arguing.

- *Electronic video surveillance and alarms.* There are video cameras and alarms in all stores nationwide. A fixed color camera is located near the front of each store with a clear view of the front door and cash register. VCRs maintain a record of all activity in the store. Each store also uses both fixed and remote activator alarm devices that transmit signals to a remote monitoring system. Store employees are encouraged to carry the remote alarm activators on their belts or in the pockets of their smocks.
- *Escape routes.* 7-Elevens are designed with only one entrance and exit. Fencing and landscaping with large bushes are used to thwart easy egress and block alleys or other escape routes that could be used by robbers.
- *Relationship with the local police.* 7-Eleven provides satellite offices for local police departments at which officers can make phone calls, complete paperwork, and meet with residents of the neighborhood they patrol. These Police Community Network Centers (PCNC) provide a dedicated telephone, drawers for storing forms and paperwork, and racks for displaying crime prevention literature. Studies have indicated that a strong police presence acts as a deterrent to robbery. Store employees and customers have consistently reported they feel safer with an increased police presence in their store and area.

SOURCE: Scott Lins and Rosemary J. Erickson, "Stores Learn to Inconvenience Robbers: 7-Eleven Shares Many of Its Robbery Deterrence Strategies," *Security Management*, November 1998, pp. 49–53.

---

lots during the hours when the mall is open, and the perimeter during the hours it is closed. In addition, police respond to malls on request to assist the private security officers in keeping order, to deal with emergencies, and to process arrests that result in a defendant being brought into the formal criminal justice system. Additionally, many stores within malls have their own security officers, generally proprietary, and their own loss prevention departments. Mall security generally cooperates with individual store security.

Research has discovered that many shopping-center managers are placing local law enforcement substations or offices on the premises. Although these tenants do not pay rent, this type of initiative affords the shopping center the benefit of increased police presence without having to pay the officers' salaries. Further recent research shows that regular police patrols had a far greater impact on mall motor-vehicle theft than did private security patrols.[27]

During the last few years, police departments around the nation have assigned officers to shopping malls, supplementing private security officers. Malls increasingly provide the police with fully equipped substations, police cars, and salaries, plus an "administrative fee." Many police officials in jurisdictions where police become involved in mall policing claim that because the mall policing is done either by additional officers hired to handle the load or by officers volunteering for overtime, the practice does not take police away from other parts of town.

Police officers first started coming into malls informally around 1992, after several highly publicized abductions in shopping malls around the country, including the 1992 abduction of Gail F. Shollar of Edison, New Jersey, who was abducted with her infant daughter at the Middlesex Mall in New Jersey and killed. In the wake of these attacks, the police started patrolling parking lots and then gradually went indoors. At about the same time, malls began offering police substations inside malls, where the police could book shoplifting suspects in less than half an hour, instead of the three hours it would take to do everything at the police station.[28]

According to a consultant on mall security, there has generally been some kind of formal partnership between the local police and shopping centers in recent years, ranging from an occasional off-duty police officer to many places where there are full-time police officers paid for by the mall. He said that the contracted municipal police supplement what is always a much bigger private security force in the mall. He said security costs at a major mall typically run $1 million a year or more, often exceeding costs for services such as maintenance, because the publicity of even one notorious incident, such as an abduction or a carjacking, could cost a mall far more in lost business and reputation.[29] "This is where the people are, so this is where we are," said one police chief.[30]

In 2000, one shopping mall was completely rewired to install a new **retail alert system**. Using the new system, Merchant Wired, which uses broadband technology that allows for simultaneous voice, video, and data transmission, merchants can immediately notify other merchants in the mall of possible shoplifters or persons passing bad checks. The former telephone alert system could take an hour for all the stores to be notified. The system allows numerous other business applications, including two-second verification of credit cards.[31]

The 2005 London subway bombings and other terrorist events have increased concerns that suicide bombers may target malls in the United States, and many private security firms are adopting methods to prevent such attacks.[32]

Industrial Facilities, Factories, and Warehouses

The major security concerns at industrial facilities, factories, and warehouses are property protection, theft, security of proprietary or classified information, fire protection, safety, traffic control, sabotage, and internal theft. Many industrial facilities employ a large proprietary security department under the direction of a security manager, which provides a myriad of services, and some use a mix of proprietary and contract security. Alarms and access control technology are used in these premises, and electronic video surveillance is frequently used in areas prone to theft. Security officers generally are stationed at entrances and cargo docks. They also patrol by making rounds of buildings, particularly after closing hours, using computerized security guard tour systems that were discussed in Chapter 3.

Office Buildings

The major security problems for commercial office buildings are after-hour burglaries and thefts, unauthorized visitors, and incidents of internal theft. Security personnel from a central station, using electronic video surveillance, can effectively monitor large commercial office buildings. Contract security personnel, whose duties include access control, motoring surveillance systems, and making regular security checks or rounds throughout the building, generally provide security at office buildings.

According to the *National Real Estate Investor*, office-building security has been evolving steadily since 9/11, from relatively open access to much stricter environments through the use of electronic barriers, individual identification, monitoring, and vehicle control.[33] Security professionals report that security measures start outside the building itself at the perimeter and moves into the building, applying in ever-increasing layers or levels.

retail alert system Program in which businesses in the same area notify each other immediately in the event of a crime; alerts can be done by telephone, voice, video, or data transmission.

Experts suggest that all buildings today use turnstiles to control traffic moving through the lobby to the elevators. Before 9/11, one could enter a building and encounter moderate security, and specific security needs were handled at the floor level by tenants. Today, security begins before or as one enters the building.[34]

In a major recent survey, it was reported that the private sector spent about $76 billion on homeland security upgrades in 2003 alone. Beefing up security at locations such as building lobbies has been the most visible display of increased security. Also, many financial services firms have shifted employees and operations to backup trading sites outside of major urban centers in order to continue their operations in the event of a future terrorist attack.[35]

Temporary badging for visitors, contractors, and others temporarily visiting a building is an important factor in office-building security. The technology of **expiring time badges** allows visitor badges to change colors when the badge is no longer valid, showing that the wearer is no longer authorized to be in the building. The technology can set expiration for various time periods, such as half-day, one day, one week, one month. This technology is used in thousands of facilities worldwide, including government agencies, hospitals, schools, corporations, and airports, and can be customized to a particular company. This technology also can provide temporary-badge visitor management system software for visitor management and can issue predesigned reports of daily visitors, signed-in visitors, preregistered visitors, visitor log by date, auto signed-out reports, and emergency evaluation reports. The emergency evacuation report automatically prints a report of all visitors on premise and their location in the event of the need to evacuate the building for an emergency. The system also can print similar-type parking permits.[36]

Public and Private Utilities

Public utilities provide gas, telephone, electricity, water, and other services to the public. They generally have large plants and service areas. Most public and private utilities have a proprietary security staff supplemented by contract security guards. The major security problems affecting public and private utilities are terrorism, sabotage, destruction of property and assets, thefts of services and assets, and personal protection of employees. Nuclear facilities present additional security and safety problems. Security at nuclear facilities is closely supervised and monitored by the federal government. The following paragraphs detail some particular risks concerning dams, oil and chemical facilities, and nuclear facilities.

Dams The Army Corps of Engineers conducts studies of possible security problems at dams. In a recent study, it determined that a terrorist attack against the Kensico Dam in Westchester County, New York, which holds back the Kensico Reservoir, a 30.6-billion-gallon basin, would be catastrophic, causing extensive flooding in Westchester and threatening New York City's drinking water. About 90 percent of the city's water supply flows through the Kensico Reservoir. New York City, which owns the reservoir and dam, stations full-time police officers at the dam and surrounding areas and uses barriers, enhanced lighting, and security cameras.[37]

Oil Facilities The Houston, Texas, area, with two of the four largest oil refineries in the United States and much of the infrastructure used to transport oil and natural gas around the country, has been mentioned as one of the most sensitive potential targets for terrorist attacks. The city of Houston is also the intellectual and financial center for the global energy industry. According to a spokesperson for the East Harris County Manufacturers' Association, which represents 125 industrial concerns along the Houston Ship Channel, among them refineries, shipping companies, and petrochemical plants, "A possible attack is absolutely a concern for us. It's something to worry about night and day."[38] Oil companies provide extensive proprietary and contract security for their property and assets.

Chemical Facilities The chemical industry engages in security measures, and most firms generally operate proprietary security department and also use contract security services at their facilities. However, in 2004, the Congressional General Accounting Office (GAO) reported that there were problems with the chemical industry's vulnerability to terrorist attacks. It reported that 123 chemical

temporary badging Process of identifying visitors, contractors, and others temporarily visiting a building or other facility.

expiring time badges Temporary identification system for visitors, contractors, and others temporarily visiting a building or other facility; these badges change colors when the badge is no longer valid, showing that the wearer is no longer authorized to be on the premise.

plants across the country could each expose more than 1 million people to serious health issues if a chemical release occurred. Another 600 facilities could endanger between 100,000 and 1 million people.[39]

In 2004, the fertilizer industry, in concert with the Bureau of Alcohol, Tobacco, Firearms, and Explosives, began urging sellers of ammonium nitrate—which has been the main ingredient in at least half-a-dozen major terror attacks in the United States and abroad—to track sales and require buyers to show identification. Nevada and South Carolina have laws requiring such tracking. Both the 1993 World Trade Center attack and the 1995 Oklahoma City federal building bombings involved truck-size batches of ammonium nitrate.[40]

Nuclear Plants Nuclear power facilities generally have proprietary security departments with well-trained security officers, and many also use contract security services to assist their regular security services. Nuclear facility security is closely monitored by the Nuclear Regulatory Commission (NRC), which also closely regulates the companies that run the nuclear facilities. Since 9/11, the NRC has required the nation's 104 commercial nuclear power plants to engage in drills to repel possible attackers. The Wackenhut security firm has been hired to train the workers who will conduct mock attacks on plants in triennial drills.[41]

Hospitals and Healthcare Facilities

Some of the major security problems facing hospitals and healthcare facilities are the protection and safety of patients and employees; order maintenance; and the prevention of thefts, fraud, and internal employee theft. The issue of healthcare fraud is covered extensively in Chapter 10 of this textbook.

Security is responsible for preventing unauthorized persons from entering the facility or patients' rooms (visitor control). In addition, security problems are often encountered in the hospital's emergency rooms due to unruly, disruptive, emotionally disturbed, and intoxicated patients and visitors. Many hospitals station a uniformed security officer in the emergency-room area. Security personnel are also responsible for security at receiving locations, offices, cafeterias, supply rooms, and locker rooms, as well as for parking and traffic control. Particular attention is given to areas where drugs are stored.

Hospitals and healthcare facilities generally use both proprietary security and contract security agencies. Security methods include alarms, access control systems, electronic video surveillance, and uniformed security personnel. Security personnel generally maintain a presence at hospital entrances and may also have a security desk at the entrance. Hospital visitors are generally controlled by a pass system; however, many hospitals use volunteers to administer the system. Hospital and healthcare facilities usually use a badging system for employees. Generally, at night, all main entrances and exits are locked and alarmed, and all employees and visitors must use the main entrance. Special attention is also addressed to security at psychiatric wards.

Three measures are usually useful to help decrease loss and thefts of drugs at a hospital or healthcare facility: internal reporting and monitoring, investigations, and employee education. Nurses dispensing drugs carefully account for and record the removal and use of all drugs from the pharmacy on special inventory forms, and outgoing and oncoming supervisory nurses do an inventory of all stored drugs. The security department and the head of pharmacy immediately investigate all cases of missing or unaccounted-for drugs, and employees are educated on the importance of security of drugs.[42]

The International Association of Healthcare Security and Safety (IAHSS) is a professional trade organization dedicated to healthcare security. It works to improve and professionalize security and safety in healthcare facilities through the exchange of information and experiences with healthcare security and safety executives. It has developed the Certified Healthcare Professional Administrator (CHPA) credential. The CHPA credential signifies professional competence and is recognized nationally by healthcare security personnel and healthcare human resources directors. It also offers basic certification and training for healthcare security officers—Certified Healthcare Security Officer (CHSO)—and healthcare security supervisors—Certified Healthcare Security Supervisor (CHSS). It also publishes the *Journal of Healthcare Protection Management* and has a website.[43]

Hotels and Motels

The primary security problems associated with hotels and motels are the personal safety of guests, thefts from guest's rooms, thefts of and from autos in parking lots, and vandalism to the property of the hotel. Other major concerns are fire safety;

order maintenance; and safety in pools, exercise rooms, and recreation areas.

Methods of security include alarms, access control, electronic video surveillance, and uniformed and plainclothes security officers. Security services are generally provided by a proprietary staff supplemented by a contract security firm. Larger hotels have a security manager for decision making and supervision of security staff. Most hotels with multiple entrances and exits lock and secure all doors except the main entrance during nighttime hours.

The American Hotel and Lodging Association (AH&LA) is a professional trade association representing the lodging industry in the United States. It offers its members assistance in numerous matters, including risk management and safety and fire protection.[44] AH&LA has a loss prevention committee that assists the industry and members in achieving more effective security, safety, and fire protection programs by working with appropriate federal, state, and local governments.[45]

The AH&LA has an affiliate organization, the Educational Institute (EI). EI is the world's largest source of training and education for the lodging industry. It offers three certifications for hotel and motel security personnel: the Certified Lodging Security Director (CLSD), the Certified Lodging Security Supervisor (CLSS), and the Certified Lodging Security Officer (CLSO). These certifications recognize education and experience in the hotel and motel security profession.[46] Another trade association, the International Hotel and Restaurant Association (IH&RA), provides industry members with crime prevention and travel safety education.[47]

Banks

The major security concerns at banks are the protection of assets and information, the protection of employees and patrons, and the prevention of crimes at their facilities. Computer crime and financial and other "white-collar" crime is also a major concern at banks and other financial institutions and will be covered in Chapters 9 and 10. Generally, banks have large proprietary security departments that provide a myriad of corporate security services, including investigations. Banks that use uniformed guards at their branches generally hire them from contract guard agencies. Banks also use contract armed guards and armored car services for money transfers.

There are three traditional security methods used by banks to prevent robberies: uniformed security officers, cash control procedures, and dye packs.

- Security officers—There is widespread debate within the banking industry regarding the effectiveness of uniformed security officers, both armed and unarmed. While they may have some deterrent value in thwarting the amateur robber, there is little evidence they deter the professional or experienced robber. Often, even, one-on-one robberies (between the robber and a teller) often occur without a security guard being aware that they are taking place. However, there are advantages in having uniformed security officers because they offer a sense of security for customers and they are credible witnesses for the police.

- Cash control—Banks place strict limits on the amount of cash permitted in the bank vault safes and individual teller stations. Once the cash level reaches its limit at individual teller stations, the teller must return the excess money to the vault.

- Dye packs—Dye packs are objects attached to a pack of money that is supposed to be given to the robber by the teller. After the robber leaves the bank, the packs explode, and the money and person carrying it are covered in ink. The dye packs render the money useless and clearly identify the carrier. There are transmitters used to activate the dye packs, and they must be properly positioned so that the packs do not detonate until after the robber has left the facility.

Other robbery prevention devices that are seeing more recent use at banks are metal-detection portals and customer-assisted depositories. Metal-detection portals are located in the foyer of the bank branch and are constructed of bullet-resistant material. If a weapon is detected at the portal, an alarm goes off, and the inner doors to the bank lock. Once the doors lock, no one can get in unless buzzed in. If no weapon is detected, the inner doors open. Security personnel must use care in setting and adjusting the metal-detection sensors, so they will activate for weapons but not for objects such as keys and cellular phones. If not adjusted properly, the alarms will become a nuisance, and employees will eventually open the door for anyone who does not appear suspicious. Customer-assisted depositories are similar to standard night-deposit drops. These are units deployed inside the branch for use by commercial businesses for daytime deposits. The customer deposits the money into the drop and receives a receipt from the deposit machine. There is a digital transaction camera that photographs the person making the deposit and the person removing the bag.

Banks also make extensive use of robbery analysis and risk-assessment measures to design proper precautions against robbery. When doing robbery analysis, security managers study past robberies and use statistical analysis to identify trends and potential problem areas in need of improvement. They compare branch statistics with those that other banks have reported to local law enforcement and the FBI. Security managers use risk-assessment measures by gathering historical information for each branch and using the statistical data and information from bank-robbery studies to create a branch risk-assessment form to survey and rate the bank's facilities. Developing a scoring system and a rating-factor process allows security to assign a risk-assessment score to each facility. This information is then used to determine how to reduce the rating to an acceptable level through methods such as additional equipment, increased training, and new procedural controls.

Banks use their risk analysis and robbery survey results to prepare proper training for bank employees in robbery deterrence. Statistical analysis has revealed a significant correlation between training and robbery activity. It has been found that monetary losses and the number of robberies temporarily decrease following intensive employee-training programs. The heightened alertness and vigilant adherence to procedure apparently has an impact. However, as time passes, robbery activity usually returns to, or near, previous levels.

Also related to banks are the security problems related to automatic teller machines (ATMs). There have been numerous incidents of assaults, robberies, rapes, abductions, and other crimes at these units located at banks, stores, malls, street corners, and other locations. Many jurisdictions have enacted laws regarding ATM security requiring surveillance cameras and other security methods. Exhibit 5.3 covers some basic ATM site security measures.

Government Buildings and Facilities

Federal buildings are operated and managed by the General Services Administration (GSA). Since 9/11, the **Federal Protective Service** (FPS) of the

---

EXHIBIT 5.3   **Some Basic ATM Site Security Measures**

- Persons inside ATM enclosure areas should have an unobstructed view of the surrounding area.
- Shrubbery and vegetation should not provide means of cover or concealment for possible criminals.
- Adequate lighting is essential at all times.
- There should be visible video surveillance coverage.
- Emergency signal devices should be available.

Department of Homeland Security has guarded these buildings. The FPS provides law enforcement and security services to over 1 million tenants and daily visitors to all federally owned and leased facilities nationwide. It maintains this security by managing and overseeing over 10,000 armed private contract security guards.[48] States and other governmental jurisdictions have security departments that have jurisdiction over their buildings or contract out these services to private security guard agencies.

As a result of terrorist acts against government buildings, including the first bombing of the World Trade Center in 1993 and the Oklahoma City federal building in 1995, elaborate security barriers have been erected in front of and around the perimeter of many government buildings. These enormously heavy concrete barriers are intended to prevent vehicles from ramming into the buildings or parking right in front of them.

Prior to 9/11, security at federal buildings, or more specifically, the lack of security at these buildings, had received much scrutiny from Congress, the media, and the public.[49]

The U.S. Capitol and its grounds, including numerous buildings, parks, and thoroughfares, are protected by the U.S. Capitol Police, whose numbers have increased to almost 2,300 officers from 1,200 officers before 9/11. They have officers at the entrances of all buildings, many carrying assault rifles. They also conduct periodic traffic checkpoints around Capitol Hill and have instituted horse patrols for crowd control. The Capitol police budget increased 32 percent for the fiscal year of 2004 over the previous year, for a total cost of $230 million. In 1998, two Capitol police officers were killed by a deranged gunman. The Capitol police also are

Federal Protective Service A unit of the Department of Homeland Security that hires security officers to guard federal buildings.

responsible for protecting members of Congress and their families throughout the entire nation and its territories and possessions.[50] Despite all the improved security efforts at the U.S. Capitol, in September 2006 an armed man was able to enter and run throughout the building before being apprehended.[51]

There has been much criticism regarding security at federal laboratories, especially the Los Alamos National Laboratory in New Mexico. In 1999, Wen Ho Lee, a former nuclear scientist at Los Alamos National Laboratory, was arrested and charged with mishandling nuclear secrets. He had moved classified data regarding nuclear weapons from a computer at the lab onto ten private portable computers. After this incident, new rules have been imposed involving close scrutiny of scientists' contact with foreign nationals, polygraph tests, and limitations on scientific collaborations.[52]

However, even after the tightened security, a pair of computer hard drives containing nuclear secrets were discovered missing from a secured vault at Los Alamos and then were found later behind a copying machine under conditions that were highly suspicious. The drives contained data on nuclear weapons and were intended for emergency use by the government's Nuclear Emergency Search Team to respond to nuclear accidents and terrorist threats. They were missing from a secure area of the Lab's X Division, where nuclear weapons are designed.[53] Even after these incidents, Los Alamos has continued to be plagued with security problems.

Private contract security firms are also being used at military installations around the nation. The reason for the privatization of security at military installations is to free up soldiers from doing garrison support to do what they are trained to do. As the U.S. military shipped thousands of military police to Iraq in 2004, it needed to replace those who were doing security duty at important military installations around the country, including Fort Bragg in North Carolina, and West Point in New York. The 4,100 soldiers who were shipped overseas were replaced by 4,385 private security guards. The military contracted with two large private security firms, Wackenhut Services and Vance International, for $194 million to provide security guards to protect forty military properties. So far, there have been no complaints about the performance of the private guards who protect gates and patrol army bases. Vance International has received several high-profile assignments in the recent past, including the Athens Olympics and the Republican and Democratic National Conventions. Wackenhut Services is a subsidiary of Group 4 Securicor based in London.[54]

Other nations seem to have security problems in their government buildings, as the following security lapses in 2004 show:

- Two men dressed as the comic-book figures Batman and Robin climbed unnoticed to a Buckingham Palace ledge, where they hung signs to try to gain national attention for fathers' rights.

- A reporter from a Scottish newspaper walked unchallenged into Queen Elizabeth's residence in Edinburgh disguised as a construction worker.

- Protesters trespassed onto the balcony of the House of Commons and lobbed condoms filled with purple flour at Prime Minister Tony Blair.

- An investigative reporter used fake references to get a parliamentary job and then smuggled in fake bomb-making materials.

- A person said he had been allowed to take his penknife into the visitor's gallery of the House of Commons but had a banana confiscated by a guard.[55]

Educational Facilities

This section will focus on security operations at educational facilities, including schools, libraries, museums, and archives.

Schools

School security has become a major issue in the United States in the wake of numerous high-profile school shootings in the 1990s, particularly the 1999 shooting at Columbine High School in Littleton, Colorado. Chapter 7 of this text provides extensive coverage of school shootings and violence prevention at schools.

Colleges College campus security officers engage in a wide variety of tasks, including investigation of serious crimes; enforcement of parking regulations; alarm monitoring; building lockup; medical center, stadium/arena, and nuclear facility security; personal safety escorts; and traffic enforcement.

As one example of college security, Drexel University, a 17,000-student campus in West Philadelphia, uses a mix of proprietary security and contract security to ensure safety on campus. Its

Office of Public Safety consists of a senior associate vice president of public safety, an executive director, an associate director, an assistant director of investigations and victim support, a campus investigator/crime-prevention officer, a systems coordinator, five contractual supervisors, nine dispatchers, a director of contract services, and seventy-five private security officers contracted from Allied Security. It provides a comprehensive public safety program consisting of target patrols, strong access controls, electronic video surveillance, and emergency call boxes. Its security officers are required to perform targeted patrol and clock into a wand guard tour system at designated times and places. More than 60 percent of all university buildings, including residence halls and computer labs, are protected by a card access system. Students must scan their photo identifications at one of the card readers to obtain access to buildings. The university has more than 170 surveillance cameras that are monitored at the security control center, and the video feed from all the cameras is digitally recorded. The campus also has seventy emergency call boxes with strobe lights that are monitored in the control center.[56]

The federal Clery Act mandates that colleges and universities that receive federal funds must report crime data to inform the public about crimes on campus. These reports are forwarded to the U.S. Department of Education for 6,000 U.S. institutions of higher learning.[57] The Clery Act was named after Jeanne Clery, a freshman who was raped and killed in her dorm at Lehigh University in Bethlehem, Pennsylvania. Her parents accused Lehigh of covering up crime and lobbied for a law requiring more accountability from colleges.[58]

Secondary and Elementary Schools Many school districts comprised of elementary and secondary schools have their own security departments focusing on order maintenance, student safety, access control, crime control and prevention, and vandalism. Many schools employ contract security guards to police their schools. Schools are using metal detectors, surveillance cameras, and numerous other attempts to increase security.

Increasingly, camera surveillance is becoming prevalent in high schools and is seen as helpful in reducing crime. In a 2004 study, Stephen F. Garst, a school safety coordinator, reported that 75 percent of the schools in Texas that he surveyed reported using surveillance cameras, and most of them reported that they had reduced crime and had solved some recorded crimes.[59]

Museums, Libraries, and Archives

The major security concerns at museums, libraries, and archives are the protection of valuables, access control, perimeter protection, vandalism, order maintenance, and crowd control. These institutions have valuable collections of art, artifacts, books, manuscripts, and other treasures that can never be replaced.

While there are no reliable figures on the extent of art theft, Interpol estimates that it is exceeded in dollar value only by drug trafficking, money laundering, and arms dealing.[60] The largest art robbery in recent history occurred at the Isabella Stewart Gardner Museum in Boston in 1990, when two men dressed as police officers entered the museum and overpowered two unarmed security guards. They then made off with twelve master works, including paintings by Rembrandt, Vermeer, Degas, and Manet. In 2004, two men wearing dark ski hats over their faces burst into the Munch Museum in Oslo, Norway, and stole the world-famous painting *The Scream* by Edvard Munch and another famous painting by Munch, *Madonna*. One of the men held the guards at gunpoint, ordering them to the floor while the other used a wire cutter to clip the framed paintings off the wall. A silent alarm alerted the police, who arrived in one minute, but the thieves had already left. Two hours later, less than a mile away, police found shattered wooden frames and glass from the stolen works, causing fear that the two treasures might have been damaged. Art experts said it would be impossible for the robbers to sell the paintings to another gallery or legitimate collector because of the fame of the photos. Officials thought that the thieves might demand ransom. Law enforcement agencies around the world were alerted to the robbery through Interpol.[61] In August 2006, the paintings were recovered in relatively good condition in Norway.[62]

In 1994, another version of *The Scream* had been stolen from the National Gallery in Oslo, when burglars entered a window before opening time. Three months later—after the government refused to pay a $1 million ransom demand—four Norwegian men were arrested in an elaborate sting operation in which British undercover agents from Scotland Yard posed as representatives of the J. Paul Getty Museum in Los Angeles and offered to pay hundreds of thousands of dollars to secure the painting and return it to the national gallery in Oslo.

Often, stolen artworks are quickly returned, as in the case of twenty van Goghs stolen from and quickly returned to the Vincent van Gogh Museum in Amsterdam, in 1991. Sometimes, as with Titian's long-lost *Rest on the Flight into Egypt*, recovered in Britain in 2002, precious artworks emerge from the criminal underworld years after being stolen, when an investigator gets a legitimate tip or an intermediary contacts another intermediary, who contacts the original owner looking for a reward. The Titian was stolen from a grand English country estate in 1995.[63] Oddly, in 1995, a man walked out of New York City's Museum of Modern Art with Marcel Duchamp's famous *Bicycle Wheel*, outran guards, and later dumped the artwork in pieces in the museum's sculpture garden.[64]

Experts say that some art thieves are low-level criminals who are likely to bungle the operation and dispose quickly of the works, often for a fraction of their value; others are members of organized gangs who use the paintings as collateral or bartering chips in underworld drug deals or for forged documents and weapons. In such cases, recovering the paintings, if they are recovered at all, can take years, even decades. There are private firms that help track down stolen works, such as Art Recovery Limited.[65] Interpol produces a semi-annual *Most Wanted Works of Art* on CD-ROM, profiling nearly 20,000 stolen artworks. It also provides daily updates to this on its website.[66]

Protecting collections without impeding the public's ability to enjoy them is a delicate balancing act. Large museums, libraries, and archives generally have a proprietary security department and make extensive use of security guards at entrances and in exhibits. Guards also engage in order maintenance regarding unruly patrons. They use a variety of devices to prevent entry and prevent theft of art, such as motion detectors, infrared sensors that monitor a room's temperature and can see the shapes of warm bodies moving through it, ultrasonic sensors that trigger an alarm if their sound waves strike a foreign object, and microwave sensors hidden within walls.[67]

Formerly, museum display cases holding valuable art had metallic strips that sounded an alarm when the glass was broken, but it was felt that they took away from the attractiveness of the display. Now museums use acoustic sensors that can be as small as a quarter and set off an alarm when they detect glass breaking or being cut.

A camera trained on a specific object can be programmed to sound an alarm at any shift in the object's outline. Some institutions are even considering a sort of lojack system for artwork: little wireless transmitters that could track the location and movement of every object in their collections. Conservators, though, are often wary of affixing anything to old works of art.

To protect against insider thefts, museums check employees' backgrounds carefully; issue card keys to restrict access in buildings; guard storage rooms, which hold the bulk of most collections; enforce strict rules for signing objects in and out; and teach guards to watch their fellow employees as closely as they watch strangers. With today's tiny, high-resolution video cameras and Internet technology, museum security officials and other administrators can even view the galleries and their guards from a central control room or other remote location.

In 2004, despite the violent theft of the Munch masterpieces in Oslo, the directors of New York's Metropolitan Museum of Art and Museum of Modern Art said they had no plans to increase security or change their procedures. Officials there said even the most well-guarded art institution might be unable to prevent the kind of robbery that occurred in Oslo. "At the end of the day, it's just art, and you would not want someone to take a bullet for it," one gallery official said. The Metropolitan Museum of Art does have some armed guards, but most are not armed. However, officials declined to specify what security methods they have in place except to say they are very confident in the security of the art and visitors at all times.[68] The American Museum of Natural History in New York City is very careful about security and even uses about a dozen security guards to patrol every corner of the museum's twenty-five interconnected buildings during the overnight (midnight to 8 A.M.) shift.[69]

Most museum security systems are made to thwart burglaries, especially after hours, the most frequent type of art heist. Museums have installed security cameras and mechanisms that make it harder to detach extremely valuable paintings and sculptures from walls and floors. Many museums conduct mandatory inspection of bags at the entrance to prevent would-be thieves from getting weapons or tools into the museum. Extensive videotaping exists. In cases of armed robberies, museum's security policies generally follow those used in banks, in which guards are instructed not to put themselves or bystanders in any danger by trying to stop thieves with guns. Increasingly, private galleries are also hiring guards when they are showing extremely valuable artworks.[70]

One of the most frequent problems at museums is the visitor who feels he or she must touch the art. Some museums use electric-eye–type sensors that beep or play recorded messages when people get too close to the art. Others place artworks behind railings or behind glass. Some museums rely on psychology: A strip of brass along the floor, about a foot and a half from the wall, has been effective in keeping people from getting too close to the displays. However, the most ubiquitous security concern may be the visitors for whom "Do Not Touch" signs are a challenge rather than a warning.

Libraries and archives have propriety security departments and often hire contract guard services to supplement them. These institutions use electronic markings on books and other valuables that trigger electronic sensors at exits to reduce thefts. The Association of College and Research Libraries (ACRL), a division of the American Library Association, has a security committee that gives specific advice on library security. The ACRL has established two sets of security guidelines: *Guidelines Regarding Thefts in Libraries* and *Guidelines for the Security of Rare Books, Manuscripts, and Other Special Collections.*[71]

In 2006, after a man was sentenced to prison after stealing over $3 million in maps from some of the world's finest libraries, the curator at the special collections department at Northwestern University stated,

> He ripped part of the fabric of our society in the same manner as any other criminal and while the results might not be as visible, they are felt and the damage has been done. Policies of access will now change, more institutions will now have security cameras and guards, collectors who might have become friends of institutions will now shy away and most of us will trust all a good deal less.[72]

Houses of Worship and Cemeteries

Although it is disturbing to think so, churches, synagogues, temples, mosques, other places of worship, and cemeteries can suffer from burglary, vandalism, arson, theft, and many other crimes. Many houses of worship have valuable property, such as ancient scrolls and documents and valuable artifacts. Today, the majority of houses of worship are locked and alarmed when they are not in use. Some very large ones have a proprietary security department, and others hire contract security services. Police and private security have been especially vigilant and protective of houses of worship after the terrorist attacks of 9/11.

The major security problems at cemeteries are vandalism and desecration of graves and tombstones. In order to deter vandalism, cemeteries use perimeter protection, such as fencing. Some large cemeteries may have a proprietary security force or contract security out if necessary.

Security experts admit that cemeteries are poorly secured areas and recommend installing lights to deter thieves and having a caretaker's house on the property. One cemetery sells annual memberships to dog walkers who, while roaming the cemetery, serve as a sort of security patrol. Today, criminals take plaques, stained glass windows, urns, and other ornaments and sell them to antique dealers, auctions, and flea markets. Two organizations, the National Cemetery Conservation Foundation and the National Trust for Historic Preservation, are seeking to create a register of funerary items, so they can be tracked when stolen.[73]

Transportation Facilities

This section will focus on security at transportation facilities in the United States, including airports, bus and train stations, ports, cargo depots, trucks, and parking lots and garages. The tragic events of 9/11 dramatically changed the face of transportation security in this nation.

In addition to renewed and improved efforts by the private sector to secure its facilities, the creation of the cabinet-level Department of Homeland Security (DHS) brought about dramatic changes in travel and transportation security. DHS assumed the responsibility of coordinating, through a number of governmental agencies, the security for many modes of travel and transportation, including trains, trucks, cruise ships, buses, airplanes, maritime activity, and ports. ASIS International offers several professional training courses in transportation security issues.[74]

You Are There!

Arson Prevention for America's Churches and Synagogues

In the aftermath of numerous suspicious fires at churches and synagogues, the International Association of Arson Investigators offers the following advice to proprietors of churches and synagogues.

External Security

- Illuminate the exterior and entrances. Arsonists, like burglars, fear light.
- Use motion-activated lighting near doors and windows.
- Keep shrubbery and trees trimmed so buildings can be observed by passing patrols.
- If in a rural setting, ensure crops are far enough away to allow proper illumination of the area.
- Do not allow church signs to block the view of the building.
- Many churches have basement entries that are hidden from view; these should be secured with locking ground-level doors when church is not in use.
- Ladders, external stairways, and fire escapes allowing access to the roof should be secured.
- Painting the building white or constructing it with light-colored brick makes a human figure more readily seen at night.
- Consider fencing the areas or sides that are not readily visible to patrols or neighbors.

Internal Security

- Use properly installed deadbolt locks on all exterior doors.
- Windows that can be opened should have adequate locks on them.
- Consider decorative or wrought-iron protection for windows. (Windows used as emergency exits must still be able to be opened in an emergency.) Doors should have similar protection.
- Consider installing a combination burglar and fire alarm with a phone dialer.

- If there is a private security firm in your area, consider a contract with them because they will check the building at unscheduled intervals.
- Keep a current list of all individuals who have access to church keys, and change locks periodically.

Community Awareness and Cooperation

- Keep church leaders informed of problems.
- Be aware of individuals who may be disgruntled or likely to cause damage to church property through arson or vandalism.
- Be aware that vandalism may precede arson!
- Open avenues of communication with fire and law enforcement officials about the arson problem churches are facing.
- Appoint a person from the church to be a liaison with law and fire officials.
- Promote neighborhood watches and educate the neighbors with the lighting arrangements (motion lights and so on).
- Initiate an arson hotline.
- Educate neighbors on recognizing unusual activities.
- Encourage neighbors to make note of strangers spending time in the neighborhood, either on foot or in vehicles. Write down the license plate numbers of suspicious vehicles and inform the proper authorities.
- Have all guests register, and remove register from church each night.
- Raise public awareness through the news media that the problem exists.
- Be aware that individuals may pose as service technicians to get into the church.
- Arsonists may carry a liquid accelerant in an inconspicuous container, such as a beverage container.
- Do not advertise on church signs or bulletins when church will not be in use.
- Involve your insurance agent.

SOURCE: International Association of Arson Investigators, "Arson Prevention for America's Churches and Synagogues." Retrieved April 23, 2007, from http://www.firearson.com/ef/arsons/index.asp.

Airports

Air travel is a major part of modern life. It has been estimated that over 1 billion passengers fly each year. The major threats to airports and airlines are terrorism, skyjacking, smuggling, air cargo thefts, access control, property and facility protection, crowd control, and order maintenance.

Prior to 9/11, most airport management providers employed proprietary security to perform security management functions in their airports and facilities and hired contract security firms for access control and baggage and passenger checking. Airlines and airports generally have proprietary security departments and use contract security firms for many security services. Chapter 13 of this

You Are There!

The Value of Good Lighting, Fences, and Gates

Good lighting deters criminals and provides a sense of safety for users and the ability to observe the premises. Sodium lights are best because they provide ten times the light of an incandescent bulb with the same electrical wattage. Lights should always be on.

Fences, gates, and other perimeter barriers do not keep out all those who are determined to get in, but they do perform four important functions:

- They delineate the boundaries and define any unauthorized persons within as trespassers.
- They discourage wanderers and opportunistic thieves.

- They delay penetration for an amount of time sufficient for police or security to respond.
- They channel legitimate traffic to a limited number of entrances and exits that can be managed by security and access control equipment.

Fences can be secured with intrusion sensors that provide immediate electronic indication of people attempting to get over or under them.

SOURCES: Dan M. Bowers, "Assigning a Place for Parking Security," *Security Management*, December 1999, pp. 63–67; and Terry Pristin, "A Push for Security Gates That Invite Window Shopping," *New York Times*, August 1, 2000, p. B8.

textbook fully discusses airport and airline security in the wake of 9/11.

Tremendous attention began to be directed toward airport and airline security in the 1960s when numerous incidents of skyjacking (armed passengers commandeering airliners and forcing them to detour the flight and land in a certain airport—Cuba became the most commonly demanded destination) led to a national panic. This led to increased security in airports and airlines, much of it mandated by the federal government's Federal Aviation Administration (FAA). This additional security consisted of increased access controls at airports and on planes, screening of passengers, screening of baggage by x-ray detection and physical search, development of psychological profiles of skyjackers, metal and explosive detectors, and the use of sky marshals (armed federal agents) on high-risk flights.

In 1973, after an increase of hijackings further alarmed the nation, **security screening points or checkpoints** were set up in all U.S. airports under the control of the FAA and were guarded by armed police officers. However, in 1978 the FAA and the airline industry agreed to end the practice of using armed police at the security screening points or checkpoints, in part because they considered their use more dangerous than the possibility of a gunman forcing his or her way through the checkpoint area. The reasoning for the removal of the armed officers was the fear of a shootout in such a crowded area as an airport. Security at the screening points was turned over to private security officers, mostly hired from contract security service firms.[75] The 1988 terrorist bombing of Pan American Flight

103 over Lockerbie, Scotland, that killed hundreds led to even more security at airports; however, contract private security personnel continued to be the primary checkers of all passengers and luggage.

Over the years, airport security remained porous and was subject to much congressional and press criticism. In the years just prior to 9/11, inspections of airport security by the FAA and others revealed numerous cases of inept security. The following are some examples of what was discovered:

- Screeners at airport security checkpoints consistently missed weapons that undercover testers hid under their clothing or noticed them and did not do anything.
- Airport employees did not pay attention to certain factors that could have indicated possible terrorism, such as passengers buying one-way tickets for cash at the last moment.
- Ground crews left planes unlocked and unattended.
- Undercover investigators gained unauthorized entry to restricted areas on numerous occasions. It was found that the most common problem regarding access at airports was **"piggybacking"** (unauthorized persons closely following authorized employees into restricted areas).

security screening points or checkpoints Checkpoints set up in 1973 at all the nation's airports to screen all travelers.

piggybacking When unauthorized persons closely follow authorized employees into restricted areas; also known as tailgating.

- Airlines and airport operators did not follow access control procedures to control access to certain areas, including aircraft and baggage holding rooms.

- Airports had poor security training programs.

- Loopholes in the personnel screening process allowed convicted felons to get security jobs at airports without fingerprint or background checks.[76]

On September 11, 2001, the system of passenger screening at the nation's airports failed miserably, and armed al-Qaeda terrorists were able to board airliners.[77]

As a result of the 9/11 tragedy, the president signed into law the **Aviation and Transportation Security Act**, which, among other things, established a new **Transportation Security Administration (TSA)** to protect the nation's transportation systems and ensure freedom of movement for people and commerce. This new agency assumed the duties formerly provided by the FAA. The newly established TSA recruited thousands of federal security personnel to perform screening duties at commercial airports and significantly expanded the federal air marshals program. It also created the positions of **federal airport security directors** to be directly responsible for security at airports, developed new passenger boarding procedures, trained pilots and flight crews in hijacking scenarios, and required all airport personnel to undergo background checks. The TSA was eventually placed under the administrative control of the **U.S. Department of Homeland Security (DHS)**.[78]

Since 9/11, no area of American life has been subjected to more intense scrutiny than air travel, and the federal government has continued imposing tougher rules for screening employees, passengers, and luggage for the estimated 730 million people who travel on commercial aircraft each year. It has installed powerful x-ray machines to screen baggage that cost about $1 million apiece. Officials reported that the number of guns and knives seized at airport checkpoints nationwide had more than tripled since 9/11. Before 9/11, fewer than 2 percent of checked bags were inspected; since then, all of the more than 700 million pieces of baggage are either x-rayed, swabbed for explosive traces, or both. Before 9/11, there were only thirty-seven federal air marshals assigned to riding airliners undercover; as of 2004, there were thousands, according to airport officials. Domestic security officials also began using computer equipment that recognizes fingerprints and other features to verify the identities of foreign visitors as they enter and depart the United States.[79] About 15 percent of the estimated 2 million daily passengers are chosen for secondary screenings, including pat-downs. This number does not count people who are automatically wanded (physically inspected with a hand-held metal detector) after they set off metal detectors when passing through security.[80] In 2006, the DHS imposed added security measures on air travelers by banning liquids and gels in carry-on luggage due to a thwarted terrorist incident in England.[81] Also in 2006, the TSA began to do random searches of workers at airports, including baggage handlers, janitors, and food vendors.[82]

The three major security operations that have been instituted at airports to guard against passengers carrying explosives, weapons, or other contraband onto airplanes include access control, profiling, and explosive detection.

- Access control: Access control technology and practices attempt to ensure that unauthorized persons do not enter airplanes and secured airport areas. All employees are required to wear identifying badges and are limited to specific parts of the airport for which they are authorized. All access points to nonpublic parts of the airport or airfield are alarmed, guarded, and controlled. All passengers must show their travel vouchers and subject themselves to an electronic and perhaps personal search prior to entering the gate areas of the airport.

- Profiling: **Profiling** of passengers is an attempt to identify possible terrorists and smugglers and

Aviation and Transportation Security Act Bill passed in the aftermath of the 9/11 terrorist attacks that established the Transportation Security Administration (TSA) to protect the nation's transportation systems and ensure freedom of movement for people and commerce.

Transportation Security Administration (TSA) Federal agency established in the aftermath of the 9/11 terrorist attacks to protect the nation's transportations systems and ensure freedom of movement for people and commerce.

federal airport security director Position directly responsible for security at the nation's airports; established in the aftermath of the 9/11 terrorist attacks.

U.S. Department of Homeland Security (DHS) Federal cabinet-level department established in the aftermath of the 9/11 terrorist attacks.

profiling Use of a person's characteristics to assess the likelihood of criminal activity or wrongdoing.

to prevent them and their baggage from getting onto airliners. Airlines develop personality profiles of the traits of terrorists and smugglers and attempt to match persons to the profile. If a person is identified as matching the profile, he or she is detained and subjected to additional searches and questioning, if appropriate.

■ Explosive detection: Detection of possible explosives being put into airline baggage is conducted by profiling, visual and physical inspection, and the use of dogs trained to recognize explosive vapor. Airports use various types of sophisticated x-ray and explosive-odor detection devices.

Despite drastic improvements since 9/11, there are still numerous problems regarding airport security.[83] After 9/11, the government began to create a computer system of "virtual borders" intended to identify would-be terrorists entering the United States. This system, "U.S.-Visit" will capture fingerprints and other profile information of hundreds of millions of people who enter or leave the United States each year. The system, which investigators estimate could cost as much as $15 billion over ten years, is intended to help officials determine who should be prohibited from entering the country, to identify visitors who have overstayed or violated the terms of their admission, and to help law enforcement agencies track those who should be detained. Supporters of the system argue that the database would have provided the means to apprehend some of the 9/11 terrorists who were known to the FBI but, they say, could not be located before the attack. It is intended as an early warning, providing customs and border officials with instant access to a web of databases storing intelligence and law enforcement watch lists, profile data, and information from foreign governments. This system might detect individuals who appear in law enforcement or intelligence databases but provides little protection against attackers not known to the government.[84]

While acknowledging that it is almost impossible to catch terrorists without previous records or matching intelligence data, the DHS said the system was intended to minimize the risk. Regarding fears about false positives, DHS says it has processed more than 4 million travelers since January 2004 using photos and prints, and the false positive rate was less than one-tenth of 1 percent.

Thefts at airports are also a major concern for travelers. Airport security personnel patrol passenger areas of airports to watch for suspicious persons and possible crimes in progress; however, travelers must be constantly vigilant over their belongings. According to the leading insurance provider for computers, its clients reported 319,000 laptop computers stolen in 1999. Many of these laptops were stolen at airports, sometimes by organized rings of thieves (see Exhibit 5.4).[85]

Bus and Train Stations

The major security problems at bus and train stations and on trains and buses are terrorism, order maintenance, crowd control, protection of company property and equipment, vandalism, and theft. Major train and bus companies operate their own proprietary security departments, and many hire contract security guards for some security services. The nation's largest passenger service, Amtrak, has its own police department. Firms use proprietary and contract security guards, perimeter barriers, high-tech fencing, enhanced lighting, and intrusion detection equipment to secure their facilities.

The tragic events of 9/11 increased the security consciousness of railroads and transit systems. The DHS is now cooperating with the Department

---

EXHIBIT 5.4 Watch Your Laptop at the Airport

Over 300,000 laptop computers were stolen in the United States in 1999. Many of these thefts occurred at airports by organized teams of thieves. The teams operate this way:

> A two-person team waits by a busy security checkpoint for someone carrying a laptop. When they see him or her (the mark), they then line up at the machine in front of the mark. One of the thieves passes through the metal-detector gate without incident. The other waits until the mark has placed the laptop onto the conveyor belt, and then walks in front of the mark and through the gate in a way that deliberately causes a backup since he or she is carrying sufficient amounts of metal on his or her person to set off the alarm. As the alarm sounds, the security person asks him or her to step back, empty his or her pockets, and go through the device again. In the meantime, the targeted computer has already emerged on the other side, where the first thief simply walks off with it, while its owner waits to get through the gate and get his or her laptop from the belt. By then, both the first thief and the laptop are gone.

Source: Joe Sharkey, "A Rising Number of Laptop Computers Are Being Stolen at Airports by Organized Rings of Thieves," *New York Times*, March 29, 2000, p. C10.

of Transportation (DOT) and other federal agencies and has taken significant steps to enhance rail and transit security in partnership with the public organizations and private firms that own and operate the transit and rail systems.[86] The Federal Railroad Administration and the DHS focused on the security vulnerabilities in the system with the cooperation of the American Association of Railroads. New assessments and security enhancements were made to ensure security among all modes of rail transportation, including rail and transit lines.[87] Since the London subway bombings in 2005, many mass transit facilities use the police to conduct random bag searches of passengers.

Ports, Cargo Depots, and Trucks

Ports, cargo firms, cargo depots, and trucking firms generally have a proprietary security force to deal with major thefts and use contract security firms for other security services at fixed locations such as terminals. The major security problems for ports, cargo companies, depots, and trucking firms are terrorism, cargo theft, hijacking, and employee theft.

Since the creation of DHS, the U.S. Coast guard has operated under its administrative control and plays an integral role in maintaining the operations of U.S. ports and waterways by providing a secure environment for mariners and people to operate freely. It implements the Maritime Transportation Security Act regulations that enhance security at ports, facilities, and vessels nationwide. It maintains maritime safety security teams in major vital ports and can conduct rapid, nationwide response by ground or sea.[88] The DHS has published an informative brochure entitled *Secure Seas, Open Ports: Keeping Our Waters Safe, Secure and Open for Business* that details the many layers of new security measures that secure our nation's ports. It emphasizes that there is now a system of security measures that ensure security from one end of a sea-based journey to the other. These measures are enforced by the U.S. Coast Guard, Customs and Border Protection, the private sector, and state and local authorities.[89]

Ninety-five percent of all international commerce enters the United States through its roughly 360 public and private ports; but nearly 80 percent of that trade moves through only 10 ports, with the biggest loads passing through Los Angeles, Long Beach, and Oakland in California, and New York.[90] In 2006, a U.S. Senate homeland security subcommittee reported that the number of high-risk cargo containers inspected before entering the United States is "staggering low" and that government efforts to keep terrorists from exploiting the systems are riddled with blind spots.[91]

Traditional security controls for the safety of truckers and their cargo are timed and specialized routes and driver call-ins to company dispatch centers. Modern electronic computerized tracking and communication systems have enhanced security's ability to immediately and accurately geographically track and communicate with truckers and ensure their safety and the safety of their cargo.

The American Trucking Associations (ATA) is a professional organization representing the trucking and cargo industry. The ATA's Safety and Loss Prevention and Security Council offers prevention programs to combat cargo theft and to give security advice, industry news, and other services to truckers, and trucking and cargo companies across the nation. It also publishes a monthly newsletter, *Safety Bulletin*; a bimonthly newsletter, *Security News*; and a quarterly magazine, *The Informer*. The ATA also awards the Certified Cargo Security Professional (CCSP) credential that denotes that the holder has voluntarily demonstrated knowledge and skill in the design, implementation, and administration of security protection within the cargo/transportation industry.[92] ASIS International also offers several professional development training courses regarding cargo, port, and ship security.[93]

Parking Lots and Garages

The major security problems at parking lots and garages are assaults, robberies, personal thefts, and thefts of and from autos. Security at parking garages is difficult due to the fact that they usually have low ceilings, making it difficult to provide adequate observation inside them via electronic video surveillance. In addition, these facilities usually are difficult to light and often have architectural trouble spots, such as nooks, crannies, stairwells, and elevators that can serve as hideouts for attackers. Parking facilities underneath buildings also create opportunities for terrorists, such as the one that occurred in New York City's former World Trade Center in 1993 where a terrorist bomb exploded. The bomb was transported into the building's parking garage in a vehicle.[94]

Parking lot and garage security usually includes bright lighting, perimeter fencing, call stations that activate an alarm and provide a location when used during an emergency, electronic video surveillance, access control, patrols, and awareness training. Access control devices in parking lots and garages include card readers that trigger swinging-arm barriers. Similarly, activated doors or turnstiles can be installed at pedestrian entrances. Automatic vehicle-identification systems (AVID) use a system similar to a smart card or access control card that is attached to the vehicle and automatically sensed at the entry lane, raising the barrier.

Many corporations use awareness training of employees and security escort services. Parking lots and garages place signs in garages such as "Do not leave personal property in your vehicle," or "These premises are under camera surveillance at all times." Some evaluations showed reductions in car-related crimes by adding security guards to parking lots.[95] Exhibit 5.5 offers some security tips to follow when using a parking facility.

EXHIBIT 5.5   **Some Security Tips When Using a Parking Facility**

- When entering the parking lot, have your car keys out and ready.
- Check under the vehicle before approaching it and look inside it before getting in.
- Avoid parking next to a van or panel truck (assailants may lurk within unseen).
- Try to enter and exit the garage when there are other people present.
- If entering during low-traffic hours, always use the company's security escort service.
- Avoid window decals and bumper stickers that attract unwanted attention.

Source: Dan M. Bowers, "Assigning a Place for Parking Security: Through a Combination of Physical Security, Officer Patrols, and Security Awareness Training, Any Parking Facility Can Provide a Safe Mooring for Its Users," *Security Management*, December 1999, p. 67.

Entertainment Facilities

This section will focus on security operations at entertainment facilities in the United States, including sporting arenas and ballparks, movies, theaters and clubs, pools and beaches, amusement parks, cruise ships, and casinos.

Sporting Arenas and Ballparks

Security problems at sporting arenas and ballparks include order maintenance, crowd control, illegal entry, vandalism, and theft of property from patrons and vendors. Security at stadiums also includes the area surrounding the stadium.

Most major arenas employ a proprietary security department and supplement it with contract security for games and other major events. Many hire off-duty local police officers to moonlight as security officers. The public police generally patrol the exterior of the stadiums but in exceptional cases may actually provide extensive police coverage within the stadium itself. A major example of the regular public police being used at a sporting event was during the 2004 baseball season's American League playoff between the New York Yankees and the Boston Red Sox, at Yankee Stadium in New York. The NYPD had to assign scores of uniformed officers on the field, at the foul lines, to deter unruly fans who were throwing bottles and other objects at the players.

Access control is very important at stadiums to ensure that only persons who have paid for a ticket are granted access. Traditional access control at stadiums has involved handing a ticket to a ticket-taker and then passing through a turnstile while security personnel are on hand in the event of any gatecrashers or other unruly fans. Today, many stadiums are using new technologies that speed entry and improve security. This technology includes electronic ticket readers or optical scanners, in which a fan enters the stadium by scanning a ticket under a reader or inserting a ticket into a machine that reads the bar code and records the seat number, time of entry, and other information. These devices can detect counterfeit tickets, prevent people from passing stubs to friends outside, and aid management in monitoring patron flow. The Toronto Blue Jays and Baltimore Orioles

You Are There!

Security at the Staples Center

The Staples Center, which opened in Los Angeles in October 1999 as home of the National Basketball Association's Lakers and Clippers, the National Hockey League's Kings, and the arena football Avengers, features a high-tech security system that includes sophisticated access control systems, and video surveillance.

Some of the components of Staples' security include the following:

■ Security was designed up front, as the building was being planned and built. Therefore, management was able to incorporate sophisticated access control systems, such as door contacts, infrared sensors, alarms, video surveillance, and other equipment, in a more coherent manner and at a lower cost than would have been the case if security issues had only been addressed after completion of the facility.

■ Access control is coordinated with other functions, such as lighting, fire alarms, and computer

access, in a single system. Thus, the same central monitoring location is used to monitor all building management systems and security systems.

■ The security staff monitors ninety cameras for the seating area alone from the central monitoring system.

■ All workers (fulltime, parttime, hourly, and contract) are funneled through a single entrance and exit. The security command center approves each arriving employee and a camera outside of the loading dock records the license plates of all approaching vehicles. Lost entry cards can be deactivated with a few clicks on a keyboard. If a person is terminated, his or her manager can have security deactivate the card without the employee having to turn it in.

SOURCE: Michael A. Gips, "Sporting a New Look: Access Control Trends at New Sports Arenas Show That Security Is Experiencing a Winning Season," *Security Management*, February 2000, pp. 48–56.

---

use such systems. In certain venues, such as Madison Square Garden and Radio City Music Hall in New York, ticket collectors use hand-held scanners to process each ticket. In all of these systems, if a ticket is counterfeit or already used, the turnstiles lock and security personnel intervene and investigate.[96] In 2006, the Cleveland Cavaliers began to eliminate paper tickets for season-ticket holders. The team's new "Flash Seats" technology aims to control the resale of tickets. Admission to their arena, the Q, is gained by electronically matching a ticket holder's ID—either a driver's license or credit card—to the one on the Flash Seat's account.[97]

As of 2005, Titans Coliseum in downtown Nashville, Tennessee, home of the Tennessee Titans football team, was an example of state-of-the-art security. It uses 128 sophisticated surveillance cameras, a central control room for security personnel, and an in-stadium surveillance security team. It also has a door alarm system, multimedia access control, asset tracking, two-way voice communications, and video management. The video surveillance system, in addition to servicing security functions, has helped supply evidence for numerous incidents in the stadium. It has the capability to access and retrieve video quickly for police reports and accident/injury claims. Microphones in areas where cash is handled are able to

pick up what is being said in case of a robbery or another potential emergency situation.[98]

Violence control is also a major issue in sports arena security. Some professionals report that violence is on the rise at sporting events. An example of a security breakdown occurred at the Staples Center in Los Angeles, after the Los Angeles Lakers won the National Basketball Association (NBA) championship series in June 2000. Two police cars were set on fire, two TV news vans were damaged, and nearly two dozen auto and garbage fires were reported. Looters invaded a computer store, glass storefronts were shattered, and at least seventy-four vehicles at seven car dealerships were damaged. Eleven people were arrested, and four police officers suffered minor injuries during a rock- and bottle-throwing melee. The Los Angeles mayor blamed the problems on a few hundred hoodlums out of the 30,000 people in and around the Staples Center. The violence erupted among an estimated 10,000 people who had watched the game on a jumbo screen outside Staples Center.[99]

Also, in 2004, a major security breakdown occurred at the Palace of Auburn Hills in Michigan, during which fans began to throw full beverage cups at a member of the Indiana Pacer's basketball team. That player, joined later by other players, rushed into the stands, punching and assaulting

You Are There!

Security at the 2004 Summer Olympics in Athens, Greece

The Greek government spent more than $1.2 billion for security at the 2004 Summer Olympic Games in Athens, Greece. All 70,000 people attending the opening parade of athletes in the main Olympic stadium at the opening of the games, and others attending subsequent events at all venues, had to walk through a bank of metal detectors; six helicopters hovered above with blinking lights; and a 200-foot blimp, crammed with surveillance cameras and microphones, watched over the crowd and the stadium. Officials deployed 60,000 police officers, firefighters, coast guard officers, and volunteers as part of the security network. Another 40,000 soldiers were called in to help guard the event sites, state

communications and utility facilities, railroad depots, and border crossings.

In addition to mobilizing personnel, Greece bought a $325 million security package from a California company that is a major provider of security systems for the U.S. military. This system collected and managed data from hundreds of surveillance cameras, underwater sensors at ports, vehicle-tracking devices, motion detectors fastened to fences around the many Olympic venues, and images captured by the blimp.

SOURCE: Susan Sachs, "The Games Begin, Cautiously; Olympians Make Their Entrance, with a Heavy Force Watching," *New York Times*, August 14, 2004, pp. D1, D2.

fans. Eventually, officials had to end the game with forty-six seconds remaining as the rumble in the stands extended onto the court. Nine fans were hurt. The NBA commissioner suspended several players, and law enforcement officials indicted several players and fans for assault.[100] In 2006, a fan threw a hypodermic syringe at the San Francisco Giant's Barry Bonds at Petco Park in San Diego. In response, the San Diego Padres baseball team management imposed stricter security measures.[101]

Security's goal regarding fan violence is to keep these overzealous fans, or any weapons or projectiles they might be carrying, on the outside. Some stadiums subject entering fans to a body and package search. Some teams also often threaten season-ticket holders with confiscation of their tickets for violent or abusive behavior. Weapons detection is a contentious issue among security professionals. Most stadiums do not have weapons-detection equipment and shy away from it for fear of the image that the detectors might project and the delays they might cause. However, in 2006, metal detectors were installed at Memorial Stadium at Nebraska University. The detectors were purchased with a DHS grant.[102] DHS grants have also been used by Oklahoma, Ohio State, Michigan, and Louisiana State Universities to improve security at their football stadiums.[103]

In England, in order to reduce the traditional violence and hooliganism at soccer stadiums, major stadiums have been rebuilt with all standing-room terraces removed. Family-friendly regulations and drinking restrictions have been

put in place, stewards are positioned at entrances, and security cameras have been installed to permit visual checks of every seat. Opposing fans sit apart from one another during the game and are steered away from one another as they exit the parks by mounted police officers.[104]

In addition to violence control and order maintenance, stadiums and other large places of assembly must worry about the overcrowding of events. A good example of overcrowding leading to tragedy occurred at the 2000 Roskilde festival, just outside Copenhagen, Denmark, at a Pearl Jam concert. Many fans among the 50,000 young people caught up in the enthusiasm began pushing forward, leaving some up front screaming and climbing on top of each other to get air. By the time the crush subsided, eight fans had been trampled to death and twenty-five more were injured. There had been barriers erected to prevent spectators up front from being pressed by those behind them, and dozens of security staff were positioned to help squeezed spectators escape, but these tactics failed. In 1979, at a Who concert in Cincinnati, Ohio, eleven fans were killed in a crowd stampede.[105] Also, in 1985, in Brussels, thirty-nine fans were killed in the panic surrounding a soccer game, and in 1989, in Sheffield, England, one hundred fans died in a crowd-control disaster at another game.[106]

Movies, Theaters, and Clubs

The major security problems at movie houses, theaters, and clubs are order maintenance, crowd

©Keith Levit/First Light

The major security problems at movie houses, theaters, and clubs are order maintenance, crowd control, illegal entry, and thefts from patrons and vendors. Many of these premises hire contract security guards and station them in the lobby to be available in case of trouble. Large theaters maintain a proprietary security force and supplement it with contract guards when necessary.

others by an audience member. Some promoters report that they take special security precautions at concerts they promote. One promoter insists that door staff search all backpacks and conduct pat-downs and that bouncers inside scan the crowd for suspicious activity, as well as having employees monitor patrons via security cameras. The purpose of security, promoters say, is to stop trouble before it escalates. These promoters say they beef up their security plans when more aggressive fans are expected, scheduling extra staff and metal detectors. Some promoters say their security staffers at large-scale concerts are trained to look for certain types of people in the audience who may cause trouble and are usually briefed beforehand about fans who have tried to communicate with performers. They say that security is tighter at heavy-metal and hip-hop shows.[107]

Security arrangements at Radio City Music Hall in New York City, which can seat over 6,000 patrons, are based on a coordinated effort that focuses on quality personnel, good procedures, and ongoing public liaison. Security department personnel include a director, three supervisors, three managers, and an in-house staff of forty-one officers who provide 24-hour coverage in three shifts. In addition, a minimum of two emergency medical technicians is on hand at each show, as well as a special response team consisting of a supervisor and four security officers. Radio City uses pre-employment screening for all personnel, which includes a background investigation and a credit and criminal record check. The security officers' training program is based on a two-hundred-page manual of goals and procedures, on which personnel are periodically retested. Radio City security prides itself on its high-quality personnel, well-rehearsed procedures, and coordination with local fire and police departments in circumstances requiring additional expertise, such as fire inspections, bomb threats, ticket scalping, and media relations.[108]

Pools and Beaches

The major security concerns at pools and beaches are order maintenance, crowd control, parking, and the safety of users and employees. The primary means of deterring bathers at times when lifeguards are not present are signs saying, "Swimming prohibited when lifeguard not on

control, illegal entry, and thefts from patrons and vendors. Many of these premises hire contract security guards and station them in the lobby to be available in case of trouble. Very large theaters maintain a proprietary security force and supplement it with contract guards when necessary. Often, promoters staging large events, such as rock concerts, boxing matches, and the like, provide their own security to protect participants and complement the security the venue provides.

At a club in Ohio in 2004, "Dimebag" Darrell Abbott, a heavy-metal guitarist for the band Damageplan, was gunned down along with three

duty." Most drownings occur when lifeguards are off duty.[109]

Amusement Parks

The major security concerns facing amusement parks are order maintenance, crowd control, access control, parking, and the safety of visitors and employees. Almost all amusement parks operate a proprietary security department and hire extra contract security guards when necessary.

As an example of amusement park security, the Walt Disney World Resort near Orlando, Florida, employs a 500-person unarmed security force that is responsible for security and crime control for its 34,000 employees and the more than 135,000 people who visit the resort daily. This force handles between fifteen and thirty criminal incidents per day, including embezzlement, retail theft, auto theft, burglary, and occasionally, violent crime.[110]

There are numerous fairs, exhibits, and events throughout the nation at public and private centers, fairgrounds, and other large open areas. The major security concerns are order maintenance, crowd control, prevention of thefts of exhibits and other valuable property, parking, and the safety of visitors and employees. Many of these centers have a proprietary security force, while others hire a contract agency whenever the center is in use. Also, as with other major assemblages, often promoters staging large events, such as rock concerts, boxing matches, and the like, provide their own security to protect participants and complement the security the venue provides.

Cruise Ships

Crimes at sea often fall into a jurisdictional no-man's-land of law enforcement. Generally, if the ship is in the waters of a foreign country, the crime is reported to the officials of that nation and to the embassies of the parties involved. The criminal law of the nation under whose flag the ship flies generally does not apply, unless the ship is actually in that country's waters at the time of the incident. Although crimes are reported to a particular country, they are not necessary investigated by that country. As an example, Royal Caribbean ships are required to contact the FBI when a crime occurs in international waters and the local police when in U.S. waters. When in the Caribbean, criminal incidents are also reported to officials at the next port of call. Guests can bring civil suits against cruise lines for

crimes that occur aboard a cruise ship. Therefore, all cruise lines investigate criminal incidents on their ships and may take action against offenders.[111]

All major cruise lines have security managers and security officers on each ship, and generally each ship has a central station that monitors and controls all security activities, such as video monitoring and access control. Cruise-line security departments must meet regulations established by the International Maritime Organization. These regulations outline specific security measures that ships must implement, including preparing security plans, restricting access to certain areas of the ship, establishing identification systems, and screening passengers and crews. Incidents of serious criminal activity on cruise ships remain relatively rare but are an ongoing concern. The major issues confronting cruise line security personnel are illegal drug smuggling, sexual assaults, stowaways, piracy, and terrorism. DHS conducts luggage checks at all U.S. ports, and many cruise lines work with it to prevent drug smuggling on board. In addition, in the aftermath of 9/11, cruise lines conduct pre-employment and random drug screening of all employees. The typical cruise line may have a few stowaways each year due to a lapse of security at the dock; however, most are prevented due to access control systems.

Reports of sexual assault are the most common criminal allegations aboard cruise ships. The Carnival line recently faced two lawsuits from victims of sexual assaults, and the cases were settled out of court. There is no centralized database of sexual assault reports on cruise ships. However, Carnival reported that from 1994 to 1999, there were 108 reports of sexual assaults, including 32 rapes among the more than 6.5 million passengers they carried. Carnival terminated forty employees as a result of these incidents. Carnival gives a training course to each employee including information regarding sexual harassment, inappropriate behavior, and investigation of sexual assault allegations. It estimates that there are about two cases of sexual assault for every 100,000 passengers.

Terrorism is always a concern with international cruising. The hijacking of the Italian cruise ship, the *Achille Lauro*, in the Mediterranean in 1985, terrorized

terrorism The unlawful use or threat of force or violence against individuals or property to intimidate or coerce a government, the civilian population, or any segment thereof, in furtherance of political, religious, ideological, or social objectives.

many travelers. The terrorists who took over the ship killed an American passenger. The *Achille Lauro* was a small ship in a remote area of the world, but its victimization completely changed cruise industry security. Major lines hire security consultants and contract security agencies to monitor activities in various ports. These security consultants and contract security agencies provide intelligence and help devise risk-management strategies. Carnival conducts three-day terrorism awareness seminars for new employees and conducts security searches each week on every ship. All cruise lines get monthly government briefings on terrorist activity.

ASIS International offers professional development training courses regarding ship security.[112]

Casinos

There are numerous security concerns at casinos, including the safety of patrons and employees, protection of assets of the casino from robbery and theft, order maintenance, and crowd control. Casinos generally operate a proprietary security department and hire some contract security guards for certain duties. Casinos use sophisticated access control and video surveillance systems and make extensive use of armed security guards.

Casino gaming areas are usually monitored from the casino's control center, which is staffed by security personnel with gaming security backgrounds. The casino camera operators are educated in all forms of cheating and scams associated with each game. Training is conducted by the casino, the police, and the appropriate state gaming control board. A security booth is prominently situated next to the cage, the area where chips are cashed and other monetary transactions take place. Security controls all entrances to the cage area. Officers accompany personnel during movements of money anywhere on and off site. Officers escort employees whenever necessary. They also will escort any patrons upon their request. Security uses security checkpoints, video cameras, and sophisticated access control systems to separate the public and back-of-the-house areas, such as loading docks, money rooms, employee-only areas, and the like.

Security officers are trained to constantly look for possible victims while patrolling the casino floors, such as people who leave a purse at a slot machine or display large amounts of money inappropriately. They try to take a quiet approach to moving drunks and other disorderly persons without raising the awareness of regular patrons.

In Las Vegas, all casino and other private security departments exchange updates and network at monthly meetings of the Las Vegas Security Chiefs Association, which includes representatives from the Las Vegas Metro Police and all police units involved with tourist security and safety.

The Venetian Casino in Las Vegas has more than four hundred security personnel. The majority are patrol officers. There are usually about ninety officers on duty during a normal shift, with the number increasing on weekends and during special events. It has an investigations unit, which conducts background checks on all employees, due diligence probes, and other investigations. When hiring security personnel, the casino looks for candidates possessing casino security experience or experience in law enforcement, the military, or private security. All employees must pass drug testing and thorough background reviews. All Venetian officers are trained in casino operations; first aid including the use of portable defibrillators, CPR, and water rescue; as well as other normal security functions and duties. The security department maintains a close liaison with the police and other security departments.[113]

The Venetian has more than 1,200 video cameras in place, which are pan/tilt/zoom, inside domes, or track cameras, allowing for joystick manipulation. According to the director of security, the cameras monitoring the casino can zoom down and count the freckles on someone's hand. The Venetian has one central monitoring and dispatch area for the hotel and a second for the casino. Both operate around the clock, documenting occurrences inside the resort and casino. There are always at least two monitoring officers on duty at each station.

Most casinos engage in information sharing with other casinos in the same geographic area because the same criminals usually frequent all casinos in an area. As an example, two casinos in Connecticut, the Mohegan Sun Casino and the Foxwoods Casino, share visual information about criminal activities on gaming floors, by using digital image transmission systems, so the two security departments can quickly compare visual notes and step in and stop a crime in progress. When security at either casino spots a suspicious individual on the floor, live digitized video can be transmitted immediately to the other casino.[114] More than 140 casinos in the United States and throughout the world partake in the Surveillance Information Network (SIN), through which they send warnings to other casinos. In a recent incident, the surveillance department at the Borgata Casino and Spa in Atlantic City was able to help a casino in Lithuania identify a group of international roulette cheaters that had recently passed through the Borgata.[115]

Caesars Palace in Las Vegas uses a key control system for its 45,000 square foot hotel and casino with 5,500 employees, using an automated system to distribute high-security keys used for maintaining and filling slot machines, the money or cashier cage, and accessing guest rooms. The keys are enclosed inside a locked housing unit, each key secured inside the unit by steel holding rings, which attach to tamper-proof key rings that hold the keys in position. The housing units are secured by a keypad that requires each user to enter a personal identification number (PIN). Access to the key housing units are also controlled by a hand-geometry technology reader. The hand reader measures the unique characteristics of each hand and plots seventy points on the top of the hand to form a template. The reader recognizes a variety of data unique to living flesh, such as blood pressure, so a severed hand, for example, would not be recognized. Security controls employee access privileges by controlling which readers recognize each employee's handprint. It can also run user audits to see who has entered an area and when the access occurred. The system can identify all employees who accessed the keys or the secured area at any given moment.[116]

The hand-reader database constantly updates the templates as it takes new reads of a user's hand to account for minor fluctuations in a user's hand composition. If an employee is out of work for an extended time, however, the system may not recognize that person when he or she returns. Also, this happens when a person loses or gains a significant amount of weight, such as during pregnancy and after childbirth. The hand reader works together with the keypad. Employees must first enter their PIN and then place one hand on the reader. The hand reader uses the PIN to locate the user's original handprint template stored in the database and compares it to the current handprint. If they match, it verifies the user's identity. If employees have not picked up keys when they should or returned them on time, an alarm message is sent to the supervisor who is responsible for tracking the employee and retrieving the keys.

The Borgata Casino and Spa in Atlantic City uses a 2,000-camera video network surveillance system integrated with the casino and hotel's operational technology. The system is integrated with a gaming industry–specific facial recognition program, the Viisage Visual Casino System, which matches database images of known cheats against stills captured by the surveillance cameras. Casino security has uncovered and stopped several scams, including a $20,000-marker scam and a mini-baccarat scam using false shuffles in which one employee was arrested. In another case, a craps dealer was caught stealing gaming chips and was arrested. The casino operates both a surveillance center and a security control room, which are staffed at all times by multiple officers with the same capability. The surveillance control room also receives input from the alarms, fire, life-safety, and access control systems, as well as sensor readings from the Borgata's more than fifty elevators and escalators.[117]

Homeland Security and Premise Security

In the aftermath of 9/11, there have been tremendous changes in security in the United States. The U.S. government totally revamped its governmental structure to create the cabinet-level Department of Homeland Security (DHS) to prioritize safety in the United States. It passed numerous new laws and regulations affecting the security of the nation's travel operations, including airports and planes, trains, trucks, cruise ships, and buses, as well as the security of U.S. ports. This chapter has discussed some of these new issues, and Chapter 13 will provide extensive information on the area of terrorism and private security.

Additionally, many companies have taken serious steps for increased security and spent millions of dollars on scanners, turnstiles, and other security measures. Many large companies erected **security barriers** around their buildings, some using concrete barriers or huge potted flowerbeds that limit access. As an example, Morgan Stanley in New York ringed its corporate headquarters with forty-one 8-foot-long concrete planter tubs and sixteen cylindrical planters. At some places, the tubs are barely more than 1 foot apart. According to Peter DiMaggio of the American Institute of Architects, these standoff barricades are important because one of the most effective tools a designer has against a high-explosive terrorist attack is to

security barriers Standoff barricades used to protect buildings from attack.

force the terrorist to detonate the explosives as far from the building as possible.[118]

However, Thomas E. Cavanagh of the Conference Board spent three years studying how corporations responded to the 9/11 attacks and found in a study of one hundred midsize companies—including potentially vulnerable industries like transportation, financial services, utilities, and telecommunications—that almost half had not increased annual spending on security at all after 9/11. Forty percent of the executives said security was an expense that should be minimized, and a quarter of the companies said their chief executives had not met with their security chiefs in the last year.[119]

Some say that since there have been no serious incidents since 9/11, a sense of complacency may have set in, and corporations are now more concerned about rising costs and bottom lines and lack a sustained focus toward security. Although many of the companies studied by Cavanaugh have relaxed their ambitious plans and have removed many security devices, he still found that 40 percent of larger firms, with 1,000 or more employees, had established off-site emergency operations centers.

Summary

- Property crime and premise crime are serious problems in our nation. The most recent data published by the FBI indicated that approximately 10.4 million serious property crimes, including 2.15 million burglaries, 7.02 million larcenies/thefts, and 1.26 million motor vehicle thefts, were reported to the police in the latest reporting year.

- Although the police arrested about 291,000 persons for burglary; 1.15 million persons for larceny or theft; about 16,000 persons for arson, 273,000 for vandalism; and 127,000 for receiving, buying, or possessing stolen property in the latest reporting year, they are limited in their ability to prevent premise and property crime due to their limited jurisdiction, personnel, and other duties.

- Among the premises seriously affected by crime in our society are residential places, including neighborhoods, private residences, and public housing developments; businesses, including retail stores, convenience stores, fast-food restaurants, shopping centers and malls, industrial facilities, factories and warehouses, office buildings, public and private utilities, hospitals and healthcare facilities, hotels and motels, and banks; government buildings and facilities; and educational facilities, including schools, museums, libraries, and archives. Other premises seriously affected are houses of worship and cemeteries; transportation facilities, including airports, bus and train stations, ports, truck and cargo depots, and parking lots and garages; and entertainment facilities, including sporting arenas and ballparks, movies and theaters, pools and beaches, amusement parks, cruise ships, and casinos.

- A major contribution to security in recent years is the Business Improvement District (BID) concept that involves the combined efforts of the business community and the private security industry with the cooperation of the public police. BIDs are private organizations funded by local businesses that oversee critical services, such as sanitation and security for businesses in their area.

- The National Association of Convenience Stores (NACS) is a major professional trade association for employees, owners, and others who have an interest in retail security. The major methods it recommends to maintain security and reduce crime are cash control; visibility, including clear sight lines into stores, prominent position of cash registers in the front of the stores, and balanced exterior and interior lighting; eliminating escape routes; electronic video surveillance; alarms; and employee training, particularly "robbery-deterrence" training.

- Shopping malls and shopping centers offer many opportunities for criminal activity and for problem people to loiter. Many malls, and the stores within them, have their own proprietary security, and many others hire contract guard services. The public police also frequently patrol and respond to shopping malls.

- Codes of conduct, consciously posted, are extremely important in maintaining order and reducing crime in shopping malls.

- Public and private utility facilities, including gas, electricity, water, telephone, oil, and nuclear, present major security problems, including terrorism, sabotage, destruction and theft of property and assets, and personal protection of employees.

■ Several professional associations, including the International Association of Healthcare Security and Safety (IAHSS) and the American Hotel and Lodging Association (AH&LA), offer training and certification problems for security employees who work in their industries.

■ The major security methods used by banks to ensure security are robbery analysis and risk assessment, security officers, cash control procedures, employee training, and security devices such as dye packs and metal detection portals.

■ In the aftermath of the 9/11 terrorist bombings, transportation facilities, including airports and mass transportation, have been the subject of intense security interest, including the efforts of the federal government's Department of Homeland Security, local authorities, and private security professionals.

■ Sports and entertainment venues have significant problems in terms of access control and violent fan or patron behavior. Private security professionals are beginning to implement improved security measures to deal with this problem.

Learning Check

1. Discuss the extent of property crime in the United States.

2. Identify some of the methods the police use to deal with property and premise crime.

3. Identify and discuss some of the changes in security brought about as a result of the 9/11 terrorist attacks against the United States.

4. Discuss the concept of business improvement districts.

5. Identify and discuss several methods used by homeowners to protect their homes and businesses.

6. Identify four major recommendations by the National Association of Convenience Stores (NACS) to ensure security by its member stores.

7. Identify and discuss several methods used by shopping malls to ensure security.

8. Identify and discuss three professional organizations that assist their members in security.

9. Identify the major security problems at (1) office buildings, (2) hospitals and healthcare facilities, (3) hotels and motels, (4) banks and other financial institutions, and (5) sporting arenas and ballparks.

10. Provide a brief history of security checkpoints at airports.

Application Exercise

Arrange for a visit to the security director at your school or university or a large shopping mall or other business in your area. Explain to him or her some of the information you have learned in this chapter regarding security threats and concerns at the particular type of institution you are visiting. Ask the security director to explain what the security department is doing to address these threats. Prepare a five- to six-page paper, double-spaced, discussing the information that you received.

Web Exercise

Find a site on the Internet that discusses programs involving deterring crimes in retail stores such as conveniences stores. Prepare a list of the major recommendations suggested on the site and discuss them in a five- to six-page double-spaced paper.

Key Terms

Aviation and Transportation Security Act, p. 132
"broken windows" theory, p. 113
business improvement districts (BIDs), p. 116
cash control, p. 118
community crime-prevention programs, p. 115
community policing, p. 115
expiring time badges, p. 122
federal airport security directors, p. 132
Federal Protective Service, p. 125
piggybacking, p. 131
profiling, p. 132
retail alert system, p. 121
security barriers, p. 141
security screening points or checkpoints, p. 131
temporary badging, p. 122
terrorism, p. 139
Transportation Security Administration (TSA), p. 132
U.S. Department of Homeland Security (DHS), p. 132

Retail Security and Loss Prevention

©Samuel Ashfield/Getty Images

GOALS

- To introduce the concept of shrinkage, including internal and external shrinkage.
- To introduce methods used to reduce the shrinkage problem.
- To explore the effectiveness of the various methods used to deal with the shrinkage problem.
- To describe the academic and professional research in loss prevention.
- To explore special issues in retail shrinkage.
- To discuss the effects retail security and loss prevention have had on homeland security.

Introduction

Theft is a serious problem in retail establishments in the United States and throughout the world. The losses from theft and the cost of the security methods to reduce this theft are eventually passed on to shoppers by way of increased prices for everything they purchase.

This chapter will discuss the retail shrinkage problem, including internal and external theft, and methods used to deal with this problem, including management policies; CPTED (crime prevention through environmental design); audits; store detectives or loss prevention specialists; loss prevention technology, including current technology such as electronic video surveillance systems, closed-circuit television (CCTV), electronic article surveillance (EAS), and benefit denial systems, and emerging technology such as source tagging, computerized inventory control, radio frequency identification (RFID), and DNA tagging; and peer reporting. It will also discuss academic and professional research in loss prevention, as well as special issues in retail security, including racial profiling and false arrests, and the effects retail security and loss prevention have had on homeland security.

The Retail Shrinkage Problem

Shrinkage is one of the most serious problems facing retail stores, with estimated annual losses of between $12 and $40 billion.[1] Retailers use the term *shrinkage* to describe the difference between inventory on hand at the beginning of the year and inventory on hand—minus sales—at year end.[2] Thus, shrinkage can be said to be goods that a store or business purchased with the intent to resell that are lost, typically due to theft, throughout the year. Researchers have said that shrinkage refers to those losses attributed to shoplifting, employee theft, vendor fraud, and administrative (paperwork) error.[3] Researcher data suggest that the average retail firm loses 1.7 percent of its gross sales revenues to inventory shrinkage.[4]

The Crime Prevention Service for Business of Rutgers University School of Criminal Justice defines *shrinkage* as the difference between the inventory a business should have and what the business actually does have. It says most businesses do inventories to calculate this difference and that shrinkage is the result of four main factors: administrative and bookkeeping errors, employee theft, vendor or delivery-person theft, and shoplifting. According to Rutgers, higher-than-normal shrinkage levels are associated with stores with persistent overstocks and higher markdown ratios; multifloor stores with many entrances and exits; stores with supplementary storerooms and warehouses; sparsely staffed stores open long hours; stores with high personnel turnover rates; mall stores with a combination of individual assistance, self-service, and central checkout counters; and stores with inadequate screening of employees.[5]

Rutgers reports that the cost of shrinkage to a business is directly related to its profit margin. For example, if a store has a 10 percent profit margin and someone steals a $2 item, the store will have to sell $20 in merchandise to make up for that loss. Some stores have very low profit margins and suffer greatly because of shrinkage. Grocery stores often have profit margins of around 1 percent. Thus, if someone steals a steak worth $7.50, the store must sell goods worth $750 to recover the loss.[6]

Shrinkage results in numerous losses, including a revenue shortfall, an inventory shortage, loss of the cash invested in the merchandise, freight charges, productivity on the part of the people processing the shipments, and a portion of any other fixed or variable costs incurred to sell the items.[7]

The annual **National Retail Security Survey** for the latest reporting year reports an average U.S. shrinkage rate of 1.65 percent. Previous U.S. shrinkage rates varied between 1.72 percent and 1.95 percent. Most shrinkage is attributed to

---

shrinkage The reduction in inventory due to theft or diversion.

National Retail Security Survey Annual shrinkage report prepared by the University of Florida for loss prevention specialists and executives.

JOBS IN SECURITY

Loss Prevention Positions

DIRECTOR OF LOSS PREVENTION

PUBLIX, the largest employee-owned supermarket chain in the nation, employs a Director of Loss Prevention at its corporate office in Lakeland, Florida.

The primary responsibilities for this position include providing executive direction and oversight to the Loss Prevention Department; overseeing functions including strategic initiatives, business plan, policy development, and loss prevention programs and systems; providing leadership regarding inventory shrinkage reduction programs, physical security systems, and risk and liability avoidance; and directing security personnel, executive protection, and asset protection of the entire organization, including company associates, patrons and suppliers, stores, distribution centers, manufacturing plants, offices, and other facilities.

Qualifications include a bachelor's degree in criminal justice, business, or another field that provides technical, business, or managerial skills; a minimum of ten years of management experience within a retail loss prevention environment; three years of experience as the top loss prevention manager responsible for at least two-hundred geographically dispersed locations;

a minimum of one year of experience in a position of "responsible charge" of a business location, handling expense control, customer service, personnel management budgeting, financial performance, and similar responsibilities; prior operating or supervisory responsibility of a round-the-clock uniformed security force; and possession of the following certificates: CPP, CST, CFI, and CFE.

LOSS PREVENTION AGENT

GAP Inc. employs a loss prevention agent at its store in Annapolis/Bowie, Maryland. Primary responsibilities of this position include applying safety policies to all store associates and customers; assisting store personnel with any safety issues, for example, confrontations and shoplifter apprehensions; recovering assets; making safe apprehensions when theft has clearly been established; and training all new hires on loss prevention policies and procedures under the direction of loss prevention managers.

SOURCE: LPInformation.com, "Job Information, Listing 152." Retrieved January 25, 2005, from http://www.lpinformation.com.

---

retailers' own employees through employee theft and return fraud (47 percent). The remainder of shrinkage is attributed to customer theft, 32 percent; supplier or vendor theft, 6 percent; and administrative or paperwork error, 15 percent. The survey reports the cost of security as 0.51 percent of turnover (sales).[8] Figures show that shrinkage is a $34 billion-per-year problem in the United States[9] and a $28.9 billion problem in Western Europe.[10]

The National Retail Security Survey has determined that men shoplift more often than women do, that 8 percent of shoppers who enter a store will steal something, and that the typical shoplifter falls between the ages of 35 and 54.[11]

Survey of Supermarket Theft A survey to determine the amount of theft that occurs within supermarkets based on the survey's respondents.

The annual **Survey of Supermarket Theft** for the latest reporting year, from the loss prevention consultant firm, Jack L. Hayes International, showed that 35,532 employees of the twenty-four respondent supermarket groups studied were apprehended for theft or fraud (4 percent of total employee count). The average monetary cost of items stolen by apprehended staff was $551, and by customer thieves, $137. The total losses for these twenty-four retail groups were almost $2 billion.[12]

According to Richard Mader, executive director of the Association for Retail Technology Standards, "Nearly half of retail shrinkage is due to internal employee theft and of that, approximately 50 percent of the loss is through the cash register. Traditional methods of monitoring and reviewing these registers are extremely time-consuming; however emerging loss prevention technology can flag incidents electronically, allowing for faster investigations and timely resolution."[13]

You Are There!

What Is Shrinkage? A Financial Analysis of the Problem

Retailer News gives the follow hypothetical example to illustrate the concept of shrinkage:

A branch store of a men's clothing chain has ordered twelve navy blue men's sport coats. The wholesale cost of each coat is $100, and the selling price is expected to be $150. Freight charges from the manufacturer amount to $10 for each coat. The shipment arrives at the warehouse and is sent to the store, where the coats are put on the sales floor.

If four coats in the most common sizes are stolen, then the most obvious financial cost is the cost of the items ($100 each) and the freight charges ($10 each). Also, there are costs incurred to process them, move them from the warehouse to the sales floor, and otherwise prepare them for sale—these costs are difficult to assign precisely to the coats and are often called "soft costs." The wholesale cost and the freight cost are called "hard" costs.

Since the coats were stolen instead of sold, the opportunity to sell them at a profit is lost as well. If all twelve coats had been sold, maximum sales volume would have been $1,800 (twelve coats times $150 selling price). Since only eight coats remain, maximum sales value is $1,200. In order to make up the sales shortfall, another procurement of coats will have to be purchased [in] order to generate the sales volume of the original twelve.

The additional procurement means another round of freight charges and other "soft" charges. If the coats cannot be replaced, or if the remaining coats must be marked down, maximum sales volume potential is still lower, while the costs to generate the sales are higher than normal.

In summary, the shrinkage of the coats results in the following losses:

- Revenue shortfall
- Inventory shortage
- Loss of the cash invested in the merchandise
- Freight charges
- Productivity on the part of the people processing the shipments
- A portion of any fixed or variable costs incurred to sell the coats

SOURCE: Robert L. DiLonardo, "The Financial Impact of Shoplifting," *Retailer News*. Retrieved February 7, 2005, from, http://retailernews.com/399/unise399.html.

Loss prevention is a serious concern for retail businesses in the United States because shrinkage reduces their profits. Most large retail businesses have a propriety security department that performs numerous duties in loss prevention, safety, and internal auditing. Since the 9/11 terrorist attacks, many of these security departments have also adopted homeland security duties. Smaller businesses and stores may have a proprietary security employee on duty or may hire a security guard from a contract guard service.

To further exacerbate the problem, many sources, including the National Crime Victimization Survey (NCVS) of the U. S. Department of Justice (DOJ) and the Australian Institute of Criminology, report that a large number of crimes committed against businesses go unreported to the police and that shoplifting and employee theft are significantly underrepresented in crime data.[14] The NCVS indicates that roughly two-thirds of all thefts go unreported to the police. Also, because the NCVS statistics only include thefts against persons and not businesses, they ignore shoplifting entirely.[15] There are also other problems with statistics regarding shoplifting. Surveys by retail loss prevention professionals reveal that industry insiders are unable to determine what proportion of missing inventory is directly attributable to shoplifting—the best estimate is somewhere in the neighborhood of 40 percent of the total loss.[16] Researchers have consistently reported that shoplifing is one of the most underreported and misreported crimes.[17]

Some studies on shrinkage reveal the following:

- Much of retail shrinkage is attributable to employee theft.

- Shoplifting is the single largest crime affecting U.S. retailers, with annual losses totaling over $2 billion.

- In the year 2000, about 5,400 persons were arrested or detained for shoplifting every day, and up to 69 million acts of shoplifting occurred, most going undetected.

- Experts report that the costs of shrinkage, including employee theft, are business failures, lost jobs, lower tax revenues, and higher prices passed on to consumers.

- Most retail theft is detected by audits rather than witnessed, so it is not always clear whether the theft is perpetrated by customers, staff, or suppliers.

- It has been estimated that a 2 to 3 percent loss of sales to shrinkage can amount to an approximate 25 percent loss in profit. For some smaller businesses or those on otherwise tight margins, retail theft can not only affect productivity and competitiveness but can actually threaten economic survival. This crime affects not only the businesses but also other consumers, who subsidize store losses by paying elevated prices.[18]

Loss prevention (LP) refers to the use of methods to reduce the amount of shrinkage in retail stores. Loss prevention methods and techniques include management policy and operations; CPTED (crime prevention through enviromental design) techniques; internal and external audits; the use of store detectives or loss prevention specialists; peer reporting of suspicious or criminal activity; and loss prevention technology, such as closed-circuit television (CCTV), electronic article surveillance (EAS), benefit denial systems (ink tags), source tagging, computerized inventory control, radio frequency identification (RFID), and DNA tagging. Nontechnological loss prevention equipment includes observation mirrors (that allow store clerks to see throughout the store), locking antitheft cables and wires, security bars, wire lanyards, and other devices. Security guards are also part of a store's loss prevention program. Loss prevention efforts can be overt or covert. Overt security means that security efforts are obvious to all shoppers, such as locking equipment, visible cameras and tags, and uniformed security officers. Covert security includes hidden cameras and plainclothes store detectives or loss prevention specialists.

Some shrinkage researchers report that it is hard to tell what percentage of shrinkage is due to shoplifting and suggests that stores can get a rough estimate of it based on how many shoplifters are apprehended and how much merchandise is recovered. Stores can also look for signs of shoplifting activity, such as hangers and ripped price tags lying around, merchandise placed where it should not be, and product packages disposed of in hidden spaces. In addition, certain categories of stores have more shoplifting because their merchandise is more desirable by thieves, and stores in cities tend to have a bigger problem than those in suburbs and rural areas.[19]

Internal Shrinkage

As the previous section of this chapter discussed, internal shrinkage has consistently been reported as more serious than external shrinkage. Internal shrinkage is theft caused by a store or employer's own employees. It includes theft by employees, collusion between employees and others (generally friends or relatives), suppliers and vendors, and administrative errors.

This is a worldwide problem. A 2005 study from the United Kingdom Center for Retail Research found that employees in the United Kingdom stole merchandise worth £1.5 billion from their employers in 2004. The same study reported that Iceland had an even worse employee theft problem.[20]

External Shrinkage

External shrinkage is caused by theft by outsiders, generally shoplifters. In a study analyzing 166,000 shoplifting incidents submitted by 101 retail firms, it was discovered that CDs, over-the-counter medications, and health and beauty products are among the most frequently stolen items. (See Exhibits 6.1 and 6.2 for a more complete list.) According to the study, discount, department store, and supermarket retailers reported the highest apprehension rates of shoplifters.[21]

Security executives report that at least one-third of their inventory losses result from shoplifting incidents, and their apprehension data indicates that the average shoplifter gets caught with about $200 worth of merchandise. When one extrapolates this data to the entire U.S. retail industry (the National Retail Federation estimates that the industry generates $1.8 trillion in revenues each year), the retail industry suffers somewhere in the neighborhood of about $10 billion in losses due to shoplifting each year.[22]

loss prevention (LP) The use of methods to reduce the amount of shrinkage in retail stores.

EXHIBIT 6.1	Products and Items Most Likely to be Shoplifted

Type of Retailer	Merchandise
Auto parts	Hard parts
Bookstores	Electronics, CDs, cassette tapes
Consumer electronics	Portable CD players, car alarms, cell phones
Department stores	Clothing—shirts
Discount stores	Undergarments
Drug stores/pharmacies	Cigarettes, batteries, over-the-counter remedies
Fashion merchandise	Sneakers
General merchandise stores	Earrings
Grocery stores/supermarkets	Over-the-counter remedies, health and beauty aids, cigarettes
Home centers/hardware stores	Assorted hand tools
Music stores	Compact discs
Shoe stores	Sneakers
Specialty stores	Bed sheets
Toy stores	Action figures
Video stores	Video games

SOURCE: Crime Prevention Service, Rutgers University, School of Criminal Justice, "What Items Are Shoplifted the Most." Retrieved January 19, 2005, from http://www.crimeprevention.rutgers.edu.

Shoplifters use numerous common techniques:

■ Palming, or grabbing the product by hand, is the simplest and most common method used for shoplifting. Palming is often aided by the use of a package, handkerchief, or glove. An accomplice may stand in front of the shoplifter to screen him or her from observation.

■ Purses and pockets are common places to conceal shoplifted items. Thieves also use shopping bags and boxes from other stores, umbrellas, schoolbooks, knitting bags, strollers, baby carriages, sample cases, briefcases, overnight bags, and lunch boxes.

■ By placing stolen objects between their legs under a loose coat or a full skirt or dress,

EXHIBIT 6.2	Hot Items to Shoplift

Some products are considered hot because they are either craved (C-R-A-V-E-D), easy to resell, or enjoyable enough to steal.

CRAVED

C = Concealable
R = Removable
A = Available
V = Valuable
E = Enjoyable
D = Disposable

Easy to Resell

Jewelry
Car stereos
Cigarettes
CD players
TV sets
Jeans
CDs
Latest basketball sneakers

Enjoyable Enough to Steal	Not Enjoyable Enough to Steal
Cigarettes	Nicotine patches
Whiskey	Rubbing alcohol
Condoms	Antifungal cream
DVD players	Food processors
Trendy basketball sneakers	Plain white sneakers
Movie videos	Books on physics
Designer jeans	Polyester stretchy pants
Steak	Spinach
Latest hip-hop CD	Barney the Dinosaur's Greatest Hits CD
Snowboards	Snow shovels

SOURCE: Crime Prevention Service, Rutgers University, School of Criminal Justice, "Preventing Employee Theft." Retrieved January 19, 2005, from http://www.crimeprevention.rutgers.edu

a professional thief can "**crotch-carry**" as much as a 25-pound ham or eight cartons of cigarettes.

■ Another technique is wearing shoplifted hats, gloves, scarves, coats, or sweaters, or carrying purses out of the store.

crotch-carry A method of shoplifting in which the criminal carries stolen items between his or her legs, usually under a loose coat or full skirt or dress.

©Bill Aron/PhotoEdit

Shoplifting is the single largest crime affecting U.S. retailers, with annual losses totaling over $2 billion. CDs, over-the-counter medications, and health and beauty products are among the most frequently stolen items. What methods discussed in this chapter could this store use to reduce external shrinkage?

- Some thieves throw coats or sweaters over items and then pick them up with the merchandise concealed inside.

- Jewelry and other accessories can be dropped into clothing or inserted into the hair.

- In fitting rooms, tight or closely fitting garments can be put on under street clothes.

- Packages and purses can be rearranged to conceal the addition of a dress or blouse.

- Shoplifters may cause intentional confusion with merchandise, such as handling so much clothing or so many products that sales personnel lose track, or an accomplice or other party might distract sales personnel.

- Also common is price switching—taking a price tag from one product with a higher price and relabeling it with a lower price tag.

- Shoplifters may step around the end of the counter, using the excuse of wanting to see something, in order to steal expensive articles from the unlocked side of a showcase.

- Shoplifters may distract sales personnel with persistent bell ringing while an accomplice steals merchandise.

- Another common method involves removing small items from a display case and hiding them in another part of the store for later retrieval by an accomplice.

- A customer may enter a market with an empty paper bag in her purse, fill the bag with merchandise, then exit through an unmanned checkout lane. If questioned, she assures the clerk that she has already checked out.

- Boxed items that are easily opened and reclosed may have more valuable items inside them.

- Supermarket shoplifters have been known to open an expensive package of tea and pour the contents into a pocketbook, where it settles at the bottom.

- A customer may place an item in her purse and at the checkout counter ask for credit, explaining that another member of the family bought the item by mistake. If the clerk refuses the refund because the shoplifter does not have a receipt, the shoplifter wins. The shoplifter, of course, also wins if the store grants the refund.

Exhibit 6.3 provides a more detailed list of shoplifting methods.

The latest research in 2005 indicates baby formula has long been an attractive item for shoplifters, who sell it on the black market at a reduced price or use it to cut drugs. Sometimes people steal it and bring it to another store and "return it" for cash. Millions of dollars worth of powdered formula are stolen every year. Weis Markets, which operates 156 stores in Pennsylvania and five surrounding states, said its

EXHIBIT 6.3   Common Shoplifting Techniques

Hiding the Merchandise

- A large open bag—a common shoplifting tool, it is placed at the thief's feet and objects are usually dropped into it.
- The "bad bag"—a paper bag that is dirty and wrinkled.
- Shopping bags not from local stores.
- Purses to hide stolen items.
- Baby carriage or stroller—merchandise can be hidden under blankets, toys, and other things in strollers (including the baby). Some thieves have built false bottoms in baby carriages.
- Using a newspaper to hide small objects.
- Umbrellas with handles—thieves keep the umbrella closed but not snapped, on their elbows, or leaning against a counter and then drop items into it.
- Crotch-carrying—used by women wearing full skirts and dresses and men and women wearing long coats. Thieves place the merchandise between their thighs and walk away. Thieves have been known to steal hams, computers, and other large objects this way.
- Using baggy clothes to hide stolen items—some thieves have extra pockets or hooks sewn into coats and jackets. Some thieves keep one hand in a coat pocket and some have cut slits in the pocket lining, so they can reach for items without being seen.

Brazen Approach

- Some shoplifters just grab items and walk out with them, relying on the gullibility and slow response of the sales staff.
- Some thieves commonly grab garments from racks closest to the door and run off.
- Some thieves simply walk out of the store brazenly with large items that are not ordinarily put in bags.
- Often thieves steal garments by putting them on under their own clothes in a fitting room and wearing them out of the store.

Distract Store Personnel

- People may enter the store in large groups, then separate into smaller groups to make it difficult for employees to watch all of them.
- A pair of shoppers comes in, and while one distracts the sales clerk with questions, the other shoplifts.
- A single shopper sends the only employee in the store into the back room to find something and then steals items and leaves before the employee comes back.

SOURCE: Crime Prevention Service, Rutgers University, School of Criminal Justice, "Common Shoplifting Techniques." Retrieved January 19, 2005, from http://www.crimeprevention.rutgers.edu.

efforts to deter this type of theft include placing the formula section under video surveillance, teaching employees what to look out for, and placing cases behind the cash register.[23]

The Food Marketing Institute, an industry group that maintains a list of the fifty most stolen items from supermarkets, said that Similac powdered formula ranked number seventh and cans of Similac ranked eighth. In 2005, police made two traffic stops along interstate highways and netted more than 4,500 cans of stolen Similac and Enfamil powdered formula. In North Carolina, seven people were arrested last year for conspiring to steal and resell more than $14 million in baby formula.

Reducing the Shrinkage Problem

Methods of controlling retail theft range from relatively simple store practices, such as putting fewer items on display or placing stickers on packages, to sophisticated electronic surveillance mechanisms. This section will discuss methods of reducing retail shrinkage, including management policy; CPTED; audits; store detectives or loss prevention specialists; peer reporting; and loss prevention technology, including current technology and emerging technologies.

Management Policy

Aggressive management policies that emphasize employee awareness and participation in dealing with the problem are valuable in reducing shrinkage.

In a 2003 article in *Security Journal*, Adrian Beck, Charlotte Bilby, and Paul Chapman detail methods for management to develop strategic plans for investigating, addressing, and preventing merchandise shrinkage. They advocate applying holistic and systematic principles to the issue of stock loss, and they argue for a process-oriented approach as the most effective technique for mapping and measuring retail shrinkage. They tested the mapping and measuring process for retail shrinkage using supply chains from Gillette in the United Kingdom to customers in both Sweden and Hungary. They found that the stock loss reduction roadmap is an effective tool for organizing supply data in order to develop strategic approaches to combat the problem of retail shrinkage.[24]

Interviews of 1,500 shoplifters conducted by loss prevention expert Read Hayes for the Loss Prevention Research Council and the University of Florida revealed that "active, random threats to shoplifters like moving, alert staff . . . can be very effective in preventing shrinkage." The interviews indicated shoplifters are less likely to steal from a store if management applies certain policies, such as having motivated store personnel regularly approach and acknowledge customers and keeping display areas organized. Shoplifters also indicated that they will avoid stealing from stores if they know that plainclothes store detectives or loss prevention specialists are working there.[25] Exhibit 6.4 offers more shoplifting prevention measures.

Mark Lippman, owner of Guardsmark Inc., a leading contract security provider, and W. R. McGraw write that employee theft cannot be eliminated, but it can be controlled by good management techniques and the intelligent use of acceptable security procedures. They mention four ways for retailers to do this:

1. Honest people, for the most part, stay honest; dishonest people tend to stay dishonest. Employers should conduct complete background investigations, including previous employment records, and should carry out in-depth applicant interviews.

2. Employees should be made to feel that they are part of the firm and that their contributions are important to its future. Disgruntled and disaffected employees represent the greatest threat for theft and vandalism. Employers should also pay well. The most important control against employee theft is a good salary or wage. It will not stop the confirmed thief, but there is little doubt that more stealing goes on where employees are underpaid than where they are overpaid.

3. An unequivocal company policy or code of ethics should be impressed on all employees at an initial orientation. The policy must clearly indicate the ethical standards expected of the employees, as well as the consequences of violating those standards. The penalties must not be applied

EXHIBIT 6.4   Shoplifting Prevention Measures

The following are some ideas that experts recommend for stopping shoplifting. Some are easy and relatively cheap; others are more intensive and cost more money.

- Greet all customers when they walk into the store.
- Ask customers if they need any help.
- Keep counters and tables neat and orderly.
- Return unsold merchandise to displays quickly.
- Offer to hold merchandise at the sales counter for browsing customers.
- Limit the number of garments a customer can take into the fitting room, and count the garments.
- Call to customers in the fitting room and ask if they need anything.
- If selling pairs of something (like shoes), only display one.
- Alternate the direction of hangers so they lock when grabbed.
- Post signs warning of the consequences of shoplifting.
- Put only the cheaper products by the door and expensive ones away from the door.
- Organize merchandise so it can be easily viewed by more than one salesperson.
- Do not stack merchandise so high it blocks the view of salespeople.

- Arrange merchandise so customers must pick it up; otherwise, a thief can push items from the counter into some sort of container or bag.
- Keep fitting room doors locked, which forces customers to ask a salesperson to open them.
- Offer rewards to staff that detect and apprehend shoplifters.
- Widen the space between displays.
- Install more mirrors throughout the store.
- Install convex mirrors on the ceiling.
- Improve lighting so there are no dark corners in the store.
- Install fake video cameras.
- Use fake electronic article surveillance tags.
- Elevate the sales counter work area.
- Use ink merchandise tags.
- Install video cameras.
- Install an electronic article surveillance system.
- Hire a security guard.

SOURCE: Crime Prevention Service, Rutgers University, School of Criminal Justice, "Shoplifting Prevention Measures." Retrieved January 19, 2005, from http://www.crimeprevention.rutgers.edu. Reprinted by permission.

selectively, and the company must itself operate according to a high ethical standard.

4. Adequate security measures must be taken. The security measures range from sophisticated computer security systems to undercover investigations.[26]

As a recent example of a strong proactive management policy on security, the University of Central Florida, in order to prevent increasing internal theft, implemented a policy on security and internal theft reduction emphasizing timely incident reports, management awareness of employees' suspected involvement in criminal activity, proper inventory controls, improved hiring practices, background checks, credible wages, benefits, and an aggressive well-communicated management policy emphasizing intolerance

to theft. Management also directed the security department to utilize preventive tools, such as pinhole surveillance cameras and antitheft powders that are hard to see and remove from skin and clothing.[27] Exhibit 6.5 further discusses methods of preventing employee theft.

A telephone survey of sixty senior-level retail loss prevention executives from fifty-nine U.S. retail companies revealed that they recognized that theft, violence, and loss are a function of operational, demographic, process, and execution issues in the workplace, not simply a crime problem. They reported that the changing mission of their jobs included recognizing shrinkage issues and employing measures for containing it, including going into proactive, cooperative partnerships with store operations managers, finding effective ways to manage dishonest staff

---

EXHIBIT 6.5   **Preventing Employee Theft**

THEFTS AT THE POINT OF SALE
Cash registers are vulnerable areas in many stores.

- Watch out for loose change, matchsticks, or bits of papers with markings on them around the cash register area. These are often used by cashiers to help them remember the amount of extra money that they may pocket later. For example, a nickel means five dollars, a penny one dollar, and so on. If questioned about the loose change, the cashier can simply say a customer forgot her change. Matchsticks and bits of paper can be dismissed by cashiers as trash.

- Be extra suspicious of cashiers who keep a small calculator close to the cash register. This can help them keep a running total of the amount of extra money in the till.

- Make sure customers can see the amount rung up on the cash register. If the display is turned away from their view or is covered, this could mean the cashier is underringing purchases in order to pocket money later.

- Look out for an excessive number of "No Sales." These can be used as a way of opening up the drawer when there is no one around to take out money and pocket it.

- Watch out for an excessive number of "Voids." This could mean the cashier is canceling transactions that actually occurred in order to pocket that amount of money.

REFUND FRAUD
- People steal merchandise from the store and then return it for a refund (same store or other stores of the same business).

- Staff members keep the receipts from previous sales and use them to process refunds later on.

- People buy merchandise at sale prices and then return it for a full-priced refund at a later date.

- People buy products or merchandise, use them, and then return them for a refund. For example, someone buys an expensive dress, wears it, and then returns it as if she had not worn it.

SALES FLOOR
Watch for employees who do the following:

- Wander around, apparently aimlessly
- Go into the staff lounge area when it is not their assigned break time
- Socialize with employees in other areas when they are supposed to be working
- Bring their bags or purses out into the sales area

THEFTS FROM WAREHOUSES
The biggest threat to warehouses is collusion between two dishonest people—an employee inside the warehouse and another person outside.

Source: Crime Prevention Service, Rutgers University, School of Criminal Justice, "Preventing Employee Theft." Retrieved January 19, 2005, from http://www.crimeprevention.rutgers.edu.

members, and developing and implementing loss prevention performance measures and evaluation techniques.[28]

CPTED (Crime Prevention through Environmental Design)

Researchers have reported that the modern retail environment provides would-be shoplifters adequate cover to conceal their acts of thievery, including many shelves, signs, displays, and secluded areas that make it easy to hide shoplifting activity from others.[29]

The concept of **crime prevention through environmental design (CPTED)** assumes that crime is related to daily routines and activities in the area, such as traffic and pedestrian flow, and also that criminals want to avoid being observed when they are committing their crimes and thus avoid arrest. CPTED involves using and designing the space inside and outside of buildings, entrances, exits, landscaping, and lighting to present the least opportunity for a criminal to avoid detection. The three main strategies used for CPTED are natural surveillance, natural access control, and territorial reinforcement.[30]

Natural surveillance involves designing windows, lighting, and landscaping to improve the ability to observe what is going on inside and around the business. Natural access control refers to the use of doors, fences, and gates to control access to the business or property and to make the business look like a riskier crime target. Territorial reinforcement uses sidewalks, landscaping, and process to create a border between private and public property to create a feeling of territoriality and send a message to offenders that the property belongs to someone and the offender should keep out.

Using CPTED, businesses can create conditions that make it much more difficult for a criminal to avoid detection. Many of the concepts and issues raised in this chapter to deter shrinkage and retail loss involve CPTED concepts. Good examples of

crime prevention through environmental design (CPTED) Methods used to deter crime through manipulation of architectural design.

crime reduction through product design (CRPD) Methods used to deter crime by implementing security features into products.

CTPED are the studies and suggestions used by the National Association of Convenience Stores (NACS) mentioned in Chapter 5. As you may recall, these studies and suggestions concerned crime reduction design in such areas as store layout, parking lots, lighting, staffing, signage, and many other issues

A closely related concept is **crime reduction through product design (CRPD)**. According to the Australian Institute of Criminology, CRPD involves the integration of protective features into products in order to reduce their potential to become targets of criminal activity (such as theft, fraud, and damage), as well as preventing their use as instruments of crime. Some of the theft countermeasures that are now widely accepted and used in retail security, such as the electronic article surveillance (EAS) and benefit denial systems attached to retail merchandise and are mentioned in this chapter, are examples of CRPD concepts.[31]

Audits

Audits and inventories are extremely important in loss prevention efforts. Inventories of products and equipment on the store's shelves and in its warehouses and audits of financial assets can be internal (conducted by the store's own personnel) or external (conducted by firms or people hired by the company). Audits and inventories will reveal the amount of shrinkage occurring in the store and often can give clues as to who is responsible for such losses and thefts. The more often audits are conducted, the quicker the business will detect and investigate shrinkage. Many stores using cashiers do audits of each cashier's drawers at least daily.

As an example of an effective use of inventories to decrease theft, a discount electronics and appliance retailer had been experiencing unacceptable levels of theft, and a study of the problem by its security department revealed that the items most at risk of being stolen were camcorders and VCRs. These items were securely locked and were guarded by security guards and CCTV. The retailer had warehouses in four stores and a much larger one in its distribution center. All of the warehouses had numerous entrances and exits, and many employees had access to the locked storage area where the camcorders and VCRs were kept. Inventory was not taken frequently enough to link thefts with any particular person; for example, if an inventory was taken in March and again in April, and in that month ten camcorders disappeared, too many persons had access to them to determine the identity of the thief. The security director decided to order a daily inventory of all camcorders and VCRs. This "preventive audit survey" worked well because workers knew that any missing items could be linked to staff working that shift and that all would be suspect to suspicion. The result of the security director's efforts was the elimination of the theft of camcorders and VCRs and a reduction of employee theft of other nontargeted merchandise.[32]

Store Detectives/Loss Prevention Specialists

As indicated earlier, many large businesses have security or loss prevention departments and employ loss prevention or security directors or managers at their corporate offices and at their individual stores or branches. These loss prevention or security directors or managers are usually in the middle- or upper-management level in the corporate or business structure. They supervise and manage loss prevention or security programs and conduct **loss prevention investigations**, including investigations of both internal and external theft of assets. These employees are ultimately responsible for finding and apprehending employees and customers who steal merchandise or cash, destroy property, or conduct other crimes in stores and businesses (Exhibit 6.6 discusses the clues to shoplifting these professionals look for). They also may inventory and audit stock and other company possessions and assets.

Dan Doyle, chairperson of the National Retail Federation Loss Prevention Council, says that loss prevention professionals today serve as a type of internal police force for retailers. He indicates that about one-third of loss prevention professionals now have a college degree.[33]

It was reported in 2005 that organized retail theft rings have become so prolific and are causing so many losses that several large retailers, including Wal-Mart, Lowe's, and Walgreen's, have formed their own organized crime divisions. According to the head of Walgreen's organized crime unit, Jerry Biggs, organized professional retail thieves are called "boosters" and can take anywhere from $50 to $200 worth of merchandise out of a store and hit six to twelve stores a day. He says they tend to steal high-demand items that can be sold in bulk, including diabetic test strips, toothpaste, hair-care products, and over-the-counter medicine. He says a booster can make $10,000 to $20,000 a day.

EXHIBIT 6.6   Clues to Shoplifting

- Dress: Wearing heavy clothes in summer; wearing no coat in winter; wearing very worn clothing that can be switched for stolen clothes; not wearing shoes; wearing baggy clothes or full and pleated skirts.
- Actions: Enter the store in pairs, and while one distracts clerks, the other roams around; take quick glances around (scoping); do not seem interested in items they ask clerks about; are nervous, flushed, or dry-lipped or are sweating when it is not hot; hold quick conversations with other suspicious people; do not seem to know what they want and interchange articles frequently; are shopping right after opening or right before closing.
- Movements: Leaves an area of the store very quickly; tugs at a sleeve, adjusts socks, rubs the back of the neck, or makes other odd movements that might help in hiding items; reaches into a display counter or walks behind a sales counter; keeps one hand in an outer coat pocket all the time; moves quickly from displays to the fitting rooms; walks in an unusual way; pushes a baby carriage or stroller; roams around aimlessly, waiting for a friend who is shopping.
- Carrying: Carries wrinkled or dirty shopping bags (bad bags), plastic garbage bags, or backpacks; takes a lot of garments into the fitting room at once; takes more than one garment of a particular pattern into the fitting room at once; carries a large open purse; carries bags, bundles, boxes, coats slung over arms, briefcases, newspapers, umbrellas, or has an arm in a sling.

SOURCE: Crime Prevention Service, Rutgers University, School of Criminal Justice, "Spot the Shoplifter." Retrieved January 19, 2005, from http://www.crimeprevention.rutgers.edu

Boosters sell their bounty to fence operations posing as a legitimate business, where it is cleaned up and repackaged for sale over the Internet, in flea markets, or to wholesalers. One Houston ring Biggs followed stole more than $68,000 in merchandise in only three days. He also says he has tracked a group of six professional thieves from Colombia who stole $10 million worth of goods during a six-month boosting spree through the Midwest.[34]

According to a recent article by Robert L. DiLonardo, more and more retail loss prevention executives are using financial analysis techniques to determine how best to attack shortage problems. He mentions Walter E. Palmer, director of loss

loss prevention investigations Investigative programs to detect and prevent retail theft; can be proprietary or contract.

You Are There!

Shoplifting and Fencing: Operation American Dream

In the mid-1990s, a Pakistani criminal syndicate ran a large-scale shoplifting–fencing–repackaging business in the Atlanta metropolitan area. They targeted stores in and on the outskirts of the city, stealing over-the-counter medicines, pharmaceuticals, razors, health and beauty aids, computers, DVDs, stereos, TVs, clothing, shoes, and household goods from nationally recognized retail stores.

The Georgia Bureau of Investigation (GBI), after a six-month investigation, arrested the participants and closed down the operation. But within a few weeks, the gang simply regrouped and was back in operation. At this time, private security investigators for the Dayton Hudson Corporation, the owners of nationally known retail stores like Target, began to investigate the group. They discovered that its operation expanded far beyond Atlanta.

Operation American Dream was then established with the private security investigators, the GBI, the Atlanta Police Department, the Immigration and Naturalization Service, the Internal Revenue Service, and the FBI. The investigation disclosed that the principals in the Atlanta fencing operation were conspiring with other foreign nationals in Baltimore, New York, and Pakistan, to fence and repackage millions of dollars of stolen merchandise. In addition to fencing stolen items, they had been involved in money laundering,

illegal alien smuggling, auto theft, interstate transportation of stolen goods, and attempted murder.

The leaders of the operation, thirty predominantly illegal Pakistani nationals who operated convenience stores that were receiving the stolen merchandise, recruited a group of over two hundred professional shoplifters and illegal Pakistani immigrants. The shoplifters, also called boosters, would steal from retail stores primarily in small towns where store security was minimal. They would operate in groups of four or five, often using distraction techniques to steal merchandise. The group leaders supported them with vehicles and legal help if they were arrested. The stolen merchandise would later be taken to a warehouse, where it was repackaged and shipped to coconspirators in New York, Baltimore, and Pakistan. The merchandise would then be resold to retail stores.

In October 1999, a 214-count indictment resulted in the arrests of numerous subjects for multiple counts of conspiracy, money laundering, and interstate transportation of stolen property. Over $1.6 million in stolen retail merchandise and half a million dollars in currency were seized.

SOURCE: Federal Bureau of Investigation, "Major Investigations, Operation American Dream." Retrieved April 25, 2007, from http://www.retailindustrynetwork.com.

prevention for Toys "R" Us, who is a strong believer in using financial analysis to help him determine where and how to spend his loss prevention capital. Palmer believes that a thorough understanding of the capital budgeting process helps loss prevention executives make correct decisions about what to buy, how much to buy, and where to best deploy their loss prevention assets.[35]

Retail security expert Read Hayes conducted a survey of sixty loss prevention executives representing fifty-nine retail companies. Many said that in addition to their loss prevention and security duties, they are assigned a broad scope of responsibility for dealing with noncrime issues

that may ultimately dilute their loss control effectiveness. For example, almost two-thirds of the respondents were required to supervise safety and other nonsecurity functions. They reported that they worked with other corporate partners in fulfilling their duties, including store operations, inventory control, human resources, internal audit, and information technology.[36] Loss prevention executives also play a strategic role in their companies by specifying, testing, and recommending loss prevention systems. These executives also projected that their future loss prevention concerns were employee deviance, including theft, harassment, violence, and tardiness; customer theft; online computer crime; parking lot crime; and other acts of violence.

Many stores use **store detectives** or **loss prevention specialists** to deal with external and

store detective/loss prevention specialist A private investigator who investigatives retail pilferage and theft.

internal theft. The goal of the store detective or loss prevention specialist is to protect business assets and apprehend people stealing property or money from the store. After apprehending the shoplifter, the store detective retrieves the stolen property. In many cases the police are called in to arrest the violator and process him or her through the criminal justice system. Some stores use sophisticated camera equipment to scan the store for people stealing merchandise, whereas other stores rely on the store detective "roaming" the store, appearing to look like an ordinary shopper.

Many college students work their way through college with jobs as store detectives or loss prevention specialists. Being a store detective is also a good entry-level job in private security from which employees can work their way up to security management.

The United States Department of Labor's *Occupational Outlook Handbook* describes the functions of store detectives or loss prevention officers as safeguarding the assets of retail stores by apprehending anyone attempting to steal merchandise or destroy store property and preventing theft by shoplifters, vendor representatives, delivery personnel, and store employees. They also conduct periodic inspections of stock areas, dressing rooms, and restrooms and sometimes assist in opening and closing the store. They prepare loss prevention and security reports for management and testify in court against persons they apprehend. The Department of Labor considers some of the work store detectives engage in to be stressful and dangerous, as it is often confrontational. Most employers look for individuals with ingenuity, persistence, assertiveness, and the ability to communicate well and think on their feet.[37]

The Department of Labor's Bureau of Labor Statistics reports that there is keen competition for these jobs because they attract many qualified people, including relatively young retirees from law enforcement and military careers. It reports that those seeking store detective jobs have the best prospects with large chains and discount stores. It also reports that the employment of store detectives is expected to grow faster than the average for all occupations through 2014. In addition to growth, replacement of those who retire or leave the occupation for other reasons should create many job openings.[38]

Loss prevention personnel are typically responsible for interviewing suspected shoplifters and internal theft suspects. Several training programs

PRIVATE SECURITY CONNECTIONS

Some Professional Organizations for Retail Loss Prevention

Retail Loss Prevention Exchange
Loss Prevention Concepts Ltd.
Greater Cincinnati Loss Prevention Association
LP Information.com
Wicklander-Zulawski & Associates

are available to assist personnel in interviewing techniques, including the Wicklander-Zulawski Associates Inc. program, which is designed to help private-sector professionals improve their ability to obtain the truth through proper interviewing techniques. "Participants are taught the interpretation of verbal and nonverbal behavior, interrogation, and nonaccusatory interviewing."[39]

In a survey of forty U.S. retail stores employing store detectives, most retailers reported that they currently assign their store agents to patrol for shoplifters, audit store asset protection initiatives, and create loss prevention awareness among all store staff. They select new store detectives primarily on ethical and decision-making criteria. The use of force is the highest-ranked training topic, for liability purposes. Finally, more than 66 percent of the survey participants indicated that concerns about civil liability had caused them to change their training programs for store detectives.[40]

Read Hayes conducted a study analyzing more than two-hundred store detectives through written tests and supervisory evaluations to determine what makes a proficient and productive employee. According to the evaluations, the best performers tended to be less dogmatic and more open to new concepts than poor performers. However, the more experience that loss prevention personnel had before working for their current employers, the lower their ratings were in overall job performance, shoplifter apprehension, and promotion potential. For the study, Hayes developed a job performance instrument that measured three factors: overall performance assessment scores of each detective's job performance criteria over the past year; ability to apprehend thieves, deter theft, and recover merchandise; and potential as a future leader based on supervisory ratings. Hayes found that the best-performing detectives were

You Are There!

Loss Prevention at Macy's

As an example of loss prevention, in 2003 the department store Macy's detained and processed for shoplifting more than 12,000 persons in 105 Macy's stores nationwide, including more than 1,900 at their Manhattan store alone. Only 56 percent of these people were processed by the police, although 95 percent of the persons detained confessed to shoplifting and quite a few paid an in-store penalty before leaving. The Manhattan store alone lost $15 million to theft in 2002.

The Macy's Manhattan store's security includes one-hundred security officers, four German shepherds, hundreds of cameras, and a sophisticated closed-circuit television center. Plainclothes store detectives roam the ten selling floors, keeping in contact with uniformed guards by radio. The movement and activities of shoppers are tracked by over three-hundred cameras, some controlled by joysticks, as security workers watch images on dozens of closed-circuit television monitors. Macy's spent approximately $28 million on security in 2002—$4 million at their Manhattan store alone.

Macy's policy is to call the police if anyone requests legal representation or asks to be set free immediately, but most people prefer to settle the matter privately. Private security is not legally required to provide the same safeguards as are the police. Retailers are held to a standard known as the merchant's privilege or shopkeeper's privilege that allows stores to detain people on suspicion of shoplifting without police involvement. These laws also provide civil recovery statutes, allowing retailers to hold shoplifters liable for the cost of catching them and for the losses they cause, charging penalties even if an item is recovered in perfect condition. In New York State, retailers are allowed to demand five times the value of the item stolen as civil recovery.

Critics of private security procedures such as Macy's say, whether guilty or not, accused shoplifters are often deprived of some of the basic assurances usually provided in public law enforcement proceedings, including the right to legal representation before questioning and rigorous safeguards against coercion.

Wal-Mart's policy, in contrast, is to always contact the police when they detain a suspected shoplifter, according to a company spokesman. According to Donna Lieberman, executive director of the New York City Civil Liberties Union, "The issue of private security guards is a difficult one. On the one hand, stores have an interest in protecting their business. But on the other hand, security guards have neither the training nor the same legal obligations as police officers and the danger of interfering with individual rights is huge."

SOURCE: Andrea Elliott, "In Stores, Private Handcuffs for Sticky Fingers," *New York Times*, June 17, 2003, pp. A1, C14.

---

more responsive to emotions, indicating that they are more in tune with the culture and mood of the store managers and staff. The most negative traits were anger and hostility. The two most significant predictors for apprehending thieves were assertiveness and trust. The higest-performing detectives generally believed people are honest and therefore focus strongly on the behavior indicators of theft, rather than just believing everyone is probably a thief. Leadership potential was strongly predicted by the trait of deliberation and higher IQ scores.[41]

Private security officers generally are not restricted by the provisions of the U.S. Constitution in their duties, as the public police are. Private security officers do not have to give suspects *Miranda* warnings before questioning, and the exclusionary rule does not apply to the evidence they seize. However, they must be very careful in their operations because they and their employers can be sued and suffer monetary losses. Chapter 4 of this textbook fully discussed these issues.

The legal justification for the use of store detectives is the common law doctrine of the **shopkeeper's privilege**, or **merchant's privilege**. Under this theory, a storekeeper or shopkeeper can reasonably

shopkeeper's privilege/merchant's privilege Common-law doctrine that holds that a merchant or shopkeeper can reasonably detain and question a person if she or he has a justified suspicion that the person is committing an illegal act.

detain and question a person if the shopkeeper has a justified suspicion that an illegal act, such as theft, has taken place on the shop's premises. This doctrine holds that even if it is later found that no crime took place, the detention is proper if based on the following conditions:

■ Detention: Detention does not need to be physical restraint—it may arise out of words, conduct, gestures, or threats as long as the detainee believes that he or she is not free to leave the premises.

■ Probable cause: The detention of the subject must be based on probable cause—significant facts that would cause a reasonable person to believe than an offense has occurred and that the detained subject committed it.

■ Reasonableness: The detention of the subject must be reasonable considering the factors of physical surroundings, physical contact, and the type and level of any threats.

■ Consistency: Retailers must have policies that are applied evenhandedly without regard to the subject's race or other personal characteristics.[42]

Many security experts recommend that security personnel in retail stores avoid physical contact that could conceivably result in physical injury to suspected shoplifters, including striking, tackling, or sitting on suspects. Joseph LaRocca, the vice president of National Retail Federation's loss prevention, reports, "Most retailers have a policy of not going into a [foot] chase or getting into a combative fight with someone." LaRocca says that most retailers have a policy of letting combative shoplifters go and following up by calling police.[43]

As an example of the legal aspects of the shopkeeper's or merchant's privilege, the Iowa Court of Appeals, in 2003, considered a lawsuit by two shoppers detained by Wal-Mart on suspicion of shoplifting. The court decided that Wal-Mart was justified in detaining the shoppers; however, it left undecided the issue of whether the detention time of two-and-a-half hours was reasonable and decided that the case should be decided by a jury.[44]

In this case, in 2001, Angie Jacobson dropped off her friend Brittany Van Zante at the Wal-Mart store in Coralville, Iowa. Van Zante purchased cosmetics and a date planner. Jacobsen returned to the store to pick up her friend, and the two reentered the store and each purchased more items. Van Zante was told by store personnel that as long as

she retained her receipt, she could take the items she purchased previously into the store. While the two shopped, another shopper, a loss prevention employee at another company, heard the two shoppers ripping open packages. He reported this action to the store's two security guards, who were off-duty police officers hired by the store. After Jacobson and Van Zante left the store, they were stopped by the two security officers, who asked and received permission to search the car Jacobson was driving. While searching the car, the officers took all the items that could have been purchased from Wal-Mart. The officers matched the items in the car with the receipts. The two suspects were also frisked in case they had hidden merchandise on their persons. The two women were then escorted back to the store, where they were placed in separate rooms and questioned. Van Zante admitted to opening items within the store but contended that these were items she had purchased earlier. During the questioning, a store clerk checked the items the officers found against the receipts and found no discrepancies. After two-and-a-half hours, the two shoppers were released.

Jacobson and Van Zante sued Wal-Mart, claiming they were falsely imprisoned and detained. Wal-Mart argued that its personnel were justified in detaining the women because of the suspicion of shoplifting. The defendants filed a motion for a summary judgment (a hearing based on the facts of a case without a trial). The Iowa District Court for Johnson County granted the summary judgment, ruling that Wal-Mart was entitled as a matter of law to detain suspected shoplifters. The plaintiffs appealed the decision, and the Iowa Court of Appeals overturned and remanded the case, ruling that while Wal-Mart was legally justified in its initial detention of the suspects, the court was unclear in its interpretation as to whether the officers had detained the women for a reasonable period of time and ruled that the final question must be decided by a jury.

Company officials must consider all the ramifications of their shoplifting enforcement efforts and carefully study them to ensure that they are cost effective and achieving the results they expect. As a recent example, a consultant was hired by a large retailer in a major metropolitan city to analyze its loss management program. He conducted a multistep analysis to consider all aspects of the program, including interviews of store executives, loss prevention officers, and local prosecutors, as well as analyses of store and court records. His interview of store executives disclosed that they believed the store's policies were effective in preventing shoplifting but were dissatisfied with the court's practice of allowing most of the arrestees to plead their cases down to misdemeanors and receive little or no official punishment. They also believed their policies were effective in preventing future offending and recidivist offenders because none of the persons arrested had previous apprehensions at the store. He analyzed approximately four-hundred case files prepared by the store detectives and scrutinized each to determine how each case was handled by the prosecutor's office. He then met with the local district attorney to discuss the results of his analysis and to improve the relationship between the store and the prosecutors.[45]

The review of the store's and prosecutor's records revealed that the store's records contained numerous legal and reporting inaccuracies, the majority of the cases were misdemeanors and only nine cases exceeded the felony threshold, and only seventy-two of the cases were actually prosecuted. The typical defendant received a $45 or $90 fine. The records also disclosed that each of the offenders was listed as a firsttime offender by the store's officers and that in every case the merchandise was recovered. The consultant determined that, contrary to the perception of company executives, prosecutors were not being given strong felony cases that they then pled down to misdemeanors; in fact, most cases simply did not meet the felony prosecution threshold. In addition, many problems in the paperwork caused prosecutorial problems. For example, many of the arrestees were indeed recidivists who gave different names to the arresting officer (in one case, an arrestee had twenty-seven prior apprehensions).

Thirty-two of the arrests involved employee theft and averaged losses of about $2,000. These cases received harsher punishments than those levied against the conventional shoplifters. Thus, the consultant determined that serious cases did receive more attention by the prosecutor.

The consultant worked with the company executives and the security department to improve record keeping, introduce computer programs, and

improve relationships and procedures between the security department and the prosecutor.

In some cases, retail stores avoid bringing shoplifters into the formal criminal justice system, which is often initiated by calling the police and having the shoplifters arrested. Instead, many use **civil recovery** or **civil demand programs**, which began in the 1980s. Using these programs, the store initiates civil court proceedings against thieves to recover monetary damages. In civil recovery remedies, the store is a direct party to the action (as opposed to its role in the criminal justice process, where the public prosecutor is not required to consult the store in any plea-bargaining negotiations) and thus can gain some control of the process to recover lost revenues and deter future theft. Forty-nine states have some version of civil recovery law. Most of these proceedings are pursued at the same time criminal hearings are being held and involve three stages after an incident in which someone is taken into the store's custody: the inquiry, the letter or demand stage, and the lawsuit. Civil recovery generally entitles the merchant to recover the value of damaged or unrecovered merchandise; the time and money spent in pursuing the property, including employee, security, and investigative costs; and any related expenses.[46]

Only a small fraction of all shoplifters are turned over to law enforcement officers, and an even smaller proportion are formally booked.[47] Two researchers reported in 2002 that retailers participating in a national survey indicated they only prosecute 24 percent of all shoplifters they apprehend.[48]

Some businesses will contract private investigative firms to help them in their loss prevention programs. Two of these programs are shopping services and internal intelligence programs. Shopping services use "integrity shoppers" or "mystery shoppers" to make discrete observations in stores to deter inventory shrinkage; detect dishonest employees; provide evidence for prosecuting employees caught stealing; and observe the performance and operations of store personnel, including attitude, courtesy, approach, appearance, knowledge, and salesmanship. These services are provided by "shoppers"—actually, undercover agents from these investigative firms who pose as customers. The undercover agents then prepare reports that are forwarded to the businesses for appropriate action. Internal intelligence programs involve private investigators from the investigative firm being planted in the corporation's business

civil recovery/civil demand programs Programs in which retail stores instigate civil court proceedings against shoplifters to recover monetary damages.

operations to make observations and report back to the investigating service, which then reports to the business. These programs are designed to combat theft of funds and merchandise, use of alcohol or drugs on the job, gambling, sabotage, or other illegal activity. Chapter 11 covers information regarding these programs.

Researchers are critical of current loss management efforts. In a 2004 article in *Justice Quarterly*, the journal of the Academy of Criminal Justice Sciences, the authors report that modern retailers are forced to work within tight budgets and therefore usually choose not to deploy a large antishoplifting security force. They report that in-store security staff are expensive and challenging to train, seldom stay on the job for long periods of time, and frequently bring personal biases to the job. Retailers increasingly try to leverage technology, such as security tags and CCTV, to cut their loss prevention costs while still monitoring shoplifters. These systems, however, according to the authors, require staffing to be successful (that is, a person to staff the video monitor or respond to the alarm), and the effectiveness and efficiency of the shoplifting prevention and apprehension effort falls largely on the shoulders of store-level sales associates and their managers. Often, associates are unmotivated, minimum-wage employees, and their managers are too busy with a myriad of other responsibilites to provide antishoplifting interdiction training.[49]

Peer Reporting

A 2004 study indicated that peer reporting is one of the most effective techniques to detect and prevent employee theft. **Peer reporting** involves employees monitoring and reporting suspicious, illegal, or unethical behavior by other employees within the company. The research disclosed that many large retail businesses encourage their employees to report dishonesty they witness in the workplace, and most businesses in the survey reported they used toll-free hotlines to facilitate it. One-half of the companies that promote peer reporting indicated that they use financial incentives to encourage such reporting.[50]

Several major security services companies assist company peer reporting programs. For example, Pinkerton Investigative Services offers its "AlertLine Ethics and Compliance Hotline," and Wackenhut offers its "Safe2Say Hotline Service." Businesses contract these companies to provide this service for their employees. The services then report any information received back to the company.[51] See Chapter 11 for more information on this area.

Loss Prevention Technology

Loss prevention technology has been used for decades in retail security. This technology can be separated into current technology, including electronic video surveillance systems, CCTV, electronic article surveillance (EAS), and benefit denial systems (ink tags); and emerging technology, including source tagging, computerized inventory control, radio frequency identification (RFID), and DNA tagging. Nontechnological loss prevention equipment includes observation mirrors (that allow store clerks to see throughout the store), locking antitheft cables and wires, security bars, wire lanyards, and other locking devices. These locking devices work to keep merchandise from being stolen, but retail experts say they are a poor way to display merchandise because they make it difficult for people to examine items and try on garments. They require a clerk to unlock the item so someone can examine it, and because many shoppers are in a hurry, this might cause shoppers to move on to a store where items are more accessible. The Security Industry Association, a Virginia-based trade group, reports that electronic security is a $30 billion-a-year industry.[52]

Most of the time, the antitheft technologies deployed in retail are visible because stores want them to be a deterrent to people looking to shoplift, in addition to actually catching shoplifters.[53]

A professional association for people interested in loss prevention technology is the Association for Retail Technology Standards (ARTS), dedicated to reducing the costs of technology through standards.[54]

Current Technology

As mentioned, the most common current technologies are electronic video surveillance systems, CCTV, EAS, and benefit denial systems (ink tags). Electronic surveillance video systems, including CCTV, are discussed extensively in Chapter 3.

peer reporting Programs in which employees monitor and report suspicious, illegal, or unethical behavior by other employees.

Closed-Circuit Television (CCTV) Among the earliest technological tools used to combat shoplifting, **closed-circuit television (CCTV)** is a private video system within a building, complex, or store used to visually monitor a location for security or industrial purposes. Tapes can be recorded and viewed on-site or viewed remotely using telephone lines. Most CCTV systems consist of CCD (charged couple device) cameras, monitors, time-lapse video recorders, control units, and some other types of equipment.

The modern CCTV camera is available in monochrome (black and white) and color and can be set in fixed positions or placed on pan/tilt/zoom devices that allow the camera to move up, down, left, and right. Using a zoom lens allows a closer view of the desired image. Monitors are similar to standard television sets; however, they lack the electronics to pick up regular television. They are also available in monochrome and color. The video recorders used in the security industry generally have the ability to record up to a week of video on one tape. A coaxial cable is the standard means of transmitting video in a CCTV system (similar to the type of cable used by cable companies to send television into the home). There are control units used to control each video signal going to the VCR and the monitor.[55]

CCTV cameras can be mounted in smoke detectors, sprinkler heads, thermostats, or clocks. Many stores mount the cameras in ceiling domes (they are bubble-like and tinted, so no one can see where the camera is pointed). From this vantage point, a pan/tilt/zoom camera can swing about and follow someone around the store. However, if security is not monitoring and operating the camera, it can be set up to pan automatically but will not follow a particular person around the store.[56]

A store or business can have security officers view the monitors in real time from a control room or the security office, and the viewer can contact a security person on the floor by radio if there is evidence of shoplifting. The floor person may then further observe subjects and apprehend them, if necessary.

Over the years, retailers have updated from analog video surveillance systems (tape cassettes) to digital video. Experts say these systems can detect movement and switch to high resolution, allowing a user to zoom in to produce a clear, crisp image. A system by Florida-based ADT, which owns the antitheft company Sensormatic, allows a regional headquarters to access digital video surveillance networks at stores and narrow down hours of footage to ten or fifteen seconds. A spokesperson for Home Depot said the chain's digital closed-circuit system has made "a world of difference over analog in terms of clarity and speed."[57]

The latest in CCTV technology is remote transmission that allows a CCTV system to be monitored from a professional central monitoring station anywhere in the world. Some argue that this gives companies the ability to "look in" on inventories, points-of-sale displays, and employees.[58]

It is important to realize that CCTV cannot be used in bathrooms and fitting rooms. Companies that have done this have been sued by customers for violation of privacy. (See Exhibit 6.7 for more information on fitting room security.) Also, there are certain areas in the workplace where taping employees is questionable, and companies should seek legal advice prior to doing this.[59]

A 2004 survey of CCTV operations commissioned by a major food retailer that focused on seventeen stores outfitted with the same CCTV system revealed that stores with more CCTV operators reaped more benefits in terms of security, higher theft discovery rates, higher stock recovery rates, and reduced loss.[60]

Rutgers' Crime Prevention Service for Business reports that CCTV can prevent and deter crime because of one or more of the following reasons:

- Deterrence—Potential burglars and thieves may see the camera and decide the store is too much of a risk and therefore not a good target.

- Prosecution—Thieves and shoplifters may be observed on camera, and this can help catch them and prosecute them.

- Fear reduction—If everyone knows that there is a camera, they may feel safe in or around the store, thus preventing potential criminals from attacking.

- Monitoring and intervention—If there is a security guard monitoring the area through CCTV systems, he or she may act on any suspicious behavior and thus prevent a crime from occurring. Security guards may also deploy employees to a particular location or near a person detected on the monitors.[61]

closed-circuit television (CCTV) A private video system in a building, store, or geographic area for security monitoring.

EXHIBIT 6.7	Fitting Room Security

Fitting rooms are havens for shoplifters because merchants are not allowed by law to watch people when they are in them. There are two main things merchants can do to reduce loss as the result of fitting rooms: restrict access to the rooms and monitor the clothes going in and out.

Restrict Access
- Small stores: Keep the fitting room doors locked when no one is using them.
- Big stores: Put an attendant outside the fitting rooms. This person can assist with customers' selections and monitor the clothes people take in and out of the fitting rooms.

Monitor Clothes
- Count how many items people are taking into the fitting room, and make sure they come out with the same number.
- If you have a busy store, give customers going into the fitting room a prenumbered tag corresponding to the number of garments they have. This keeps the attendants from having to remember details about each person.
- Limit the number of garments that can be taken into the fitting room at one time.
- Be sure to check the fitting rooms frequently for garments left behind. Pay attention to price tags and hangers left around—these may be evidence that shoplifting has occurred.

SOURCE: Crime Prevention Service, Rutgers University, School of Criminal Justice, "Fitting Rooms." Retrieved January 19, 2005, from http://www.crimeprevention.rutgers.edu.

There are three main types of CCTV cameras:

- Dome cameras—These cameras are usually placed inside a dark dome and cannot be seen from the outside, so the thief will not know whether the camera is pointing his or her way or not. These cameras may turn or may be fixed.

- Wall cameras—These are big, visible cameras. They may be simple or have many options, such as being waterproof, bulletproof, or equipped with infrared lighting or zoom capability.

- Hidden cameras—These small, covert cameras are hidden inside other objects and are not easily detectable.[62]

There are also different types of monitors and VCRs. If a store wants to prosecute people, it needs a video recorder so it can record evidence.

If it wants to be able to use CCTV to watch people and intervene before or after something happens, it needs monitors. In addition, businesses need to consider what they want to achieve using CCTV, for example, monitoring the interior or exterior of the building; during business hours or all of the time; the whole area or just certain spots; general movement or detailed images of faces or license plates; and so forth.

Electronic Article Surveillance (EAS) Electronic article surveillance is a modern, effective method of reducing shoplifting and other retail crime. *Electronic article surveillance (EAS)* is the term used to describe antishoplifting protection systems for both apparel and packaged products. EAS is a technology used to identify articles as they pass through a gated area in a store. An alarm goes off to alert staff if anyone is removing items from the store without paying for them. It involves an electronically detectable element (tag) pinned onto a garment or affixed by means of an adhesive to an item. Transmitters and receivers are placed at magnetic portals, gates, pedestals, or sensors at store exits to detect the presence of the tags as shoppers leave the stores. At the point of purchase, these tags are either removed or rendered inoperative by store staff so that the purchaser may exit the premises without setting off an alarm. The tags can be disposable paper tags and labels or reusable hard plastic tags (commonly called "alligators") that can be attached to apparel.

Some stores even use dummy or inactive EAS tags and systems to deter shoplifting by giving the appearance that the products are protected. It has been reported that one company sold over 20 million of these dummy tags at one-third cent each in one year alone.[63]

Gordman's Department Stores, headquartered in Omaha, Nebraska, with forty-five locations in ten states, decided to adopt EAS in the mid 1990s when the technology was exploding and there was intense competition. It selected two companies for a nine-month trial and has stayed with one of them since then because it believed the company provided good follow-up and service. Inventory shrinkage immediately started to decline as internal theft was

electronic article surveillance (EAS) Antishoplifting protection systems for both apparel and packaged products; an alarm sounds if a product is taken from a store without being purchased.

sharply curtailed. Its director of asset protection estimates that shrinkage would be 0.5 to 0.75 points higher without EAS.

Benefit Denial Systems (Ink Tags) Although **benefit denial systems** (most commonly, **ink tags**) are attached to apparel in the same way as EAS tags, these, if tampered with, will break and stain the garment (usually with colored indelible ink). A warning to this effect is printed directly on the tag. A garment with an ink stain can be neither worn nor sold, so shoplifters cannot gain any benefit from stealing it. The ink tags now available are compact (little more than 1 inch in diameter), reusable, and easily removed by store clerks with a special tool at the point of sale.

Numerous studies have reported reductions in crime or shrinkage after implementation of EAS and ink tag systems in particular stores.[64]

Emerging Technology

As mentioned earlier, the most common emerging technologies in loss prevention are source tagging, computerized inventory control, radio frequency identification (RFID), and DNA tagging.

Source Tagging A newly developing practice is source tagging, where manufacturers attach tracking tags to products before they reach stores. This saves retailers from installing them. **Source tagging** is the imbedding of disposable security labels at the point of manufacture or packaging. On the retail side, source tagging can reduce or eliminate labor costs for in-store tagging,

reduce training requirements, and discourage employee theft.[65]

Computerized Inventory Control Stores are now turning to a new tool to fight shrinkage: computer models that help them predict which items are prone to theft. This type of software, marketed by firms like SPSS and Security Source, uses historical data on sales, returns, voided transactions, and inventory to identify suspicious patterns.

This type of software helped Chase-Pitkin, a home-improvement chain in upstate New York, realize that outdoor merchandise like gas grills and Christmas trees were disappearing, an anomaly it ordinarily would not have caught until doing a post-holiday inventory. Now motion detectors and extra staffers keep those items from being stolen. The software also helped specialty retailer Brookstone determine that a particular piece of home audio equipment was likely to vanish. Now front-of-the-store displays contain just empty boxes; full boxes feature a security tape over the handle that can be removed only by cashiers, making it difficult for thieves to carry bulky items out of the store.[66]

The nation's largest convenience store chain, 7-Eleven, is using a wireless NEC corporation handheld computer that reduces excess inventory and theft and dramatically boosts sales by eliminating one of the retailing industry's worst problems—running out of hot-selling items. This technology tells the operator exactly how many items are in stock and where they are.[67]

Radio Frequency Identification (RFID) Distinctive information can be written to **radio frequency identification** (RFID) devices or tags and retrieved by RFID scanners. Some have described these tags as a kind of combination bar code, computer chip, and mobile phone. Unlike traditional bar codes that this technology aims to replace, RFID gives every tagged object a unique identification (a bar code describes only a class of objects, such as cans of a particular brand of soda). Companies hope to use RFID to track trillions of objects that circulate the world every year from factories, onto transportation vehicles, into warehouses, onto store shelves, through checkout counters, and into homes and offices. Accurate tracking should eventually save business hundreds of billions of dollars a year because it improves distribution, reduces theft, cuts labor costs, and shrinks inventories.[68]

Radio tagging (RFID) has been spreading through the economy for decades in applications

---

benefit denial system Antishoplifting system in which a tag is attached to an article that will damage or stain the article if it is taken from the store without purchasing it.

ink tag Antishoplifting device in which an ink-filled tag that will break and stain the article if it is removed from the store without being purchased is attached to an article.

source tagging Antishoplifting tags that are attached to products by manufacturers before they reach stores.

radio frequency identification (RFID) Antishoplifting tags or devices that contain the specific information about the target; if they are taken from the store without being purchased an alarm will sound; also called radio tagging.

like automated toll collection (E-Z passes), tracking tags for animals, and wireless cards controlling access to buildings. Rapidly increasing in retail, it is revolutionizing the way stores track inventory, experts say. Its use is expected to continue exploding in the next few years. Checkpoint Systems Inc., which earned $13.9 million on $370 million in revenue in the first half of 2004, has been working since the late 1990s on trying to fit more and more data on smaller and smaller RFID chips and cutting the price manufacturers pay for the tags.[69] As of 2004, it was estimated that about 20 million Americans were using RFID every day. According to a spokesperson for the National Retail Federation, RFID technology is still in its earliest stages for retail use.[70]

The tags contain an antenna and microchip encased in plastic that receive query signals from scanning devices called readers. Using the energy captured from those signals, they broadcast a snippet of code identifying the goods to which they are attached. The tag stores data on a chip—anything from a serial number to information about where and when the object was manufactured. The tags derive their power from the RFID reader, which generates a low-powered radio signal. When the RFID tag passes near a reader, that signal activates the tag's chip and causes it to transmit information through the small antenna back to the reader. RFID tags have many advantages over bar codes, which are line-of-sight devices that must be seen directly by a laser to be read. Bar codes also need to be clean and placed on the surface of the packaging. Radio tags, however, can be embedded inside the packaging or even incorporated into the item itself. Also, large numbers of tags can be read at once rather than individually by a machine.[71]

In January 2005, Wal-Mart directed its top one-hundred vendors and thirty-seven smaller manufacturers to begin shipping it products in cases equipped with RFID tags. When these cases are unloaded from trucks and pass through doors at Wal-Mart's loading docks, special electronic readers will register the information. For now, they will tag only cases and not individual items. The tags currently cost from 19 cents to 40 cents each, but prices are expected to go down as their use increase. This wireless system will enable the company to know how many items of a certain product are in the store and where they are—on the floor or in the stock room. Target stores, Albertson's grocery chain, electronics retailer Best Buy, and even the Pentagon have also begun to require suppliers to start using RFID tags. The Food and Drug Administration has indicated that it would encourage an RFID tracking system to better follow pharmaceuticals from manufacturers to retail outlets. These efforts are said to be crucial to creating a pervasive RFID system throughout corporate America by the end of the decade.[72] One writer predicted that RFID tags may reach 5 cents each within the next five years and that the technology may allow tags to be reused without buying new ones.[73] RFID, as we will see later in this chapter, is now being used for improved homeland security at our nation's border crossings.

RFID technology has also been incorporated into credit or debit cards. As of 2006, 20 million Americans had these cards that allow the cardholder to make a purchase by waving the card in front of a contactless card reader instead of sliding the card through a magnetic reader or handing it to a sales clerk. Cell-phone makers are also building RFID chips into their phones.[74]

Some privacy groups are concerned that when RFID devices are placed by manufacturers or retailers in their products, it will enable them to trace consumers by matching a surreptitious scan of a product after it has been purchased to purchase records, thus obtaining consumer contact information.[75] In 2004, on the Internet technology site, CNET, columnist Declan McCullagh expressed his fears about RFID technology:

> It becomes unnervingly easy to [imagine] a scenario where everything you buy that's more expensive than a Snickers will sport RFID tags. That raises the disquieting possibility of being tracked through our personal possessions.[76]

In 2006, the National Science Foundation awarded a $1.1 million grant to a consortium of academics and industry representatives to study the privacy and security implications of RFID technology.[77]

DNA Tagging **DNA tagging** is an example of the possible future of technological advances in loss prevention technology. In the 1990s, Jun-Jei Sheu, a Taiwanese scientist, began research using microscopic fragments of DNA embedded into everyday objects, as a security and anticounterfeiting tool. The mathematical possibilities offered

DNA tagging Antishoplifting or anticounterfeiting technology that uses miscroscopic fragments of DNA.

EXHIBIT 6.8 Some of the Approaches Retailers Use Most Often to Stop Theft

	Percent of Retailers Using
Burglar alarms	94.4
Visible closed-circuit TV	73.3
Check-approval systems	61.9
Armored-car pickups	56.8
Cables, locks, chains	51.7
Hidden TV/digital video recording	50.8
Observation mirrors	49.2
Data software	49.2
Secured display fixtures	48.3
Drop safes	46.6
Mystery shoppers	45.8
Electronic security tags	42.4
Antishoplifting signs	41.5
Uniformed guards	37.3
Ink/dye denial tags	36.4
Silent alarms	32.2

SOURCE: Monty Phan, "Fight vs. Shoplifters Goes High-Tech," *Newsday*, January 16, 2005, p. A24; and Richard C. Hollinger and J. L. Davis, *2002 National Retail Security Survey*, Gainesville: University of Florida, 2002.

by DNA's long and apparently random sequences of four-amino-acid "base pairs" would make such a marked item entirely unique, if embedded into product labels. As of 2004, a company called Applied DNA Sciences was working on putting this technology into smart cards and other items.[78]

As another example of emerging technology, the company Data Video Systems installs and maintains machines that recognize faces, eyes, or fingerprints and cameras that can be hidden in nearly anything, including smoke alarms or exit signs. In 2004, it received its first million-dollar contract—a job for the U.S. Department of Energy hanging high-power transmission and fiber-optics lines between substations and hydroelectric generation plants at dams. Its business includes installing and maintaining everything from commonplace

National Retail Federation World's largest retail trade association.

card readers to biometric identification of eyes and facial scans.[79]

Exhibit 6.8 provides a summary of the approaches retailers use most often to stop theft.

Academic and Professional Research in Loss Prevention

Several professional associations and academic services provide retail security professionals with research on loss prevention.

The **National Retail Federation (NRF)** is the world's largest retail trade association. Its membership includes the leading department, specialty, independent, discount, mass merchandise, catalog, and Internet stores in the United States and fifty other nations around the world. NRF represents an industry with more than 1.4 million U.S. retail establishments, more than 23 million employees (about one in every five American workers), and recent yearly sales of $3.8 trillion. As an industry umbrella group, it represents more than one hundred state, national, and international retail associations.[80]

More than 250 loss prevention executives serve on NRF's several loss prevention committees. The following are some of these committees:

- NRF Loss Prevention Advisory Council: This council includes representation from the largest specialty stores, including The Gap, The Limited, to name just two. The council directs the development of services and programs in the loss prevention area.

- NRF Food Industry Prevention Advisory Council: This council meets twice a year as needed via conference call and focuses on loss prevention and security issues unique to food retailers.

- National Investigators Network: This group meets annually as an entire group and three to four times yearly within its six regions. The group also hosts conference calls when needed. It allows retail investigators to network with each other on critical issues and cases at local, regional, and national levels. Membership is comprised of corporate executives with primary responsibility for the investigation of major cases for retailers. The regional meetings have been held in Dallas; Columbus; New York City; Washington, DC; Anaheim; and Miami.

- Organized Retail Crime/Theft Task Force: This ad hoc group meets as needed to discuss legislative remedies to the growing organized retail crime problem.
- Women in Loss Prevention Caucus: This group meets annually and by conference call quarterly to discuss the issues that some members face in advancing their careers in retail loss prevention. The network is open to female security executives in loss prevention divisions of retail companies.
- NRF–FBI Intelligence Network: This group meets as needed to build stronger relationships between retail loss prevention executives and the FBI.[81]

The NRF sponsors an annual Loss Prevention Conference and Exhibition, where loss prevention executives for all segments of retail security, including asset protection; fraud; information systems; inventory shortage; loss prevention; operations; safety; security management; shortage control; special investigations; and regional, district and store management gather to learn, network, and share best practices. Over 1,200 retailers from the loss prevention, asset protection, and risk management arenas generally attend this three-day event. Highlights include keynote presentations, networking opportunities, and exhibits from more than 150 leading service providers presenting their products and technologies. The 2005 annual conference and exhibition was held in San Diego and included educational forums and sessions on many topics, including organized retail crimes, fraud, leadership skills, online auction fraud, vulnerability assessments, investigative trends and techniques, cargo theft, and internal and external thefts.[82]

The **Loss Prevention Research Council (LPRC)** is a professional organization whose mission is to evaluate and develop innovative crime and loss control techniques that can improve the performance of its members (see Exhibit 6.9). It provides objective, science-based information, analyses, training, and solutions to its members. Its members and research partners are made up of leading retail and supplier corporations. It uses field experimentation, offender interviews, focus groups, surveys, and quantitative analyses to conduct its studies and makes specific recommendations or action models to its members.[83] Some of its members include such

---

EXHIBIT 6.9 **Research Activities of the Loss Prevention Research Council (LPRC)**

- Analysis of data from shoplifters and apprehensions
- Extensive shoplifter and fence video interviews
- Content analysis of offender interview data
- Tracking the flow of high-risk merchandise through supply chains
- Sales-floor consumer and employee behavior analysis
- Surveying merchandise protective practices
- Employee and consumer focus groups
- News media retail crime reporting content analysis
- Developing methods for selecting top-performing LP specialists
- Studying employee hotline programs
- Evaluating trends in industry LP reports
- Protective display and packaging analysis
- Offender interview thematic analyses
- Delphi research on future patterns
- Conducting a North American study of organized retail crime
- Crime event mapping and patterns
- Predicting loss levels based on internal and external factors
- Extensive RCTs and pilot field experiments

SOURCE: Loss Prevention Research Council, "Homepage." Retrieved January 23, 2005, from http://www.lpresearch.org.

---

large companies as Gillette, Barnes and Noble, Bloomingdale's, Polo, Ralph Lauren, Walgreen's, Disney, Home Depot, and CVS/pharmacy.[84]

LPRC has initiated the **StoreLab program** to codevelop and test innovative store/facility layouts, work processes, and technologies to maximize productivity, sales, and profit while minimizing losses and crime. This program is open to retailers, product suppliers, and solution developers. StoreLab research and development (R&D) can take place throughout the entire supply chain from manufacturer, through distribution, and on to the point of sale in stores. All R&D

Loss Prevention Research Council (LPRC) A professional organization that evaluates and develops innovative crime and loss control techniques to improve the retail performance of its members.

StoreLab program Academic and industrial program to codevelop and test store and facility layouts, processes, and technologies to maximize productivity, sales, and profit while minimizing losses and crime.

You Are There!

Academic Studies Aid Loss Prevention Personnel

Numerous academic studies have provided loss prevention personnel with information to help them design security programs to reduce shoplifting. Some of these are as follows:

■ Professional shoplifters—those who steal to derive all or part of their income—are the minority of shoplifters, but they tend to steal more items and take items of greater value than do amateurs. The best strategies against these professional thieves are CCTV systems, EAS devices, displaying high-priced items inside a locked showcase or securing them to shelves with merchandise cables, and deploying many sales representatives and undercover agents on the sales floor.

■ The best strategies to deter amateur shoplifters are the use of very visible CCTV cameras or very obvious EAS devices; overt security, including signs warning of the penalties for shoplifting; and notification of parents of teenagers who shoplift.

■ A shoplifting prevention experiment conducted in Great Britain indicated that store redesign and electronic tagging were effective short-term solutions to the problem of shoplifting.

■ A study of shoplifters in Stockholm, Sweden, revealed that males stole more electronic items and females stole more clothing, perfume, and cosmetics. However, the value of the goods stolen was about the same. The most common times for being caught were Monday through Thursday, as well as late afternoons. Most of the shoplifters were unemployed.

■ A study on the effectiveness of increasing the frequency with which articles at great risk of theft are inventoried revealed a 100-percent reduction in shrinkage of the target articles and an 85-percent reduction in nontarget item shrinkage. In this study, employees knew about the increased inventory counts but shoppers did not, thus leading the researcher to assume that the reduction in shrinkage was due to deterrence of employee theft.

SOURCES: Read Hayes, "Tailoring Security to Fit the Criminal," *Security Management*, July 1999, pp. 110–116; D. P. Farrington, "Measuring, Explaining and Preventing Shoplifting: A Review of British Research," *Security Journal*, *12*(1), 1999, pp. 9–27; E. Sarasalo, B. Bergman, and J. Toth, "Repetitive Shoplifting in Stockholm, Sweden," *Criminal Behavior and Mental Health*, *8*(4), 1998, pp. 256–265; Barry Masuda, "Displacement vs. Diffusion of Benefits and the Reduction of Inventory Losses in a Retail Environment," *Security Journal, 3,* 1992, pp. 131–136.

---

initiatives take into account three critical integrated factors: enhancing consumer sales conversion rates, facilitating long-term employee productivity and execution, and maximizing location and product protection. As of 2005, LPRC was working on seven StoreLab projects with major retailers and product suppliers.[85] There are three stages in StoreLab projects:

■ Laboratory testing: Processes and technologies are tested in a lab setting that provides for confidential testing as well as superior control.

■ Local field testing: The practical usability, durability, efficacy, and tactical use of current or developing efforts are tested in particular retail locations.

■ Field experimental testing: Here, more rigorous testing of the actual efficacy and financial benefits of the refined innovations is conducted. Sampling, measurement, control, and statistical analyses are designed carefully for these evaluations.

The LPRC research efforts use a customized combination of field experiments, quantitative modeling, video review, Delphi surveys, failure mode effects analysis, surveys, and expert and offender interviews to shape and test hypotheses and best methods. Participating retailers may provide stores under the StoreLab program (digital video connections) to allow for continuous improvement testing. Promising ideas can then be more rigorously tested. LPRC also maintains a panel of recent or active offenders for initial testing.

In addition to studies for all members, LPRC project specialists work with retailers and manufacturers to develop proprietary near-term and strategic research projects, including identifying goals, uses of the findings, research methods, data access, analysis, and timelines. An LPRC project manager is assigned to conduct the project and to maintain ongoing communications. Staff are also available for data entry or to help manage large data sets.

The LPRC partners with the **Loss Prevention Research Team (LPRT)** at the University of Florida, a team of professors, research scientists, practitioners, and graduate students whose mission is to conduct retail research by providing actionable information to real-world businesses. The LPRT works with retailers and others to form and test hypotheses regarding the impact of innovative store spatial solutions, workplace procedures, selection and training methods, and current and emerging technologies on employee, customer, and store behavior and performance. It includes faculty and research coordinators and a research staff. It is located in the University of Florida's College of Design, Construction, and Planning in order to provide direct access to store and facility design and layout expertise. It also works with faculty from the University of Florida's David Miller Center for Retailing Education and Research, the Florida Survey Research Center, and the Center for Criminology and Law. Its research focus is on asset protection/loss prevention.[86]

The LPRT emphasizes a total store concept and works with the LPRC on the StoreLab R&D program to explore the effects of inventive store design, in-store process, and evolving technologies on consumer buying, employee productivity, asset loss, and margin and sales enhancement. LPRT also works with retailers on student internships and solicits sponsored research projects for graduate students.

The **Security Research Project** at the University of Florida studies various elements of workplace-related crime and deviance with a special emphasis on the retail industry. Its principal research activity is the National Retail Security Survey, a nationwide annual study now in its eleventh year, comprising the most recent empirical data on retail loss prevention, asset protection, and security activities.[87]

Rutgers University's School of Criminal Justice has created the **Crime Prevention Service for Business of Rutgers University, School of Criminal Justice** that works with small businesses in Newark and the rest of northern New Jersey to find workable, inexpensive crime prevention measures geared toward individual businesses. Its goal is to reduce crime using simple and low-cost or no-cost methods. It offers programs and information in the following areas: preventing specific crimes against businesses, including break-ins and burglary, fraud, employee theft, robbery, shoplifting, vandalism and property damage, violence, and cargo theft; crime prevention cases studies; and special

topics, including crime prevention theory, CPTED, CCTV, and lighting.[88]

A leading trade magazine for loss prevention professionals is *LossPrevention* magazine, which offers articles of interest to retail loss prevention management professionals. Its topics range from investigations to technology to financial skills.[89]

Homeland Security and Retail Security and Loss Prevention

Homeland security has become a central concern for our government, private security professionals, law enforcement personnel, and our citizens. Although retail security and loss prevention do not directly affect homeland security, some of their features have positively enhanced it.

One example is the increased security at retail establishments in our transit facilities, including airports, rail and bus stations, shopping malls, and business areas. The extra overt security sets a proactive environment to deter terrorists. In addition, the increased training that retail security personnel receive includes homeland security training and helps them to be more vigilant and better observers.

Furthermore, technology created for retail security and loss management, including electronic surveillance systems and RFID systems, has been put into place in homeland security systems. Electronic video surveillance systems, which have been used in retail establishments for years, are now also being used extensively in transit systems and buildings and on the street to help ensure homeland security.

In 2005, it was reported that RFID technology could help airports improve airline baggage

---

Loss Prevention Research Team (LPRT) A team of professors, research scientists, practitioners, and graduate students who conduct retail research and provide actionable information to businesses.

Security Research Project University of Florida program that studies various elements of workplace-related crime and deviance with a special emphasis on the retail industry.

Crime Prevention Service for Business of Rutgers University, School of Criminal Justice University program that works with small businesses to find workable, inexpensive crime prevention measures.

handling; however, major airlines would each have to invest tens of millions of dollars to adopt RFID luggage tracking. In tests, RFID systems have accurately identified bags when they passed a scanner 95 percent of the time. These results suggest this system could eliminate more than two-thirds of lost baggage problems.[90]

Also in 2005, the U.S. Department of Homeland Security (DHS) reported that it was exploring the use of RFID technology in its US-VISIT program, which is part of a continuum of security measures that begins outside U.S. borders and continues through a visitor's arrival in and departure from the United States. US-VISIT is designed to enhance security for our citizens and visitors while facilitating legitimate travel and trade across our borders, simplifying the entry and exit process, and enhanc-

ing the integrity of the immigration system while respecting the privacy of our visitors.[91] Chapter 13 of this textbook will fully discuss US-VISIT.

In August 2005, DHS reported that it had begun testing RFID technology at five U.S. land border ports, including Nogales East and Nogales West in Arizona, Alexandria Bay in New York, and Pacific Highway and Peace Arch in Washington State. It will use RFID to more efficiently record the entries and exits of visitors. RFID tags are now embedded in Customs and Border Forms 1-94A, the standard arrival and departure record issued at ports of entry.[92]

Due to arrests made by local and state law enforcement, the FBI has linked stolen baby formula to terrorism, saying proceeds from black market sales have been used to support such terrorist organizations as Hamas and Hezbollah.[93]

Summary

- Shrinkage is one of the most serious problems facing retail stores, with estimated annual losses of between $12 and $40 billion. Retailers use the term *shrinkage* to describe the difference between inventory on hand at the beginning of the year and inventory on hand—minus sales—at year end.

- The annual National Retail Security Survey for the latest reporting year reports an average U.S. shrinkage rate of 1.65 percent. Most shrinkage is attributed to retailers' own employees through employee theft and return fraud (47 percent). The remainder of shrinkage is attributed to customer theft, 32 percent; supplier or vendor theft, 6 percent; and administrative or paperwork error, 15 percent. The cost of security was reported as 0.51 percent of turnover (sales).

- Loss prevention (LP) refers to the use of methods to reduce shrinkage in retail stores.

- The concept of crime prevention through environmental design (CPTED) assumes that crime is related to daily routines and activities in the area, such as traffic and pedestrian flow, and that criminals want to be avoid being observed when they are committing their crimes and thus avoid arrest.

- Crime reduction through product design (CRPD) involves the integration of protective features into products in order to reduce their

potential to become targets of criminal activity (such as theft, fraud, and damage), as well as preventing their use as instruments of crime.

- Many stores use store detectives or loss prevention specialists to deal with external and internal theft. The goal of the store detective or loss prevention specialist is to protect business assets and apprehend people stealing property or money from the store.

- Private security officers generally are not restricted by the provisions of the U.S. Constitution in their duties, as the public police are. Private security officers do not have to give suspects *Miranda* warnings before questioning, and the exclusionary rule does not apply to the evidence they seize.

- Many security experts recommend that security personnel in retail stores avoid physical contact that could cause physical injury to suspected shoplifters, including striking, tackling, or sitting on suspects.

- Civil recovery or civil demand programs entitle merchants to recover the value of damaged or unrecovered merchandise; the time and money spent in pursuing the property, including employee, security, and investigative costs; and any related expenses.

- Peer reporting involves employees monitoring and reporting suspicious, illegal, or unethical behavior by other employees.

- Closed-circuit television (CCTV) is a type of electronic video surveillance system that uses a private video system within a building, complex, or store to visually monitor a location for security or industrial purposes.

- *Electronic article surveillance (EAS)* is the term used to describe antishoplifting protection systems for both apparel and packaged products.

- Benefit denial systems are attached to apparel in the same way as EAS tags, but with these, if tampered with, fluids—usually colored indelible ink vials—break and stain the garment.

- Radio frequency identification (RFID) is an emerging EAS technology that is packed in tiny tags or devices and can be read without being in line of sight.

- The Security Research Project at the University of Florida studies various elements of workplace-related crime and deviance with a special emphasis on the retail industry. Its principal research activity is the National Retail Security Survey, a nationwide annual study comprising the most recent empirical data on retail loss prevention, asset protection, and security activities.

Learning Check

1. Define *shrinkage* in the context of inventory.
2. Discuss the extent of the retail shrinkage problem in the United States.
3. Identify three major ways retail businesses can deal with the shrinkage problem and discuss them.
4. What is CPTED? Give two examples of it and discuss them.
5. Define *peer reporting* and discuss it.
6. Identify three major types of technology used to detect shoplifting and discuss them.
7. What is RFID? Discuss it.
8. What is a store detective or loss prevention specialist? Describe her or his duties.
9. Identify three sources of academic and professional research in loss prevention and discuss them.

Application Exercise

Your professor, an adjunct member of the faculty who is the manager of loss prevention for a major department store branch in your area, has invited students to attend the annual convention of the National Retail Federation with her and present a student panel on retail security. She has assigned the topic "A Model Policy for Shrinkage Control at a Department Store" for anyone willing to attend. Prepare an outline detailing the major topics you will cover in your ten-minute presentation and an abstract summarizing your presentation.

Web Exercise

You have been hired as the assistant loss prevention director at a new national chain of department stores. Your boss, the Director of Loss Prevention, asks you to research some major professional and academic groups that study loss prevention. He asks you to prepare a report identifying at least four such groups, indicating their websites and a synopsis of the coverage of loss prevention each covers on its website.

Key Terms

Personal Security

©Reuters/Dario Pignatelli/Landov

GOALS

- To provide you with an overview of personal crime in the United States and attitudes toward personal safety.
- To acquaint you with private security efforts for personal security.
- To introduce you to the industry and methods of assessing travel risk.
- To familiarize you with methods of self-protection.
- To alert you to certain special issues regarding personal security.

Introduction

Imagine that you are sitting on a plane headed to Las Vegas for a fun vacation. Just as you get buckled up to await takeoff, you hear screaming and yelling. People start rushing off the plane, and you see a little girl being trampled in the aisle during the rush. You try to retrieve some of your things from your seat, but someone yells to you, "Get off the plane! Your life is more important than your stuff!" As you exit the plane, you find out that a man armed with a handgun had run past security and onto your plane, entered the cockpit, and taken the pilot and copilot hostage, demanding to be taken to Antarctica, where he had to destroy an alien military base.

This is a true story. A mentally disturbed man armed with a 10-millimeter automatic pistol ran past the metal detectors at Gate 33 at JFK International Airport, dashed onto an elevated jetway, and boarded a National Airlines Boeing 757 set to fly to Las Vegas. He then took the pilot and copilot hostage. Police responded in approximately three minutes, and heavily armed officers from a special unit boarded the plane and helped the last of the 143 passengers to escape—many by sliding down an inflatable chute in the rear of the plane, which had been opened earlier by a quick-thinking flight attendant. For approximately three hours, police engaged in hostage negotiations with the disturbed gunman, who first demanded that the pilot take him to Miami. He later changed his mind and demanded to be taken to Buenos Aires, and last, to Antarctica. Finally, the man surrendered to the police.[1] Threats to our personal safety are terrifying.

We had generally taken the issue of personal safety for granted as we went about our daily routines. Then we were shocked out of our complacency as we read about the Columbine High School shootings, the tragic events of 9/11, and then the Virginia Tech

University massacre. These incidents and numerous other acts of terrorism and crime have demonstrated some of the risks we face at work, commuting, at school, in the community, and at home. The tragic events contained in this text have shaken most of us out of our lethargy and complacency. Today, most people, sadly and correctly, are very concerned about their personal protection.

Crime and fear of crime are significant issues in U.S. society, and the police perform admirably in their efforts to prevent crime, apprehend offenders, and ensure a sense of public security. However, the police are often overwhelmed with their many duties and are hampered by jurisdictional and legal restrictions. The private security industry attempts to fill the gap by offering protective services to its clients.

This chapter will first discuss the extent of personal crime we experience as a society and our attitudes toward personal safety. Then it will discuss the many efforts of the private security industry to ensure its clients' personal safety, including antiterrorism efforts, and the concepts and operations of executive protection and bodyguards or personal protection specialists. It will also cover the important function of assessing travel risk to ensure the personal safety of business and leisure travelers. Additionally, the chapter will discuss several methods of self-protection, including personal alarms and devices, cell phones, protective vests and garments, personal self-defense training, and protective vehicles. Also, attention will be paid to certain special issues regarding personal security, such as kidnapping, workplace violence, domestic violence and the workplace, stalking, school shootings and other acts of school violence, and violence against taxi drivers. The chapter will conclude with a discussion of homeland security and personal security.

Personal Security in the United States

Crimes against persons have always been a serious societal problem and engendered serious concern by citizens. Since the tragic events of 9/11, the issues of personal security have risen higher in our consciousness.

For the latest reporting year, the FBI's *Uniform Crime Reports* indicated that over 1.39 million serious personal crimes were reported to the police in the United States, including about 16,700 murders or nonnegligent manslaughters; 93,900 forcible rapes; 417,000 robberies; and 863,000 aggravated or felonious assaults. Also, it indicated that the public reported about 10.2 million serious nonpersonal or property crimes to the police in the same

JOBS IN SECURITY

Personal Protection

Several professional associations offer training and job networking in personal protective services.

- Richard W. Kobetz & Associates provides protective services for corporations and private families. It runs the Executive Protection Institute, which offers various courses in personal protection.
- The International Association of Personal Protective Specialists is a professional association for personal protection professionals and offers various courses in personal protection.
- Gavin de Becker & Associates provides protective services for a diverse group of clients, including media figures, government agencies, media companies, giant corporations, police departments, religious leaders, champion athletes, politicians, battered women's shelters, and children's schools. It offers training services, employment opportunities, and many other security services and employs the following three positions:

Security Staff Agent
Duties: Provides protective coverage to public figures at residential and commercial locations, public appearances, movie locations, live-audience television studios, and political events and during foreign travel.

Entry-Level Investigator
Duties: Supports case managers and senior investigators by conducting investigations related to threats of violence and inappropriate pursuit, pre-employment screening, vulnerability reduction, and other high-stakes investigations.

Threat-Assessment Case Manager
Duties: Supports senior staff in the Threat Assessment and Management Division by conducting assessments of cases of inappropriate pursuit, including public-figure pursuit, domestic violence, interpersonal violence, and workplace violence.

- Major private security contract service corporations offer personal protection services, careers, and training.

Sources: Executive Protection Institute, "Protective Agents Available." Retrieved October 14, 2005, from http://www.personalprotection.com; International Association of Professional Protection Specialists, "About Us." Retrieved October 14, 2005, from http://www.iapps.org; and Gavin De Becker & Associates, "About Us." Retrieved October 16, 2005, from http://www.gavindebecker.com; and Gavin De Becker & Associates, "Employment Opportunities: Protective Security Division." Retrieved October 17, 2005, from http://gavindebecker.com/application.

---

year, including about 2.2 million burglaries, 6.78 million larcenies/thefts, and 1.24 motor vehicle thefts.[2] The *UCR's Crime Clock* indicates that, on average, there is one murder every 31.5 minutes, one forcible rape every 5.6 minutes, one robbery every 1.3 minutes, and one aggravated assault every 36.5 seconds.[3] Also, for the latest reporting year, the FBI reported that the police made about 603,500 arrests for violent felony crimes, including murder and nonnegligent manslaughter, forcible rape, robbery, and aggravated or felonious assault; 1.3 million crimes for misdemeanor assaults; and 1.6 million arrests for felony property crimes. The police made about 11 million arrests for other crimes not listed.[4]

For the latest reporting year, the *Gallup Poll Monthly* reported that about 38 percent of respondents reported they feared walking alone at night in their own neighborhood; 67 percent believed there was more crime in the United States now than a year ago; and 47 percent believed there was more crime in their own area now than last year.[5]

Clearly, violence, crime, and fear are endemic to American life.

Private Security Efforts for Personal Security

As indicated in Chapter 1 of this text, the inability of local, state, and federal police agencies to protect individuals and corporations from terrorist attacks, kidnappings, and other serious crimes has led to the development of a growth industry in private security. Many businesses and organizations protect their employees by maintaining a safe environment and offering them special protection and escorts when necessary. These security escorts may include escorting employees carrying money or valuables to banks and escorting them after work into parking lots and garages or to mass transit facilities. Corporations also provide protection against workplace violence situations and in possible domestic violence situations at the workplace. This section will discuss antiterrorism efforts, executive protection, and bodyguards or personal protection specialists.

Antiterrorism Efforts

Terrorism has a long tradition in world history and has been used frequently by radical and criminal groups to influence public opinion and to attempt to force authorities to do their will. Terrorists have criminal, political, and other nefarious motives. Chapter 13 of this text will discuss the history of terrorist acts and describe in detail public and private efforts against it.

Most major U.S. firms have been targeted by terrorists in some format. Political extremists and terrorists use the violence and suspense of terrorist acts, such as bombing, kidnapping, and hostage situations, to exert pressure on those in authority to comply with their demands and cause the authorities and public to recognize their power. Also, they use their activities to obtain money for their cause, to alter business or government policies, or to change public opinion. Attacks against executives are common in Latin America, the Middle East, and Europe and have spread to the United States. Successful terrorist techniques employed in one country spread to other countries. Governments and corporations have developed extensive plans to deal with terrorism. Members of corporate executive protection departments and others concerned with personal protection pay constant attention to terrorist possibilities and develop plans to deal with these eventualities in this country and abroad.[6]

Private industry has made major efforts to protect their businesses, premises, assets, and personnel against terrorism. Numerous other chapters of this text also discuss the many antiterrorism efforts of the private security industry, including Chapter 5, Chapter 9, Chapter 12, and Chapter 13.

Executive Protection

The security departments of many major corporations have personnel assigned to particular executive protection duties, including protecting high-level executives and other key personnel at work, at home, and while traveling. Their duties also include personal safety at major corporate events, such as annual meetings. In response to increased targeting by terrorist groups, many multinational businesses have developed executive protection programs as part of their overall corporate security plan. Such programs may include personal protective services, kidnap and ransom insurance, risk and threat assessment studies, creation of crisis response committees, and formulation of crisis management plans and policies. In selecting an executive protection specialist, corporations give special attention to extraordinary qualifications. In addition to being unobtrusive in the executive's environment, the specialist has training in intelligence collection and evaluation, advance preparations, and travel planning. The average protection specialist also may have experience as a working bodyguard or personal protection professional. While some employers feel that individuals retired from government protection programs have the necessary expertise, their experience may be too specialized or limited.[7]

During 2004, there were 4,000 kidnappings in China, 2,000 in Mexico, and 400 in Argentina. Also, a recent travel warning from the U.S. State Department reported that from September 2004 to April 2005, more than 30 Americans were murdered or kidnapped in the Mexican state of Tamaulipas, and even more were robbed while riding in taxis and buses.[8]

Most multinational corporations have detailed executive protection plans, crisis management teams, and threat assessment strategies.[9] Companies without security departments or those with smaller security departments often use major contract security companies to provide their corporate and executive security services. These contract companies generally emphasize strategic prevention and conduct threat assessments before establishing prevention plans. Executives without corporate security or executive protection specialists may hire private investigators to advise them on matters of personal security or as personal bodyguards or personal protection specialists to accompany them on their travels and in the course of their business and social activities.

The primary goals of **executive protection (EP)** are to protect the **principal** (the executive or other company employee to be protected) from kidnapping and intentional or accidental injury and to minimize the possibility of the principal encountering the many hazards that exist in today's world, both at home and abroad. Security personnel trained in executive protection are known as **executive protection specialists (EPS)**. Often, an unstated goal of the EPS is also to protect the principal and the corporation from public embarrassment. Generally, executive protection programs include target hardening, bodyguard operations, and training sessions teaching executives how to avoid being identified as targets and what they can do if they do become a target. The key to success in executive protection is preplanning for a possible attack or incident. One of the major problems encountered by the EPS is the reluctance of some executives to be protected. Often the EPS is also charged with the protection of the executive's family and residence and the installation of home security systems.

Employee protection specialists educate work and home staff regarding terrorism techniques and threats, as well as other security risks and the necessity of prompt reporting of any suspicious occurrences. One of the important precautions executives can take is the avoidance of predictable patterns. The kidnapping and murder cases of Exxon executive Stanley Reso and famous Italian politician Aldo Moro illustrate the vulnerability of executives, politicians, and other VIPs and the need for their security directors to try to protect them.

Some of the methods used by an EPS are the threat assessment, the advance survey, and the actual protection. The **threat assessment** is the collection of facts to develop plans for the protective assignment. EP specialists use peer networking, trade publications, and news media analysis, as well as the Internet, to accomplish this function. The EPS researches and anticipates any threats or emergencies and has contingency plans in effect. Many hate groups or radical groups have sites on the Internet where they advertise their intentions. The assessment includes the political climate and regional conditions around the company's facilities and areas frequented by company personnel.[10]

The **advance survey** (advance work) involves a dry run of the area to which the principal will be escorted. EP specialists travel to the area before the principal's arrival and map out probable routes and alternatives and assess potential problems that will ensure a safe and smooth passage. The EPS checks out hospitals and law enforcement agencies. The Internet provides many sites to assist with maps and finding locations. The Internet also makes contact with peers easier than the telephone. The actual protection involves escorting and protecting the principal and ensuring site security and similar functions. The protection may involve the assignment of additional protective personnel and equipment.

Technology has become increasingly important in executive protection. Thermal imagers and infrared technology can help EP specialists detect intruders in low light or other obstructing conditions, such as fog, mist, smoke, and the presence of foliage and other obstructions. Portable, wireless alarm and electronic video surveillance technology is being used to temporarily protect hotel rooms, vehicles, and other locations. Panic buttons, motion detectors, door switches, and motion switches can also be integrated into executive protection to provide space and perimeter protection. Since most of this technology is wireless, it provides comprehensive coverage even if electrical power goes out due to weather conditions, emergencies, or attacks. Other advanced sophisticated technology, such as digital cameras for documentary purposes and graphic information and global positioning systems are used in all phases of executive protection.

executive protection (EP) Program to protect corporate executives or other employees from kidnapping and intentional or accidental injury.

principal Person being protected in an executive protection program or other personal protection program.

executive protection specialist (EPS) Persons employed to protect corporate executives or other employees from kidnapping and intentional or accidental injury; could be a proprietary or contract employee.

threat assessment Common tool in private security to determine who would want to attack a particular company or business and why and how they would do so. Also known as a threat evaluation, facility characterization, or target value assessment.

advance survey Performing practice exercises or dry runs of an area where a principal will be escorted.

You Are There!

To Keep Yourself Safe, Change Your Routine

THE SIDNEY RESO AND ALDO MORO MURDER CASES

One of the most important lessons a VIP, a high-level corporate executive, a celebrity, or any other kidnap-at-risk person can learn is to alter his or her routine in order to avoid becoming a creature of habit. Both Sidney Reso and Aldo Moro unintentionally and inadvertently made their kidnappers' job easier by being creatures of habit.

Sidney Reso was a high-level executive for the Exxon Corporation who lived in suburban New Jersey. In 1992, a husband-and-wife kidnapping team watched Sidney Reso and carefully noted all his actions for almost thirty days before they attacked. Sitting in a van parked down the street from Reso's house, the couple documented his daily routine, learning his habits and identifying his vulnerabilities. Then, one morning, the couple abducted Reso in his driveway as he retrieved his newspaper, something they had seen him do every morning at the same time. He was shot in the struggle and died several days later in captivity—a victim of a kidnap-for-ransom scheme that had gone tragically awry.

Aldo Moro, the famous Italian politician, was also a creature of habit. He would leave his home every morning to attend mass at a nearby church. Then, shortly after 9 A.M., he would leave for his office using the same route each morning. The rest of his daily activities were also matters of routine. Although five armed men guarded him that morning, terrorists using military precision attacked him. They blocked Moro's vehicle and a following police car on a narrow street, and four gunmen hiding behind a hedge opened fire. Eighty rounds hit the police car. Three policemen, Moro's driver, and a bodyguard were killed. Moro was dragged by his feet from the car. Almost two months later, Moro was found dead in a car in Rome.

In the aftermath of these incidents, much attention was given to the development of a counter-surveillance program as part of executive protection measures. In the Reso case, a countersurveillance team may have noticed the couple's van parked outside the executive's house and traced the license-plate number back to the person who had leased the vehicle: a disgruntled former Exxon employee. In the Moro case, a countersurveillance program would have checked the travel route prior to Moro's travel to observe any suspicious conditions or circumstances.

SOURCES: Joseph Autera and Michael Scanlan, "Seeing through Enemy Eyes: Countersurveillance That Seeks Out the Attacker's Perspective Is the Key to Good Corporate Executive Protection." Retrieved July 11, 2000, from http://www.securitymanagement.com/library/000663.html; and Philip P. Purpura, *Security and Loss Prevention: An Introduction*, 3rd ed. (Boston: Butterworth-Heinemann, 1988), p. 432.

The area of executive and personnel protection has provided the opportunity for a large business in areas such as bullet-resistant garments, defensive-driving schools, bomb control, explosive detectors, personal alert safety systems, personal protection devices, protection training, risk-assessment services, and vehicle and travel security.

Many businesses and institutions have **crisis management teams (CMTs)** in place to immediately deal with threats or actual emergencies regarding their executives. The CMT consists of senior executives, security executives, attorneys, financial and medical specialists, terrorism experts, and police liaisons. The team also generally has a communications specialist onboard to deal with communications and negotiations between the terrorists or kidnappers and the company. The CMT engages in preplanning and prepares plans for all scenarios. In the event of an emergency, the team goes into action.

EP specialists also consider emergency medical procedures for their principals, have documents that include the principal's medical history and other important information, identify all medical facilities in the city where the executive will be traveling, make contact with key security and medical personnel there, and conduct a security and medical survey of those facilities that might have to be used during a health-related emergency.[11] Some carry an automatic external defibrillator (AED) that can deliver electrical shocks to restore normal heart-beating patterns to victims of sudden cardiac arrest.

Insurance companies offer executive protection policies that not only provide money for ransom

crisis management team (CMT) Team of corporate executives and specialists prepared to immediately deal with threats or actual emergencies.

but also pay for such things as the fees of kidnap negotiators and follow-up psychiatric treatment for victims and their families. America's biggest multinational corporations have carried coverage against kidnapping for years.[12] In 2006, it was estimated that at least 60 percent of America's largest five hundred companies carry kidnapping, ransom, and extortion insurance (known in the industry as K&R).[13]

Security experts recommend that corporations institute a **countersurveillance** program as part of its executive protection measures. A countersurveillance operation is an ongoing process by which security personnel put themselves in the frame of mind of a potential attacker. They observe and document the executive's daily routine and all usual activity near the executive's home, on travel routes, and close to the office and other regular stops. This operation is based on the theory that criminals first conduct surveillance themselves before launching an attack against a corporate executive. If executive protection personnel know where the likely attack points are and assign security personnel to watch those areas, they can often uncover possible future crimes before they occur. Countersurveillance measures are very important when an executive has received a specific threat, works in a high-profile controversial industry, maintains a high profile, or is about to travel into a high-risk area.[14]

In 2005, security experts warned that business travelers should always make their lodging and transportation plans well in advance, arriving in modest vehicles and making sure to take a taxi that has been arranged through the hotel or host country. They also warn that arriving in a corporate jet and wearing expensive clothing and jewelry are invitations to kidnapping and that eating at the hotel restaurant is safer than going to night spots where Americans tend to congregate. They also advise that travelers carry two wallets, with one wallet full of enough cash, but no credit cards or identification, to placate a robber.[15]

The risk to foreigners in Iraq is serious. Since 2004, more than two-hundred foreign civilians have been kidnapped and more than thirty have been killed in Iraq.[16] In 2006, the American embassy in Baghdad estimated that between five and thirty persons, mostly Iraqis, have been abducted every day in Iraq since the fall of Saddam Hussein.[17]

As of 2005, executive protection has become important for companies that do business in Colombia because of the kidnapping problem there. There are many types of kidnappings in Colombia, including ransom kidnappings, kidnappings to apply political pressure, kidnappings to obtain information from victims, group kidnappings, and "express" kidnappings to force victims to withdraw money from an ATM.[18] **Express kidnappings** are ones that involve a target of opportunity with little preparation and planning on the part of the criminal. One can avoid being an express kidnapping risk by avoiding behavior that indicates that one is wealthy.[19]

Many companies today are hiring **employee assistance professionals (EAPs)** who are familiar with kidnapping crimes, negotiating tactics, and the methods kidnappers use in particular nations. These professionals will try to prevent employees from being kidnapped or help them survive a kidnapping by providing helpful information to the employees and their families. As an example, an EAP may advise employees not to lie to kidnappers because if the lie is discovered, kidnappers are likely to become enraged and also not to resist the kidnappers because resistance is likely to cause the kidnappers to become more violent.[20]

As an example of private security efforts in executive protection, Pinkerton Consulting and Investigation Services offers "executive protection/close protection services" to its clients. It develops low-profile awareness and protection programs for corporate personnel and offers armed or unarmed specially trained agents that can provide physical security for an individual, group, or location, 24 hours a day. It can provide security drivers trained in evasive driving techniques and arrange ground transport in advance for pick-up and drop-off to client destinations. It also can provide state-of-the-art armored vehicles with specially trained drivers to provide secure transport and chartered private jet services to provide a safe and secure mode of air travel.[21] It also provides its customers with a comprehensive guide for executive travel security, which includes advice to senior executives in the following areas: preparation before travel; travel planning; advice on luggage, dress, money

countersurveillance The practice of avoiding surveillance or making surveillance difficult.

express kidnapping Kidnapping involving little preparation and planning on the part of the criminal.

employee assistance professionals (EAPs) Professionals who try to prevent employees from being kidnapped or help them survive kidnapping by providing helpful information to the employees and their families.

EXHIBIT 7.1   **ASIS International Professional Development Course in Executive Protection**

OVERVIEW

Corporate executives, celebrities, government leaders, and other prominent individuals are frequently in situations that demand exclusive personal protection. Executive protection specialists must be equipped with a thorough understanding of both the assessment of risk and the areas of vulnerability to ensure the highest level of security for their client. The ASIS International Executive Protection Program covers procedures required for professional protection.

PROGRAM HIGHLIGHTS

This two-day instructional course is intended for audiences with a range of professional experiences and interests, from entry-level to seasoned practitioners. Faculty members include preeminent specialists who share proven and insightful techniques for handling any executive protection situation.

WHO SHOULD ATTEND

Professionals responsible for personal protective services and those interested in becoming employed in this security specialty.

PROGRAM BENEFITS

■ Learn the fundamentals of the underlying philosophy of executive protection and the mindset that drives

both the protection specialist and the professional protection program.

■ Understand what it takes to succeed in this highly specialized security profession and how to prepare for an entry-level position.

■ Develop an understanding of the benchmarks of a thorough advance survey.

■ Discover what is meant by the "choreography of protection" and understand its critical significance.

■ Review residential, workplace, and transportation security elements and current, real-world issues.

■ Gain a thorough understanding of the elements of threat assessment and risk analysis.

■ Learn the latest techniques and advance procedures for protective operations.

■ Investigate educational and career opportunities in the private sector and what it takes to succeed in this security specialty.

SOURCE: ASIS International, "Professional Development Course Details: Executive Protection." Retrieved October 17, 2005, from http://www.asisonline.org/store/program_detail.xml?id=6350.

---

and valuables, personal effects, information that should be left at the office or home, security at the airport and on the aircraft, ground transportation, the hotel, traveling inside the areas of destination, motor vehicle security, secure driving techniques, checking cars for car bombs, action to be taken on being threatened, emergency procedures, and confidential contact lists. It also provides information for companies regarding establishing a company travel policy, insurance coverage, and incident response procedures.[22]

Female executives, like their male counterparts, frequently travel or live abroad for business. When they do so, they are often more at risk than their male peers. A study by the Travel Data Center found that women represent a disproportionate number of victims of violent crime, especially personal assault. Avon Products Inc. introduced a global "Women and Security" program designed to raise awareness of the dangers of overseas travel and to train female associates to reduce their vulnerability to those dangers. Avon started this project by doing a risk assessment. After the risk

assessment, a program was designed with the following components: brochures, self-defense training, and one-on-one evaluations. The one-on-one evaluations involve a security staff member observing the daily routine of an executive and then comparing it to the national risk assessment to determine which practices need to be changed. Feedback has indicated that women traveling for Avon now have an overall feeling of increased security and reduced anxiety. The women also state that their productivity is higher.[23]

As of 2005, several hotels, including ones in the United Kingdom, Dubai, South Africa, and Mexico City, have designated floors or wings specifically for women who are guests. The hotels have enhanced security with peepholes and chains on the doors and, in some cases, surveillance cameras in the hallways. Generally only waitresses provide room service for these rooms, and often the members of the engineering and housekeeping staff are women.[24]

Exhibit 7.1 gives details on ASIS International's professional development course on executive protection.

Bodyguards or Personal Protection Specialists

Many persons in our society hire **personal protection specialists (PPS)** or **bodyguards** to escort them throughout their regular daily activities or to escort them on special events, such as business trips or vacations. These people use bodyguards for the actual physical protection they provide and also the sense of security they give. People who use bodyguards include business executives, celebrities, VIPs, politicians, wealthy persons, or just about anyone else who has the financial resources to pay for such services. Sometimes these bodyguards are called **chauffeurs** because they drive the principals throughout the day to their various activities, in addition to providing myriad other duties for them.

Sometimes bodyguards are hired on a regular basis or often just for a specific purpose, such as serving as a bodyguard or courier to accompany someone or money or other valuables to a destination or to pick up and deliver someone to a destination. Many former law enforcement officers or military personnel work as bodyguards, as individual contractors, or as members of a contract bodyguard service. Bodyguard agencies and independent operators acting as bodyguards advertise in the yellow pages, through business and professional publications, and through networking. Many have their own websites. Bodyguards become familiar with the laws and customs in different places where they might be living or traveling to with their principals and are able to fit into the principal's work and play schedule. The bodyguard is also responsible for the maintenance and inspection of vehicles used by the subject to ensure that they are serviceable and have not been tampered with.

There are many schools teaching bodyguard skills. Many of the instructors are former law enforcement or military personnel. They teach skills such as the use of weapons, defensive and evasive driving techniques, and hand-to-hand combat. They also give specialized instruction in alarm systems and video surveillance operations. The schools also teach students skills in protocol and dress.

One example of such a training program is the Executive Protection Institute, operated by Richard W. Kobetz & Associates Ltd., a Virginia-based corporation established in 1978 to provide protective services. Its services include providing personal protection specialists for corporations and private families on a continuing or emergency basis through a worldwide network. It operates full- and parttime teams involved in the protection of recognized world leaders, corporate executives, dignitaries, and celebrities. Its concerns include travel, as well as family and residential protection. It arranges for stockholder meetings and conference and convention protective services and can coordinate executive travel domestically and internationally. It offers a position-placement network for full- and parttime positions, newsletters, information sources, resources, regional networking socials, and annual conferences. It also offers international certification as a PPS.[25]

Working as a bodyguard can be a difficult job that involves long hours spent away from family and friends and the constant pressure of always being on duty. Former practitioners write that there are six basic principles involved in a bodyguard operation:

- Guarding the principal
- Knowing the principal's world
- Preceding the principal into an area to check it
- Taking command
- Planning for and guarding against the worst
- Making life difficult for the opposition[26]

Celebrity security is particularly difficult because it involves the combination of famous people, high-profile events, and intense media coverage. Security managers and personnel in this specialty deal with the complex web of businesses that make up the entertainment industry and the types of threats each faces. Celebrity protection specialists generally have strong public relations skills that allow them to enforce security procedures diplomatically when dealing with highly successful entertainers. In addition, they handle large crowds and differentiate between well-meaning fans and tourists and persons who may have a more sinister agenda. Procedures for providing security at special events focus on

personal protection specialist (PPS)/bodyguard Person employed to provide personal protection for a person.

chauffeur A person employed to drive a car or limousine that transports passengers.

You Are There!

Moshe Alon—Security Chief for Jennifer Anniston and Brad Pitt's Wedding

Moshe Alon, the long-time bodyguard of actress Elizabeth Taylor, was the security chief for the Brad Pitt–Jennifer Anniston wedding in August 2000. Pitt and Anniston spent over $100,000 for more than seventy armed guards, issued special pins for entry passes, and made wedding staffers wear balloon-adorned armbands, while helicopters patrolled the sky to keep the paparazzi from their wedding. Their efforts were successful at their $1 million affair.

Alon worked three-and-a-half years in security details in the Israeli military and five years in the Israeli secret service. He first came to the United

States in 1984 for the Los Angeles Summer Olympics as a guest and consultant of the LAPD. He founded his own seven-hundred-employee company, Pacific Security Consultants. Alon said the men and women he hires—typically former police officers and military personnel—have to do a lot more planning and thinking than beating up. He says, "We're not hired guns. We don't work with goons. You need more common sense and good, sharp thinking than anything else."

Source: David K. Li, "Israeli Goes from Secret Service to Celeb Service," *New York Post*, August 6, 2000, p. 7.

protecting the celebrity, securing the site, and access control to prevent incidents by overzealous fans and gate-crashers. There are numerous manuals for bodyguards written by former practitioners.[27]

The International Association of Professional Protection Specialists (IAPPS) is a professional organization for bodyguards and security personnel involved in the protection of executives, dignitaries, celebrities, and others, as well as those acting as couriers and other professional protectors. The IAPPS provides services and products to assist professional protection specialists in performing their duties (see Exhibit 7.2 for a list of IAPPS training classes).[28]

As an example of how large security firms provide assistance in personal protection, Kroll

Risk Consulting Company provides immediate response to threats against corporations, their employees, and private individuals by assessing the nature of the threat and designing appropriate intervention strategies to deter violent behavior and protect people at risk. These strategies may include investigations, coordination with law enforcement and mental health professionals, executive protection, and threat management training. Kroll offers the following specialized protective services and training for its clients:

- Individual protection—including threat assessment and investigations, long-term threat management, executive protection, site advances for proprietary protective details, event security, technical surveillance countermeasures, personnel background screening, and 24-hour crisis hotline

- Training for corporations and individuals—including travel and employee security seminars, tactical driving, abduction avoidance, combative skills, executive surveillance detection, and workplace violence prevention

- Training for security professionals—including protective detail training, firearms training, combative skills, less-lethal weapons instruction, surveillance detection, apprehension avoidance, tactical driving, and certification[29]

Kroll trains security professional at corporations' local sites or at their operational facility, the Crucible, an 88-acre facility in Northern Virginia,

EXHIBIT 7.2 Training Classes Offered by the International Association of Professional Protection Specialists

Introduction to Celebrity/VIP/Executive Protection (2 days)
Executive Protection One (4 days)
Executive Protection Master Class (7 days and nights)
Introduction to Fugitive Recovery/Bail Enforcement (Bounty Hunting) (2 days)

Source: International Association of Professional Protection Specialists, "Certified Training, Conferences and Seminars." Retrieved October 22, 2005, from http://www.iapps.org/seminars1.html.

which features multimedia classrooms, small arms ranges, defensive driving courses, and defensive tactics training areas. It trains protective details assigned to the U.S. Department of Defense, the U.S. State Department, and U.S. intelligence agencies, as well as local, state, and federal law enforcement organizations.

Security While Living or Traveling Abroad

Living or traveling abroad can be particularly dangerous, considering the threats of terrorism and corporate and personal kidnapping. This section will discuss danger abroad and assessing travel risk abroad.

Danger Abroad

Those who run businesses in the more dangerous parts of the world face a bewildering range of threats to the safety and health of their employees. As *The Economist* reports,

> Indeed, there are many more disagreeable places to choose from than there were a generation ago. In the days of the Cold War, there was usually a government to deal with, or at worst a rebel authority. These days, a growing number of countries, or large tracts of them are run (if at all) by shifting coalitions of warlords or local bullies. Such power vacuums create potentially lethal uncertainty.[30]

As an example, in July 2004, an aid group that specializes in sending medical staff to countries in conflict shut down all its programs in Afghanistan after five of its staff were killed in a deliberate attack on a clearly marked aid vehicle. The Taliban (one of the groups competing for power in Afghanistan) spokesman justified the murders by saying that aid organizations were helping the Americans.[31]

More than 4,000 industry representatives attended a recent annual convention of the National Business Travel Association. The two major topics of discussion at the convention were global security and the growing importance of internal online booking systems. These internal online systems can provide a network where the traveler, travel manager, security director, and other company executives can maintain close contact for security reasons. They also provide tools for risk assessment, keyed to specific destinations.[32] The importance of security today is evidenced by the following statement by one of the attending corporate travel managers: "On 9/11, it took us thirty-one minutes to find everyone, but now we can do it in maybe thirty seconds."[33]

A recent survey by the World Travel and Tourism Council found that most business travelers are willing to travel even when there is a threat, as long as they think the destination they are going to and the people they are working for are taking measures to mitigate that threat.[34]

Assessing and Addressing Travel Risk Abroad

The U.S. Department of State's Bureau of Consular Affairs pays particular attention to the safety of Americans traveling abroad for business and pleasure. The Department of State studies the risks of traveling to every country in the world and issues travel warning "don't-go" lists for countries that it considers too dangerous to travel to.[35] Its website provides access to its travel information and services section, which offers travel warnings and consular information sheets (see Exhibit 7.3). One can click on any country and obtain the following information regarding safe travel in that country:

- Description of the country
- Entry requirements for U.S. citizens
- Customs regulations
- Safety and security
- Crime information
- Criminal penalties

EXHIBIT 7.3	Services Available from the U.S. Department of State for U.S. Citizens Traveling Abroad

The U.S. Department of State's Office of American Citizens Services and Crisis Management (ACS) serves Americans traveling or residing abroad. Its primary goal is to meet the needs of American citizens while providing them with premier customer service. ACS administers the Consular Information Program, which informs the public of conditions abroad that may affect their safety and security. It supports the work of the overseas embassies and consulates in providing emergency services to Americans in cases of arrest, death, crime victimization, repatriation, medical evacuation, temporary financial assistance, and welfare-and-whereabouts cases.

It assists in nonemergency matters of birth, identity, passport, citizenship, registration, judicial assistance, and estates. ACS can facilitate the transfer of funds overseas to assist U.S. citizens in need, repatriate the remains of loved ones who have died overseas, assist with medical bills, assist victims of crime, and help U.S. citizens who are detained in foreign prisons. It administers a repatriation loan program to bring home destitute Americans, operates a 24-hour duty officer program and crisis response teams who work on task forces convened to deal with natural or man-made disasters.

The U.S. Department of State offers the following services on its website:

- **Travel Warnings**   Travel warnings are issued when the State Department decides, based on all relevant information, to recommend that Americans avoid travel to a certain country. Countries where avoidance of travel is recommended will have travel warnings, as well as consular information sheets and specific country background notes.

- **Public Announcements**   Public announcements are a means to disseminate information about terrorist threats and other relatively short-term and/or transnational conditions posing significant risks to the security of American travelers. They are made any time there is a perceived threat that has identified Americans as a particular target group. In the past, public announcements have been issued to deal with short-term coups, bomb threats to airlines, violence by terrorists, and anniversary dates of specific terrorist events.

- **Consular Information Sheets**   Consular information sheets are available for every country of the world. They include such information as the location of the U.S. embassy or consulate in the subject country, unusual immigration practices, health conditions, minor political disturbances, unusual currency and entry regulations, crime and security information, and drug penalties. If an unstable condition exists in a country that is not severe enough to warrant a travel warning, a description of the condition(s) may be included under an optional section entitled "Safety/Security." On limited occasions, the State Department also restates any U.S. embassy advice given to local employees. Consular information sheets generally do not include advice but present information in a factual manner, so the traveler can make his or her own decisions concerning travel to a particular country.

- **Background Notes**   Background notes are factual publications that contain information on all the countries of the world with which the United States has relations.

Source: U.S. Department of State, Bureau of Consular Affairs, *Travel.State. Gov.* Retrieved October 22, 2005, from http://travel.state.gov.

- Medical facilities
- Medical insurance
- Other health information
- Traffic safety and road conditions
- Aviation safety oversight
- Registration/embassy and consulate locations
- Consular access
- Rules on firearms and penalties
- Currency regulations
- Photography restrictions[36]

One may also obtain a list of the countries that the Department of State recommends that Americans avoid visiting. The list remains current and may change over time.[37] The Bureau of Consular Affairs also publishes numerous information tips for safe travel for U.S. citizens abroad. These travel warnings are available in brochures, in information sheets, and online.[38]

Private corporations are also involved in assessing travel risk. As an example, Real World Rescue is one of the leading companies that teach travel safety to government and humanitarian agency workers, business travelers, and increasingly, leisure travelers. Many leisure travelers enjoy roaming the Third World and sometimes run into trouble, such as kidnappings, that is not ordinarily covered in travel guides. According to the chief consultant for the company, tourists over the last few years have been primary targets for crime. Special-interest travel, such as adventure travel, ecotourism, and journeys to exotic locales, is one of the fastest-growing segments of the U.S. travel market, according to industry estimates. In addition to top business people, some leisure travelers now take their trips accompanied by travel escorts (bodyguards or personal protection specialists).[39] Another private company involved in travel risk assessment is iJet Travel Risk Management, a travel-risk–management services firm.[40] Travel businesses, travel publishers, and the media frequently produce books and other advisories regarding crime threats while traveling.[41]

As an example of assessing and addressing travel risk, Wackenhut Consulting and Investigation Services provides advice, support, and protection for key executives and other employees who travel or relocate to foreign countries and face potential threats to their safety and security. It can provide qualified protection specialists and professional drivers to limit exposure to dangerous or unpleasant situations around the clock. It also can provide 24-hour intelligence, threat analysis, and monitoring for virtually anywhere in the world.[42] Through World Watch, Airline Insider, and HotSpots travel security databases, Wackenhut can give clients the most current analysis of security conditions and preventive-step recommendations necessary to conduct business and travel with minimum risk. Hotspots is a weekly briefing that delivers a complete picture of incidents that could impact personal well-being, business, or travel. These databases provide international social, economic, and political news and weather, often not covered in the mainstream media and geared to business travelers, pilots, and security professionals.[43]

Exhibits 7.4 and 7.5 offer safety tips for people traveling, abroad or domestically.

---

personal alarms Alarms carried by persons to summon assistance in an emergency.

panic devices Buttons placed throughout a premise for the use of a person to summon assistance in an emergency.

mobile security devices (MSDs) Devices placed in vehicles for persons to summon assistance in an emergency.

telematics The science of two-way communications using global positioning satellite (GPS) technology.

Self-Protection Efforts

This section will cover some major areas of personal protection, including personal alarms and devices, cell phones, protective vests and garments, personal self-defense training, and protective vehicles.

Personal Alarms and Panic Devices

It has been reported that millions of **personal alarms**, also known as **panic devices** and **mobile security devices (MSDs)**, are in use. Many are found in motor vehicles (as part of a road service/directions feature), but many are carried by individuals and are connected to their pagers and other small electronic devices. These communications are also known as the science of **telematics**—two-way wireless communications using global positioning satellite (GPS) technology.[44]

When using a MSD or panic device, a person, with the press of a button, can transmit his or her precise location via GPS. It has been reported that many police departments fear being overwhelmed by inappropriate calls from these devices, such as calls for car towing and false alarms. Police also worry that these devices might cause users to take unnecessary risks, thinking that help may be just a push of a button away.

Other personal alarms or panic devices not connected to a MSD or telematics technology generally make an ear–splitting, high-pitched siren when activated that can be heard a very long distance away to attract attention to the user or to scare an attacker away. Some manufacturers advise that they are useful for civilian personnel working in correctional and mental therapy environments because the alarm sound will echo through hallways and doors, alerting security personnel to the sender's location. Most of these are battery operated and have a flashing light. Some also have a flashlight and can be attached to a key chain. These are advertised for as little as $10. Other personal alarms can be placed between a door and the doorframe or to a window or personal property. Many of them allow the user to program delay times of three, six, or twelve seconds. When the door or window is opened or the personal property is moved, the alarm will sound with a piercing noise.[45]

Many corporations and institutions install emergency phones or panic devices in their

EXHIBIT 7.4   Top Ten Tips for U.S. Citizens Traveling Abroad

The U.S. Department of State Bureau of Consular Affairs offers the following top-ten tips for U.S. citizens traveling abroad.

1. Make sure you have a signed, valid passport and visas, if required. Also, before you go, fill in the emergency information page of your passport!
2. Read the consular information sheets and public announcements or travel warnings, if applicable, for the countries you plan to visit.
3. Familiarize yourself with local laws and customs of the countries to which you are traveling. Remember, the U.S. Constitution does not follow you! While in a foreign country, you are subject to its laws.
4. Make two copies of your passport identification page. This will facilitate replacement if your passport is lost or stolen. Leave one copy at home with friends or relatives. Carry the other with you in a separate place from your passport.
5. Leave a copy of your itinerary with family or friends at home so that you can be contacted in case of an emergency.

6. Do not leave your luggage in public areas. Do not accept packages from strangers.
7. Prior to your departure, you should register with the nearest U.S. embassy or consulate through the State Department's travel registration website. Registration will make your presence and whereabouts known in case it is necessary to contact you in an emergency.
8. To avoid being a target of crime, try not to wear conspicuous clothing and expensive jewelry, and do not carry excessive amounts of money or unnecessary credit cards.
9. In order to avoid violating local laws, deal only with authorized agents when you exchange money or purchase art or antiques.
10. If you get into trouble, contact the nearest U.S. embassy.

Source: U.S. Department of State, Bureau of Consular Affairs, "Tips for Traveling Abroad." Retrieved October 22, 2005, from http://travel.state.gov/travel/abroad.html.

EXHIBIT 7.5   Hotel and Motel Traveler Safety Tips

- Don't answer the door in a hotel or motel room without verifying who it is. If a person claims to be an employee, call the front desk and ask if someone from the staff is supposed to have access to your room and for what purpose.
- When returning to your hotel or motel late in the evening, use the main entrance of the hotel. Be observant and look around before entering parking lots.
- Close the door securely whenever you are in your room and use the locking devices provided.
- Don't needlessly display guestroom keys in public or carelessly leave them on restaurant tables, at the swimming pool, or other places where they can be easily stolen.
- Do not draw attention to yourself by displaying large amounts of cash or expensive jewelry.
- Don't invite strangers to your room.
- Place all valuables in the hotel or motel's safe deposit box.
- Do not leave valuables in your vehicle.
- Check to see that any sliding glass doors or windows and any connecting room doors are locked.
- If you see any suspicious activity, report your observations to the management.

Source: American Hotel and Lodging Association.

buildings or on their grounds that allow employees and others direct access to security personnel by picking up the handset or activating the device.[46] Many security consultant and security firms offer advice and technical assistance with personal alarms and other panic devices.

Cell Phones

Cellular or cell phones have proven to be extremely helpful in personal protection. A recent federal report noted that the sense of security offered by **cellular (cell) phones** is a major factor in the accelerated growth of the industry. Nearly half the owners of cell phones say they have used the phones to report crime, car trouble, drunk drivers, or medical emergencies. Additionally, cell phones are now used extensively by law enforcement and security personnel as the primary means of communicating with their supervisors while out in the field. Many localities have given free preprogrammed cell phones to domestic violence victims, taxi and delivery drivers, citizen patrol members, and other at-risk citizens.[47] Also, many parents give their children cell phones for self-protection.

cellular (cell) phone A portable telephone that uses wireless cellular technology to send and receive phone signals.

The increasing use of photo and video technology on today's cell phones also increases their potential for security uses.

Many consider the use of cell phones by persons while driving to be dangerous. The city of Brooklyn, Ohio, became the first city in the United States to prohibit the use of cell phones while driving, in a municipal ordinance passed in 1999.[48] Today, several states have enacted laws prohibiting the use of cell phones while driving.

Although cell phones may be highly effective ways of communicating, it must be remembered that they might not work in some areas lacking mobile access or in urban subways or tunnels. Also, as happened during the July 2005 terrorist bombings on the London subway system, mobile networks may become unusable because millions of frantic people overloaded the system by using their mobile phones to call friends and family. The chief executive of the London Ambulance Service, Peter Bradley, warned that mobile phones are not a reliable communications tool during large emergencies. Some experts believe that mobile networks should be purposely shut down during terrorist attacks to prevent terrorists from using mobile phones to detonate bombs.[49]

Protective Vests and Other Garments

Since the 1970s, when the first bullet-resistant vest appeared on the law enforcement scene, there has been a constant evolution of fibers, materials, and vest design. Ballistic engineers can choose from polyethylene to microfilament fabrics to create hybrid vests that offer the best ballistic protection in a lightweight and comfortable design. Different materials offer different performance against different ballistic threats. It is important that protective vests be wearable, or they will not be worn.[50]

Body armor is also available to the general public. The director of research for Second Chance, a major developer of body armor, reported that light jackets made from ballistic fibers are currently available but are expensive. Today's bullet-resistant vests are designed to defeat bullets only, and multithreat vests are designed to protect from ice picks or commercial knives. Manufacturers are constantly working to create an all-purpose vest that protects wearers against multiple threats and prevents body trauma.[51]

Body armor is intended to absorb energy from the bullet and disperse the impact of the bullet. There are more than ninety manufacturers worldwide, using one or more man-made fibers. When building a vest, developers must accomplish three things: capture the bullet, disperse the energy from the bullet, and minimize trauma to the wearer.[52] Security consultants and security consulting firms offer professional advice regarding protective wear.

Personal Self-Defense Training

Many Americans are interested in personal self-defense tactics to ensure their own safety. There are numerous self-defense classes for all ages in all parts of the United States run by private operators or sometimes by school districts as adult education courses. These courses and classes range from formal martial arts instruction to basic self-defense or street survival courses.

Self-defense/assertiveness training for women attempts to prevent violence against them by strengthening their capacity to stand up for and defend themselves. A recent article reports that the National Survey of International Gender Relationships examined the role of self-defense/assertiveness training in the lives of over 3,100 college women and determined that women with such training reported fewer traits of negative expressiveness than did women without this training. It concluded that this training might help to counter women's traditional gender-role socialization, as women with training have more traits of positive instrumentality.[53]

Another recent study indicated that feminist self-defense training positively affects women's lives, including changes in the way they deal with potentially dangerous situations. Moreover, it indicated that the benefits of the training extend beyond dangerous situations to influence many different aspects of women's daily lives, including their interactions with a range of others and their self-confidence. These self-defense classes teach women the skills needed to prevent and respond to violence, including verbal, physical, and sexual violence.[54]

Many businesses offer personal security courses for their employees, and many colleges in urban areas offer new residential students orientation classes in urban survival.

Protective Vehicles

Armored and bullet-resistant vehicles have been a popular life-saving measure for people at constant risk of assassination and abduction. These high-tech **protective vehicles** are designed to resemble ordinary passenger vehicles but come equipped with protective features.

Protective vehicles are used extensively in executive protection and bodyguard operations because security experts report that 80 percent of attacks on dignitaries occur while they are in transit. Customizing cars to keep things and people out is a big business today. Purchasing an armored vehicle involves three assessments: the threat, the technology, and the manufacturers. A threat assessment will determine what kind of attackers might pursue the principal and what sorts of weapons they are likely to use. A technology assessment involves considering what type of armor is required (for example, transparent, fibrous, alloy, ceramic, compost) and how heavily the vehicle should be armored, as well as considering the need for other protective equipment, such as air scrubbers, non-explosive fuel tanks, remote starters with bomb scans, ram bumpers, deadbolt locks, fire-suppression systems, and special tires. Assessing vehicle manufacturers includes determining whether the company's vehicles and armoring systems have been independently tested to validate quality and integrity and determining if they can provide timely worldwide service.[55]

The largest passenger-vehicle armoring company in the United States is O'Gara-Hess & Eisenhardt, which produces commercial armored passenger vehicles, military armored vehicles, and armor system integration to customers around the world. It engineered its first bullet-resistant car for U.S. President Harry S. Truman during World War II and has since provided vehicles for more than sixty international heads of state, diplomats, and corporate executives around the world. It offers vehicles in the following categories of protection: handgun protection, assault-rifle protection, armor-piercing protection, and explosion-resistant protection. It takes vehicles such as Chevrolet Suburbans, Lexuses, Jeep Grand Cherokees, Toyota Land Cruisers, and GM Hummers and reskins them with armor plating, ballistic glass, run-flat tires, and beefed-up mechanicals—engines, suspension, brakes—to accommodate the extra weight. It also has one of the largest ballistic databases in the world.[56]

As of 2005, Brazil's armored-vehicle industry was booming due to a surge in violent crime and kidnappings that have targeted Brazil's upper classes over the past decade. Its vehicle-armoring industry has overtaken Mexico and Colombia as the biggest in the world and is now aiming at the lucrative market for armored vehicles in Iraq. The Brazilian companies refit cars and SUVs with steel plating, bulletproof windows, and other defenses and equip the vehicles with more proactive defensive measures, such as the capability to shoot tear gas or discharge oil slicks during high-speed chases.[57]

Unfortunately, many of these protective vehicles did not have the extreme level of protection needed for modern explosive devices until very recently. This was a serious problem because 50 percent of recent attacks on VIPs are related to explosive devices. In order to address this problem, the Royal Canadian Mounted Police's Armoured Systems Engineering Section, in conjunction with O'Gara-Hess & Eisenhardt, has joined forces to construct armored vehicles capable of defeating explosive threats. The backbone of the new technology is two layers of steel—one to absorb or repel the energy and the second to prevent any shrapnel from getting inside the vehicle and injuring the passengers if the first layer fails to defeat the blast. This integrated design system provides maximum protection against grenade munitions, pipe bombs, and large quantities of nondirectional dynamite explosions.[58]

Darren Flynn, North American sales manager for O'Gara-Hess & Eisenhardt, says, "You have to be able to assure a client exactly what our systems will defeat, what will happen in worst-case scenarios, and realistic standards." He also says the goal of the armored vehicle and driver is the same: "Get your passenger out of the danger zone. That's what all of the expense of the armored vehicle buys you—a couple of seconds to get away." He says the two major rules for armored vehicles are first that they must blend into the environment and second, to never let anyone know what level of protection the vehicles has.[59]

Private security firms and consultants offer their clients professional and technical advice regarding protective vehicles, and many will provide these vehicles and expert drivers for their clients when necessary.

protective vehicles High-tech vehicles designed to protect persons in personal protection situations.

You Are There!

Terrorist's Guide to Kidnapping

An al-Qaeda training manual on kidnapping reveals the following advice to terrorists:

- Upon kidnapping a group of people, execute any security forces immediately. This prevents others from showing resistance.
- Before attempting to abduct people from a building, conduct a thorough study of the fences around the building, as well as the security protection teams and systems. Review the plans of the building and information on its partitions. Use cars that enter the building without inspection to smuggle in equipment.
- Target victims on connecting flights rather than the first flight. Look for homing devices on VIPs.

- Resist negotiators' delay tactics; in case of any stalling, start to execute hostages immediately.

The manual includes examples of various historical abductions. As one example, it noted that the Red Army's takeover of the Japanese embassy in Lima, Peru, in 1996 failed because the hostage situation dragged out for more than a month. This gave rescuers a chance to dig tunnels under the embassy, from which they carried out their rescue mission.

SOURCE: "A Terrorist's Guide to Kidnapping," *Security Management*, August 2004, p. 16.

Special Issues Regarding Personal Safety

The private security industry is heavily involved in responding to special issues regarding personal security. Security consultants and security consulting firms are often hired to advise individuals and corporations on methods to deal with personal safety. In addition, private investigators and private security employees frequently provide security services in this area. This section will discuss several special issues regarding personal safety, including kidnapping, workplace violence, domestic violence and the workplace, stalking, school shootings and school violence, and violence against taxi drivers.

Kidnapping

Kidnapping is a major problem in our society, and although it is the responsibility of the police to officially report, investigate, and apprehend violators of this crime, private security firms and private

security employees become involved in these cases and offer assistance and ancillary investigative services to the police and to their clients.

Kidnapping is the seizure and abduction of a person by force or threat of force and against the victim's will. There are several types of kidnapping incidents, including abduction by family members, child abduction, corporate kidnapping, and illegal trafficking of people.

Abduction by Family Members Although most of us think of child abduction as the act of a stranger, research indicates otherwise. Studies have found that abductions by family members represent the most prevalent type of child abduction. Children from birth to 5 years generally have a greater risk of victimization by parents or other trusted caregivers. In contrast, more-independent school-age children who experience lapses in supervision by caretakers are more often victimized by acquaintances or strangers outside their homes.[60]

Family abductions are defined as a family member wrongfully abducting a child. The National Center for Missing and Exploited Children has issued a comprehensive 250-page prevention and response guide to family abduction. This publication offers a family-abduction action checklist to summarize steps a parent can take to prevent an abduction or to recover a missing child; tips on how parents and other family members can safeguard children at risk; civil court remedies once a child is abducted; criminal remedies in family

kidnapping The transportation or confinement of a person without authority of law and without his or her consent or the consent of his or her guardian, if a minor.

abduction cases; information on searching for a missing child, including contact information for organizations specializing in missing children; legal methods of child recovery in the United States; law and procedures including the Parental Kidnapping Prevention Act and the Hague Convention on the Civil Aspects of International Child Abduction; and much more information.[61]

Child Abduction The *Second National Incidence Studies of Missing, Abducted, Runaway, and Thrownaway Children (NISMART-2)* reported the following kidnapping statistics for the latest reporting year:

■ There were an estimated 115 stereotypical kidnappings (defined as abductions perpetrated by a stranger or slight acquaintance and involving a child who was transported fifty or more miles, detained overnight, held for ransom or with intent to keep the child permanently, or killed). In 40 percent of these stereotypical kidnappings, the child was killed, and in another 4 percent the child was not recovered.

■ There were an estimated 58,200 child victims of nonfamily abduction (defined more broadly to include all nonfamily perpetrators and crimes that involved lesser amounts of forced movement or detention than the more serious crimes of stereotypical kidnappings).

■ Fifty-seven percent of children abducted by a nonfamily perpetrator were missing from caretakers for at least one hour, and police were contacted to help locate 21 percent of the abducted children.

■ Teenagers were by far the most frequent victims of both stereotypical kidnappings and nonfamily abductions.

■ Nearly half of all child victims of sterotypical kidnappings and nonfamily abductions were sexually assaulted by the perpretrator.[62]

Research has indicated that subjects who abduct children usually are not first-time offenders, but are serial offenders who often travel during the commission of multiple sexual offenses against children. Interstate travel by the offender could predicate prosecution under Title 18 USC, which makes it a federal violation for a person to travel in interstate commerce for the purpose of engaging in any sexual act with a person under eighteen years of age.

One help to families whose children may be subject to abduction are **kidnapping kits**. These kits contain forms and guidelines on what to have available for law enforcement should a child be abducted. They include fingerprint cards, space for current photos, descriptions of birth marks and the like, and a place for DNA evidence (usually hair) to be enclosed.

Corporate Kidnapping Corporate kidnapping is a serious problem in the business world. Corporate kidnapping in the twenty-first century is all about money—large sums demanded by kidnappers who know what international corporations have been willing to pay to save their workers. The employers, in turn, take out large insurance polices to defray this cost of doing business in the developing world.[63]

Wackenhut Consulting and Investigation Services offers a kidnapping and extortion program for its clients. It reports that managing an extortion or kidnapping requires a highly professional and carefully orchestrated response. For companies operating in regions that have significant risks of extortion, Wackenhut provides training specifically designed to respond to this risk. Its briefings of the crisis management team lay out the details of managing extortions, the criticality of communications and initial actions, and key strategy decisions. It conducts realistic training exercises to prepare team members for the stress of managing an extortion and provides on-site advice and logistical assistance during actual extortions, as well as a cadre of experienced and fluent consultants who provide advice and support at company headquarters and the scene of the incident. Its personnel provide the key element of hands-on experience that helps make sense of unusual situations and aids in building and implementing a strategy to end the incident.[64] Its crisis management and response services offer evacuation and incident-response services to assist companies in preparing emergency evacuation plans and to assist them in evacuations from hazardous situations in all regions of the world. Its evacuation plans are based on risk assessment and preplanned actions in a phased, flexible evacuation process.[65]

Corporations can also maintain kidnapping kits (similar to those used by parents) for their

kidnapping kit A child safety kit whereby vital information (name, age, address, weight, height, etc.) can be stored; usually includes a fingerprint kit and a place to store DNA samples (i.e., hair).

personnel who travel. These kits contain forms and guidelines on what to have available for law enforcement, including the information normally maintained for children, as well as personal and medical information plus family contact information. These kits might improve the determination of proof of life after a kidnapping.

People Trafficking People traffickers generally lure their victims—many of whom suffer from poverty, unemployment, and gender discrimination in their home countries—to the United States with false promises of employment opportunities. Once these victims reach this country, however, traffickers force them to work as sweatshop laborers, domestic servants, agricultural workers, or prostitutes.[66] In 2006, it was estimated that there were approximately 12.3 million people in forced labor, bonded labor, forced child labor, and sexual servitude.[67]

Congress passed the Victims of Trafficking and Violence Protection Act of 2000 to counter the growing problem faced by the United States and the world of international trafficking of people. It offers assistance to foreign, state, and local law enforcement agencies in dealing with this problem.[68]

The scope of this crime is wide and varied, but it typically involves victims entrapped in commercial sexual exploitation such as prostitution or labor exploitation in sweatshops, domestic servitude, and construction and agricultural settings. The United States is primarily a destination country for people trafficked from other countries. Under the authority of the Trafficking Victims Protection Act of 2000 and the Trafficking Victims Protection Reauthorization Act of 2003, the United States established comprehensive programs, training mechanisms, and processes for combating trafficking in persons both domestically and abroad, as well as for assisting victims.[69]

Workplace Violence

A man with a violent past and a failing marriage who was angry over a repossessed car entered a GMAC auto-finance loan office in southern Florida, and within two minutes shot and killed eight workers and a customer and wounded four others with twenty-eight bullets from a .30-caliber carbine.[70] In San Leandro, California, a sausage factory owner who had complained he was being harassed by the government over heath violations shot and killed three meat inspectors, one from the U.S. Department of Agriculture and one from the state, who had come to the plant to perform inspections.[71]

These are just two of the hundreds of apparently senseless acts of workplace violence experienced every year in the United States (see Exhibit 7.6 for more examples). According to the U.S. Bureau of Labor Statistics, nearly 1,000 workers are murdered and 1.5 million are assaulted in the workplace every year. According to the Workplace Violence Institute, companies lose $36 million annually to workplace violence, and the U.S. Department of Labor reports that workplace violence accounted for 15 percent of all work-related fatal occupational injuries.[72]

Workplace violence is one of the most serious problems facing American society. It is being studied by many researchers and public and private agencies, including the National Institute for Occupational Safety and Health (NIOSH), the Occupational Safety and Health Administration (OSHA), the National Center for the Analysis of Violent Crime, and the Workplace Violence Research Institute. The Workplace Violence Research Institute is a full-service provider in workplace-violence prevention programs, including consulting, training, incident prevention, crisis response, and program maintenance. It is comprised of acknowledged experts in this specialized field and is able to bring unique experience to the business community, industry, and public agencies. It conducts ongoing research to identify vulnerabilities of occupational risks and provide effective solutions to those exposures.[73] Many corporations across the nation are also working on this problem and developing strategies and procedures for dealing with it. There have been numerous books, studies, and articles devoted to this issue.[74] NIOSHA released a DVD on preventing work-related homicides. Among other material, it contains a training program and OSHA guidelines.[75]

Workplace violence was once narrowly defined as physical misbehavior, ranging from heated arguments to homicide, occurring between coworkers at their place of employment, but the definition has been extended in recent years to include any criminal misbehavior committed against people in the workplace.[76]

Workplace violence includes fights between coworkers; threats of assault made by one against

---

workplace violence Any criminal misbehavior committed against people in the workplace.

EXHIBIT 7.6   **Some Major Workplace-Violence Incidents**

- April 2006, Pine Bluff, Arkansas—A Tyson Foods Inc. employee who had just been suspended from his job returned to the production plant carrying two pistols and opened fire, wounding a coworker before he was shot by the police.

- May 2006, Cobb County, Georgia—A contractor walked into a carpet warehouse and opened fire on an employee, killing the man before shooting and killing himself.

- September 2002, New York City—An executive with a major healthcare firm's corporate offices near Times Square killed two coworkers with semiautomatic weapons after one of the workers ended an affair with him by e-mail. The executive called the two workers into his office and shot them before turning the gun on himself.

- June 2002, Providence, Rhode Island—An employee shot a coworker to death and wounded another at a newspaper production plant. He then killed another employee in a nearby suburb before he was found dead in a burned-out car.

- June 2002, Los Angeles—Sheriff's deputies found a cache of unregistered firearms stockpiled in a house and a storage unit belonging to a recently fired nuclear power plant worker, who was arrested for allegedly threatening to kill his coworkers.

- December 2001, St. Mary's County, Maryland—A construction worker stormed a construction site and shot his supervisor and the supervisor's brother, killing both men. After firing at a state trooper while trying to escape, the worker held a 52-year-old woman hostage overnight in a trailer home. He surrendered after the woman managed to escape.

- December 2001, Goshen, Indiana—An employee of a simulated wood products company burst onto the factory floor and opened fire with a shotgun, killing one man and wounding six other people before he killed himself.

- February 2001, Melrose Park, Illinois—A Navistar International worker, fired for conspiring to steal engine parts, entered his former factory with an assault rifle. He killed four workers and injured four others before killing himself. The attack took place one day before the worker was to have begun a prison sentence relating to the conviction on the theft charges.

- December 2000, Boston, Massachusetts—A software tester for a Boston-area Internet technology consulting firm killed seven coworkers during a shooting rampage at the firm. The worker repeatedly shot his colleagues at close range with a 12-gauge shotgun and an assault rifle fed with a 60-round magazine.

SOURCES: Pinkerton Consulting & Investigations, "Workplace Violence Incident Timeline." Retrieved November 13, 2004, from http://www.ci-pinkerton.com; "Officials: Tyson Worker Shoots Co-Worker," *Associated Press*, April 20, 2006; and Suzanne Marques, "Contractor Kills Manager, Self." Retrieved October 13, 2006, from http://www.11alive.com.

---

another; the wanton destruction of property; the subtle intimidation of one employee by another; the harassment of a new worker by older workers; and the covert sabotage of work equipment, data, or records by a disgruntled employee.[77]

NCAVC, the National Center for the Analysis of Violent Crime of the U.S. Department of Justice, has identified four major types of workplace violence: (1) violent acts by criminals who have no connection with the workplace; (2) violence against employees by customers, clients, patients, students, inmates, or any other person for whom an organization provides services; (3) violence against coworkers, supervisors, or managers by a current or former employee; and (4) violence in the workplace by someone who does not work there but has a personal relationship with an employee, such as an abusive spouse or domestic partner.[78]

Some of the direct costs involved with workplace violence are medical costs, lost productivity, property damage, lost sales, worker's compensation claims, insurance costs, employee counseling, the cost of added security, and litigation expenses. Some of the indirect costs are psychological trauma, loss of valued employees, loss of morale, loss of customers, and negative impact on a company's image.[79]

Some feel that workplace violence is rooted in the subculture of a particular workplace, so much so that preventing it requires an assessment of the dynamics of an organization and its impact on employees. One article states that in order to determine if workplace violence is endemic to the organization, the organization should focus on steps for building or rebuilding a professional organization that will create a climate that reduces the risk of workplace violence. It suggests the selection of someone from outside the organization to act as the facilitator for a series of in-house meetings to collect input about creating a professional organization, then hiring an organizational development consultant who will work with the department to help create a culture that will attract, retain, and produce a healthy organization.[80]

According to a recent report, the number of workplace shooting incidents, as well as the number of people killed in these incidents, has increased significantly. Today, more than 75 percent of all workplace homicides are committed with firearms. The study also revealed that in at least 13 percent of the cases, the shooter had a publicly known history of mental health concerns; 92 percent of the shooters were male; 79 percent of the guns used were handguns; and 81 percent of the handguns were semiautomatics.[81]

Regarding stranger workplace violence, the U.S. Department of Justice reported that for the latest reporting year there were 609 workplace homicides. The vast majority of them (469) were shooting incidents.[82] A 2005 report from the University of North Carolina reported that North Carolina employers that allow employees to carry weapons are three times more likely to have a homicide in the workplace than are employers who ban all types of weapons. This risk of a homicide doubled when the weapons are guns. Furthermore, there was a nearly sevenfold increase in the risk of a worker being killed in workplaces that allowed guns and other weapons.[83]

The U.S. Bureau of Labor Statistics, in a study of workplace-violence incidents, reported that the following professions were at higher-than-normal risk of being attacked at work: convenience-store employees, teachers at junior high schools and high schools, bartenders, cab drivers, and nurses. Forty percent of the robberies committed during that period were committed against transportation workers or retail sales workers, including taxi drivers and clerks. It also reported that cab drivers are ten times more likely to be killed on the job than the average worker, and security guards and police also have higher-than-normal chances of being murdered while working.[84]

In addition to individual corporate programs addressing this serious concern, private security consulting firms are also heavily involved. Wackenhut Consulting and Investigations Services offers customized workplace-violence prevention and training programs for companies to deal with this problem and the resultant disruption of business.[85]

Pinkerton Consulting and Investigative Services offer its clients a workplace-violence protection program. It helps companies develop programs that address volatile situations that might lead to violent incidents. The comprehensive program includes information regarding corporate policy and planning, employee awareness and training programs, intervention techniques, incident review, team-reporting programs, and threat management. Its services include the following:

■ Screening new hires—performing all aspects of a thorough background investigation

■ Physical security—recommending effective and efficient safeguards to appropriately increase the level of security by evaluating and installing additional safeguards, for example, access and egress controls; interior movement control; barriers; alarms; "know-when-to-run," "know-where-to-run" programs; security officers; security equipment; and electronic security systems

■ No tolerance—implement no-tolerance policy, hard fast rules, and work practices that support security, for example, prohibit hostile or intimidating behavior, prohibit even veiled threats, and prohibit weapons

■ Awareness training—promote two-way communications, hazard identification, correcting problems, reporting channels and training employees to use conflict-resolution techniques, recognize pre-attack behavior, and avoid an assault

■ Reporting—execute a plan of reporting incidents, for example, set up a hotline for employees to report weapons, any threat, situations that could lead to violence, domestic abuse victims in the workforce, and outsider threats

■ Incident management—implement early intervention programs, establish police liaison and crisis-management plan

■ Recovery—mitigate liability, offer counseling and support, handle press, and replace rumors with facts[86]

It also offers workplace-violence seminars.

In a 2004 article, Frank E. Rudewicz, a senior managing director and counsel at Decision Strategies in Connecticut and chairman of the ASIS International Safeguarding Proprietary Information Council, discusses the continuum of workplace violence and the need for corporations to take proactive efforts to detect early signs of impending violence so that preemptive measures can be taken before a problem gets out of control. He asserts that people do not typically "snap" and become violent; rather, violence occurs on a continuum, often beginning with minor harassing behavior and becoming increasing threatening to the point of violence. He describes this continuum of escalating violence as the HARM Model: harassment, aggression, rage, and mayhem.[87]

He states that workplace violence may begin with irritating behavior on an employee's part that is inappropriate conduct for the workplace, such as acting in a condescending way to a customer, slamming an office door, glaring at a colleague, playing frequent practical jokes on a particular employee, and the like. At the next level, aggressive hostile behaviors may become harmful to another person or the company, such as spreading damaging rumors about a coworker, damaging someone's personal belongings; shouting, and the like. The next stage along the continuum is rage. Rage is manifested through intense behaviors that often cause fear in others and that may result in physical and emotional harm to people or damage to property. It is inappropriate behavior that is physical and visible, ranging from pushing or shoving to sabotaging another worker. The final stage is mayhem, which is physical violence against people or the violent destruction of property. Activity in this category can range from slapping a customer or ransacking and destroying a facility to shooting a coworker to death.

Rudewicz recommends that corporations establish threat-assessment teams to deal with early warning signs of threatening or potentially violent behavior as it occurs along the HARM continuum and to assist management to avoid later incidents, and he suggests numerous steps management can take to deal with the issues. He also recommends that companies adopt a strong zero-tolerance policy and address any violations of this policy with termination of the violating employee, if necessary. The major elements of this policy should include prohibitions against aggressive or hostile behavior that creates a reasonable fear of injury to another person; racial or cultural epithets or other derogatory remarks; harassing or intimidating statements, phone calls, or e-mail messages, or those that are unwanted or deemed offensive by the receiver; physical assault, threat of assault, or stalking of an employee or customer; and carrying weapons on company-owned or leased property.

In a 2005 article, Karen Karr, an attorney who represents employers in labor relations and employment matters, advises that to facilitate quick,

decisive action in response to a threat of harm, employers should enact a general policy prohibiting violence, threats of violence, and possession of weapons on company property and that employers should then assess their work force and devise a plan for responding to danger. She writes that a ban on violence, threats, and weapons must be consistently enforced in a nondiscriminatory manner.[88] She suggests the plan include the following:

- Assessing and improving security measures
- Providing reporting requirements and methods
- Establishing investigation procedures for verifying and assessing the seriousness of a threat
- Creating a relationship and emergency plan with psychologists, attorneys, and law enforcement
- Training supervisors and managers to identify potential triggers of violent behavior
- Providing access to an employee-assistance program
- Devising evacuation and reporting procedures for catastrophic events
- Developing a system of accountability for plan implementation
- Compiling a list of numbers for contacting appropriate police and medical assistance
- Giving all employees a call-in number to account for their safety
- Designating one place for everyone to meet in case of a catastrophic event
- Providing medical and psychological counseling for employees exposed to violent incidents

Paul Viollis and Doug Kane wrote in 2005 that high-risk employees for workplace violence are usually younger males who have poor stress-management skills and a tendency to complain. Signs of possible future violence are making threats or being prone to physical or verbal outburst. They write that since many instances of violence occur when a high-risk employee is fired or laid off, considerable care should be taken to make sure that the termination notice be made in such a way that there is little room for argument and that a high level of security be available if necessary. They report that only slightly over 25 percent of companies have conducted a formal risk assessment of the potential consequences of workplace violence.[89]

The State of Hawaii Department of Labor has a policy that it may deny jobless benefits to a worker fired for misconduct. In 2005, the Hawaii Supreme

Court ruled that this misconduct can also include joking that clashes with company policy designed to protect workers from violence in the workplace. In this case, a women who had worked for twenty-two years as a hostess at a hotel was fired after she jokingly placed her hands around the throat of a coworker and shook her for about five seconds. She was fired and filed for unemployment benefits but was turned down by the state. She appealed, and the court found that because her employer had a zero-tolerance policy against violence in the workplace and the woman knew about it, she should not have even joked about assaulting a coworker. The court's opinion held that "her conduct was in deliberate disregard of the standards of behavior which the employer had a right to expect of an employee."[90]

Although many firms are proactively involved in workplace-violence identification and response, unfortunately, in a recent survey conducted by the American Society of Safety Engineers, 80 percent of the respondents reported that they do not have a written workplace-violence policy. About a quarter of respondents said they planned to develop such a policy.[91]

Michael J. Witkowski, a professor of criminal justice and director of the graduate program in security administration at the University of Detroit–Mercy, reports that companies must be aware of the risks posed by gangs that may expose them to incidents of workplace violence and crime. Considering that there are about 31,000 known gangs with an estimated 846,000 members in the United States and that adults are involved in about 46 percent of gang incidents, it is no surprise that gang members enter the workplace with no intention of leaving behind their gang life and its related violence and criminal activity. These gang members can victimize businesses with internal theft, fraud, computer crime, and large-scale drug dealing. He cites numerous examples, such as gang members penetrating companies and allowing fellow gang members access to proprietary information and access to company facilities and services. He suggests that companies adopt proactive measures to ensure that gang members are kept out of their organizations.[92]

Many professional associations and organizations, such as ASIS International (see Exhibit 7.7) and MOAB Training International, based in Harleysville, Pennsylvania, offer workplace-violence prevention training. MOAB (management of aggressive behavior) teaches individuals how to handle aggressive behavior. These techniques are based on sound psychological principles and empirical data.[93]

Domestic Violence and the Workplace

Domestic violence, including spousal abuse and lover abuse, is one of the most serious problems for U.S. families and society in general. For the latest reporting year, the U.S. Department of Justice's "Homicide Trends in the United States" reports that 1,545 persons (385 males and 1,159 females) were killed by their spouse (784), boyfriend or girlfriend (706), or ex-spouse (57),[94] and the FBI's latest *Uniform Crime Reports* reported that a total of 1.56 million cases of family violence that involved injury were officially reported to the police during the preceeding five years. Of these incidents, the most prevalent relationship was boyfriend/girlfriend, followed by spouse.[95]

It has been estimated that approximately 25 percent of absenteeism, lower worker productivity, and medical benefits claims stem from domestic violence. Domestic violence has been described as a pattern of learned behavior used to gain and maintain power and control over another.[96] It has also been estimated that nationwide, employers lose $36 billion per year due to domestic violence.[97]

In 2005, it was reported that the economy of Tennessee loses millions of dollars per year due to domestic violence, which directly affects businesses in the form of absenteeism, reduced productivity, health care, lost wages, sick leave, and security costs. Domestic violence also costs the Tennessee healthcare system $32.9 million a year.[98]

Domestic violence has a long history in all cultures, but it is only during the last twenty years or so, and only in some advanced industrial nations, that this type of human conflict has gotten the attention and reactions of society.[99] This violence can also take place in the workplace.

Considering that one out of three women will experience domestic violence in her life, any midsize to large company is certain to have employees who are dealing with this problem daily. This inevitably impacts their productivity and poses security problems for the employer while the employee is at work. One authority advises that

domestic violence Violence in the family or between husband and wife or partners.

EXHIBIT 7.7   **ASIS International Professional Development Course in Enhanced Violence Assessment and Management**

Violence assessment is a specialized form of risk assessment that focuses on the violence and potential violence that may occur between human beings and seeks to understand the immediate risk of physical harm posed by the behavior of individuals and small groups. Once the level of risk is assessed, then the knowledge of human behavior and individual perspective can be used to effectively deter the individual/s from acting in a violent way toward a population.

The program provides a clear understanding of how individuals decide to act violently toward others. It offers a practical, proven methodology to assess the behavior of these individuals and manage them away from violent acts toward specific targets. The focus is on practical case assessment and management regardless of the environment or elements of a case, whether domestic violence, school violence, workplace violence, or domestic terrorism.

How an Attendee Will Benefit

■ Learn quick case triage for better, immediate resource allocation.

■ Practice a direct, state-of-the-art method for violence assessment.

■ Understand what case facts are the most critical for violence assessment and learn how to obtain them.

■ Find the balance in case interventions for best results.

■ Understand how to get significantly more information per interview with only a small amount of additional time.

Who Should Attend

■ Security professionals who are responsible for violence assessment and management.

■ Investigative professionals who want to enhance their understanding of violence dynamics and improve their skills at interviewing.

■ Human resource professionals who have a direct or shared responsibility to provide violence assessment and incident management for their organizations.

Sessions

■ Neuropsychological, Psychological, and Behavioral Foundations of Violence

■ Information Gathering and Analysis

■ Enhanced Cognitive Interviewing

■ Use of Assessment Tools for Enhanced Violence Assessment

■ Effective Intervention Methods

SOURCE: ASIS International, "Professional Development: Enhanced Violence Assessment and Management." Retrieved October 17, 2005, from http://www.asisonline.org/store/program_detail.xml?id=3444587.

---

employers should develop a policy that addresses this issue. She says this policy should explain how an employee who is a victim can get assistance and describe how the employer has taken steps to ensure a safe working environment. The policy should define the roles of the director of security, the director of human resources, and employee supervisors and should be disseminated to all employees through the employee handbook, brochures, a company-produced video, and employee training. Supervisors should be trained to recognize the warning signs of domestic abuse and, when abuse is suspected, should tactfully raise the issue with the employee. The situation should be addressed as soon as possible because of the tendency for domestic violence to escalate. The company should obtain all the facts of the patterns of abuse and the status of the relationship between the victim and the abuser, the abuser's behavior pattern, the existence of orders of protection, any threats of suicide by the abuser, the possession

of guns, substance abuse, and whether violence has previously been committed in a public place. Victims should be encouraged to develop a safety plan, and employees and supervisors who screen those who enter the workplace should have knowledge of all domestic violence situations, copies of protection orders, and photographs of abusers.[100]

One organization has developed a six-step guide for creating a domestic violence workplace policy. It suggests the following:

1. Creating interest among an existing group or committee to take on the task of developing the policy

2. Researching other workplace policies on domestic violence, including local government policies, in order to understand their basic components

3. Engaging human resources staff in participating or leading the policy development process

4. Drafting the policy

EXHIBIT 7.8 Workplace-Violence Protection Tips

PROTECTING EMPLOYEES

Some workers, such as those who exchange money with the public; deliver passengers, goods, or services; or those who work alone or late at night are at increased risk. All employees need certain protections. Experts agree that a zero-tolerance policy provides the best protection. OSHA suggests that employers offer additional protections, such as the following:

- Conduct a security assessment.
- Perform pre-employment background investigations in the hiring process.
- Implement safety/awareness training.
- Secure the workplace with video surveillance, extra lighting, and alarm systems and limit access with badges, electronic keys, and security guards.
- Limit the amount of cash on hand.
- Equip field staff with cellular phones.
- Keep employer-provided cars properly maintained.
- Instruct employees not to enter a location where they feel unsafe.

EMPLOYEES PROTECTING THEMSELVES

Employees need to take charge of their own protection in order to avoid becoming victims. Certain steps are important in reducing the odds:

- Learn to recognize and avoid violent situations by attending personal-safety training programs.
- Alert supervisors to any concerns about safety or security.
- Challenge unknown persons in the workplace.
- Avoid traveling alone into unfamiliar locations when possible.

- Carry only minimal money and required identification.
- Do not allow unknown persons to follow you into the worksite.
- Do not allow unknown persons into restricted areas, especially if they do not have an access control badge.

WHAT TO DO AFTER AN INCIDENT

Prompt, appropriate response is critical following an incident of workplace violence. Leading experts suggest the following:

- Encourage employees to report and log all threats.
- Provide prompt medical evaluation and treatment.
- Report violent incidents to local police promptly.
- Inform victims of their legal right to prosecute perpetrators.
- Discuss the circumstances of the incident with staff members. Encourage employees to share information about ways to avoid similar situations in the future.
- Offer stress-debriefing sessions and posttraumatic counseling services to help workers recover from a violent incident.
- Investigate all violent incidents and threats, monitor trends in violent incidents by type or circumstances, and institute corrective actions.

SOURCES: U.S. Occupational Safety and Health Administration, "Workplace Violence Protection Tips." Retrieved November 14, 2004, from http://www.osha.gov; and Pinkerton Consulting and Investigations, "Workplace Violence Protection Tips." Retrieved November 14, 2004, from http://www.ci-pinkerton.com/workplace/wkViolenceTips.html.

---

5. Gaining support for the policy from key stakeholders in the organization

6. Training the staff on the new policy[101]

Numerous different panic alarm devices can be installed in a victim's home or worn on a victim's body that can immediately summon the police in the event of a possible attack. Often, like stalking victims, some abuse victims hire bodyguards to escort them to prevent attacks.

stalking Repeated harassing, and threatening behavior by one individual against another, which might involve following a person, appearing at a person's home or place of business, making harassing phone calls, leaving written messages or objects, or vandalizing a person's property.

Security firms and private security officers become involved in this specific area of violence and frequently provide consulting and protective services to affected individuals and corporations.

Exhibit 7.8 provides a list of workplace-violence protection tips for both employees and employers.

Stalking

Stalking (repeated harassing, and threatening behavior by one individual against another, which might involve following a person, appearing at a person's home or place of business, making harassing phone calls, leaving written messages or objects, or vandalizing a person's property) is a serious problem in our society. It sometimes leads to serious crimes of violence and almost always terrifies, alarms, and annoys the person being stalked. The police attempt to help victims of stalking but often cannot obtain the evidence needed to prosecute stalkers because most stalking laws require that the perpetrator make a credible threat of violence against the victim or members of the victim's immediate family. Also, the police cannot escort the stalking victim throughout his or her day to prevent such activity. Therefore, private security firms and private security officers frequently become involved in antistalking activities, investigations, and prevention.

Stalking is widespread. Nearly one in twelve women and one in forty-five men are stalked at least once in their lifetime. It is estimated that more than a million women and nearly half a million men are stalked in the United States each year. The overwhelming majority (78 percent) of victims are women, and the majority of offenders (87 percent) are men.[102]

Most victims know their stalkers. Even though we often hear reports of fans stalking celebrities, survey evidence indicates that less than a quarter of female victims and a third of male victims are stalked by strangers. Sixty percent of female victims and 30 percent of male victims are stalked by current or former intimate partners. Behaviorally, stalking is similar to domestic violence in that it is a crime of power and control. It is estimated that 25 to 35 percent of stalking cases involve violence, and when stalking leads to violence, it is often a precursor to lethal violence. In 75 percent of completed and attempted female homicides by intimates, the offenders stalked the victims in the year prior to the offense.

Victims of stalking may experience anxiety, depression, guilt, helplessness, and symptoms of posttraumatic stress disorder. Stalking is a serious offense often perpetrated by mentally disturbed offenders, and it can cause major mental health consequences, of which society often has little understanding.[103] In 2005, a study of female college undergraduates who identified themselves as victims of stalking following the termination of a romantic relationship revealed that almost 63 percent experienced threats of violence while being stalked, and 36 percent actually were physically attacked.[104]

Stalking has received attention from state legislatures. The first antistalking law was passed in 1990 in California. Since then, all fifty states have enacted antistalking laws. The U.S. Congress enacted the first federal stalking law in 1996.[105] Relevant federal laws include Interstate Stalking, Interstate Violation of a Protection Order, Federal Domestic Violence Firearm Prohibitions, Interstate Communications, and Harassing Telephone Calls in Interstate Communications.[106]

There are numerous handbooks and manuals for stalking victims, which describe the psychology and tactics of stalkers, prestalking warning signs, safety tips, and practical and legal options for stalking victims. Safety planning in these cases must include safety in the home, in the car, at work, and in public and, unfortunately, possible relocation.[107]

Many stalking victims, including noted celebrities and regular citizens, hire bodyguards on a fulltime or parttime basis to protect themselves against stalkers.

Corporations can also help in incidents involving employees receiving annoying, hostile, or obscene phone calls from a stalker. Often, victims in these cases become afraid to answer the phone. One professional security manager and professor suggests a method that a corporation can use to deal with this. He says that to limit the stalker's impact on an employee's well-being and productivity, he would have the employee be given a new number and the employee's old number segregated so that only he could access it, and he would monitor the calls to obtain information in order to identify the caller.[108]

School Shootings and School Violence

School violence has been defined as "any intentional verbal or physical act producing pain in the recipient of that act while the recipient is under the supervision of the school."[109]

Prior to April of 2007, the most deadly act of school violence in U.S. history occurred at Columbine High School in Littleton, Colorado, in April of 1999. In this incident, two students, Eric Harris and Dylan Klebold, armed with an arsenal of weapons stormed into Columbine High School in Littleton, Colorado, and killed twelve other students and one teacher and wounded twenty-one others before killing themselves.[110] For the latest reporting year, the U.S. Department of Justice Statistics reported that a total of 764,000 violent crimes were committed against students age 12 to 18 at school, including rape, sexual assault, robbery, and assault.[111]

An injured student is carried out of Norris Hall in the aftermath of the school shooting at Virginia Tech University in 2007, where a lone student killed himself and thirty-three other instructors and students. Unlike most elementary and high schools, college campuses are spread out, making it difficult to cordon off large areas. In the aftermath of the Virginia Tech massacre, parents and students were outraged that the school took so long to notify students that a gunman was on the loose—some two hours after the first reports of gunshots on campus.

In 2006, citizens were again shocked by a series of school shootings, including the shooting of ten female students and the killing of five of them at an Amish one-room school house in West Nickel Mines, Pennsylvania; the taking of six hostages and killing of one of them at a high school in Bailey, Colorado; the shooting of nineteen students at a junior college in Montreal; the shooting of two teachers at an elementary school in Essex, Vermont; and others.[112] (See Exhibit 7.9 for more major school shooting incidents.) In response to these shootings, the President of the United States convened a conference on school shootings in October 2006. At the conference he said, "All of us in this country want our classrooms to be gentle places of learning—places where people not only learn the basics—basic skills necessary to become productive citizens—but learn to relate to one another."[113]

Bullying is also a problem in schools. Bullying has been defined as "intentional, repeated hurtful acts, words, or other behavior with a real or perceived power imbalance between bully and victim" and "repeated, unprovoked behavior intended to cause harm or distress (oppression) to a victim who is vulnerable due to a real or perceived imbalance of power." Bullying can be physical, verbal, emotional, or sexual. It has been associated with violence in school.[114] The U.S. Department of Justice has indicated that about 7 percent of students

age 12 to 18, for the latest reporting year, reported that they were the target of bullying behavior; almost 12 percent reported that they were the target of hate-related words; about 36 percent saw hate-related graffiti; and over 21 percent observed street gangs at their school.[115]

Crime is also a problem at colleges. Statistics indicate that one in three students will become a crime victim while studying at a college or university.[116] At approximately 7:00 A.M. on Monday, April 16, 2007, a lone gunman, Cho Seung-Hui, a 23-year-old Virginia Tech University English major from South Korea, walked into West Ambler Johnston Hall Dormitory on the Virginia Tech campus, a campus of 26,000 students, and shot and killed two students and injured more than a dozen others. Campus police, along with the Blacksburg Police, began to search for the "person of interest" immediately after receiving the initial 911 phone call at 7:15 A.M. Approximately two hours later, a 911 caller reported more shooting across campus in Norris Hall. Campus police, along with local, state, and federal law enforcement officers, arrived at Norris Hall to find that the gunman had chained the doors from the inside of the building, preventing immediate access to the hall that had become the focal point of his shooting rampage. In the aftermath of the nation's deadliest school massacre, thirty-two students and faculty lay dead, and countless others were injured. It was later determined that the shooter died of a self-inflicted gunshot wound to the head. Later that day, Virginia Tech President Charles Steger poignantly addressed the nation concerning the mass shooting, describing the massacre as a "tragedy of monumental proportions."[117]

According to Criminal Justice Professor Michael Pittaro, such violence places our students in harm's way, disrupts the harmonious balance of the normally positive academic environment, and jeopardizes the stability and cohesiveness of the community, which in turn naturally influences the creation and direction of social policy designed to ensure the safety and security of our nation's students. Pittaro states, "The school shooter's

EXHIBIT 7.9   **Some Major School Shooting Incidents**

2007	Blacksburg, Virginia—A Virginia Tech student shoots nearly two-hundred rounds into several classrooms, killing thirty-two fellow students and faculty and wounding many others before taking his own life.
2006	West Nickel Mines, Pennsylvania—A man shoots ten female students, killing five, at an Amish one-room school house.
2006	Bailey, Colorado—A man takes six girls hostage and kills one at a high school. He then fatally shoots himself.
2006	Montreal, Canada—A man with a semiautomatic rifle shoots and kills one and wounds nineteen others at a junior college.
2006	Essex, Vermont—A man shoots two teachers, one fatally, at an elementary school.
2006	Rural Wisconsin—A student fatally shoots the principal a day after the principal gave him a disciplinary warning for having tobacco on school grounds.

2006	Joplin, Missouri—A student in a green trench coat and a mask carried an assault rifle into school, pointed it at students, and fired a shot into a ceiling before the weapon jammed.
2005	Red Lake Indian Reservation, Minnesota—A student shoots and kills five schoolmates, a teacher, and an unarmed guard at a high school.
2004	Philadelphia, Pennsylvania—A student fatally shoots one student and wounds three others at a high school.
2003	Cold Spring, Minnesota—A 15-year-old student shoots and kills two fellow students with a .22-caliber semiautomatic handgun.
2001	Santee, California—A student kills two fellow students and wounds thirteen others.
1999	Littleton, Colorado—Two students shoot and kill fourteen classmates and a teacher.
1997	West Paducah, Kentucky—A student kills three students and injures five others.

behaviors and actions are often similar to that of the domestic terrorist who sets out to redress the perceived wrongs of society, or in most cases, a select few who have ridiculed, belittled, demeaned, or even ostracized the individual to the point where revenge or retaliation are the primary motivators for the attack."[118]

Many schools and school districts throughout the nation hire private security officers to patrol their schools and property. In addition, many schools and school districts employ security directors who oversee all security operations and manage school safety personnel as part of their administrative staff. Also, many hire private security consultants or private security firms to assist them in preparing plans to ensure safety in their schools. Unlike most elementary and high schools, college campuses are spread out, making it difficult to cordon off specific areas. In the aftermath of the Virginia Tech massacre, parents and students were outraged that the school took so long to notify students that a gunman was on the loose, and when the announcement was finally made— some two hours after the first reports of gunshots on campus—the warning was delivered silently via e-mail. It appears that campus police officers thought the initial shootings in the dorm were an isolated incident. However, school officials could have used existing technology to warn students

much sooner, enabling them to get behind locked doors. The University of North Carolina at Charlotte is one of ten schools using Digital Acoustics' high-tech intercom system, which can immediately broadcast a message to a single classroom, the entire campus, or any combination of the two. Johns Hopkins University also uses cutting-edge technology; every few weeks, campus safety officers from yet another school come by to check out the new system, which places "smart" video cameras around campus that rely on computer algorithms to detect suspicious activity. The university is about to install another camera (bringing the total to 102 on its main Homewood campus) that will alert a security officer if it films someone climbing a fence, walking down an alley late at night, or lingering by a windowsill, although the software is not yet able to determine whether a person is carrying a gun.

Sophisticated technology does not come cheap, and neither do highly trained campus security officers. In the past, says Steven Healy, public safety director at Princeton University, campus security officers have had to fight for limited resources at many schools by "asking people to imagine the unimaginable."[119]

Schools throughout the nation are upgrading security to counter attacks like those at Virginia Tech and Columbine, as well as terrorist attacks that may impact schools. The following are some recent examples:

- The Metropolitan School District of Washington Township in Indianapolis equipped its 120-bus fleet with sensors and GPS units that track all bus movements.

- The School of the Future, a new high school in Philadelphia, requires each student to swipe a smart card at every entrance, exit, and classroom entrance to track all student movements.

- Brittan Elementary School in Sutter, California, started using radio-frequency identification tags to track students. However, after complaints by a few parents with the assistance of the American Civil Liberties Union of Northern California that the program was demeaning, the school dropped the program.[120]

As a specific example of a comprehensive school security program, the Newark, New Jersey, School District, which serves a population of approximately 285,000, of whom about 45,000 are school age, and administers eighty-two schools spread over a 21-square-mile urban area, has developed a comprehensive physical security program. It has metal detectors at the entrances of its fourteen high schools, and all students, staff, teachers, administrators, and visitors are required to pass through them. (In one recent year, security officers confiscated about one-hundred bladed objects, including razors, knives, and box cutters and four firearms.) All other doors have magnetic locks and are kept closed. Many of the schools have alarms, motion detectors, and video cameras. All high schools and forty-four of the elementary and junior high schools have cameras placed in hallways, stairwells, auditoriums, gymnasiums, cafeterias, exterior locations, and other areas. The cameras are monitored on site by security officers, some of whom also patrol school property around the clock. According to New Jersey law, each high school has at least one security officer on school property for every 225 students, and junior high and elementary schools also have security officers in place. Each school has designated entrances for students, staff, and visitors. All visitors must sign in and receive a visitor badge and wear it while on school property. All students receive color-coded ID cards that tell security officers which floors or areas of the school they are allowed in. Also, all contract employees must wear special temporary IDs, which they can only obtain after they undergo a criminal background check. Regular checking of student,

visitor, and administrator IDs has become a fixed security ritual.[121]

The FBI's Behavioral Science Unit has sponsored a series of seminars to better understand and counter the school shooter. Generally, school shooters are described as white males under the age of 18. Most come from troubled families and view themselves as different compared to the general student population at their schools. Some were apparently bullied and may have exhibited signs of depression. In some instances, a significant event, such as an embarrassing interaction with classmates, a breakup of relationship, or a conflict with a parent occurred just prior to the shooting. Recommendations from the seminars are that schools should take any threats seriously. They also recommend creating an anonymous tip line.[122]

Experts recommend that school officials establish a threat-assessment team that includes representatives from various disciplines and include the school nurse, head custodian, school security personnel, teachers, and counselors. When a threat is received, all members should assemble to discuss the facts. The evaluation should focus on the type of threat, the persons involved, the capacity of the person making the threat to actually execute it, and the ramifications of the various responses being considered.[123]

The National Institute of Justice has released a list of Internet resources to assist school personnel with preparation, response, and resolution with regard to school critical incidents. This list of public and private resources focuses on threat assessments/site surveys, emergency-plan development, interagency cooperation, recovery from and dealing with post-traumatic stress disorder, and organizations dealing with school violence.[124] One of the resource sites is National School Safety and Security Services, which is a private, independent national consulting firm specializing in school security and crisis preparedness training, security assessments, and school safety. It offers school security assessments that provide proactive and practical recommendations for school safety and crisis preparedness planning, heightened school security for terrorist threats, school security and school police staffing, and other issues pertinent to individual schools and school districts.[125]

Violence against Taxi Drivers

Taxi or cab drivers are frequently the victims of serious crime because they ply their trade at all hours of the day and night and travel in all types of

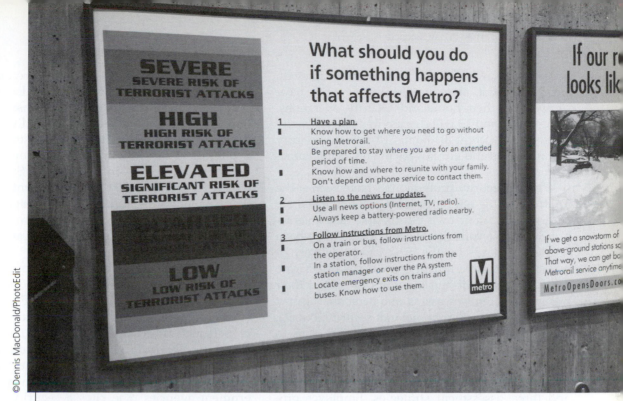

This sign posted in a metro rail service station advises passengers of the proactive protective measures they should take in the event of an intensified terrorist threat level. Signs similar to this one have been posted in airports, railway stations, bus terminals, and other areas related to transportation in the United States.

neighborhoods. Also, they tend to have ready cash available while out on the streets. The police pay particular attention to crimes committed against taxi drivers and frequently stop cab drivers to inquire about their safety. However, crimes against taxi drivers continue to be a major problem. Many security consultants and security firms are hired to advise taxi companies on methods to help themselves. Situational crime-prevention measures, such as partitions between drivers and passengers, video cameras, and GPS are possible solutions that can reduce the risk to drivers.[126] The most recent statistics from the U.S. Bureau of Labor Statistics reported that cab drivers are ten times more likely to be killed on the job than the average worker.[127]

Two Australian researchers have estimated that taxi drivers have up to fifteen times the average exposure to occupational violence and that the high incidence of assaults on taxi drivers compared with other workers was consistent over time and increasing. Risk factors for violence against taxi drivers included evening and night work, intoxicated young male passengers, a driver's inability to speak fluent English, working alone, inadequate driver knowledge of an area, and customers with limited funds.[128]

An article in *Security Journal* reported that women entering the workforce as taxi drivers face gender-dominated forms of victimization, as well as the same security concerns as male drivers. The results of a study of British taxi drivers in a particular large town revealed that female and male drivers reported similar levels of physical attack and verbal abuse; however, women were significantly more likely to be sexually harassed and to consider leaving their jobs due to violence at work. The women were more likely than male drivers to report physical attacks to the police. The drivers were interviewed regarding security methods they used, and they reported two-way radios in the car, cell phones, CS (2-chlorobenzalmalononitrile) gas sprays, weapons, and verbal skills. No partition screens or in-car security cameras are used due to their expense.[129]

Homeland Security and Personal Security

The tragic events of 9/11 brought the issues of homeland security and personal security to everyone's attention. The Federal Department of Homeland Security was established to provide homeland security for our citizens and businesses, and other local, state and federal agencies have stepped up their homeland security operations. Chapters 12 and 13 will discuss in detail the many efforts and accomplishments of private security organizations and employees in enhancing homeland security.

Private security professionals have been at the forefront in the efforts to keep our homeland secure through their own efforts and their interaction with government agencies. Often, they have set the standards for the professional delivery of services that government should follow. Private industry has made major efforts to protect their businesses, premises, assets, and personnel against terrorism and other homeland security threats. Corporations have developed extensive plans to deal with the personal safety issues of homeland security. Most corporations have detailed executive-protection plans, crisis-management teams, and threat-assessment strategies. Employee protection specialists educate employees regarding terrorism techniques and threats, as well as other security risks and the necessity of prompt reporting of any suspicious occurrences.

Companies without security departments or those with smaller security departments often use major contract security companies to provide their corporate security services. These contract companies generally emphasize strategic prevention and conduct threat assessments before establishing prevention plans. These firms also provide immediate response to threats against corporations, their employees, and private individuals by designing appropriate intervention strategies to deter violent behavior and protect people at risk. As one example, iJET Intelligent Risk Systems offers services to over 350 corporate clients to assist them in monitoring, protecting, and responding to emergencies and crises responses. It provides real-time intelligence and clear communication channels during emergencies.[130]

The devastation and problems brought about by Hurricane Katrina in 2005 in the Gulf Coast areas of Louisiana, Mississippi, and Florida tested the ability of society to respond to the needs of personal safety and security. Security industry writer Sherry L. Harowitz reported that private industry was much quicker in helping their employees in Hurricane Katrina than were government agencies. She cites a security director: "First and foremost, in a disaster situation, you have to make sure your people are safe, and then you have to protect your property." She quotes another security director who set up a number of employee hotlines for companies so that their employees could call in: "We would check people off, get their health status, understand what their needs were, where they were, and did they know about other employees."[131]

Summary

- Personal crime is a serious problem in the United States. For the latest reporting year, the FBI indicated that over 1.39 million serious personal crimes were reported to the police in the United States, including about 16,700 murders or nonnegligent manslaughters, 93,900 forcible rapes, 417,000 robberies, and 863,000 aggravated or felonious assaults.

- For the latest reporting year, police made about 603,500 arrests for the most serious violent crimes, including murder and nonnegligent homicide, forcible rape, robbery, and aggravated assault. The police made about 1.3 million arrests for misdemeanor assaults. The police also made about 11 million arrests for other crimes not listed here.

- The inability of local, state, and federal police agencies to protect individuals and corporations from terrorist attacks, kidnappings, and other serious crimes due to their limited jurisdiction and personnel has led to the development of a growth industry in private security.

- Private security personnel are involved in efforts for antiterrorism, executive protection, personal protection, assessing travel risk, workplace violence reduction, domestic violence prevention, stalking, and school violence.

- The security departments of many corporations have personnel assigned to executive protection duties, including protecting high-level executives and other key personnel at work, at home, and while traveling. Many corporations without security departments hire contract security services to provide these services.

- Many persons in our society hire personal protection specialists or bodyguards to escort them through their regular daily activities or to escort them on special events, such as business trips or vacations.

- The U.S. Department of State's Bureau of Consular Affairs pays particular attention to the safety of Americans traveling abroad for business and pleasure. The Department of State studies the risks of traveling to every country in the world and issues travel warning "don't-go" lists for countries that it considers too dangerous to travel to.

- Many people in our society use personal alarms, also known as panic devices and mobile security devices (MSDs), for self-protection. Many of these are found in motor vehicles (as part of a road service/directions feature), and many are carried by individuals, connected to their pagers and other small electronic devices. These communications are also known as the science of telematics—two-way wireless communications using GPS technology.

- Corporate kidnapping is a serious problem in the business world. Corporate kidnapping in the twenty-first century is all about money—large sums demanded by kidnappers who know what international corporations have been willing to pay to save their workers. The employers, in turn, take out large insurance polices to defray this cost of doing business in the developing world.

- Workplace violence is one of the most serious problems affecting U.S. business and society. During the latest reporting year, there were 609 workplace homicides, and the majority involved shootings. Private security professionals are addressing this problem.

- Domestic violence is a major corporate problem in that about a quarter of employee absenteeism, lower productivity, and medical benefit claims result from domestic violence. Private security professionals are involved in helping corporations and citizens deal with this problem.

- Private security professionals are increasingly becoming involved with the serious crime problems, violence, and bullying behavior in our nation's schools.

Learning Check

1. Discuss the extent of personal crime in the United States.

2. Discuss the extent of fear in the United States.

3. Name and discuss three methods corporations use to protect their executives.

4. Discuss some of the methods personal security professionals use to protect persons they are hired to protect.

5. Discuss the assistance provided by the U.S. Government to protect its citizens when traveling abroad.

6. Name and discuss some personal safety devices.

7. Discuss the extent of workplace violence in the United States.

8. Discuss some of the methods corporations can use to deal with the problem of workplace violence.

9. Discuss some methods that corporations can use to deal with issues of domestic violence.

10. Discuss some of the methods used to prevent school violence.

Application Exercise

You have been hired as a summer intern by a dot-com corporation in your area. The corporation has grown significantly in the past decade and is preparing to extend its operations to several foreign countries in Europe, South America, and Asia. Your manager asks you to prepare a report for her discussing the major problems company executives may face when traveling overseas and the measures the corporation can take to ensure their safety.

Web Exercise

In order to celebrate your graduation from college, your parents have offered to take you on a week's vacation to the country of your choice anywhere in the world. They are concerned about their travel safety and ask you to research whatever country you wish to travel to and determine the following:

- Description of the country
- Entry requirements for U.S. citizens
- Customs regulations
- Safety and security

- Crime information
- Criminal penalties
- Medical facilities
- Medical insurance
- Other health information
- Traffic safety and road conditions
- Aviation safety oversight
- Registration/embassy and consulate locations
- Consular access
- Rules on firearms and penalties
- Currency regulations
- Photography restrictions

Key Terms

Employment-Related Security

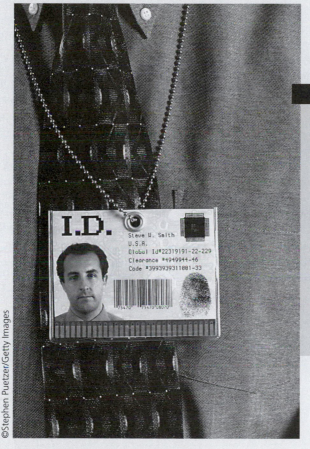

©Stephen Puetzer/Getty Images

GOALS

- To make you aware of the necessity for employment-related security in the workplace.
- To provide an overview of employment-related security in the workplace.
- To introduce you to background investigations.
- To familiarize you with employment-related drug testing or drug screening, sexual harrassment in the workplace, employee monitoring, and employee-misconduct investigations.
- To discuss homeland security and employment-related security.

Introduction

Consider the following scenario:

> You are a hospital patient and see a doctor approaching your bed. You observe him inject something into your intravenous tube. You awaken several days later, find out you had suffered a seizure, had been critically ill, and are lucky to be alive. You tell hospital officials your story about the doctor, but they do not believe you. Thirteen years later, you read in the newspapers that the doctor you suspected of harming you has been accused of being a serial killer who used his medical knowledge and job opportunities to kill numerous patients in the United States and around the world.

This is a true story. Dr. Michael Swango, while a medical student, was nicknamed Double-O Swango by his fellow students, who joked that he had a license to kill because of the large number of his cases that ended in death. During his tenure as a hospital intern, besides the incident involving the near-fatal attack just descibed, a 19-year-old woman mysteriously died after a fatal injection caused her heart to stop. Several years later, he was convicted of attempting to kill some coworkers by lacing their doughnuts and coffee with an arsenic-based pesticide. He served two years in prison.

> Then, after release from prison, he obtained a job as a doctor in a Veterans' Affairs hospital. During his three months there, three of his patients died after being administered lethal injections. Subsequently, he practiced medicine in Zimbabwe, Africa, where it was charged that he poisoned seven patients, five

of them fatally. At the time of his arrest, he was on his way to Saudi Arabia to be a doctor in another hospital.

Why was Dr. Swango allowed to continue his reign of serial murder for thirteen years? Why did he land job after job despite his history? Perhaps the answer lies in the fact that no one at any of his jobs conducted an extensive pre-employment background investigation to determine his work experience and background before they hired him. They just took him at his word. Employment-related security and pre-employment background investigations are among the most important investigations performed by private sector investigators. Failure to conduct a proper pre-employment background investigation can subject a corporation or business to enormous financial liability judgments. It can also, as in Dr. Swango's case, result in deaths.

This chapter will discuss the necessity for employment-related security; background investigations, including pre-employment screening and other background investigations; employment-related drug testing or drug screening; sexual harassment in the workplace; employee monitoring; employee-misconduct investigations; and homeland security and employment-related security.

For more specific information regarding these issues and these types of investigations, students are encouraged to research the scholarly and professional sources noted in the chapter paying special attention to information offered by the professional associations with a presence on the Internet.

Need for Employment-Related Security

In order to lead and manage an effective organization, managers and supervisors need to know the essential information about their employees, both permanent and temporary,

that might impact their job performance. It is equally as important for management to have similar knowledge about their vendors, suppliers, and those working as private contractors with their business. This knowledge is important because it enables the organization to properly use its human resources to make the enterprise effective and successful and to prevent the company from being destroyed within its own ranks.

You Are There!

He Was a Serial Killer But Continued Getting Jobs as a Doctor: The Michael Swango Case

When Michael J. Swango was a medical student at Southern Illinois University, classmates called him Double-O Swango, joking that he had a license to kill because of the large number of his cases that ended in deaths.

In 1984, when he was a medical resident at Ohio State University Hospital, Swango was accused of causing a patient to have a seizure after injecting something into her intravenous tube. The patient survived and told hospital officials about the attack, but they did not believe her. An investigation by the hospital cleared him, but Swango was not allowed to continue his residency there for a second year.

He returned to his native Illinois and worked as an emergency medical technician with the Adams County Ambulance Service. While there, he was convicted of lacing his coworkers' doughnuts and coffee with an arsenic-based ant killer. Five people became ill, but no one died. He was sentenced to five years in prison but served only two.

When he was released from prison, Swango used false names and documents to try to get a number of medical positions. He was hired by a veterans hospital in South Dakota but fired when his past became known.

In 1993, Swango was hired as a medical resident by the Stony Brook Health Sciences Center, in Stony Brook, New York, after lying to the admissions office and saying that his previous conviction for poisoning stemmed from a "barroom brawl." As a Stony Brook intern, he was assigned to the Veterans Affairs Medical Center in Northport, New York. During his tenure there, three of his patients died after being administered lethal injections. Another of his patients fell into a coma after being given an injection of a paralyzing medication; the man subsequently died.

After he had worked there for three months, Stony Brook officials learned about his criminal past, which had been featured in newspapers and on national television, and fired him. However, officials at the time said they had determined that no harm had come to the 147 patients he treated there.

After being dismissed by Stony Brook in 1993, Swango went to practice medicine in Zimbabwe, Africa. Subsequently, authorities there issued a warrant for his arrest on charges that he poisoned seven patients, five of them fatally.

He was arrested in 1997, while stopping over in Chicago en route to a new job as a doctor in Dhahran, Saudi Arabia, charged with making a false statement to Stony Brook officials, and began serving a three-and-a-half-year prison sentence.

Finally, in July 2000, after exhuming the bodies of the three patients found dead at the Northport Veterans Affairs Medical Center and finding the poisons in their bodies, federal investigators charged Swango with the 1993 murders. He was also charged with the 1984 murder of a 19-year-old patient at the Ohio State University Hospital by giving her a potassium injection that caused her heart to stop.

As of 2000, the FBI, the Department of Veterans Affairs, and prosecutors around the world were investigating and building other cases against him. In September 2000, Swango pled guilty to the three murders at the Northport Veterans Hospital and was given three life sentences.

Sources: Michael Cooper, "Former Doctor Charged in Death of Three Patients," *New York Times*, July 12, 2000, p. B1; James B. Stewart, *Blind Eye: The Terrifying Story of a Doctor Who Got Away with Murder*, New York: Simon & Schuster, 1999; and Charlie LeDuff, "Prosecutors Say Doctor Killed to Feel a Thrill," *New York Times*, September 7, 2000, p. B1.

Management has a moral and fiduciary obligation to its shareholders to manage and supervise employees, so they positively improve the firm's business performance. It also has an equally important obligation to its employees to ensure their coworkers operate in the best interests of the firm.

Employee-related security includes **background investigations**, including pre-employment screening and other background investigations; employment-related drug testing or drug screening; sexual harassment in the workplace;

background investigations The process of acquiring information on an individual through third-party services, government organizations, and private individuals in the hopes of making a determination on the future actions of an individual based on past actions.

JOBS IN SECURITY

Careers in Background Investigation

NATIONAL ASSOCIATION OF PROFESSIONAL BACKGROUND SCREENERS (NAPBS)

The National Association of Professional Background Screeners (NAPBS), founded in 2003, is a nonprofit trade association representing the interest of companies offering employment and background screening. It affords the opportunity for qualified companies to participate in shaping the body of knowledge and reputations impacting our futures.

NAPBS promotes ethical business practices and compliance with the Fair Credit Reporting Act and fosters awareness of issues related to consumer protection and privacy rights within the background screening industry. It provides relevant programs and training aimed at empowering members to better serve clients and to maintain standards of excellence in the background screening industry.

BACKGROUND INFORMATION SERVICES INC.

The following are two positions employed by Background Services Inc.

■ Sales executives: Responsibilities include calling on human resources and loss prevention managers at current and prospective client businesses. The position requires five years of sales experience.

■ Entry-level sales position: This position requires a bachelor's or associate's degree.

Sources: National Association of Professional Background Screeners (NAPBS), "Homepage." Retrieved December 18, 2005, from http://www.napbs.com; and Background Information Services Inc., "Available Jobs." Retrieved December 18, 2005, from http://www.employeescreen.com/web/careers.htm.

---

employee monitoring; and employee-misconduct investigations.

The Privacy Rights Clearinghouse, a nonprofit consumer organization interested in consumer information and consumer advocacy, located in San Diego, California, reports that employers must investigate potential and current workers for several reasons:

■ Negligent-hiring lawsuits are on the rise. If an employee's actions hurt someone, the employer may be liable. A bad hiring decision can wreak havoc on a company's budget and reputation.

■ Current events, including child abuse and child abductions, the 9/11 terrorist attacks, and major business scandals such as Enron and other major corporate scandals of the early 2000s, have caused an increase in the scrutiny of corporations and their employees and thus caused an increase in the need for **employment-related security.**

employment-related security Knowing the essential information about employees, both permanent and temporary, that might impact their job performance, breach security, or subject to the organization to liability.

■ False or inflated information supplied by job applicants seems to be on the rise, with estimates that 30 to 40 percent of all job applications and resumes include some false or inflated facts.

■ New federal and state laws require that background checks be conducted for certain jobs. Many of these jobs include working with children, the elderly, or the disabled.

■ Our current information age has made employment-related security and investigations easier to conduct with the availability of computer databases containing millions of records of personal data.[1]

Another recent concern causing increased employment-related security is the current extent of drug usage among employees. Studies have shown that, on average, 10 to 12 percent of the workforce in any given company abuse drugs, and about 50 percent of job-site accidents are caused by illegal drug use. The effects of on-the-job accidents resulting from drug abuse are deaths and injuries, high insurance payouts, and increased health-benefit utilization and worker's compensation claims. Injured employees are lost to their employers for considerable lengths of time and drive up insurance premiums. High accident rates can also damage a company's reputation and severely affect an organization's ability to remain competitive. It has been reported that the construction industry has one of the highest rates of drug use among its workers, with approximately 25 percent of all laborers and supervisors abusing drugs.[2]

Chapter 4 discussed the critical problems of civil and criminal liability involving workers. Businesses are increasingly being held liable for injuries that their employees inflict on third parties. Many states hold companies liable for negligent hiring and negligent retention, asserting that the companies have a duty to investigate employees' backgrounds properly to determine if they have harmful character traits.

Negligent hiring means that an employer has hired someone without properly confirming that the information on his or her application is accurate and factual. Lawsuits for negligent hiring or retention can be based on negligence in conducting a pre-employment investigation, failing to conduct an investigation, or hiring with knowledge of a dangerous propensity. If no facts were available before hiring an employee but became known during the course of employment, a case for **negligent retention** can be made. Companies who serve the public have an added responsibility to exercise due caution in their hiring practices.[3]

The U.S. Department of Commerce has reported that 30 percent of all business failures are the result of poor hiring practices, that embezzlement costs industry $4 billion a year, and that other employee crime, both blue and white collar, costs another $45 to $50 billion annually. Statistics also indicate that most people who steal, cheat, defraud, or embezzle are never detected by their former employers and that over a quarter or more of job applicants stretch the truth or lie on their employment applications.[4]

To underscore the importance of employee-related security, Mark Lippman, owner of Guardsmark Inc., a leading contract security provider, and W. R. McGraw write that while employee theft cannot be eliminated, it can be controlled by good management techniques and the intelligent use of acceptable security procedures. They report that honest people, for the most part, stay honest; dishonest people tend to stay dishonest; and employers should conduct complete background investigations, including previous employment records, and should carry out in-depth applicant interviews.[5]

As an example of the importance of employment-related security, in 2004, the Mississippi Office of the Attorney General, in its *Workplace Violence Prevention Guide*, stated that among the signs of potentially violent employees were previous threats of violence against others or threats of suicide; numerous conflicts with customers, coworkers, or supervisors; statements of extreme desperation over marital, family, or relationship difficulties; extreme financial hardship; and alcohol or drug abuse. For these reasons, it recommends that efforts to prevent workplace violence should include pre-employment screening and drug and alcohol testing.[6]

The federal government is intensely interested in employee-related security, including background investigations and other personnel and investigative matters affecting the massive federal workforce. In the wake of an alarming number of espionage cases involving U.S. employees in the early to mid-1980s, then Secretary of Defense Caspar Weinberger established the Department of Defense (DOD) Security Review Commission to examine DOD policies and procedures to prevent further damaging losses of classified information. The commission recommended that a personnel security research center (think tank) be established. In 1986, the Defense Personnel Security Research and Education Center (PERSEREC) was established in Monterey, California. Today, it is known as the **Defense Personnel Security Research Center** but still carries the acronym of **PERSEREC**.[7]

PERSEREC's mission is to improve the effectiveness, efficiency, and fairness of the DOD personnel and industrial security systems, and it conducts long-term programmatic research for the security and intelligence communities. Its work is directed toward improving personnel security, investigations, adjudications, due process, continuing evaluation of personnel, and security awareness. Its vetting systems area covers a wide range of personnel security processes, including the process of evaluating personnel for their suitability for access to national security

negligent hiring Hiring an employee without properly confirming that the information on his or her employment application is accurate and factual.

negligent retention Retaining an employee after negative information is discovered after her or his hiring.

Defense Personnel Security Research Center (PERSEREC) The federal government's think tank for background investigations and other personnel and investigative matters affecting the federal workforce.

information. It covers prescreening, investigations, and adjudications.

Employment-related investigatory services in the private sector are provided by proprietary security departments in corporations and businesses, large and small contract security investigative services companies, and independent private investigators.

Most large corporations and businesses have their own proprietary (in-house) security departments that provide a wide range of security services, including investigations. Some of these large corporations and businesses may also use major contract (outside) security service companies to conduct all or some of their investigating services. Some corporations use a combination of in-house and outside investigators. Many smaller companies and businesses hire independent private investigators, often one- to two-person firms, to conduct investigations.

■────────────────────────────

Background Investigations

Background investigations are extremely important in the workplace and include pre-employment screening and other background investigations, including the investigation of vendors, private contractors, temporary workers and other companies. Often, the background investigations process for selecting personnel and evaluating them for the best use of their employment is called **vetting.**

It is legal for job applicants, existing employees, and volunteers to be asked to submit to background checks. For some jobs, background screening is required by federal or state law. The Privacy Rights Clearinghouse reports that the current emphasis on security and safety has dramatically increased the number of employment background checks conducted. It says that some people may be uncomfortable with the idea of an investigator poking around in their personal history because they fear that an in-depth background check could unearth information that is irrelevant, taken out of context, or just plain wrong or include information that is illegal to use for hiring purposes or that comes from questionable sources.[8]

vetting A process of examination and evaluation. Specifically, performing a background check on someone before giving him or her an award or honor or offering him or her a position.

EXHIBIT 8.1   Employment-Related Services Provided by Some Major Contract Security Services Firms

Kroll Inc.
Background Screening Services
- Background investigations
- Substance abuse testing
- Credit screening
- International background screening
- Vendor screening
- Employment reference database

Pinkerton Consulting and Investigations
Background investigations/employee vetting

Wackenhut Consulting and Investigation Services
Pre-employment background screening

SOURCES: Kroll Inc. Retrieved October 7, 2004, from http://www.krollworldwide.com; Pinkerton Consulting and Investigations Services. Retrieved October 7, 2004, from http://www.ci-pinkertons.com; and Wackenhut Consulting and Investigation Services. Retrieved October 14, 2004, from http://www.ci-wackenhut.com.

Wackenhut Consulting and Investigation Services describes its background investigations as follows:

> These services include applicant checks, comprehensive backgrounds, and technical backgrounds. Applicant checks are intended for entry-level positions and positions in which no money is handled. They include driving records, civil and criminal court records, social security number verification, credit reports, and past employment verification. Comprehensive backgrounds are intended for higher-level positions, or jobs that involve handling money or sensitive information. These backgrounds include the basic checks and can also include verification of identity, education and professional credentials, contact and interviews of listed references, and exploration of resumes.[9]

Exhibit 8.1 provides a listing of some background investigative services provided by three major contract investigating services firms.

One employment background screening company reports that it conducts the following background screening services:

- Online employee background screening
- Executive-level background checks

- Employee background update reports
- Business asset searches
- Business background checks
- International background checks
- Drug testing and medical examinations[10]

The Privacy Rights Clearinghouse reports that there are many companies specializing in employment screenings and that these companies fall into several broad categories, ranging from private investigators to companies that do nothing but employment screening.[11]

Craig Gilbert, a CPP and independent security consultant, recommends that when a company considers hiring a background screening provider or vendor, it should thoroughly check out the vendor to make sure it is reliable and thorough. The company should ensure that the screening vendor offers basic background screening services, such as employment verification, criminal history check, educational verification, work-related references, and if permitted by law, credit checks.[12]

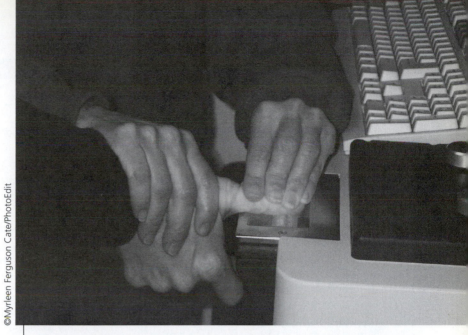

©Myrleen Ferguson Cate/PhotoEdit

Many corporations conduct extensive pre-employment background investigations before they hire in order to screen out dishonest or disreputable applicants. Fingerprints are required for those seeking jobs in a wide variety of fields, and this has spawned a cottage industry of electronic fingerprint capturers, who gather prints by computer or convert old-style inked print cards to electronic images. Here a fingerprint is captured using Live Scan. The fingerprints are electronically scanned and transmitted to the Department of Justice (DOJ) for a criminal record check. Digitizing the fingerprint minutiae (the characteristics that make fingerprints unique) enables the electronic transfer of the fingerprint image data in combination with personal descriptor information to central computers at the DOJ in a matter of seconds, instead of the days required to send hard-copy fingerprint cards through the mail.

Pre-Employment Background Screening

Recall the Dr. Michael Swango case from the opening text of this chapter. Swango was a serial murderer who went from one medical job to another, killing patients as he went along. Yet he continued to be hired, and no employer conducted an examination of his background before hiring him. **Pre-employment background screening** is among the most important types of investigations conducted in the private investigations sector.

Today, for reasons indicated earlier in this chapter, many corporations conduct extensive pre-employment background investigations before they hire in order to screen out dishonest or disreputable people. These background investigations may be conducted by in-house personnel, contract investigating firms, or independent private investigators.

As an example of corporate pre-employment background investigations, the National Football League (NFL) and its teams use intensive pre-employment background examinations of graduating college players entering the pro football draft every year. They check criminal records; interview law enforcement officials at the players' colleges; and speak to coaches, friends, and the players themselves. In one draft year, 68 of the 323 draft-eligible players had "reportable information," meaning that there was some aspect of the players' background that raised eyebrows on the league's security staff, ranging from speeding tickets to drug possession, fights, and violations of NCAA rules. An increasing number of individual teams are combining their security personnel with the league's resources to ensure that nothing is missed.[13]

pre-employment background screening Screening of potential employees.

As another example, Richard Seldon, president of Sterling Testing in New York, reports that he works with 6,000 businesses nationwide, including the NFL's Washington Redskins, to perform background checks. He said that 7 percent of all background checks done by his company reveal some type of criminal behavior.[14]

The National Basketball Association and most other major professional sports teams also conduct background checks for every draft-eligible player in whom they are interested. Teams use their own scouts or hire outside investigative firms.

A recent example of a background investigation causing a management-level Major League Baseball employee to lose his job occurred in 2004. Former New York Mets second baseman, Wally Backman, was hired to manage the Arizona Diamondbacks, but within four days, Blackman was fired after a background investigation revealed that he had pleaded guilty to a misdemeanor harassment charge after a domestic altercation, had a driving-under-the-influence conviction, and had filed a bankruptcy case.[15]

The ADP Employer Services Hiring Index indicated that for the latest reportable year, employers conducted 4.4 million pre-employment background checks. This is three times higher than the number of checks conducted eight years previously. The number of checks has been increasing due to the realities of 9/11, increased federal scrutiny of corporate governance, and a desire by companies to avoid ethics breaches. David Hagaman, editor of the *Georgia Employment Law Newsletter,* explains, "If I hire you and you had an unfit past, and I never checked, and you come to work with me and strike a customer, I might be liable for negligent hiring."[16]

The ADP Employer Services Hiring Index determined that 9 percent of the background checks turned up negative information or inaccuracies about criminal, driving, and credit records; worker compensation claims; and reference checks. Of the criminal records checked, 5 percent had an infraction of some sort, and 50 percent of the employment, credential, and education checks uncovered discrepancies in the information that the applicant provided to employers. Also, nearly 30 percent of the applicants had at least one conviction or violation on their driving records, and 45 percent of the credit records checked revealed a bankruptcy, judgment, lien, or report to a collection agency.[17]

Pre-employment checks have increased, not just because of security concerns but also due to the

EXHIBIT 8.2 What Is Included in a Background Report?

Driving records
Vehicle registration
Credit records
Criminal records
Social security number
Education records
Court records
Worker's compensation records
Bankruptcy information
Character references
Neighborhood interviews
Medical records
Property ownership
Military records
State licensing records
Drug-test results
Past employers
Personal references
Incarceration records
Sex offender lists

SOURCE: Privacy Rights Clearinghouse, "Employment Background Checks: A Jobseeker's Guide." Retrieved December 3, 2005, from http://www. privacyrights.org.

increased ease with which background information can be obtained and lower costs for this information. Background checks are not limited to new employees—many companies are rechecking their employees on an annual basis, says Jason Morris, president of a background investigations firm.[18]

According to the Society for Human Resource Management, 96 percent of businesses surveyed in 2004 indicated that they conduct reference and background checks on job applicants. Larger companies conduct checks 99 percent of the time, while small companies report doing them 92 percent of the time. It was also reported that criminal checks are done to some degree by 87 percent of companies, and 61 percent say they always or occasionally do credit checks. Education records, military discharge information, and motor vehicle department checks are also growing in importance.[19]

Pre-employment screening generally includes, at a minimum, criminal history, verification of prior employment, education, and social security number. The applicant's driving record, credit report, and professional licenses are also generally reviewed.[20] Exhibit 8.2 lists the categories generally included in a background report.

Another important part of pre-employment investigations might include military records, if appropriate. Applicants should be asked for a copy of their DD-214, the standard document given to all U.S. military personnel on their discharge from the service. This form provides dates of entry and separation from the service and all locations where the service person was assigned, in addition to other information. A military record search from the military records facility of the National Personnel Records Center can also be done.

Regarding educational records checks, often a deceptive applicant with a computer and printer technology skills can create realistic-looking diplomas. Applicants can be asked to have all schools they attended mail a copy of their official transcript to the investigator. The investigator can also personally check each school. If a school has closed down, its records are generally sent to the state's Department of Education, and the investigator can check there. Legitimate degrees from distance-learning educational institutions can be checked through the Distance Education and Training Council that evaluates and accredits such colleges.

A survey of *Security Management* readers shows that of all pre-employment selection tools, criminal records checks are most common, with 93.6 percent of respondents routinely checking them. Other often-used pre-employment screening methods mentioned included employment history, 91.1 percent; education records, 75.2 percent; drug screens, 71.5 percent; and integrity tests, 14.5 percent.[21]

Some corporations are turning to personnel service companies to recruit, screen, and hire new employees. In addition to identifying potential job candidates, these services conduct extensive background investigations that include everything from criminal records checks to drug tests.[22]

In 2005, Arizona expanded the state's program requiring that background checks be completed for anyone seeking employment with agencies that care for the infirm, such as nursing facilities, healthcare centers for the mentally retarded, adult residential care facilities, and adult daycare centers. Applicants for jobs as personal care attendants in a supervised independent-living program or in a hospice must also undergo a background check. Applicants who are found to have been convicted of crimes of violence will be barred from employment in these facilities.[23]

An example of a small firm that conducts pre-employment background checks is the Timberline VIP Shuttle, started in 2003 to provide transportation between Springerville, Arizona, and Phoenix. Although it employs only three drivers, it conducts criminal and motor vehicle checks on all prospective drivers. The firm's president says, "We're entrusting them with a fairly expensive piece of equipment as well as with the safety of many people.[24]

Businesses generally must get written permission from job applicants to conduct background investigations through an outside pre-employment checking agency, but they do not need written permission for checks done by in-house staff.[25]

When conducting background checks, employers should be fully aware of all laws related to what information may be obtained and what is confidential. The best place to start with a background check is often with a candidate's former employer. However, due to possible liabilities for defamation, many employers are reluctant to give detailed information about a past employee's performance. Often, if the former employer does not say anything outright, nonverbal cues may help in determining what the employer actually thinks about the applicant. Asking specific questions rather than simply making a general request for information may yield better information. Education records, driving records, and criminal record checks are good sources of potentially important information. To reduce possible liability claims, employers should use the same process to investigate the background of each candidate for a position.[26]

The federal **Fair Credit Reporting Act (FCRA)** sets national standards for employment screening. However, the law under the FCRA only applies to background checks performed by an outside company, called a **consumer reporting agency (CRA).** It does not apply in situations where the employer itself conducts background checks in-house.[27]

Three companies—Trans Union, Experian, and Equifax—maintain **consumer credit reports** on anyone who has ever used a credit card, held a mortgage, taken out a car loan, bought insurance, or used credit in any other way. Each agency offers two types of credit reports. The first is used by banks and other lenders to determine whether

Fair Credit Reporting Act (FCRA) Federal law designed to promote accuracy and ensure the privacy of the information used in consumer reports.

consumer reporting agency (CRA) Business that conducts and maintains credit reporting information; also known as a credit bureau.

consumer credit reports Records on anyone who has ever used credit in any way.

You Are There!

What Is the Fair Credit Reporting Act (FCRA)?

If one has ever applied for a charge account, a personal loan, insurance, or a job, he or she has a credit file. These files contain information on where people work and live, how they pay their bills, and whether they have been sued, arrested, or filed for bankruptcy.

Companies that maintain and sell this information are called Consumer Reporting Agencies (CRAs). The most common type of CRA is the **credit bureau.** The information CRAs sell to creditors, employers, insurers, and other businesses is called a consumer report.

The Fair Credit Reporting Act (FCRA), enforced by the Federal Trade Commission, is designed to promote accuracy and to ensure the privacy of the information used in consumer reports. Some important provisions of the FCRA include the following:

▪ Creditors, employers, or insurers cannot get someone's report that contains medical information without that person's approval.

▪ A CRA cannot supply information about people to their employers, or to prospective employers, without their consent.

▪ Only businesses with a legitimate business need, as recognized by the FCRA (for example, if someone applies for credit, employment, or insurance or to rent an apartment), can get a copy of a credit report.

There are three major national credit bureaus:

Equifax
PO Box 740241
Atlanta, GA 30374-0241

Experian
PO Box 2104
Allen, Texas 75013

Trans Union
P.O. Box 1000
Chester, PA 19022

SOURCES: Federal Trade Commission, and the Fair Credit Reporting Act (FCRA), 15 USC @1681 *et seq.*

a person has strong enough credit to obtain a loan. The second is used by potential employers to check an applicant's credit history. The employee credit report usually contains the following types of credit activity: trade lines (a record of all the credit accounts the person has ever had), credit balances, the highest amount ever owed, and payment history. It also contains some civil records and judgments, including bankruptcies and liens.

Whenever a company plans to use a credit report in a hiring decision, it must follow the requirements of the FCRA, which are enforced by the Federal Trade Commission (FTC).[28] The FCRA is a law designed to protect the privacy of **consumer report information** and guarantee that the information supplied by consumer reporting agencies is as accurate as possible. Under FCRA rules, an employer is required to notify the job candidate

if a **consumer report** will be requested. Also, if the company decides to take an **adverse action** against the candidate (that is, not offer the person the job) because of the information in the credit report, it must notify the applicant in advance, give the applicant a copy of the report, and provide a written explanation of the candidate's rights under the FCRA. The applicant is then allowed to dispute any inaccurate information in the report.

Corporations must be careful when using preemployment credit checks to make hire and no-hire decisions. Various court cases, federal law, and FTC opinions have established a series of precedents that govern when a credit report can and cannot be used to deny someone employment. Many companies have been sued by rejected applicants for making erroneous hiring decisions based on credit reports.[29]

Experts recommend that if a report indicates a job applicant has bad credit, it should not be taken at face value. The company should investigate any mitigating factors, such as catastrophic family illnesses, that might explain the bad credit history.

Pre-employment background screening agencies generally charge between $25 and $200 for a background screen. Factors that affect the price include

credit bureau The most common type of CRA.

consumer report information Credit history information maintained and disseminated by consumer reporting agencies.

adverse action A refusal to offer a person a job because of information on the person's credit report.

You Are There!

How Does the Fair Credit Reporting Act (FCRA) Affect a Pre-employment Background Report?

The federal Fair Credit Reporting Act (FCRA) sets national standards for employment screening. However, the law only applies to background checks performed by an outside company, called a consumer reporting agency, under the FCRA. The law does not apply in situations where the employer itself conducts background checks in-house.

Particular states may have more-restrictive employment-screening laws, and many state labor codes and state fair-employment guidelines limit the content of employment checks.

The FCRA reports that the following information cannot be reported to prospective employers:

- Bankruptcies after ten years
- Civil suits, civil judgments, and records from arrest, from date of entry to after seven years
- Paid tax liens after seven years
- Accounts placed for collection after seven years
- Any other negative information (except criminal conditions) after seven years.

Again, states might have more restrictive laws, particularly regarding arrest information.

The FCRA does not prohibit employers from asking certain questions on employment applications; however, state employment laws may limit the questions an employer asks on a job application. The FCRA also permits a prospective employer to perform investigative reports and question an applicant's neighbors, friends, or associates about one's character, general reputation, personal characteristics, or mode of living. The subject of an investigation is entitled to know the nature and scope of an investigative consumer report but has to request such information. The law also permits other questions, such as age and marital status.

The FCRA requires an employer to obtain a candidate's or employee's permission to obtain private records regarding the following:

- Education records—A school can release "directory information," which can include name, address, dates of attendance, degrees earned, and activities, unless the student has given written notice otherwise.
- Military service records—The military may release name, rank, salary, duty assignments, awards, and duty status.
- Medical records—The Americans with Disabilities Act allows a potential employer to inquire only about one's ability to perform specific job functions.

A potential employer can contact an applicant's past employers, who then can say anything (truthful) about the former employee's past job performance. However, most employers have a policy of only confirming dates of employment, final salary, and other limited information. Also, for certain jobs, such as truck driver positions, that fall under the regulations of the Federal Department of Transportation, employers are required to accurately respond to an inquiry from a prospective employer about whether a candidate took a drug test, refused a drug test, or tested positive in a drug test with a prior or current employer.

Under the FCRA, an employer must obtain an applicant's written authorization before a background check is conducted. The authorization must be on a document separate from all other documents, such as employment applications. If an employer uses information from the consumer report for an adverse action, such as denying the job applicant, terminating the employee, rescinding a job offer, or denying a promotion, it must do the following:

- *Before* the adverse action is taken, the employer must give the applicant a "pre-adverse action disclosure." This includes a copy of the report and an explanation of the consumer's rights under the FCRA.
- *After* the adverse action is taken, the individual must be given an "adverse action notice" that contains the name, address, and phone number of the employment screening company and a statement that this company did not make the adverse decision, rather that the employer did, and a notice that the individual has the right to dispute the accuracy or completeness of any of the information in the report.

Source: Privacy Rights Clearinghouse, "Employment Background Checks: A Jobseeker's Guide." Retrieved December 3, 2005, from http://www.privacyrights.org.

the employee's responsibility level and how much business the screener does with the client.[30]

As mentioned earlier, if employers decide not to hire a job applicant because of information revealed by the background check, they are required by the FCRA to inform the applicant of this. However, a spokesperson for the Privacy Rights Clearinghouse says that many managers fail to comply with this requirement and instead simply tell applicants that they were not as qualified as another candidate. An employment attorney writes that in some cases where job applicants have been denied a job because of incorrect information in their background records, they may have no legal options unless they can prove that the background screening company or employer acted with willful misconduct or negligence.[31]

Lately, fingerprints are required for those seeking jobs in a wide variety of fields. Some recent examples include applicants for a janitor's job at the Bruggenmeyer Memorial Library in Monterey, California; liquor store owners in Telluride, Colorado; and school-bus drivers throughout Illinois. Insurers also require some companies to do background investigations, including fingerprints, for some categories of workers they are hiring.[32] This has spawned a cottage industry of electronic fingerprint capturers, who gather prints by computer or convert old-style inked print cards to electronic images. Once taken, the prints are sent to state authorities, who forward them to the FBI Fingerprint Center in Clarksburg, West Virginia. In 2006, Florida made electronic fingerprinting checks mandatory for applicants for a real-estate sales associate or broker's license.[33]

In 2004, the FBI performed 9 million checks for private employers, up from 3.5 million in 1992. Half of all fingerprint checks today are employment related. Formerly, job applicants went to law enforcement agencies to get fingerprints taken; now many private companies do it themselves. As an example, National Background Check, a Columbus, Ohio, company with twelve offices around the state, digitally fingerprints thousands of job applicants each month and usually processes the prints within twenty-four hours.[34]

Many scam operations provide false pre-employment background information to prospective employers. Sometimes friends pose as corporate executives or other professional references, but other scams can be more elaborate. Some sham corporations have been established that receive information from a dishonest job seeker and then supply that information in response to a basic employment verification call. Also, some individuals sell illegitimate college degrees to job seekers and establish fake offices that investigators can call to verify the information.[35]

Considering the growing proliferation of scam operations, good pre-employment investigators go beyond the normal methods of checking applicants' backgrounds. Previously, many employers verified a job applicant's previous five-year work history by relying on the names and telephone numbers of references supplied by the applicant; however, today investigators often ensure these references are legitimate by verifying them through the particular company's human resources department. In addition, the investigator must verify the legitimacy of the company itself by checking the local chamber of commerce, business reference books, and the state government's corporate business department. If the applicant claims that a business he or she has worked for has closed, the investigator can verify this through state corporate records, old business directories, or phone books. The applicant can be required to provide tax documentation (W-2s) as proof of employment.

Although registering of **sexual offenders** has been required since 1994 by the Jacob Wetterling Act and community notification was required as of 1996's Megan's Law, it has taken several years for states to comply with both laws, and the public record researcher or investigator who wants to examine these records faces two major challenges. First, many states have not consolidated all records for public access—many states use the Internet for public notification; other records are still held by local law enforcement and are released only after an assessment of need. Second, each state has its own classification of offenders, with up to three levels possible. Level-one offenders are considered low risk, and their records may be released only to law enforcement. Level-two offenders are considered medium risk, and their records are released to those who work with children or individuals with reduced capabilities. Level-three offenders are high risk and may be reported to the public.[36]

These levels may also dictate what is released on Internet sites, so researchers should be aware that the public list on the Internet might be incomplete. When doing background checks for certain

sexual offender Person convicted of a sexual offense against another person.

Laws Affecting Workplace Discrimination

The U.S. Equal Employment Opportunity Commission (EEOC) was established by Title VII of the Civil Rights Act of 1964. It enforces the following laws:

- Title VII of the Civil Rights Act of 1964 which prohibits employment discrimination based on race, color, religion, sex, or national origin. (42 USC § 2000)

- Equal Pay Act of 1963, which protects men and women who perform substantially equal work in the same establishment from sex-based wage discrimination. (29 USC § 206)

- Age Discrimination in Employment Act of 1967, which protects individuals who are 40 years of age or older. (29 USC § 621)

- American with Disabilities Act of 1990, which prohibits employment discrimination against qualified persons with disabilities in the private sector, and in state and local governments. (42 USC § 12101)

organizations, such as daycare centers, with more extensive rights to offender information, record researchers may need to check with local law enforcement.

A significant problem regarding sexual offender registration ensued in the wake of Hurricane Katrina in 2005, as authorities had no idea where most of the 4,500 registered sex offenders who left Louisiana and Mississippi went after the hurricane. Convicted sex offenders are required by law to register so authorities can keep track of them and notify officials in other jurisdictions when they move. Tracking sex offenders is the responsibility of each offender's home state, but because of the chaos surrounding the hurricane, that did not happen. A nationwide private background screening service company that does background checks for businesses did find five of them in Arizona. The company had offered a free Katrina sex offender search to law enforcement. Four of the five offenders located by the company had criminal histories involving offenses against juveniles. The company found the individuals in Arizona by tracking personal information when they opened bank accounts or set up utilities, then cross-referenced the dates and patterns of that information with their centralized nationwide database of sex offenders.

A spokesman for the company said most of the information was indexed back to a social security number, which he said his service can legally only share with law enforcement.[37]

Traditionally, many corporations had used **polygraph (lie detector) examinations** in pre-employment screening and internal investigations. However, the 1988 **Employee Polygraph Protection Act (EPPA)** prohibited the use of pre-employment polygraph examinations in the private sector except for government employers, law enforcement agencies, and certain critical industries. Many of the corporations involved in these areas, as well as many law enforcement agencies, still use polygraph examinations in their pre-employment background examinations.

Criminal records are another important part of background searches. In 2004, Wal-Mart developed a policy of conducting criminal checks on all qualified job applicants as a result of being sued for negligence in South Carolina related to a minor's accusation that a worker fondled her. The suit alleges that Wal-Mart failed to disclose that the accused employee had two convictions for indecent exposure.[38]

Frederick G. Giles, a CPP and Vice President of Research Services for the Wackenhut Corporation, wrote in 2004, citing a former Connecticut Attorney General, "The single most reliable predictor of criminal behavior is the fact of a prior criminal history."[39] Indeed, criminal record checks are an essential part of background investigations.

Criminal record checks have generally been conducted through examinations of a jurisdiction's public records, and today many corporations are paying to obtain state police or FBI records. Multi-state criminal records databases can be a useful tool in checking previous criminal records.[40] Although **multistate criminal records databases** can be useful tools for background investigations, there are limitations and legal risks involved in using them.

polygraph (lie detector) examination Test using a scientific instrument (polygraph machine, also known as a lie detector) to measure credibility.

Employee Polygraph Protection Act (EPPA) A 1988 law that prohibits the use of pre-employment polygraph examinations in the private sector except for government employers, law enforcement agencies, and certain critical industries.

multistate criminal records databases Computerized databases used by background investigators to conduct criminal record checks.

You Are There!

The Employee Polygraph Protection Act of 1988 (EPPA)

Formerly, the polygraph was used extensively in private industry for screening job applicants and preventing employee theft. Its use in pre-employment screening was severely limited by the Employee Polygraph Protection Act (EPPA), signed into law in June 1988. In addition to limiting the use of the polygraph, this law, which is enforced by the U.S. Department of Labor under the authority of the Secretary of Labor, banned the use of any other lie detector tests in the workplace, except for the polygraph. Such lie detector machines include psychological stress evaluators, deceptographs, and voice stress analyzers.

The EPPA prohibited random polygraph testing by private sector employers and the use of the polygraph for pre-employment screening. The law provides that an employer cannot ask or tell job applicants to take a polygraph as part of the job-interviewing process and that an employee under investigation may not be fired for refusing to take a polygraph examination nor solely on the basis of the test results. The law exempts the U.S. government or any state or local government from its provisions and restrictions.

The EPPA allows the use of the polygraph for pre-employment screening for employers whose primary business is the provision of certain types of security services; companies that manufacture or dispense controlled substances; and businesses doing sensitive work under contract to the federal government, such as nuclear plants, power facilities, water companies, and the like. The law also provides that other private industries can still request employees to take a polygraph test as part of an internal criminal investigation but that the firm must justify a reasonable suspicion that the employee was involved in the alleged offense. The suspected employee must be notified in writing forty-eight hours in advance of the test and may have a lawyer present during the testing.

SOURCES: F. Lee Bailey, Roger E. Zuckerman, and Kenneth R. Pierce, *The Employee Polygraph Protection Act: A Manual for Polygraph Examiners and Employers* (Severna Park, MD: American Polygraph Association, 1989); James J. Kouri, "Federal Polygraph Law: A Blow to Private Security," *The NarcOfficer*, May 1989, pp. 37–39; Hugh E. Jones, "The Employee Polygraph Protection Act: What Are the Consequences?" *The NarcOfficer*, May 1989, pp. 41–42; and Norman Ansley, "A Compendium on Polygraph Validity," *The NarcOfficer*, May 1989, pp. 43–48.

Despite these risks, some security directors are turning to these databases because they cover a much wider geographical area than the traditional search conducted at county courthouses. However, multistate databases are often inaccurate for a number of reasons. Not all states provide criminal records to these databases, and those that do may not provide all the records they have. The candidate may also have a record in these databases under another name or variation of name. One author states that considering the inaccuracies and legal dilemmas they present, Internet criminal records checks should not replace traditional searches but should be used in conjunction with them.[41]

In 2005, the *Dallas Morning News* ran an article discussing problems with people who have been wrongfully listed in the Texas Department of Public Safety's criminal record database, resulting in them losing job offers. The man erroneously listed in the state's criminal database, Quinton Graham, had been trying to clear his name since 1999. His brother, who has a physical likeness and, of course, knowledge of his personal data, including his birthday, had fraudulently used his identity

when cited for a traffic violation in the early 1990s. Graham discovered the erroneous records in 1999, when a job offer was abruptly withdrawn. Graham appealed numerous times to the Texas authorities, but the problem was not corrected. Since 2001, the Department of Public Safety has processed 127 claims of misused identity and expunged 284 records because of misuse. These numbers present only a small portion of the problem because not all people know they are erroneously listed.[42]

According to Jay Foley, co-executive director of the Identity Theft Resource Center, a nonprofit organization based in California, clearing a criminal record is complicated because once the data is entered, it is sold and resold to private companies who make the erroneous information easily accessible on the Internet. Even if the originating agency corrects the record, there is no guarantee the private companies will. "It's sort of like tracing a raindrop, because you have no idea where the rain is going to fall—you just know that it will. Information, once it's put into the system, bought from the system, transferred all around—there's no telling where it's going to end up."[43]

PRIVATE SECURITY CONNECTIONS

Some Professional Associations Concerned with Privacy Rights

Privacy Rights Clearinghouse
American Civil Liberties Union (ACLU)

Often, background investigations may be conducted, but they are not done correctly. As an example, the U.S. General Accounting Office reported that an analysis of 530 background investigations of employees of the U.S. Department of Defense were woefully inadequate. All 530 of these people received top-secret clearance even though investigators had not always verified such basic information as residency, citizenship, or employment. At that time, the agency responsible for conducting the DOD investigations faced a backlog of more than 600,000 cases. The backlog was due to failed management reforms and inadequate oversight.[44]

In 2004, Carl Pergola, national director of First-Global Investigations of BDO Seidman, said he often finds companies that either do not run background checks or run them poorly. He said one company that retained his firm had hired a woman who had been convicted of embezzlement and permitted to serve her time on weekends; therefore, she had no gap in her employment history.[45]

Other Background Investigations

Most companies perform background checks for regular employees to avoid being liable for the actions of these employees or being the victims of their criminal actions; however, a company can also be found liable for the actions of a temporary or contract employee who harms someone on company property or company time (see Exhibit 8.3 for information on an ASIS International professional development course regarding this topic.). The most common types of nonregular employees are independent contractors, including vendors and consultants. About 1.2 million U.S. employees, or 1 percent of the workforce, are temporary employees, and about 6.5 percent of the workforce are independent contractors, including vendors and consultants. Most courts have held that an employer–employee relationship exists for these temporary and independent

EXHIBIT 8.3 ASIS International Professional Development Course

Virtual Forum: Safe Hiring Audit: Implementing and Measuring Due Diligence
Employers that fail to exercise due diligence in their hiring practices risk hiring criminals or unqualified workers, workplace violence, theft or litigation. This session presents a safe hiring audit that evaluates a firm's due diligence in the hiring process, reviews best practices, provides strategies that can be implemented immediately at little or no cost, and assists in demonstrating due diligence in the event an employer must defend its hiring practices in court.

Source: ASIS International, "Professional Development Course, Virtual Forum: Safe Hiring Audit: Implementing and Measuring Due Diligence." Retrieved October 16, 2005, from http://www.asisonline.org/store/program_detail.xml?id=2153906.

contractors, and the hiring company has the right to control and direct the person who is working for them. Thus, the company hiring these persons can be held liable for their conduct.[46]

As one example, a manufacturer was found liable when its distributor's independent door-to-door salesperson sexually assaulted a female customer in her home. The court found that the manufacturer had a duty to take reasonable precautions to prevent the assault because it retained control over how the salespeople operated; it was the manufacturer who required the sales staff to perform in-house demonstrations of its products.[47]

N. Alexander Erlam, the general counsel of a leading provider of background screening services to companies worldwide, recommends that any firm hiring temporary workers or private contractors should conduct background screening on these employees themselves to avoid liability.[48]

Erlam's advice is particularly important in Florida. A law enacted in 2005 requires all employees of companies that have working contracts with Florida school districts, including employees of vendors and contractors, to be subject to fingerprinting and a detailed criminal background check before being allowed to work on school property when children are present. (The Jessica Lunsford Act was enacted in Florida after a convicted sex offender kidnapped and killed a 9-year-old girl in February 2005. The girl was killed by a man who had worked as a subcontractor at her school.) Many types of workers are affected by the law, including

You Are There!

Recent Court Decisions on Pre-Employment Background Screening

FENJE v. FELD

Dr. Paul Fenje was accepted into a residency program at the University of Illinois based on his own representations about his exemplary background. After Fenje began working, his supervisor found that Fenje had lied about his past. Fenje was fired. He then sued the University of Illinois and his supervisor for violating his due process rights. The court found that the university was within its rights to fire him because Fenje obtained the job under false pretenses.

MORAN v. MURTAUGH, MILLER, MEYER, & NELSON

Gene Moran was hired as a paralegal in a law firm. However, in conducting a background check after he began work, the company learned that Moran had several felony convictions. The company requested Moran's resignation. Moran asked for the records the company had used to make its decision, citing the California Investigative Consumer Reporting Agencies Act (ICRA), and the company mailed him this information a day after receiving the request. Moran filed a lawsuit claiming that the firm violated the ICRA by not providing him with the information before it made its decision. A state appeals court found in favor of the firm, ruling that it had acted in good faith and had provided the information to Moran in a reasonable amount of time.

KARRAKER v. RENT-A-CENTER

A federal appeals court ruled that the Minnesota Multiphasic Personality Inventory, a test that measures personality traits as well as psychiatric disorders, is a medical test under the Americans with Disabilities Act (ADA). In this case, Rent-A-Center was sued because it was using this test to determine whether employees should be promoted to management positions. The court ruled against Rent-A-Center, holding that under the ADA, medical tests may not be used to determine whether an individual will be employed or promoted to a new job.

BROWNE v. SCR MEDICAL TRANSPORTATION SERVICES

SCR Medical Services (SCR), under a contract with the Chicago Transit Authority, provides transportation via van to disabled people who are unable to use the city's main rail and bus services. It hired Robert Britton to drive one of the company's vans. Prior to hiring him, SCR conducted a criminal background check through the Illinois State Police. The background check showed that Britton had no prior convictions. A year later, a disabled woman filed a complaint with SCR, saying that an SCR driver whom she could not identify exposed himself to her and attempted to kill her. Britton was a suspect because he was the driver of the vehicle transporting the woman that day. Britton denied the allegations, and the woman was unable to pick him out of a lineup.

Four months later, another woman, who suffered from cerebral palsy, accused Britton of sexually assaulting her twice, once in the vehicle in which he was driving her and once inside her home. The woman filed criminal charges against him, and he was arrested. A complete police record check submitted at trial revealed that Britton had a long history of arrests but no convictions.

The victim filed a lawsuit against SCR, claiming that the company negligently hired Britton and should have known that he was a danger to customers. The Circuit Court of Cook County dismissed the case, and the woman appealed the decision. The Illinois Court of Appeals upheld the lower court, ruling that SCR was not negligent in hiring or retaining Britton. The court ruled that there was no way SCR could have known about Britton's arrests because only convictions are reported. The court ruled also that SCR did investigate the previous claim of inappropriate behavior made against Britton but that he could not be implicated.

SOURCES: *Fenje v. Feld*, U.S. Court of Appeals for the Seventh Circuit, No. 04-1056, 2005; *Moran v. Murtaugh, Miller, Meyer, & Nelson*, in Teresa Anderson, "U.S. Judicial Decisions," *Security Management*, September 2005, p. 196; *Karraker v. Rent-A-Center*, U.S. Court of Appeals for the Seventh Circuit, No. 04-2881, 2005; *Browne v. SCR Medical Transportation Services*, Illinois Court of Appeals for the Third Division, No. 96L12925, 2005; and Teresa Anderson, "U.S. Judicial Decisions," *Security Management*, May 2005, p. 104; October 2005, pp. 102 to 104; April 2005, p. 98.

contracted laborers, roofers, delivery drivers, trash collectors, baseball umpires, and soda vendors.[49] The law does not determine who pays for the costs of fingerprinting, and in many cases districts are forcing contractors to pay them. Some fear that these costs will end up being redirected back to taxpayers through higher construction costs.[50]

Florida school officials applaud the intention of the law but also fear that the scope of the law will make it difficult to implement and comply with. In the Santa Rosa School District, the assistant super-intendent for human resources says that the issue of ensuring that workers have had the background checks will be the responsibility of the contractors. However, she says that schools will also bear some of this responsibility and will have to be responsible for making sure that a person does not come on cam-pus without some type of identified clearance.[51]

Some report that the Jessica Lunsford Act is wreaking financial havoc for contractors in Florida. The president and CEO of the Florida Gulf Coast chapter of Associated Builders and Contractors, a statewide advocacy organization, complains of the fingerprinting cost of $65 and the amount of time workers must stand in line to get printed.[52]

Employment-Related Drug Testing or Drug Screening

Numerous reports over the past decade by govern-ment organizations, such as the U.S. Department of Health and Human Service's Substance Abuse and Mental Health Services Administration (SAMHSA), the National Institute on Drug Abuse (NIDA), the U.S. Department of Labor, and numerous others, indicate that substance abuse is a serious problem in the workplace. Substance-abusing workers have been found to be less productive and have higher absenteeism rates, higher worker's compensation claims, higher turnover rates, and higher accident rates than those who do not abuse drugs. Other costs of drug abuse in the workplace are diverted supervisory and managerial time, friction among workers, damage to equipment, poor decisions, and damage to the company's public image.[53]

According to data from SAMSHA's latest National Household Survey on Drug Use and Health (NSDUH) (see Exhibit 8.4), about 46 percent of the

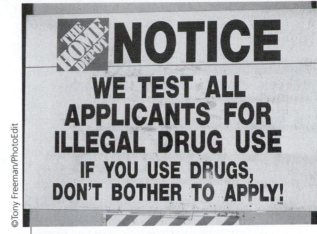

©Tony Freeman/PhotoEdit

Substance-abusing workers have been found to be less productive and have higher absenteeism rates, higher worker's compensation claims, higher turnover rates, and higher accident rates than those who do not abuse drugs. In order to withstand legal challenges, drug-testing policies must be created fairly and be well documented, professionally administrated, and effec-tively communicated to employees and management.

U.S. population (110 million Americans) age 12 or older reported that they had used illicit drugs at least once in their lifetime; 15 percent reported personal use of an illegal drug within the past year; and 8 per-cent reported such use within the past month.[54] The latest statistics from SAMHSA's Drug Abuse Warn-ing Network (DAWN) revealed there were over 670,000 drug-related visits to hospital emergency departments nationwide in the latest reported year.[55]

In 2006, it was reported that illegal drug use among workers fell to its lowest level in nearly two decades, in part due to tougher drug-testing

EXHIBIT 8.4	National Survey on Drug Use and Health: National Findings, 2004

Drug Use	Percent of Population Aged 12 or Over
Current illicit-drug users	7.9
Current drinkers of alcohol	50.3
Current users of a tobacco product	29.2
Currently substance-dependent or abusive of substances	9.4

SOURCE: U.S. Department of Health and Human Services, Substance Abuse and Mental Health Services Administration, *2004 National Survey on Drug Use and Health: National Findings* (Washington, DC: Author, 2005).

measures. Quest Diagnostics, which performs 7.3 million drug tests a year, reported that testing positive for drugs fell to 4.1 percent.[56]

Workplace-related **drug testing or drug screening** is completely legal. The **Federal Drug-Free Workplace Act** of 1998 was passed to provide employers and employees with the right to work in a drug-free workplace. The majority of federal and state guidelines and laws support drug policies and drug-testing programs. The federal government firmly supports drug-testing programs in the workplace.[57]

In order to withstand legal challenges, drug-testing policies must be created fairly and be well-documented, professionally administered, and effectively communicated to employees and management. The U.S. Department of Justice maintains that employers must be fully aware of the legal liabilities associated with drug testing sought by job applicants who are eventually not hired and by current employees who refuse to take a drug test or who are fired or disciplined for testing positive on a drug test.[58]

Recent court decisions have shown that companies face an enormous liability when they do nothing or do the wrong thing when confronted with clear evidence of drugs or alcohol use in the workplace. If corporations ignore drug or alcohol problems in the workplace, severe safety and legal problems can ensue.[59]

In 2005, it was reported that the drug-testing industry receives an estimated $737 million in revenue from approximately 20 to 25 million drug tests administered annually to Americans. Today, a majority of companies in the United States administer pre-employment drug tests to job applicants.[60]

Employers have cited four primary reasons for employee drug testing:

▪ Concern over the economic costs of drug abuse, including increased healthcare costs, absenteeism, and on-the-job accidents

▪ Fear of liability for injuries caused by employee drug use

▪ Belief that drug use increases the amount of employee theft

▪ Desire to control conduct of employees[61]

drug testing or drug screening Analysis of employees or candidates for illicit drug use.

Federal Drug-Free Workplace Act Federal legislation that requires some federal contractors and all federal grantees to provide drug-free workplaces as a condition of receiving a contract or grant from a federal agency.

According to the executive director of the Institute for a Drug-Free Workplace, "Employers have the single most effective weapon in the war on drugs: a paycheck."[62]

In 2005, SAMHSA indicated that a comprehensive work drug-testing program involves pre-employment tests, random tests, reasonable suspicion/cause tests, postaccident tests, return to duty tests, and follow-up tests. See Exhibit 8.5 of this chapter for a complete explanation of each of these tests.[63]

To ensure accuracy and reliability, the U.S. Department of Health and Human Services has issued technical and scientific guidelines for employee drug testing. Standard procedures involve an initial screening assay followed by a confirmation assay. The National Institute on Drug Abuse offers a laboratory certification program.

Seriously affecting the validity of drug testing is the proliferation of numerous cottage industries supporting efforts to foil detection in drug tests, including using others' urine (clean urine) as a substitute for one's own and using urine adulterants to fool the test by producing a negative reading for drugs. In 2005, SAMHSA issued a comprehensive report describing the background of attempts by individuals to cheat on drug tests, particularly urine testing (urinalysis), as well as instructions for personnel at collection sites to collect urine for each type of drug test and instructions to employers for scheduling these tests.[64]

Traditionally, drug testing has been done by urine analysis; as of 1995, for example, urine testing was the most common form of employee drug testing, and the average cost per person tested was $35. However, drug testing by hair analysis is gaining popularity. Much of the research on hair testing is being conducted by the National Institute of Justice, in collaboration with the National Institute on Drug Abuse. Because hair analysis and urine testing address different time periods of illicit drug use, hair testing should not be expected to replace urinalysis. However, it offers promise as a supplementary technique. Because it detects exposure over prolonged periods of use, it can also be done less often than urinalysis and could potentially reduce testing costs. Exhibit 8.6 covers testing methods for employment-related drug testing or drug screening.

Experts recommend that employers should include in their employee handbook a clear policy on employee drug abuse and the employer's procedure for addressing it, and also recommend

EXHIBIT 8.5	Reasons for Employment-Related Drug Testing or Drug Screening

The Division of Workplace Programs of the Substance Abuse and Mental Health Services Administration of the U.S. Department of Health and Human Services reports that a comprehensive workplace drug-testing program should include the following tests:

- Pre-employment test—An individual is required to provide a specimen during the job application process. Generally, a negative drug result is required before an employer may offer employment to an individual.

- Random test—An employer selects, using a truly random selection process, one or more individuals from the employees included in the employer's workplace drug-testing program. A random selection process precludes an employer from attempting to preselect a particular employee for a drug test.

- Reasonable suspicion/cause test—An employee is required to provide a specimen when there is sufficient evidence to indicate that the employee may have used an illicit substance. Typically, the evidence is based on direct observations made by supervisors

or coworkers that an employee has used or possesses illicit substances, exhibits physical symptoms of being under the influence, and has patterns of abnormal or erratic behavior.

- Post-accident test—An employee is required to provide a specimen after being involved in an accident or incident on the job. The results of such a test may provide evidence as to the cause of the accident or incident.

- Return to duty test—An employee is required to provide a specimen to ensure that the employee is drug-free before being allowed to return to work.

- Follow-up test—An employee is tested at random intervals after returning to work to ensure that the employee remains drug-free.

Source: U.S. Department of Health and Human Services, Substance Abuse and Mental Health Services Administration, Division of Workplace Programs, "Reasons for Drug Testing—February 2005." Retrieved November 23, 2005, from http://dwp.samhsa.gov/index.aspx.

that components of a comprehensive employer effort to counter employee drug abuse should include a needs assessment, policy development, employee education, supervisor training, employee assistance, and drug testing. Because employee drug testing is a controversial and sensitive issue, the experts say it requires careful planning, consistently applied procedures, strict confidentiality, and provisions for appeal.[65]

Employers suspecting that an employee is abusing drugs or alcohol should document how the employee's work has been affected, including the numbers of times the suspected employee has reported late to work, fallen asleep on the job, been belligerent, or slurred words. Employers should also develop a program of counseling and discipline for suspected drug or alcohol abusers, as would be the case for any employee who has not been performing as expected on the job. The employer should not attempt to diagnose the cause of the employee's job-performance problem, and responses to poor workplace performance should be designed to improve job performance and retain the employee.[66]

A corporate or vendor medical review officer (MRO) must certify all drug-testing results in order for them to be legally binding. According to the

U.S. Department of Health and Human Services, a MRO is defined as "a licensed physician responsible for receiving laboratory results generated by an agency's drug testing program who has knowledge of substance abuse disorders and has appropriate medical training to interpret and evaluate an individual's positive test result together with his or her medical history and any other relevant biomedical information." A MRO meets with the employee suspected of drug use to determine if there are any pre-existing medical conditions to consider or if he or she is currently taking any prescription drugs that could alter the test's outcomes. In order for an employee to be terminated from her or his job, an MRO must agree with the results of the drug test. Failure to have agreement from an MRO can subject an employer to adverse legal actions.[67]

Although illegal drugs or controlled substances, particularly opiates, cocaine, marijuana, amphetamines, and others, receive much attention, alcohol is by far the largest substance-abuse problem in society. A report by the Bureau of National Affairs estimated that one in twelve American workers abuses alcohol, more than double the abuse rates of marijuana, cocaine, and amphetamines combined. Financial estimates of alcohol-related losses sustained by U.S. employers range from $9 billion to

| EXHIBIT 8.6 | Testing Methods for Employment-Related Drug Testing or Drug Screening |

The most current testing methods for employment-related drug testing or drug screening include urine, oral-fluid, hair, sweat, or blood testing. Drug testing or drug screening can be conducted in a laboratory setting or on-site.

URINE

Urine-based testing is the most widely used method of drug testing. It is currently considered the industry standard and is approved by the U.S. Department of Transportation and the Substance Abuse and Mental Health Services Administration of the U.S. Department of Health and Human Services.

The urine-collection process must be closely observed, and the testing requires specialized laboratory facilities for analysis. Urine-test results can take from twenty-four to ninety-six hours to return from the lab and are costly and can be easily adulterated. Generally, it can take several hours for traces of marijuana to appear in urine; therefore, someone who is tested thirty minutes after using the drug will test negative.

ORAL-FLUID

The oral-fluid procedure typically involves collecting the fluid in one's mouth using a prepackaged swab to test for the drug. Oral-fluid–based testing is a small but growing method of drug testing. It is relatively easy to administer and can be done on-site with immediate results. Oral-fluid testing has not been accepted for federal employee testing and can only detect THC (the active controlled substance in marijuana) for up to twenty-four hours.

HAIR

Hair testing is another method for drug testing that is becoming more prevalent. It can detect past drug use for a longer time period than other testing methods, but it is costly and can take several days for results to be returned.

SWEAT

Sweat testing is the least proven method for drug testing and is not widely used. The testing process is relatively noninvasive, but results can take several days to come back.

BLOOD

Drug testing using blood is almost exclusively restricted to hospital and/or clinical use. It is the most accurate sample for detecting current usage but is highly invasive and costly and requires expensive laboratory equipment.

LABORATORY vs. ON-SITE TESTING

Urine, blood, or hair testing must be analyzed in a laboratory. These samples must be obtained by a trained professional who can ensure that proper collection procedures are followed. It requires that persons being tested leave their place of employment, taking time away from their jobs.

On-site tests, typically oral-based, can be done at the place of employment. This takes up less time and allows employers to immediately test employees whom they suspect of being under the influence of a drug. It also reduces the chances of adulteration, as the employees must submit to the drug test as soon as they are notified.

SOURCE: Peter Cholakis, "How to Implement a Successful Drug-Testing Program," *Risk Management*, November 2005, p. 24.

as much as $150 billion annually. The U.S. Department of Health and Human Services has reported that alcohol is the leading cause of accidental death through motor vehicle crashes, falls, and fires. Alcohol abuse also leads to absenteeism, tardiness, higher healthcare costs, increased accidents and injuries at work, and reduced productivity. Some companies do screen prospective employees for intoxication.[68]

Prior to the U.S. Supreme Court decision in *Board of Education v. Earls* (2002),[69] about 7 percent of public school districts used drug testing (5 percent for student athletes and an additional 2 percent for students engaged in other extra-curricular activities). It is estimated that private schools, which are unaffected by the *Earls* ruling, use drug testing more often than public schools. Legal precedents underlying *Earls*, notably those that have focused on school athletes, have considered the risks of drug abuse while playing sports as involving a decreased expectation of privacy, an unobtrusive search, and a severe need that is met by the search.[70] In *Earls*, the U.S. Supreme Court cautioned that the desirability and wisdom of drug testing is an issue to be decided by local school boards, but in this case *(Earls)*, "Testing students who participate in extracurricular activities is a reasonably effective means of addressing the school district's legitimate concerns in preventing, deterring, and detecting drug use."[71]

You Are There!

Recent Court Decisions on Drug Testing and the Workplace

THOMAS J. TOW v. TRUCK COUNTRY OF IOWA, INC.

The Iowa Supreme Court has ruled that a company cannot require an employee to pay the cost of his drug test. In this case, Truck Company of Iowa, Inc. hired a new employee, Thomas Tow, on the condition that he pass a background check and drug test. Tow's drug test was inconclusive. The company told Tow that he would have to pay for a new test before he would be hired. Tow sued the company. The court ruled that, in Iowa, a company must pay for such tests.

ROBERT RELFORD v. LEXINGTON-FAYETTE URBAN COUNTY GOVERNMENT

A federal court of appeals ruled than an employee's arrest for the possession of drug paraphernalia, together with his abuse of sick-leave policy and his refusal to submit to a drug test, is sufficient grounds for requiring the employee to undergo ongoing, random drug screening.

In 1997, Robert Relford was working as an electrician for the Lexington-Fayette Urban County Government in Kentucky. One evening after work, he was arrested for possession of drug paraphernalia. Because he was incarcerated, Relford was unable to report to work the next day. Instead of telling his supervisor the truth, Relford convinced a coworker to lie and tell the supervisor he was sick. However, the supervisor found out Relford had indeed been incarcerated. Relford was suspended for five days and ordered to submit to a drug test. He refused, claiming the county did not have reasonable suspicion, a requirement under its own policy, to test him for drugs. In turn, the county fired him.

Relford then brought a complaint before the county's civil service commission. The commission found that the county's action was reasonable but that its policy had confused Relford, and it ordered him to be reinstated but required him to consult with the county's employee assistance program and submit to random drug tests. Relford returned to work but appealed the commission's decision, arguing that he should not be required to submit to random drug testing. While his appeal was pending, Relford was chosen to undergo a drug test. He tested positive for illegal narcotics and was fired. Relford filed a lawsuit with the U.S. District Court for the Eastern District of Kentucky, claiming he was unlawfully fired because of a drug test that violated his Fourth Amendment rights. The District Court found that the county had reasonable suspicion to require a drug test. Relford appealed the decision.

The U.S. Court of Appeals for the Sixth Circuit affirmed the lower court's decision, ruling that Relford's prior arrest for drugs, coupled with his dishonesty and his attempt to cover up the incident, did suggest the use of illegal drugs, and thus the county was within its rights to subject him to random drug testing.

SOURCES: *Thomas J. Tow v. Truck Country of Iowa, Inc.*, Supreme Court of Iowa, No. 04-0462, 2005; *Robert Relford v. Lexington-Fayette Urban County Government*, U.S. Court of Appeals for the Sixth Circuit, No. 03-5600, 2004; and Teresa Anderson, "U.S. Judicial Decisions," *Security Management*, August 2005, p. 94; April, 2005, pp. 98, 100.

Researchers have studied the effectiveness of the U.S. military's aggressive workplace drug-testing policy and discovered that since the imposition of its policy, the rate of illicit drug use among military personnel has become significantly lower than civilian rates.[72]

Large and small companies are involved in drug testing. In Arizona, in 2005, it was reported that about 30 percent of small companies have drug policies in place, compared with 87 percent of companies with five hundred or more workers and virtually all of the Fortune 500 companies.[73]

Sexual Harrassment in the Workplace

Sexual harassment, which can be defined as unwarranted and unwelcome sexual attention, is a serious social problem. A 2004 article estimated that approximately one-half of all women will be sexually harassed during the course of their academic or working

sexual harassment Unwanted and uninvited sexual contact or advances.

You Are There!

Landmark U.S. Supreme Court Cases on Sexual Harassment in the Workplace

MERITOR SAVINGS BANK v. VINSON

Ms. Vinson, after being dismissed from her job at a Meritor Savings Bank, sued Sidney Taylor, the vice president of the bank, charging that he had constantly sexually harassed her and thus created a hostile work environment.

In this case, the U.S. Supreme Court ruled that Title VII of the Civil Rights Act of 1964 prohibited any disparate treatment of men and women in employment and that discrimination by sex produced a hostile work environment.

ONCALE v. SUNDOWNER OFFSHORE

Joseph Oncale, a male, claimed that he was sexually harassed by coworkers and his supervisor on an offshore oil rig on several occasions; once when he was restrained by coworkers while another coworker placed his penis on Oncale's neck; on another occasion when he was threatened with homosexual rape; and then again, when a bar of soap was forced into his anus in the shower room. Oncale complained to supervisory personnel, but they took no remedial actions.

Upon hearing the case in December 1997, the U.S. Supreme Court ruled unanimously that the prohibition against sex discrimination, set out in Title VII of the Civil Rights Act of 1964, also applied to same-sex sexual harassment. It reasoned that Oncale's lawsuit was actionable because he was placed in a disadvantageous working condition.

FARAGHER v. CITY OF BOCA RATON

After resigning as a lifeguard employed by the City of Boca Raton, Florida, Beth Ann Faragher brought an action in U.S. District Court against the city and her immediate supervisors, alleging that they had created a sexually hostile atmosphere by touching her and commenting about her. She complained that the actions of her supervisors were serious violations of her lives. Sexual harassment has negative consequences for both individuals and organizations, and victims experience serious negative effects on their health, psychological well-being, and job satisfaction.[74]

conditions of employment and constituted an abusive working atmosphere. The District Court upheld her lawsuit.

Upon appeal to the Court of Appeals, that court held that Faragher's supervisors were not acting within the scope of their employment when they engaged in the harassing conduct and that the city could not be held liable for negligence in failing to prevent it.

Upon appeal to the U.S. Supreme Court, the Court found that the city was indeed vicariously liable under Title VII of the Civil Rights Act of 1964 for actionable discrimination caused by a supervisor and that it failed to disseminate its policy against sexual harassment when its officials made no attempt to control the conduct of its supervisors.

BURLINGTON INDUSTRIES, INC. v. ELLERTH

Kimberly Ellerth worked for Burlington Industries for fifteen months and then resigned, claiming that she allegedly suffered sexual harassment by her supervisor because of his sexual advances toward her. Ellerth refused the supervisor's advances but did not suffer any tangible retaliation and was, in fact, promoted once. Moreover, she remained silent about the supervisor's conduct despite her knowledge of the company's policy against sexual harassment. Ellerth brought an action against Burlington Industries, claiming that the employer was responsible for the supervisor's actions, which constructively led to her resignation.

The U.S. Supreme Court upheld Ellerth's claims and held that employers are vicariously responsible for supervisors who create hostile working conditions for those over whom they have authority.

SOURCES: *Meritor Savings Bank v. Vinson*, 477 U.S. 57 (1986); *Oncale v. Sundowner Offshore*, 523 U.S. 75 (1998); *Faragher v. City of Boca Raton*, 524 U.S. 775 (1998); and *Burlington Industries, Inc. v. Ellerth*, 524 U.S. 742 (1998).

sexual harassment in the workplace Unwanted and uninvited sexual contact or advances in a workplace.

hostile environment sexual harassment A workplace that promotes or tolerates sexual harassment.

The U.S. Supreme Court has decided several cases on **sexual harassment in the workplace** in the past few decades. The general rule the Court has established is that employers can be held liable for both actual sexual harassment in the workplace and **hostile environment sexual harassment**.[75]

In the 1970s, courts first acknowledged that employees were within their rights to sue their employer when they were subjected to unlawful sexual harassment in the workplace. Then,

You Are There!

Recent Court Decisions on Sexual Harassment in the Workplace

NINA BENJAMIN v. JERRY ANDERSON AND JOKER'S WILD BAR AND RESTAURANT

Nina Benjamin was employed as a cocktail waitress at Joker's Wild Bar and Restaurant in Missoula, Montana, from September 1998 to March 1999, and was supervised by Jerry Anderson, a manager, and Darinda Williams, the owner. The restaurant owners had no sexual harassment policy. In August 1998, prior to Benjamin's employment, a female employee had complained that Anderson had sexually assaulted her after driving her home from a party in August 1998. The employee had complained to Williams and offered a written statement that Anderson's actions were unwelcome; however, no investigation was ever conducted.

After a Christmas party in December 1998, Anderson offered to drive Benjamin, who later admitted to having had too much to drink, home and she agreed. Several times during the ride home, Anderson attempted to initiate sexual contact with Benjamin, who was drifting in and out of consciousness. Several days later, Benjamin told Anderson that she wanted to make it clear that there would be no intimate contact between them. Anderson told her that it had already happened on the ride home after the party.

Rumors began to circulate in the workplace about the alleged sexual relationship between Benjamin and Anderson. Benjamin told another supervisor about Anderson's actions, and he said that he was sorry that it had occurred and that he would take care of it. The supervisor then approached Anderson and told him that his actions with Benjamin were inappropriate. No other actions were taken.

Subsequently, Anderson began arranging shifts at the workplace so that Benjamin always worked with him. He brushed against her and made inappropriate comments during these shifts. During one shift, Benjamin rebuffed Anderson for touching her. After the shift, Anderson reported to Williams that Benjamin had treated a customer rudely and had not been performing her duties well. Benjamin was fired a few days later.

Benjamin sued the restaurant for sexual harassment. A Montana circuit court ruled in favor of Benjamin, finding that the restaurant had allowed an employee to engage in a pattern of abuse and that it had no sexual harassment policy in place to counter such abuse. At trial, Williams, the owner, testified that employees were supposed to figure out what to do on their own in such cases. The restaurant appealed the circuit court's decision.

The Montana Supreme Court upheld the lower court's decision. The court pointed out several critical factors that led to the restaurant's liability, including that the restaurant had no sexual harassment policy and the fact that, even after Benjamin reported the incident, restaurant management allowed Anderson to set Benjamin's schedule and supervise her. The court also ruled that the company acted inappropriately by not investigating the prior assault Anderson allegedly had committed. Both assaults reportedly occurred in exactly the same way, which should have alerted the restaurant to the possibility of future incidents.

MILLER v. DEPARTMENT OF CORRECTIONS

A male prison warden was found guilty of conducting four simultaneous affairs with woman employees and using his authority to get the women special treatment, such as promotions and perks.

In this case, the California Supreme Court ruled that widespread sexual favoritism in the workplace can create a hostile workplace environment. While an isolated case of favoritism would not be grounds for a harassment charge, ruled the court, employees may sue if the message conveyed in the workplace is that women are sexual playthings or that they must engage in sexual conduct with supervisors to get ahead.

SOURCES: *Nina Benjamin v. Jerry Anderson and Joker's Wild Bar and Restaurant*, Montana Supreme Court, No. 03-757, 2005; *Miller v. Department of Corrections*, Supreme Court of California, No. S114097, 2005; and Teresa Anderson, "U.S. Judicial Decisions," *Security Management*, November 2005, p. 124; September 2005, pp. 194–196.

and continuing today, the U.S. Supreme Court has held that Title VII of the Civil Rights Act of 1964 prohibits sexual harassment in the workplace. The Court has continued to define various types of behavior that constitute actionable sexual harassment. In 1998, the Court decided several landmark cases that dramatically changed the legal underpinnings for sexual harassment law. These cases established new and broader standards for holding employers liable when management-level employees engage in conduct that creates a hostile environment for subordinates. Also in the same term, the Court found that same-sex harassment can create employer liability and declared that sexual harassment does not differentiate between genders and that males could be held liable for sexual harassment of males, and women for women. This ruling has pervasive implications for all sorts of workplace conduct, such as all-male "horseplay" and all-female talk. Evolving and expanding sexual harassment law underscores the importance of employers' continual and effective management training. Employers must ensure that their workplace harassment prevention policies and all other policies are up to date and that they are effectively communicated to each employee. Employers, the Court ruled, should clearly define what constitutes harassing behavior, reinforce a zero-tolerance response to it, and outline the range of disciplinary consequences for harassers.[76] Some courts have applied these decisions to other unlawful forms of harassment, such as racial, religious, ethnic, and disability harassment.[77]

In 1999, the Equal Employment Opportunity Commission (EEOC) issued a series of guidelines for businesses to clarify what employers need to do to comply with the 1998 Supreme Court decisions. These guidelines mandate the following:

- Establish a sexual harassment policy.
- Post the policy.
- Investigate all cases promptly.
- Offer remedies to injured parties.
- Train employees to avoid harassing others.
- Create safeguards to prevent incidents of sexual harassment.

The EEOC stipulates that the investigation of all sexual harassment complaints should start within twenty-four hours after a complaint is received and should be completed as quickly as possible. At a minimum, the investigative process should include interviews with the victim, the alleged harasser, and all witnesses identified by either party. It also requires that copious notes documenting the investigative procedures and all results should be made and kept in an investigation file separate from employee personnel files. The company must report the results of the investigation in a timely manner to the employee who made the complaint.

The courts have emphasized that agencies must use care to prevent and correct sexual harassment. The courts have mandated that employers must establish, disseminate, and enforce an antiharassment policy and complaint procedures and take other reasonable steps to prevent and correct harassment. Further, they have said, employers must create multiple reporting channels, stop harassment once it starts, have follow-up procedures in place, and ensure that no tangible job benefits are withdrawn from a harassed employee.[78]

Employee Monitoring

Recent technology enables employers to monitor many aspects of their employees' jobs, particularly on telephones and computer terminals, through electronic and voice mail, and on the Internet. When they conduct **employee monitoring**, employers, unless employer policy dictates otherwise, may listen, watch, and read most of an employee's workplace communications.[79]

Monitoring Phone Calls

Employers may monitor calls with clients or customers for reasons of quality control. Federal law allows unannounced monitoring for business-related calls. However, when an employer realizes a call is personal, he or she must immediately stop monitoring the call, but when employees are told not to make personal calls from specified business phones, the employee takes the risk that calls on those phones may be monitored. Telephone numbers dialed from business extensions can be recorded by a "pen register," which allow the employer to see a list of phone numbers dialed and the length of each call. This information may be used to evaluate the amount of time spent by employees with clients.

Monitoring Computer Use

Employers can use computer software that enables them to see what is on the screen or stored in an employee's computer terminal and hard disks. They can also monitor Internet usage, such as web surfing and e-mail. Some companies also

employee monitoring The monitoring of employees' phone and e-mail usage by an employer.

use **keystroke monitoring systems** that record how many keystrokes per hour an employee is performing. Another computer-monitoring tool allows employers to keep track of the amount of time an employee spends away from the computer or idle time at the terminal.

According to a 2006 survey, more than 38 percent of companies employ staff to read or analyze outbound e-mail. Close to a third of all companies have fired an employee and more than half have disciplined an employee in the past year for violating an e-mail policy. About 80 percent of companies have a written e-mail policy.[80]

Employers own the computer network and the terminals and thus are free to use them to monitor employees. Sometimes, however, union contracts in collective bargaining procedures may limit the employers' right to monitor, and the Fourth Amendment prohibition against unreasonable search and seizure may apply to public sector employees.

Employees should realize that electronic and voice mail systems retain messages in memory even after they have been deleted. They are often permanently backed up on magnetic tape, along with other important computer data.

Employee-Misconduct Investigations

Often, employers must conduct internal investigations of employee misconduct. These investigations must be for legitimate business purposes or else they can become a source of corporate liability if it is later found they were initiated for an improper motive or if the investigative procedures or results are mishandled. These investigations may include misconduct relating to an employee's job performance when it is against company policy and subject to discipline as defined in employer's codes of conduct or in collective bargaining agreements; financial misdeeds or other misuse of company assets; abusive behavior toward supervisors, coworkers, or business contracts; current drug or alcohol use; violation of federal, state, or local laws and regulations; violations of pre-existing written employers' policies; or noncompliance with the rules of self-regulatory organizations overseeing the employer's business.

John Goemaat, an employment and labor attorney, writes that in order to minimize the risks of problems in an investigation, it must be conducted in a professional manner through agents of the employer who are well trained and aware of the legal standards involved. He says these investigations must be conducted properly to respect the interests of the complainant, witnesses, and the accused and to avoid potential liability.[81]

Goemaat writes that among the laws that apply to **employee-misconduct investigations** are the general federal and state antidiscrimination laws that protect employees from termination of employment because of characteristics that include their race, gender, national origin, religion, age, disability or handicap, sexual preference or orientation, and marital status. A decision to conduct an investigation may be challenged if it appears to be based on one of these protected characteristics.

Collective bargaining agreements can also affect an employer's right to investigate. Employees can challenge an investigation that has employed techniques contrary to the provisions of the labor agreement or contract. For example, the National Labor Relations Board has ruled that investigative techniques or procedures that a company might use on union members who are employees are a mandatory subject of collective bargaining.

Goemaat also noted that certain types of internal investigations are mandated by law, for example, harassment charges. When an employee alleges harassment based on a characteristic protected by antidiscrimination laws (for example, sexual harassment, as discussed earlier in the chapter), the employer must prove to the court that it did not condone such harassment, that it had a policy against it, and that it took action to prevent or correct the harassment.

Investigations of employee misconduct during off-duty hours may present significant problems, and the employer must ensure that it is following state law in these cases. Some of these issues may relate to alcohol and tobacco use and political activities.

Recent amendments to the FCRA, known as the Fair and Accurate Credit Transactions Act of

---

keystroke monitoring system Automated system that records how many and which keystrokes an employee is performing on the computer.

employee-misconduct investigation An internal investigation into allegations of employee misconduct, which, if warranted, could result in the employee's termination, criminal prosecution, or other disciplinary measures.

2003 or FACTA, set a new standard for employee-misconduct investigations. FACTA affects investigations by a third party that an employer may hire to investigate employee misconduct. This section was adopted to make it clear that, as opposed to background investigations, employers do not have to get permission to conduct a misconduct investigation.[82]

FACTA ensures that an employer does not need to give notice or to get permission to conduct a misconduct investigation if it hires an outside party, such as law firms or other investigators, to conduct the investigation. However, employees covered by collective bargaining agreements may still have the right to file a grievance for adverse personnel actions, and their union may be entitled to some disclosure of investigative results during grievance and arbitration proceedings. Terminated employees may also bring agency or court actions challenging their termination and be entitled to discovery of the information on which the employer made its decision.

Homeland Security and Employment-Related Security

Employment-related security is extremely important for continued homeland security. All DHS employees, as well as all federal, state, and local government employees, are carefully and thoroughly subjected to pre-employment background screening and continual screening to discover any conditions in their lives that may impact the quality of the work they perform. In addition, nongovernment persons working as temporary employees, private contractors, volunteers, or vendors for these critical homeland security functions are carefully screened. The screening not only produces the best employees with the best histories of past employment and the absence of criminal histories but also ensures that these people are loyal to the United States of America and not in sympathy with terrorists or others seeking to destroy the quality of American lives.

Critical infrastructure facilities, including utilities, are particularly vulnerable to homeland security threats. As one example, Americans consume more than 340 billion gallons of water each day, according to the American Water Works Association, and although there has never been a confirmed terrorist attack on a water utility, the industry is vulnerable. At Aqua America, which provides water for more than 2.5 million residents of thirteen states, employees are subject to background screening during the hiring process.[83]

In its "Preemployment Background Screening Guidelines" issued in 2006, ASIS International recommends that background screening procedures should involve the checking of terrorist watch lists. They suggest that employers check with Interpol and the U.S. Treasury's Office of Foreign Assets Control.[84]

The Private Security Officer Employment Authorization Act of 2004, discussed in Chapter 1 of this text, increased the ability of private security employers to perform background checks by giving them the opportunity to request FBI criminal background checks on persons applying for or holding positions as private security officers.

Since 9/11, background investigations, including pre-employment and ongoing screening, have increased exponentially in the private sector to ensure that its workers are as qualified as government-sector employees.

Summary

- Employee-related security includes background investigations, including pre-employment screening and other background investigations, employment-related drug testing or drug screening, sexual harassment in the workplace, employee monitoring, and employee-misconduct investigations.

- The Privacy Rights Clearinghouse, located in San Diego, California, reports that employers must investigate potential and current workers for several reasons, including the fact that negligent hiring lawsuits are on the rise. If an employee's actions hurt someone, the employer may be liable. A bad hiring decision can wreak havoc on a company's budget and reputation.

■ Our current information age has made employment-related security and investigations easier to conduct with the availability of computer databases containing millions of records of personal data.

■ It is legal for job applicants, existing employees, and volunteers to be asked to submit to background checks. For some jobs, background screening is required by federal or state law.

■ Employers conducted 4.4 million pre-employment background checks in the latest reportable year. This number is three times higher than the number conducted just eight years ago. The number of checks has been increasing due to the realities of 9/11, increased federal scrutiny of corporate governance, and a desire by companies to avoid ethics breaches.

■ The federal Fair Credit Reporting Act (FCRA) sets national standards for employment screening. However, the law only applies to background checks performed by an outside company, called a consumer reporting agency, under the FCRA. The law, however, does not apply in situations where the employer itself conducts background checks in-house. Whenever a company plans to use a credit report in a hiring decision, it must follow the requirements of the FCRA.

■ Numerous reports over the past decade by government organizations, such as the U.S. Department of Health and Human Service's Substance Abuse and Mental Health Services Administration (SAMHSA), the National Institute on Drug Abuse, the U.S. Department of Labor, and numerous others, indicate that substance abuse is a serious problem in the workplace. Substance-abusing workers have been found to be less productive and have higher absenteeism rates, higher worker's compensation claims, higher turnover rates, and higher accident rates than those who do not abuse drugs. Other costs of drug abuse in the workplace are diverted supervisory and managerial time, friction among workers, damage to equipment, poor decisions, and damage to the company's public image.

■ Workplace-related drug testing or drug screening is completely legal. The Federal 1998 Drug-Free Workplace Act was passed to provide employers and employees with the right to work in a drug-free workplace.

■ Sexual harassment can be defined as unwarranted and unwelcome sexual attention and is a serious social problem.

■ The U.S. Supreme Court has decided several cases on sexual harassment in the workplace in the past few decades. The general rule the Court has established is that employers can be held liable for both actual sexual harassment in the workplace and hostile environment sexual harassment.

■ Employers, unless employer policy dictates otherwise, may listen, watch, and read most of an employee's workplace communications, including phone calls and computer use.

■ Often, employers must conduct internal investigations of employee misconduct. These investigations must be for legitimate business purposes or else they can become a source of corporate liability if it is later found that they were initiated for an improper motive or if the investigative procedures or results are mishandled. These investigations may include misconduct relating to an employee's job performance when it is against company policy and subject to discipline as defined in employer's codes of conduct or in collective bargaining agreements; financial misdeeds or other misuse of company assets; abusive behavior toward supervisors, coworkers, or business contracts; current drug or alcohol use; violation of federal, state, or local laws and regulations; violations of pre-existing written employers' policies; or noncompliance with the rules of self-regulatory organizations overseeing the employer's business.

Learning Check

1. Describe some of the reasons why it is important to conduct employment-related security testing.

2. Name and discuss the major forms of employment-related security.

3. Identify and discuss the basic information that is verified in a pre-employment background investigation.

4. What is the Fair Credit Reporting Act? How does it affect pre-employment background investigations?

5. Is employment-related drug testing legal? If so, under what conditions could an employer require an employee to submit to drug testing?

6. Discuss the extent of drug screening in industry.

7. Define *sexual harassment*. What law affects sexual harassment in the workplace?

8. Describe the steps you would take to investigate an allegation of sexual harassment at your business.

9. Name some of the ways that employees may have their workplace communications monitored. Discuss how this can be done. Is this legal? Discuss why it is legal or not.

10. Do employees need to be notified by their employers that they are subject to investigation of their possible employee misconduct? Discuss your answer.

Application Exercise

You are the regional manager of pre-employment background investigations for a major contract security services company. Your company is under consideration to be hired by a large hospital in your area to conduct background investigations of all personnel they intend to hire. The hospital administrator tells you that the hospital has suffered significant liability damages in the past for misconduct and unprofessional conduct committed by employees. Several employees last year were arrested by the local police on charges of drug sales, drug possession, driving while intoxicated, and larceny. In addition, the hospital is suffering significant losses in its cafeteria and gift shop operations.

The hospital administrator asks you to prepare a brief report for her detailing the type of pre-employment background investigations you will perform if hired.

Web Exercise

Surf the Internet and find some pre-employment screening services agencies in your local area. Contact two of them and find out the extent of the background information they screen for and the price they charge for their services.

Key Terms

adverse action, p. 214
background investigations, p. 207
consumer report information, p. 214
consumer reporting agency (CRA), p. 213
consumer credit reports, p. 213
credit bureau, p. 214
Defense Personnel Security Research Center (PERSEREC), p. 209
drug testing or drug screening, p. 222
employee monitoring, p. 228
Employee Polygraph Protection Act (EPPA), p. 217
employment-related security, p. 208
employment-misconduct investigations, p. 229
Fair Credit Reporting Act (FCRA), p. 213
Federal Drug-Free Workplace Act, p. 222
hostile environment sexual harassment, p. 226
keystroke monitoring system, p. 229
multistate criminal records databases, p. 217
negligent hiring, p. 209
negligent retention, p. 209
polygraph examination, p. 217
pre-employment background screening, p. 211
sexual harassment, p. 225
sexual harassment in the workplace, p. 226
sexual offender, p. 216
vetting, p. 210

Information and Computer Security

©Tek Image/Photo Researchers, Inc.

GOALS

- To introduce you to the many security problems associated with the use of computers in business and at home.
- To alert you to the many forms of cybercrime and cyberproblems.
- To familiarize you with the methods used by organizations today to control and regulate computer use and maintain security.
- To show you how investigators investigate computer crime.
- To introduce you to methods that you can use to maintain the security and integrity of computer use.
- To discuss homeland security and information and computer security.

Introduction

Computer technology has facilitated the speed and ease of business transactions, personal communications, and information sharing as well as lowering their costs, but it has also enabled sophisticated criminals and others to tap into these legitimate uses and victimize computer users and society itself.[1] Consider these recent incidents:

- In 2006, a U.S. Congressman from Florida, Mark Foley, was forced to resign from his position after it was disclosed that he had sent a series of sexually explicit e-mail and text messages to congressional pages.[2]

- Also in 2006, a deputy press secretary for the U.S. Department of Homeland Security was charged with using a computer to seduce a child. The official had found a teenager's profile online and began having sexually explicit conversations with her on the Internet. He also sent her pornographic movie clips and instructed her to perform a sexual act while thinking of him.[3]

- In 2005, a series of vicious and hate-filled e-mail messages calling for violence flooded French cyberspace. These messages preceded the worst series of riots and public disorder in recent French history. Some of these messages stated: "Go to the nearest police station and burn it." "I want to kill the cops." "God bless France, because war is about to begin." "All the housing projects should rise. The wait is over. Friday, November 11, a meeting under the Eiffel Tower. At 2 P.M. Show up, it's important."[4]

- In 2005, a U.S. Department of Justice report indicated that crooks have recently sent phony e-mails, including claiming to be FBI agents asking for help in an identity theft case; claiming to be a bank director from London offering access to money left behind by someone murdered in the London terrorist bombings; and claiming to be representatives of charities involved in helping the victims of hurricanes Katrina and Rita.[5]

- A 2005 poll of information technology (IT) security professionals revealed that a third of large enterprises had been victims of intrusions to their office networks and office servers in the last two years, although more than 92 percent of these firms have installed a network firewall. Forty percent of very large companies having 20,000 or more employees indicated they had fallen victim to hackers during the same time period.[6]

- In 2003, one identity theft ring, by itself, was charged with stealing identities from at least 30,000 people and using them to make tens of millions of dollars in profit. In that year also, about 9.9 million people were victimized by identity thieves, businesses and financial institutions suffered about $48 billion in losses because of identity theft, and victimized consumers paid more than $5 billion in out-of-pocket expenses to regain their financial identities.[7]

- A computer financial news service advised investors that a California manufacturer of fiberoptic communications equipment planned to restate its earnings for the last two years and that its chief operating officer had resigned. Investors rushed to sell their

The Computer Crime Problem in Business and Society

Growing criminal use of the computer has caused significant harm to U.S. businesses, as the following surveys show.

- In a survey of two-hundred companies, more than 25 percent reported they had suffered data loss from a computer virus in the last year. More than 70 percent indicated they currently used virus detection systems. In addition, 15 percent reported hacking attempts; 10 percent, system intrusion; 7 percent, data alteration or defacing; and 4 percent, data theft.[12]

- A 2004 survey, by the National Cyber Security Alliance (NCSA) and the Internet service provider America Online, of adults using either dial-up or broadband Internet access found that although 77 percent of those surveyed thought they were either "very safe" or "somewhat safe" from online threats, 67 percent did not have currently updated antivirus software. Actually, it was determined that 80 percent of the computers of the persons surveyed were infected with spyware, and almost 20 percent of the machines had viruses. The study also determined that two-thirds of all the computer users surveyed did not have firewall protection, and more than half

shares, and the stock plunged from $103 to $45 in fifteen minutes. The drop stripped more than $2 billion from the company's market valuation before the NASDAQ stock market halted trading in the stock at about 10:30 A.M. The freefall dragged down stocks of several companies in similar businesses and the NASDAQ as well. The report was false.[8]

■ A 15-year-old New Jersey schoolboy racked up almost $273,000 in illegal gains by buying penny stocks and then hyping them up in a barrage of false e-mail messages to various web bulletin boards that made the stocks seem hot. He sold the stocks as soon as the price rose.[9]

■ A 45-year-old Louisiana woman was charged by the St. Tammany's Parish sheriff's office with trying to turn her 11-year-old daughter into an Internet porn star—doping the child and training her to perform sex shows for cyberpedophiles. Among the evidence were e-mails in which the woman boasted how she fed the girl Valium and White Russians to relax her inhibitions in front of the camera.[10]

■ The Love Bug virus caused billions of dollars in damage around the world, mostly to big corporations that were forced to shut down their internal communications to stamp it out. It came as an e-mail titled "ILOVEYOU" with an attachment that, if opened, infected the computer and e-mailed itself to everyone in the user's Microsoft Outlook address book. Later that year, the "Pokey" virus hit. The cartoon character mutated on the web and spread itself via e-mails, wrecking PCs it got into by wiping out their system files. Kids were the targets of this virus. It appeared as an e-mail with the title "Pikachu Pokemon" and the message "Pikachu is your friend."[11]

After reading about these incidents, you may think that criminals have taken over the Internet and we are all facing doom. The good news, though, is that computer crime can be investigated, the persons who commit these crimes can be prosecuted, and with proper knowledge and precautions, we can protect ourselves from computer crime.

This chapter will introduce you to the many security problems associated with the use of computers in business and at home and to the methods used to maintain the security and integrity of computer use. It will cover many forms of cybercrime and cyberproblems, including fraud, identity theft, cyberterrorism, web attacks, computer hacking, cyberstalking, computer use by pedophiles, computer viruses, spam, spyware, software piracy, and data security. It will familiarize you with the many types of computer viruses and other computer assaults and show how people and businesses can protect themselves from such attacks. The chapter will also cover the methods organizations use to maintain computer security and methods used by investigators to investigate computer crime. It will also discuss homeland security in relation to information and computer security.

said they did not understand what a computer firewall is or how it works. (A firewall, either software or hardware, protects a computer from unauthorized access over a network).[13] The NCSA is a public–private partnership focused on promoting cybersecurity and safe behavior online and providing awareness and response to pressing cybersecurity issues. Its website provides information needed to secure one's computer; tips on how to safeguard a system; a self-guided cyber security test; and educational materials and other Internet resources to empower home users, small businesses, schools, and universities to stay safe online.[14]

Computer crime problems have also plagued the U.S. government.[15] In 2000, more than a quarter of the government's major agencies failed a computer security review, showing significant problems in allowing unauthorized access to sensitive information. The auditors were successful in almost every test in readily gaining unauthorized access that would allow intruders to read, modify, or delete data for whatever purpose they had in mind.[16]

In addition to causing problems for business and government, computer crime affects the fabric of life in the United States. Almost every day, in almost every newspaper in the country, there are stories of children being propositioned by pedophiles on the net, people being stalked by predators on the net, and other such problems.

Computer technology generally overtakes itself with a new generation about once every three years. Meanwhile, increasingly sophisticated and

JOBS IN SECURITY

Information and Computer Security Positions

SPECIALIST—SYSTEM/DATA SECURITY

The Bank of America employs a specialist in system/data security. Responsibilities include electronic data recovery and cybercrime investigations. Data-recovery duties include coordination with bank associates, outside legal counsel, and regulators that require access to electronic data. Investigative duties include coordinating high-tech cybercrime investigations related to, or directed against, the bank network from both internal and external sources and facilitating coordination with law enforcement, regulators, corporate security, and corporate audit to ensure investigative issues are resolved completely.

Qualifications include significant experience associated with cybercrime investigations and the forensic recovery of electronic data and qualification to testify as an expert in the processes to recover and search electronic data while maintaining the integrity of the original version of the data. Also required is experience in the time and resource management of an incident response team required to respond to provide investigative experience 24/7 and experience in the investigation of hacking and other unauthorized activity that might occur on a global network.

INFORMATION SECURITY ANALYST

The Children's Hospital of Philadelphia employs an information security analyst. Responsibilities include the overall development and implementation of identified information security solutions, developing security event monitoring strategies, conducting security investigations, monitoring designated systems, coaching and developing IS personnel, and working directly with IS clients to identify and reduce security risks.

Requirements are three years of related field experience and knowledge of information security regulations, standards, and leading practices. Must be proficient with Windows, UNIX, Lawson, and Clinical Applications and have knowledge of information systems risk-management practices, including system management and change control practices. A bachelor's degree in a related field and certification as an Information System Auditor, Information Security Manager, or Information Systems Security Professional are preferred.

SOURCES: High Technology Crime Investigation Association, "Job Bulletins." Retrieved October 31, 2004, from http://www.htcia.org/job-bulletins/jb_bofa.htm; and Information Systems Security Association, "Careers." Retrieved October 31, 2004, from http://www.issa.org/careers/opps/chop.html.

computer-literate criminals employ new technologies virtually as soon as they appear. Government and industry have attempted to deal with these problems. As one example, working in partnership with federal, state, local, and international law enforcement agencies, the U.S. Department of Justice has developed the National Cybercrime Training Partnership (NCTP). The NCTP works with all levels of law enforcement to develop and promote a long-range strategy for high-tech police work in the twenty-first century, to improve public and political understanding of technology problems and solutions, and to ensure that technology solutions are fully implemented.[17]

The spread of the wireless data technology known as **Wi-Fi** has reshaped the way millions of Americans go online, letting them tap into high-speed Internet connections at home and in many public places. Sophisticated criminals use the unsecured Wi-Fi networks of unsuspecting consumers and businesses to help cover their actions in cyberspace and hack into neighbors' networks.[18] A 2005 study reported that 14 percent of wireless network owners have accessed their neighbors' connection, and anecdotal evidence suggests more and more people are logging on for free.[19]

The cybercrime problem does not only affect the United States; cybercrime occurs in every nation in the world and can involve transnational operations using information and communication technologies. The Internet operates without borders and provides a vehicle to criminals to ply their trade across national borders; cybercrime knows no borders. The global proliferation of new

Wi-Fi Stands for Wireless Fidelity, a brand originally licensed by the Wi-Fi Alliance to describe the embedded technology of wireless local area networks (WLAN).

Top Ten Security Tips for Computer Users

10. Never give out your social security number, online or off. This information in the wrong hands is a license to steal.
9. Use a paper shredder. Don't just throw out unsolicited credit card applications. Shred them.
8. Don't use the same password over and over. Make new variations.
7. Watch your laptop at the airport. Be especially careful at passenger screening stations, which is where most laptop thefts occur.
6. Keep your antivirus software up to date. Hackers never rest. Every e-mail attachment can contain a possible virus, so scan it before you open it.
5. Use the latest versions and software patches for your e-mail and your browser. New security loopholes are constantly being discovered.
4. Don't accept cookies. If you have to, delete them when you are finished surfing.
3. Use a password to log onto your computer. Most operating systems let you set a password. It's a good idea to establish such a password and to change it regularly.
2. Turn off your computer when you are not using it. It's the only sure way to keep hackers out.
1. Never send an e-mail that you wouldn't want your spouse, or your boss, to read.

Source: John R. Quain, "Top Ten Security Tips," *Newsday*, August 16, 2000, pp. C16, C17.

information and communication technologies has spawned even more forms of computer-related crimes that threaten the confidentiality, integrity, and availability of computer systems, as well as the critical infrastructure of every nation on the globe. Variations in the levels and degrees of technological adaptation to the computer age have created a "digital divide" that makes some regions more vulnerable to cybercrime than others.[20]

Many experts believe that new levels of investigative expertise are required to trace criminal activity and its effects through a myriad variety of Internet service providers (ISPs) and across national borders. Dealing with transnational cybercrime is a challenge that must be handled by international cooperation, particularly regarding legal, procedural, and regulatory accords and academic, law enforcement, and private-sector participation that transcends national borders.

Exhibit 9.1 offers the top ten security tips for computer users.

Cybercrime and Cyberproblems

There are many definitions of computer crime or **cybercrime** (see Exhibit 9.2 on page 239). L. E. Quarantiello defines computer crime as "any illegal act in which knowledge of computer technology is used to commit the offense."[21] Martin L. Forst defines cybercrime as "all illegal activities that are committed by or with the aid of computers or information technology or in which computers are the targets of the criminal enterprise."[22] The Business Software Alliance (BSA) defines cybercrime as,

> Any illegal behavior directed by means of electronic operations that targets the security of computer systems and the data processed by them. In a wider sense, "computer-related crime" can be any illegal behavior committed by means of, or in relation to, a computer system or network, however, this is not cyber-crime.[23]

The BSA is a professional organization dedicated to promoting a safe and legal digital world. It represents the world's commercial software industry and its hardware partners before governments and in the international marketplace. BSA fosters technology innovation through education and policy initiatives that promote cyber security, copyright protection, trade, and e-commerce.[24]

Cybercrime falls into three categories: (1) a computer is the target of criminal activity; (2) the computer is the tool used or is integral to the commission of the crime; and (3) the computer is only an incidental aspect of the crime. Cybercrime is a relatively new phenomenon and affects services such as telecommunications, banking and finance, transportation, electrical energy, water supply, emergency services, and government operations that depend on computers for control, management, and interaction among themselves.[25] Cybercrime would be impossible without the Internet. Most businesses in the United States have Internet sites, and over half of them conduct electronic commerce on the Internet.

The Cyber-Crime and Intellectual Property Theft program of the Business Software Alliance collects and disseminates data and research on six categories of cybercrime that directly impact

cybercrime An illegal act committed through the use of computer technology.

YOU CAN CLICK BUT YOU CAN'T HIDE

I | ILLEGAL DOWNLOADING
Inappropriate for All Ages

If you think you can get away with illegally swapping movies, you're wrong. Illegally trafficking in movies is not just a dirty little secret between you and your computer. You leave a trail. The message is simple: if you are downloading copyrighted movies without proper authorization, you are breaking the law. You face serious consequences if you illegally swap movies. The only way not to get caught is to stop.

Pursuant to the Copyright Act (17 U.S.C. Section 504(c)), statutory damages can be as much as $30,000 per motion picture, and up to $150,000 per motion picture if the infringement is willful.

© 2004 Motion Picture Association of America, Inc.

©Michael Newman/PhotoEdit

Cyberpiracy can be defined as the act of copying copyrighted material and/or the use of the Internet to market or distribute creative works protected by copyright. Piracy has become a major concern for the music, television, and movie industries, which are especially vulnerable to the illegal distribution of their products, and recently they have instituted more proactive efforts to stop piracy.

citizens and consumers, and educates these groups on the scope and depth of the problem, as well as current policies and research aimed at addressing the issue. The categories of cybercrime it addresses are financial, piracy, hacking, cyberterrorism, online pornography, and cybercrime in schools.[26]

According to a report by the Bureau of Justice Statistics of the U.S. Department of Justice, the Computer Security Survey conducted by the Bureau of Justice Statistics and the U.S. Census Bureau revealed that 74 percent of businesses reported being a victim of cybercrime. Nearly two-thirds of the businesses had been victimized by a computer virus; a quarter had experienced denial-of-service attacks, such as the degradation of Internet connections due to excessive amounts of incoming information; and about a fifth reported that their computer systems had been vandalized or sabotaged.[27]

This section will discuss some of the most common crimes and problems on the Internet, including

fraud, identity theft, cyberterrorism, web attacks, computer hacking, cyberstalking, computer use by pedophiles, computer viruses, spam, spyware, software privacy, and data security, and some of the methods being used by law enforcement and businesses to deal with these problems.

Fraud

The Internet presents many opportunities for various types of fraud, particularly securities fraud. Because of the Internet's amorphous nature, companies are more susceptible to insider trading and dissemination of misinformation on it that can undermine an orderly market.[28]

In an attempt to deal with these problems, accounting firms are increasingly hiring former law enforcement people to investigate computer crime and are establishing forensic units (scientific examination of evidence) and investigative services units.[29]

In 2000, the FBI teamed up with the U.S. Department of Justice and the National White Collar Crime Center to establish the Internet Fraud Complaint Center to address fraud committed over the Internet and to serve as a vehicle to receive, develop, and refer criminal complaints regarding cybercrime. In 2003, the Internet Fraud Complaint Center was renamed the **Internet Crime Complaint Center (IC3).** The IC3 provides victims a convenient and easy-to-use reporting mechanism that alerts authorities to suspected criminal or civil violations. IC3 also offers law enforcement and regulatory agencies a central repository for complaints about Internet crime, works to quantify patterns, and provides timely statistical data of current fraud trends. This site lets those who have been bilked online to register a complaint with law enforcement. Analysts reviewing a complaint determine its jurisdiction, conduct necessary investigative work, and distribute the information to the appropriate law enforcement agencies. Through such online reporting, the IC3 tracks trends and new fraud schemes.[30]

The Internet Crime Complaint Center's 2005 report, *IC3 2004 Internet Fraud Crime Report*, indicated that Internet auction fraud was by far the most reported offense, comprising over 71 percent

Internet Crime Complaint Center (IC3) Department of Justice and National White Collar Crime Center reporting mechanism that addresses fraud committed over the Internet and serves as a vehicle to receive, develop, and refer criminal complaints regarding cybercrime.

EXHIBIT 9.2   **Cybercrime Definitions**

Computer virus A hidden fragment of computer code that propagates by inserting itself into or modifying other programs.

Cyberterrorism The effect of acts of hacking designed to cause terror. Like conventional terrorism, its intent is to cause violence against persons or property or at least cause enough harm to generate fear.

Denial of service The disruption or degradation of an Internet connection or e-mail service that results in an interruption of the normal flow of information. Denial of service is usually caused by other events, such as ping attacks, port scanning probes, and excessive amounts of incoming data.

Embezzlement The unlawful misappropriation of money or other things of value by the person to whom it was entrusted (typically an employee) for his or her own use or purpose.

Financial cybercrime Crimes that disrupt businesses' ability to conduct e-commerce (or electronic commerce).

Fraud The intentional misrepresentation of information or identity to deceive others, the unlawful use of a credit/debit card or ATM, or the use of electronic means to transmit deceptive information in order to obtain money or other things of value. Fraud may be committed by someone inside or outside the company.

Hacking The act of gaining unauthorized access to a computer system or network and in some cases, making unauthorized use of this access. Hacking is also the act by which other forms of cybercrime (for example, fraud, terrorism) are committed.

Online pornography Using the Internet as a medium to violate 18 USC 2252 and 18 USC 2252A, Possessing or Distributing Child Pornography, or 47 USC 223, Distributing Pornography of Any Form to a Minor.

Phishing or spoofing The sending of e-mail messages to members of online payment accounts, such as banks, credit-card companies, and online payment services, to update their records. In the spoofed or phished phony message, account holders are warned that failure to update the records will result in account suspension. Recipients are asked to update their e-mail address, credit-card number and expiration date, billing address, phone number, birth date, and mother's maiden name. The recipient is then automatically transferred to an "updating your account screen," which resembles the screens provided by the legitimate company. If a recipient enters information, it is sent on to a criminal operation.

Piracy The act of copying copyrighted material; the use of the Internet to market or distribute creative works protected by copyright.

Theft of proprietary information The illegal obtaining of designs, plans, blueprints, codes, computer programs, formulas, recipes, trade secrets, graphics, copyrighted material, data, forms, files, lists, and personal or financial information, usually by electronic copying.

Vandalism or sabotage The deliberate or malicious damage, defacement, destruction, or other alteration of electronic files, data, web pages, and programs.

SOURCES: Ramona R. Rantala, *Cybercrime against Businesses* (Washington, DC: U.S. Department of Justice, Bureau of Justice Statistics, 2004), p. 8; Business Software Alliance, "Cybercrime." Retrieved October 26, 2004, from http://www.global.bsa.org/cybercrime/cybercrimes; and Alice Dragoon, "Foiling Phishing." Retrieved October 29, 2004, from http://www.csoonline.com/read/100104/phish.html.

---

of referred complaints. Among those complaints that reported a dollar loss, the highest median dollar losses were found among check fraud ($3,600), Nigerian letter fraud ($3,000), and confidence fraud ($1,000). The report also indicated that almost 75 percent of offenders and 67 percent of victims were male and that e-mail and web pages were the two primary mechanisms by which the fraudulent contact took place.[31]

As one example of a successful investigation, the FBI launched a major investigation of the Internet auction site eBay after a Sacramento lawyer tried to bid up the cost of a painting he had offered for sale by using at least five different Internet names to make bids. Self-bidding, also known as shill bidding, is forbidden by eBay rules and is illegal in the traditional auction world. Participation in a shill-bidding ring is a violation of federal laws prohibiting mail fraud and wire fraud.[32]

Chapter 10 of this textbook will discuss numerous types of fraud, including credit-card fraud, insurance fraud, and medical and healthcare fraud, much of which is committed through the Internet.

Identity Theft

Although **identity theft** is not new—criminals have been doing it for ages—the Internet is making it one of the signature crimes of the digital era. Websites sell all sorts of personal information, and

identity theft The criminal act of assuming another person's identity.

You Are There!

Some Types of Internet Auction Fraud

■ *Failure to deliver:* A buyer pays for an item but never receives it from the seller. About 80 to 90 percent of the complaints the Federal Trade Commission receives pertain to this kind of fraud.

■ *Misrepresentation:* A buyer receives an item that is less valuable than what was described.

■ *Shill bidding:* A seller or an associate, posing as a buyer, places a fake bid intended to drive up prices.

Source: Deborah Kong, "Internet Auction Fraud Increases," *USA Today*, June 23, 2000, p. B3.

by using that information, criminals can acquire credit and make purchases.[33]

In 2006, the U.S. Bureau of Justice Statistics reported that 3.6 million households, representing 3 percent of households in the United States, discovered that at least one member of the household had been the victim of identity theft during the previous six months. These cases of identity theft involved authorized use or attempted use of existing credit cards; unauthorized use or attempted use of other existing accounts, such as checking accounts; and misuse of personal information to obtain new accounts or loans or to commit other crimes. The estimated loss reported by the victims totaled $3.2 billion, and the average loss was $1,290.[34]

The U.S. Department of Justice defines identity theft and identity fraud as those types of crimes in which someone wrongfully obtains and uses another individual's personal data in a way that involves fraud or deception, typically for economic gain.[35] The Identity Theft and Assumption Deterrence Act of 1998[36] made identity theft a federal crime and enabled law enforcement agencies to investigate identity-theft crimes and the associated fraud that often results. The Identity Theft Penalty Enhancement Act of 2004[37] added aggravated and terrorism provisions to the law and increased sentences for violating it.

dumpster diving Scavenging through garbage to retrive personal identification material.

Analysts say that several factors combine to made identity theft a hard crime to deter, including the growth of the Internet, e-commerce, and digital finance; expanding consumer credit worldwide; the fragmentated nature of local and federal law enforcement; and the inadequate regulations governing the credit industry. Anyone can be targeted by identity thieves, including children and the dead. A growing number of thieves now assume the identity of entire companies, adopting the companies' employer identification numbers to secure commercial loans, corporate leases, or expensive products.

The Federal Trade Commission (FTC) provides a website for information on how to proceed and file an identity theft complaint. The site also has links to useful information from other federal agencies, states, and consumer organizations. The information provided to this site becomes part of a secure database that law enforcement officials across the nation use to help stop identity thieves. It also has a toll-free identity-theft hotline.[38]

The targets of identity thieves are often creditworthy consumers whose financial status may be assumed from the specific neighborhoods in which they live. The stolen identities can then be used to apply for driver's licenses, telephone numbers, car loans, and charge cards. They can also be used to steal benefits, such as pensions and social security payments.[39]

Identity thieves use a variety of tactics to obtain personal information. Besides the simple act of stealing a wallet or purse, they scavenge garbage, steal mail, and read credit reports and personnel records by using the Internet to access computerized personal information. The following are some of the common ways these thieves have worked:

■ *Dumpster diving:* Identity thieves scavenge through garbage to retrieve discarded material of value. They obtain account numbers, addresses, and dates of birth from financial, medical, and personal records, all of which can be used to assume an identity.

■ *Mail theft*: Identity thieves check mailboxes, looking not only for new mail but also for paid bills or credit-card payments that people leave in their mailboxes for the postal carrier to collect. They use information from these items to obtain credit or purchase products and services in the victim's name. Also, by working with cooperative postal employees, they can steal mail from mail processing areas. Identity thieves can

You Are There!

These Are Identity Thieves

In 2000, two people were arrested in Queens, New York, for using mail they had stolen from thousands of homes in Queens and Long Island neighborhoods to help them steal more than $1.5 million from banks and credit-card companies. For eighteen months, starting in 1998, the two combed through hundreds of thousands of pieces of mail to retrieve credit-card applications, checks, and personal information like social security numbers and driver's license numbers. They set up a computer database of all the information they collected, applied for credit cards, and cashed stolen checks. A list of two-thousand names was found in the computer database.

Identity-theft crimes involving the postal system have been increasing rapidly.

SOURCE: Edward Wong, "Two Charged in $1.5 Million Mail-Theft Scheme," *New York Times*, June 8, 2000, p. B8

also attempt to complete a change-of-address card in order to divert a victim's mail to a rented mailbox.

▪ *Internal access:* Identity thieves can obtain personal information illegally from a computer connected to a credit reporting bureau or from an employee accessing a company's database that contains personal identification information.[40]

The latest technique in identity theft is phishing or spoofing. **Phishing** or **spoofing** involves the sending of e-mail messages to members of online payment accounts, such as banks, credit-card companies, and online payment services, to update their records. In the spoofed or phished phony message, account holders are warned that failure to update the records will result in account suspension. Recipients are asked to update their e-mail addresses, credit-card number and expiration date, billing address, phone number, birth date, and mother's maiden name. The recipient is then automatically transferred to an "updating your account screen," which resembles the screens provided by the legitimate company. If a recipient enters information, it is sent on to a criminal operation, which might access the account to send spam, steal the person's identity,

make fraudulent purchases, or otherwise falsely use another's identity.[41]

The FTC estimates that 75 million to 150 million phishing e-mails are sent every day in the United States and that in 2005, these messages resulted in $920 million in consumer losses and $2 billion in business losses. These losses affected 1.2 million victims.[42]

Phishing and identity theft are not just a problem in the United States. A 2005 report from the Australian Institute of Criminology reported that in February 2005 alone, it detected over 13,000 new distinctive phishing e-mails from over 2,600 separate phishing sites, a dramatic increase from just over 100 in December 2003.[43] Also in 2005, Toronto, Canada, law enforcement officials reported that tens of thousands of bank accounts had been hacked by a "state-of-the-art" identity theft ring capable of churning out near-flawless passports and identification and credit cards.[44]

According to the director of the Privacy Rights Clearinghouse, a nonprofit group, a good percentage of identity theft is caused when people do not destroy unused credit applications or when these are stolen out of the mail.[45]

A survey of identity theft victims conducted by the California Public Interest Research Group and the Privacy Rights Clearinghouse explored the problems that the victims face.[46] According to the survey:

▪ The average victim learned about the identity theft fourteen months after it occurred.

▪ More than half the victims considered their cases to be unsolved at the time of the survey, with their cases having been open an average of forty-four months.

▪ Victims spent an average of 175 hours actively trying to clear their names.

▪ The average total fraudulent charges made on new and existing accounts of survey respondents was $18,000.

▪ Respondents found out about the identity theft in one of two ways: They were denied credit or a loan because of a negative credit report created by fraudulent accounts or a creditor or

phishing or spoofing The sending of fraudulent e-mail messages to members of online payment accounts, such as banks, credit-card companies, and online payment services, to update their records.

debt-collection agency contacted them about lack of payment.

■ Most of the respondents were victimized by "true-name" fraud, in which the thief uses identifying information to open new accounts in the victim's name, or "account takeover," in which the thief makes fraudulent charges to a legitimate existing account.

■ Most victims expressed dissatisfaction with police and credit bureau assistance.

In October 2004, more than forty people in the United States and abroad were charged with operating one of the largest websites ever for trafficking in stolen identity information and credits cards. The site had about 4,000 members who dealt with at least 1.7 million stolen credit-card numbers and caused more than $4 million in losses. The website offered instructions on a variety of crimes, including electronic theft of personal identifying information, credit-card and debit-card fraud, and the production and sale of false identification documents.[47]

Banks have been pressured by government officials to improve their password protection for online banking. In 2005, the Federal Financial Institutions Examination Council, an umbrella group of regulators that includes the Federal Reserve and Federal Deposit Insurance Corporation, told banks that single-factor authentication, such as a user name and password, is not enough to protect against account fraud and identity theft.[48]

In 2006, it was reported that one of the most common forms of identity theft involved illegal immigrants using fraudulent social security numbers to obtain jobs.[49]

ASIS International offers a virtual forum education program on identity theft that discusses new legislation and information for dealing with this problem.[50]

Cyberterrorism

Cyberterrorism involves the use of computer networks, including the Internet, to steal, damage, and

---

PRIVATE SECURITY CONNECTIONS

Professional Resources for Persons Interested in Combatting Identity Theft

Identity Theft Resource Center (ITRC)
Privacy Rights Clearinghouse
U.S. Federal Trade Commission (FTC)
California Public Interest Research Group (CALPIRG)
Credit Reporting Agencies
    Equifax
    Experian (formerly TRW)
    Transunion Corporation

---

alter information. These incidents are on the rise and pose a real and present danger to the United States' **critical information infrastructure.** Sometimes these crimes can be financially motivated, or sometimes a person may attempt to hack into private and government networks for peer recognition or to make a statement. A review of military literature indicates that the critical information infrastructure and the **defense information infrastructure** are under constant, organized, and repetitious attacks from other nations, as well as from within the United States.[51] Control systems for many of our nation's critical infrastructures are computerized, including natural gas distribution and drinking-water systems, and thus are vulnerable to cyberattacks. A cyberattack could bring the nation to a standstill.[52] The U.S. Congress reports that greater coordination among critical infrastructure entities and the government is essential to the security of our nation's control systems.[53]

Louise I. Shelly states that transnational organized crime and terrorist groups have made use of information technology to plan and implement their criminal activities. She states that in our information technology age, messages can be transmitted without leaving a trace; massive wire fund transfers can occur across multiple jurisdictions in an hour, and international plotting can occur within chat rooms and protected communications within a computer system. Even traditional systems of underground banking have been revolutionized by the ability to provide almost instantaneous instructions on the delivery of funds. Both terrorist and transnational criminal organizations have used the full variety of information technology to achieve their desired results, including the

---

cyberterrorism Terrorism that initiates, or threatens to initiate, the exploitation of, or attack on information sources.

critical information infrastructure All control systems for the nation's infrastructure, including utilities, banks, and the like; mostly computerized.

defense information infrastructure All control systems for the nation's defense capability; mostly computerized.

use of cell phones, satellite phones, computers, and virtual private networks.[54]

In 2005, a Philadelphia-based nonprofit organization, the Cyber Incident Detection Data Analysis Center (CIDDAC), developed a new weapon in protecting sensitive electronic data from cyberterrorism. The CIDDAC system can detect a cyberintruder in real time, alert the company or agency immediately, trace the location and the cyberintruder, and alert law enforcement without revealing the name of the victim organization. The type of system not only allows for real-time detection and action but protects the privacy of organizations that would rather not publicize the fact that they were victimized by cyberterrorism.[55]

Web Attacks

Web attacks have been a serious problem on the Internet. For example, over three days in 2000, hackers or cybervandals attacked web giants Yahoo, eBay, CNN, and several others. Users could not connect to these sites or suffered extremely long delays. The attackers used a variation of a so-called "Smurf assault" that resulted in a denial of service. A **denial-of-service (DOS) attack** is a deliberate attempt to shut down a network operation by overloading it. The attack was launched through at least fifty locations. Attackers directed thousands of calls at the computer sites in a very short time, overloading them.[56]

The Computer Security Institute's Computer Crime and Security Survey reported that DOS attacks are the computer security incidents that cost companies the most money. The report found that DOS attacks are often combined with viruses.[57] The Computer Security Institute is a membership association and education provider for the information security community. It helps security professionals protect their organizations' valuable information assets through conferences, seminars, and publications. It produces the Computer Crime and Security Survey in conjunction with the FBI's Computer Intrusion Squad.[58]

Computer Hacking

Computer **hacking** is the willful and malicious penetration of a computer system to achieve some purpose. Once a hacker breaks into the system, he or she can use application programs in the system to retrieve information, change data, obtain access to accounts, disable internal computer systems, and damage the reputation of companies and agencies.

Research has revealed that typical computer hackers are white males between 15 and 34 years of age; they begin using the computer for illegal purposes between the ages of 10 and 25. Hacking tools and methods are readily available on the Internet, and many require little technical expertise. Some of the reasons for hacking are financial motivation, a quest for status among other hackers, or just for the challenge and fun of it. Today, hackers often boast of their exploits, and they leverage the knowledge accumulated by other, earlier hackers to break into various computer systems for malicious purposes. Because hackers are able to alter critical files and use application programs without authorization, companies continue to implement and improve various security measures, such as passwords, to restrict unlawful access and protect system integrity.[59]

Another type of hacker is known as a **"hacktivist."** These people commit DOS attacks, disseminate spam, and deface websites, believing they are carrying out acts of civil disobedience. They attempt to call attention to an issue by their crimes. In one example, a group defaced the official website of the Ku Klux Klan, replacing it with content from the website of Hate Watch, a civil rights group. Some consider hacktivists to be similar to freedom fighters and see their actions as a form of protest. But others say they commit criminal acts of vandalism.[60]

A report by an information technology consulting firm reported that websites that provide instructions on how to crack computer systems and commit technology-related frauds have cost businesses more than an estimated $1 trillion a year in preventive maintenance, recovery, theft, and unrealized revenue. The report focused on the free or low-cost software tools provided by these

---

web attack Large amount of hostile activity targeted at one particular company.

denial-of-service (DOS) attacks Deliberate attempts to shut down a computer network operation by overloading it.

hacking The willful and malicious penetration of a computer system.

hacktivist People who commit denial-of-service attacks, disseminate spam, and deface websites, believing they are carrying out acts of civil disobediance.

EXHIBIT 9.3   How to Avoid Getting Hacked on the Internet

If you are connected to the Internet, you are vulnerable to intruders. The following are some ways to keep your data safe:

1. Use antivirus software and update it often to keep destructive programs off your computer.
2. Don't allow online merchants to store your credit-card information for future purchases.
3. Use hard-to-guess passwords that contain a mix of numbers and letters, and change them frequently.
4. Use different passwords for different websites and applications to keep hackers guessing.
5. Use the most up-to-date version of your web browser, e-mail software, and other programs.
6. Send credit-card numbers only to secure sites; look for a padlock or key icon at the bottom of the browser.
7. Confirm the site you are doing business with. Watch your typing.
8. Use a security program that gives you control over "cookies" that send information back to websites.
9. Install firewall software to screen traffic if you use DSL or a cable modem to connect to the net.
10. Don't open e-mail attachments unless you know the source of the incoming message.

SOURCE: "How to Keep from Getting Hacked," *Time*, February 21, 2000, p. 44.

websites that allow people with little technical knowledge (so-called **script kiddies**) to become instant system crackers, to defeat filtering software, to steal credit-card numbers, and to cheat telephone companies.[61]

Exhibit 9.3 gives tips to keep from getting hacked on the Internet.

Cyberstalking

While the Internet has transformed communication on a global level, it has also created a medium for stalking. Experts report that the typical cyberstalker is an emotionally disturbed loner for whom **cyberstalking** provides anonymity and the opportunity to conceal gender and identity. Although activities in cyberspace are protected by the First Amendment, computer users must abide by state and federal legislation. The free-speech issues

script kiddies   Hackers with little technical knowledge; they follow directions prepared by someone else.

cyberstalking   The harrassment of others by computer.

pedophiles   Sexual offenders who receive gratification from sexual contact with children.

resulting from the use of cyberspace include anonymity, accountability, defamation, discrimination, harassment, obscenity, and the liability of online services and Internet service providers. Numerous states have enacted laws against electronic harassment, and law enforcement is constantly detecting and arresting offenders. According to Michael Pittaro, professor of criminal justice at Lehigh Valley College, law enforcement at the federal, state, and local level must unite, share, and disseminate intelligence information. Pittaro recommends that law enforcement form a cooperative partnership with Internet service providers (ISPs), since both are ultimately working towards the same goal, eradicating online harassment.

In addition, organizations such as Women Halting Online Abuse and the CyberAngels have formed to educate the community about online harassment and to protect individuals from these crimes.[62]

Computer Use by Pedophiles

Internet-related crimes involving children include obscene material, child pornography, **pedophile** networking, and hate propaganda.

As indicated in the introduction to this chapter, two troubling incidents involving high-level government officials occurred in 2006.[63] A National Institute of Justice research survey on Internet victimization of youth indicated that as many as one in five children fell victim to Internet crime during a one-year study period, and concluded that Internet crime is increasing and that children are particularly vulnerable to online advances. The study focused on four types of online victimization: sexual solicitation and approaches, aggressive sexual solicitation, unwanted exposure to sexual materials, and harassment.[64]

Numerous law enforcement agencies are dealing with this problem by creating proactive units investigating such crimes. For example, Marty Kolakowski, an investigator for the Wayne County Sheriff's Department in Detroit, goes online with a fictitious screen name as bait for pedophiles who prey on naïve, rebellious kids from broken homes. Kolakowski is not alone. He is one of thousands of cops from local, state, and federal law enforcement agencies nationwide who pose as potential victims of pedophilia, eventually meet the seducer, and arrest and bring him or her to prosecution.[65] A 2005 Australian government report indicates there has been a steady stream of police operations that have targeted online child pornography, and the findings of studies of these operations indicate they serve to disrupt the notion of anonymity endemic to Internet crimes.[66]

The FBI indicates that some of the signs that a child may be at risk include his or her spending large amounts of time online, the parents' finding pornography on the child's computer, and the child's receiving phone calls from men the parent does not know or making phone calls to numbers the parent does not recognize. If they suspect their child is being victimized, the FBI recommends that parents take the following actions: Openly discuss their suspicions with the child, review what is on the child's computer, use their caller-ID service to determine who is calling the child, and purchase a device that shows telephone numbers dialed from the home phone. To prevent online exploitation, parents should talk with their children about sexual victimization and potential online dangers, keep the computer in a common room in the house, use blocking software or other parental controls, and maintain access to the child's online account.[67]

Experts say that some children try to fill emotional holes and find companionship through online relationships. "Many children are gullible and impressionable," said Dr. Bela Sood, professor of psychiatry and pediatrics at Virginia Commonwealth University Health Systems. Referring to the dangers of the Internet to these gullible and impressionable children, Sood says, "Imagine stretched arms and fingers climbing into your bedroom if you allow them to."[68]

In 2006, the social networking Internet site MySpace.com hired a former federal prosecutor to patrol the service and launched ads warning kids about Internet predators. MySpace offers its members, primarily young people, the ability to create detailed profile pages featuring music, photos, and other attractions to show the online world.[69]

© AP Photo/Jim Cole

Tim and Helen Remsburg pose in their home in Hudson, NH, with a photo of Helen's daughter, Amy Boyer. Liam Yovens, who murdered Boyer, had chronicled his obsession with her and his plot to kill her on a website, and he paid Docusearch Inc., the Internet information broker, about $150 to get her social security number and other information, including her work address. The Remsburgs fought for Internet privacy by arguing that their daughter's death could have been prevented if her personal information was kept private and not for sale. The outcome of the case has impacted the field of private investigation: The industry regulates itself more carefully, even turning in investigators who illegally obtain information.

Computer Viruses

Computer viruses wreak havoc in direct damage and disruption and in confusion and misinformation. Viruses are also known as "malware" (short for "malicious software"). A **computer virus** can

computer virus Malicious software program written to damage or harass other computer systems.

You Are There!

Freedom on the Net: Anything Goes

RENO v. AMERICAN CIVIL LIBERTIES UNION

In June 1997, the U.S. Supreme Court in *Reno v. American Civil Liberties Union*, in a sweeping endorsement of free speech on the Internet, declared unconstitutional a federal law making it a crime to send or display indecent material online in a way available to minors.

The seven-to-two decision was the Court's first effort to extend the principles of the First Amendment into cyberspace. The Court's decision, written by Justice John Paul Stevens, struck down the 1996 Communications Decency Act, ruling that the Internet is entitled to the highest level of First Amendment protection, similar to the protection given to books and newspapers. The Court has continuously held that more-limited First Amendment rights apply to speech on broadcast and cable television, where it has tolerated a wide array of government regulation. The Court's action upheld a 1996 decision by a three-judge federal district court in Philadelphia that had struck down the decency law in 1996 shortly after its passage.

The decision made it unlikely that any government-imposed restriction on Internet content would be upheld as long as the material has some intrinsic constitutional value. The Court held that the indecent material at issue in the case was not precisely defined by the 1996 law but was merely referred to in one section of the statute as "patently offensive" descriptions of "sexual or excretory activities."

Here is an excerpt from Justice Stevens' decision:

> It is true that we have repeatedly recognized the government interest in protecting children from harmful materials. But that interest does not justify an unnecessarily broad suppression of speech addressed to adults. . . . [T]he government may not reduce the adult population to only what is fit for children. [In a previous case], we remarked that the speech restriction at issue there amounted to "burning the house to roast the pig." The [law] casting a far darker shadow over free speech, threatens to torch a large segment of the Internet community.
>
> As a matter of constitutional tradition, in the absence of evidence to the contrary, we presume that governmental regulation of the content of speech is more likely to interfere with the free exchange of ideas than to encourage it.

SOURCE: *Reno v. American Civil Liberties Union*, 117 S.Ct. 2329 (1997).

---

be defined as a program that can "infect" other programs by modifying them to include a copy—possibly evolved—of itself. *Infect* means that the program inserts itself into the chain of command so that attempting to execute a legitimate program results in the execution of the virus instead or as well.

Viruses rely on users unwittingly spreading them from one computer to another, but some viruses, usually using the Internet, find their own way to spread. There are various types of viruses and other malicious programs, including boot sector infectors, file infectors, macro viruses, worms, Trojan horses, and memetic (or meme) viruses.[70]

worms Self-replicating computer programs that use a network to send copies of themselves to other nodes (computer terminals on the network), often without any user intervention.

Trojan horse Type of computer virus that claims to do something desirable but instead does something destructive.

- Boot sector infectors infect the master boot record or DOS boot record, which contains the programs used to start up the computer. They may be spread by the exchange of diskettes.

- File infectors infect executable files and spread quickly through file systems and on networks. They may be spread by the exchange of diskettes.

- Macro viruses infect macro programming environments. (A macro is an automated program that helps users avoid repetitive tasks.) These spread rapidly and account for the majority of virus incidents.

- **Worms** copy themselves across systems and networks without attaching to a host program. They usually use the Internet and find their own way to spread.

- **Trojan horses** replicate themselves and claim to do something desirable but instead do something the victim does not expect or does not want

You Are There!

Police Put Away Cyber-Perv

Anthony Correnti, age 26, a schoolteacher who had taught in a private Manhattan high school and in a Long Island public school district, had prowled the Internet for years. He began stalking one of his victims online when she was only 11 years old. He pursued her even after she changed her screen name. He sent e-mail messages of "Let's get together" and "You're so hot, I want to go out with you" to this child. Later, he sent her nude photographs of himself.

When the girl's mother discovered what was transpiring, she immediately contacted local police. The Suffolk County Police Department's Computer Crime Section traced e-mails sent to the minor to Correnti's computer. Upon examining Correnti's computer, authorities discovered that he had one of the most extensive pornography collections ever found, including pictures of adult men having sex with girls as young as 4 years old. Some of the photographs in his collection included nude students right in his own classroom.

Correnti was arrested. In addition to the computer crime charges, he was charged with sexually abusing five girls, 13 to 16 years old. In 2001, he pleaded guilty to using a child in a sexual performance, possessing a sexual performance by a child, and providing indecent material to a minor, and to counts of third-degree rape and third-degree sodomy. He was sentenced to ten to thirty years in prison.

SOURCE: Laura Stiles, "Teacher Used Internet to Prey on Children," *Suffolk Life*, October 3, 2001, pp. 23, 24.

EXHIBIT 9.4 Common-Sense Tips for Protecting Yourself from Internet Viruses

■ **Do nothing:** Ignoring a file that arrives from the net is one of the best ways to stop a virus in its tracks. Keep your curiosity in check. Do you really need to see everything that is sent to you? Maybe you should wait until you read the next day's newspapers before you open any new files.

■ **Update your virus software:** Most antivirus programs won't recognize an entirely new virus. However, you can keep old ones from attacking by frequently updating the programs.

■ **Make backups:** Antivirus programs can clean an infected machine, but they can't restore files that have been infected. Back up any important stuff on floppy disks.

SOURCE: Jared Sandberg, "How to Protect Yourself: Common-Sense Tips for Keeping Internet Viruses at Bay," *Newsweek*, May 15, 2000, p. 44.

thousands of corporations unhooked their computer systems from the Internet and began the laborious process of purging the program internally. The virus also attacked government agencies, including the White House, the Pentagon, Congress, and the British House of Commons. The Love Bug virus, like the earlier 1999 Melissa virus, was activated when a user clicked on an e-mail attachment, and it was propagated automatically to all the e-mail addresses found on the user's computer.[71]

The best way to avoid infection is to not open e-mail attachments from unknown sources and to keep antivirus software up to date (see Exhibit 9.4). Once a computer is infected, special software may be needed to repair any damaged files.

Spam

It has been reported that spam represents 65 percent of all e-mail. **Spam** or junk mail is unsolicited e-mails, usually for a commercial purpose.[72]

The fighters against spam include software engineers who try to identify and block spam from e-mail in-boxes, investigators in private industry, and an increasing number of prosecutors and law

to happen. Trojans are often subdivided into two classes: password stealers and programs that do direct damage to files and file systems.

■ **Memetic viruses** includes virus hoaxes (sometimes called metaviruses) and other types of chain letters, erroneous security alerts, accurate but not very useful alerts, and vendor hype alerts.

As mentioned in the introduction to this chapter, one dangerous virus, the Love Bug, was sent around the world on May 4, 2000. This rogue software program, borne by an e-mail message proclaiming "ILOVEYOU," jammed and crashed e-mail systems, destroying data on hundreds of thousands of computers. To defend themselves,

memetic viruses Computerized hoaxes, chain letters, erroneous alerts.

spam Unwanted and uninvited computer messages.

enforcement agents who are learning how to combine traditional detective work with cybersleuthing. The Direct Marketing Association has paid $500,000 to hire fifteen investigators who work alongside agents from the FBI and other government agencies in a program known as Project Slam-Spam.[73]

Using information provided by Internet providers, along with their own decoy computers and e-mail accounts, these investigators have built a database of more than one-hundred spammers. Increasingly, they are actually purchasing advertised products and responding to offers of get-rich-quick schemes to track down the spammers. Initially they started to work backward from the e-mail and found that to be a frustrating route. This did not lead to a live body, and now they have started to go the other way and follow the money trail.

The project has built cases against forty spammers, and it has started to refer these cases to federal and state prosecutors. In May 2004, Howard Carmack, who sent 825 million junk e-mail messages from his home in Buffalo, was sentenced by New York State to at least three-and-a-half years in prison in a 2003 case for violations of identity theft and business records. As in most criminal investigations, the use of an informant familiar with the operation was one of the most powerful investigatory tactics.

Sterling McBride, who formerly hunted down escaped prisoners for the U.S. Marshals Service, is now an investigator for Microsoft. He carefully watches for tidbits of data that link some of the two-billion pieces of junk e-mail that Microsoft's Hotmail service receives each day with the people who send them. Once he finds an electronic key to a spammer's identity—a real name, address, or phone number, McBride uses all the tools of a regular detective, including trailing suspects, subpoenaing their bank records and looking for disgruntled former associates to become informers.[74]

The big Internet service providers, including America Online, have been steadily suing spammers for the last few years, using trespass and computer crime laws. Microsoft's two-year-old "digital-integrity" unit, which also fights online fraud, identity theft, and spyware, employs more

than one-hundred people around the world and has a $100 million annual budget. Many of their investigators, like McBride, were former law enforcement officers and prosecutors hired originally to track down software counterfeiters who have shifted their attention to spam.[75]

Internet providers are also filing "John Doe" suits in which the identity of the defendant is not known and thus are able to subpoena records from banks and others to determine the identity of spammers. One investigator says, "The most useful information is who pays for various aspects of the spam operation. To spam, you need four or five things—a hosting service, a domain name, mailing software, mailing lists, and so on. Each one you have to purchase from someone." Another investigator said, "The real key is trying to figure out how to connect the virtual world with someone you can hold responsible for this. Once you have the link, you can use all the tools of a normal investigation."

A 2005 report by a computer software maker disclosed that the entertainer Britney Spears tops the list of famous people whose names are used in mass e-mail messages to entice readers to download damaging viruses. A typical scenario of this scam involves a spam e-mail that either contains the virus program as an attachment or includes a link to a website that can infect the reader's computer with a Trojan-type virus. Other famous names the creators of these viruses often use include Jennifer Lopez, Paris Hilton, and Bill Gates. Often, criminals use phony news events surrounding well-known individuals such as Osama bin Laden or Michael Jackson to lure readers to click onto the virus link.[76]

Spyware

In 2004, the Federal Trade Commission reported that it had filed its first assault on spyware. **Spyware** is bits of computer code that surreptitiously install themselves on the computers of Internet users to track their activities, push them to websites, barrage them with advertisements, and otherwise wreak havoc with their machines.[77]

The suit, which seeks an injunction against a New Hampshire company, claims it exploited vulnerabilities in Microsoft's Internet Explorer web browser, the most widely used browser, to seize varying amounts of control over users' computers. It also charges that the spyware deployed by the company changed users' home pages, installed

spyware Bits of computer code that surreptitiously install themselves on the computers of Internet users to track their activities, push them to websites, and barrage them with advertisements.

advertising and software programs on the users' computers, and caused a deluge of pop-up windows to appear on computer screens—without the users' consent. In some instances, the complaint says the codes caused computers to malfunction, slow down, crash, or cease working properly.

It is difficult to measure the problem of spyware, but Microsoft complained that nearly half of the system failures reported by users of its Windows operating system were traceable to spyware infestation. Also, a representative of Dell Computers said that complaints about spyware had eclipsed all other problems on its technical help lines.

In 2005, it was reported that spyware was a growing concern among security professionals due to its ability to compromise sensitive data and destroy IT resources and was listed as the top concern of over 87 percent of respondents to a survey.[78]

Software Piracy

A Business Software Alliance survey revealed that in 2003, more than $50 billion was spent globally on commercial software. However, almost $80 billion worth of software was actually installed. The difference represents the size of the software piracy market. The study showed that China, Vietnam, the Ukraine, Indonesia, and Russia are the top-five pirating countries. Stronger copyright laws have been countered by increasing online piracy via spam, auction sites, and peer-to-peer systems.[79]

Data Security

The security of data is always under attack. In 2006, the U.S. Department of Veterans Affairs reported that personal information belonging to 26.5 million U.S. veterans, including their social security numbers and dates of birth, was stolen. This information was contained on a laptop stolen from one of their data analysts' homes.[80]

Also in 2006, in a report issued by the U.S. House of Representative's Government Reform Committee, it was reported that nineteen federal agencies have reported the loss of sensitive personally identifiable information since January 2003. Among the agencies reporting such losses were the Department of Veterans Affairs, the Department of Agriculture, the Department of Commerce, the Department of Defense, and the Department of the Treasury. The report indicated that only a

small number of the data breaches were caused by hackers breaking into the system. Most of the data losses, instead, stemmed from the theft of laptops, drives, and disks, as well as unauthorized use of the information by employees and contractors.[81]

In 2004, a magnetic tape with information about 120,000 Japanese customers of Citigroup's Citibank division disappeared while being shipped by truck from a data management center in Singapore. The tape held names, addresses, account numbers, and balances. In 2005, an entire box of tapes in the care of the United Parcel Service, with personal information on nearly 4 million American customers, disappeared.[82] In 2005, Time Warner disclosed that personal information, including names and social security numbers for 600,000 current and former employees, had gone missing on a truck while in the care of a data-storage company.[83]

Tens of thousands of Americans' data, including social security numbers, addresses, and drivers' license numbers, were stolen in March 2005 from three leading data brokers, ChoicePoint and LexisNexis, Bank of America, and Westlaw. Westlaw reported that it was changing its policies so that 85 percent of subscribers who once had access to full social security numbers will no longer have such access.[84] LexisNexis has restricted access to individuals' social security and drivers' license numbers. ChoicePoint made similar restrictions. LexisNexis said the only customers who will continue to receive full social security and drivers' license numbers are government law enforcement agencies, investigative and claims departments of insurance companies, investigative and debt-collecting units of financial institutions, and debt-collection companies.[85]

In 2005, MasterCard International reported that more than 40 million credit-card accounts of all brands might have been exposed to fraud through a computer security breach at a payment-processing company, the largest case of stolen consumer data to date. A pattern of fraudulent charges were traced to an intrusion at CardSystems Solutions of Tucson, Arizona, which processes more than $15 billion in payments for small to midsize merchants and financial institutions each year. About 20 million Visa and 13.9 million MasterCard accounts were compromised in addition to American Express and Discover cards. The accounts affected included credit cards and certain kinds of debit cards. An intruder had placed a computer code or script on the CardSystems network to steal the data and was able to obtain cardholders' names, account numbers, and expiration dates, as well as the security code, which is typically three or four digits printed on the credit card. Cybercriminals can use the account numbers to purchase stolen goods or secure cash advances or can sell the numbers in bulk at underground sites on the Internet.[86]

Some private investigators and data brokers favor access to commercial databases to assist clients, arguing that civilian investigators, like insurance brokers, employment screeners, and other businesses, have a legitimate need for some sensitive information. A 1993 decision by the Federal Trade Commission allowed credit-reporting companies to sell header information to the data-brokering industry, which also amasses data from public information sources like court filings and criminal records. (Header information is the commonly entered entries made on applications, such as loan or mortgage applications. It includes such information as names, addresses, and the like). The Gramm-Leach-Bliley Act of 2002 reversed the credit header rule and prohibited credit reporting agencies from selling header information outside the rules set out by the Fair Credit Reporting Act, but it did not specify what data brokers and their subscribers could do with information already in their systems.[87]

How Organizations Maintain Computer Security

Today, automated or computerized data is the primary method of collecting, storing, processing, and analyzing corporate and organizational information of all types. In the business and government area, information processing that used to take decades to do is now accomplished in seconds. Most large agencies or businesses have separate **information technology (IT)** departments to control and study the information managed by their computers. Generally, these organizations assign a high-level executive, called variably the IT manager, IT officer, or chief information officer, to command the IT department. These senior executives

information technology (IT) Department that controls and studies the information managed by a business' computers.

PRIVATE SECURITY CONNECTIONS

Professional Associations for Persons Interested in Computer Security

Direct Marketing Association
Computer Security Institute (CSI)
Information Systems Security Association (ISSA)
International Association for Computer Information Systems (IACIS)

---

are responsible for all aspects of their company's information technology and systems. They direct the use of IT to support the company's goals in terms of both technology and business process. They usually report to the company's chief executive officer or chief operating officer and usually oversee technology purchases and services provided by the information systems department.[88]

Many organizations have given their chief security officer (CSO) the additional function of information systems security officer (ISSO) to oversee IT security as well as all security responsibilities. Many of these individuals have a military, FBI, or Secret Service background. The typical CSO or ISSO oversees and coordinates security efforts across the company, including information technology.[89]

A survey of security professionals by the Business Software Alliance and the Information Systems Security Association (ISSA) revealed that business leaders were certainly aware and prepared for any eventuality. The ISSA is the largest international nonprofit association in the world specifically for security professionals. Its more than 10,000 worldwide members include practitioners at all levels of the security field in a broad range of industries, including communications, education, healthcare, manufacturing, finance, and government.[90]

Specifically, the survey results revealed that most security professionals say the risk of a major cyberattack on their organization is likely, their organization is prepared to defend itself, and their organization's ability to defend itself has improved over the past twelve months. The survey also indicated most organizations have in place a formal security program function; access controls; a written information security policy; and regular monitoring, reviewing, and auditing. Most respondents also indicated that they have antivirus software, firewalls, e-mail filtering, network intrusion detection systems, e-mail attachment blocking, and Internet website blocking.[91]

Most corporations, businesses, agencies, and institutions use computer security methods to help maintain the integrity and security of their computer infrastructure, including systems control, encryption, computer-use monitoring, computer emergency or computer incident response teams (CERTs or CIRTs), early warning systems, and biometrics. The information in this section is provided to help you understand the importance of computer security methods and to give you insights into how computer security can be violated.

Systems Control

According to a article on protecting computer networks, corporate security managers protect their computer networks without diminishing the level of efficiency by asking and answering the same types of questions they ask about physical security: What needs protection? Who might attack? How will they do it? How can risk be managed?[92]

What Needs Protection? All aspects of the corporate computer environment need protection, including web servers, mail servers, firewalls, and individual workstations.

Who Might Attack? There are several primary types of attackers: hackers, business rivals, foreign intelligence gatherers, and insiders.

- *Hackers:* These are a diverse group ranging from programming geniuses who study the inherent weaknesses and vulnerabilities in software and networks to script kiddies, as described earlier in this chapter.
- *Business rivals:* Competitors may try to obtain information illicitly through virtual back doors.
- *Foreign intelligence gatherers:* Some countries are known to have active industrial espionage efforts against U.S. corporations.
- *Insiders:* Outsiders—people without any legitimate access—account for fewer than half of the reported information security incidents in the United States. Most incidents of hacking are committed by people with some degree of legitimate access, ranging from employees to former employees, customers, and contractors. Insiders may be doing it for their own enjoyment,

or they may be working for rivals or foreign intelligence agencies. Former insiders also may take advantage of their knowledge of the system to retain access to the network. Sometimes, they continue to use access privileges that the company failed to terminate at the end of their employment.

How Will They Do It? Attackers try to enter the network by probing for information and locating IP addresses, services, and sources of more information by using any of the following methods.

- *Finding holes:* Once a target has been identified, attackers can employ freely available tool kits (programs) that find and exploit a wide range of problems in the computer system. They may also begin their search for network vulnerabilities in the physical world by looking in dumpsters for documents that contain company phone lists with e-mail addresses that are also user names. Hackers use deception to get user names and passwords by convincing unaware employees to divulge their password or other security-related information.
- *Covering tracks:* Once attackers have a preliminary foothold into the system, their next step is to cover their tracks by using programs that cloak their activities and open a back door to the system so they can return. Now the attacker can probe the system for information or use it as a platform to attack other systems.
- *Attacking from within:* As already noted, insiders account for most security incidents. Generally, they attack in the same way described here.

How Can Risk Be Managed? Once systems managers understand their company's exposure and level of threat, they have a good idea of the specific risks that must be managed and mitigated. They must find ways to balance the need for security with usability through policy and tools.

The purpose of an information system security policy is to communicate that information security is a priority and that all employees are responsible and accountable for maintaining it (see Exhibit 9.5 for guidelines for protecting a work laptop when traveling, for example). Such a policy also involves controlling privileges. Policies are generally complemented by a layered defense designed to prevent those with limited privileges from easily gaining access to restricted parts of the network. The system administrator

---

EXHIBIT 9.5   **Guidelines for Protecting a Laptop when Traveling**

- Never put your laptop into airline baggage systems.
- Insure it. A typical insurance policy for a laptop will cost $75 for $3,000 worth of loss, theft, or damage.
- Think negative! If something bad can happen, it will happen. Have backups of all data; encrypt all sensitive information.
- Have identifying information on your computer, in the event you lose it.
- Carry your laptop in a nontypical carrying case. It makes it less obvious that it is a computer, and makes it and you less a mark. Try a padded backpack.

SOURCE: Peter H. Lewis, "Have Laptop, Will Travel, With Extreme Care," *New York Times*, July 13, 2000, pp. G1, G3.

---

generally regulates each user's rights and permissions to file access and takes appropriate security measures, such as additional log-in requirements for particularly sensitive areas.

Regular use of security tools can help system administrators do their jobs more efficiently and improve the overall security of the network. These tools include firewalls, virtual private networks (VPNs), hacker tools, intrusion detection, and people.

- *Firewalls:* **Firewalls** are the basic building blocks of restricting network traffic, such as between the Internet and the internal systems, and allow a system administrator to separate functional groups while still permitting required traffic in the area. They also provide an audit trail of authorized and blocked traffic, which may allow staff to spot probe attempts or other unauthorized activity.

- *Virtual private networks:* VPNs provide transmission security—protection from passive observation of a data stream and from insertion attacks, where the attacker injects information into an established data stream.

- *Hacker tools:* Software such as security scanners or vulnerability assessment tools helps system administrators view their networks from an

attacker's perspective, so they can take corrective action.

- *Intrusion detection:* Intrusion detection systems detect malicious activity, either by listening to the network wire or by monitoring logs. They compare the activity flagged to an internal database of attack signatures.

- *People:* Computer security is not just a technical problem. People are the most important part of the security system—from the system and network administrators who have day-to-day operational responsibility of the system to all the people involved in the security loop.

Some IT professionals are backing off the typical advice of creating a complicated alpha-numeric password. This is because they feel that people will just write down the password, jeopardizing its confidentiality. They claim this creates more of an opportunity for compromise than password cracking does.

In 2005, Chevron oil company employees, with 1,800 offices in two-hundred countries around the world, began to use their Chevron SmartBadges to access the corporate network and log on to their desktop workstations. Using this two-factor authentication, employee smart cards plus a PIN, Chevron is taking the lead in corporate cyber security.[93]

Encryption

Another method of ensuring computer security is **encryption**—that is, using algorithms to scramble the information on a computer so that the information is not usable unless the changes are reversed. The growing use of computers and networks requires businesses, most notably those in financial services, to secure their computerized transactions and proprietary information. In response to these needs, widely available and sophisticated encryption technologies have been developed. The trend is to integrate robust digital encryption technologies into commercial desktop applications and networks. These are generally easy to use and unbreakable.[94]

The RSA encryption algorithm was widely used for more than a decade to protect the privacy of digital commerce and communication. It was originally awarded a U.S. patent in 1983. This technology, also known as public key cryptography, makes it possible for two people who have never met to exchange information securely. The RSA encryption algorithm was placed into the public domain in September 2000, permitting programmers to incorporate the technology into their products.[95]

---

firewall A software program that prevents unauthorized entry into computer networks.

encryption A method of encoding information to prevent illegal use.

Computer-Use Monitoring

Another way to ensure computer integrity is to monitor computer use. A 2005 Proofpoint survey determined that over 36 percent of companies employing more than 1,000 employees analyze outbound e-mail, and another 27 percent are planning to implement e-mail analysis in the near future. Larger companies conduct even more e-mail monitoring.[96] In 2005, according to an American Management Association and ePolicy Institute study, 55 percent of companies surveyed admitted to monitoring employee e-mails.[97]

As an example, at Ritvik Toys, near Montreal, a systems manager monitors every website that his employees browse and every e-mail message they send or receive. This company is one of thousands of companies that are looking at workers' correspondence on a routine basis. Reasons companies give for monitoring their employees' computer use is that such use overloads networks, slows computers, could allow staff to leak intellectual property or trade secrets, could allow attackers to steal valuable information, and could crash the system. Companies also monitor e-mail to ensure compliance with financial disclosure.[98]

The following is a good example of the positive results of successful computer monitoring. Managers at a New York City import–export company suspected it was being victimized by two employees. The company installed a software program called *Investigator* that retails for about $99 a copy. It furtively logs every single stroke entered onto a computer. The program revealed that the two employees were deleting orders from the corporate books after they were processed, pocketing the revenues, and building their own company from within. The program picked up on their plan to return to the office late one night to swipe a large shipment of electronics. As the suspects gained entry to the office, they were arrested by police hiding in the rafters of the firm's warehouse. They were charged with embezzling $3 million over two-and-a-half years.[99]

In offices around the United States, managers are installing software that monitors their employees' computer activity, both online and offline, every message sent, every website visited, every file formatted, and every key stroked— even if the activity was not saved or was deleted. According to the American Bar Association, employers are free to monitor an employee's use of their networks as long as they do not violate labor and antidiscrimination laws by targeting union organizers, for example, or minorities.

In 2005, it was reported that many major companies, including Delta Air Lines, Wells Fargo, and Google, are firing and disciplining employees for what they say about their jobs on their **blogs.** (Blogs are personal computer sites that often contain a mix of frank commentary, freewheeling opinions, and journaling.) More than 8 million adults in the United States have created blogs as of 2005, and 32 million Americans are blog readers. About 20,000 new blogs are created daily. These blogs link to create what is now known as a **blogosphere,** a series of collective Internet conversations that is one of the fastest-growing areas of new content on the web.[100]

CERT Teams

After an infamous incident involving a Cornell University graduate student, security professionals recognized a need for quick response to security incidents on the Internet. At that time, the **computer emergency response team (CERT)** at Carnegie Mellon University was instituted as a central clearinghouse of computer security information and as a technical adviser on incident response for companies and government agencies. Today, many companies and institutions have established their own CERTs to deal with hacking problems on their networks. These teams evaluate computer security programs, establish policy, and respond to and correct the damage caused by hacking incidents. For example, when hackers broke into Stanford University's system, stealing more than 4,500 passwords, the university's CIRT responded by patching the system and getting passwords changed. The team also counseled students and faculty about good password selection and protection behavior.[101]

---

blog Personal computer sites that often contain a mix of frank commentary, freewheeling opinions, and journaling.

blogosphere A series of collective Internet conversations that is one of the fastest-growing areas of new content on the web.

computer emergency response team (CERT) Team of specialists who deal with hacking problems on company and institutional computers; also known as computer incident response team (CIRT).

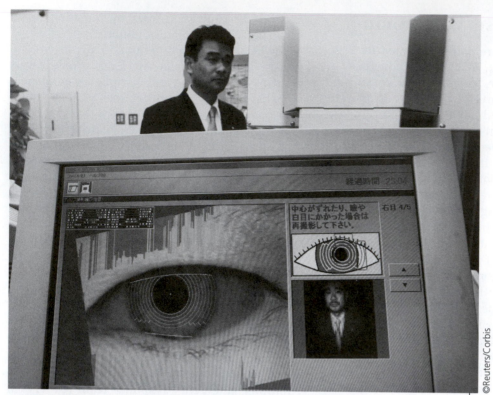

©Reuters/Corbis

Biometric security systems store digital images of users' fingerprints, earlobes, irises, hand shapes, and other unique biometric characteristics. Here a man registers an imprint of his iris using Takefuji Corporation's iris-scanning automatic teller machine. Iris scans analyze the features that exist in the colored tissue surrounding the pupil, which has more than 200 points that can be used for comparison, including rings, furrows, and freckles. The scans use a regular video camera and can be done from further away (up to 2 feet) than a retinal scan. They can scan the iris through glasses and have the ability to create a measurement accurate enough that it can be used for identification purposes, not just verification.

Early Warning Systems

In October 2004, International Business Machines (IBM) released a monthly report of threats to computer networks, the "Global Business Security Index," in an effort to establish an indicator similar to the federal government's Homeland Security Advisory System. It gives computing managers early warning of a range of computer vulnerabilities, like attacks by malicious hackers, automated software, viruses, and worms. It is generated from data gathered by 2,700 IBM information security employees and a global network of about half a million sensors—software programs and security hardware distributed to its customers and its own networks in thirty-four countries. It routinely detects 100 million suspected or actual attacks against IBM customers each month.[102]

The federal government also maintains an early warning system through its **National Cyber Alert System (US-CERT)** program, which provides all citizens, from computer security professionals to home computer users, with free, timely, and actionable information to better secure their computer systems.[103] US-CERT provides two types of documents or services, technical documents and nontechnical documents. Technical documents include technical cybersecurity alerts that provide real-time information about current security issues, vulnerabilities, and exploits; and cybersecurity bulletins that provide weekly summaries of security issues and new vulnerabilities. These cybersecurity bulletins, which are intended for technical audiences, also provide patches, work-arounds, and other actions to help mitigate risk. Nontechnical documents include cybersecurity alerts

National Cyber Alert System (US-CERT) Federal government early warning system that provides citizens with timely and actionable information to secure their computer systems.

that provide real-time information about current security issues, vulnerabilities, and exploits. They are released in conjunction with technical cyber-security alerts when there is an issue that affects the general public. Cybersecurity alerts outline the steps and actions that nontechnical home and computer users can take to protect themselves from attack. Cybersecurity tips describe common security issues and offer advice for nontechnical home and corporate computer users. Although each cybersecurity tip is restricted to a single topic, complex issues may span multiple tips. Each tip builds on the knowledge, both terminology and content, of those published prior to it.

Biometrics for Computer Access

Another way to make computer systems more secure is to use **biometrics** for computer access. Biometric security systems store digital images of users' fingerprints, earlobes, irises, handshapes, and other unique biometric characteristics. How does it work? Computer scans identify a person's unique biometric characteristics, then digitally store the scans. A computer uses video cameras and sensors to match those templates with the patterns of would-be system users. The computer may still recognize a password, but the biometrics will validate identity. The system can lock in on a person as well as a user ID. Fingerprints can be verified in two seconds or less by a device rigged to a personal computer's keyboard. Sperm banks, childcare centers, and San Francisco International Airport have used security systems that recognize hand geometry, and Canada's public health system uses thumb scans to block unauthorized access.[104]

Investigating Computer Crime

Law enforcement and private industry are involved in numerous programs to prevent and investigate computer crime. Many were discussed earlier in this chapter. This section will focus on particular areas of computer crime investigation, including the basic investigation, specialized technical techniques, proactive investigative techniques, electronic surveillance and interception, and services provided by major investigative firms.

The Basic Investigation

In a 2003 article, David Griffith reports that almost every major municipal or county law enforcement agency in the United States has a computer crime or cybercrime investigator. He reports that one of the basic skills needed to become a cybercrime investigator is a thorough knowledge of how the technology works. The typical cybercrime investigation begins like most other investigations, with a citizen's complaint that he or she has been the victim of a crime.[105]

The first investigative step is to find the Internet protocol (IP) address of the individual that defrauded the complainant. (An IP address is a series of numbers and letters attached to every piece of data that moves on the Internet.) The next step is to work with the Internet service provider's (ISP) security people to gain access to the IP address used by the person that committed the crime. (Most major dot-com companies have their own security specialists.) The ISP is a subscription service that grants the user access to the Internet. ISPs have records of everything a subscriber does on the Internet. One of the most important weapons in a cybercrime investigator's arsenal is a letter requesting that the ISP preserve the data until the investigator can secure a subpoena, warrant, or court order requiring the ISP to turn over its records. Often, the investigation is likely to involve another agency. After a suspect's computer and various hard drives have been seized, it is time for the computer forensic specialist to make a "true copy" or "mirror copy" of the hard drive. The true copy of the data can then be examined using a qualified computer forensic analyst and a number of computer forensics software programs.[106]

The New York City Police Department (NYPD) maintains a computer crime squad with twenty-five officers who have significant computer and investigative skills. It handles all sorts of cases, from a network intrusion at a Wall Street financial company to "if a little old lady calls because some spam put porn on her computer." It also handles all types of computer intrusions, terrorist leads, organized crime cases, murders, and lesser crimes. The NYPD online forensic investigations are conducted in a controlled environment, the secure room, where everything a detective does online is monitored in order to produce results that will be admissible in

biometrics Digital capture of physical characteristics and conversion into data for storage. The data are used to validate identity.

court. Here, the detectives surf terrorist sites, look for money trails, or conduct proactive investigations looking to investigate and arrest sexual predators by posing as preteen boys and girls.[107]

Specialized Technical Techniques

The keys to solving computer crimes are the traditional investigative skills and techniques, including establishing evidence of a crime, determining how the crime occurred, identifying likely suspects, and developing the case for prosecution. Investigators also need to be knowledgeable about information security and fraud on the Internet, how to preserve evidence from attacks on computer hardware, environmental support systems, and computer hardware.[108] However, there is a difference between handling traditional, tangible evidence and computer evidence, and that difference is the fragility of computer evidence. It can be altered, damaged, or destroyed simply by turning a computer on or off at the wrong time. This means that the field of computer forensics requires special training and skills.

The FBI's Computer Analysis Response Team programs take a two-pronged approach to computer forensic examinations. First, field examiners help FBI agents with investigations and support state and local law enforcement agencies. Second, highly trained personnel at FBI headquarters conduct laboratory examinations of digital evidence that field agents are not trained to do.[109]

Sophisticated, highly technical procedures are involved in the investigation of computer crime. The International Association of Computer Investigative Specialists (IACIS) is made up of law enforcement professionals who are dedicated to education in the field of forensic computer science. Its members include federal, state, local, and international law enforcement professionals who are trained in the forensic science of seizing and processing computer systems. Their training incorporates forensic methods for searching seized computers, along with the rules of evidence and the laws of search and seizure. Investigators look for evidence that has been hidden, concealed, encrypted, or protected with passwords. They also look for software time bombs, Trojan horses, TSRs, and other destruction devices that could destroy the evidence, the physical computer, or both.[110]

The IACIS also offers two certification programs: Certified Electronic Evidence Collection Specialist and Certified Forensic Computer Examiner. It provides an opportunity to network with other law enforcement officers who are trained in computer forensics. The IACIS has published a set of forensic examination procedures to deal with the special problem of computer evidence. Exhibit 9.6 provides a description of these procedures.[111]

In 2004, the National Institute of Justice prepared and published *Forensic Examination of Digital Evidence: A Guide for Law Enforcement*, an extensive set of instructions for members of the law enforcement community who are responsible for the examination of digital evidence. Also, the NIJ has published *Electronic Crime Scene Investigation: A Guide for Law Enforcement*, which deals with common situations encountered during the processing and handling of digital evidence. These guides offer agencies and investigators rules that can be used to develop their own policies and procedures.[112]

Another organization providing networking for computer investigators is the International High-Technology Crime Investigation Association, which encourages, promotes, aids, and interchanges data, information, experience, ideas, and knowledge about methods, processes, and techniques relating to investigations and security in advanced technologies among its members.[113]

Another professional organization is the Computer Crime Research Center (CCRC). The CCRC, created in 2001, is a nonprofit, private scientific research organization that collaborates with major universities, institutes, and research centers to conduct research in legal criminal and criminological problems of cybercrime with the purpose to render scientific and methodical aid and consulting. It performs analysis of the results of scientic practical research in counteracting and preventing computer crimes.[114]

Proactive Investigative Techniques

Most proactive online law enforcement investigative techniques focus on cybersex offenders. Online investigations of cybersex offenders usually focus on the distribution of child pornography and online solicitation of children for sex, as well as meetings with children for the purposes of sex. Using proactive investigative techniques, investigators present themselves as children with appropriate victim profiles.[115]

Former Attorney General Janet Reno, while addressing the General Assembly of the

International Association of Chiefs of Police, stated that the most cost-effective way for law enforcement to investigate cybercrime, including cybersex offenses, is to organize law enforcement resources on a national and regional basis so that not every jurisdiction has to purchase the expensive equipment required to detect and investigate it.[116]

Electronic Surveillance and Interception

The nation's communications networks are routinely used to commit serious criminal activities, including espionage. Organized crime groups and drug-trafficking organizations rely heavily on telecommunications to plan and execute their criminal activities. It is important for law enforcement agencies to be able to conduct lawful electronic surveillance of criminal communications to acquire evidence. Such electronic surveillance requires legal court orders, called interception orders, issued by high-level courts. Interception orders are limited to certain specified felony offenses.

In recent years, the FBI has encountered an increasing number of criminal investigations in which the criminal subjects use the Internet to communicate with each other or with their victims. Because many ISPs lack the ability to discriminate communications to identify a particular subject's messages to the exclusion of all others, the FBI designed and developed a sophisticated electronic surveillance and monitoring device called **DCS1000,** a digital collection system formerly called "Carnivore." This device provides the FBI with a "surgical" ability to intercept and collect communications that are the subject of a lawful court order while ignoring those which they are not authorized to intercept.

This type of tool is necessary to meet the stringent requirements of federal wiretapping statutes. If a court order provides for the lawful interception of one type of communication (for example, e-mail) but excludes all other communications (for example, online shopping), DCS1000 can be configured to intercept only those e-mails being transmitted either to or from the named suspect. In effect, DCS1000 limits the messages viewable by human eyes to those included in the court order. The ISP's knowledge and assistance are legally required to install the device.[117]

The FBI's use of the DCS1000 system is subject to intense oversight from internal FBI controls, the U.S. Department of Justice, and the courts.

There are significant judicial penalties for misuse of the tool, including exclusion of evidence, as well as criminal and civil penalties. The system is not susceptible to abuse because it requires expertise to install and operate, and such operations are conducted, as required in the court orders, in close cooperation with the ISPs. The FBI shares information about DCS1000 with industry to assist companies in their efforts to develop open standards for complying with wiretap requirements.

In 2005, law enforcement suffered severe criticism and judicial setbacks from privacy advocates relative to Internet and cellular-phone surveillance. New Federal Communications Commission (FCC) rules, scheduled to take effect in May 2007 and making it easier for law enforcement to monitor e-mails and Internet-based phone calls by requiring broadband ISPs, including universities and libraries, to pay for redesigning their networks to make them more accessible to court-ordered wiretaps, were challenged by privacy, high-tech, and telecommunications groups in federal court. These FCC rules would make broadband Internet providers and voice-over Internet protocol companies subject to the 1994 federal law, the Communications Assistance for Law Enforcement Act, which requires telecom carriers to design their networks so they can quickly intercept communications and deliver them to the government when presented with a court order.[118]

Also in 2005, federal judges in Texas and New York denied FBI requests for court orders that would have forced wireless carriers to continuously reveal the location of a suspect's cell phone as part of an ongoing investigation. The judges said the FBI may not track the locations of cell-phone users without showing evidence that a crime occurred or is in progress, saying that to do so would violate long-established privacy protections. In these cases, the two federal courts approved FBI requests for other information from the wireless carriers, including logs of numbers a cell-phone user called and received calls from but said the requests for the cell-site locations amounted to the ability to monitor someone's movements, and the FBI needed probable cause for that.[119] Depending on a wireless phone's capabilities, carriers can determine either precise or rough locations of users when they make or receive calls, a feature primarily used for

DCS1000 A device used by the FBI to intercept information through the Internet while ignoring what it is not authorized to collect; formerly known as "Carnivore."

EXHIBIT 9.6	**Forensic Examination of Computers and Digital Media**

The IACIS has developed the following as a guide for forensic computer and digital evidence examinations.

All computer and digital media examinations are different. The examiner must consider the totality of the circumstances as he/she proceeds. So, then, not all components here may be needed in every situation, and examiners may need to adjust to unusual or unexpected conditions in the field.

Cases involving computers and other electronic devices are borderless. Multiple jurisdictions and agencies may be involved in investigative and analytical activities, and each agency or jurisdiction may employ specific procedures. This document, then, is not intended to supercede [sic] or conflict with jurisdiction or agency policies or procedures. Rather it is a foundation document that outlines general principles.

GUIDE FOR FORENSIC EXAMINATIONS

Computer system components and other electronic devices (including digital and electronic media) are items of evidence just like any other items of evidence. As such it is incumbent upon the examiner to follow agency procedures for documenting the receipt and handling of the items.

The computer system and/or the media should be examined physically and an inventory of hardware components noted. Documentation should include a physical description and detailed notation of any irregularities, peculiarities, identifying markings, and numberings.

When examining a computer the system date and time should be collected, preferably from the BIOS (Basic Input/Output System) setup. The date and time should be compared to a reliable known time source and any

differences noted. If the BIOS setup information is accessible then drive parameters and boot order should be noted. Depending on the BIOS, other information such as system serial numbers, component serial numbers, hardware component hashes, etc. should be noted.

Examination of media should be conducted in a forensically sound examination environment. A forensically sound examination environment is one which is completely under the control of the examiner. No actions are taken without the examiner permitting them to happen; and when the examiner permits or causes an action he/she can predict with reasonable certainty what the outcome of the action will be.

Examiners may choose to employ a forensically sound operating system. The use of physical write-blocking devices or software write-blocking devices may be used in operating system environments that are not forensically sound.

Conducting an examination on the original evidence media should be avoided. Rather examinations should be conducted on a forensic copy of the original evidence, or via forensic evidence files.

Properly prepared media should be used when making forensic copies to insure no commingling of data from different cases. Properly prepared media is that which has been completely overwritten with a known character.

Regardless of whether the examiner performs a direct device-to-device copy of the media or creates forensic evidence copies for examination or restoration, the copy process should be forensically sound.

Examination of the media should be completed logically and systematically by starting where the data of evidentiary value is most likely to be found. These

---

emergencies.[120] These rulings came as controversy continued to mount over the government's ability to conduct domestic surveillance under the USA Patriot Act, enacted after the 9/11 terrorist attacks.

Services Provided by Major Investigative Firms

Some of the major private investigative services firms offer services to business and industry in computer technology and computer investigations.

For example, Kroll Inc., in an effort to help attorneys review massive amounts of computerized text and data, locates, analyzes, and organizes key evidence in preparation for client cases. Its Kroll Ontrack electronic discovery specialists help attorneys and litigators at corporations, law firms, and government agencies gather and filter electronic documents for use in legal proceedings, regulatory matters, and investigations. It also recovers, restores, and protects electronic data that has been erased, reformatted, or lost and investigates the sources of technology and data tampering.[121]

locations will vary depending on the nature and scope of the case. Examples of items to be noted might include:

- If the media is a hard drive, the number and type of partitions should be noted.
- If the media is an optical disc, then the number of sessions should be noted.
- File systems on the media should be noted.
- A full directory listing should be made to include folder structure, filenames, date/time stamps, logical file sizes, etc.
- Installed operating systems should be noted.
- User created files should be examined using native applications, file viewers, or hex viewers. This includes such files as text documents, spreadsheets, databases, financial data, electronic mail, digital photographs, sound and other multimedia files, etc.
- Operating system files and application created files should be examined, if present. This would include, but is not limited to: boot files, registry files, swap files, temporary files, cache files, history files, log files, etc.
- Installed applications should be noted.
- File hash comparisons may be used to exclude or include files for examination.
- Used and unallocated space on each volume should be examined for previously deleted data, deleted folders, slack space data, intentionally placed data. Previously deleted filenames of apparent evidentiary value should be noted. Files may be automatically carved out of the unallocated portion of the unused space based upon known file headers.
- Keyword searches may be documented to identify files or areas of the drive that might contain data of evidentiary value and to narrow the examination scope.
- The system area of the volume (i.e., FAT, MFT, etc.) should be examined and any irregularities or peculiarities noted.

- Examination of areas of the media that are not normally accessible such as extra tracks or sectors on a floppy disk, or a host-protected area on a hard drive may be required.
- To facilitate examination of data, user settings, device and software functionality, etc., the computer may be booted using either a copy of the boot drive or by using a protected device on the original device to determined functionality of the hardware and/or software.
- The forensic software used during the examination should be noted by its version and should be used in accordance with the vendor's licensing agreement. The software should also be properly tested and validate for its forensic use by the examiner or the examiner's agency.

At the conclusion of the examination process, sufficient notation of any discovered material of an apparent incriminating or exculpatory evidentiary nature should be made.

Sufficient documentation should be made of all standard procedures and processes initiated as well as detailed notation of any variations made to the standard procedures.

Any output of the recovered data should be properly marked with appropriate identifiers in accordance with policies from the examiner's agency.

SOURCE: International Association of Computer Investigative Specialists, "Forensic Procedures: Forensic Examination of Computers and Digital and Electronic Media." Retrieved November 22, 2005, from http://www.iacis.info/iacisv2/pages/forensicprocprint.php.

Pinkerton Consulting and Investigations uses its e-commerce search engines to assist clients in protecting their property by identifying and locating potential theft, counterfeiting, diversion, and infringement on the Internet. It also assists corporations in conducting business intelligence and verifying distributors, products, licenses, and prices.[122]

Wackenhut Consulting and Investigation Services also provide Internet monitoring to help clients track down counterfeiting, theft, and infringement on the Internet.[123]

Homeland Security and Information and Computer Security

Today, the computer and other forms of information technology are used by criminals, terrorists, and others to disrupt our domestic tranquility and homeland security.

One of the most serious potential problems in ensuring homeland security is the country's dependence on automated systems controlling critical infrastructure, including energy, food, and other necessities chains, and communications systems. A terrorist takeover of only one of these systems could bring our way of life, as we know it now, to a halt.

Terrorists and other demented persons are constantly online, planning their crimes and soliciting others to join them. A good recent example of the use of computer and information technology to disrupt homeland security occurred in France during October and November 2005. Beginning October 27, 2005, a series of riots, spreading like a virus, engulfed more than three-hundred cities around Paris, resulting in murders, injuries, arsons, and untold amounts of property damage. On one night alone, 1,100 cars were burned. Hackers took over the official website of a northern Paris suburb and dispatched thousands of fake e-mails calling for more violence. Local gangs used the computer and text messaging on their cell phones as early warning systems to alert their members about the movements of riot police during operations in their communities. The website of a French radio station popular among young people had to shut down its most provocative blogs after the exchanges became increasingly vile and bloggers used the forum to call for a violent gathering at the Eiffel Tower: "All the housing projects should rise. The wait is over. Friday, November 11, a meeting under the Eiffel Tower. At 2 P.M. Show up, it's important." "God bless France, because war is about to begin," "I want to kill the cops," and "Go to the nearest police station and burn it."[124]

Another homeland security and computer problem is the issue of steganography. Steganography is the art and science of writing hidden messages in such a way that no one apart from the intended recipient knows of the existence of the message; this is in contrast to cryptography, where the existence of the message itself is not disguised, but the content is obscure. Steganography is a way to conceal a coded message inside an innocuous-looking photograph, document, or other bit of media. A person can observe a photo on a particular website of a person wearing a certain type of uniform; it could contain microdots spelling out a call for a jihad, and one can only find them if he or she is trained to look at the image correctly.

In order to protect society, local, state, and federal law enforcement agencies, together with private security personnel, help to secure cyberspace and to maintain computer security. Public and private investigators investigate cybercrimes and detect, intercept, and close down these threats. Private security professionals have always taken the lead in technological crime investigation and will continue to do so.

Summary

- The growing criminal use of the computer has caused significant harm to U.S. businesses, citizens, and the government. Computer crime negatively affects the fabric of life in the United States.

- Some of the major cybercrime and cyberproblems include fraud, identity theft, cyberterrorism, web attacks, computer hacking, cyberstalking, computer use by pedophiles, computer thefts, computer viruses, spam, spyware, software piracy, and data security.

- Identity theft or identity fraud occurs when someone wrongfully obtains and uses another's personal data in a way that involves fraud or deception, typically for economic gain.

- Cyberterrorism is the use of computer networks, including the Internet, to steal, damage, and alter information. Cyberterrorism poses a real and present danger to U.S. critical information infrastructure.

- A denial-of-service attack (DOS) is a deliberate attempt to shut down a computer network operation by overloading it.

- Computer hacking is the willful and malicious penetration of a computer system to achieve some purpose.

- A "hacktivist" is a computer hacker who commits DOS attacks, disseminates spam, and defaces websites, believing she or he is carrying out acts of civil disobedience.

- Computer viruses wreak havoc, damage, disrupt, and cause confusion and misinformation on computers. Viruses are malicious programs that can infect other programs by modifying them to include copies of themselves.

- Spam represents about 65 percent of all e-mail. Spam or junk mail is unsolicited e-mails, usually for a commercial purpose.

- Most corporations, businesses, agencies, and institutions use security methods to help maintain the integrity and security of their computer infrastructure, including system control, encryption, computer-use monitoring, computer emergency or computer incident response teams, early warning systems, and biometrics, to control access.

- Firewalls are the basic building blocks for restricting computer network traffic, such as between the Internet and internal systems. They provide audit trails of authorized and blocked traffic.

- A basic computer investigation involves finding the Internet protocol (IP) address of the suspect; working with the Internet service provider (ISP) security personnel to gain access to the suspect's IP address; requesting the ISP to preserve the suspect's data until the investigator secures a subpoena, warrant, or court order requiring the ISP to turn over its records; seizing the suspect's computer and hard drives; making a "true or mirror copy" of the suspect's hard drive; and then conducting a computer forensics examination on the hard drive.

Learning Check

1. Identify and discuss three examples of the computer crime problem in business and society.

2. Name and discuss three specific types of cybercrime and cyberproblems.

3. What is identity theft? Describe and discuss three ways identity thieves acquire victims' information.

4. What is a computer virus? Describe and discuss three types of viruses.

5. What is cyberstalking? Discuss several ways in which it is done.

6. What are some ways pedophiles use the Internet? Discuss some of them.

7. List and discuss some of the methods used by organizations to maintain computer security.

8. Discuss several reactive and proactive methods used by law enforcement to investigate computer crime.

9. What is DCS1000?

10. Name three professional associations involved in helping to maintain computer security, and discuss how each one helps in this process.

Application Exercise

The principal of a local high school hires you to assist with a problem occurring at her school. The school has a large computer lab and provides access to the Internet to all students. In addition, each student is assigned an e-mail account that can be accessed at school or at home. Several students have contacted the principal and informed her that they have received offensive and stalking-type e-mail messages. The principal wants you to investigate and determine who is sending the inappropriate e-mail. Prepare a brief report to the principal describing how you will investigate this case.

Web Exercise

Contact your local Internet service provider and determine if it provides security advice to its users. If so, obtain the advice and prepare a report detailing this advice. Also, ask the server to provide you with the precautions it takes to maintain the security and integrity of data on its systems.

Key Terms

biometrics, p. 255
blog, p. 253
blogosphere, p. 253
computer emergency response team (CERT), p. 253
computer virus, p. 245
critical information infrastructure, p. 242
cybercrime, p. 237
cyberstalking, p. 244
cyberterrorism, p. 242
DCS1000, p. 257
defense information infrastructure, p. 242
denial-of-service (DOS) attacks, p. 243

Investigative Security

Photofest

GOALS

- To introduce you to the three major forms of private-sector investigations.
- To provide you with an overview of the major types of investigations conducted by private-sector investigators.
- To introduce you to the many noncriminal investigations and services conducted by the private sector.
- To acquaint you with the many types of criminal investigations conducted by private-sector investigators.
- To make you aware of information sources for private-sector investigators to introduce you to the problem of "pretexting" for private-sector investigators.
- To discuss homeland security and investigative security.

Introduction

Your 18-year-old daughter never appears at home after school. You report the case to the police, and they conduct a preliminary investigation as well as an immediate search of the area between her school and your home. They also conduct a canvas of people in the neighborhood. The preliminary investigation discloses that your daughter had indicated to some friends that she hated school, hated home, and was intending to run away with her 19-year-old boyfriend. The police go to the home of the boyfriend and his parents, and the parents tell them that they have not seen their son in a week and that they are happy about that. They say that their son, a high school dropout, is lazy and doesn't have a job, and they don't want him to come back home. After some more investigative steps, the detectives tell you it appears your daughter has voluntarily left home, and it is not apparent that her disappearance involves foul play. They tell you that they are closing the investigation and that they will notify you if any further information comes in. You are annoyed. Do you have any options in continuing this investigation and finding your daughter?

This chapter will discuss private-sector investigations, including proprietary security investigations, contract security investigations, and independent private investigations.

Among the main noncriminal investigations and services performed by private-sector investigators and discussed in this chapter are financial investigations, product-liability investigations, finding people/missing persons, personal injury, wrongful death, medical malpractice, domestic/marital, and other miscellaneous investigations and services.

Among the many criminal investigations performed by these private-sector investigators and discussed in this chapter are violent and property crimes; corporate crime; internal theft; fraud, including business and credit-card fraud; insurance fraud, including worker's compensation and medical and healthcare fraud; counterfeiting or theft of intellectual property rights; and industrial espionage.

The chapter will also discuss information sources for private-sector investigators and the problem of "pretexting," and will discuss homeland security and investigative security. The important issues of background investigations, drug screening, and sexual harrassment in the workplace were discussed fully in Chapter 8.

Some of the material presented here on methods of investigation is quite general. For more specific methods for each type of investigation, I urge students to research the scholarly and professional sources noted here, paying special attention to information offered by the professional associations with a presence on the Internet. Most importantly, I urge students to interact closely with those true experts, both academic and professional, who have done or are doing the real work of investigating and to listen to their advice and learn from their experience. A textbook can never replace the real lessons one can learn from these true experts.

Major Forms of Private-Sector Investigations

Investigatory services in the private sector are provided by proprietary security departments in corporations and businesses, large and small contract security investigative services companies, and independent private investigators.

Private security expert Robert D. McCrie, of John Jay College of Criminal Justice at City University of New York, provides this commentary on the current role of private investigators:

Organizations use the services of outside investigators for many reasons: [P]re-employment screening (vetting), internal investigations, executive protection, and the testing of controls are the principal reasons. Many organizations today have their own internal investigative departments. But the need for external investigators—the term *detective* is dated—always exists. The use of outside investigators has increased considerably in recent years, in part because the need for in-house investigations has grown due to legal and insurance requirements. Further, in-house departments have sometimes been downsized. Investigators generally provide excellent value to their clients. In some instances, the use of

JOBS IN SECURITY

Investigative Security Positions

INSURANCE INVESTIGATIONS
Insurance Investigator

Anthem Blue Cross Blue Shield in Denver, Colorado, employs an investigator. The position's duties include collecting, researching, and validating bills and claims data in order to detect fraudulent, abusive, or wasteful activities and practices. Qualifications are a bachelor's degree and two to three years related experience or an equivalent combination of education and experience. Strong writing and oral communication, PC, research, and problem-solving skills are required.

Special Investigative Unit Insurance Investigator

American International Group Inc. in Phoenix, Arizona, employs an SIU investigator. The position requires field investigations in the area. Qualifications are a bachelor's degree, knowledge of multilines of insurance, extensive white-collar crime investigative experience, and computer literacy.

Claims Investigator

International Claims Specialists of Voorhees, New Jersey, employs a parttime qualified claims investigators in the Baltimore area. Qualifications include experience in taking statements, interviewing skills, and report-writing techniques.

FRAUD INVESTIGATIONS
Investigator—Internal Audit

Michael Page International in New York City employs an investigator/internal auditor. Responsibilities include reducing financial fraud and abuse losses by investigating, preventing, detecting, analyzing, reporting, and recovering losses. Qualifications include

being a CPA or CFE with comprehensive investigative experience in financial fraud investigations.

Internal Audit Manager—Forensic Accounting

The Masco Corporation in Taylor, Michigan, employs an internal audit manager/forensic accounting position. Responsibilities include leading and managing a global effort in the detection, prevention, and deterrence of financial fraud or abuse. Qualifications include a minimum of ten years of experience in public accounting, internal auditing, or law enforcement or investigative fields; a bachelor's degree in accounting, law enforcement, or a related field; CFE and CPA or CIA designations are preferred.

Fraud Detection Analyst

The Advanta Corporation of Horsham, Pennsylvania, employs a fraud detection analyst. Responsibilities include preventing and detecting fraudulent activity on MasterCard accounts issued by Advanta Business cards. Qualifications and skills desired include analytical skills; knowledge of Microsoft Windows, Excel, and Word; and an excellent understanding of credit-card products and operations, including collections and customer service. Also preferred are fraud experience in a credit-card operations environment; experience making outbound calls using Falcon; knowledge of organized credit-card rings; FDR and Microsoft Access knowledge; and a two-year degree in criminology or equivalent experience in law enforcement and investigations.

Sources: International Association of Special Investigations Units, "Insurance Jobs." Retrieved October 11, 2004, from http://www.iasiu. org; and Association of Certified Fraud Examiners, "Career Center." Retrieved October 11, 2004, from http://www.cfenet.com.

investigative expertise would have saved much time and money for organizations. But finding a competent investigator is not easy. One has to evaluate the individual for his or her ability, appropriateness, and efficiency for a given assignment. The care and feeding of those uncommon superior investigators involves keeping in touch and giving regular assignments or paying a modest retainer.[1]

This section will include a description of each of the forms of private-sector investigations and give

some examples of the investigations and services provided by each one.

Proprietary Security Investigations

Most large corporations and businesses have their own in-house (proprietary) security departments that provide a wide range of security services, including investigations. Sometimes, some of these large corporations and businesses may also use major

©Reuters/Carlos Duarte/Landov

The Wackenhut Corporation is a leading provider of security-related and diversified human resource services to business, industry, and government agencies on a worldwide basis. These services can be dangerous: Investigators inspect the crime scene of an armed robbery of a Wackenhut truck, September 2006. The armed robbers escaped with over $8 million after seizing and subduing the security officers to gain control of the armored vehicle. ■

contract (outside) security service companies to conduct all or some of their investigating services.

Most **proprietary security investigations** conducted by in-house security personnel concentrate on such matters as pre-employment background checks for new employees, as discussed in Chapter 8; internal crime and loss prevention; insurance cases; credit applications; and civil litigation cases.

Contract Security Investigations

Many large corporations and businesses, as well as many smaller ones, use the services of contract security companies, which provide numerous security services and investigations. Also, many private individuals use the services of these companies. Some of these contract investigation firms are local and small, while others are large and national or international in scope. One of the largest **contract security investigation** companies is Pinkerton Consulting and Investigation, which

is a leading provider of global security services, including investigations, consulting, business intelligence, security systems integration, and employee selection services. Pinkerton Consulting and Investigation conducts services for thousands of businesses worldwide, including more than 80 percent of the Fortune 1000. This centuries-old company is today a subsidiary of Securitas Inc., based in Stockholm, Sweden, which is the largest security company in the world, with annual revenues of $6 billion and 220,000 employees in more than thirty-two countries throughout North and South America, Europe, and Asia. Securitas Inc., under its subsidiary, Securitas USA, also owns and operates the former Burns International Services, American Protective Services, and First Security Services.[2]

Some of the following specialized services are offered by Pinkerton Consulting and Investigation, in addition to the background or pre-employment investigations previously covered:

■ *Fraud investigations:* These involve the investigation of questionable insurance claims; they unearth the facts of the claim and present them in a manner that is comprehensive, documented, and understandable. They include worker's compensation, disability, property, casualty, or product-liability claims.

proprietary security investigations In-house corporate or business security investigations.

contract security investigations External companies hired to provide investigative security services.

■ *Undercover investigations:* These involve confidential **undercover operations** and inquiries that can detect and develop evidence of theft, embezzlement, bribery, kickbacks, harassment, conflicts of interest, sabotage, and substance abuse. These investigations may attempt to prevent illegal acts by employees, business associates, or outside individuals.

■ *Claims investigation/surveillance:* These services help insurance companies and the self-insured fight fraudulent claims by detecting fraud and providing detailed, reliable reports and admissible evidence. The methods used include activity checks, surveillance, claimant and witness interviews, reviews of medical and autopsy reports, skip tracing, and records searches. The records searched include Department of Motor Vehicle, previous employment, education, professional credentials, neighborhood checks, and the like. Claims investigated include property and casualty claims, worker's compensation, liability, malpractice, theft or burglary, contestable death, accidental death, and dismemberment and disability.

■ *Executive protection:* These include programs for the prevention of terrorism, kidnapping, extortion, and bodily harm to individual executives and businesses.

■ *Due diligence/asset searches.* These include verification of deeds and titles, litigation, liens, assets, or personal or corporate reputations to minimize the risks involved in lending or underwriting.

■ *Intellectual property protection:* This involves searching for and protecting trademarks, patents, and copyrights to prevent and recover losses due to counterfeit products.

Another major contract security service company is the Wackenhut Corporation, a leading provider of security-related and diversified human resource services to business, industry, and government agencies on a worldwide basis, including the United States and over fifty other countries on six continents. Wackenhut Consulting and Investigation Services deals with business crime of every kind, at every level, across the country and overseas.[3]

Some of the specialized investigative services, in addition to background investigations, provided by Wackenhut Consulting and Investigations Services include the following:

■ *Shopping services:* Professional shoppers conduct integrity, efficiency, and facility analyses,

---

which help identify losses, curt or abrasive behavior of some employees, and poor conditions leading to customer dissatisfaction.

■ *Hotline programs:* These include various hotline reporting programs staffed by trained investigators around the clock, every day of the year. These hotlines encourage the reporting of criminal activity, drug dealing, drug use, gambling, misconduct, sexual harassment, discrimination, weapons possession, safety violations, fraud, or ethics and compliance violations.

Another leading financial investigating firm in the United States is Kroll Inc., which is headquartered in New York City. During the merger mania of the 1980s, Kroll was Wall Street's major "private eye," specializing in digging up dirt in heated takeover battles. When the merger mania of that decade cooled, Kroll kept its grip on the top rung of financial investigating by continuing to do financial investigations for the U.S. government, foreign governments, and large corporations. Clients pay an average of $1,500 a day for the services of a Kroll agent, and the company's employees are well-paid by industry standards. Senior managers earn $100,000 to $300,000 a year, and top executives make as much as $500,000 a year. Kroll recruits former federal and state prosecutors; former agents from the FBI, CIA, and IRS; and former diplomats and Congressional aides to be agents.[4]

Independent Private Investigations

Independent private investigators are generally self-employed persons or members of small one- or two-person firms. Many smaller companies and businesses hire independent private investigators to conduct investigations. Private individuals requiring investigatory services also use private

undercover operations Covert activities designed to catch criminals.

EXHIBIT 10.1   **Things Private Investigators Do**

- Assist attorneys in case preparation
- Reconstruct accidents for insurance companies and attorneys
- Review police reports for attorneys (many private investigators are former members of police departments and can offer attorneys an "inside look" at police terminology and jargon)
- Do surveillance and observations for insurance companies and attorneys
- Do background investigations of possible spouses
- Do background investigations of potential employees
- Do criminal investigations of cases the police do not because of a lack of resources
- Run credit checks
- Do financial resources checks
- Investigate missing persons cases the police cannot put enough resources into

- Investigate missing persons cases that are not police cases (no crime involved)
- Check into conduct of spouses or lovers
- Investigate suicides
- Offer personal protection
- Offer executive protection
- Offer premise or meeting protection
- Create travel itineraries
- Do honesty or "shopper" testing
- Investigate insurance or worker's compensation fraud
- Reconstruct auto accidents
- Work undercover for private firms to uncover criminal activity, drug use, and work-rule violations
- Investigate product-liability cases
- Serve subpoenas

investigators. Independent private investigators generally charge from $35 to over $100 per hour.

The media image of the private investigator has always been a rather poor one. As depicted in movies, television shows, and novels, and perhaps in real life, private investigators are rather sleazy individuals who either operate illegally or on the fringes of the law. This image has changed recently, according to Sam Brown and Gini Graham Scott in their book, *Private Eyes: The Role of the Private Investigator in American Marriage, Business, and Industry:*

> The stigma through the last half-dozen decades of the PI image has been that of an aloof, alcoholic, uneducated ex-cop who followed errant wives and husbands. Today's private investigation business is a whole other ballgame. State regulatory agencies plus continuing education plus professional associations have made the PI a respected member of the community. New steps are constantly taken in the industry to increase ethical standards and commitment to excellence.[5]

A review of popular magazines and newspapers reveals that private investigators are involved in the following broad areas: investigating art thefts,[6] investigating terrorism cases,[7] investigating kidnapping cases,[8] following lovers and spouses,[9] helping Hollywood stars clear their names of damaging gossip,[10] conducting financial investigations for corporations and foreign governments,[11] checking out prospective mates (with the threat of AIDS,

this could be very important),[12] attempting to free wrongly convicted convicts,[13] exposing defense fraud,[14] investigating business fraud,[15] working for corporate clients, investigating corporate drug rings, tracing stolen goods, tracking lost assets,[16] finding lost pets,[17] investigating insurance fraud, and serving subpoenas.[18] Exhibit 10.1 of this text provides a sample of some of the varied investigative services offered by independent private investigators.

In most states, private investigators are required to be licensed by the state. Licensing requirements generally include state residency, U.S. citizenship, training or work experience as a police officer or investigator, or apprenticeship under a licensed private investigator. Many also require a clean arrest record, passing a background investigation, and passing an oral or written examination. A few states have no regulations. See Chapter 2 of this text for a full discussion of the latest selection, hiring, licensing, and training standards for private investigators.

A professional trade association for private investigators is the National Association of Investigative Specialists (NAIS). NAIS concentrates on marketing investigative services, developing new investigative techniques, providing training programs for those in practice or those wishing to enter the profession, developing positive media coverage of the investigative profession, and acting as a center for case referrals and publicity for members.[19] Another professional association for private investigators is the International Private Investigator's Union, which provides for its members an interactive community where they can discuss and promote all aspects of the profession, including the expertise of private investigations, training principles, legal reviews, statutes, services, education, referrals, and technical strategies that enhance the value of the profession.[20] There are other investigative professional organizations dedicated to specific investigatory skills, such as the American Medical Investigator's Association, the Criminal Defense Investigation Training Council, the National Association of Fire Investigators, and others.[21]

A major trade magazine for private investigators is *PI Magazine: Journal of Professional Investigators.*[22] Also, ASIS International offers professional certification and credentialing for private investigators through its **professional certified investigator (PCI)** designation, and the International Foundation for Protection Officers offers certification through its Crime and Loss Investigation Program.[23] See Exhibits 10.2 and 10.3 for information about these certifications.

Overview of Private-Sector Investigations

There are several ways we can categorize the investigations and services provided by private-sector investigators. For example, authors Pamela A. Collins, Truett A. Ricks, and Clifford W. Van Meter categorize these investigations and services as follows:

■ *Legal investigations:* These investigations involve the courts, including both criminal and civil litigation. In these cases, the investigator locates witnesses; conducts interviews; gathers and reviews testimonial, documentary, and physical evidence; takes photographs; and testifies in court.

■ *Corporate investigations:* These involve investigating criminal or other misconduct in the workplace. They might involve the investigation of theft of company assets, drug abuse in the workplace, and myriad other conditions. Some of these investigations may involve undercover operations.

■ *Financial investigations:* These involve accounting and finance skills and tend to focus on uncovering and developing cases against employees or clients who are suspected of

---

PRIVATE SECURITY CONNECTIONS

Some Professional Associations for Private Investigators

World Association of Detectives (WAD)
World Association of Professional Investigators (WAPI)
Council of International Investigators
National Association of Investigative Specialists (NAIS)
National Association of Legal Investigators (NALI)
International Private Investigators Union (IPIU)
National Association of Professional Accident Reconstruction Specialists (NAPARS)
Association of Professional Investigators and Security Providers (API-SP)
Criminal Defense Investigation Training Council (CDITC)
National Association of Fire Investigators (NAFI)
National Alliance of Gang Investigators (NAGI)
National Association of Professional Process Servers (NAPPS)
National Construction Investigation Association (NCIA)
National Defender Investigators Association (NDIA)
Traffic Accident Reconstruction Origin (TARO)
United States Professional Investigators Network (USPI)

---

embezzlement or fraud. They generally involve developing confidential financial profiles of persons or companies who may be parties to large financial transactions and often involve working with investment bankers and accountants to determine the how's and who's of thefts. Often these investigators have the Certified Fraud Examiner (CFE) designation described later in this chapter.

■ *Loss prevention investigations:* These are generally conducted for retail organizations and include investigations of both internal and external theft of assets. These investigators are responsible for finding and apprehending employees and customers who steal merchandise or cash or destroy property. They also may audit stock and other company possessions. (This area was also covered extensively in Chapter 6 of this textbook.)

---

professional certified investigator (PCI) ASIS International board certification accepted as the international standard of competence in security investigations; a positive indicator of state-of-the-art knowledge of investigations applications and best practices.

EXHIBIT 10.2   **ASIS International Professional Certified Investigator Designation**

ELIGIBILITY

Candidates wishing to take the PCI examination must first satisfy the following requirements:

1. Nine years of investigations experience, at least five years of which shall have been in case management; OR

2. An earned Bachelor's Degree or higher from an accredited institution of higher education and seven years of investigations experience, at least three years of which shall have been in case management.

3. The applicant must not have been convicted of any criminal offense that would reflect negatively on the security profession, ASIS International, or the certification program.

PCI EXAMINATION STRUCTURE AND CONTENT

The PCI examination consists of multiple-choice questions covering tasks, knowledge, and skills in subjects identified, by professional investigators, as the major areas involved in this field. All exam questions come from the official reference books. No questions on the exam are taken from any other source.

The subjects are:

Case Management

A. Evaluating cases on continuing basis for potential ethical conflicts
   - Elements of conflict resolution
   - Nature/types/categories of ethical issues related to cases (fiduciary, conflict of interest, attorney–client)
   - Applicable aspects of laws, codes, and regulation

B. Determining needs and developing strategies by reviewing options
   - Negotiation process
   - Investigative methods
   - Cost-benefit analysis
   - Applicable aspects of law, codes, and regulations

C. Implementing strategies by utilizing the investigative resources necessary to address case objectives
   - Investigative resources (e.g., staffing, scheduling)
   - Time management
   - Quality assurance process
   - Chain-of-custody procedures
   - Change analysis/management

Evidence Collection

A. Conducting surveillance by physical and electronic means in order to obtain relevant information
   - Methods of surveillance
   - Types of surveillance

- Types of surveillance equipment
- Pre-surveillance routines
- Applicable aspects of laws, codes, and regulations

B. Conducting interviews/interrogations of subjects to obtain relevant information
   - Interview techniques (electronic, face-to-face, telephonic)
   - Techniques for detecting deception (e.g., non-verbal communication)
   - Methods and techniques of eliciting admission and/or confession
   - Composition and content of witness/subject statement
   - Applicable aspects of laws, codes, and regulations (e.g., individual rights, privacy, interrogation)

C. Collecting and preserving objects and data for future assessment and analysis
   - Requirements of chain of custody
   - Methods/procedures for preserving various types of evidence
   - Forensic opportunities and resources
   - Applicable aspects of laws, codes, and regulations (e.g., rules of evidence and discovery)

D. Conducting research by physical and electronic means and analyzing data to obtain relevant information
   - Physical resources
   - Electronic resources
   - Applicable aspects of laws, codes, and regulations

Case Presentation

A. Preparing reports to substantiate investigative findings
   - Critical elements and format of an investigative report
   - Investigative terminology
   - Logical sequencing of information
   - Applicable aspects of laws, codes, and regulations

B. Preparing and presenting testimony by reviewing case files, meeting with counsel and presenting relevant facts
   - Witness preparation
   - Types of testimony
   - Applicable aspects of laws, codes, and regulations (e.g., applicable privileges, hearsay, rules of procedure)

SOURCE: ASIS International, "Professional Certified Investigator." Retrieved November 5, 2005, from http://www.asisonline.org.

EXHIBIT 10.3 International Foundation for Protection Officers' (IFPO) Crime and Loss Investigation Program

The IFPO Crime and Loss Investigation Program is a comprehensive distance-education course designed for home or work study. The program is interactive, with web-based learning exercises, and teaches the essential components of investigation within both public law enforcement and the rapidly expanding field of security/loss prevention. The topics covered include interviewing, report writing, surveillance, intelligence, undercover investigation, background investigations, and crime-scene procedures. These core competencies are covered in two texts as well as a series of online papers.

Students successfully completing the program qualify for IFPO certification.

Source: International Foundation for Protection Officers, "Crime and Loss Investigation Program." Retrieved November 3, 2005, from http://www.ifpo.org.

- *Insurance fraud investigations:* These investigations generally involve fraud against insurance carriers, such as automobile, worker's compensation, disability, healthcare, life, homeowners, and others.

- *Computer fraud investigations:* These investigations involve developing evidence to prove computer or cybercriminal activities; sometimes this type of investigation is called computer forensics. (Computer security was covered extensively in Chapter 9 of this textbook.)

- *Core investigations:* These investigations involve the entire panoply of investigative services for businesses or individuals, including crimes or wrongs committed or threatened; background investigations of people and businesses; pre-employment background checks of job applicants; conduct and honesty of employees, agents, contractors, and subcontractors; incidents and illicit or illegal activities by persons against companies or company property; retail shoplifting; internal theft by employees or other employee crime; the truth or falsity of statements or representations; the whereabouts of missing persons; the location or recovery of lost or stolen property; the causes, origin of, or responsibility for fires, libel or slander, losses, accidents, injuries, or damages to property; the credibility of informants, witnesses, or other

persons; and the security of evidence to be used before investigating committees or boards of award or arbitration, or in the trial of civil or criminal cases and the preparation thereof.[24]

The fundamental difference between the private-sector investigator and the police investigator is the investigative objective. Whereas police investigators are primarily concerned with the interests of society, the private investigator serves organizational and individual interests.

Many private investigators are former police detectives or federal agents. Similar to the public investigation, the private investigation may overlap into a criminal area. However, the private investigator has no authority by state law to investigate a legally proscribed crime and should in all cases involving criminal violations inform the appropriate law enforcement agency.

Major Types of Private-Sector Noncriminal Investigations

Numerous types of private-sector noncriminal investigations not only provide important services for society but also provide job opportunities for persons interested in investigations.

All private-sector noncriminal investigations, as well as most criminal ones, involve the search for and collection and analysis of significant amounts of information. Information is the goal of the investigation. This information is contained in numerous written records maintained by government, private, and media information repositories. Much of it today is contained in enormous electronic databases. Also, significant amounts of information can be obtained through interviews and observations.[25]

This section will discuss the following noncriminal investigations conducted by private-sector investigators: financial investigations, product liability, finding people/missing persons, personal injury, wrongful death, medical malpractice, domestic/marital, and miscellaneous investigations and services. Pre-employment and other types of background screening, as well as drug screening, and sexual harassment in the workplace, were covered in Chapter 8 of this textbook.

You Are There!

"The Best Surveillance People I've Ever Had …"

"The best surveillance people I've ever had were females who did not have a law enforcement background," said Richard "Bo" Dietl, head of Bo Dietl and Associates Security and Investigations. He said that at least 40 percent of the investigators in his agency are women. "They're great on surveillance. No one suspects a woman is following them. They're also great on eavesdropping for the same reasons."

According to the managing director of Kroll Inc., "We need people with legal expertise, computer expertise, forensics experts. Those people come in all genders, shapes, and sizes."

Among the women profiled in a *New York Post* special on "Breaking through Gender Barriers" are these:

- A 25-year-old Brown graduate who spends her workdays hunting down information behind multi-million-dollar business deals. She is a former book publisher.

- A 28-year-old former junior-high teacher.
- A 28-year-old former employee of an art firm.
- A 25-year-old who graduated from Harvard and studied Romance poetry at Oxford. Her biggest case was an investigation into art stolen from Holocaust survivors during World War II. The probe led to major New York art galleries and former members of the Office of Strategic Services, the forerunner of the CIA.
- A Columbia Law School graduate and former assistant U.S. attorney, who worked for several years at the prestigious law firm of Cravath, Swaine and Moore. Last year, while providing services to Madison Square Garden, she helped bust a major ticket-scalping ring, resulting in the firing of seven employees.

SOURCE: Todd Venezia, "These Tough Gals Are Private Eye-Openers: Charlie's Angels Have Nothing on New Breed of Supersleuths," *New York Post* (July 19, 2000), pp. 20–21.

Financial Investigations

Financial investigations are conducted by proprietary investigating departments, contract investigative services, and private investigators. Many involve financial crimes and fraud and are covered later in the chapter. Others involve credit applications. Here are three examples of these investigations:

- *Due diligence investigations:* These investigations involve giving due diligence advice to companies contemplating entering into a business contract with another company or individual. (Due diligence means careful attention to details so that a company cannot be held liable for negligence.) These cases may involve a venture capitalist giving a loan to a prospective business, a franchisor lending money to a franchise, or a firm considering merging with another firm. The investigator checks out the subject's financial background, bill-paying history, and other financial dealings. In order to find this information, the investigator normally uses credit-reporting agencies and national computerized databases.

- *Postjudgment collection:* These cases involve an attempt to locate financial assets, such as bank accounts, real estate, securities, and motor vehicles, that the client can attach to settle a legal judgment prior to obtaining a writ of execution from the court to start a collection process.

- *Prejudgment investigation:* This occurs when an attorney is evaluating whether or not to take a case based on the possible damages that may be recovered. The investigator attempts to uncover the assets owned by the person the attorney's client wants to sue.

Product Liability

Corporations and private investigators investigate **product liability cases**—that is, lawsuits in which a client claims to have been injured by a certain product. A good recent example of product liability is the large number of lawsuits against Merck Pharmaceuticals over the possible negative effects of its Vioxx medication. As of 2005, Merck was subject to thousands of lawsuits over improper marketing and liability by users of the Vioxx drug that was taken by 20 million Americans between 1999 and 2004. Merck stopped selling it after a clinical trial linked the drug to heart attacks and strokes in patients taking Vioxx for eighteen months or longer.[26]

product liability cases Lawsuits in which a client claims to have been injured by a certain product.

Another case involved Ford Motor Company and the Bridgestone–Firestone Tire Company and resulted in the recall of 6.5 million tires. Investigators believe that three specific brands of Firestone tires caused accidents that left forty-six people dead and more than eighty injured. The tires were original equipment on 2-million Ford Explorer sport utility vehicles. Investigators discovered that these tires were produced at Firestone's Decatur, Illinois, factory by replacement workers during a union work dispute.[27]

The investigator's job is to determine whether the product was up to current safety standards and if anyone involved with the product was negligent. Whether the product was defective depends on the current state of the art, and negligence depends on whether those involved in the product—from the manufacturer to the distributor to the retailer—did something they should not have done or did not do something they should have done.

The investigator reviews the facts of the case to determine what happened and why it happened. The investigator also seeks to discover whether the product was involved in product liability complaints in the past. Because the product liability field can be quite technical and specialized, investigators often bring in experts or specialists in these cases. In addition, some investigators with previous experience in specialized fields, such as aviation or engineering, specialize in these cases.

Finding People / Missing Persons

Often investigators are hired to find people who are missing, have dropped out of sight, or are trying to hide. The police do not have the resources to fully investigate all missing persons cases and generally concentrate their efforts on cases that are suspicious or indicate foul play and on cases involving missing children and senile or disabled persons.

A private investigator may also be hired by a parent to locate a child taken in a custody dispute by the ex-spouse and removed to another jurisdiction outside of the court that is supervising the custody agreement. In these cases, the investigator may obtain a custody order from the court and proceed to attempt to locate the child, then travel to that location and execute the court order.

In a typical missing persons case, one of the first steps the investigator might take is to simply use the white pages of the telephone directory to see if there is a listing in the area where the person might be or might have fled to. Investigators also do name searches through public records to attempt to locate addresses and sometimes names of relatives, personal contacts, and business associates who might provide leads to the person's whereabouts. Some of these records may be marriage, divorce, voter registration, lawsuit, and real property records that are accessible to all members of the general public, including investigators. Many investigators also access this information through national computerized databases, also known as information brokers, from their personal computers.[28]

Personal Injury

In personal injury cases, the percentage of liability is determined by a jury or an expert, and evidence related to the extent of damages is presented using medical records and expert and victim testimony. The job of actually determining who was at fault often belongs to the private-sector investigator hired by the attorney or insurance company.

In these cases, investigators search for and interview witnesses, take photographs, and seek out additional information related to the incident. For example, in an auto accident, the investigator looks for evidence of faulty road conditions, such as faulty paving, traffic signs blocked by overgrown trees, snow or ice conditions, improper lane markings, and the like. In cases involving injury while operating certain equipment or machinery, the investigator attempts to identify the owner of the equipment and its manufacturer and any defects present. The investigator looks for facts that might have been missing from the police report and for witnesses that the police may have missed.

In vehicle accident cases, investigators engage in accident reconstruction analysis in an attempt to duplicate the events leading to the accident. The task of accident reconstruction has been simplified and enhanced in recent years with the help of computer simulations, which can be presented in a court hearing. Two professional associations may be helpful to investigators in these type of cases: the Traffic Accident Reconstruction Organization and the National Association of Professional Accident Reconstruction Specialists.[29]

Wrongful Death

Often, people who do not believe a police or coroner's official report that someone's death was from natural causes or an accident or suicide will hire a private-sector investigator to reopen the case. In these cases, the investigator will attempt to find new witnesses and sources, reinterview persons involved in the case, and do a much larger investigation than the public agency had time to do. The investigator may also hire a private forensic pathologist to reexamine the official reports. In cases involving accidental deaths in or by motor vehicles and other vehicles or those involving the operation of equipment, the investigator might solicit the assistance of a specialist to determine if there was product liability involving the vehicle or machinery for which the manufacturer, distributor, or retailer might be accountable.

Medical Malpractice

Private investigators may be hired by attorneys handling medical malpractice cases for a patient, doctor, or hospital. The investigator attempts to discover who is at fault for the malpractice. Could it be the doctor, hospital staff, paramedics? Could it be the result of an existing condition of the person? Could it be the result of an improper diagnosis by the doctor? In order to answer these questions, the investigator interviews all persons involved in the case and reviews all the official documents and the past histories and records of the persons involved. The investigator might also hire medical experts to determine if the care given to a person was consistent with the current standard of medical care required for people with that particular medical condition.

Domestic/Marital

Often, people who believe that their spouses may be having an affair or cheating on them with another person hire private investigators to confirm these beliefs or to obtain evidence for a legal action. Generally, private investigators conduct surveillance of the subject and attempt to obtain photographic evidence of the activities of the person and anyone with whom he or she is in contact.

Many investigators do not like to become involved in domestic or marital investigations because the cases can become very emotional and also involve an inordinate amount of time in surveillances and stakeouts. Furthermore,

participating in such investigations can be a little like stepping into the middle of a soap opera.

Miscellaneous Investigations and Services

Private investigators often become involved in numerous varied types of investigations and services for their clients, including security advice and crisis management, guard and patrol services, and service of subpoenas.

Security Advice and Crisis Management Very often, private-sector investigators, because of their experience and expertise, are hired as consultants by firms or individuals seeking advice in implementing security and contingency plans in the event of emergencies or crises. Consultants are problem solvers who generally bring a great deal of experience and competence to an assignment. Their contacts, resources, and independence contribute to their usefulness to clients.

Guard and Patrol Services Many private-sector investigators combine their investigative services with guard and patrol services. The guard and patrol service is the largest component of the security industry in terms of revenue and personnel employed. More people are employed as private security guards than are employed by the public law enforcement sector. The security guard and patrol services market has grown steadily in the past two decades. Current growth comes from companies switching from proprietary security officers to those provided by an outside contractor. In recent years, the decline of law enforcement services relative to demand has encouraged further growth of this industry. Many of these firms also offer investigative services and alarm and armored-car services. Chapter 3 of this text covered the area of guard and patrol services.

Service of Subpoenas Often, courts or other government offices will hire a local private investigative firm to serve subpoenas to individuals requiring them to appear in court or at another government hearing. The local private investigator's knowledge of the community greatly assists him or her in locating and serving these subpoenas. Generally, the investigator is paid a fee for each subpoena served.

Meet Kat Albrecht—A Pet Detective

At least 4 million pets are lost annually, according to data from U.S. animal shelters. However, the actual figure may be much higher because some lost pets are never reported missing, and others may be found before a shelter is notified.

Kat Albrecht, a former police officer, has worked to find many missing pets and now is training others to do so. She is a pet detective. Albrecht served eight years as a search-and-rescue officer in Santa Cruz, California. In 1998, when a back injury caused her to leave the department, Albrecht became a full-time pet detective. She applied the same technologies, principles, and theories, such as profiling, search probability theory, and analysis of physical evidence, that she had used to find missing persons to find missing pets. She had trained Rachel, her Weimaraner, to track and recover pets.

Albrecht retired from active pet detective duty in 2001 and has since focused on training other pet detectives and establishing a national network for the recovery of lost pets. Her website, Missing Pet Partnership, offers advice and methods for finding missing pets and links to other pet detectives. Albrecht's agency also offers training programs and certification for other pet detectives.

Albrecht also wrote *The Lost Pet Chronicles: Adventures of a K-9 Cop Turned Pet Detective* (Bloomsbury USA, 2004).

SOURCES: Robert Mortiz, "A Pet Sleuth to the Rescue," *Parade*, July 11, 2004, pp. 8, 9; *Missing Pet Partnership*. Retrieved October 14, 2004, from http://www.lostapet.org; and Kathy Albrecht, *The Lost Pet Chronicles: Adventures of a K-9 Cop Turned Pet Detective*, Bloomsbury USA, 2004.

Major Types of Private-Sector Criminal Investigations

Crime is a significant fact of life in the United States. Chapters 5 and 7 of this textbook discussed the numbers and types of crime occuring in the United States. Our society relies on the police to deal with the issues of crime because crime is considered a violation of the greater society's values and norms; however, the private sector does get involved in investigating some particular crimes.[30]

Although crimes and criminal investigations generally fall under the jurisdiction of the public police, private-sector investigators often conduct criminal investigations for their corporations, businesses, or clients, corporate or private. In this section, we will briefly discuss private-sector investigations in the following criminal areas: violent and property crimes; corporate crime; internal theft; fraud, including business and credit-card fraud and counterfeiting; insurance fraud, including worker's compensation and medical and healthcare fraud; and industrial espionage.

Violent and Property Crimes

The police are generally called in to investigate serious violent and property crimes in the workplace. However, often, a defense attorney will hire a private investigator to reinvestigate the police investigation that resulted in the arrest of the attorney's client. In these situations, the private investigator canvasses the area where the crime took place in an attempt to find new witnesses. He or she also re-interviews police witnesses and victims, as well as the defendant. Private investigators seek access to all of the police reports in a case through the discovery or disclosure process. They review the reports and look for inconsistencies and mistakes. Often, they attempt to re-create the crime scene to test certain theories or hypotheses. They are not allowed, however, to be present at crime scenes while they are still active.

In addition, corporate investigation departments, contract security service companies, and private independent investigators may also investigate these crimes to apprehend the violator and to prevent a reoccurrence. These investigators only supplement the investigations done by police investigators and do not replace them.

The following is one recent example of how independent, licensed private investigators help their clients investigate crime:

> A couple who suspected their house cleaners were stealing their property after a $30,000 antique bracelet disappeared hired Thomas Ruskin, a former NYPD detective and president of CMP Group Inc., who set up a sting. Ruskin placed cameras in the couple's bedroom. The cleaners were caught on the tape stealing a video camera and several blank checks as the couple and the private investigators watched from a neighbor's apartment. The investigators then swooped in to the apartment where the cleaners admitted to the thefts and to other thefts from other clients.[31]

Corporate Crime

Corporate crime is various crimes committed by corporations, their employees, and their representatives for the benefit of, or on behalf of the corporation. These crimes include economic crime (money laundering, bribery, price fixing), misrepresentation in advertising, production and sale of unsafe products, deceptive packaging, environmental crime, and also crimes against persons, including crimes causing injury or death.[32]

Corporate crimes also include those committed against corporations by officers, directors and employees (fraud, theft, embezzlement, corruption), crimes committed against corporations by external forces (robbery, burglary, larceny, piracy), and crimes committed for corporations by internal forces (regulatory noncompliance, tax evasion, bribery, and false financial statements).

In 2002, as the result of numerous corporate financial scandals in the last decade, including those connected with Enron, Tyco International, and WorldCom, Congress passed the federal **Sarbanes-Oxley Act** (the Public Company Accounting Reform and Investor Protection Act of 2002) to protect investors by improving the accuracy and reliability of corporate disclosures. This law covers such issues as establishing a public company accounting oversight board, auditor independence, corporate responsibility, and enhanced financial disclosure.[33] The Sarbanes-Oxley Act has caused renewed public interest in

reducing corporate crime and crime committed by corporate officials. Many companies, however, report having problems complying with the requirements of the new law.

The complex and expensive requirements of the Sarbanes-Oxley Act, regarding reporting and management of internal business controls, have received much high-profile attention in addition to becoming the basis for an industry of compliance-management products and services. It involves important processes that businesses must implement in order to minimize the risk of declines in shareholder value. It mandates that executive compensation and loans follow a prescribed code to ensure that such transactions benefit the shareholders and not solely individual employees. It requires companies to notify executives when stock trading is suspended so that they can avoid making illegal transactions during such a period. It also requires the implementation of an ethics code, made available to all employees, that makes clear the nature of unacceptable conduct and requires employees to report such conduct; and it also establishes rules for retention of sensitive documents and penalties for unauthorized document destruction.[34]

Internal Theft

Internal theft and fraud are serious problems affecting U.S. businesses, and private security professionals are actively involved in dealing with these problems.

Theft of corporate assets can be devastating to businesses. It can include theft by outsiders or insiders. As indicated in Chapter 6 of this textbook, employee theft can have a more devastating effect on retail businesses than victimization by burglars, robbers, and shoplifters.

Internal theft in the workplace can generally start in the mail room, but workplace theft is costliest when committed by high-ranking employees who have access to large amounts of funds.[35]

Specific measures to prevent employee theft are a drug-free workplace, pre-employment screening, crime-prevention and loss awareness, and employer–employee communications. Other crime-prevention measures are inventory and money controls, target hardening (use of security devices, such as locks, gates, alarms, and the like), and use of professional consultants and vendors to enhance physical security. Companies also use aggressive undercover operations and proactive measures to deal with this crime.

Sarbanes-Oxley Act Federal law enacted in 2002 to protect investors by improving the accuracy and reliability of corporate disclosures; also known as the Public Company Accounting Reform and Investor Protector Act.

You Are There!

The Sarbanes-Oxley Act

The Sarbanes-Oxley Act, officially titled the Public Company Accounting Reform and Investor Protection Act of 2002 (PL 107-204, 116 Stat. 745) and also commonly called SOX or SarBox, was signed into law in July 2002 by President George W. Bush. It was created to protect investors by improving the accuracy and reliability of corporate disclosures. The law covers such issues as establishing a public-company accounting oversight board, auditor independence, corporate responsibility, and enhanced financial disclosure. It was designed to review dated legislative audit requirements, and some consider it the most significant change to U.S. securities law since the New Deal in the 1930s. President Bush stated that it included the most far-reaching reforms of American business practices since the time of Franklin Delano Roosevelt. It seeks to make corporate accounting and financial disclosure by companies much more transparent to investors.

The new law came about in the wake of a series of corporate scandals in the 2000s, including Enron, Tyco International, and WorldCom. As one example, in 2002, WorldCom revealed it had overstated its earnings by more than $3.8 billion during the last year, primarily through improper accounting methods. The act is named after its sponsors, Senator Paul Sarbanes and Representative Michael G. Oxley.

Some of the law's major provisions include the following:

- Certification of financial reports by CEOs and CFOs
- Ban on personal loans to any executive officer or director
- Accelerated reporting of trades by insiders
- Prohibition on insider trades during pension-fund blackout periods
- Public reporting of CEO and CFO compensation and profits
- Additional disclosure
- Auditor independence, including bans on certain types of work and precertification by the company's audit committee of all other nonaudit work
- Criminal and civil penalties for violations of security laws
- Significantly longer jail sentences and larger fines for corporate executives who knowingly and willfully misstate financial statements
- A requirement that publicly traded companies furnish independent annual audit reports on the existence and reliability of internal controls relating to financial reporting

SOURCES: Elisabeth Bumiller, "Bush Signs Bill Aimed at Fraud in Corporations," *New York Times*, July 31, 2002, p. A1; *Sarbanes-Oxley Act*. Retrieved November 6, 2005, from http://en.wikipedia.org/wiki/Sarbanes-Oxley-Act; and *The Sarbanes-Oxley Act Community Forum*. Retrieved November 6, 2005, from http://www.sarbanes-oxley-forum.com.

Fraud, Including Business and Credit-Card Fraud and Counterfeiting

Fraud, in general, is defined as theft by the intentional use of deceit or trickery. Fraud is an enormous problem for U.S. businesses. This section will discuss business fraud, credit-card fraud, and counterfeiting or the theft of intellectual property rights.

Business Fraud The American Institute of Certified Public Accountants maintains auditing standards, detailing the auditor's responsibility to detect and report material misstatement in financial statements due to fraud.[36] The two relevant types of misstatements are misstatements arising from fraudulent financial reporting and misappropriation of assets. Other considerations in preventing and detecting corporate fraud include managerial controls, employee screening, forensic accounting, and others.[37] Also, as mentioned earlier in this chapter, the Sarbanes-Oxley Act, passed in 2002, is designed to help prevent corporate fraud.

Private businesses use financial controls, preventive methods, and internal investigative teams to combat all types of fraud. Private security professionals can offer substantial assistance to public law enforcement officials by providing comprehensive and accurate investigative reports of incidents, and public law enforcement officials can also help businesses by providing suggestions on how to conduct investigations.[38]

fraud Larceny committed by trickery or deceit.

A survey of 5,000 businesses, government agencies, and nonprofit agencies revealed the following average loss for each respondent as a result of employee fraud:

■ Check fraud by employees, including forgeries and mail-room theft, resulted in an average loss of $624,000.

■ Theft of company bank accounts by employees using ATM cards resulted in an average loss of $300,000.

■ Theft and misuse of company credit cards resulted in an average loss of $1.1 million.

■ Loss from employee expense-account abuse resulted in an average loss of $141,000.[39]

As an example of internal fraud, a mail-room clerk at a nonprofit foundation stole $650,000 in checks over three months, pawning them off to an intermediary for pennies on the dollar. The foundation did not know anything was wrong until students who had been awarded research grants started calling from schools around the world, asking when the money would arrive. The mail-room clerk took the checks to a teller at a bank, who deposited them into false accounts.[40]

Banks use fraud investigators to look into merchant fraud, and businesses hire fraud investigators to look into fraud by customers. For example, the First Data Corporation of Atlanta, which processes credit- and debit-card transactions, as well as information related to financial transactions over the Internet, by check, and via wire transfer, aggressively investigates fraud with its own proprietary investigating department. In addition to their security investigations for First Data, these security investigators conduct field investigations for retailers and merchant fraud investigations for banks on a contract basis.[41]

Security professionals report that, in some ways, workplace thieves have become easier to catch through technology such as video cameras, decoys, and other tools. But computers, modems, and the Internet also offer employees new ways of tampering with financial records, transferring funds, and covering their tracks. Security professionals report that there are several reasons why fraud is increasing. In the 1990s, for example, as labor shortages threatened growth, some companies

eliminated pre-employment screening to speed up hiring. Another reason is that with pressure to post record earnings quarter after quarter, many businesses have cut back on departments like accounting and security that help detect theft but do not generate revenue because management often looks at internal controls as cost centers, not profit centers.[42]

Fraud examiners also attribute much of the recent wave of office criminality to the stock market boom that created hordes of overnight millionaires and some employees' resultant impatience with their occasional pay raise. In addition, there is a widening gap between executive and worker compensation. Corporate chief executives earn an average of four-hundred times what their regular employees do. The disparity in pay has fueled discontent and eroded loyalty to such a degree that stealing on the job is often seen as acceptable behavior.

The Association of Certified Fraud Examiners (ACFE) reports that companies usually lose 6 percent of their annual revenues to employee theft. One consequence of the growth in employee theft has been a large gain in the number of fraud investigators. The number of members in ACFE confirms this gain.[43]

ACFE is dedicated to fighting fraud and white collar crime. With offices in North America and Europe and chapters around the globe, ACFE responds to the needs of antifraud professionals. It certifies qualified individuals as **certified fraud examiners (CFEs),** who are trained in the highly specialized aspects of detecting, investigating, and deterring fraud and white collar crime. Each member of the association designated as a CFE has earned certification after an extensive application process and after passing the uniform CFE examination. ACFE also conducts numerous seminars and conferences.

These fraud examiners come from various professions, including auditors, accountants, fraud investigators, loss prevention specialists, attorneys, educators, and criminologists. They gather evidence, take statements, write reports, and assist in investigating fraud in its varied forms. They are employed by most major corporations and government agencies and provide consulting and investigative services. CFEs have investigated more than 1 million suspected cases of civil and criminal fraud.

Major U.S. financial institutions are also working to set up a new defense against insider fraud: a database of employees known to be scam risks.

certified fraud examiner (CFE) Investigator who is certified to conduct fraud investigations.

Credit-card fraud is an international criminal activity increasingly run by organized crime syndicates that often have industry insiders on their payrolls. Here the evidence from an undercover operation by the Spanish police displays high-quality "fake" credit cards, video consoles, mobile phones and other goods seized. The operation resulted in the arrests of twenty-three people suspected of using a sophisticated scheme to produce false credit cards.

In 2005, it was reported that a consortium of one hundred of the largest U.S. financial institutions, including JPMorgan Chase and Wachovia, are developing the new database listing information on employees at financial institutions who were fired because they compromised customer data or knowingly caused financial losses.[44]

Credit-card fraud An international activity, **credit-card fraud** is increasingly run by organized crime syndicates that often have industry insiders on their payrolls. The basic types of credit-card fraud are point-of-sale fraud, card-not-present fraud, e-commerce fraud, ATM fraud, and identity theft. Card-not-present fraud involves setting up a fake or ghost operation to qualify for card-reader installations and using stolen card data to make fraudulent purchases over the telephone or via the Internet. Credit-card Internet fraud has ballooned as online e-commerce has become more widespread. Lost or stolen cards are usually fraudulently used before the owner reports the card loss. ATM-related credit-card fraud occurs most often when consumers write down their PIN and keep it in their wallet or purse.[45] The area of identity theft is also a major form of commercial

fraud and was covered in depth in Chapter 9 of this text.

In a 2005 article, it was reported that many retailers that sell through the Internet and cable television channels use fraud investigators and high-tech computers to monitor orders for signs of fraud. Some of the things these investigators look for might include a suspect address that customers want goods sent to or the speed of orders from one place. Major credit-card companies have invested millions of dollars in high-tech fraud-detection systems, giant computers that process up to 5,000 transactions a second during busy times, doing real-time pattern analysis to detect billing-address anomalies and other signs that something is not right with a credit-card order.[46]

One firm uses seventeen investigators assigned a large caseload of orders flagged by the computers. Most of the flagged orders involve a check of address databases or a call to the address verification

credit-card fraud Fraud involving the use of credit cards, including point-of-sale fraud, card-not-present fraud, e-commerce fraud, ATM fraud, and identity theft.

279

hotline at the credit card's issuing bank. About 8 percent of orders turn out to be fraudulent.

In "card-not-present" transactions, duped retailers lose out on merchandise fraudulently ordered if it is never recovered. They also lose the money they paid to process and ship the items, and they have to pay a fee to the credit-card issuer for reversing the charge.

The International Association of Financial Crimes Investigators (IAFC) is a professional organization created in 1968 as the International Association of Credit Card Investigators (changed to IAFC in 1996). It is comprised of law enforcement officers and investigators from credit–card companies, banks, airlines, telecommunications firms, petroleum processors, and transporter agencies that provide an environment within which information about financial fraud, fraud investigation, and fraud prevention methods can be collected and exchanged.[47]

Counterfeiting Another type of business fraud is the theft of **intellectual property rights** or counterfeiting. The manufacture and sale of **knock-off or copycat** (counterfeit) **goods** create health and safety problems for consumers, economic losses for trademark owners, and criminal problems for society.

In order to protect consumers, to safeguard the intellectual property rights of trademark owners, and to ensure product integrity, companies and industry representatives maintain alliances with law enforcement officials around the world in addition to other efforts they make to combat this problem. For example, the Calvin Klein Cosmetics Company uses aggressive countermeasure programs, including lobbying, to gain enforcement support. The company distributes product identification information to the worldwide law enforcement community to facilitate identification of suspected counterfeit products related to its registered trademarks. Organizations such as the World Customs Organization, the World Trade Organization, the World Intellectual Property Organization, and others assist in seeking effective legislative and enforcement protection for intellectual property rights worldwide.[48]

Insurance Fraud, Including Worker's Compensation and Medical and Healthcare Fraud

Insurance investigations are a major part of the private-sector investigating industry. Insurance company investigators and private investigators hired by insurance companies investigate all types of insurance frauds, including casualty, worker's compensation, and medical and healthcare fraud. They often conduct surveillances on persons who may be engaged in **insurance fraud**. For example, a person may claim an injury from a work-related action and go on disability or worker's compensation or sue an employer. The investigator may follow the subject or conduct a clandestine surveillance in an attempt to gain evidence that the subject is not suffering from any work-related or accident-related injuries. Often, investigators are able to photograph a subject performing some action, like mowing a lawn or dancing at a club, that would not be possible if the individual were actually suffering from the results of the alleged injuries. Chapter 11 of this textbook will discuss surveillance tactics.

An excellent source for insurance fraud investigations is the National Insurance Crime Bureau (NICB). The NICB provides investigative services for insurers and law enforcement agencies in the investigation and prosecution of organized rings and persons or companies perpetrating insurance fraud.[49]

The National Society of Professional Insurance Investigators (NSPII) is an organization established to provide recognition, encouragement, and support to individuals involved in conducting insurance investigations. The NSPII sponsors seminars and workshops offering case management concepts and principles for fraud detection and prevention. It keeps its members aware of relevant legislative issues and actions and recent court decisions. It also serves as a resource center, providing technical and legal information to the industry as it becomes available. Members include independent investigators, insurance company personnel, forensic accountants, and attorneys.[50]

intellectual property rights An umbrella term for various legal entitlements that attach to certain names, written and recorded media, and inventions.

knock-off or copycat goods Counterfeit products.

insurance fraud Fraud in insurance claims, including disability, worker's compensation, auto, medical, health care, and other types.

You Are There!

Some Examples of Successful Work by Insurance Fraud Special Investigations Units (SIUs)

■ The insured's husband was driving the insured vehicle when he caused a three-car accident. One person was taken to the hospital as a result of the accident. A claim was filed against the insured of $10,000.

The investigation by the SIU revealed that the insured's policy was uploaded at 5:22 P.M. on the same date as the loss. However, the police report showed that the accident was called in at 5:05 P.M., seventeen minutes prior to the inception of the policy. When the claimants were interviewed, they stated that the insured's wife was in the car at the time of the accident but exited the vehicle and walked down the street prior to the arrival of the police. It was determined that the insured's wife had gone into an agent's office and purchased a policy after the accident and before the arrival of the police.

■ An insured stated that he let someone hold the keys to his auto when he went to the restroom. When he came out, the vehicle was gone. The insured claimed that he only knew the suspect's first name and pager number. The vehicle was recovered with all windows broken out, the steering column stripped, and damage to the right front fender. The suspect was apprehended and interviewed by the police. He stated that the insured gave him the vehicle in exchange for drugs.

When confronted with this information by the SIU, the insured voluntarily withdrew his claim. This case is being reviewed for prosecution.

SOURCE: Phyllis Van Wyhe, "Special Investigations Units (SIUs)," *Fraud and the Agent.* Retrieved October 11, 2004, from http://insurancece.com.

Many insurance companies have established highly trained **special investigative units (SIUs)** as part of their insurance fraud control or claim security programs. The SIU's role is to train claim representatives in dealing with routine fraud cases and to thoroughly investigate more serious fraudulent activities. These teams often include former law enforcement officers, attorneys, accountants, and claims experts. Many of them have had previous extensive claim investigation or law enforcement experience. SIUs dramatically impact the bottom line of many companies. It has been reported that while results vary from company to company, on average, companies save $10 for every dollar they invest in SIUs.[51]

The International Association of Special Investigation Units (IASIU) is comprised of insurance industry fraud investigators dedicated to promoting a coordinated effort within the insurance industry to combat insurance fraud and provide education/training and high professional standards of conduct among insurance investigators. IASIU offers an accrediting process for individuals with the specialized skills required to detect, investigate, and prevent insurance fraud. Qualified individuals may earn the designation of **certified insurance fraud investigator**.[52]

The Insurance Information Institute is a professional organization provided by the insurance industry to allow consumers to obtain information on various types of insurance and insurance company information, such as hot topics, facts and statistics, and the latest studies.[53]

Worker's Compensation Fraud Worker's compensation fraud is an ongoing problem that can cost businesses enormous sums of money if not handled properly. Management must act quickly after detecting the first signs that an employee may be lying about a workplace injury to collect benefits. Waiting even a month or two can make it impossible to gather enough evidence. If the investigation is delayed, critical time-sensitive evidence of fraud through proper video surveillance will be missed. In addition, witnesses will no longer have fresh memories of the incident. Key elements of the

special investigating units (SIUs) Teams used by insurance companies to train claim representatives in dealing with routine fraud cases; they also investigate more-serious fraud cases.

certified insurance fraud investigator Investigator who is certified to conduct insurance fraud investigations.

investigation are the interview of witnesses, documentation of all injuries and conditions at the site of the injury, document analysis, and surveillance. All reports prepared by the complainant, including medical and government reports, are analyzed to determine if any inconsistencies exist.[54]

Medical and Healthcare Fraud An extremely serious problem, **medical or healthcare fraud** can be committed by a healthcare provider, a patient, or both. Billions of dollars are lost each year in frauds against Medicare, Medicaid, and insurance and health maintenance organizations. As an example, in 2000, a well-known fertility specialist with a busy, celebrity-studded practice, had his medical license suspended by the New York State Department of Health, which declared him "an imminent danger to public health." He was charged with numerous counts of negligence, incompetence, fraudulent practices, and moral unfitness. He has also been prosecuted by the federal government for a fraud scheme in which he billed insurance companies for gynecological cases that actually involved fertility procedures.[55]

Since the early 1990s, heathcare fraud, the deliberate submittal of false claims to private health insurance plans and/or tax-funded health insurance programs such as Medicare and Medicaid, has been viewed as a serious and still-growing annual healthcare outlay, which in 2000 alone amounted to $1.3 trillion. Every year, more than 4 billion health insurance benefit transactions are processed in the United States. The National Health Care Anti-Fraud Association (NHCAA) reported in 2002 in its Anti-Fraud Management Survey that fifty-nine of its member insurers collectively recovered or prevented payment of just under $326 million as a direct result of their antifraud activities. NHCAA estimates that of the nation's annual healthcare outlay, at least 3 percent—or $39 billion—is lost to outright fraud.[56]

The following are the most common types of fraud committed by dishonest providers:

■ Billing for services that were never rendered

■ Billing for more expensive services or procedures than were actually provided or performed—upcoding

---

PRIVATE SECURITY CONNECTIONS

Information Centers for Fraud Investigators

National Insurance Crime Bureau (NICB)
National Fraud Information Center and Internet Fraud Watch (NFIC)
Insurance Information Institute (III)

■ Performing medically unnecessary services solely for the purpose of generating insurance payments

■ Misrepresenting noncovered treatments as medically necessary covered treatments for purposes of obtaining insurance payment[57]

A 2004 article in the *Prosecutor* focuses on billing for nonrendered services, fraudulent coding for a service that is more expensive than the one actually rendered, the mischaracterization of a service to make it qualify for insurance coverage, the performance of unnecessary medical services, quackery and sham cures, and kickbacks. In these cases, prosecutors establish a liaison with the SIUs of insurance companies that do business in the state. The SIUs act as in-house fraud detection and investigation units for insurance companies. In addition, state and private worker's compensation bureaus often have an intelligence base regarding suspect providers and can supply evidence that would form the basis for a criminal charge.

Prescription fraud, which is also known as pharmaceutical diversion, is the illegal acquisition of prescription drugs for personal use or profit. Methods for committing prescription fraud include the forging of prescriptions, going to several doctors to obtain multiple prescriptions, and altering prescriptions to increase the quantity. A significant amount of prescription fraud is undetected because it is not a high law enforcement priority. The prescription drugs most often involved in fraud include Valium and Vicodin, as well as Xanax, Oxycontin, Lorcet, Dilaudid, Percocet, Soma, Darvocet, and morphine.[58]

The NHCAA is a private/public partnership against healthcare fraud and an excellent resource because it provides a variety of investigative support resources, as well as a number of education and training programs geared toward the prosecution and investigation of healthcare fraud.[59]

The NHCAA has established the NHCAA Institute for Health Care Fraud Prevention, which holds

---

medical fraud Fraud committed by a healthcare provider, patient, or both.

healthcare fraud Deliberate submittal of false claims to private health insurance plans and/or tax-funded health insurance programs, such as Medicare and Medicaid.

Some Professional Associations for Fraud Investigators

Association of Certified Fraud Examiners (ACFE)
International Association of Financial Crimes Investigators (IAFCI)
National Society of Professional Insurance Investigators (NSPII)
National Health Care Anti-Fraud Association (NHCAA)
NHCAA Institute for Health Care Fraud Prevention (NHCAA Institute)
International Association of Special Investigation Units (IASIU)

annual training conferences to spotlight emerging schemes, current issues, and best practices on the healthcare and disability fraud forefront. The annual conference is attended by industry and law enforcement professionals. It also provides education and training in the form of interactive CDs that provide a substantive basic education in the nature, scope, and impact of healthcare fraud. It grants the professional designation **accredited healthcare fraud investigator (AHFI)** to individuals who meet certain qualifications related to professional experience, specialized training, formal education, and demonstrated knowledge in the detection and investigation and/or prosecution of healthcare fraud.[60]

Industrial Espionage

Espionage is the practice of spying to acquire information. The term *industrial espionage* refers to the practice of obtaining business or technological information through surreptitious means. This practice has long existed and is a growing concern today, especially in the defense, aerospace, manufacturing, microelectronics, and computer industries.

Corporations can obtain information about each other's business, operations, and technology legally through the Freedom of Information Act; by reading technical or business publications; or by attending trade shows and business conventions. They can obtain information semilegally through employees who change jobs and illegally through bribery or blackmail. Although the practice of industrial espionage is most commonly ascribed to industry, theft of scientific ideas and technological advances has been a problem among governments as well.

According to a 2006 article in the *San Francisco Chronicle,*

Corporate espionage is a fact of life. Some form of snooping is relatively commonplace at all kinds of companies, experts say. And in the electronic age they are becoming even more so. Corporate spying may be as simple as a company president visiting competitors' stores to see what's on sale, as elaborate as engaging outside experts to learn about a rival's business or as high-tech as hiring a hacker to try to breach a company's own security measures to identify weaknesses.[61]

Industrial espionage is generally easy to carry out. Agents can install wiretaps or bugs; steal, buy, or transcribe documents; steal equipment; or simply observe with their own eyes. (A wiretap is a device put on a telephone system to intercept telephone conversations. A bug is a microphone that can intercept conversations in a room or other location.) Sometimes the agent is a plant—a person who is positioned in a target organization for an extended period of time—or an insider—a member of the targeted organization who has shifted loyalties and who produces information on a regular basis.

Many firms employ disreputable people to surreptitiously and illegally record or intercept phone calls or conversations in corporate meetings. In today's world, where business contracts are awarded with a "winner-take-all" mentality, some domestic companies and foreign corporations will go to any measure, including criminal activity, to ensure that they are awarded the contract. Disgruntled employees are the most sought-after asset by a competitor because of the corporate knowledge they possess. Also, because today's marketplace is unstable, many employees do not feel a sense of loyalty to their employer, and this can lead to industrial espionage.[62]

Foreign intelligence services are also a threat to business. In a 2002 article in *Security Journal*, Peter R. J. Trim discussed the role of China in industrial espionage and a network of Chinese agents

accredited healthcare fraud investigator (AHFI)
A unique professional designation granted by the National Health Care Anti-Fraud Association to individuals who meet certain qualifications related to professional experience, specialized training, formal education, and demonstrated knowledge in the detection, investigation, and/or prosecution of healthcare fraud.

industrial espionage Covert collection of industrial secrets or processes.

established in American corporations. He reported that China conducts an information warfare strategy via the Internet and stressed the need for businesses wishing to protect sensitive and confidential data and information to establish a corporate intelligence unit to act as liaison between the company and its constituent parts and between the company and various government agencies.[63]

Trim also reported that cyberattacks against companies require the expertise of several specialists to defend against such attacks. He concluded that the establishment of a corporate intelligence unit levels the playing field for business competition and allows a company to concentrate on developing and launching marketable products and services.

The other side of espionage is **counterespionage**, which is the prevention and thwarting of hostile espionage. Counterespionage uses some of the same methods as espionage itself. One method of disabling an adversary's espionage program is by planting one's own agent (a mole) into the adversary's espionage organization. Another method of thwarting espionage is **sweeping** any locations where important meetings and discussions are held, which includes using electronic means to locate and remove any wiretaps or bugs that might be present and using electronic devices to prevent the surreptitious recording of conversations. Sweeping operations have opened a new field of employment for private security investigators with electronic or technical expertise. Also, counterespionage needs have developed a new industry providing space-age products in such areas as audio and video surveillance.

It may sometimes be easy to obtain sensitive proprietary technical and personnel information as a result of a company's insufficient access control and security procedures. An author, while doing research on a series of novels he intended to write on high-technology espionage, conducted an experiment in which he personally visited twelve high-tech companies of various sizes in a certain area in a northwestern state. In eleven of the twelve companies, he was able to penetrate the facilities and had numerous opportunities to steal sensitive proprietary information. He was able to roam the hallways and offices of the companies

and freely chatted and received important proprietary information from employees and security guards. He was able to view important documents on workers' computers and on their desks. In only one company was he challenged by an alert receptionist who denied him entrance to the workplace. The author concluded that small companies need to take security more seriously:

> Throughout this project, I could have been stopped by a skeptical receptionist who need only have asked probing questions about the nature of my business and who I was there to see. A visitor sign-in program and a requirement that all visitors be escorted by the person with whom they have an appointment would also have deterred me. In addition, I would have been thwarted by an electronic access control system in which doors to various suites were locked.[64]

In 2006, a major case of industrial espionage shocked the business world. The computer maker Hewlett-Packard (HP) was accused of using illegal methods to obtain phone records of board members, journalists, and others in order to investigate leaks of confidential information by corporate board members about the company's corporate strategy. In September 2006, the company's chairwoman Patricia C. Dunn and other major corporate executives resigned. Among the major issues discovered was the use of "pretexting" by investigators—impersonating someone else to obtain that person's calling records from a phone company. (Pretexting is discussed later in this chapter.) It was disclosed that HP had hired a team of independent investigators who had misrepresented themselves as the board members and journalists to their phone companies in order to obtain their phone records. Dunn, another corporate official, and three outside investigators were indicted on felony charges by the California Attorney General.[65]

Information Resources for Private-Sector Investigators

Obtaining information is the primary goal of the investigator. Information leads to the discovery of facts that may explain crimes and other

---

counterespionage Efforts made to prevent and thwart hostile espionage.

sweeping Checking of a premise for electronic surveillance devices.

occurrences in which the investigator is interested. Investigators obtain information from a multitude of sources. In today's society, from birth until death, people leave a plethora of facts about themselves and their activities through numerous sources, including other people and records.

Some have described the world we are living in as the "Information Age." Much of the information discussed in this chapter can be found in computer files and on the Internet, both of which can be accessed easily by the average person. Often, investigators can obtain necessary information by making a telephone call or visiting the source of the information.

Numerous sources of information are available to investigators, including both people and records. People can be classified as regular sources (victims and witnesses) and cultivated sources (informants and confidential informants). Records can originate with law enforcement sources; government sources at the federal, state, and local levels; and private sources, including business organizations, public utilities, credit-reporting agencies, and the local public library. Numerous books and directories, as well as the Internet, are good sources of information.

Some of the numerous information searches available to investigators and the public on the Internet include names, ages, birth dates, addresses, phone numbers, background checks, criminal checks, court records, public records, marital/divorce records, and the like. Some of these sites allow people to do a search by themselves, and some provide an assisted search for a fee.

Corporate contract investigative services and private independent investigators use the Internet to find information they are interested in by accessing large computerized databases. By entering certain **header information** into the appropriate database, an investigator can obtain additional information regarding the subject. Header information can be a name, address, social security number, or any of the many types of information that the average person enters onto forms—for example, when requesting a car loan, registering at a college, obtaining a telephone company or utility company account, or simply filling out a coupon to win a free turkey at the local supermarket.

Some important major sources of information are entered into **computerized databases** kept by informational brokers. Information brokers purchase their information from both public and private agencies that collect this information constantly. **Information brokers** are private persons or corporations that provide detective or computerized databases to private-sector investigators throughout the nation. Detective databases are specialized information resources designed to help detectives, attorneys, skip tracers, and other interested parties locate people, find assets, uncover motor vehicle records, and trace college transcripts, credit histories, phone numbers, forwarding addresses, references, and other related data. Private investigators using their personal computer and a modem can contact any number of these databases online.

Information brokers obtain their information from numerous sources, including public records, news sources, corporate mailing lists, and marketing lists. They also access and catalogue header information. Certain information, such as financial records, bank account information, and social security numbers, cannot be provided to information brokers.

Some information brokers and investigators may use a form of trickery known as **pretexting** to get private information like bank accounts and phone numbers. They call a bank, phone company, or other business and claim to be the customer whose records they are seeking. This often works because customer service representatives are trained to provide help to customers.

Another ruse to obtain information is the so-called Trojan check. The information broker sets up a dummy corporation and sends a check for a small amount of money to the target of his investigation, either as a supposed rebate or award. When the target deposits or cashes the check, information about the target's bank account is imprinted on the canceled check. The broker can then use the information to approach the bank.

Private investigator James J. Rapp is one notable example of how to use ruses such as pretexting to obtain personal information. Rapp, who claimed

---

header information Databased personal information that is sold to marketers.

computerized databases Databases containing huge amounts of personal information from public and private sources, maintained by information brokers who sell information to investigators or other interested persons; also known as detective databases.

information broker Private person or corporation that provides detective databases to private investigators throughout the nation.

pretexting Pretending to be someone else to obtain information about that person.

on his web page that he could quickly get anyone's private telephone records or bank account balances for as little as $100, became the subject of a lawsuit by the Federal Trade Commission (FTC) in 1999. In the lawsuit it was claimed that his employees would call banks, pretending to be doddering and confused customers in order to obtain social security numbers and other information—like the maiden name of an account holder's mother.[66]

Rapp was also indicted by a Golden, Colorado, grand jury for providing confidential information to news organizations about the JonBenet Ramsey murder investigation. He was also charged with giving the media private information about the victims of the Columbine High School shooting and using subterfuge to get everything from unlisted telephone numbers to bank records.[67]

Rapp was accused of using deception to ferret out personal information to build a $1 million business. It has been reported that he obtained information on murder victim Ennis Cosby's credit-card records; home addresses of organized crime detectives in Los Angeles; visits by television's *Ally McBeal* star, Calista Flockhart, to a Beverly Hills, California, doctor when the tabloids were filled with articles saying she suffered from eating disorders; and the phone records of Kathleen E. Willey, the former White House volunteer who claimed that former president Bill Clinton made unwanted sexual advances toward her.

The case against Rapp was the biggest test of whether practices that on their face are deceptive are also illegal. Formerly, it had not been illegal to lie about identity, except when impersonating a police officer or government official. Until this case, deceptions by private investigators and information brokers had not been prosecuted, and no federal law specifically prohibited impersonating someone to get confidential information.

The Rapp case and numerous other cases have caused significant changes in the methods used by some information brokers in seeking information. Rapp and others settled with the FTC and federal courts and were fined and precluded from ever again obtaining or selling private financial information.[68] Additionally, a federal law, the Gramm-Leach-Bliley Act, was passed by Congress in 2002 to prohibit any person from obtaining financial information by making false, fictitious, or fraudulent statements to a bank or other financial institution. It also prohibited the use of lost, forged, counterfeit, or stolen documents to get sensitive financial information. Subsequent to the passing of the Gramm-Leach-Bliley Act, the FTC monitored and screened more than 1,000 websites, identified almost 200 companies that offered to obtain and sell nonpublic confidential financial information for fees ranging from $100 to $600, and prosecuted them. The FTC has been active in bringing cases to halt the operations of companies and individuals that allegedly practice pretexting and sell consumers' financial information.[69]

■

Homeland Security and Investigative Security

As mentioned throughout this textbook, private-sector investigators, including proprietary security departments, contract security providers, and independent private investigators, are important resources in our nation's efforts for homeland security.

Some of the investigations engaged in by private-sector investigators involve issues that impact on international organized crime rings and other organizations or individuals that often could also be involved in terrorist activities. Some examples are corporate crime, many types of insurance fraud, and especially, industrial espionage. Many terrorist organizations finance their operations through crime.

Additionally, federal, state, and local agencies, including the Department of Homeland Security, contract the services of private-sector employees or investigators to perform many homeland security duties.

Gramm-Leach-Bliley Act Federal law enacted in 2002 prohibiting any person from obtaining financial information by making fictitious or fraudulent statements to a bank or other financial institution.

Summary

- Investigatory services in the private sector are provided by proprietary security departments in corporations and businesses, large and small contract security investigative services companies, and independent private investigators.

- Most large corporations and businesses have their own proprietary (in-house) security departments that provide a wide range of security services, including investigations. Sometimes some of these large corporations and businesses may also use major contract (outside) security service companies to conduct all or some of their investigation services.

- The major noncriminal investigations conducted by private-sector investigators include financial investigations, product liability, finding people/missing persons, personal injury, wrongful death, medical malpractice, domestic–marital, and miscellaneous investigations and services. In addition, the private sector engages in pre-employment and other types of background screening, as well as drug screening and investigation of sexual harassment in the workplace.

- The major criminal investigations conducted by private-sector investigators include violent and property crimes; corporate crime; internal theft; fraud, including business and credit-card fraud and counterfeiting or intellectual property theft; insurance fraud, including worker's compensation and medical and healthcare fraud; and industrial espionage.

- Product liability cases are lawsuits in which a client claims to have been injured by a certain product.

- Fraud is theft by the intentional use of deceit or trickery.

- Credit-card fraud is an international criminal activity increasingly run by organized crime syndicates that often have industry insiders on their payrolls.

- Counterfeiting of goods and products, also known as the theft of intellectual property rights, is a serious problem in society. The manufacture and sale of knock-off or copycat goods create health and safety problems for consumers, economic loss for trademark owners, and criminal problems for society.

- Medical and healthcare fraud is an extremely serious problem that can be committed by a healthcare provider, a patient, or both.

- Many insurance companies have established highly trained special investigative units (SIUs) as part of their fraud control or claim security programs. The SIU's role is to train claim representatives in dealing with routine fraud cases and to thoroughly investigate more serious fraudulent activities. These teams often include former law enforcement officers, attorneys, accountants, and experienced claims experts. SIUs can dramatically impact the bottom line of many companies.

- The term *industrial espionage* refers to the practice of obtaining business or technological information through surreptitious means.

- The other side of espionage is counterespionage, which is the prevention and thwarting of hostile espionage. Counterespionage uses some of the same methods as espionage.

- Sweeping is the use of electronic means to locate and remove any wiretaps or bugs to prevent the surreptitious recording of conversations.

- Information brokers are persons or businesses that provide computerized database information for investigators.

- Pretexting is a form of trickery to get private information like bank accounts and phone numbers. Pretexters call a bank, phone company, or other business and claim to be the customer whose records they are seeking. The Gramm-Leach-Bliley Act, passed in Congress in 2002, makes it illegal to obtain financial information by making false, fictitious, or fraudulent statements to a bank or other financial institution. It also prohibits the use of lost, forged, counterfeit, or stolen documents to get sensitive financial information.

Learning Check

1. Describe some of the major duties of a proprietary corporate security department's investigating unit.

2. Identify three types of investigative services or activities performed by a typical contract security services provider and give a brief description of each.

3. Identify five services provided by independent private investigators.

4. How do investigators investigate product liability cases?

5. What is medical or healthcare fraud? What are some of the methods used to commit medical and healthcare fraud?

6. What is the major effect of insider theft to a business or corporation?

7. Name and describe some of the miscellaneous investigations and services provided by private-sector investigators.

8. Define *industrial espionage* and give an example of it.

9. Name and describe the functions of three professional associations concerned with fighting insurance fraud.

10. What is pretexting? How does one do it? Is it legal? Explain your answer.

Application Exercise

You have been hired by a local insurance company as a consultant to advise the company on insurance fraud. Based on your understanding of this chapter, prepare an eight- to ten-page report listing the major effects of insurance fraud on business and society and some of the methods investigators and insurance companies use to investigate this fraud.

Web Exercise

Search the web and find a professional organization or agency responsible for certifying and/or licensing private investigators (armed or unarmed) in your state. In addition to licensing requirements (if any), what education, experience and/or training do you need to become a private investigator?

Key Terms

accredited healthcare fraud investigator (AHFI), p. 283

certified fraud examiner (CFE), p. 278

certified insurance fraud investigator, p. 281

computerized databases, p. 285

contract security investigations, p. 266

counterespionage, p. 284

credit-card fraud, p. 279

fraud, p. 277

Gramm-Leach-Bliley Act, p. 286

healthcare fraud, p. 282

header information, p. 285

industrial espionage, p. 283

information broker, p. 285

insurance fraud, p. 280

intellectual property rights, p. 280

knock-off or copycat goods, p. 280

medical fraud, p. 282

pretexting, p. 285

product liability cases, p. 272

professional certified investigator (PCI), p. 269

proprietary security investigations, p. 266

Sarbanes-Oxley Act, p. 276

special investigative units (SIUs), p. 281

sweeping, p. 284

undercover operations, p. 267

Surveillance and Undercover Operations

©Reuters/Corbis

GOALS

- To introduce you to the concept of surveillance and its importance in private security.
- To explain the preparations and techniques necessary to conduct an effective surveillance.
- To show you how undercover operations fit into the general role of private security.
- To acquaint you with the many purposes, techniques, and types of undercover operations.
- To show you the many job opportunities available in undercover operations.

Introduction

Did you ever watch television detective shows or movies and envision yourself participating in those exciting and dramatic events, being like those fictional heroes and heroines? I hope you realize that most surveillances and undercover operations are not similar to their television and movie representations. Most surveillances and undercover operations are in fact quite boring—but can also be very dangerous.

Do you know someone who may be tempted to engage in criminal activities at her workplace, such as stealing or taking drugs? Did you realize that most of corporate America is constantly taking precautions against such events?

Surveillance and undercover operations are often critical parts of the private security process. Surveillance may be quite costly in both personnel and equipment. If conducted improperly, it can tip off the subject to the fact that he is being watched. But sometimes, surveillance is the only possible option

available for obtaining information in a case. Undercover work, or playing the role of another person to conduct an investigation, also has a vital role in private security.

This chapter discusses the reasons and preparation for surveillance, as well as the surveillance itself, various types of surveillances, effective surveillance techniques, methods used to record and debrief the surveillance, and technological surveillance devices.

The chapter also looks at the purposes and types of undercover operations, the qualities needed to be an effective undercover agent, the preparations necessary to carry out an undercover assignment, and tactics that can be used by the undercover agent. It discusses the dangers endemic to undercover investigations, including the problems inherent in participation in illegal activity by the agent. The chapter ends in a discussion of homeland security and surveillance and undercover operations in private security.

Definition and Purposes of Surveillance

A **surveillance** is the **covert** observation of places, persons, and vehicles for the purpose of obtaining information about the identities or activities of subjects. The word *covert* means secret or hidden. The person conducting the surveillance is generally called a **surveillant**. The person being watched is generally called the **subject**. The U.S. Department of Labor defines the job of a surveillant as observing a site, such as the home of a subject, from an inconspicuous location, using still and video cameras, binoculars, and a cell phone, until the desired evidence is obtained.[1] Surveillance is

used extensively in private security for a variety of reasons.

Although no longer the primary reason for surveillance, domestic cases remain a large part of private investigation surveillance. According to Sam Brown and Gini Graham Scott:

> Sometimes the spouse just wants to know. He or she already suspects something, and really just seeks some confirmation. It can be hard to know the truth, but for many people, that's really better than being up in the air, guessing, suspecting, but never really knowing. They realize where they stand now and can deal with that.[2]

As we saw in Chapters 8 and 10 of this textbook, surveillance is used in many private security non-criminal investigations, such as domestic/marital cases, child custody cases, and pre-employment checks. It is also used in many private security criminal cases, such as insurance fraud, corporate fraud, and industrial espionage.

In domestic cases, investigators follow spouses or other significant people and report their actions to their clients. Often they attempt to get photographic evidence. In insurance fraud cases, the investigator tries to observe and possibly take photographs of persons who have filed insurance claims for injuries. Often, insurance companies

---

surveillance The covert observation of places, persons, and vehicles for the purpose of obtaining information about the identities or activities of subjects.

covert Undercover; secret.

surveillant The person conducting the surveillance.

subject The person being watched in a surveillance.

JOBS IN SECURITY

Mystery Shoppers

The website for the Mystery Shopping Providers Association recently advertised the following two job opportunities:

ONGOING BANK SHOPS

The client is looking for detail-oriented individuals who have experience with banking-related mystery shops. Shoppers must be reliable, observant, organized, and objective. Teller transactions with the bank will be necessary, as well as interviews with customer service representatives and loan representatives. Telephone calls to the bank will also be needed. Out-of-pocket expenses, including mileage, are reimbursed. Shoppers must be able to write well-written narratives as well as answer ten to thirty Yes/No questions. Forms will be provided by e-mail. All forms and necessary paperwork are sent by e-mail in PDF format. The ability to open PDF files using Adobe Acrobat Reader is a must. Computer and e-mail knowledge are essential.

ONGOING GROCERY STORE SHOPS

Ongoing grocery store shops—these stores are shopped three to four times every four weeks. The fee/reimbusement is $11/up to $3.00 for a required purchase. You should spend at least twenty minutes in the store. The assignment specifics include observing the facility, customer service of employees, checking for item availability from the store sales flyer, and cashier and bagger evaluation.

Source: Mystery Shopping Providers Association, "Homepage." Retrieved October 24, 2005, from http://www.mysteryshop.org.

have investigators on their staffs to conduct these surveillances, or they may hire local private investigators to conduct them. The investigator attempts to obtain photographic evidence of the claimant performing certain physical activities that would be impossible to perform if he were actually suffering from the claimed injuries. For example, he might be mowing the lawn, dancing at a club, or walking without the cane that he now claims he needs.

In corporate espionage cases and other corporate cases, the investigator may try to track the activities of company executives to observe whom they meet and determine what they discuss. In today's highly competitive business world, a disloyal executive can make a fortune by trading or selling company secrets to a competitor. Generally, the best method to use in corporate surveillance is to follow the executive from the company parking lot around lunchtime. Often, these secret meetings occur in a restaurant at lunchtime, just like other business meetings. It is best to obtain photographic and audio evidence, if at all possible. In some cases, criminal charges may be brought. However, in most cases, the presentation of evidence to the subject is sufficient for the person to admit guilt, resign, or make restitution.

Surveillance is also used in child custody cases to obtain evidence for use in a legal proceeding to show that a person is an unfit parent or to find a child who has been kidnapped by a noncustodial parent or who is not taken home after a visitation. Custody cases can be difficult, especially if the subject takes the child a distance from the legal residence.

In addition, store detectives or loss prevention specialists, shopping services, and mystery shoppers, who conduct integrity, efficiency, and facility analyses that help identify losses, curt or abrasive behavior of some employees, and poor conditions leading to customer dissatisfaction, use surveillance techniques. Chapter 6 of this textbook covered surveillance and undercover operations in retail security.

Preparation for the Surveillance

Surveillance is demanding work. Grady Dublin, an International Association of Chiefs of Police instructor who teaches a forty-hour surveillance course, puts it this way:

> It's not like the movies. It's hours and hours of boredom, of tedious watching, and waiting. And then, all of a sudden, all hell can break loose. . . . You need people who can shift gears quickly if something goes sideways. . . . They need to be predictable in their responses, [and need to] know the plan, stick with it, and not try to improvise.[3]

You Are There!

A Child Custody Surveillance Case

A former night-school student of this author's, a middle-aged woman who worked for a PI, told this story. One night, her assignment was to follow a woman—let's call her Irene—and attempt to make observations about her character. She was involved in a custody fight with her husband over their two children. The husband alleged she was an unfit mother who abused alcohol and drugs. The student picked the subject up at her home and tailed her to a local bar that she went to every Friday evening. The student had researched the case and knew where the subject would take her, so she was dressed appropriately for the Friday-night club scene. After a short time, the student, who was standing at the bar close to the subject, turned to her and asked her, "Do you have a cigarette? I stopped smoking, but I'm having a hard time, particularly when I'm drinking." The subject gave her a cigarette, and the two started to exchange small talk about how difficult it is to break bad habits. Eventually, the student mentioned that she was trying to stop using cocaine but was finding it impossible. The subject then asked the investigator if she would like to purchase some blow—cocaine—from her and use it in the ladies' room. At this time, the student graciously turned her down and left the bar to write her observations and the dialogue in her notebook. People love to talk.

Comparing the reality of surveillance to its television depiction, a licensed private investigator said, "For example, take Tom Selleck in Magnum PI. He does his surveillance in a red Ferrari. Now, what private investigator would do that? The idea is to fade into the landscape, to be discreet, not stand out and announce yourself."[4]

Effective surveillance takes not only skill but also preparation. The preparation involves doing your homework, being prepared, having a cover story, checking equipment, having a temporary headquarters or a telephone base, notifying the local police, blending, and being aware of convoys.

Do Your Homework Investigators must know their facts before conducting surveillance. They must know the subject's habits, her daily routine, when she leaves for work, where she goes, whom she meets. They should have her photograph or complete description, know the car she uses and other cars available to her, know entrances and exits for buildings the subject may enter. They should do a test run of the surveillance a day or two before it will occur. They should know the streets, the terrain, any detours, any hazards.

Lois Pilant writes that investigators conducting surveillances must have the following skills:

▪ Show exceptional common sense and good judgment

▪ Be able to operate both independently and as a team member

▪ Show strong leadership qualities

▪ Demonstrate presence of mind and have a proven track record of dependability in times of high stress

▪ Be extremely patient

▪ Be street savvy and have the gift of gab[5]

Be Prepared A surveillance can go on for a long period of time, and it may be difficult to drop the surveillance to attend to personal needs. Before the surveillance, the investigator should avail himself of food, drink, and a toilet. One of the benefits of using a van for surveillance is that a portable toilet can be installed in the rear for emergency use, curtained off to ensure privacy.

If the surveillance could involve following a person on foot in an urban area, the surveillant should have exact change or the token or fare card necessary to follow the subject onto a bus, subway, or other means of public transportation. It is important to have several different articles of clothing that can be changed rapidly to deter recognition by the subject. Most importantly, the surveillant should answer the following questions before beginning: Do I have a map for the area or areas that will be involved in the surveillance? Do I have sufficient gas in the vehicle? Do I have extra gas and water in the event of a breakdown?

Have a Cover Story The surveillant should have a **cover story** if challenged by the subject or an

---

cover story A fictitious explanation for one's presence or activity.

associate and should have cover articles, such as a newspaper or paperback book, that he could look at to appear as if he is not watching the subject.

Check Equipment Any equipment that is going to be used in the surveillance, including the vehicle that will be used, should be thoroughly inspected beforehand. The vehicle should be checked for mechanical problems. Recording equipment, including transmitters, should be checked before leaving the office. Batteries should be tested to ensure they are fully charged. Only virgin (new and never used) batteries and recording tapes should be used in most recordings and transmissions. If a case is important enough to spend resources on surveillance, why trust a used battery or tape? And never assume a virgin battery that has just been taken from the factory wrapping is fully charged—it too should be tested.

Have a Temporary Headquarters or Telephone Base The surveillance team should have a temporary headquarters in which to assemble for debriefing if the surveillance is terminated, if the subject appears to be staying put for a long time, or for any other reason. The team should also have a telephone base with a common number where they can call the base operator to leave a message for the other team members or to receive messages from them.

Notify the Local Police Private investigators should consider notifying the local police of their presence in the area they are conducting their surveillance. If the police respond to calls of suspicious persons, their activity may blow the investigator's cover.

Blend Surveillants must be able to **blend** in wherever they are assigned to conduct a surveillance: They should be of average size, build, and appearance and have no noticeable peculiarities in either appearance or mannerism. They should dress like those living or working in the area of the surveillance. For example, in a financial section of a city, the surveillant should be dressed in a business suit and carry a briefcase. In an industrial area, the surveillant should be dressed more casually.

Surveillants cannot appear to be just hanging out. They should be involved in some normal activity for the area, such as talking in a corner telephone booth or sitting on a park bench during lunch hour—eating a hot dog and reading the local paper.

Some surveillance involves locations, such as nightclubs, expensive restaurants, or dances or social events, where the surveillant will look more in place if accompanied by a date. Although it might save money for an investigator to bring along a friend as a partner, this is not recommended. One should avoid using amateurs for a professional's job. Investigators must also consider the issue of confidentiality. The friend might tell everyone he knows about the interesting evening he had and compromise the confidentiality of the investigation.

Be Aware of Convoys A convoy is a deliberate attempt to evade a surveillance and often involves prior knowledge that a surveillance will occur. People or vehicles similar in appearance to the people or vehicles believed to be the subject of the surveillance are sent out in the hope that the surveillants will follow one of the convoys rather than the subject under investigation.

■

The Surveillance

There are two primary types of surveillance: the stationary surveillance and the moving surveillance. This section discusses both types, as well as what a surveillant should do if a tail is made, common mistakes in maintaining surveillances, testing tails, and practicing surveillances.

The Stationary Surveillance

In a **stationary surveillance**, the investigator generally watches a particular house or building and notices who comes in and out, possibly taking photographs or videos. If it is an important case, the surveillant might rent a house or apartment in the immediate vicinity. This way, there is a place to store equipment and a window from which to observe with binoculars, telescope, cameras, and night-vision devices. In addition, the surveillant has access to necessities such as telephone, water, food, and a bathroom.

In stationary surveillances, it is extremely important that surveillants relieve each other properly at the end of shifts. They must also be

---

blend To become part of a surrounding environment or culture.

stationary surveillance Surveillance from a fixed location.

Two private investigators engaged in a stationary surveillance keep the target in view from an adjacent building using field binoculars and a wide-angle camera lens to take pictures that will be used as evidence in the investigation.

©Antonio Mo/Getty Images

which people on the outside cannot see. Some of the best surveillance vans have periscopes that permit the investigator to watch and photograph areas in a 360-degree circumference from the van.

If costs preclude the use of high-tech surveillance vans, taxis or business vehicles are good alternatives. When using local business trucks, investigators must know how many workers are usually assigned to the vehicles and the clothing or uniforms they wear. They must appear to blend into an area. Always consider a gender mix when using an auto for a stationary surveillance. A young male and a young female sitting together in a car will rarely seem suspicious.

Whether the investigator is working alone or with a partner, the stationary surveillance can be a challenge. As one licensed private investigator put it:

You just can't leave your car or your post when you're on a surveillance, because that could be the very moment when the subject suddenly decides to leave himself. And then you've missed him, and you may not even know it. So you absolutely have to stay there and you have to stay awake, which sometimes can be hard to do. . . . And then there's the boredom and the loneliness. . . . Plus another problem can be just going to the bathroom or eating, because you can't get out, and you can't leave anything on the street. You have to bring any food into the car with you before the surveillance, and if you have to go to the bathroom, well, you have to improvise, say, by urinating into a milk carton. . . . When the subject suddenly appears or leaves, the investigator has to be ready to take off too, call of nature or not.[6]

careful about blending to ensure they look like the type of people who would live on such a block.

In most stationary surveillance cases, it would not be cost-effective to rent a house or an apartment. Instead, they are conducted by investigators sitting in private cars at a discreet distance from the location. Investigators should consider using a business-type vehicle (for example, phone company or utility company trucks) or, if at all affordable, a surveillance van. Modern surveillance vans generally have windows to look out of and take photos and videos through but into

The Moving Surveillance

There are three basic types of **moving surveillances** or tails: the **rough tail**, the **loose tail**, and the

close or **tight tail**. The rough tail is used in cases where it is not of utmost importance to keep the subject from knowing about the tail. Organized crime individuals and other professional criminals know they are under constant surveillance. In the rough tail, it is usually unnecessary to take extraordinary means to remain undetected. In contrast, in a loose tail it is of utmost importance to remain undetected and less important to keep the subject under constant surveillance. In the close or tight tail, it is of extreme importance not to lose the subject but equally as important not to be detected. Moving surveillances can be conducted by foot or by automobile.

Foot Surveillance A one-person tail, also known as a **shadow**, is the most undesirable way of following someone by foot. The risk is too great that the subject will detect the one-person tail. It is better to use as many persons as possible.

A typical foot surveillance can be conducted by three persons, using the **ABC method**. The A surveillant is closest to the subject. The B person follows the A person, usually on the same side of the street. The C surveillant may be on the opposite side of the street or may be in front of the subject. All three surveillants can at prearranged intervals shift positions in many different manners. For example, A can move ahead of the subject, with C taking the position following the subject and B moving to the other side of the street. This constant moving will reduce the likelihood that the subject will "make" the tail.

Prearranged signals should be used if any of the surveillants believes that the subject has made the tail. The signals should indicate if a surveillant is dropping out of the tail or if another surveillant should drop out.

Precautions should be taken when turning corners or entering buildings so that the closest surveillant does not appear to be following the subject. If the subject boards a public bus or train or goes into the subway, at least one of the surveillants should enter the public vehicle and sit behind the subject on the same side of the vehicle. The other surveillants may try to get ahead of the bus and board at a later stop. If the subject enters a taxicab and the surveillants have access to a vehicle, they should follow the taxi; if they have no access to a vehicle, at least one of the surveillants should attempt to hail another taxi and follow the subject's taxi. In all cases, a member of the surveillance team should record the license plate and name of the taxi company and the time and place at which the trip began, so they can check the records of the company

for the final destination in the event the cab cannot be followed.

Automobile Surveillance Maintaining a successful auto surveillance is extremely difficult considering highway conditions, traffic-control devices, driving habits, and other problems associated with auto traffic in the United States.

It is always better to have more than one vehicle in the surveillance team. If there is only one vehicle, it makes the chances of detection or losing the subject vehicle that much greater. Although it is better to have several vehicles in a moving surveillance, it cannot always be done. Budgetary considerations often dictate that only one vehicle can be used. When several cars are used, surveillants can drop back and change positions, much as they do in foot surveillance. With autos, this is actually easier to do because the surveillants can transmit directions and suggestions using portable radios. Radio transmissions are also crucial during an auto surveillance so that all members of the surveillance know the location of the subject. If two cars are used, it is best to have one serve as a lead car, driving in front of the subject, with the second car following. With two cars, the surveillants can also **leapfrog**, changing positions to lessen the chance of the subject making the surveillance. If three or more surveillance vehicles are available, the third and fourth cars can maintain surveillance on parallel blocks and be ready to fall into the lead or follow the auto if the subject makes a turn from his route.

The type of vehicle used by the surveillance team is also important. If a nondescript blue Chevy has been behind you for a few miles and then turns off at a highway exit and another nondescript blue Chevy appears behind you three exits later, it may not seem to matter. However, if a very distinctive car appears behind you again and again, you will probably notice it. The investigator conducting a surveillance that could last several days might consider using a rental car and changing it daily.

close/tight tail A person is under constant surveillance and the surveillant remains undetected.

shadow A one-person surveillance.

ABC method A three-officer or three-vehicle surveillance tactic in which the A surveillant is closest to the subject; the B surveillant follows the A person, usually on the same side of the street; and the C surveillant is on the opposite side of the street or in front of the subject.

leapfrog The process of surveillants changing positions during a surveillance to deter observation by the subject.

When following a car, it is best to stay one or two car lengths back. If it is affordable, two surveillants should be in the surveillance car so that one can concentrate on driving and the other can make observations.

If the subject pulls into a parking spot on the street or in a parking lot, the surveillance team should park as far as possible from the subject and follow his movements through binoculars, resuming the surveillance when he returns to the car.

Nighttime surveillance is usually more difficult because with their headlights and taillights on, many cars look similar in the dark, and investigators may find themselves tailing the wrong car. The solution is to mark the subject car, if possible, beforehand—spray some fluorescent paint onto the license plate, rear fender, or taillight.

An effective method of making auto surveillance easier is to place a vehicle tracking system on the subject auto. The vehicle tracking system emits electronic beeps or signals to a receiver in the surveillance car. Unfortunately, vehicle tracking systems are expensive and difficult to retrieve because the surveillant cannot just walk up to the subject auto to retrieve the system, particularly if the car is parked on private property (see the discussion of vehicle tracking systems later in this chapter).

Finally, investigators need to drive carefully and defensively to avoid a traffic accident. In the event of an accident, the surveillant could not only suffer injury but blow the operation.

What If the Tail Is Made?

If the surveillant has good reason to believe he has been "**made**" (the subject has detected the surveillance), she should immediately discontinue the surveillance and make evasive moves designed to prevent the subject from turning the surveillance back onto the surveillant. The surveillant must ensure that the subject does not follow her to her home or office.

Common Mistakes in Maintaining Surveillances

Investigators can make many mistakes when maintaining surveillances. One of the biggest is to make any of the following assumptions:

made When a surveillant is discovered or identified by a subject.

- The subject has checked into a hotel or motel at 2300 hours (11 P.M.). This means he is going to spend the night.
- The subject has entered a store in a mall. He will leave using the same entrance.
- The subject has returned to his home or apartment. He will probably stay for a long time or the night.
- The subject begins to run or to speed. This means he has made the tail.

Some other mistakes an investigator can make include staying parked in the same spot for too long; using a conspicuous car; having two surveillants in the front seat for an extended period of time; approaching the parking position furtively; parking in a prohibited zone, thereby attracting attention; failing to manage the changeover to a relieving team unobtrusively; and telephoning repeatedly from the same store or other phone location.

Testing a Tail

Many subjects who anticipate a tail or who have had experience with surveillance will attempt to test a tail. On a public transit conveyance such as a bus, taxi, subway, or railroad, the subject may board and then wait until the moment when the doors begin to close to exit the conveyance. If in a car, the subject may circle a certain block two or three times and then return to the place where he began. In a building, the subject may walk through the front door and then make an immediate U-turn and exit the building, looking to see if he will "bump into someone." The same technique can be used in a store in a mall. Investigators conducting a surveillance should be aware of these tricks in order to avoid detection.

Surveillance Requires Practice

A surveillance is a complicated undertaking, particularly if there are a number of investigators involved. When investigators have the time, they should conduct mock foot and auto surveillances. These mock events should involve investigators who normally would work together; other investigators should evaluate their effectiveness.

Recording the Surveillance

All surveillances should be recorded in writing and may also be recorded with videos. When using photography in a surveillance, agents should use both still and video cameras. Still cameras produce superior quality photos and can more easily be fitted with a zoom lens. Plus, photos can be viewed without a monitor or VCR. On the other hand, video records action and audio that still cameras cannot capture.[7]

Written Notes

Written notes are essential in a surveillance. What did the subject do? Where? When? With whom? How? Why? If possible, the notes should be taken as the event unfolds. If it is not possible to record the notes contemporaneously, the investigator should record them as soon as possible after the event.

Photographs

Surveillances may require taking photographs. When taking photos, it is always best to take as many as possible and from as many different angles and distances as possible. Each photo should be backed up, including the following information: date, time, location of photographer, and subject; camera, lens, lens setting, and frame number of the photo; and identification of subject and any associates. In addition, the investigator's written reports should include the brand, model, and serial number of the camera used and the brand, name, speed, and so on, of the film.

It has become standard for investigators to use the 35-millimeter camera for surveillance purposes. However, there is now a tremendous variety of automatic (point-and-shoot) cameras on the market that take good photos and have attachments such as telephoto lenses available. These cameras require no training or sophisticated knowledge of photography.

Many believe that current digital photography is superior to conventional photography, and the conversion from conventional to digital photography has not posed any significant evidentiary problems. A variety of authentication methods can ensure the integrity of a photo in the face of any challenge that alleges manipulation has occurred.[8]

Also available are a vast array of night-vision devices that can be attached to cameras or scopes, enabling an investigator to see and take photographs in virtual darkness. Because these devices are quite expensive, investigators should get the best possible technical advice before purchasing them to ensure they get the best value for their money.

Often, photographs serve as leverage in a case. When confronted with a photo depicting them at a particular time or event, subjects may feel compelled to stop evading and tell the truth.

Video

The use of video cameras to record pertinent moments can be very effective in a surveillance, particularly a stationary surveillance. In many cases, a video camera can be put in a hidden location and turned on, letting the investigator perform other duties. These types of hidden cameras are used extensively at banks and department stores. The investigator must practice using this equipment before taking it on a surveillance.

Debriefing the Surveillance

After every surveillance, the members of the surveillance team should hold a meeting and debrief the surveillance. What did we do right? What did we do wrong? People learn by their mistakes, and if the mistakes are brought out and thought about, they might not occur again. Even if the surveillance was a success and no obvious mistakes were made, the team members should still hold the debriefing and brainstorm alternatives to some of the methods they used. There is never only one way to conduct a surveillance. In unsuccessful surveillances, the debriefing will focus not only on mistakes but possibly on a new plan or new techniques.

Technological Surveillance Devices

Today's advances in technology provide us with more surveillance devices than ever before. Formerly, surveillance equipment might have consisted of a broken-down van used to store a camera and a pair of binoculars. Today's investigators have high-tech state-of-the-art listening, recording, and viewing devices, high-tech surveillance vans,

A technician sweeps a boardroom to detect and eliminate suspected eavesdropping and surveillance devices, particularly bugs, wiretaps, and hidden cameras. Sophisticated advancements in technology that make illegal "bugging" of businesses and corporations easier have made it more challenging to protect corporations from such clandestine tactics.

vehicle tracking systems, night-vision devices, surveillance aircraft, and global positioning systems, among other innovations.[9]

Many technology and equipment companies offer an interesting and informative website for anyone interested in technology equipment for private security. They discuss light intensification systems (such as night-vision goggles, night-vision scopes, night-vision pocket scopes, and infrared illuminators), thermal imaging systems, surveillance systems (such as wireless video and audio systems, miniature pinhole board cameras, miniature microphones, miniature video and audio recorders, miniature video and audio transmitters and receivers, covert body video and audio systems, and long-range cameras and lenses), and vehicle tracking systems.[10]

A 2005 article discusses the latest in "tactical viewing" systems. The shrinking sizes of cameras and fiber-optic technology have allowed the development of this mobile tactical viewing equipment that can be passed under doors, around corners, and into dark areas through the use of night-vision cameras. This equipment includes a telescoping-pole camera device; an underdoor remote viewing scope; a viewing device that can be tossed, rolled, or dropped into rooms, stairwells, hallways, or under vehicles; cameras for distance viewing in total darkness; and devices that can be slipped under doors and

manipulated to view an entire room while officers view it on a monitor at a safe location.[11]

Often, many people find undercover technological surveillance improper. In a recent case, nurses at the Good Samaritan Hospital in Los Angeles objected to the use of hidden cameras in clocks throughout the hospital. The nurses objected to the placement of the cameras in break rooms, a fitness center, and other areas because they believed the cameras invaded their privacy. They said people often changed clothes in those areas. As a result, a technical consulting firm was hired, as part of an agreement made by the unions and the hospital in a mediation meeting, to investigate these charges. The company found no evidence that anyone watched footage on the recorder connected to the cameras in these areas.[12]

Listening, Recording, and Viewing Devices

In today's technically advanced world, there is no limit to the number of affordable devices that allow people to listen electronically to, record, or view incidents in real time. Generally, devices that can record conversations are called recorders. Some are as small as a matchbook and can be concealed in an area or worn by a person. Other devices, called transmitters, are designed specifically to be worn on a subject's body.

They transmit conversations to a listening post where other investigators are stationed. The investigators can follow the conversation and perhaps intervene if the investigator wearing the transmitter is in danger. The investigators manning the listening post can also record the conversation on a recorder.

Electronic surveillance generally uses three basic components: transmitter, receiver, and recorder. Additional requirements are an antenna and a power supply. In many cases, all these components are built into a kit. Factors that affect the system's quality and versatility are the sensitivity of the receiver, the quality of the transmitter, the versatility of the recorder, and the number of internal and external power supplies and accessories. Audio Intelligence Devices, a subsidiary of Westinghouse Electric, is one of the largest suppliers of electronic surveillance equipment. It supplies intelligence kits, body transmitters, tracking systems for vehicle and cargo, "bug" detectors, telephone intercept devices, miniature cameras, video transmitters and receivers, and pinhole lens cameras, as well as an entire line of night-vision equipment, surveillance vans, and training equipment.[13]

"Bugs" are miniature devices that can be placed at a location to transmit conversations held at that location to a listener who can be quite a distance away. Very often these bugs are used in corporate espionage and are illegal. Also available are parabolic and shotgun microphones or bionic ears, which can monitor conversations from outside a premise. The use of such bugs has led to the birth of an industry, often referred to as "sweeping," where technicians check or sweep rooms, residences, or telephones for these illegal devices.

Investigators also have at their disposal a tremendous amount of miniature still and moving cameras and camcorders that can be used to record any selected event. These devices are advertised in investigative and security trade magazines and at trade shows or conventions nationwide.

Surveillance Vans

A vehicle specialist describes today's state-of-the-art surveillance van: "When talking about surveillance vehicles today, . . . we tend to think of a van whose interior looks slightly less complex than the bridge of Star Trek's *USS Enterprise*."[14]

This specialist describes the ideal surveillance van's equipment:

. . . power periscopes operated by a joystick; six cameras to cover 360 degrees of a van's exterior, plus a periscope-mounted observer's camera; videotape decks to record everything happening on the street; quick-change periscope camera mounts; portable toilets; video printers; motion detection cameras; night vision cameras; cellular telephones; AM/FM cassette entertainment systems; CB radio, police radio, police scanners; and other personalized equipment.[15]

No matter how technologically advanced a surveillance van is, if it is out of place for the location of the surveillance or if surveillants are moving about in it, it will blow the surveillance.

Vehicle Tracking Systems

Vehicle tracking systems, also sometimes referred to as transponders, bumper beepers, or homing devices, enable investigators to track a vehicle during a surveillance. These systems are actually transmitters that can be placed on a subject's vehicle. The tracking system consists of the transmitter on the subject's vehicle and a receiver, which picks up the signal from the transmitter.

Night-Vision Devices

Among the most sophisticated surveillance devices in use today are enhanced **night-vision devices**, including monocular devices small enough to hold in one hand, which can be adapted to a still or video camera.

Perhaps an automobile slowly approaches you in the dark with its lights out. With a normal night vision scope you can see it clearly—but you can't see through the windshield to see who's driving the car. Switch on the infrared (IR) laser, and it illuminates a spot through the windshield so you can identify the operator. In another case, at night a man lurks on the porch of a mountain cabin. In normal mode only the cabin and porch are clearly visible. The IR laser illuminates a spot to show the person waiting in the shadows.[16]

As far back as 1800, Sir William Herschel discovered the fact that every object emits thermal

---

bugs Concealed electronic devices placed in a premise to transmit conversations.

vehicle tracking system Transmitters that enable investigators to track a vehicle during a surveillance; also called transponders, bumper beepers, or homing devices.

night-vision devices High-tech devices used to aid vision in the dark.

energy in the infrared (IR) wavelengths. His son, Sir John Herschel, took the first IR photographs of the sun approximately forty years later. Infrared surveillance systems appeared toward the end of World War II as a covert way to observe the enemy at night. The Germans were the first to use IR systems as impressive nighttime tank killers. The Soviets developed IR systems in the 1960s and 1970s. Since then, these systems have been used by the United States during the Korean, Vietnam, and Gulf Wars and during Operation Iraqi Freedom.[17]

A more sophisticated form of infrared technology is thermal imaging (TI), which does not require any light at all. Traditional night-vision equipment requires minimal light, such as from the moon. Thermal imaging can see not only through darkness but also through fog, mist, and smoke. It is especially useful in penetrating many types of camouflaging. Thermal imaging takes advantage of the infrared emission but does it passively, so only the user knows when it is in operation, not the subject.[18] IR and TI systems can be mounted on vehicles and pan possible subjects in all directions. Display screens can be mounted in investigators' cars, and joysticks can be used to direct the panning of the cameras.[19]

Surveillance Aircraft

Airplanes are also used in the arsenal of surveillance devices, including short take-off and landing aircraft that do not require extensive landing fields and have proved to be very successful in surveillance operations, fixed-wing aircraft, and rotorcraft. Advanced electronic and computer systems for aircraft now include real-time video downlinks and low-light surveillance.[20]

As of 2005, about a dozen companies were developing portable **unmanned aerial vehicles (UAVs)** that can be equipped with cameras to transmit live video feeds to agents on the ground, miles away. While larger and more sophisticated unmanned aircraft have been in use by the military for years, this new breed of UAV is small enough to be transported in the trunk of a car and then assembled and put into the air. One company's official said he expects to sell his "Kite Plane," which has a wingspan of about 4 feet and weighs less than 5 pounds, for $5,000. UAVs could be much cheaper than using piloted planes or helicopters for surveillance. It has an exoskeleton made of foldable graphite composite poles, similar to tent poles, and a skin of parachute cloth that creates the wings of the airplane. Its frame makes it durable and flexible, allowing for a soft landing sliding onto dirt or into the arms of someone waiting to catch it. Its propeller shuts off before landing, and it carries a video surveillance camera that is aimed toward the ground; the video is transmitted wirelessly at thirty frames per second. It is piloted much the same way a toy remote-controlled car or airplane would be, with a hand-held joyskick. It can fly as high as 1,000 feet and has a top speed of thirty miles per hour, but its rechargeable battery can only last for twenty minutes. Companies are working on larger, more sophisticated versions that have programmable autonomous flight capability (they would not have be be guided by someone with a remote control).[21]

Global Positioning Systems (GPS)

Global positioning systems (GPS) are the most recent technology available to help investigators. GPS is a network of twenty-four satellites used by the U.S. Department of Defense to pinpoint targets and guide bombs. These satellites are equipped with atomic clocks and equally accurate position-measuring telemetry gear. GPS has been used for everything from helping hikers find their way through the woods to guiding law enforcement officers to stolen vehicles. When GPS is combined with geographic information systems and automatic vehicle locations, investigators can tell where they are on a map and a dispatch center can continuously monitor their location. GPS is also used by fleet operators to track fleets for routing purposes and for rolling emergencies. It can be used to track the route over time and to monitor the vehicle's speed.[22]

Definition and Purposes of Undercover Operations

An **undercover operation** may be defined as a form of investigation in which an investigator assumes a different identity in order to obtain information

---

unmanned aerial vehicle (UAV) Portable flying device that can be equpped with cameras to transmit live video feeds to surveillants on the ground.

global positioning systems (GPS) A satellite system used to locate any position on the map.

undercover operations Covert activities designed to catch criminals.

or achieve another investigatory purpose. In other words, the **undercover investigator/operator/ agent** (often simply called the **undercover**) plays the role of another person.

An undercover operation is similar to a surveillance yet is also quite different. In a surveillance, the investigator's primary purpose is to follow a subject or observe what is going on in a particular area or involving a particular person or persons. In an undercover operation, the investigator may be merely observing. However, he may also be performing certain actions designed to get other people to do something or react to or interact with the investigator in a certain way. The primary function of the investigator in these cases is to play a role without anyone realizing that he is playing a role.

Undercover operations are used in many private security noncriminal investigations, such as domestic/marital cases, child custody cases, and pre-employment checks. They are also used in many private security criminal cases, such as insurance fraud, corporate fraud, and industrial espionage. In these cases, the investigator often creates an undercover identity and role to enable her to blend into a situation without being detected as an undercover agent.

Most undercover investigations are complicated and may incur legal challenges that can create liabilities for private investigating agencies, and even the investigator, if done improperly. In a three-part series on undercover investigations in *Security Management* magazine, Eugene F. Ferraro, a CPP and chairman of ASIS International Standing Committee on Workplace Substance Abuse and Illicit Drug Activity, describes the following stages of an undercover investigation:

- *Planning phase:* In this phase of the investigation, the objective must be established and an investigative team selected. A cover story must be established for the undercover operative, and that person must be covertly placed into the operation.
- *Case management:* In this phase, the case is managed and coordinated between the major players in the operation, including the undercover investigator, supervisors, managers, law enforcement agencies, and legal representatives.
- *Communication:* Effective communications must be developed between all of the members of the operation. Methods of communication include written reports, e-mail, telephone conversations, and case files.
- *The investigation:* This is the vehicle for achieving the objectives of the undercover operation.

- *Closure:* Eventually, the operation must be shut down when the objectives are met or when an emergency occurs that endangers the undercover.[23]

Types of Undercover Operations

Several important types of undercover investigations are covered in great detail in other chapters in this text. According to Gary T. Marx, private security undercover investigations generally involve inventory losses, pilferage, willful neglect of machinery, unreported absenteeism, "general employee attitudes," and "delicate investigations."[24] Many other categories can be added to private security undercover investigations, including criminal, marital, civil, and child custody cases, to name only a few. This section covers four important private security undercover investigations: criminal and noncriminal private security investigations, shopping services and mystery shoppers, silent witness programs, and internal intelligence programs. Recall that the store detective or loss prevention specialist was discussed in detail in Chapter 6.

Criminal and Noncriminal Private Security Investigations

As mentioned, undercover operations are used in many private security criminal and noncriminal investigations. Of particular importance is that private security is expanding into areas once the sole domain of public law enforcement by participating in complex criminal investigations and patrols of downtown districts and residential neighborhoods to ensure public safety. However, the debate as to whether private security should investigate criminal matters continues to thrive.

undercover investigator/operator/agent An investigator who disguises his or her own identity or uses an assumed identity to gain the trust of an individual or organization to learn secret information or to gain the trust of targeted individuals in order to gain information or evidence.

undercover Covert investigation of criminal activity; person who conducts undercover operations.

You Are There!

Meet Jim Jolly, the Mystery Shopper

"It's a sin in my book to be out of coffee," said Jim Jolly. Jolly is a mystery shopper—one of thousands of people who visit stores looking for things like empty shelves, misplaced goods, stale muffins, and dirty bathrooms. His employer is C&S Mystery Shoppers of North Brunswick, New Jersey, whose mission is to give store executives a view of what it is like for regular people to shop in their stores.

For a single store visit and copious notes on its condition, C&S charges about $35 and the cost of a bag of groceries, which the shopper gets to keep. Another company, Mystery Shoppers Inc. of Houston, videotapes its visits, using a hidden camera, and then plays the tapes for the store manager. A package of visits can cost as much as $1,000.

SOURCE: Jennifer Steinhauer, "The Undercover Shoppers: Posing as Customers, Paid Agents Rate the Stores," *New York Times*, February 4, 1998, pp. D1, D23.

Shopping Services and Mystery Shoppers

Private security firms offer **integrity shoppers**, **mystery shoppers**, and other shopping services to prospective business clients to test the integrity and efficiency of retail business personnel. These services are performed by "shoppers"—actually, undercover agents posing as customers—and are designed to deter inventory shrinkage, detect dishonest employees, and provide evidence for prosecuting employees caught stealing.[25]

Stores contract **shopping services**, or mystery shopping services, to make discrete observations in their stores. For a fee, a mystery shopper will visit a store and observe the performance and operations of store personnel. The shopping service then prepares a report that is sent to the store manager and corporate managers. Almost every

integrity shoppers Undercover agents who test the integrity of retail personnel.

mystery shopper Agent who visits a store and observes the performance and operations of store personnel.

shopping services Services performed by undercover agents posing as customers to test the integrity and efficiency of retail business personnel.

major U.S. retail company regularly uses mystery shoppers. Banks are tested on how hard reps work to open new accounts, restaurants are timed to see how fast service is, and a mall greeter may be monitored for the consistency of her smile. The findings reported by mystery shoppers are used to train employees for customer satisfaction.

Mystery shoppers also observe and judge other attributes of employees: attitude, courtesy, approach, appearance, knowledge, and salesmanship. Undercover agents observe the actions of the employees and question them while posing as ordinary customers. They also report on the following conditions at the business: appearance, lighting, displays, housekeeping, and the like. As an example of this, Wackenhut Consulting and Investigation Services offers a surveillance program that specializes in video documentation of suspected incidents of criminal activity or unethical behavior by employees.[26]

The Mystery Shopping Providers Association (MSPA) is a professional trade association dedicated to improving service quality using anonymous resources. It has over 150 member companies worldwide, including marketing research and merchandising companies, private investigation firms, training organizations, and companies that specialize in providing mystery shopping services. It offers training and certification programs to provide clients with standardized industry education, practices, and qualifications for mystery shoppers and sponsors an annual educational conference. The MSPA estimates that there are approximately 1.5 million mystery shoppers in the United States and 250,000 internationally.[27]

Silent Witness Programs

Private investigating firms also offer silent witness programs to prospective corporate clients. These programs provide a method for honest, dedicated employees who are concerned about wrongdoing in the workplace to volunteer helpful information without compromising themselves. They use some techniques familiar to the Neighborhood Crime Watch and media TIPS programs, making a telephone number readily available to employees throughout a facility or company. Materials explain the program and guarantee anonymity, and all calls are monitored by trained personnel in the private investigating firm's communications center.

As an example, Pinkerton Investigative Services offers its customers its "AlertLine Ethics and Compliance Hotline." This is a toll-free, third-party resource

You Are There!

Covert or Overt Investigations in the Workplace?

Covert or undercover operations should be used only when there is no other way to resolve a case. Covert operations are useful in the following circumstances:

■ There is consistent, reliable information suggesting employee misconduct or criminal activity but not enough information to prevent the activity or identify those involved.

■ Losses have occurred in a specific area, but there is no information on how the losses occurred or who is responsible.

■ There is a strong suspicion of on-the-job alcohol or drug abuse or drug dealing in the workplace but no definite evidence.

■ It is necessary to determine whether employees are following company policies and procedures, but routine auditing is impossible.

The following are not good cases for covert operations:

■ To determine the strength of a union's activity campaign by identifying workers sympathetic to the union; this is illegal and can hurt employee relations and morale

■ When the losses are too small to justify the expense of an undercover operation

SOURCE: "Covert or Overt? That Is the Question," *Security Management*, July 2000.

---

available around the clock, so employees may make confidential and anonymous reports to their agencies regarding colleagues' unethical behavior. Alert-Line serves over 1,000 companies, representing more than 8 million employees in more than 100,000 client locations throughout the world.[28] As another example, Wackenhut offers customers its "Safe2Say Hotline Service," which operates around the clock and gives employees a confidential, anonymous outlet to report concerns of fraud, theft, violence, and other workplace issues. The service is provided by highly trained, multilingual communications specialists.[29]

Internal Intelligence Programs

Another type of program offered is the internal intelligence program, in which private investigative firms plant undercover agents in the corporation's business operations to make observations and report back to the company. These programs have been used successfully to combat theft of funds and merchandise, use of alcohol or drugs on the job, gambling, sabotage, or other illegal activity.

As an example of this, Pinkerton Investigative Services offers field research and compliance audits to provide its clients with an objective overview of their facilities, employees, and markets, using services such as compliance audits and monitoring, safety and security audits, market data collection, and mystery shopping. The field research department performs Prescription Drug Marketing Act inventories, Fair Credit Reporting Act on-site verifications, and other compliance audits as well.[30]

As yet another example of this, Wackenhut Consulting and Investigation Services offers undercover services in which skilled investigators, posing as employees, are placed into an unsuspecting work force to gather information on workplace problems. Upon identifying problem areas, detailed reports are provided to assist customers in taking appropriate remedial action. The program also gives recommendations to prevent future incidents.

The Undercover Operation

The undercover operation is perhaps the most sensitive and most dangerous type of investigation. If the undercover investigator is **burned**—that is, if her true identity is discovered or her assumed identity is found to be false—not only is the investigation compromised but the life of the investigator may be in peril. Selecting which person to do the job is probably the most important part of the investigation.

The Undercover Operator

The undercover should be an experienced investigator who knows all the skills and nuances of the trade. He should be an expert in blending techniques and have above-average communication skills. He must be an intelligent, calm person capable of concealing nervousness or discomfort in threatening situations and capable of adapting to changing conditions.

burned When an investigator is discovered by the person under surveillance.

Charlie Fuller, a retired ATF Special Agent who operates a consulting firm providing week-long undercover training programs, says the traits and characteristics that embody a good undercover agent include flexibility, strong moral fiber, discipline, intelligence, and the ability to think quickly. He warns that it is easy for undercover agents to get caught up in their work and that the psychological demands of the job are enormous.[31]

The undercover investigator must have a general understanding of the type of role she will be playing. When investigators are playing the role of a drug addict or criminal, they must be familiar with the roles and know how such a person would act in every possible situation. If they are assuming the role of a person in a certain occupation, they must be thoroughly versed in that occupation. They must fit into the environment of the investigation. Speech, conversation, mannerisms, behavior, knowledge, attitude, opinions, interests, and clothing—all must match those of the undercover milieu. The ability to observe, remember, and make sound judgments is essential.

The most important consideration in selecting an undercover investigator is to ensure that the individual's true identity will not be recognized. Often, in private investigations, it is difficult to use experienced investigators in the same general geographic area where they have performed ordinary investigative duties.

Because of the inherent difficulties in using experienced—and thus possibly easily recognized—personnel in an undercover capacity, there is always a temptation to use recently hired investigators for undercover assignments. Yet this practice can be extremely dangerous. If the investigator does not have the experience and personal characteristics necessary for undercover assignments, he is likely to be uncovered.

Preparation for the Undercover Operation

Extensive and detailed preparations are necessary before conducting an undercover operation to ensure both the success of the investigation and the safety of the undercover.

Identification Undercover investigators should always have personal papers to document the role they are playing. A driver's license and credit cards in the name of the person the investigator is supposed to be are essential. If investigators are assuming certain occupational or professional credentials, they should have documentation—a union card or a wallet-size professional license or diploma, for example.

Background Records If an investigator is assuming a role and identity that could be checked through the examination of public or private records, then those records need to be created and placed at the location that might be the subject of an inquiry, such as the personnel office of a corporation. Undercover investigators should have a complete background history prepared for them, including name, current and past addresses, and past working experience.

Cover Story A fictitious personal history—a cover story—should be prepared for the undercover investigator. Investigators should have a thorough knowledge of the contents of their assumed history, and documentation should exist to prove this personal history.

Getting In Only one or two people in an organization should know that an undercover investigator is joining the organization. The security director and the head of personnel, if not subjects in the investigation, should be notified; but it must be emphasized in the strongest manner possible that this information has to remain confidential.

Knowledge of Investigation Subjects Undercovers must be thoroughly briefed on the subjects involved in the investigation. They should know in particular of the existence of possible dangers they could experience and how to avoid them.

Knowledge of Geographic Area Undercovers must have detailed knowledge of the geographic area of the investigation to ensure that they move about expeditiously and safely there. Furthermore, there is no better indication that a person may be an imposter than lack of knowledge about key buildings, highways, or other locations with which those who live in or frequent the area are familiar.

Tactics for the Undercover Operation

Undercovers must follow numerous procedures or tactics to ensure the success of the investigation and not compromise their assumed identity.

Be Prepared for Questions Undercovers must be prepared for the eventuality that someone might ask them if they are undercover operatives. They need to know how to say no in a convincing manner, such as appearing to be shocked by the question or just playing dumb. Hesitating or seeming embarrassed could be seen as an admission.

Blend In Undercover investigators must blend into the operation and act as naturally as any new worker or person would in the particular environment. They should get to know coworkers slowly; do their job effectively but no better or worse than others; and most importantly, follow the habits of coworkers. Undercovers should not be aggressive and should not ask questions. Their job is to observe and report.

Go Slow Care must be taken to conduct the undercover operation as slowly as necessary. Frequently, employees engaging in illegal conduct may be nervous and may suspect any new employee, especially a new employee who seems too eager to make friends or ask questions.

Get Out before It Goes Down Generally, it is best to take the undercover out of the operation before the arrest or exposure of the subject so that it does not seem that she had anything to do with it. Generally, if the operation has been successful in obtaining information, the security department can obtain or develop evidence to arrest the subject or bring the subject's actions to light without involving the undercover investigator.

What Not to Do Authors Wayne W. Bennett and Kären M. Hess warn undercover investigators not to write any investigatory notes that the subject may discover and read; not to carry any identification other than the cover ID; not to communicate overtly with headquarters; and not to suggest, plan, initiate, or participate in criminal activity. They offer the following checklist for the planning of an undercover assignment:

- Is there any alternative to undercover work?
- What information is needed from the assignment?
- Is adequate information about the subject available?
- Have you established a good cover?
- How will you communicate with headquarters?

- What will you do if you are arrested?
- Do you have an alternative plan if the initial plan fails?
- Do you have a plausible reason for leaving once the assignment is completed?[32]

Advice from Experts

Former FBI Special Agent Joseph D. Pistone offers agents the following suggestions on tactics to use when operating in an undercover fashion:

- First, keep your fabricated past simple and as close to the truth as possible. Construct a criminal past that allows you to work alone and without violence.

- Second, do not indicate that you have a great deal of money; that leads people to believe that you are a cop or a person who can be conned out of his or her money.

- Never keep notes or anything that could expose your identity. You can never know when you will be searched.

- Try for acceptance in the target group without drawing attention. Do not be pushy. Use brief introductions, short conversations, appearances in one place or another, or hints that show you know your way around. Try to leave a trail of credibility, but build slowly. The quickest way to be identified as a law enforcement officer is to move too fast. You have to play by the rules of the street, to show that you have the time. Let the target check you out and come to you.

- Continue to be your own person and keep your personality intact. Some undercover agents think they must drink heavily or take drugs to blend in or demonstrate their toughness, but that is a serious mistake. If you compromise your own standards and personality, smart criminals see right through the facade. An undercover agent must realize that at some point down the line he or she will have to testify in court about his or her activities. If the undercover officer took drugs or engaged in any serious wrongdoing, his or her credibility will be seriously questioned, and the effectiveness of the testimony greatly diminished.

- Not every person has the capacity to work undercover. Undercover assignments require

To Catch Cheating Husbands

Former New York City Police Department detective Gerry Palace operates Check-A-Mate, a full-service private investigation agency, which uses real-life decoys to test a man's propensity to cheat on his spouse. Palace sends female undercover agents out into Manhattan nightspots to test subjects who are suspected of being unfaithful. The agents are told to engage in conversation with the subjects and then ask key questions, such as, "So, a good-looking guy like you has to be married, right?"

All of Palace's female agents work part-time and have other jobs in film, theater, or modeling. Furthermore, every woman he employs has been a victim herself—cheated on by a man.

The agents wear hidden tape recorders to record anything said by the subjects. These recordings can then be replayed for the clients.

SOURCE: Daniel Jeffreys, "Bait and Snitch Is His Game: Ex-NYPD Detective Uses Real-Life Decoys to Catch Cheating Wall Street Men," *New York Post*, August 18, 1999, pp. 28–29.

officer in Cairo, Illinois, makes the following recommendations:

- One person is not enough. A person working alone is isolated, and the tendency for corruption is much greater.
- The primary factor in an undercover investigation is the safety of the individual conducting it.
- Undercover operations are not cost effective. They require a great deal of time and money to begin and shouldn't be attempted on a part-time basis or without adequate support.
- Agents should never go into a situation cold. There should be goals set for any operation and a basis of sound, reliable information. Secrecy is a must.
- Training is essential.
- Operations should be closely monitored by superiors and mechanisms should be available to help agents deal with stress.
- It is important to know when to end an operation. When it is not producing the anticipated results, it should be terminated.[34]

a strong, disciplined personality, capable of working alone without backup.

- While you are pretending to be somebody else, you will encounter the same personality conflicts you would find anywhere. There will be people you will like and people you will not. You must override your natural inclinations for association and learn to cultivate who[m]ever can help your investigation. You must learn to swallow your gripes and control your temper.
- Finally, undercover agents must make difficult decisions on their own, often right on the spot. You must accept the consequences of being wrong and making mistakes, because you will have nobody to hide behind on the street. You must be street-smart, disciplined to work, and willing to take the initiative.[33]

Professor James J. Ness of Southern Illinois University, who worked as an undercover police

Communicating with Supervisors

It is essential that undercover investigators have a **contact** person they can immediately call or see at any hour of the day or night. Without this contact, investigators may find themselves out in the cold with no assistance.

Telephone conversations with the contact should take place far from the undercover operation to ensure that the call is not being recorded or otherwise overheard. Investigators should make no calls from their home, for the phone may be tapped.

It is best to make any telephone calls to the contact from pay telephones far away from the operation or site of the investigation or from cell phones. The investigator should continually change the location of the telephone from which the calls are made to avoid setting a pattern. Telephone calling cards should not be used because they leave a paper trail that suspicious subjects can study.

In addition, undercovers must be careful with written reports or communications. In a sensitive case, there should be several **mail drops** to which

contact An investigator who maintains contact with an undercover officer.

mail drop A method used by undercover agents to leave information for other investigators.

they can send correspondence and from which they can receive correspondence. Personal meetings between undercover investigators and their contact should also be considered extremely dangerous. Precautions must be taken to ensure that these meetings are not observed. It is advisable for the undercover investigator to have an associate in the operation who can facilitate communications and secure help in the event of an emergency.

Recording the Undercover Operation

Record keeping and reporting are essential in undercover investigations. Collecting facts and detailed information is essential so that logical conclusions can be drawn. While assigned to the undercover investigation, investigators cannot record notes or jot down information. They cannot continually run into a bathroom or other private area to write down facts, names, phone numbers, addresses, and so on. Instead, they must memorize certain data until they have the opportunity to write it down.

Also, business receipts must be obtained, and there must be an accounting of all money spent. In some operations, agents will be expected to spend their own money and then receive compensation from their employer. In other operations, they are given a certain amount of funds to spend. In both cases, employers and supervisors expect them to account for any funds used or requested.

Danger in the Under-cover Operation and Illegal Activity

Obviously, undercover operations can be very dangerous to investigators if their cover is blown. Careful attention to the details, including the suggestions made in this chapter, will reduce the potential dangers. Furthermore, investigators should take no chances with their safety. If they have any doubt whatsoever about the integrity of their cover, they should immediately abort the mission and notify their contact from a safe location. No investigation is as important as the safety of the investigator.

Undercover investigators, even those directly involved in investigating illegal drug use, should never engage in illegal activity. Using drugs can affect their reasoning ability, conduct, and powers of observation. It can cause them to say things that they shouldn't and can compromise their testimony in court.

Of course, they must have a cover story in the event they are offered drugs. Several good stories are these: "I'm on probation, dude. No way, they test me every week. Ain't going behind bars again for nothing." "I can't do substances, man. I'm in AA, it's my last shot. If I screw up this time, my wife is leaving me. Can't take the chance."

Undercover investigators must not only avoid engaging in illegal conduct but also avoid any conduct that might compromise their status. As one private investigator who hires undercover investigators says: "The problem with letting go, with getting drunk, is the operative is likely to make a mistake. This whole undercover business involves walking a line that is so thin between who you are, and who you are supposed to be, that the longer you walk it, the easier it is to fall off."[35]

David Owens, a veteran of many years as a lieutenant in the Syracuse, New York, Police Department's Special Investigations Division supervising undercover investigations and now a professor of criminal justice, warns potential undercover agents:

> Another problem area is that you are almost constantly engaged in deceptive covert tactics. In other words, you are living a lie! This can have serious negative impact on one's health, and family life. . . . You must be able to maintain a strong sense of right from wrong. For, in the work of the undercover officer, it is easy to allow the underworld to rub off on you. Should you ever find yourself involved in an undercover assignment, it will be up to you not to let that happen. The consequences of such poor judgement could ruin your life.[36]

Homeland Security and Surveillance and Undercover Operations in Private Security

Surveillance and undercover operations are essential in terrorism and homeland security investigations and operations for observing the actions of suspected terrorists and the locations they may be targeting.

Many private security firms provide personnel to the Department of Homeland Security and other federal, local, and state agencies to help in these duties. Also, corporate security departments and contract security providers are involved in

homeland security–related surveillance and undercover operations for their firms or businesses, or the firms or businesses they are providing services for, to ensure that they are protected from terrorism incidents. Preventive steps and additional security measures, including increased security patrols, the installation of additional monitoring and surveillance devices, and the training of personnel at target sites, can identify possible terrorists and their preparatory activities and prevent other tragedies like 9/11 from occurring again.[37]

The demands for increased homeland security have also resulted in new automated surveillance and undercover antiterrorism technology, including intelligent cameras that function without operators and automated sensory devices able to detect tiny traces of biochemicals, explosives, or radiation. These innovative security surveillance systems can monitor people, as well as the environment, food and water supplies, borders, ports, and much more, to prevent terrorism.[38]

Summary

- A surveillance is the covert observation of places, persons, and vehicles for the purpose of obtaining information about the identities or activities of subjects. The word covert means secret or hidden.

- Surveillance is used in many private security noncriminal investigations, such as domestic/marital cases, child custody cases, and preemployment checks. It is also used in many private security criminal cases, such as insurance fraud, corporate fraud, and industrial espionage.

- A surveillant must have a cover story if challenged by the subject or an associate of the subject and should have cover articles, such as a newspaper or paperback book, that he or she could look at to appear as if not watching the subject.

- Surveillants must be able to blend in wherever they are assigned to conduct a surveillance.

- Written notes are essential in surveillance. If it is not possible to record them contemporaneously, the surveillant should record them as soon as possible after the event.

- Today's surveillants have high-tech state-of-the-art listening, recording, and viewing devices;

high-tech surveillance vans; vehicle tracking systems; night-vision devices; surveillance aircraft; and global positioning systems, among other innovations.

- Vehicle tracking systems, also sometimes referred to as transponders, bumper beepers, or homing devices, enable surveillants to track a vehicle during a surveillance.

- An undercover operation may be defined as a form of investigation in which an investigator assumes a different identity in order to obtain information or achieve another investigatory purpose.

- Private security firms offer integrity shoppers or mystery shoppers to business clients to test the integrity and efficiency of retail business personnel.

- Private security firms offer corporate clients silent witness programs that provide a method for honest and dedicated employees who are concerned about wrongdoing in the workplace to volunteer helpful information without compromising themselves.

- Internal intelligence programs are those in which private investigative firms plant undercover agents in a company's business operations to make observations and report back to the company.

- The undercover operation is perhaps the most sensitive and most dangerous type of investigation. If the undercover is burned, not only is the investigation compromised but her life may be in peril.
- Record keeping and reporting are essential in undercover investigations.
- Undercover investigators must not only avoid engaging in illegal conduct but also avoid any conduct that might compromise their status.

Learning Check

1. What is the primary reason for investigators to conduct a surveillance?

2. What are some of the most important preparations a surveillant should make prior to a surveillance?

3. Discuss some of the methods a surveillant may use to blend into an area.

4. Discuss some of the common mistakes surveillants may make when conducting surveillance.

5. Describe the best techniques for a surveillant to use when conducting a surveillance of a moving vehicle.

6. During a surveillance, the surveillant is "made." What should the surveillant do now?

7. Identify and discuss at least three reasons to conduct an undercover investigation.

8. Identify and describe three technological surveillance devices.

9. During an undercover investigation, the investigator is approached by subjects of the investigation, who offer him drugs. What should the investigator do? Why?

10. Describe several cover stories an undercover operator might use in the event he is approached to take drugs during an undercover operation.

Application Exercise

Test your ability to do a foot surveillance. Team up with a friend and plan the surveillance. Your friend will be the subject; you will be the surveillant. You may even form a surveillance team of three or four

friends. The rules are simple: (1) The subject starts from a prearranged location at 1300 hours (that is, 1 P.M.) or another starting time. (2) The surveillant or surveillance team is free to follow the subject and use any techniques appropriate to conduct the surveillance. (3) If the subject spots the surveillant or member of the surveillance team at any time, that surveillant must drop out of the surveillance. When all members are spotted, the surveillance is over. Members of the exercise team will reassemble at a prearranged location and debrief the operation.

Web Exercise

Use the Internet to research at least two large private security or investigating services and prepare a report discussing the services each provides in surveillance and undercover operations.

Key Terms

ABC method, p. 295
blend, p. 293
bugs, p. 299
burned, p. 303
close/tight tail, p. 295
contact, p. 306
cover story, p. 292
covert, p. 290
global positioning systems (GPS), p. 300
integrity shoppers, p. 302
leapfrog, p. 295
loose tail, p. 294
"made", p. 296
mail drop, p. 306
moving surveillance, p. 294
mystery shopper, p. 302
night-vision devices, p. 299
rough tail, p. 294
shadow, p. 295
shopping services, p. 302
stationary surveillance, p. 293
subject, p. 290
surveillance, p. 290
surveillant, p. 290
undercover, p. 301
undercover operations, p. 300
undercover investigator/operator/agent, p. 301
unmanned aerial vehicle (UAV), p. 300
vehicle tracking system, p. 299

Private and Public Partnerships for Security

©Myrleen Ferguson Cate/PhotoEdit

GOALS

- To acquaint you with the need for cooperation between the police and the private security industry.
- To introduce you to the concept of privatization of government services.
- To acquaint you with the numerous private and public partnerships developed to deal with U.S. crime and security problems.
- To acquaint you with the concepts of moonlighting.
- To familiarize you with community crime-prevention programs.

Introduction

As indicated in Chapter 1, the concept of police is rather new in world history. Since the beginnings of society, there has been a need for security and for people to protect themselves and their loved ones against crime and disorder. Over the centuries, these methods have progressed from hiding in caves, walling off cities, and engaging in hand-to-hand combat. All of these were private efforts. We do not see the concept of publicly provided systems of security until the fourteenth century in Europe. The concept of police, as we know it today, was not developed fully until the nineteenth century.

Since the middle of the nineteenth century the police have dominated the market share in security in the United States. The Civil War era began to see the emergence of private security forces. The 1940s and 1950s saw the growing popularity of private security firms in corporate and industrial America. Since the crime-ridden years of the 1960s, there has been a renewed aggressive emphasis on using both the police and the private security industry to deal with increasing crime and disorder.

In recent times, the private security industry has revolutionized our former concept of crime fighting and security. Today, private security outnumbers the police by three officers to one and spends double the amount of funds. The noted financial and public affairs publication *The Economist* writes that this revolution in private security is likely to change the way people think about the government.

> The growth of such property [private malls and gated communities] dramatically extends the private police's sphere of activity. It also changes the relationship between the police and private guards. There is no question of the private police being the junior partner in malls. They are in the front line. The old public monopoly over keeping the peace has not been replaced by a public-private partnership but, to a great extent, by the private sector. . . . In these places [private malls and gated communities], the system of maintaining order depends directly on the consent of those who live or shop in the area (after all, they have chosen to live in the gated community or shop in the mall).[1]

Today, as we are in the first decade of the twenty-first century, the emphasis on private and public partnerships has emerged as one of the leading issues in the study and practice of criminal justice.

This chapter will discuss the need for cooperation between public and private law enforcement and the concept of privatization of government services. It will discuss numerous examples of private and public partnerships to achieve security, including federal, state, and local law enforcement partnerships; bail enforcement agents' controversial role in the criminal justice system, and special private and public police partnerships to fight terrorism. It will discuss the successful concept of business improvement districts (BIDs). Additionally, the chapter will discuss police officers working for private security firms (moonlighting), private security officers working for government agencies, and private citizens policing their own communities and volunteering to work for their police departments.

Need for Cooperation

As we saw in Chapter 2 of this textbook, although the police have legal jurisdiction in the entire nation, they generally only exercise this power on public streets and thoroughfares and in other public places.

There are numerous restrictions on the police, including their limited jurisdiction, reactive role, philosophical differences, and overwhelming workload and duties. The private security industry has provided services beyond the scope of the police to its clients; these services have improved the safety and security of our nation. The lessons of history and research have taught us that neither the police nor private security can do their jobs alone. They need each other.

The private and public sectors do not have identical interests in the fight against crime, but their interests can be complementary. Private security providers owe their allegiance to their clients and employers, whereas the police work for the entire society. However, both the police and private security have a common goal: the safety and security of society. Private security personnel can provide substantial assistance to the police by providing comprehensive and accurate investigative reports of incidents. The police can provide suggestions on how to conduct

JOBS IN SECURITY

Private Security Positions for Public Entities

PINKERTON GOVERNMENT SERVICES

Pinkerton Government Services Inc. provides professional security services to government agencies. Among the minimum qualifications for these jobs is the completion of a Pinkerton Government Services background investigation. Applicants must be able to meet and continue to meet any applicable state, county, and municipal licensing requirements for security employees. Applicants selected for certain positions will also be subject to a government security investigation and must meet eligibility requirements for access to classified information.

To obtain information about these jobs, contact Pinkerton Government Services Inc. at their website or contact the Pinkerton Government Services office nearest you. You can obtain the locations of their offices at their website.

WACKENHUT NUCLEAR SECURITY SERVICES

Wackenhut Services Inc. offers professional security services to nuclear plants throughout the nation. Together with three highly successful small businesses who have a continuing presence in East Tennessee, they comprise the Oak Ridge Team, which has assumed responsibilities for protective services and security functions for the Oak Ridge Department of Energy Reservation facilities in Tennessee.

SOURCES: Pinkerton Government Services, Inc., "Career Opportunities." Retrieved October 25, 2005, from http://www.pgs-usa.com; and Wackenhut Services Inc., "The Oak Ridge Team." Retrieved October 25, 2005, from http://www.wackenhut.com.

---

investigations. Private and public resources can be combined to decrease crime and increase security.

In a 1995 article in the *Journal of Security Administration*, R. H. Moore Jr. was perhaps prophetic when he argued that in the future, private security must work more closely with the police because it will assume many of their responsibilities. He also predicted that contract security will have a greater role in the protection of government property and that private security must recognize the increasing technological sophistication and larger networks of criminal organizations. In addition, he wrote that robots, electronic sensors, and surveillance devices will perform basic guard duty and thus, private security personnel will need to be literate in computers and technology.[2] We have seen all of his predictions come true.

There has traditionally been a lack of cooperation and communication between the police and the private security industry. The reasons for this traditional problem were discussed at length at the 2004 National Policy Summit, "Building Private Security/Public Policing Partnerships to Prevent and Respond to Terrorism and Public Disorder," held in Arlington, Virginia. This summit involved about 140 executive-level representatives of local, state, and federal law enforcement agencies; security departments of major corporations; security product and services providers; professional

organizations in the law enforcement and private security field; universities; and federal agencies.[3] This lack of communication and cooperation is particularly serious in view of the constant fear of terrorist attacks on our nation, including its critical infrastructures, since the 9/11 terrorist attacks.

Since then, public law enforcement has made great strides in obtaining potential terrorist attack information; however, it has been reluctant to share this information with the private business and industrial sectors that tend to be most vulnerable to these attacks. Private corporations have complained that they do not receive timely threat information from law enforcement, yet they also fear that any information they themselves give to law enforcement may end up disseminated to the public.

Despite their similar interests in crime prevention, the fields of policing and private security have rarely collaborated. Summit participants noted that only 5 to 10 percent of law enforcement chief executives participate in partnerships with private security and that emergency response exercises designed to deal with terrorism and other national disasters and disorders tend to include police, fire, public health, and governmental authorities but leave out private security. The participants did note, however, that certain private–public operational partnerships, such as business improvement districts (discussed later in this chapter), have proven to be very successful.

In their frank discussion of the reasons for the lack of cooperation between the police and private security, the discussants found that some of it is caused by police dissatisfaction with the private security industry's lack of pre-employment screening, training, standards, certification, and regulation; and that some in law enforcement think of private security as a threat to their domain. On the other hand, they found that many private security practitioners believed the police have little understanding of the security industry's broad range of functions, capabilities, expertise, and resources and therefore fail to appreciate the importance of its valuable role in preventing and solving crime.

Another major source of conflict between the police and private security was the tremendous inherent problem of sharing information. Companies, on one hand, do not wish to let privileged business information become public knowledge, such as through the Freedom of Information Act, and many find that when they report cybercrime, police and prosecution officials seize their corporate records and computers to pursue the cases. On the other hand, law enforcement may at times be legally prohibited from sharing some information that private security desires, such as criminal histories. Also, police often feel uncomfortable sharing homeland security-related information with companies that operate in the United States but are owned by noncitizens from foreign countries.

While acknowledging that there are reasons why the police and private security have had past difficulties in cooperating, the summit found that it is in the best interests of public and private policing agencies to work together for the following reasons:

■ The police can help prepare private security to assist in emergencies (particularly important because, in many instances, security officers are the first responders). They can help to coordinate joint efforts to safeguard the critical infrastructure for which private security is responsible. The police can help train security officers and provide them with services, additional personnel resources, and expertise.

■ The police can benefit from the vast knowledge of the private sector in special areas, such as cybercrime and advanced technology; gather better knowledge of incidents through the reporting efforts of private security; obtain intelligence; and reduce the number of calls for service.

The summit found that private security also has much to gain from cooperating with the police because they can coordinate their plans in advance regarding evacuation, transportation, and other issues; gain intelligence from law enforcement regarding threats and crime trends; develop relationships, so they will know who to contact for help or to report information; build law enforcement's understanding of corporate needs, such as confidentiality; and boost law enforcement's respect for the security field.

The participants expressed a belief that with cooperation and partnerships, law enforcement agencies will be better able to carry out their traditional crime-fighting duties and their additional homeland security duties by using the many private security resources in the community. Also, they believe private security organizations will be better able to carry out their mission of protecting their companies' or clients' people, property, and information at the same time they serve the homeland security objectives of their communities.

Summit participants believed there were many current hopeful signs for possible improvement of police–private security relationships. It reported that these signs included the many retired law enforcement officials at the federal, state, and local levels obtaining jobs in private security after retirement, as well as the off-duty employment of many public police officers as private security officers. It also looked positively on the development of numerous private-sector police forces, such as college campus public-safety departments, and the many contractual arrangements in which government agencies contract with private security for services traditionally performed by law enforcement officers.

Privatization

The concept of privatization of government services has been discussed and debated for several decades. **Privatization** means turning over government-provided functions, entirely or in part, to the private sector. Proponents of privatization argue that the private sector can provide services more cheaply and more effectively than government does.

privatization Government agencies contracting out government-provided services to private agencies.

The Reason Foundation, through its Reason Public Policy Institute, has been at the forefront of the debate on privatization of government services.[4] In 1992, it established its Privatization Center, which provides practical research and analysis, how-to guides, case studies, and reports designed to inform elected officials on how to streamline government. The center specializes in government services—such as health services, social services, and public safety—and infrastructure—such as airports, electric power, highways, transit, and water/wastewater facilities. It explores how different institutional arrangements can create incentives for efficiency, improve customer service, enhance accountability, and save taxpayer dollars. It has a hotline, a monthly newsletter, and a website. It also publishes numerous special reports, as well as its *Annual Privatization Report,* a comprehensive overview of the year's most significant privatization developments in the United States.[5]

The Privatization Center reports that a variety of alternative service delivery techniques can be used entirely, or in combination, to privatize government services, including the following:

▪ **Contracting out/outsourcing**—contracting the service or part of it to a private company

▪ Management contracts—contracting the operation of a facility to a private company

▪ Franchising—granting the right to provide a service to a private company

▪ Internal markets—allowing government agencies to purchase support functions from an outside supplier

▪ Vouchers—providing government payment for the service; however, customers are given redeemable certificates to purchase the service from outside companies

▪ Commercialization (service shredding)—stopping government-provided service and allowing the open market to compete for the right to provide it

▪ Self-help—allowing community groups and neighborhoods to jointly become nonprofit companies and provide the service

▪ Volunteers—using volunteers to provide all or part of a government service

▪ Corporatization—turning government organizations into private businesses and no longer receiving government backing

The Privatization Center reports that police department budgets nationwide have been growing at about 3 percent a year, but demands for their services have increased much faster. In response, police departments are turning to privatization techniques to deal with this. Some of the methods government is using are intergovernmental contracting (for example, the Los Angeles County Sheriff's Department has entered into contracts to provide policing services to other government jurisdictions that can no longer afford to do so); using volunteers to perform nonsworn duties; civilianization by using nonsworn members to perform nonsworn duties; and outsourcing administrative, support, and other nonsworn duties to free up police to concentrate on their primary mission of protecting life and property.

It reports that outsourcing police services, such as performing funeral escorts, directing traffic, responding to burglar alarms, issuing parking citations, dispatching police vehicles, transporting and watching prisoners, watching over buildings found to be unlocked, and performing other nonemergency duties can reduce costs by up to 30 percent.[6]

Private and Public Partnerships

The Economist, reflecting on the growth of the private security business during the past two decades, reported that this growth was attributable to the desire of citizens to protect themselves from crime as well as the recent changing attitudes of the police. It reported that earlier, the public police regarded their private counterparts as a threat, whereas now they see them as partners and have delegated much of their work to them.[7]

Local, State, and Federal Law Enforcement Partnerships

In 2000, in a major emphasis on private–public partnerships, the Bureau of Justice Assistance of

contracting out/outsourcing Hiring external companies to perform duties for a company.

the U.S. Department of Justice, with the support of ASIS International, the International Association of Chiefs of Police, and the National Sheriffs' Association produced the report, *Operation Cooperation: Guidelines for Partnerships between Law Enforcement & Private Security Organizations*, as a call to action to persuade police, sheriffs, and security professionals to work together. The report offers some of the best ways to make this collaboration successful, based on years of national research and ideas from groundbreakers in public–private cooperation.[8]

The report acknowledges that over time, law enforcement agencies and private security operators (both contract security providers and corporate security departments) have increasingly come together, pooling their strengths to prevent and solve crimes. The report says these collaborative efforts, or **private–public partnerships**, work toward the protection of life and property.

Among some of the important points made by the report is a comparison of the special strengths of the police and private security. The strengths of the police are its special legal powers and extensive training. The strengths of private security are its size and its special expertise and resources, such as the use of technology to prevent and detect crime; investigation of high-tech and economic crime; and unique corporate and personal relationships that help it to address certain crimes, such as school shootings, workplace violence, or computer crime. The report indicates that successful public and private relationships can help to address joint problems, such as combating violence and drugs in the workplace, reducing false alarms, performing crisis planning, and much more.

It reported that the following are some of the benefits of law enforcement–private security cooperation:

- Networking and the personal touch.
- Collaboration on specific projects, such as urban quality-of-life issues and high-tech crime.
- Increased crime prevention and public safety.
- Cross-fertilization on techniques, such as crime prevention through environmental design, community policing, and the use of technology.
- Information sharing.
- Leveraging of resources. A law enforcement agency may be able to teach or help private security employees to do some work that law enforcement now handles, including, perhaps,

contracting out various noncrime and nonemergency tasks that do not require sworn law enforcement personnel. Also, security organizations may be able to more effectively help police reduce a variety of crimes against businesses.

- New crimes and issues. A variety of these are constantly arising that only a joint effort between the public and private sectors can help solve, for example, Internet crimes or cybercrime.

Historically, as we have seen, private security and law enforcement practitioners have not always had the best relationship. Sometimes, police have looked down on security officers, and at other times, security executives have felt the police were not interested in their concerns, such as high-tech crime, white collar crime, or terrorism. However, the trend in recent years had been toward partnerships. The major new developments that have driven this trend, according to *Operation Cooperation* staff, are the enormous growth and sophistication of private security and the mission of community policing that attempts to establish partnerships and cooperative efforts.

Operation Cooperation reports that the typical activities of collaborative programs include:

- Networking, including breakfast and lunch meetings, lectures and speeches, and directories of contacts
- Information sharing, such as local crime trends, modus operandi, incident information, shared e-mail trees, web pages, and newsletters
- Crime-prevention programs, such as joint participation in security and safety; consultation on crime prevention through environmental design and community policing; and joint efforts on local concerns, such as check fraud, video piracy, graffiti, false alarms, and neighborhood watch programs

---

Operation Cooperation Comprehensive 2000 government report, *Guidelines for Partnerships between Law Enforcement & Private Security Organizations*, prepared by the U.S. Department of Justice in collaboration with ASIS International, the IACP, and the National Sheriffs' Association and detailing public/private partnerships for security.

private–public partnerships Joint efforts between private security and public agencies to deal with crime.

- Resource sharing, including the lending of technical and language expertise, lending of computer equipment, "buy money," security devices, and the preparation of booklets listing contact information and other information

- Training, such as the hosting of special speakers and experts

- Legislation, including the drafting and supporting of laws and the tracking of important legislation

- Joint operations, such as the investigation of complex financial frauds or computer crimes; critical incident planning for natural disasters, school violence and shootings, and workplace violence; and joint sting operations on crimes such as cargo theft

- Research and guidelines, including the preparation and review of research papers and protocols regarding false alarms, workplace drug crimes, workplace violence, product tampering, mobile security devices, nonsworn alarm responders, closed-circuit television, security personnel standards, and the like.

The common elements that make a program successful, according to the report, are leadership, a facilitator or driver, structure, staff, an office, money and other resources, a clear mission or vision, uniqueness, benefits, tangible products, goodwill, shared power, and early success on a hot issue. The common reasons for failure are joint problems not being addressed or solved, chiefs losing interest, the founders or staff coordinators being reassigned or retired, personality clashes or oversized egos, inadequate funding, and/or no support staff.

Some of the major cooperative programs discussed by the *Operation Cooperation* staff include:

- APPL (Area Police/Private Security Liaison): APPL was founded by the New York City Police Department (NYPD) and prominent security directors in New York City in 1986 to enhance public/private cooperation in personal and property protection, to exchange information, and to help eliminate the credibility gap between police and private security. It began with thirty private security organizations and as of 2000, included more than one thousand. It is the largest local cooperative program between police and private security in the nation. APPL has monthly and annual meetings and engages in inventories of private-sector electronic video surveillance installations for use in criminal investigations. It also operates a specialized business crime squad in Midtown Manhattan, a radio network for door attendants, and the inclusion of private security representatives in the NYPD command-and-control center during emergencies.

- Law Enforcement and Private Security Council of Northeast Florida (LEPSCNF): LEPSCNF was established in 1996 to conduct joint training for law enforcement and private security personnel on crime-scene protection, search procedures, and coordination of evacuation plans for hurricanes, fires, and other disasters. It was developed with the assistance of the Federal Law Enforcement Training Center (FLETC).

- Federal Law Enforcement Training Center (FLETC) Operation Partnership: This partnership was originally funded by the Mobil Corporation. It now involves a two- to three-day program at the FLETC designed to teach law enforcement and private security managers how to build productive, cooperative relationships between their organizations. It is essentially a "train-the-facilitator" course that teaches police and private security managers to become advocates and facilitators for cooperative partnerships. It brings together law enforcement and security managers from a specific city, county, or region to develop a cooperative police/private security plan. Upon returning to their communities, team members collaborate to refine their plans and implement specific programs.

- California High-Technology Crime Advisory Committee: This committee was established in 1998 to assist regional high-tech crime task forces. Public-sector members include the California State Sheriffs' Association, the Police Chiefs' Association, the attorney general's office, the highway patrol, the high-tech crime investigators' association, the office of criminal justice planning, and the district attorneys' association. Private-sector members represent associations of computer hardware manufacturers, software publishers, cellular carriers, Internet-related companies, cable television providers, film producers, and telephone carriers. About half of the private-sector members have security backgrounds. It has developed a statewide strategy for combating high-tech crime and awards large grants to regional law enforcement task forces that have conducted hundreds of investigations and recovered millions of dollars in lost property.

■ Dallas/North Texas Regional Law Enforcement and Private Security Program (LEAPS): LEAPS consists of the deputy chief of the Dallas Police Department (DPD) and private security members from each of nine private business sectors. One officer from each DPD patrol division is assigned to support the program, and more than fifty private-sector organizations participate. It engages in security officer and police officer training, special-interest relationship building, and dissemination of crime information between public and private agencies. This program has enabled police to enlist the support of the private sector, whose security officers outnumber police officers by five to one in the Dallas area.

■ Virginia Police and Private Security Alliance (VAPPSA): VAPPSA has five topical sectors that include law enforcement, security alarm, private investigators/contract security, retail/mall security, and corporate security. It holds monthly meetings that focus on telecommunications fraud, electronic eavesdropping, juvenile offender programs, violence in the workplace, alarm industry trends, and public safety crisis management. It also shares crime information.

■ Center City District (CCD): The CCD was founded in Philadelphia in 1991. It combines a police substation with a private security operations firm and a sanitation firm. It performs law enforcement, security, and physical maintenance and improvement of the central business district of Philadelphia. In CCD, public and private employees share office space and work together closely. Its activities are funded through a special tax levy on businesses located within its boundaries.[9]

Some other exemplary public–private programs discussed in *Operation Cooperation*, such as Dallas's Downtown Emergency Response Team (DERT), the Financial Services Information Sharing and Analysis Center (FS/ISAC), and more information on the Dallas/North Texas Regional Law Enforcement and Private Security Program (LEAPS) are described in the You Are There! feature, "Some Examples of Private Security and Public Policing Partnerships."

Professional associations also play a major role in developing the concept of police and private security cooperation. The International Association of Chiefs of Police (IACP), the leading professional organization of police executives in the world, maintains a Private Sector Liaison Committee (PSLC). The PSLC is composed of professionals from the public and private sectors who meet to research, debate, develop guidelines, and offer advice to law enforcement and private security professionals through the guidance of the IACP. It was founded in 1986 with the mission to "develop and implement cooperative strategies for the enhancement of public law enforcement and private sector relationships in the interest of the common good." Members of the committee include police chiefs, sheriffs, federal law enforcement executives, corporate security directors, security consultants, directors of security industry associations, college professors, security company executives, military officials, and IACP officials.[10]

The PSLC had developed into a think tank for the IACP on a myriad of issues. Some of the areas in which the committee has developed protocols or guidelines include the following:

■ Product tampering

■ Drugs in the workplace

■ Combating workplace drug crimes

■ False-alarm perspectives

■ Combating workplace violence

■ Nonsworn alarm responder

■ Response to mobile security alarm devices

■ Private security officer selection, training, and licensing

■ Preventing and responding to school violence

The PSLC is currently developing the following projects designed to benefit both law enforcement and the private sector:

■ Extensive collaboration and research on the problem of technology-related crime. It is collaborating with the American Electronics Association, the International Electronics Security Group, and the RAND Corporation to study and provide useful information and training for law enforcement practitioners to help them cope with the steady rise of computer and other high-tech crime.

■ Developing a protocol for the legal and ethical use of electronic video surveillance and monitoring by public safety organizations.

You Are There!

Some Examples of Private Security and Public Policing Partnerships

THE DALLAS/NORTH TEXAS REGIONAL LAW ENFORCEMENT AND PRIVATE SECURITY PROGRAM (LEAPS)

The Dallas/North Texas Regional Law Enforcement and Private Security Program (LEAPS) began in 1995. It has more than 125 local law enforcement and corporate members who attend monthly meetings, hold seminars, and coordinate between private security and police to help deal with security problems. It addresses the critical need for police and public agencies to have good working relationships with private security. If there is an incident on private property and security officers are the first responders, police will work with them. LEAPS can activate private security groups and request they serve as civilian volunteers in a crisis, doing such tasks as search and rescue and debris removal. Also, it assists private businesses in developing appropriate security measures. Cooperative links have been forged with the fire department and hazmat teams.

Some successful applications of LEAPS include the following:

- An office-building security officer observed a car speeding through a parking lot adjacent to his building and obtained a partial license-plate number. He contacted the private security liaison at the Dallas Police Department and provided the information. The police analyzed the information and the partial plate number and linked the driver to a high-end auto-theft ring. He was arrested and prosecuted.
- In late 2003, after a robbery at a mall, the security officer called a liaison officer who put the information over the police dispatch system. The police apprehended the perpetrators before they left the mall parking lot.
- In January 2002, a man ran out of a burning apartment and began screaming at fire department

officials in Spanish. A member contacted a uniformed security officer known to speak Spanish and asked him to translate. Based on the security officer's translation, rescue workers were able to save a 9-month-old baby inside the apartment.

THE DOWNTOWN EMERGENCY RESPONSE TEAM (DERT)

In 2001, just months before 9/11, security directors in downtown Dallas formed the Downtown Emergency Response Team (DERT) for disaster-response planning. DERT oversees a thirty-person security team, a ten-member maintenance team, and a special-events division and works with the Dallas/North Texas Regional Law Enforcement and Private Security Program (LEAPS) that serves as a liaison between police and private security professionals in the greater Dallas area.

DERT consists of security directors, property managers, general contractors, and representatives of the city of Dallas. It also works with the American Red Cross, the Dallas Area Rapid Transit System, and the Building Owners and Managers Association. The group addresses natural disasters, foreign and domestic terrorism, and other emergencies and disasters. It includes a private-sector command post, pre-issued perimeter passes, onsite perimeter passes, and clearly marked helmets. In an emergency, the Dallas police set up a mobile command post several blocks away from the epicenter of the disaster that serves as the locus of communications during the crisis. The command post is shared with private-sector representatives of the affected property. Command personnel have a computer database and printout of pass numbers and individuals. Most of the costs of the program have been borne by businesses participating in DERT. The group also conducts drills.

- Producing guidelines for law enforcement response to mobile security alarm devices. These new devices incorporate alarm, global positioning, and cellular phone technology in one package. Although initially envisioned for use in motor vehicles, this rapidly growing technology has already been incorporated into handheld personal devices.
- Developing critical-incident planning for public safety agencies in the light of new threats

posed by weapons of mass destruction and the constantly evolving terrorist problem.

In another impetus for the development of public and private partnerships, the Office of Community-Oriented Policing Services prepared a guide, titled *National Business Leadership Strategies: A Guide to Engaging the Private Sector in Community Policing Initiatives*, to provide guidance in facilitating the process of police agencies engaging private-sector businesses as partners in providing security

In early 2004, after high winds blew off portions of a large water tower on top of one downtown building, DERT implemented its emergency plan. Within minutes, the details of the crisis were announced over a local radio station dedicated to emergency announcements. Also, emergency notifications went out to all DERT members via e-mail, text message, PDA, and pager. All property managers, security directors, and engineers in all downtown buildings knew what was happening and were kept abreast of the emergency as it progressed. Police closed off major thoroughfares, mass transit officials were notified, alternative routes for buses and light-rail systems were activated, and all responsible members responded to the scene. Security personnel at surrounding businesses implemented their own emergency plans. Building engineers and maintenance were able to correct the situation, and no one was hurt. Other recent incidents, such as the rupture of a 72-inch water main and a bomb threat, were also handled effectively because of Dallas's pioneering planning efforts.

THE FINANCIAL SERVICES INFORMATION-SHARING AND ANALYSIS CENTER (FS/ISAC)

The Financial Services Information-Sharing and Analysis Center (FS/ISAC) is a high-tech group designed to allow the industry's security professionals to share threat and mitigation information. It is a public–private group that provides intelligence to the financial services sector. The center's original mission was to collect information about cybersecurity threats, risks, and vulnerabilities; analyze these to assess their criticality for the financial sector; and deliver alerts to participants. After 9/11, the center expanded its focus beyond cybersecurity and now includes researching and distributing information on physical threats as well.

FS/ISAC starts by collecting an enormous amount of threat data that is then sent to analysts and analyzed. The cybersecurity and physical intelligence comes from member reports on subjects such as new virus attacks or an unusually high number of probes of particular ports, and from DHS. Once a vulnerability or incident is analyzed, it can be categorized as normal, urgent, or crisis, depending on the risk to the financial services sector, and members are notified.

FS/ISAC is managed by a board of directors from traditional financial service businesses, such as Goldman Sachs, Morgan Stanley, and Merrill-Lynch, and brings leading members of the physical and IT security worlds together. It deals with the problem that cost the New York City government $1 billion in lost tax revenue—the proliferation of hawkers selling counterfeit products like fake Fendi handbags, replica Rolex watches, and pirated DVDs. More than $23 billion in counterfeit goods changes hands in New York City each year. Forty-two percent of all counterfeit CDs seized in the United States are made within the metropolitan New York area. New York City accounts for 8 percent of the $287 billion in counterfeit goods sold in the United States. Fashion companies and law enforcement officials have been aggressively pursuing those who make and sell these cheap imitation goods.

SOURCES: "Cooperation Improves by LEAPS," *Security Management*, September 2004, pp. 48–50; Teresa Anderson, "Dallas Gets DERT on Downtown," *Security Management*, September 2004, pp. 45–55; Peter Piazza, "Intelligence Is the Best Defense," *Security Management*, September 2004, pp. 57–65; and Eric Dash, "The Handbag? Total Knockoff. The Price Tag?" *New York Times*, November 23, 2004, pp. B1, B6.

---

for the community. It provides examples of some partnership success stories across the country, including the use of business resources to establish a police substation in a mall to address crime that was hurting mall business and a partnership to target the theft of laptop computers from area businesses.[11]

In an important article in 2004, Chief Al Youngs, of the Lakewood, Colorado, Police Department and acting assistant dean of the criminal justice program at the University of Phoenix in Lakewood,

wrote that partnerships between the police and private security providers can keep crime rates low and do it with fewer resources. He reported that privatization of certain police department functions has proven to be a powerful solution to increased law enforcement at decreased costs and cites as an example that some federal agencies have saved as much as 50 percent by hiring contractors to provide services in government functions. Police today, he argues, typically spend less than

20 percent of their time on crime-related matters. He believes that in the future, police departments will be contracting out the functions that do not involve crimes or emergencies.[12]

Among the specific recommendations Youngs offers in his article are these:

■ Services with the potential to be priced should be considered as candidates for privatization or user charges.

■ To save money and to help police officers become more available to perform the tasks that only they can conduct, agencies should privatize tasks that do not require the full range of skills of police officers.

■ Private companies should provide such services as response to burglary alarms, and people with alarm systems should pay for the services they demand.

■ Private security can prove effective in a distinct geographic area and therefore, owners of apartment complexes should consider using private security agencies.

■ Agencies should consider any relatively low-skill or specialized high-skill services as candidates for transfer to private security.

■ Departments should ensure that the cost of monitoring contractor compliance and performance should not exceed the savings from privatization.

■ Agencies should request that their state legislatures consider whether the current legal status and regulations pertaining to private security are appropriate in view of the expanded role expected from them, such as emergency vehicle status and expanded powers of arrest.

■ Problem-oriented policing offers the prospect of improved police–private partnerships in dealing with specific crime problems.

■ The community-policing approach offers hope for improving police performance and the community's sense of participation. Like privatization, community policing helps society better determine the use of its scarce police resources. Further, it brings the police "back" to constituents.

Some examples of privatization cited by Youngs include the following:

■ The Fresno, California, Sheriff's Department outsourced its prisoner transport duties, saving a substantial amount of money.[13]

■ Police departments in eighteen states currently use, or plan to use, private security guards to fill support roles. One firm provides security for six major public transit systems around the country, transports prisoners, maintains booking and security for a juvenile assessment center, and supplies security for courthouses in forty states.[14]

■ Over the past several decades, privatization in law enforcement has grown to such an extent that virtually every function, including security, jails, prisons, and court-related services, is being contracted out somewhere in the United States.[15]

■ Lakewood, Colorado's, police department has contracted with outside firms for nearly ten years. In addition, it uses trained citizen volunteers for police administrative work, such as fingerprinting citizens and issuing parking tickets to violators of handicapped parking. It also uses volunteers who have graduated from its citizen's police academy to serve as surveillance units regarding specific crimes, such as graffiti. It also uses civilian investigative technicians to conduct follow-ups, question victims and suspects, and prepare affidavits. It contracts with a private security firm to guard hospitalized prisoners and to provide assistance in protecting crime scenes.

Some other important recent examples of successful public–private partnerships follow:

■ In Australia, public and private agencies established the National Motor Vehicle Theft Reduction Council (NMVTRC) to design and implement strategies to reduce Australia's high rate of vehicle theft. The NMVTRC board is composed of senior representatives from Australian police services, transport agencies, motor manufacturers, insurers, motor trades, monitoring associations, and governments. This council involves government and industry agreements, partnerships, and commitment.[16]

■ Public and private officials developed the Metropolitan Detroit Mall Fraud Task Force in 1998 to deal with retail and credit fraud. The task force combines the resources of the FBI Detroit office, the U.S. Secret Service, and the U.S. Postal Service with local police and investigators from private industry. The private security industry provides corporate-based resources, information, and expertise that law enforcement often lacks. Eighteen months after the task force investigation began, arrests were made on a multimillion-dollar fraud network. As a result of the task force efforts, the incidence of counterfeit credit cards has been drastically reduced, millions of dollars have been saved in fraud losses to industry, and countless victims have been saved from having their credit-card history attacked.[17]

■ In 2004, a group of fifty financial services companies formed the Identity. Theft Assistance Center (ITAC), a Washington-based group that works with the FBI, Department of Homeland Security, Justice Department, Secret Service, and others to pursue suspected cases of identity theft. ITAC members developed a new system aimed at helping companies to streamline the methods they use to handle cases of identity theft. The group has emphasized to companies that, ideally, customers should have to speak to no more than one company employee when reporting a suspected case of identity theft—a practice originated by Wachovia, an ITAC member. This helps to reduce the hassle and bottlenecks that customers have traditionally encountered when trying to report identity theft. Half of the fraud cases reported to ITAC involve more than one financial company, with many involving as many as nine companies.[18]

■ The Illinois Motor Vehicle Theft Prevention Council is a partnership between the insurance industry, the State's Attorney, and law enforcement agencies. It requires insurance companies to pay into a special trust fund based on the number of private passenger automobiles insured for physical damage. The trust fund earns approximately $6 million annually that is then designated for law enforcement programs that increase the investigation and prosecution of vehicle theft–related crimes. Since it began in 1991, the annual number of motor vehicle–theft offenses has decreased 40 percent.[19]

Business Improvement Districts (BIDs)

Since the early 1970s, downtowns in cities across the United States and Canada have been using the business improvement district concept as a mechanism for revitalization. In these programs, the cities levy and collect a special assessment tax on property and business owners within a defined area and then return these assessment taxes back to the business improvement district to finance a wide range of services, including such things as security, maintenance, marketing, economic development, parking, and special events. A **business improvement district (BID)** delivers supplemental services, such as sanitation and maintenance, public safety and visitor services, marketing and promotional programs, capital improvements, and beautification in a designated area.[20] In New York City, any commercial, retail, or industrial area may apply for BID status through a local sponsor; then the local community board, the city planning commission, the city council, and the mayor must approve the proposal. The city's Department of Small Business Services works with commercial property owners and businesses to assist them in forming BIDs and managing BID services on an ongoing basis. New York City, as of 2004, had forty-six BIDs, including twenty-one in Manhattan, fifteen in Brooklyn, six in Queens, and four in the Bronx.[21]

Wisconsin also has had BIDs since 1984;[22] Milwaukee has thirty-one BIDs.[23] In California, BIDs date back to 1965, and as of 2004, there were two-hundred BIDs in the state. The largest is the City of San Diego's BID program that was created in 1970 as the Downtown Improvement Area. Since that time, San Diego has created eighteen separate districts with more than 11,000 small businesses. Assessment fees for businesses in BIDs in San Diego generally range between $40 and $500 per business per year. Some of the newer BIDs charge higher fees, ranging from $490 to $1,200 per year, with some anchor businesses paying up to $5,000 to support BID-related projects.[24] Albany, New York, has three BIDs. These BIDs are designed to provide enhanced services in the area in order to reverse the deterioration of their urban business environments and to compete more effectively with suburban malls.[25]

Heather MacDonald, a Fellow at the Manhattan Institute, writes that the core functions of a BID usually include keeping sidewalks and curbs clean, removing graffiti, and patrolling the streets.

---

business improvement districts (BIDs) Private organizations that oversee critical services, such as security and sanitation, for businesses in a defined geographical area or district.

The BID movement is one of the most important developments in local governance in the last two decades. There are anywhere from 1,000 to 2,000 such districts nationwide. . . . Baltimore's downtown business leaders have dispelled the area's reputation for crime with roving patrols of uniformed "ambassadors," who assist tourists and discourage panhandlers. . . . As cities grew dirtier and unrulier, customers fled to suburban shopping malls, where they didn't have to worry about getting mugged or stepping in a pool of urine. . . . New York's Grand Central Partnership's security patrol produced a 60 percent drop in crime. . . . Most criticism of BIDs springs from a deep suspicion of private enterprise, which some people believe can be up to no good where public spaces are concerned. BIDs are disproving that belief, showing that private interest and the public good can coincide. . . . They operate without civil service rules and red tape; most important, they negotiate labor contracts from a clean slate. They can hire and fire employees based on performance, not civil service status or other government mandates.[26]

The Philadelphia Center City District, established in 1991, represents a successful collaboration between municipal police and private security to improve the quality of life in the city's downtown business district.[27] A 2002 article in *Security Journal* reports that a review of official records and direct observations of customer service representative activity in Philadelphia's Center City District BID demonstrated that it was effective in achieving crime prevention and provides a vital link between police, private security, and the public. Public surveys show public appeal for customer service representative programs. The Center City District combines public policing along with a crime-prevention specialist tasked with conducting crime-prevention training seminars and analysis of crime trends.[28]

The Reason Foundation's Privatization Center praises BIDs. It says the success of the additional security provided by BIDS in lowering local crime rates has been demonstrated many times over. It ranks two of the most noted BIDs as the Los Angeles Garment District BID, where brightly dressed security guards on bicycle have reduced crime in the area by 20 percent, and the Grand Central BID in New York City, where extensive private security patrols have produced a 60 percent drop in crime.[29]

The Privatization Center emphasizes that the growth of more sophisticated and effective private security services has also contributed to the success of BIDs and mentions that some security companies have begun to specialize in providing highly trained and better-paid guards, equipped with high-tech gear and using aggressive techniques, to deter crime. It cites a good example of this as the Critical Intervention Services (CIS) that provide security in over fifty low-income apartment complexes in Florida. CIS uses armed guards in SWAT-style uniforms with visible bulletproof vests. Their intent is to intimidate would-be troublemakers, but they also work closely with local residents and landlords to establish a rapport. The result has been an average 50 percent decrease in crime in the complexes that CIS patrols.

Bail Enforcement Agents

Bail enforcement agents, otherwise known as **bounty hunters,** are controversial persons in the private–public partnership concept in the United States. Bail is a fixed amount of money set to insure an arrested person's appearance for all future court scheduling. If a person obtains bail, she is immediately released from custody. If the person does not appear, she forfeits the bail. If a person does not have sufficient money to post cash bail, she can obtain a surety bond from a bail bondsman, who guarantees the court that he will pay bond forfeiture if the defendant fails to appear for the scheduled court appearances. The arrested party must pay a premium to the bonding company to secure the bond. Generally, the bonding company does an investigation of the arrested party and her family to be reasonably assured that the person will appear on the court dates. If the person does not show up in court, the bail bondsman has the right to apprehend or arrest the defendant and produce her to the court of jurisdiction. The bail bondsman can delegate this authority to a bail enforcement agent or bounty hunter.[30]

If a person fails to appear before the court on the specified date, a judge can designate that person an FTA (Failure to Appear) and issue a warrant for his arrest. The bondsman who provided the bail then immediately owes the court the full amount of the bond, which is insured through a surety or insurance company. The bail enforcement agent

---

bail enforcement agent/bounty hunter Person hired by a bail bondsman to apprehend persons who have skipped or forfeited bail.

(bounty hunter) is hired by the bondsman, who is licensed by the state department of insurance. The bounty hunter is a civilian who gets paid to prevent the bondsman's complete loss of money. The bail enforcement agent earns between 10 and 20 percent of the bond amount when she apprehends a fugitive.

According to the U. S. Supreme Court in *Taylor v. Taintor* (1873), people who forfeit bail bond (bail jumpers) can be arrested without a warrant or other process. It also allows a person to enter the home of another to make the arrest.[31] The Court based its decision under the Extradition Clause of the U.S. Constitution (Article IV, § 2). In *Taylor v. Taintor,* the Court wrote,

> When bail is given, the principal is regarded as delivered to the custodies of his sureties. Their dominion is a continuance of the original imprisonment. Whenever they choose to do so, they may seize him and deliver him up in their discharge; and if that cannot be done at once, they may imprison him until it can be done. They may exercise their rights in person or by agent. They may pursue him into another State; may arrest him on the Sabbath; and, if necessary, may break and enter his house for that purpose. The seizure is not made by virtue of new process. None is needed. It is likened to the rearrest by the sheriff of an escaping prisoner.[32]

Bail enforcement agents can pursue these bail jumpers into other states, break into private premises to arrest them, and engage in other conduct that sworn police officers are not allowed to do. However, it is important to note that, according to a 2000 Federal Appellate Court decision in the 6th Circuit, although a bondsman may be authorized under the law of the state where a bond is made to retrieve bail jumpers, he must abide by the laws of the state he enters to pursue his fugitive. In this case, Larry Lund, a licensed bail bond underwriter from Florida, was arrested by Ohio law enforcement officers for his actions while arresting Michael Gish, an alleged fugitive bail jumper from Florida for whom Lund and his partner and wife, Deborah Lund, had written a bail bond. In order to arrest Gish, Lund entered the house of a third party in Ohio where Gish was alone with two small children and arrested and removed Gish without making provision for the care and safety of the two children in the house.

©Getty Images

A bail bondsman is any person or corporation who acts as a surety and pledges money or property as bail for the appearance of a criminal defendant in court. This practice is almost exclusively found in the United States. If a person fails to appear before the court on the specified date, a judge can designate that person an FTA (Failure to Appear) and issue an arrest warrant. The bail enforcement agent (bounty hunter) is hired by the bondsman, who is licensed by the state department of insurance. The bounty hunter is a civilian who gets paid to prevent the bondsman's complete loss of money.

The Lunds sued the Ohio arresting officers, claiming they committed constitutional violations under 42 U.S. Code (USC) Section 1983 (Civil Action for Deprivation of Rights) and numerous common-law torts under Ohio law. The U.S. district court ruled against the Lunds and the appellate court concurred, writing that nothing in *Taylor v. Taintor* was intended to authorize a bondsman to violate the law of a state or provisions of the U.S. Constitution in an effort to apprehend a bail jumper and that the Lund's argument was wrong.[33]

The National Association of Bail Enforcement Agents (NABEA) is a professional organization for bail enforcement agents designed to promote and encourage the use of private fugitive-recovery agencies; improve conditions and regulations with courts, public offices, and law enforcement agencies; and promote legislation that will support the industry. It provides training and certification classes taught by experienced professional active bail enforcement agents, who are part of NABEA. NABEA offers a sample investigation and recovery contract between a bail bond agency and the bail enforcement agency or officer. It also offers current news and information for its members.[34]

The American Bail Coalition is a professional organization of underwriters of criminal court appearance bonds and insurance and underwriter surety companies. Its purpose is to educate local government on the benefits of commercial-bond bonding and to advance the interests of the industry. It has a national headquarters in Washington, DC. Its website offers news, surveys of bail laws, court-case searches, and various other information of interest to members.[35]

The recovery of fugitives across state lines is covered under the provisions of the federal Uniform Criminal Extradition Act (UCEA). The UCEA is a procedure whereby fugitives who have committed a crime in a state can be returned from the state in which they are located now to the state where the offense was committed. Under the UCEA, a private person can arrest a fugitive accused of a crime, for which the punishment is at least one year of confinement, in another state. But the accused must be brought before a judge or magistrate within hours of arrest, whereupon she will be confined to allow for formal extradition process from the requesting state. All states in the United States, except Missouri and South Carolina, have adopted the UCEA. Since the late 1980s, courts have said that UCEA also applies to bail fugitives. It is important to realize that the arrest by a surety is always for purposes of surrendering the fugitive back to judicial authorities.[36]

States throughout the United States have various laws regarding bail enforcement agents or bounty hunters. Some states outlaw commercial bonding, use public bail systems, or ban bounty hunting (Wisconsin, Oregon, Illinois, and Kentucky); some eliminate freelance bounty hunters but allow full-time "runners" who work for one bond agent at a time (Florida, North Carolina, and South Carolina); some require bail recovery agents to be licensed by the state (eleven states). Other states have certain particular requirements for bounty hunters, such as Oklahoma, which requires an out-of-state

bounty hunter or bond agent to be accompanied by peace officers or licensed Oklahoma bond agents when seeking to apprehend bail jumpers.[37]

Under law, the terms *bail, surety, bondsman,* and *bail bond agent* mean the same thing—the person who provides the bail to release an arrested person; and the terms *bail recovery agent, bail fugitive recovery agent, bail enforcement officer,* and *bounty hunter* have the same meaning—the person hired by the bondsman to capture a person who has skipped bail.[38]

Bounty hunters can have particular problems if a fugitive enters another country, as laws in other nations can be quite different, and capturing a fugitive might be considered kidnapping in that country.

Private and Public Partnerships against Terrorism

Since 9/11, and especially since the creation of the Department of Homeland Security (DHS), there has been unprecedented improvement in private and public partnerships and cooperation to promote homeland security. This section will explore and discuss these new vital partnerships.

The private security industry possesses an incredible body of knowledge regarding homeland defense and terrorism and has traditionally been involved in protecting much of the nation's critical infrastructure.

In 2002, the U.S. Office for Domestic Preparedness, along with Michigan State University's School of Criminal Justice, prepared a report, *Critical Incident Protocol—A Public and Private Partnership*, that discussed the necessity and benefits of the public and private sectors working together to plan for emergencies. The protocol was the product of the efforts of one hundred persons from the public and private sectors who participated in five regional meetings held throughout the State of Michigan. Their collective expertise and personal experience became the resources for the development of this protocol.[39]

Under the protocol, the term *critical incident* is defined as "any event or situation that threatens people and/or their homes, businesses, or communities." The **critical incident protocol** has five objectives:

1. To create the public and private sector's understanding of their common goal to protect lives and property while sustaining the continuity of community life

2. To encourage the public- and private-sector entities that may have engaged in the assessment and planning process in isolation to form cooperative partnerships

3. To assist those businesses and communities lacking emergency planning experience in the development of a joint emergency planning process

4. To develop an understanding of mutual goals and to understand how public and private resources can complement and support each other

5. To serve as a resource for those engaged in the joint planning process

The protocol outlines lessons learned in establishing partnerships in advance, so a critical incident can be managed and resolved with minimum loss to the community. It also provides guidance for conducting individual and joint public–private evaluations of risk factors and understanding what business functions are critical to individual businesses and the community. Further, guidance is provided for developing joint public–private–sector emergency plans, along with the identification and sharing of community resources in responding to disasters. Other topics addressed are the facilitation of business resumption and recovery, the development of training exercises, and the incorporation of mitigation of harm throughout the entire process while recognizing its significance in preventing a disaster and reducing its potential impact. It contains references, including Internet resources, a glossary, and appended supplementary aids.

Radford W. Jones reports that the critical incident protocol concept originated in 1998, when a small focus group from the public and private sectors met to discuss how well both jointly prepared for disasters. The focus group agreed there was a need for a written protocol on the best practices for communities to share, coordinate, and manage resources and expertise to resolve a critical incident, including threat of or attack using weapons of mass destruction.[40]

Also in 2002, the passage of The Homeland Security Information Sharing Act of 2002 reflected the realization that communication and shared intelligence between business, industrial, and government organizations are essential to dealing with terrorism. This bill allowed the president to establish procedures for federal agencies to share homeland security information.[41]

In 2003, the Office for Domestic Preparedness, issued *The Office for Domestic Preparedness Guidelines for Homeland Security*. These guidelines are a series of activities, objectives, and elements that organizations can use as a framework for the development of jurisdictional terrorism-prevention plans. They include specific steps jurisdictions can take to improve collaborations between and among public- and private-sector agencies, including the establishment of a system, center, or task force to serve as a clearinghouse and to prepare memorandums of understanding and formal coordination agreements between agencies.[42]

Also in 2003, the *National Strategy for the Physical Protection of Critical Infrastructures and Key Assets* was issued. This report establishes priorities for the protection of areas such as agriculture, food, water, public health, emergency services, government, defense industrial base, information and telecommunications, energy, transportation, banking and finance, chemicals and hazardous materials, postal and shipping services, national icons, nuclear power plants, dams, and skyscrapers. DHS has been working with industry groups to fund prevention programs and generate common standards, best practices, and information sharing. Security grants have gone to sectors ranging from intercity buses to ports.[43]

In 2004, in order to address the fact that the biggest obstacle to information sharing between business and the government has traditionally been the private sector's fear that any security data it supplies to the government could be subject to public disclosure under the Freedom of Information

critical incident Any event or situation that threatens people and/or their homes, businesses, or community.

critical incident protocol Procedures to address critical incidents.

Act (FOIA) or used for regulatory purposes, the DHS created the Protected Critical Infrastructure Information Program. This program was designed to safeguard critical information submitted to the government from the reach of the FOIA and regulators. Critics have warned, however, that this program might be ineffectual or counterproductive. One of the most glaring problems, they report, is that data submission is voluntary and the DHS does not clarify the particular type of data it is seeking. Critics argue that the scope of the information sought may be boundless. In short, critics do not believe the government's claim that the data submitted to DHS will be protected from FOIA or regulatory disclosure.[44]

As mentioned earlier in this chapter, in 2004, the U.S. Department of Justice's Office of Community-Oriented Policing Services, in partnership with the IACP and a broad-based group of private security and law enforcement professionals, released a comprehensive report outlining a national strategy to strengthen existing partnerships between private security and public law enforcement agencies and to assist in the creation of new ones to prevent and respond to terrorism and public disorder. The report is the outgrowth of a national policy summit on this issue and provides law enforcement executives and their private security counterparts with the tools they need to accomplish this vital task. **The 2004 National Policy Summit**, "Building Private Security/Public Policing Partnerships to Prevent and Respond to Terrorism and Public Disorder," held in Arlington, Virginia, involved about 140 executive-level representatives of local, state, federal, and other law enforcement agencies; security departments of major corporations; security product and services providers; professional organizations in the law enforcement and private security fields; universities; and federal agencies.[45]

Law enforcement representatives included municipal, county, and tribal chiefs; sheriffs; state police executives; and representatives of federal and special law enforcement agencies (such as transit police). Private security representatives included CEOs of security firms, major corporate

security directors and chief security officers, security consultants, and representatives of security service and technology consultants. Professional organization representatives included members of IACP, the Joint Council on Information-Age Crime, Major Cities Chiefs Association, National Sheriffs' Association, Police Executive Research Forum, the Security Industry Association, ASIS International, the National Association of Security Companies, and the International Security Management Association. All of these associations provided expert advice and financial support to the summit. Academic institution representatives included John Jay College of Criminal Justice, Michigan State University, Northeastern University, and the University of Washington. Federal government representatives included the Department of Defense, Department of Justice, Department of Homeland Security, Federal Bureau of Investigation, U.S. Secret Service, and Sandia National Laboratories. Representatives of the following firms also attended and helped sponsor the summit: Allied Security, Bank of America, Chevron Texaco, First Citizens Bancshares, Security Management Consulting, and Target.

Participants were assigned to working groups to deal with major problems. The working groups produced five recommendations, including formal commitments to cooperate from leaders of major public and private law enforcement and security organizations; federal funding for research and training in cooperative endeavors; a national advisory council to develop and coordinate cooperative actions; federal leadership in convening key practitioners to fuel cooperation; and consideration of summit concerns by local partnerships in setting priorities.

The summit addressed the fact that since 9/11, public law enforcement agencies have been under tremendous pressure to perform their traditional crime prevention and response activities, in addition to assuming a large amount of homeland security work, despite tight city, county, and state budget restrictions. It also addressed the similar pressure on private security operations to conduct their traditional activities to protect people, property, and information, mindful of the profitability requirements of the businesses they serve, in addition to their nationwide effort to protect the nation from external and internal terrorist threats.

The summit generated some major policy recommendations, including that the DHS and Department of Justice should fund research and training on law enforcement and private security operations and that leaders of major law enforcement and private

The 2004 National Policy Summit A joint effort by the International Association of Chiefs of Police (IACP), the Office of Community-Oriented Policing Services (COPS), the U.S. Department of Justice (DOJ), and ASIS International, that addressed the major issues concerning the history and current status of public-private partnerships in an effort to enhance communication and cooperation between the public and private sectors.

security organizations should make a formal commitment to cooperation. Among specific activities that the two groups could conduct together, according to the participants, are infrastructure protection, improvement of data interoperability, and prevention and investigation of high-tech crime. The summit participants also suggested that joint research should include such efforts as studying existing partnerships in Israel, Ireland, and Sweden and conducting cost-benefit analysis of particular security measures. The specific recommendations made by the summit are included in Exhibit 12.1.

Currently, DHS is continuing to address the crucial need for public/private cooperation in preventing and dealing with terrorism. Its Private-Sector Office works directly with individual businesses, trade associations, and other professional and nongovernment organizations to share department information, programs, and particular opportunities.[46] It has also developed the Homeland Security Information Network-Critical Infrastructure (HSIN-CI) program to share information between the public and private sectors. Private-sector members receive alerts and notifications from DHS via phone, e-mail, fax, and pager. This system targets security professionals in specific sectors of the economy and notifies them of evolving threat information. The secure network includes 24-hour contact information for members to list particular assets that they can offer in case of an emergency; for example, if a disaster occurred and a large number of bulldozers were needed, this information would be forwarded to the group. The network also allows members to report suspicious activities directly to the FBI. This information is then shared with the DHS.[47]

As an example of local cooperation, detectives from the NYPD Counterterrorism Bureau developed Operation Nexus, in which they develop and cultivate contacts with certain businesses that might become unwitting partners of a future terrorist plot. Its members visit scuba shops and hardware stores and talk to parking garage attendants, plastic surgeons, hotel managers, tool rental companies, bulk fuel dealers, and trade schools. They have spoken to trade conventions and conventioneers throughout the United States. They concentrate on particular types of businesses based on intelligence that the department has culled from sources like the al Qaeda manual for terrorist operatives and debriefings of some of the group's leaders and foot soldiers. When they visit, the detectives leave their business card and the

EXHIBIT 12.1	**Recommendations of the 2004 National Policy Summit**

I. Leaders of the major law enforcement and private security organizations should make a formal commitment to cooperation.

II. The Department of Homeland Security and/or the Department of Justice should fund research and training on relevant legislation, private security, and law enforcement–private security cooperation.
   A. Conduct baseline and ongoing research
   B. Conduct and encourage training

III. The Department of Homeland Security and/or Department of Justice should create an advisory council to oversee the day-to-day implementation issues of law enforcement–private security partnerships.
   A. Institutionalize partnerships
   B. Address tactical issues and intelligence sharing
   C. Work to improve selection and training guidelines and standards for private security personnel
   D. Market the concept of law enforcement–private security partnership
   E. Create a national partnership information center

IV. The Department of Homeland Security and/or Department of Justice, along with relevant membership organizations, should convene key practitioners to move this agenda forward in the future.

V. Local partnerships should set priorities and address key problems as identified by the summit.

Source: U.S. Department of Justice, Office of Community-Oriented Policing Services, *National Policy Summit: Building Private Security/Public Policing Partnerships to Prevent and Respond to Terrorism and Public Disorder* (Washington, DC: Author, 2004), pp. 19–27.

department's terrorism hotline number. All visits are recorded in an extensive automated database that tracks the contacts, listing the detective assigned, the type of business, hours of operation, names of people spoken to, and whether they have any security equipment, like video cameras, that can capture images of people who enter. Other jurisdictions, including the Metropolitan Police in London and the New York State Office of Public Security, have replicated the NYPD program.[48]

In 2004, the FBI entered into a partnership, the Twin Cities Security Project, with security chiefs from forty Minnesota companies and law enforcement agencies that share information with each other to gain a broader view of potential terrorist activity. In 2005, the FBI established a secure website where all parties can communicate with each other. They also share data by telephone and e-mail and meet quarterly to network. The program is valuable because what a private company may see as a single case of identity theft, law enforcement may be able to use as information to track money going to terrorism groups. According to the head of the Minneapolis FBI office, "There's a whole other world out there outside of law enforcement; this is a faster way of connecting the dots."[49]

The Pennsylvania Office of Homeland Security and the Philadelphia Chapter of ASIS International have teamed up to improve cooperation between public law enforcement and corporate security in the fight against terrorism. Together they have developed a four-pronged program designed to protect the state against terrorist threats and to foster a debate about the best ways to prevent future attacks against the nation. This joint effort includes four strategies: (1) an antiterrorism task force that facilitates formal and informal cooperation between private security and state officials; (2) an e-mail communication system that links corporate security officials directly with the state's homeland security office; (3) a joint public awareness campaign designed to increase public vigilance against terrorism; and (4) a state-level committee bringing together public law enforcement and private security to discuss tips for protecting corporations and other vital structures against future attacks. There are similar cooperative efforts underway in other states, including Iowa, California, and Florida.[50]

Police Officers Working for Private Security Providers (Moonlighting)

Many police officers throughout the United States **moonlight** (work on their off-duty hours) as private security guards for private security agencies. Almost all police departments require an officer to obtain the department's permission

before obtaining private security employment. In some departments, the officers must find their own private employer; in others, the police union serves as a broker in assigning off-duty officers to private employers. In some areas, the police department itself actually serves as the broker between the private employers and the off-duty officers.

Some of the police departments that permit officers to perform private security on their off-duty hours allow the officers to wear their uniforms. Also, many departments permit the off-duty use of other department equipment, including radios and vehicles.

As discussed earlier in this text, the use of the police as private security guards can lead to ethical and equity problems. To whom is the officer responsible—the primary employer (the police department) or the private company? Who is responsible for the officer's liability in the event she makes a mistake? Should a police department continue to pay an officer who is out on sick report due to injuries sustained while working for a private firm? If an officer is guarding a local business and she observes a crime on the street, which obligation comes first—the obligation to the private business for security or the obligation to her oath of duty?[51]

Also, the use of police working for private security agencies can lead to legal problems for the firms hiring these officers. Chapter 4 of this textbook covered this area in detail, particularly Section 1983 violations, assault and battery, negligent hiring, *Miranda* warnings, and searches and seizures.

Private Security Officers Working for Government Agencies

The traditional proprietary approach to security requires a considerable investment in personnel, training, and equipment and can distract a company or organization from its core expertise and strategic priorities. Many government agencies, particularly federal agencies, are turning to contract security services to provide guards and other security functions (see Exhibit 12.2).

Wackenhut Services Inc. is a good example of private security workers working for public law enforcement agencies. It is a world leader in providing armed and unarmed security personnel

moonlight When police officers work in private security jobs during their off-duty hours.

EXHIBIT 12.2 Security Services Provided for the Federal Government by Private Security Providers

Guard Services
Armed and unarmed security guards
National scope guard service management
Motor/bike patrol and inspection
Access control
Emergency response
EMT/first responders
Visitor escort services
Surge services

Fire Services
Firefighters/EMTs
Incident response
Fire prevention
Dispatch
Community education
Administration
Facilities and equipment

Technical Services
Performance management program
Security console operations
Project management
Canine bomb detection
Lock and key services
Facility assessments
Government compliance
Satellite launch support

Administrative Services
Reception functions
Badge and ID functions
Mailroom services
Reception functions
Document control
Government programs
Security training
Visitor management

SOURCE: Pinkerton Government Services Inc., "Services." Retrieved October 25, 2005, from http://www.pgs-usa.com/services.htm.

and specially equipped special response teams, helicopter crews, canine teams, law enforcement officers, and special nuclear-materials security couriers.[52]

Wackenhut provides extensive services in the National Capital Region, which covers three states, and the District of Columbia. Nearly nine-hundred employees, on fifteen physical security contracts, work in the region providing law enforcement services. They protect some of the nation's most essential properties; interact with senior government officials, federal law enforcement and security agencies, foreign officials, and dignitaries; and serve the general public. These security officers serve in assignments with the Drug Enforcement Administration, Department of Justice, Federal Aviation Administration, Nuclear Regulatory Commission, and the Pentagon. They serve as Justice Protection Security Officers, Washington, DC Special Police Officers, executive protection drivers, badging and security guards, and alarm station/control center operators. Most are armed and licensed.[53]

It provides threat mitigation, training and education, exercises, and prevention programs, including HazMat (hazardous materials) training, development of policies and procedures, and training in crisis and consequence management, logistical support, planning, and oversight of large-scale field and table-top exercises for police and fire departments.[54]

Wackenhut also provides Custom Protection Officers for the U.S. Armed Forces. These officers are deployed to service locations where the need for quality and well-disciplined, trained security personnel is in demand, such as in transit systems, courthouses, prisoner transport and booking operations, and residential security programs. It also has special response teams and K-9 handlers.[55]

Another very large private security provider, Securitas U.S.A., through its subsidiary Pinkerton Government Services Inc., also provides numerous security services to the federal government, including guard, fire, emergency, technical, and administrative security services. It has offices in thirty-two states and over 4,000 security specialists, most with government clearances.[56]

The United Government Security Officers of America is an international bargaining union representing security officers employed on federal, state, and local governmental contracts and domestic accounts on issues of employment, health, safety, and wages.[57]

for the U.S. government. It is the only contracted private security agency to receive the Commission on Accreditation for Law Enforcement Agencies (CALEA) accreditation, a distinction many police departments aspire to achieve. Its security officers provide services at some of the nation's most sensitive and vital government installations and secure our nation's government nuclear facilities. It has sophisticated capabilities, including highly trained

Community Crime-Prevention Programs

Closely aligned with privatization and private and public partnerships are **community crime-prevention programs**. As we saw in the introduction to this chapter, the earliest forms of crime fighting and security efforts were personal efforts and community efforts. Today, the police and the private security industry have the primary role of protecting society; however, increasingly community crime-prevention programs are very important in maintaining the peace and sense of order in our communities.

The police have an obligation to help citizens protect themselves against crime. It is obvious, however, that the police cannot solve the crime and disorder problems of the United States by itself, and it cannot let citizens take the law into their own hands. To address these problems, the police must turn to the public for its support and active participation in programs to make the streets safer and improve the quality of life. As Wesley G. Skogan has written, "Voluntary local efforts must support official action if order is to be preserved within realistic budgetary limits and without sacrificing our civil liberties."[58]

This section will discuss the following categories of community crime-prevention programs: self-policing, citizen patrols, neighborhood watch, crime stoppers, and citizen volunteers.

Self-Policing

Throughout our history as a society, citizens have banded together for common efforts to achieve security and preserve their way of life. These communal efforts still exist, but some of these programs have not been legal and in fact were harmful to society. In some of these efforts, people took the law into their own hands and violated other people's civil rights, and at times took their lives.

community crime-prevention programs Anticrime programs in which citizens participate in crime-prevention programs in thier own neighborhoods; some examples are neighborhood watch, crime watch, block watch, community alert, citizen patrols and citizen marches.

Reflecting on the a range of self-policing that it says runs from the respectable to the atrocious, an article in *The Economist* reported,

> At one end are out-and-out vigilantes: the Ku Klux Klan, the Mafia . . ., and Northern Ireland's punishment squads. These last are sectarian gangs who beat up their victims with baseball bats to suppress crimes in Loyalist or Catholic areas. They are tolerated much more than the terrorists to whom they are linked. By and large, though, there is little evidence that vigilantes are increasing in number in the West, though in the most lawless countries— South Africa, Russia, Columbia—they are rife.
>
> In practice, the main difference between vigilantes on one end of the spectrum and residential patrols at the other lies in their attitude to the law and the police. Vigilantes really do take the law into their own hands. They decide what the law is. They see themselves as alternatives to the police or as defenders of a community against police harassment. In contrast, citizen's groups carry out the law as it stands; they do not seek to define it. Hence, they do not challenge the basic view that the state should be the only authority defining law and order. Rather, they see themselves as police-support groups. By and large, this sort of group survives in societies where the law is respected, while vigilantes do not. Without some police support, self-policing tends to lose legitimacy and, eventually, money and help from the community.[59]

Self-protection is still very important in our society, despite the best efforts of public law enforcement and private security, as the following example shows. Since the unsolved murders of three older citizens in a quiet, middle-class section of Columbus, Mississippi, and other unsolved murders of seniors, the elderly citizens are taking measures to ensure they are not also victims:

> Older people are buying locksmith shops out of dead bolts and have installed security systems in houses that they once thought nothing of leaving unlocked. Pistol sales have tripled at least, and a firearms instructor at a city gun range is teaching a class for elderly residents. . . . No one seems to go out much after dark unless they are in a group, and many carry weapons of some kind, even if it is just a baseball bat.[60]

Citizen Patrols

Citizen patrols are popular in the United States. They involve citizens patrolling on foot or in private cars and alerting the police to possible crimes or criminals in the area, thus being the eyes and ears of the police. The best-known citizen patrol is the Guardian Angels. The group, founded by Curtis Sliwa in 1977 to patrol New York City subway cars and stations, now has chapters in many other parts of the United States and in seven other countries. The Angels are essentially young people in distinctive red berets and T-shirts who patrol on buses, subways, and streets. Their main function is to act as an intimidating force against possible criminals or potentially disruptive people. Many people report that the mere presence of the Guardian Angels reassures them. Despite their popularity with citizens, however, the Guardian Angels have not been welcomed by police executives, who argue that only well-trained officers can maintain order.[61]

Researcher Susan Pennell evaluated the Guardian Angels' impact on crime in San Diego and twenty other localities in the United States. The impact of the Angels on crime was inconclusive. However, the study revealed that a majority of citizens knew that the Guardian Angels were patrolling their neighborhood, and most of those who knew about the Angels felt safer as a result of their presence.[62] Recently, the Guardian Angels have developed an academy, which is licensed in New York and is working in conjunction with the DHS on efforts to keep society safe.[63]

Many police departments are now utilizing citizens as observers in more formal ways. Volunteers with training (often graduates of the Citizens' Police Academy) are uniformed and drive in department vehicles. These vehicles are marked but carefully painted differently than police cars. The citizens patrol in teams and are another set of eyes and ears for the police, guided by strict policies on noninvolvement and instructions on how to report suspicious activity. The Nashville Police Department has an active BOLO ("Be on the Lookout") patrol. Citizens are trained to make observations in their neighborhoods and report suspicious activity to patrol officers. When they are out patrolling, they wear special insignias designating they are with the BOLO program. They address quality-of-life issues, including things such as graffiti or burned-out lights. In a business–community partnership, GTE Wireless donated one-hundred phones and service to the BOLO program.[64]

©Dennis MacDonald/PhotoEdit

A Neighborhood Crime Watch sign warns potential criminals that the neighborhood's residents will report all criminal and/or suspicious activity to the police. According to the National Crime Prevention Council, Neighborhood Crime Watch is one of the oldest and most effective crime-prevention programs in the country, bringing citizens together with law enforcement to deter crime and make communities safer.

Neighborhood Watch

Citizen involvement in crime-prevention programs has increased greatly in the past few decades. These programs are designed so that people in communities watch for suspicious people, lobby for improvements like increased lighting, report crime to the police, conduct home security surveys, and generally work with the police to make neighborhoods safer.[65]

Crime-prevention programs in which community members participate have different names in various parts of the country. Examples are Crime Watch, Block Watch, Community Alert, and, most commonly, Neighborhood Watch. Neighborhood Watch groups engage in a wide range of specific crime-prevention activities, as well as community-oriented activities. Citizens watch over activities on their block and alert the police to any suspicious or disorderly behavior. Neighborhood Watch blocks have clear signs alerting people that the block is protected by a Neighborhood Watch group.

In some jurisdictions, regular service providers have gotten involved in various crime-watch programs. Providers such as postal employees, power company employees, and delivery personnel who are routinely out in residential areas are trained in identification of suspicious activity. They radio or call in this activity to their dispatchers, who in turn notify the police.

Crime Stoppers

Crime Stoppers originated in 1975 in Albuquerque, New Mexico, and quickly spread across the country. In the typical Crime Stoppers program, the police ask television and radio stations to publicize an "unsolved crime of the week." Cash rewards are given for information that results in the conviction of the offender.[66] Crime Stoppers U.S.A. reported that information provided to it as of 2006 had resulted in almost 706,000 cases being closed and 395,000 arrests being made.[67]

Similar to Crime Stopper programs are programs that provide citizens the opportunity to leave anonymous tips regarding crimes and criminals for the police. Along the same lines, there have been some television shows that focus on locating wanted persons. One show that has enjoyed great success is *America's Most Wanted,* hosted by John Walsh. The show precipitated one of its highest-profile captures on March 12, 2003. Information aired by the show led to citizens calling the police when they spotted Elizabeth Smart and her kidnappers. That call, together with good police work by the officers who responded, led to a happy conclusion. Elizabeth was a 14-year-old girl kidnapped from her bedroom as she slept in Salt Lake City, Utah. She had been missing for many months, and her captors had many contacts with people who did not recognize them.[68]

Citizen Volunteers

Citizen volunteer programs—in which citizens volunteer to do police jobs, thus freeing police officers to return to patrol duties—have become numerous and popular. Citizens perform such jobs as crime analysis, clerical work, victim assistance, and crime prevention.

The use of volunteers in police departments has increased tremendously recently. Departments have realized the value of utilizing the talents of their residents from many perspectives. A police department that does not actively seek to recruit volunteers in fact is not practicing good management. The volunteers feel a vested interest in their police department and can often be counted on for support when departments are trying to expand, start new programs, or hire additional personnel. The police officers have increased involvement with the citizens at times other than crisis situations.

Administrators can redirect sworn employees to more hazardous duties when volunteers assume nonhazardous jobs. The department may be able to try new programs they would not have ordinarily been able to attempt due to a lack of personnel. The city or county government benefits from reduced or flat expenditures and the ability to not raise taxes in these budget-strapped times. The community benefits with a more educated citizenry and an increased feeling of safety. It is a win–win situation for all involved.

How to utilize volunteers is limited only by police managers and/or volunteer imagination. Nationwide, departments use volunteers for parking enforcement, for help at special events, as crime-prevention specialists, for telephone follow-ups and pawnshop investigations, and as receptionists and in clerical positions, as well as tour guides of the police facility. They may volunteer with the Police Athletic League at community-wide safety fairs, in conducting fingerprinting, and even for role-play situations in police training.

Some retirees have special talents that prove extremely valuable to police departments, such as computer expertise, printing knowledge, writing abilities (for brochures or notices), photographic or video expertise, or even cooking or catering skills to supply refreshments for special occasions.

Departments are actively recruiting volunteers and have web pages devoted to the volunteer effort, including application forms. The Nashville, Tennessee, Police Department site has a page entitled "Get Involved: Get Involved, Help Make a Difference in Your Community." It then lists the various ways community members can get involved in the department.[69] The Glendale, California, Police Department has a page devoted to volunteers, asking for people to help at the substations, serve as docents for police facility tours, or join the Retired Senior Volunteer Patrol (RSVP). The page directs them to the Volunteer Coordinator for questions.[70] The San Antonio, Texas, Police Department site has a page entitled "Volunteers in Policing VIP" that presents various opportunities for citizens of San Antonio to get involved and assist their police department. The VIP program began in 1997 with twelve volunteers; by 2001 there were over three-hundred VIPs working in various capacities within the department. They have links to an overview of the program, job descriptions, application and training, and a calendar of activities.[71]

The city of San Diego has made volunteers an integral part of its policing programs. The San Diego Police Department (SDPD) has a volunteer workforce of approximately eight-hundred citizens and has saved more than $1.5 million worth of policing hours from volunteers, in addition to allowing police officers to focus more time on serious crimes. Also, it has caused an improvement in police–community relations.[72]

One particularly interesting volunteer program used by the SDPD is its Retired Senior Volunteer Patrol (RSVP) programs. RSVP members wear uniforms with a badge, carry police radios, and drive donated marked vehicles. They have a variety of nonenforcement duties, including vacation-house checks; visits to persons living alone to check on their welfare and security; reporting broken street lights, abandoned cars, and potholes; fingerprinting; and crime-prevention presentations. In RSVP's first three years of service in the Rancho Bernardo area, crime dropped 25 percent. Another interesting program is its Crisis Intervention Team that is composed of selected citizen volunteers who are specially trained to provide immediate emotional and practical support to victims, witnesses, and other survivors of traumatic situations.

Homeland Security and Private and Public Partnerships

Since 9/11 and the resultant emphasis on the need for homeland security, there has been a groundswell of new private and public partnerships to improve the safety of our citizens and ensure that our homeland remains secure. As we will see in Chapter 13, private security professionals perform many of the homeland security activities in our nation. Also, a significant portion of the government's expenditures for homeland security is given to private security employees.

Since 9/11, Americans are more aware than ever of the threat of terrorist attacks on our soil. In the days following the attacks, we saw immediate and selfless volunteering, blood donations, and an outpouring of support for patriotism throughout the United States. Since then, the government has established the Citizen Corps, with the support and active participation of the private sector, to organize the spirit of volunteerism that is defending our freedoms. This broad network of volunteers harness the power of the American people's individual skills and interests to prepare local communities to effectively prevent and respond to the threats of terrorism, crime, and other disasters.[73]

A major tool in our nation's efforts for homeland security is the U.S. Coast Guard, which patrols our nation's waterways and borders to prevent terrorism and other crimes. As many will remember, during the tragedy of Hurricane Katrina in our nation's Gulf Coast Area, despite the failures of local, state, and federal agencies to respond to the victims of the storm, the members of the U.S. Coast Guard performed in a truly commendable fashion, making hundreds of courageous rescues of stranded victims from their rooftops. Adding to the success of the U.S. Coast Guard in homeland security efforts are the more than 35,000 members from all walks of life who serve as members of the U.S. Coast Guard Auxiliary. These citizens provide more than 2 million voluntary hours annually to benefit boaters and ensure homeland security—certainly a major example of the private and public partnerships we need to preserve our freedoms.

Summary

- The private and public sectors do not have identical interests in the fight against crime because private security providers owe their primary allegiance to their clients and employers, whereas the public police work for the entire society.

- There has traditionally been a lack of cooperation and communication between the police and the private security industry.

- Privatization means turning over government-provided functions, entirely or in part, to the private sector. Proponents of privatization say that the private sector can provide services more cheaply and more effectively than the government does.

- Business improvement districts (BIDS) deliver supplemental services, such as sanitation, maintenance, public safety, and beautification, in many of our nation's cities.

▪ Bail enforcement agents, otherwise known as "bounty hunters," are controversial persons in private law enforcement. Pursuant to a court order, they can pursue bail jumpers into other states, break into private premises, and engage in other conduct that sworn police officers are not allowed to do.

▪ The 2004 National Policy Summit, "Building Private Security/Public Policing Partnerships to Prevent and Respond to Terrorism and Public Disorder," involved executive-level representatives of government law enforcement agencies and private security professionals. It explored reasons for the traditional lack of private and public partnerships and offered numerous suggestions for improving this relationship. It resulted in numerous private and public law enforcement partnerships.

▪ Since 9/11, there has been exponential growth in the numbers of private and public partnerships to prevent terrorism.

▪ Many police officers throughout the United States moonlight (work on their off-duty hours) for private security agencies as private security guards.

▪ Many government agencies, particularly federal agencies, are turning to private contract security services to provide guards and other security functions.

▪ There are numerous community crime-prevention programs, including self-policing, citizen patrols, neighborhood watch, crime stoppers, and citizen volunteers.

Learning Check

1. Discuss some of the reasons why there need to be cooperative partnerships between the private security industry and the police.

2. What is privatization? Discuss some the methods government agencies can use to accomplish privatization.

3. Identify and discuss some of the reasons why there has traditionally been a lack of cooperation between private security and the police.

4. What is *Operation Cooperation*? Identify and discuss some of the typical activities of collaborative programs included in the report.

5. Identify and discuss three specific private/public relationships discussed in *Operation Cooperation*.

6. What is a business improvement district (BID)? Identify and discuss some successful examples of BIDs.

7. What was the 2004 National Policy Summit, "Building Private Security/Public Policing Partnerships to Prevent and Respond to Terrorism and Public Disorder"? Identify and discuss three specific recommendations made by the participants.

8. What is moonlighting? Identify and discuss some of the ethical and legal problems inherent with moonlighting.

9. Identify and discuss three specific successful police volunteer programs.

10. What is a bail enforcement agent? Identify and discuss the legal justification behind the power of the bail enforcement agent.

Application Exercise

You have been hired as a consultant to the police commissioner of the town in which you live. The commissioner has told you that he is interested in developing some private–public partnerships with private security agencies within the city. He asks you to research this issue for him and give him a report on several such programs around the country.

Prepare a six- to seven-page written report identifying and discussing such programs for the commissioner.

Web Exercise

You have been hired as a consultant to the mayor of your city or town. The mayor has indicated to you that she is concerned about the fiscal problems facing the city and is considering privatizing the city's police department or at least some of the nonessential duties it provides. She asks you to research the issue of privatization and offer her some examples of what has been done regarding this issue around the country.

Use the Internet to research this issue and prepare a six- to seven-page written report of your
findings for her.

Key Terms

Homeland Security

©Associated Press

GOALS

- To introduce you to the concepts of homeland security and terrorism.
- To familiarize you with the rapid, unprecedented actions taken to secure the nation in reaction to 9/11.
- To explore the necessity of government and private-sector efforts to ensure homeland security.
- To acquaint you with the many sophisticated efforts by the private security industry to ensure homeland security.
- To introduce you to the role of private security firms working with the U.S. military abroad.

Introduction

On **September 11, 2001 (9/11)**, our world changed.

On 9/11, a series of unthinkable and incomprehensible events led to ultimate disasters in New York City, Washington DC, and a grassy field in Pennsylvania. Those events shocked the world and changed world history.

The swiftness, scale, and sophistication of the coordinated operation, coupled with the extraordinary planning required, made most people realize that terrorism and mass murder had hit the United States. In the immediate aftermath of 9/11 it was reported that almost 5,000 people were missing and over 400 confirmed dead. These attacks shocked us even though there had been similar events (although not as massive) before.

As the smoke cleared and the final statistics were assembled, it was revealed that 3,047 people were murdered during the 9/11 terrorist attacks: 2,823 at New York City's World Trade Center, 184 at the Pentagon, and 40 in Stony Creek Township, Pennsylvania.[1]

Terrorism was not new to the United States. For years, most Americans had believed that terrorist attacks only occurred in foreign nations, but events during the past decade had changed American's perceptions:

- In 1993, the first terrorist attack on New York City's World Trade Center killed 6 and wounded 1,000.
- In 1995, the Alfred P. Murrah Federal Building in Oklahoma City was bombed, killing 168 persons and injuring 675 others.
- In 1996, a bombing at the Olympic Games in Atlanta, Georgia, killed 1 person and wounded 111 others.

During the past decade, there were also terrorist acts committed against family-planning clinics that provide abortions and against churches, as well as many other depraved, senseless incidents.

The 9/11 terrorist attacks finally jolted Americans out of their sense of complacency, and perhaps lethargy, and made them realize that indeed they themselves were the targets of terrorism and that their lives and the lives of their loved ones were at extreme risk from brutal invaders and murderers.

This chapter will discuss the general concepts of homeland security and terrorism and briefly describe government's efforts for homeland security. Then it will discuss, in more detail, the private security industry's efforts against terrorism and for homeland security, including the importance of the private security industry to homeland security; private security industry operations for homeland security; and the Department of Homeland Security and private security cooperation. It will also discuss private security firms and the U.S. military abroad.

Homeland Security

The term *homeland security* has been used after 9/11 to describe defensive efforts within the borders of the United States. Officials use it to separate the U.S. Department of Homeland Security's (DHS) operations from those of the U.S. Department of Defense.[2] Following 9/11, the U.S. government prepared and published the *National Strategy for Homeland Security* to mobilize and organize the United States to secure its homeland from terrorist attacks. It described the strategy as a complex mission requiring coordinated and focused efforts from the entire society, including the federal government, state and local governments, the private sector, and the American people.[3] The strategic objectives of the strategy are to prevent terrorist attacks against the United States, to reduce America's vulnerability to terrorism, and to minimize the damage and to recover from attacks that do occur. The strategy provides direction to the federal government departments and agencies that have a role in homeland security and suggests steps that state and local governments, private

September 11, 2001 (9/11) Date of the terrorist attacks of the largest magnitude against the United States by al Qaeda.

homeland security Defensive efforts within the borders of the U.S. *The National Strategy for Homeland Security* and the Homeland Security Act of 2002 serve to mobilize and organize our nation to secure the homeland from terrorist attacks.

JOBS IN SECURITY

Homeland Security Positions

SEEKING A JOB WITH THE U.S. DEPARTMENT OF HOMELAND SECURITY (DHS)

Persons interested in applying for Department of Homeland Security positions should visit the USAJobs electronic portal to government-wide opportunities. From that site, they can search for current DHS employment opportunities by job category, location, salary, and more.

DHS job announcements provide important information about job qualifications, duties, salary, duty location, benefits, and security requirements. Persons can view this site to determine if their interests, education, and professional background will make them a good candidate for the job.

All DHS jobs require U.S. citizenship, and most require successful completion of a full background investigation. Applicants may also be required to submit to a drug test.

CAREER OPPORTUNITIES WITH THE DEPARTMENT OF HOMELAND SECURITY (DHS)

The DHS reports the following career opportunity areas:

- Office of the Secretary: Employees work in multiple offices contributing to the overall homeland security mission.
- Office of Management: Employees work in one of a variety of critical areas, from human resources and administration to budgeting, procurement, and information technology (IT), making certain that the right resources and systems are in place to achieve homeland security's mission.
- Office of Inspector General: Employees work side by side with special agents, attorneys, engineers, and IT experts to prevent and detect fraud, waste, and abuse in homeland security programs and operations.
- Border and Transportation Security: These employees secure the nation's air, land, and sea borders. BTS employees also protect the country's transportation systems and official ports of entry and enforce the nation's immigration laws. Four agencies carry out this mission, including U.S. Customs and Border Protection employees, who prevent terrorists and terrorist weapons from entering the United States while facilitating the flow of legitimate trade and travel; U.S. Immigration and Customs Enforcement employees, who enforce

immigration and customs laws, safeguard U.S. commercial aviation, and protect federal facilities; U.S. Transportation Security Administration employees, who help to secure the transportation infrastructure from future terrorist acts in intelligence, regulation enforcement, and inspection positions; and Federal Law Enforcement Training Center employees, who develop the skills, knowledge, and professionalism of law enforcers from over eighty federal agencies.

- Federal Emergency Management Agency (FEMA): These employees prevent losses from disasters whenever possible and assist when they do happen.
- Information Analysis and Infrastructure Protection (IAIP): Employees apply their skills and talents to help deter, prevent, and mitigate acts of terrorism by identifying and assessing threats, mapping them against vulnerabilities, issuing warnings, and supporting the implementation of protective measures to secure the homeland.
- Science and Technology (S&T): Employees plan, fund, and manage research and development programs in technical fields to ensure that federal, state, and local responders have the scientific resources to protect the homeland.
- U.S. Citizenship and Immigration Services (USCIS): Employees are responsible for adjudicating and processing the host of applications and forms necessary to ensure the immigration of people and their families to the United States, from initial stages through their transition, to permanent residence, and finally to citizenship.
- U.S. Coast Guard: Civilian and military personnel work to save lives, enforce the law, operate ports and waterways, and protect the environment.
- U.S. Secret Service: These employees have the dual missions of protecting the nation's leaders and conducting criminal investigations involving law enforcement, security, information technology, communications, administration, intelligence, forensics, and other specialized fields.

SOURCES: U.S. Department of Homeland Security, "Working with DHS: Job Seekers." Retrieved December 15, 2005, from http://www.dhs; and U.S. Department of Homeland Security, "Working with DHS: Job Seekers: Career Opportunity Areas." Retrieved December 4, 2005, from http://www.dhs.gov.

companies and organizations, and individual Americans can take to improve our security.[4]

According to Jonathan R. White, professor of criminal justice and executive director of the Homeland Defense Initiative at Grand Valley State University in Grand Rapids, Michigan,

> America has no common definition of homeland security. Issues surrounding homeland security are confused because the country is dealing with a new concept, a new meaning of conflict, and a change in the procedures used to defend the United States. In the past, military forces protected the homeland, projecting power beyond U.S. borders. . . .[5]

White, however, explains that *homeland security* simply means keeping the country safe. It protects lives, property, and infrastructure and is designed to secure the United States.[6]

According to the Homeland Security Research Corporation, an international research and professional services firm serving the homeland security market, governments and businesses worldwide were expected to spend $59 billion in 2006 to prevent terrorism and promote homeland security, nearly a six-fold increase from 2000.[7]

Terrorism

Terrorism has a long tradition in world history. Terrorist tactics have been used frequently by radical and criminal groups to influence public opinion and to attempt to force authorities to do their will. Terrorists have criminal, political, and other nefarious motives. Some may remember the terrorist activities that occurred during the 1972 Olympic Games in Munich, Germany, when terrorists attacked and took hostage the Israeli Olympic team and killed all of them; the 1988 explosion of Flight 103 in the air over Lockerbie, Scotland, killing all 270 persons aboard; the Oklahoma City Federal Building bombing; and the first World Trade Center bombing in New York City. And of course, no one will ever forget the 9/11 terrorist attacks. This section will discuss general concepts regarding terrorism.

There are many definitions of terrorism. The FBI defines terrorism as "the unlawful use of force or violence against persons or property to intimidate or coerce a government, the civilian population, or a segment thereof, in furtherance of political or social objectives." The U.S. Defense Department defines it as "the unlawful use or threatened use of force or violence against individuals or property to coerce or intimidate governments or societies, often to achieve political, religious, or ideological objectives."[8] Jonathan White sums up terrorism simply: "Terrorism uses violence or threatened violence against innocent people to achieve a social or political goal."[9] The National Counterterrorism Center defines terrorism as "premeditated politically motivated violence perpetrated against noncombatant targets."[10] According to Louis J. Freeh, former director of the FBI:

> Terrorists are among the most ruthless of criminals, but their motivation rarely stems from personal need or a desire for material gain. Unlike the majority of violent criminals, terrorists do not know their victims; in fact, one of the hallmarks of terrorism is its indiscriminate victimization. Also, unlike most serious criminal activity, terrorism invites—and even depends upon—media attention to ensure a maximum yield of terror.[11]

The **Terrorism Knowledge Base** is operated by the **National Memorial Institute for the Prevention of Terrorism (MIPT)**, a nonprofit organization dedicated to preventing terrorism on U.S. soil or mitigating its effects. The MIPT was established after the 1995 bombing of the federal building in Oklahoma City and is funded by the DHS. The Terrorism Knowledge Base is a repository of incidents arranged by type, perpetrator, date, location, and other factors. It also contains overviews of terrorist groups, legal cases involving terrorism, information resources, and other valuable materials for terrorism researchers. Users can create graphs of incidents by group, incident, and other factors, and they can search terrorist organizations by ideology, such as antiglobalization, environmental, right-wing reactionary, and other groups.[12]

terrorism The use of terrorist actions; one of the hallmarks of terrorism is indiscriminate victimization.

Terrorism Knowledge Base Professional organization dedicated to preventing terrorism on U.S. soil or mitigating its effects; maintains a database of all terrorism incidents, terrorist groups, information sources, and other materials for terrorism researchers.

National Memorial Institute for the Prevention of Terrorism (MIPT) A nonprofit, nationally recognized think tank creating state-of-the-art knowledge bases and sharing information on terrorism prevention and responder preparedness.

The new Oklahoma City federal building incorporates security measures culled from investigations into the aftereffects of the 1995 bombing. The new building design includes a defined setback perimeter as well as posts and other security devices to prevent cars from stopping too close to the building; a reinforced building structure enveloped in blast-resistant laminated glass, which does not fragment in case of a blast; and blast-resistant stone walls.

According to the Terrorism Knowledge Base, from 1968 through 2004, international terrorists most frequently targeted private citizens, businesses, and property. Of the 19,383 total incidents of terrorism around the world in that period, 3,192 hit private citizens and property. Business targets were a close second, with 3,065 incidents. Among other targets hit, transportation was victimized 831 times, utilities 554 times, and airports and airlines 798 times. After al Qaeda, the most lethal group during these years was Hezbollah, causing more than 800 deaths.[13]

The **National Counterterrorism Center (NCTC)** was created in 2004, under the Intelligence Reform and Terrorism Prevention Act to serve as the primary organization in the U.S. government for integrating and analyzing all intelligence pertaining to terrorism and counterterrorism and to conduct strategic operational planning by integrating all instruments of national power. It is under the administrative control of the Office of the Director of National Intelligence.[14]

In 2006, the NCTC reported that there were over 11,000 terrorist acts worldwide in 2005, and they resulted in the deaths of over 14,500 noncombatants. Attacks in Iraq accounted for 30 percent of the total attacks and 55 percent of the fatalities. American deaths from terrorism totaled 56. Most fatalities were the result of armed attacks and bombings; none occurred in the United States or used weapons of mass destruction. It should be noted that for the 2005 report, the NCTC significantly changed the methodology for counting terrorist attacks in order to more accurately reflect the nature of the threat posed by terrorism. Thus, the new methodology makes it difficult to compare 2005 with previous government efforts to compile terrorist statistics.

Another significant concern that falls under the umbrella of terrorism and homeland security is **cyberterrorism**, which is defined by the FBI as terrorism that initiates, or threatens to initiate, the exploitation of or attack on information systems.

National Counterterrorism Center (NCTC) The primary organization in the U.S. government for integrating and analyzing all intelligence pertaining to terrorism and counterterrorism and for conducting strategic operational planning by integrating all instruments of national power.

cyberterrorism Terrorism that initiates, or threatens to initiate, the exploitation of or attack on information sources.

EXHIBIT 13.1   Some Types of Terrorism

- Eco-terrorism: Attempts to inflict economic damage to those who profit from the destruction of the natural environment
- Cyberterrorism: Initiates, or threatens to initiate, the exploitation of or attack on information systems
- Narcoterrorism: Hiring terrorists to protect the drug cartels as well as the sale and distribution of drugs by these cartels
- Bioterrorism: Involves such weapons of mass destruction as anthrax, botulism, and smallpox

---

Bioterrorism and biological weapons are also a significant threat to our society. The anthrax attacks of 2001 caused numerous deaths and injuries, as well as significant panic in our nation. Mailed letters containing alleged anthrax paralyzed the nation's postal system and forced the government to spend billions to install sophisticated detection equipment at postal centers throughout the country. (See Exhibit 13.1 for a description of various types of terrorism.)

There are four types of biological agents than can be weaponized, including natural poisons or toxins that occur without human modification, viruses, bacteria, and plagues. The federal Centers for Disease Control and Prevention (CDC) classifies the most threatening agents as smallpox, anthrax, plague, botulism, tularemia, and hemorrhagic fever. Smallpox is a deadly contagious virus. Anthrax is a noncontagious bacterial infection, while plague is transmitted by insects. Botulism is a food-borne illness. Hemorrhagic fevers are caused by viruses—one of the mostly widely known hemorrhagic fevers is the Ebola virus.[15] The CDC have developed databases and expertise on biological agents likely to be used in a terrorism attack.[16]

In 2004, the president signed a bill creating Project BioShield to help the United States purchase, develop, and deploy cutting-edge defenses against biological weapons attacks. It authorized the expenditure of $5.6 billion over ten years for the government to purchase and stockpile vaccines and drugs to fight anthrax, smallpox, and other potential agents of bioterror. It also purchased 75 million doses of an improved anthrax vaccine for the Strategic National Stockpile.[17] Fortunately, a major drawback in the use of biological weapons is that they cannot be controlled. For example, if terrorists were to release a weaponized strain of smallpox, the disease might spread to the terrorist group and their allies.[18]

Government Efforts for Homeland Security

Because homeland security involves the participation and coordination of myriad agencies of government and the private sector, the government must play a major role. This section will discuss federal, state and local efforts for homeland security.

The two major federal agencies charged with homeland security are the U.S. Department of Homeland Security and the Federal Bureau of Investigation.

Department of Homeland Security (DHS)

After much debate, study, and planning in the aftermath of 9/11, the cabinet-level U.S. **Department of Homeland Security (DHS)** was established in March 2003.[19]

The new agency merged twenty-two previously disparate domestic agencies into one department to protect the nation against threats to the homeland. The creation of DHS was the most significant transformation of the U.S. government since 1947, when President Harry S. Truman merged the various branches of the U.S. Armed Forces into the Department of Defense to better coordinate the nation's defense against military threats. DHS represents a similar consolidation, both in style and substance. The DHS includes former duties of many agencies, including the Coast Guard, U.S. Customs Service, the Secret Service, the Immigration and Naturalization Service, and the Transportation Security Administration, along

bioterrorism The intentional release or dissemination of biological agents (bacteria, viruses, or toxins); these may be in a naturally occurring or human-modified form.

Department of Homeland Security (DHS) Federal cabinet department established in the aftermath of the terrorist attacks of September 11, 2001 to protect the nation from terrorism.

with numerous other federal communications, science, and technology agencies.

The department's first priority is to protect the nation against further terrorist attacks. The department's agencies analyze threats and intelligence, guard the borders and airports, protect critical infrastructure, and coordinate the responses of the nation for future emergencies.

The DHS's major subcomponents and agencies include the Office of the Secretary; the Bureau of Border and Transportation Security, which includes the Transportation Security Administration, Customs and Border Protection, Immigrations and Customs Enforcement, and the Federal Law Enforcement Training Center; the Bureau of Emergency Preparedness and Response, which includes the Federal Emergency Management Agency; the Bureau of Information Analysis and Infrastructure Protection; the Bureau of Science and Technology; the Office of Management; the Bureau of U.S. Citizenship and Immigration Services; the U.S. Coast Guard; and the U.S. Secret Service.

To show the importance of the DHS to homeland security, it should be noted that each year 730 million people travel on commercial aircraft, more than 700 million pieces of baggage are screened for explosives, 11.2 million trucks and 2.2 million rail cars cross into the United States, and 7,500 foreign flagships make 51,000 calls in U.S. ports.[20]

DHS controls immigration into the United States through its **US-VISIT Program**. US-VISIT is part of a continuum of security measures that begins outside U.S. borders and continues through a visitor's arrival in and departure from the United States. It applies to all visitors entering the United States. It is a top priority for DHS because it enhances security for citizens and visitors while facilitating legitimate travel and trade across borders. It helps to secure the borders, facilitate the entry-and-exit process, and enhance the integrity of the immigration system while respecting the privacy of visitors.[21]

The DHS's Transportation Security Agency (TSA) is on the front lines of the nation's efforts to secure air transportation from terrorism. Since 2002, federal rules have required that the TSA conduct security inspections of all air passengers and

US-VISIT Program A continuum of security measures that begins outside U.S. borders and continues through a visitor's arrival in and departure from the United States.

EXHIBIT 13.2 U.S. Department of Homeland Security (DHS) Organization—Major Subunits

Border and Transportation Security (BTS)
Transportation Security Administration (TSA)
Customs and Border Protection (CBP)
Immigrations and Customs Enforcement (ICE)
Federal Law Enforcement Training Center (FLETC)

Emergency Preparedness and Response (EP&R)
Federal Emergency Management Agency (FEMA)

Information Analysis and Infrastructure Protection (IAIP)
Homeland Security Operations Center (HSOC)
Information Analysis (IA)
Infrastructure Protection (IP)

Science and Technology (S&T)
Office of National Laboratories
Homeland Security Laboratories
Homeland Security Advanced Research Projects Agency (HSARPA)

Office of Management
U.S. Citizenship and Immigration Services (USCIS)
U.S. Citizenship and Immigration Services
Office of Citizenship
National Customer Service Center

U.S. Coast Guard

U.S. Secret Service (USSS)

SOURCE: U.S. Department of Homeland Security, "Homepage." Retrieved August 11, 2006, from http://www.dhs.gov.

---

air travel. As of 2006, TSA had about 43,000 security screeners. TSA's air marshals are deployed on flights around the world. The number of marshals is classified. They blend in with passengers and rely on their training, including investigative techniques, criminal terrorist behavior recognition, firearms proficiency, aircraft-specific tactics, and close-quarter self-defense measures to protect the flying public. Air marshals work in plainclothes in teams of two or sometimes more. They board airplanes before passengers, survey the cabin, and watch passengers as they walk toward their seats.[22]

U.S. Customs and Border Protection is responsible for securing our borders while also facilitating the flow of legitimate trade and travel. It protects 5,000 miles of border with Canada, 1,900 miles of border with Mexico, and 95,000 miles of shoreline.

It employs 42,000 employees, including 18,000 officers, 11,300 Border Patrol agents, 1,800 agriculture specialists, and 1,150 air and marine officers and pilots.[23]

U.S. Immigration and Customs Enforcement is responsible for the enforcement of federal immigration laws, customs laws, and air security laws. It targets illegal immigrants; the people, money, and materials that support terrorism; and other criminal activities.[24] On the front lines of the efforts in maritime security is the U.S. Coast Guard. The Coast Guard protects ports and waterways.[25]

In 2006, it was reported the DHS spent approximately $40.2 billion for homeland security.[26] See Exhibit 13.2 for a list of DHS agencies.

©AP Photo/Jacquelin Larma

A National Park Service security officer stands on duty in front of Independence Hall in Philadelphia. Each act of terrorism is essentially a local problem that must be addressed by local authorities. In the aftermath of the 2001 terrorist attacks, state and local agencies are being asked to play a bigger part as first responders to terrorist incidents and in gathering intelligence.

Federal Bureau of Investigation (FBI)

The Federal Bureau of Investigation (FBI) has traditionally been the lead federal agency in the response to and investigation of terrorism. In May 2002, in the wake of massive criticism that the FBI had failed to properly handle information that could have led to the prevention of the 9/11 attacks, FBI Director Robert S. Mueller completely reorganized and created a new strategic focus for the agency. The FBI's new focus placed the following as its three priorities: (1) protecting the United States from terrorist attack, (2) protecting the United States against foreign intelligence operations and espionage, and (3) protecting the United States against cyber-based attacks and high-technology crimes. The main organizational improvements Mueller implemented in a complete restructuring of the counterterrorism activities of the FBI and a shift from a reactive to a proactive orientation were the development of special squads to coordinate national and international investigations; a re-emphasis on the Joint Terrorism Task Forces; enhanced analytical capabilities with personnel and technological improvements; a permanent shift of additional resources to counterterrorism; the creation of a more mobile, agile, and flexible national terrorism response; and targeted recruitment to acquire agents, analysts, translators, and others with specialized skills and backgrounds.[27]

The Local Level

Although the federal government's role in responding to and combating terrorism and homeland defense is extremely crucial, we must remember that each act of terrorism is essentially a local problem that must be addressed by local authorities.

D. Douglas Bodrero, former commissioner of public safety for the state of Utah and a senior research associate with the Institute for Intergovernmental Research, writing in 1999, stated, "Every act of terrorism occurring within the United States remains local in nature."[28] Bodrero, writing again in 2002, after the 2001 terrorist attacks, reiterated his emphasis that terrorism is primarily a concern for local governments:

> The planning or execution of terrorist acts on U.S. soil are the concern of every law enforcement agency, regardless of size or area of responsibility. Every terrorist event, every act of planning and preparation for that event occurs in some local law enforcement agency's jurisdiction. No agency is closer to the activities within its community than the law enforcement agency that has responsibility and jurisdiction for protecting that community.[29]

In the aftermath of the 2001 terrorist attacks, state and local agencies are being asked to play a bigger part as first responders to terrorist incidents and in gathering intelligence. Federal funding has been made available to state and local law enforcement for the development and enhancement of law enforcement information systems relating to terrorism and homeland security with an emphasis on information sharing.[30]

The following is just one example of the many state and local initiatives on homeland security. Since New York City was the first target of international terrorists in both World Trade Center terrorist attacks, the New York City Police Department (NYPD) has been at the forefront of metropolitan efforts against terrorism. About 1,000 NYPD employees work directly on terrorism-related issues every day, including active investigations. The NYPD also has its own liaison officers working full-time in Britain, France, Israel, Canada, Singapore, Jordan, the Dominican Republic, and Australia, filing daily reports on developments there. It also has a group of highly trained civilians working on terrorism. They build profiles of possible terrorists, drawing on confidential informants, surveillance, and links with other law enforcement agencies around the world and educate the department about terrorist tactics and help search for threats in the city. The NYPD also has Arabic and Farsi linguists and dozens of detectives and liaison officers from other city and state agencies. The department's telephone terrorist tip line receives about 150 calls a day.[31]

One of the NYPD's major homeland security initiatives is its Operation Nexus Program, which is a nationwide network of businesses and enterprises designed to prevent future terrorist attacks. This program is based on a belief that terrorists may portray themselves as legitimate customers in order to purchase or lease certain materials or equipment, or to undergo certain formalized training to acquire important skills or licenses. NYPD has conducted over 25,000 visits to businesses and firms that participate in the program. Members of Operation Nexus report suspicious business encounters that they believe may have possible links to terrorism.[32]

Major police professional organizations, such as the International Association of Chiefs of Police (IACP), the National Sheriff's Association, the National Organization of Black Law Enforcement Officials, the Major Cities Chief's Association and the Police Foundation, with the cooperation of the U.S. Department of Justice, have cooperated to form the **Post-9/11 Policing Project** to help bring domestic preparedness to the top of the law enforcement agenda. Its 2005 report, *Assessing and Managing the Terrorism Threat*, describes the process that law enforcement executives are trying to master in the post-9/11 era. It reports that an effective management approach to homeland security entails the following sequential steps:

▪ Critical infrastructure and key asset inventory: This inventory includes agriculture, banking and finance, chemical and hazardous waste, defense industrial base, energy, emergency services, food, government, information and telecommunications, transportation, postal and shipping services, public health, and water. It identifies key assets as national monuments and icons, nuclear power plants, dams, government facilities, and commercial assets.

You Are There!

The National Institute of Standards and Technology (NIST)

The National Institute of Standards and Technology (NIST) was founded in 1901 as the nation's first federal physical science research laboratory.

In the aftermath of 9/11, NIST is playing a key role in enhancing the nation's homeland security. Its projects, spanning a wide range of research areas, are helping the millions of individuals in law enforcement, the military, emergency services, information technology, airport and building security, and other areas to protect the American public from terrorist threats.

It is leading efforts to develop enabling technologies for protecting dams, bridges, telecommunications networks, water systems, and the electrical power grid from terrorist attacks. It is also working on chemical, biological, and other threats; infrastructure protection and cyber security; nuclear, radiological, and explosive materials; biometrics and forensic tools; and emergency response.

SOURCE: National Institute of Standards and Technology, "About NIST." Retrieved December 12, 2005, from http://www.nist.gov.

Post-9/11 Policing Project Measures to help bring domestic preparedness to the top of the law enforcement agenda.

■ Criticality assessment: This is a systematic effort to identify and evaluate important or critical assets within a jurisdiction.

■ Threat assessment: This is a systematic effort to identify and evaluate existing potential terrorist threats to a jurisdiction and its target assets.

■ Vulnerability assessment: This is the identification of weaknesses in physical structures, personnel protection systems, processes, or other areas that may be exploited by terrorists.

■ Risk calculation and countermeasure identification: This combines all earlier assessments—criticality, threat, and vulnerability—to complete the portrait of risk to an asset or group of assets.[33]

Private Security Efforts for Homeland Security

As emphasized throughout this textbook, the private security industry in the United States has always attempted to address the issues of security in the workplace and in society. The events of 9/11 have intensified the importance of the private security industry in the nation. Although much has been reported about the numerous public servants in policing and fire and emergency response who lost their lives in the terrorist bombings of 9/11, few know that thirty-five private security personnel also met their deaths in these events. Private security employees share a particular concern about the prevention of similar incidents.

This section will discuss the importance of the private security industry for homeland security, private security industry operations in homeland defense, private security and police cooperation, and Department of Homeland Security and private security cooperation for homeland security.

Importance of the Private Security Industry for Homeland Security

Private industry owns and operates about 85 percent of America's critical infrastructure and key assets; therefore, it is incumbent on this industry to play a central and aggressive role in protecting these vital economic sectors.[34] *The National Strategy for Homeland Security* reported:

> The private sector—the [n]ation's principal provider of goods and services and owner of 85 percent of our infrastructure—is a key homeland security partner. It has a wealth of information that is important to the task of protecting the United States from terrorism. Its creative genius will develop the information systems, vaccines, detection devices, and other technologies and innovations that will secure our homeland.[35]

In 2004, the Congressional Budget Office released a comprehensive special report, *Homeland Security and the Private Sector*, at the request of the ranking member of the House Select Committee on Homeland Security, to examine the role of the private sector in responding to the threat of terrorism in the United States since 9/11. It reports that the private sector generates the vast majority of the nation's economic output, and it is in their best interest to undertake measures that can help reduce the nation's vulnerability to attack and subsequent potential losses.[36]

The report covers the essential critical industries of civilian nuclear power, chemicals and hazardous materials, electricity service, and food and agriculture. It also discusses security concerns, such as vulnerability from attack, potential losses, current programs for safety, and ideas for new approaches.

Governor Mitt Romney of Massachusetts, the leader of a national working group on safeguarding the nation, told homeland security officials in December 2004 that in order to protect America against terrorists, state and local agencies, as well as private businesses, need to gather intelligence themselves and not just rely on intelligence gathered by the federal government.[37] He said, "Meter readers, EMS drivers, law enforcement, private-sector personnel need to be on the lookout for information which may be useful."[38]

The events of 9/11 intensified the importance of private security in the workplace. According to the Business Roundtable, an association of chief executive officers of leading American corporations, "Security is now a rising star in the corporate firmament. The people responsible for security have become much more visible to the top of the business and much more important to the business itself."[39] Also, market research on the security industry reported that the global security industry has moved from a peripheral activity to center stage.[40]

The *9/11 Commission Report: Final Report of the National Commission on Terrorist Attacks upon the United States* emphasized that the mandate of the DHS does not end with the government and stated that DHS is also responsible for working with the private sector to ensure preparedness. It emphasized that unless a terrorist's target is a military or other secure government facility, the **"first" first responders** will almost certainly be civilians and national preparedness therefore often begins with the private sector. It wrote,

> The lesson of 9/11 for civilians and first responders can be stated simply: in the new age of terror, they—we—are the primary targets. The losses America suffered that day demonstrated both the gravity of the terrorist threat and the commensurate need to prepare ourselves to meet it.
>
> The first responders of today live in a world transformed by the attacks on 9/11. Because no one believes that every conceivable form of attack can be prevented, civilians and first responders will again find themselves on the front lines. We must plan for that eventually. A rededication to preparedness is perhaps the best way to honor the memories of those we lost that day.[41]

The commission wrote that preparedness in the private sector and public sector for rescue, restart, and recovery of operations should include the following: (1) a plan for evacuation, (2) adequate communications capabilities, and (3) a plan for continuity of operations.[42]

The commission was created by the President of the United States and the Congress in 2002 to investigate how the nation was unprepared for these attacks, how they happened, and how the nation could avoid such a repeat tragedy. The members of the commission met for two years, reviewed more that 2.5 million pages of documents,

and interviewed more than 1,200 individuals in ten countries. It held nineteen days of hearings and took public testimony from 160 witnesses. It made forty-one main proposals to improve homeland security and prevent future acts of terrorism against our nation; four of these recommendations involved the participation of the private sector in possible similar situations. Many of the commission's recommendations were accepted and implemented by the government. Some of the major recommendations can be found in Exhibit 13.3.

Some examples of the private security industry's post-9/11 concern for homeland security follow:

▪ In 2004, the ASIS International Foundation partnered with the Police Foundation and the Vera Institute of Justice to assess the preparedness of retail mall security to respond to terrorist acts.[43]

▪ In 2004, ASIS International created its Chief Security Officer (CSO) Roundtable, an organization of thirty top-level private security executives from some of the nation's largest companies, such as General Dynamics, Fidelity Investments, and Toyota, to lead its homeland security efforts. The Roundtable has direct channels of communication with leaders in government and business and participates in forming national policy on homeland security. At their inaugural meeting, the Assistant Secretary of the DHS identified this group as a core element of U.S. homeland security efforts.[44]

▪ Companies are making numerous efforts to improve bomb detection at their facilities. Experts say that bomb-detection technology, perimeter protection, electronic video surveillance, access control, and employee vetting are crucial to organizations' overall antiterrorism strategies.[45]

▪ Many companies have spent millions of dollars on scanners, turnstiles, and other security measures. Many large companies have erected security barriers around their buildings, some using concrete barriers, others huge potted flowerbeds that limit access. As an example, Morgan Stanley in New York City ringed its corporate headquarters with forty-one dark gray, 8-foot-long concrete planter tubs and sixteen cylindrical planters. At some places, the tubs are barely more than 1 foot apart. According to Peter DiMaggio of the American Institute of Architects, these standoff barricades are important because one of the most effective tools a

"first" first responders Concept developed by the National Commission on Terrorist Attacks upon the United States that the first responders to a terrorist attack that is not a military or other secure government facility will be civilians. The Commission reasoned that national preparedness therefore often begins with the private sector.

EXHIBIT 13.3   Major Recommendations Affecting Private Security from the *9/11 Commission Report: The Final Report of the National Commission on Terrorist Attacks upon the United States*

Recommendation: Hard choices must be made in allocating limited resources. The U.S. government should identify and evaluate the transportation assets that need to be protected, set risk-based priorities for defending them, select the most practical and cost-effective ways of doing so, and then develop a plan, budget, and funding to implement the effort. The plan should assign roles and missions to the relevant authorities (federal, state, regional, and local) *and to private stakeholders.* In measuring effectiveness, perfection is unattainable. But terrorists should perceive that potential targets are defended. They may be deterred by a significant chance of failure.

Recommendation: The TSA and the Congress must give priority attention to improving the ability of screening checkpoints to detect explosives on passengers. As a start, each individual selected for special screening should be screened for explosives. *Further, the TSA should conduct a human factors study, a method often used in the private sector, to understand problems in screener performance and set attainable objectives for individual screeners and for the checkpoints where screening takes place.*

Recommendation: As the President determines the guidelines for information sharing among government

agencies *and by those agencies with the private sector, he should safeguard the privacy of individuals about whom information is shared.*

Recommendation: *We endorse the American National Standards Institute's recommended standard for private preparedness. We were encouraged by Secretary Tom Ridge's praise of the standard and urge the Department of Homeland Security to promote its adoption. We also encourage the insurance and credit-rating industries to look closely at a company's compliance with the ANSI standard in assessing its insurability and creditworthiness. We believe that compliance with the standard should define the standard of care owed by a company to its employees and the public for legal purposes. Private-sector preparedness is not a luxury; it is a cost of doing business in the post-9/11 world. It is ignored at a tremendous potential cost in lives, money, and national security.*

Note: Emphasis added.

SOURCE: National Commission on Terrorist Attacks upon the United States, *9/11 Commission Report: Final Report of the National Commission on Terrorist Attacks upon the United States* (New York: W.W. Norton & Company, 2004), pp. 391, 392, 394, 398.

---

designer has against a high-explosive terrorist attack is to force the terrorist to detonate the explosives as far from the building as possible.[46]

■ Since 9/11, about $5.6 billion have been invested throughout the world to protect airports from terrorism.[47]

■ About 400,000 people, mostly commercial truck drivers, have been trained since 2004 to spot suspicious activity on highways. This program is run by the American Trucking Association with funds from the DHS.[48]

The **American National Standards Institute (ANSI)** has developed a national standard for preparedness for the private sector. The American National Standard on Disaster/Emergency Management and Business Continuity Programs established a common set of criteria and terminology for preparedness, disaster management, emergency management, and business continuity programs.[49]

Dean C. Alexander, author of the 2004 book *Business Confronts Terrorism: Risks and Reponses*, reports that terrorism weakens industry and society through the manipulation of economic system components, such as companies, nonprofits, labor, capital, and technology. He states that integrating the concept of terrorism in relation to its effects on business, both in theory and in practice, is a growing post-9/11 trend. This book focuses on three key issues in the relationship between terrorism and business: (1) terror threats and the role that terrorists and their sympathizers play in the economic system, (2) business responses and public–private

American National Standards Institute (ANSI) An agency that serves as the coordinator of the U.S. voluntary standards system, a unique and diversified federation that includes industry, standards-developing organizations, trade associations, professional and technical societies, government, and labor and consumer groups.

| EXHIBIT 13.4 | Joint Public and Private Information-Sharing Initiatives Critical to Homeland Security Efforts |

The following are examples of some programs showing how private- and public-sector security professionals have been marshaling their technology and networking skills to bridge the knowledge gap regarding terrorist threats to the nation's infrastructure.

■ InfraGard: InfraGard was developed in 1996 to fight cyber and physical threats to critical infrastructures. It has about 10,000 members and 80 local chapters comprising industry and FBI representatives around the country. A national board links the chapters together. Members say the program works well because much of the information exchange is conducted in person at chapter meetings and events. All InfraGard members have been subjected to an FBI background check, and information is "sanitized" to remove identifying characteristics to further increase the comfort level to enhance information sharing among members.

■ ISACs: Information Sharing and Analysis Centers (ISACs) were established in 1998 and link public and private officials in certain particular areas of critical infrastructure (such as water, transportation, banking, or telecommunications) to facilitate information sharing on possible security-related vulnerabilities, threats, and breaches. The DHS represents the government in ISACs. It has formed an ISAC Council that encourages crossfertilization of ideas among sectors and a data-sharing protocol. Also, the council develops analytical methods to assist the ISACs.

■ IAIPD: The Information Analysis and Infrastructure Protection Directorate (IAIPD) is part of DHS. It serves as a center for the collection, assessment, and dissemination of information about cyber and physical threats and how to respond to them. Its information-sharing role involves sending information bulletins to the private sector and distributing summaries of relevant news articles. It also coordinates ISAC activity.

■ ATIX: The Antiterrorism Information Exchange (ATIX) serves as a conduit for the FBI, DHS, and other agencies to distribute security alerts via mail on a need-to-know basis to certain private industry groups, the public health community, school systems, and emergency management agencies.

■ GuardNet: GuardNet is the Army National Guard's broadband network that allows real-time communication among 2,700 National Guard facilities across the country. During the 9/11 attacks, this network was pressed into service for communications among the fifty states.

■ Intelink: Intelink is a CIA-operated intranet designed to link classified databases held by the CIA, FBI, Secret Service, National Security Agency, and other U.S. intelligence agencies. It is divided into user categories for different groups, such as the military. The sensitive content also calls for a multilayered security approach that includes strong cryptography and authentication through a public key infrastructure.

---

efforts to reduce these threats, and (3) terrorism's impact on business.[50]

Security experts emphasize that prevention is more cost effective than disaster recovery and thus corporations should emphasize prevention by developing proactive programs to detect, prevent, and respond to terrorist attacks. Such programs involve threat assessments, countersurveillance, formalized intelligence sharing, information protection, and security awareness training.[51]

Threat assessment, often called "threat evaluation," "facility characterization," or "target value assessment," is a common tool in private security

and is effective in determining who would want to attack a particular company or business and why. It starts with an analysis of the organization, its people, and its facilities to assess whether any of these elements might be seen as social, cultural, or economic icons whose destruction would serve terrorist goals. In this process, firms also focus on exploitation of infrastructure attacks whereby terrorists attempt to use an organization's assets to strike another target. For example, chemical plants, nuclear power plants, utilities, airlines, and other similar industries must ensure that their equipment and hazardous materials are not stolen for use against others. Even sporting goods companies who sell scuba tanks should be aware of their possible use in underwater terrorist activities. Other examples are delivery companies and uniform suppliers whose vehicles and goods could be stolen to conduct terrorist operations.

threat assessment Common tool in private security to determine who would want to attack a particular company or business and why and how they would do so. Also known as a threat evaluation, facility characterization, or target value assessment.

- CEO COM Link: The Critical Emergency Operations Communications (CEO COM) Link allows business and government to trade information on imminent threats for the purpose of response and recovery. It was formed in the wake of 9/11 and is a project of the Security Task Force of the Business Roundtable (an organization of 150 top chief executive officers who cumulatively operate a substantial percentage of U.S. critical infrastructures). Its goal is to help ensure that these companies and government officials can obtain real-time situational information in an emergency. The link, a secure dialup network, can be activated by the CEO of the Roundtable or a high-ranking member of DHS with CEO COM Link credentials. If the system is activated, member CEOs are alerted to dial into a secure conference call at a certain time, at which time they are personally briefed by the Secretary of Homeland Security. Additionally, information is also passed on when necessary to other organizations in the chemical, water, and financial services industries. A similar system, BITS, is a nonprofit consortium of the 100 largest U.S. financial institutions and has a similar information-sharing system called Crisis Communicator. It involves a high-speed, automated alert system bringing together CEOs, CIOs, crisis management executives, and government officials in a matter of minutes.
- GEWIS: The Global Early Warning Information System (GEWIS) is operated by DHS and deals with threats to or intrusions into computer networks and systems. It measures traffic flow and activity on the net and reports potential cyberattacks or disruptions to government and industry.
- CWIN: Closely associated with GEWIS is the Cyber Warning Information Network (CWIN), a vehicle for government and business to share cyber alerts and warnings over a secure network. It links about seventy-five operational centers in the United States, sixty of which belong to the private sector.
- SHARE: The Secret Service, under the authority of the USA Patriot Act, has established the Systematic Homeland Approach to Reducing Exploitation (SHARE) as a nationwide network of electronic crimes task forces. Thirteen cities now have such task forces. They are authorized to investigate computer attacks, identity fraud, and other incidents with and without homeland security implications. These task forces have focused on the financial community but are a good source of information for other industries. Under SHARE, the Secret Service and U.S. Immigration and Customs Enforcement conduct joint semiannual meetings with executive members of the financial and trade communities impacted by money laundering, identity theft, and other financial crimes.

SOURCE: Michael A. Gips, "Shared Intelligence Makes Everyone Smarter," *Security Management*, January 2004, pp. 53-63.

In addition to threat assessment, companies also engage in countersurveillance of potential targets or terrorism threats. They do this through regular uniform security personnel and undercover countersurveillance teams. Many private firms also are involved in information sharing through the **Information Sharing and Analysis Centers (ISACs)** established in 1998, as well as other public and private information-sharing initiatives. (The ISAC concept is discussed in Exhibit 13.4.) Many industry ISACs have created standardized procedures and reporting mechanisms. Companies also identify and protect key information security against terrorists. All employees, not just security and particularly those involved in executive or business travel, are generally trained in awareness of terrorism indicators. They look at everything through the eye of a potential attacker and are trained in basic countersurveillance methods, such as testing and shaking tails.

To emphasize the importance of cooperation and communication between the public and private sectors, public and private managers, professionals, and intelligence collectors have developed some important public and private information-sharing initiatives critical to homeland security efforts. These initiatives, described in Exhibit 13.4, are examples of how cooperation, technology, and networking skills can bridge the knowledge gap regarding terrorist threats to the nation's infrastructure.[52]

Information Sharing and Analysis Centers (ISACs) Centers established in 1998 to provide information sharing and analysis between the government and businesses.

| **EXHIBIT 13.5** | **ASIS International Professional Development and Training Courses Related to Terrorism and Homeland Security** |

TERRORISM AND HOMELAND SECURITY

- Disaster Management: The Incident Response Plan
- Crisis Management: The Incident Response Plan
- Assets Protection Course I: Concepts and Methods
- Assets Protection Course II: Practical Applications
- Assets Protection Course III: Functional Management
- Government Industry Conference on Global Terrorism and Political Instability
- Securing the Global Workplace
- Security Force Management
- Facility Security Design
- Executive Protection
- How to Conduct a Professional Investigation
- Physical Security
- Effective Facility Security (Virtual Forum)
- Managing Your Physical Security Program
- Anti-Terrorism Considerations for Protecting Facilities (Virtual Forum)
- Annual Bioterrorism Conference
- Closed Circuit Television—From Cameras to Contractors
- Issues in Transportation Security

BIOTERRORISM, WEAPONS OF MASS DESTRUCTION, AND THE SECURITY PROFESSIONAL

The ASIS International's "Bioterrorism, Weapons of Mass Destruction (WMD), and the Security Professional"

course is a concentrated, one-and-a-half-day program designed to allow participants to think globally and act locally, focusing on protecting people, protecting facilities, and protecting the function of the organization. It discusses pre-event preparation, event response, post-event restoration, and lessons learned to improve future preparation.

Sessions include:

- Introduction to Bioterrorism, Emerging Infectious Threats, and WMD
- Terrorism: Past, Present and Future
- Facility Preparedness and Vulnerability Assessment, Planning for WMD
- Economics and Terrorism
- Resources in a WMD Emergency, including Poison Information Centers and the Role of the Military
- Table-Top Exercises
- Introduction to Personal Protective Equipment (PPE)
- Live-Time Demonstration of Decontamination

SOURCES: ASIS International, "Professional Development: 2005 Professional Development Calendar." Retrieved October 17, 2005, from http://www.asisonline.org; and ASIS International, "Professional Development Course Details: Bioterrorism, Weapons of Mass Destruction, and the Security Professional." Retrieved October 17, 2005, from http://www.asisonline.org.

A major terrorism threat to our nation is terrorism directed at the food supply, including farms and livestock. Farmers, farm interest groups, academics, and farm industry personnel are working together with government agencies, such as the Animal and Plant Health Inspections Service of the U.S. Department of Agriculture, to prevent **agroterrorism** and strengthen U.S. farm, livestock, and poultry security. The Extension Disaster Education Network (EDEN), a private association of educators in the United States who share disaster-management experiences and strategies, reports that agriculture is a vital component of the U.S. economy and that producers face threats to crop production through natural disasters, as well as deliberate acts by individuals or groups wishing to harm consumers or the U.S. economy. Protecting the food chain is vital,

particularly at the borders, on the farm, and in government laboratories. Common security measures include border security, farmer education, disease diagnosis and surveillance, rapid reporting, disease containment, and lab security. Cattle, pigs, sheep, or other animals infected with diseases could erode public confidence in food safety and devastate the U.S. agricultural industry, which relies heavily on the foreign import of their goods. The U.S. livestock industry alone is worth an estimated $100 billion. Bacterial, viral, and toxic pathogens are retained in 450 repositories located in 67 countries throughout the world and can be transmitted by air, water, and food in the event of a security breach.[53]

A survey of farmers by EDEN indicated that only 13 percent of respondents believed that they were prepared for agroterrorism, and almost two-thirds said that they either lacked access to educational information on agroterrorism or were uncertain about whether they had access or not. To deal with this, the American Farm Bureau

agroterrorism Terrorism aimed at livestock and agriculture.

Federation reports that it has been advising farmers to increase security, keep track of who is on their property, and create ties with local law enforcement and prosecutors to speed their response to potential problems on farms. In order to promote efforts against agroterrorism, EDEN sponsors a plant biosecurity management course and an annual meeting.[54]

Increased awareness of terrorist threats is not just limited to private businesses in the United States. Thirty-six percent of security managers at large British companies expect to be targeted by terrorists, according to a joint survey conducted by RAND Europe, Janusian Security Risk, and the *Financial Times*, compared to 24 percent the previous year. Terrorism ranked first in a list of crime concerns in the survey, and three-quarters of respondents indicated that they were more concerned about al Qaeda than about traditional domestic terrorism.[55]

ASIS International provides professional development and training programs related to terrorism, bioterrorism, and homeland security (see Exhibit 13.5).

Private Security Industry Operations for Homeland Security

The following description in the media gives a sense of the intensity of private security industry operations for homeland security in the New York City region at the onset of Operation Iraqi Freedom (U.S. attack of Iraq) in 2003:

> As the United States wages war on Iraq, New Yorkers and others across the region are witnessing an extraordinary state of heightened security. No one can live or work in the region without having noticed the proliferation of armed security guards, surveillance cameras, handbag searches, metal detectors, electronic access cards and bomb-sniffing dogs, all of which have multiplied from Pennsylvania Station to the Metropolitan Museum of Art.[56]

Members of corporate security departments pay constant attention to homeland security issues and develop plans to deal with these problems. Since 9/11, private security practitioners have added homeland efforts to the top of their agenda to

©Associated Press

Since 9/11, private security practitioners have added homeland efforts to the top of their agenda to protect the interests and assets of their organizations and clients. These efforts include engaging in planning responses to actual terror events, such as staged evacuation drills; securing their computer networks; and increasing protection around their critical infrastructure assets like nuclear power plants.

protect the interests and assets of their organizations and clients. These efforts include engaging in planning responses to actual terror events, such as staged evacuation drills; securing their computer networks; and increasing protection around their critical infrastructure assets.[57]

Most multinational corporations have detailed security plans, crisis-management teams, and threat-assessment strategies to deal with homeland security issues. As one example, the Wells Fargo Insurance Company maintains Enterprise Incident Management Teams, a group of experts who guide emergency managers through incidents. Every Wells Fargo office is trained in uniform emergency procedures for every type of disaster. These teams receive ongoing education in emergency management, team facilitation, communication, decision making, and problem solving.[58]

Companies without security departments or those with smaller security departments often hire large contract security companies, such as Wackenhut, Kroll Inc., or Securitas, to provide corporate security services. These companies emphasize strategic prevention and conduct threat assessments before establishing their prevention plans. Other companies often hire security consultants to advise them on matters of personal and corporate safety.

Some examples of the private security industry's post-9/11 operations for homeland security follow:

- ASIS International conducts numerous professional development and training programs for security management professionals, relating to terrorism and homeland security. Also, its annual seminar and other conferences it hosts, such as its International European Security Conference and its Asia-Pacific Security Conference, also focus on terrorism and homeland security issues.[59]

- Many private corporations and businesses are formally training their private security personnel for homeland security threats. For example, the University of Findlay's Center for Terrorism Preparedness in Ohio has trained more than 2,000 private security personnel, law enforcement agents, and other first responders since 1999. Other universities across the nation have also begun to offer similar training to private security personnel. Major courses in these curriculums include vulnerability assessment, threat-assessment management, and actual field operations. As an example of private industry participation and support in this training, Ross Laboratories (a division of Abbott Laboratories of Chicago) has hosted homeland security training for both security personnel and law enforcement.[60] Chapter 1 of this text discussed the numerous private security college and educational programs that have been developed since 9/11.

- With religious hostility more evident since 9/11 and violent attacks at houses of worship in Iraq, Turkey, Pakistan, Tunisia, India, and elsewhere, some high-profile U.S. religious facilities or symbols have added security director positions. About twenty of them have banded together in a group called the Gatekeeper's Alliance to share and discuss security information and suggestions. The heightened threat has spurred the Anti-Defamation League to produce a security guide for Jewish institutions and the Council on American-Islamic Relations to issue a security checklist for mosques. Back-office access control, security control rooms, and even plainclothes security are now typical at the largest churches, and even some smaller houses of worship. Churches with more than five-hundred weekly congregants tend to have electronic video surveillance systems.[61]

Some examples of effective security operations at some specific companies follow:

- The South Florida Water Management District (SFWMD) protects the water quality, flood control, natural ecosystems, and water supply for about 18,000 square miles (40 percent of Florida's land, including Lake Okeechobee). Its operations are a prime example of the homeland security activities at some of the most important businesses in the nation's critical infrastructure system. SFWMD has two administrative buildings, a shipping and receiving center, seven regional field stations, forty-two pump stations, and about two-thousand water-control structures. It also has more than 1,700 employees. Five security officers patrol the administrative buildings during normal business hours, and at all other times, two officers patrol. Each field station has a rapid impact assessment team composed of field personnel to respond to any emergencies. SFWMD uses a $250,000, proximity-based access control and intrusion system; metal detectors for visitors; and access control cards for all employees. It also uses electronic video surveillance systems and perimeter gates at all buildings and field stations. X-ray detection is used for all incoming mail and packages. Management conducts intensive background screening for all new hires, and all employees receive safety and security training.[62]

- HSBC Bank scans persons and baggage brought into work by staff, contractors, and visitors, for explosives. Another investment bank also recently established its own bomb-detection canine units to help its security managers determine whether a suspect package is a bomb without having to wait for the police and evacuate a site unnecessarily.[63]

■ At George Bush Intercontinental Airport near Houston, Texas, the Houston Airport Rangers, a volunteer security force, patrols the perimeters of the 11,000-acre airport under the supervision of the airport's security office, looking for suspicious activity. There are more than eight-hundred certified Houston Airport Rangers who patrol on horseback.[64]

■ The ASIS International's Council on Gaming and Wagering Protection recently surveyed a sample of casino security chiefs and other security experts and found that physical security and surveillance at their premises were more prevalent since 9/11. Among the measures they found were live monitoring of property areas never focused on prior to the terrorism bombings, the use of proprietary explosives-detection dogs, and the inauguration or enhancement of employee awareness training programs. Also, it discovered that security monitoring and patrols and the deployment of surveillance cameras and upgrading of access control systems significantly increased. Security personnel at these facilities were seeking ways to ensure more reliable and effective communications.[65]

■ Firms are making architectural design changes to new high-rise buildings as a result of the Okalahoma City federal building and World Trade Center bombings. Special attention is being given to underground garages because in the event of an explosion in an underground garage, a whole building could come down. Building owners are strengthening the columns in their garages and instituting various levels of perimeter protection, such as access control. Also, new blast-resistant and fire-resistant building materials and wider stairwells to facilitate mass evacuation are being used in buildings.[66]

■ In England following the 2005 terrorist subway bombings, businesses and restaurants in Leeds, including local McDonald's and Starbucks stores, have heightened their terrorism awareness. Employees examine the restaurants' trash bins for bombs every thirty minutes. Businesses in Birmingham and Bradford are conducting the same regular checks. McDonald's reports that they have site-specific security systems in all their stores and that management teams are trained in security procedures.[67]

■ Many firms, such as Exxon Mobil Chemical Company and other companies, have established alternative or background locations for their operations and have disaster recovery plans to ensure that their businesses continue to run in the event of a catastrophe.

As discussed fully in Chapter 12, the 2004 National Policy Summit, "Building Private Security/Public Policing Partnerships to Prevent and Respond to Terrorism and Public Disorder," held in Arlington, Virginia, made numerous important suggestions to improve private security and police cooperation for homeland security. It involved about 140 executive-level representatives of local, state, federal, and other law enforcement agencies; security departments of major corporations; security product and services providers; professional organizations in the law enforcement and private security fields; universities; and federal agencies.[68]

In a 2005 article in *Crime and Justice International*, James F. Pastor emphasized the importance of private security and public policing cooperation when he wrote that the threat of future terrorism will change the nature of policing, transitioning it from a community policing model toward alternatives, specifically a private policing model. He writes that this fundamental shift in policing emphasizes tactical methods, technology, and alternative service providers, such as private security personnel. He predicts that the use of private security within public environments is likely to be increased in direct relation to the level of terrorist threats. He warns, however, that in this time of redefining the nature of policing, the delicate balance between security and liberty cannot be lost.[69]

Department of Homeland Security and Private Security Cooperation for Homeland Security

Since 9/11, and especially since the creation of the DHS, there has been an unprecedented improvement in public and private partnerships to improve homeland security. Chapter 12 of this textbook discussed numerous studies and partnerships between DHS and the private security industry. Exhibit 13.4 on page 348 highlights some shared intelligence and communication programs that enhance these partnerships.

The DHS maintains a private-sector office that works directly with individual businesses, trade associations, citizens, and other professional and non-government organizations to share information, programs, and particular opportunities. It assists businesses with contracts, grants, small-business opportunities, and research and development. It also provides preparedness planning to citizens and opportunities for citizens to provide tips and leads about suspicious activities.[70]

The homeland security industry includes chemical, biological, and radiological detection, as well as airport, border, rail, seaport, industrial, and nuclear plant security. In the 22-month period ending in August 2006, the DHS spent $28 billion on security-related goods and services while issuing more than 115,000 contracts.[71]

The SAFETY Act—The Support Anti-Terrorism by Fostering Effective Technologies Act of 2002—encourages the development and deployment of antiterrorism technologies that can substantially enhance the safety and preparedness of the nation. The DHS is responsible for approval of applications for designation and certification of **qualified antiterrorism technologies (QATTs)** under the SAFETY Act. This law protects potential developers of technology that could significantly reduce the risk of, or mitigate the effect of, acts of terrorism from liability claims. QATTs include products, software, services, and various forms of intellectual property.[72] In a 2004 article, two private security officials, one a former White House official and the other a former Department of Justice official, reported that the DHS spent more than $10 billion in procurements and more than $4 billion on grants during the latest fiscal year, eight times more than the previous year. The article advises companies on the rules and procedures of the DHS and other government agencies to facilitate their planning and bidding efforts.[73]

Michael A. Gips wrote in 2004, that the DHS provides lucrative opportunities for technology companies to develop and sell homeland security technology. He reported that DHS is anxious to purchase refined sensor technology for biological detection, radiation detection, cargo screening, bioagent detection, and radiological and nuclear detection devices. He reported that radiological detection portals, currently a $40 million industry, will reach $1 billion in a few years; and cargo and handheld baggage screening technology, which is currently a $300 million industry, will rise to a $2.6 billion industry. Scientists say that "fused technologies" will prevail over single-use technologies. For example, local first responders want one scanner that can identify multiple pathogens so that they will not have to use multiple scanners. Ricin-detection equipment is also in demand.[74]

Financial-market consultants say most of these innovations will come from small firms because they are much more nimble than their larger counterparts. One consultant says homeland security is "probably the fastest-growing investment in our lifetime."[75]

The DHS has also developed the Homeland Security Information Network-Critical Infrastructure (HSIN-CI) program to share information between the public and private sectors. Using this program, private-sector members receive alerts and notification from DHS via phone, e-mail, fax, and pager. The program targets security professionals in specific sectors of the economy. It notifies high-level people in the public and private sectors of evolving threat information. The secure network includes 24-hour contact information for members to list particular assets that they can offer in case of an emergency; for example, if a disaster occurred and a large number of bulldozers were needed, a possible supplier would know quickly. The network also allows members to report suspicious activities directly to the FBI.[76]

The DHS has designated six research universities as Centers of Excellence and has funded them with over $80 million. These centers are consortia of researchers who gather data, prepare computer models, and analyze findings on topics relevant to the mission of the DHS. Multidisciplinary teams from such disciplines as medicine, economics, engineering, and the social and behavioral sciences collaborate on the research, which relies heavily on risk-management principles. The results are used by DHS decision makers to weigh options on such issues as the spread of infectious diseases, the economic effects of port security, and the formation of terrorist groups. A key focus of the research efforts is to train future educators about homeland security issues.[77]

---

qualified antiterrorism technologies (QATTs) Designation and certification that protects potential developers of technology that could reduce the risk of terrorism from liability claims. Protected items can include products, software, services, and other forms of intellectual property.

Private Security Firms and the U.S. Military Abroad

The private security industry also performs vital protective services for corporations, the U.S. military, and the military of friendly countries abroad. Most average Americans did not know of these services until March 2004, when four Americans working as private security contractors for an American security company in Iraq were killed. They were ambushed in Fallujah, and their dead bodies were dragged through the streets and hung from a bridge over the Euphrates River. Those killed, who worked for Blackwater Security Consultants, were part of a lucrative but often dangerous occupation—private security operatives working for corporations and governments in the toughest corners of the world. Although companies such as Blackwater are called private security companies or private security contractors, some think of them as private paramilitary companies because they are replacing government troops in dangerous conflicts around the globe, from South America to Africa and the Middle East.[78]

In an emphasis on streamlining their operations, the American and British militaries have outsourced many tasks in Iraq to private security companies. According to the *London Times*, as of November 2006, there were anywhere from 10,000 to 30,000 private security contractors (PSCs) in Iraq. It describes their tasks as providing security at bases, protecting diplomats, and protecting convoys carrying rebuilding material. It describes the British PSC market as being worth £1.8 billion per year, with the industry ten times larger now than it was a decade ago.[79] According to *The Economist*, in 2006, private security companies had grown into the second-largest military contingent in Iraq, after American forces.[80]

Some of these security companies have formed their own "Quick Reaction Forces" and have their own intelligence units that produce daily intelligence briefs with grid maps of "hot zones." One company has its own helicopters, and several have even made diplomatic alliances with local clans. The Pentagon is relying on these private security companies to perform crucial jobs formerly entrusted to the military. In addition to guarding reconstruction projects, private companies provide security for the chief of the Coalition Provisional Authority in Iraq and other senior officials, escort supply convoys through hostile territory, and defend key locations. The U.S. Department of Defense and the Pentagon have pushed aggressively to use these companies to outsource tasks.

These private security companies operate for and alongside our military, but there is no central oversight of the companies, no uniform rules of engagement, and no consistent standards for vetting or training new hires. Some security guards complain bitterly of going into combat without adequate firepower, training, equipment, and inadequate communication links with military commanders. These security companies generally charge the government from $500 to $1,500 a day for their most skilled officers. Senior enlisted members of the Army Green Berets and the Navy Seals are leaving the military for these private security positions and making salaries between $100,000 and $200,000 a year. Private security contractor executives argue that their services have freed up thousands of troops for offensive combat operations. Some military leaders, however, are complaining that the lure of these salaries is siphoning away some of their most experienced special operations people at the very time their services are most in demand.

New security companies aggressively compete for lucrative contracts, and many security guards are hired as independent contractors by companies that, in turn, are subcontractors of larger security companies, which are themselves subcontractors of a prime contractor, which may have been hired by a U.S. agency.

ASIS International's Military Liaison Council provides a forum for military personnel and security contractors to address common issues that arise when the two groups interact on or near military installations worldwide. The purpose of the liaison council is for members of both groups to learn from each other as they work with the U.S. State Department and coalition partners.[81]

Homeland Security, Terrorism, and Private Security

Homeland security, the methods used to protect lives and the property and infrastructure of the United States, has been a consistent theme throughout this text. In the aftermath of the 9/11 terrorist

You Are There!

Profiles of Some Major Security Companies Serving the U.S. Military in Iraq

- Blackwater Security Consultants is a U.S. company that provides a wide spectrum of support to military, government agencies, law enforcement, and civilian agencies and firms in training, logistics, and operations. It recruits from special operations forces and intelligence and law enforcement communities to fulfill operating commitments in medium- to high-risk environments. It specializes in hostage rescue, close-quarter battle, structure penetrations, intelligence collection, explosive-ordinance disposal, forward observer/call for fire, reconnaissance and surveillance, sniper/countersniper operations, counternarcotics, counterterrorism operations, raid conduct and training, and other duties. It has played a major role in Operation Iraqi Freedom.

- DynCorp International has a long history of supporting the U.S. government as a private contractor in nation-building and personal protective services. It is one of the largest U.S. defense contractors and has played a major role in the United States and Colombian counternarcotics operations.

- Halliburton has managed extraordinary operations and projects around the world for over seventy-five years, responding to worldwide emergencies and crises, both natural and manmade, including intelligence analysis, security assessment, design, engineering, construction, physical security, operations, and maintenance. It provides services in more than fifty locations worldwide, to all branches of the U.S. military and other government agencies, that allow troops to focus on their primary mission.

- Global Risk Strategies is a British firm established in 1998 as a client-oriented political and security risk-management company in the areas of defense, energy, and aviation. It provides services in Iraq, Afghanistan, Pan Africa, Mozambique, and Central Asia.

- The Steele Foundation is a San Francisco–based multinational risk-management company involved in business investigations, executive security, information security, and crisis management operations around the world.

- Erinys International was founded in 2001 as an international security services and risk-management firm in sub-Saharan Africa and the Middle East. It has served a major role in Operation Iraqi Freedom, recruiting, training, equipping, and managing 14,000 Iraqi security guards to protect the national oil infrastructure of Iraq.

- MVM of Vienna, Virginia, provides protection services to U.S. government and corporate interests in war-torn countries like Iraq, Bosnia, and Haiti. It uses employees with military experience. In addition to former U.S. and NATO Special Forces, it also hires third-country nationals and, in some cases, Iraqis to work with their protection teams.

- Kroll Inc., a large U.S. security provider, uses personnel with either extensive U.S. or U.K. Special Forces experience to anchor their security teams. The other members of the team have at least six years of military experience with operational overseas experience. Each of Kroll Inc.'s protection teams also includes someone trained in battlefield first aid.

Sources: Blackwater Security Consultants, "Homepage." Retrieved September 18, 2004 from http://www.blackwatersecurity.com; DynCorp International, "Homepage." Retrieved September 18, 2004 from www.dyncorprecruiting.com; Halliburton, "Homepage." Retrieved September 18, 2004, from http://www.halliburton.com; The Steele Foundation, "Homepage." Retrieved September 19, 2004, from http://www.steelefoundation.com; Erinys International, "Homepage." Retrieved September 19, 2004, from http://www.erinysinternational.com; The Center for International Policy's Columbia Program, "Dyncorp in Colombia." Retrieved September 19, 2004, from http://www.ciponline.org/colombia/dyncorp.htm; David Baker and Robert Collier, "S.F. Agency Has Guns, Will Travel with Guards and Investigators for Hire, Steele Foundation Keeps Busy in Iraq," *San Francisco Chronicle*, June 25, 2004. Retrieved September 19, 2004, from http://www.sfgate.com; Oliver Poole, "70 a Week for Taking on the Oil Saboteurs," *News Telegraph*, May 17, 2004. Retrieved September 19, 2004, from http://www.telegraph.co.uk/news/main; and Marta Roberts, "Working in a War Zone," *Security Management*, November 2004, pp. 45–53.

attacks, government agencies, private businesses, and average citizens have been involved in numerous proactive efforts to secure the nation against terrorism and ensure homeland security. Federal law enforcement agencies have been completely restructured to deal with the importance of the homeland security mission, and state and local law enforcement agencies have put new emphasis on it. Private corporations have also added homeland security to their security mission. As indicated earlier in this chapter, 85 percent of this nation's critical infrastructure and key assets are owned and operated by the private sector, and it generates the vast majority of the nation's economic output. The private sector is a key partner in homeland security with federal, state, and local government agencies.

Although most of the academic study of homeland security and most of the public attention it has received have been concerned with the actions of government agencies, the 9/11 commission confirmed that nongovernment personnel (civilians) may be the primary targets of future terrorists and that civilians will be on the front lines of efforts to deal with these possible events.

Summary

- 3,047 people were murdered during the 9/11 terrorist attacks: 2,823 at the World Trade Center in New York City, 184 at the Pentagon in Northern Virginia, and 40 in Stony Creek Township, Pennsylvania. About 35 private security employees and professionals also met their deaths in these attacks.

- The term *homeland security* has been used since 9/11 to describe defensive efforts within the borders of the United States. Officials use it to separate the Department of Homeland Security's operations from those of the Department of Defense.

- Following 9/11, the U.S. government prepared and published the *National Strategy for Homeland Security* to mobilize and organize the United States to secure its homeland from terrorism attacks. It described the strategy as a complex mission requiring coordinated and focused efforts from the entire society, including the federal government, state and local governments, the private sector, and the American people.

- Terrorism has a long tradition in world history. Terrorist tactics have been used frequently by radical and criminal groups to influence public opinion and to attempt to force authorities to do their will. Terrorists have criminal, political, and other nefarious motives.

- Terrorism is the unlawful use of force or violence against persons or property to intimidate or coerce a government, the civilian population, or a segment thereof, in furtherance of political or social objectives. Terrorists target civilian populations—noncombatants.

- The Department of Homeland Security (DHS) is at the forefront of our nation's efforts to ensure homeland security. The department's first priority is to protect the nation against further terrorist attacks. The department's agencies analyze threats and intelligence, guard our borders and airports, protect our critical infrastructure, and coordinate the responses of our nation for future emergencies.

- The FBI is the lead federal agency in the response to and investigation of terrorism.

- Although the federal government's role in responding to and combating terrorism and promoting homeland security is extremely crucial, each act of terrorism is essentially a local problem and must be addressed by local authorities and private security professionals.

- Private industry owns and operates about 85 percent of America's critical infrastructure and key assets; therefore, it is incumbent on this industry to play a central and aggressive role in protecting these vital economic sectors. Members of corporate security departments pay constant attention to terrorist possibilities and develop plans to deal with these eventualities in this country and abroad. Since 9/11, private security practitioners have added homeland security to the top of their agenda to protect the interests and assets of their organizations and clients.

- In 2004, the *9/11 Commission Report: The Final Report of the National Commission on Terrorist Attacks upon the United States* was released. It made forty-one major recommendations to improve homeland security and prevent future acts of terrorism against our nation; four of these recommendations involved the participation of the private sector in possible similar situations. It noted that unless a terrorist's target is a military or other secure government facility, the "first" first responders will be civilians; the report concluded that national preparedness therefore often begins with the private sector.

Learning Check

1. Discuss the meaning of *homeland security*.
2. What are the objectives of the *National Strategy for Homeland Security*?

3. Define *terrorism.*

4. Discuss the latest statistics on terrorist incidents around the world.

5. Name the two federal law enforcement agencies primarily concerned with terrorism and homeland security. Discuss their efforts to deal with these issues.

6. Define and discuss the role of some of the major subunits of the Department of Homeland Security in ensuring homeland security.

7. Why is it important for the private sector to be at the forefront in preparations to prevent and respond to future terrorist attacks?

8. Cite and discuss some examples of private security efforts to ensure homeland security.

9. Name and discuss several joint public and private information-sharing initiatives crucial to our homeland security efforts.

10. Identify and discuss the role of private security firms in assisting the U.S. military abroad.

Application Exercise

You have been hired as the assistant security director of your local gas and electric company. It serves 120,000 customers in several counties in your area. The security director tells you he has heard that there are some cooperative programs with the federal government to share security news regarding homeland security threats. He asks you to research this and prepare a report for him on any cooperative programs your company can engage in.

Web Exercise

Use the Internet to obtain the latest statistics regarding terrorist acts.

Key Terms

agroterrorism, p. 350
American National Standards Institute (ANSI), p. 347
bioterrorism, p. 341
cyberterrorism, p. 340
Department of Homeland Security (DHS), p. 341
"first" first responders, p. 346
homeland security, p. 337
Information Sharing and Analysis Centers (ISACs), p. 349
National Counterterrorism Center (NCTC), p. 340
National Memorial Institute for the Prevention of Terrorism (MIPT), p. 339
Post-911 Policing Project, p. 344
qualified antiterrorism technologies (QATTs), p. 354
September 11, 2001 (9/11), p. 337
terrorism, p. 339
Terrorism Knowledge Base, p. 339
threat assessment, p. 348
US-VISIT program, p. 342

Glossary

A

ABC method A three-officer or three-vehicle surveillance tactic in which the A surveillant is closest to the subject; the B surveillant follows the A person, usually on the same side of the street; and the C surveillant is on the opposite side of the street or in front of the subject.

access control The use of qualifying devices or identification methods at various points to control the passage of people and vehicles into or out of an area or structure; limits access to people who have authorization to enter through selected points.

accredited healthcare fraud investigator (AHFI) A unique professional designation granted by the National Health Care Anti-Fraud Association to individuals who meet certain qualifications related to professional experience, specialized training, formal education, and demonstrated knowledge in the detection, investigation, and/or prosecution of healthcare fraud.

advance survey Performing practice exercises or dry runs of an area where a principal will be escorted.

adversarial system The defense and prosecution in a legal case present their respective sides as vigorously as possible.

adverse action A refusal to offer a person a job because of information on the person's credit report.

agroterrorism Terrorism aimed at livestock and agriculture.

alarm systems Electronic warning and intruder alert systems.

American National Standards Institute An agency that serves as the coordinator of the U.S. voluntary standards system, a unique and diversified federation that includes industry, standards-developing organizations, trade associations, professional and technical societies, government, and labor and consumer groups.

applets Computerized micro programs that carry out individual applications; used in smart card technology.

ASIS International Professional organization of private security professionals.

ASIS International Employment Survey Yearly survey of managers and professionals in the private security industry regarding salaries paid to proprietary and contract security employees.

Aviation and Transportation Security Act Bill passed in the aftermath of the 9/11 terrorist attacks that established the Transportation Security Administration (TSA) to protect the nation's transportation systems and ensure freedom of movement for people and commerce.

B

background investigations The process of acquiring information on an individual through third-party services, government organizations, and private individuals in the hopes of making a determination on the future actions of an individual based on past actions.

bail enforcement agent/bounty hunter Person hired by a bail bondsman to apprehend persons who have skipped or forfeited bail; also known as a bounty hunter.

benefit denial system Antishoplifting system in which a tag is attached to an article that will damage or stain the article if it is taken from the store without purchasing it.

biometrics Digital capture of physical characteristics and conversion into data for storage. The data are used to validate identity.

biometric identification systems Computerized systems that capture physical characteristics and convert them into data for identification purposes.

bioterrorism The intentional release or dissemination of biological agents (bacteria, viruses, or toxins); these may be in a naturally occurring or human-modified form.

blend To become part of a surrounding environment or culture.

blog Personal computer sites that often contain a mix of frank commentary, freewheeling opinions, and journaling.

blogosphere A series of collective Internet conversations that is one of the fastest-growing areas of new content on the web.

bodyguard See personal protection specialist.

bounty hunter See bail enforcement agent.

Bow Street Runners Private investigative unit formed by Henry Fielding in mid 1700s in England.

"broken windows" theory Theory that unrepaired broken windows or disrepair indicate that members of a community do not care about the quality of life in their neighborhood; consequently, disorder and crime will thrive.

bugs Concealed electronic devices placed in a premise to transmit conversations.

burned When an investigator is discovered by the person under surveillance.

business improvement districts (BIDs) Private organizations that oversee critical services, such as security and sanitation, for businesses in a defined geographical area or district.

C

cash control Methods used to safeguard cash in commercial businesses and institutions.

cellular (cell) phone A portable telephone that uses wireless cellular technology to send and receive phone signals.

central station monitoring Remote alarms or detection devices installed in houses and businesses that automatically transmit alarm signals to a central office that is monitored twenty-four hours a day.

certified fraud examiner (CFE) Investigator who is certified to conduct fraud investigations.

certified insurance fraud investigator Investigator who is certified to conduct insurance fraud investigations.

Certified Protection Professional (CPP) Professional certification awarded to security professionals by ASIS International.

chauffeur A person employed to drive a car or limousine that transports passengers.

civil demand programs See civil recovery program.

civil law Law that governs the relationships between individuals in the course of their private affairs, including such matters as contracts, property, wills, and torts.

civil liability Legal responsibility for conduct; includes intentional tort, negligence, and strict liability.

civil recovery programs Programs in which retail stores instigate civil court proceedings against shoplifters to recover monetary damages.

closed-circuit television (CCTV) A private video system for security monitoring in a building, store, or geographic area.

close tail A person is under constant surveillance and the surveillant remains undetected; also known as a tight tail.

command center (or control center) A management and control unit that monitors all security functions, including alarms, electronic video surveillance, and security guard operations; also known as control centers.

common law Unwritten legal precedents created through everyday practice and supported by court decision.

community crime-prevention programs Anti-crime programs in which citizens participate in crime-prevention programs in their own neighborhoods; some examples are neighborhood watch, crime watch, block watch, community alert, citizen patrols and citizen marches.

community policing Philosophy of empowering citizens and developing a partnership between the police and the community to work together to solve problems.

computer emergency response team (CERT) Team of specialists who deal with hacking problems on company and institutional computers; also known as computer incident response team (CIRT).

computerized databases Databases containing huge amounts of personal information from public and private sources, maintained by information brokers who sell information to investigators or other interested persons; also known as detective databases.

computerized guard tour systems Record the patrol activities of guards and the time and location of each visit they make.

computer virus Malicious software program written to damage or harass other computer systems.

consumer credit reports Records on anyone who has ever used credit in any way.

consumer report information Credit history information maintained and disseminated by consumer reporting agencies.

consumer reporting agency (CRA) Business that conducts and maintains credit reporting information; also known as a credit bureau.

contact An investigator who maintains contact with an undercover officer.

contracting out/outsourcing Hiring external companies to perform duties for a company.

contract security External companies hired to provide security.

contract security investigations External companies hired to provide investigative security services.

Council on Licensure, Enforcement and Regulation (CLEAR) Professional organization involved in licensing and regulatory reform in the private security industry.

counterespionage Efforts made to prevent and thwart hostile espionage.

countersurveillance The practice of avoiding surveillance or making surveillance difficult.

cover story A fictitious explanation for one's presence or activity.

covert Undercover; secret.

covert security Undercover security operations.

credit bureau The most common type of CRA.

credit-card fraud Fraud involving the use of credit cards, including point-of-sale fraud, card-not-present fraud, e-commerce fraud, ATM fraud, and identity theft.

Crime Prevention Service for Business of Rutgers University, School of Criminal Justice University program that works with small businesses to find workable, inexpensive crime prevention measures.

crime prevention through environmental design (CPTED) Methods used to deter crime through manipulation of architectural design.

crime reduction through product design (CRPD) Methods used to deter crime by implementing security features into products.

criminal liability Responsibility for criminal action.

crisis management team (CMT) Team of corporate executives and specialists prepared to immediately deal with threats or actual emergencies.

critical incident Any event or situation that threatens people and/or their homes, businesses, or community.

critical incident protocol Procedures to address critical incidents.

critical information infrastructure All control systems for the nation's infrastructure, including utilities, banks, and the like; mostly computerized.

cross examination Questioning by the opposing attorney in a judicial proceeding for the purpose of assessing the validity of the testimony.

crotch-carry A method of shoplifting in which the criminal carries stolen items between his or her legs, usually under a loose coat or full skirt or dress.

cybercrime An illegal act committed through the use of computer technology.

cyberstalking The harrassment of others by computer.

cyberterrorism Terrorism that initiates, or threatens to initiate, the exploitation of, or attack on information sources.

D

DCS1000 A device used by the FBI to intercept information through the Internet while ignoring what it is not authorized to collect; formerly known as "Carnivore."

defense information infrastructure All control systems for the nation's defense capability; mostly computerized.

Defense Personnel Security Research Center (PERSEREC) The federal government's think tank for background investigations and other personnel and investigative matters affecting the federal workforce.

denial-of-service (DOS) attacks Deliberate attempts to shut down a computer network operation by overloading it.

Department of Homeland Security (DHS) Federal cabinet department established in the aftermath of the 9/11 terrorist attacks to protect the nation from terrorism.

digital video recorder (DVR) Directly records images to a conventional computer hard drive as bits of data, instead of recording analog images to a moving medium like VHS tape.

direct testimony Statements made under oath by a witness. After a witness testifies, the other party has the right to ask questions on cross-examination.

DNA tagging Antishoplifting or anticounterfeiting technology that uses miscroscopic fragments of DNA.

domestic violence Violence in the family or between husband and wife or partners.

drug testing or drug screening Analysis of employees or candidates for illicit drug use.

dumpster diving Scavenging through garbage to retrive personal identification material.

dynamic video surveillance system (DVSS) The latest state-of-the-art digital video recording system used in electronic video surveillance systems.

E

electronic access control The use of electronic card readers, keypads, biometric devices, or a combination of technologies that restrict the passage of persons or vehicles from one point to another.

electronic article surveillance (EAS) Antishoplifting protection systems for both apparel and packaged products; an alarm sounds if a product is taken from a store without being purchased.

electronic video surveillance Systems that allow recording of events, including surveillance and security cameras and closed circuit television (CCTV) systems; can passively record or play back video at certain intervals, be actively monitored, or be used in a combination of these methods.

employee assistance professionals (EAPs) Professionals who try to prevent employees from being kidnapped or help them survive kidnapping by providing helpful information to the employees and their families.

employee-misconduct investigation An internal investigation into allegations of employee misconduct, which, if warranted, could result in the employee's termination, criminal prosecution, or other disciplinary measures.

employee monitoring The monitoring of employees' phone and e-mail usage by an employer.

Employee Polygraph Protection Act (EPPA) A 1988 law that prohibited the use of pre-employment polygraph examinations in the private sector except for government employers, law enforcement agencies, and certain critical industries.

employment-related security Knowing the essential information about employees, both permanent and temporary, that might impact their job performance, breach security, or subject to the organization to liability.

encryption A method of encoding information to prevent illegal use.

ethics The practical, normative study of the rightness and wrongness of human conduct.

ethics codes or values statements Formal statements of businesses or organizations representing their ethical and values standards.

evidence All the means by which an alleged fact is established or disproved.

exclusionary rule An interpretation of the U.S. Constitution by the U.S. Supreme Court that holds that evidence seized in violation of the U.S. Constitution cannot be used in court against a defendant.

executive protection (EP) Program to protect corporate executives or other employees from kidnapping and intentional or accidental injury.

executive protection specialist (EPS) Persons employed to protect corporate executives or other employees from kidnapping and intentional or accidental injury; could be a proprietary or contract employee.

expiring time badges Temporary identification system for visitors, contractors, and others temporarily visiting a building or other facility; these badges change colors when the badge is no longer valid, showing that the wearer is no longer authorized to be on the premise.

express kidnapping Kidnapping involving little preparation and planning on the part of the criminal.

F

Fair Credit Reporting Act (FCRA) Federal law designed to promote accuracy and ensure the privacy of the information used in consumer reports.

federal airport security director Position directly responsible for security at the nation's airports; established in the aftermath of the 9/11 terrorist attacks.

Federal Drug-Free Workplace Act Federal legislation that requires some federal contractors and all federal grantees to provide drug-free workplaces as a condition of receiving a contract or grant from a federal agency.

Federal Protective Service A unit of the Department of Homeland Security that hires security officers to guard federal buildings.

firewall A software program that prevents unauthorized entry into computer networks.

"first" first responders Concept developed by the National Commission on Terrorist Attacks upon the United States that the first responders to a terrorist attack that is not a military or other secure government facility will be civilians. The Commission reasoned that national preparedness therefore often begins with the private sector.

fraud Larceny committed by trickery or deceit.

G

global positioning systems (GPS) A satellite system used to locate any position on the map.

Gramm-Leach-Bliley Act Federal law enacted in 2002 prohibiting any person from obtaining financial information by making fictitious or fraudulent statements to a bank or other financial institution.

guard force management The concept of managing security guards by effectively supporting all the technical security that a company uses in its security operations.

H

hacking The willful and malicious penetration of a computer system.

hacktivist People who commit denial-of-service attacks, disseminate spam, and deface websites, believing they are carrying out acts of civil disobedience.

Hallcrest Reports Two comprehensive reports commissioned by the U. S. National Institute of Justice concerning the private security industry in the United States.

header information Personal information that is sold to marketers.

healthcare fraud Deliberate submittal of false claims to private health insurance plans and/or tax-funded health insurance programs, such as Medicare and Medicaid.

homeland security Defensive efforts within the borders of the U.S. *The National Strategy for Homeland Security* and the Homeland Security Act of 2002 serve to mobilize and organize our nation to secure the homeland from terrorist attacks.

hostile environment sexual harassment A workplace that promotes or tolerates sexual harrassment.

I

identity theft The criminal act of assuming another person's identity.

Industrial Defense Program Federal program established in 1952 to oversee, advise, and assist defense-related facilities; now known as the National Industrial Security Program.

industrial espionage Covert collection of industrial secrets or processes.

information broker Private person or corporation that provides detective databases to private investigators throughout the nation.

Information Sharing and Analysis Centers (ISACs) Centers established in 1998 to provide information sharing and analysis between the government and businesses.

information technology (IT) Department that controls and studies the information managed by a business' computers.

ink tag Antishoplifting device in which an ink-filled tag that will break and stain the article if it is removed from the store without being purchased is attached to an article.

insurance fraud Fraud in insurance claims, including disability, worker's compensation, auto, medical, health care, and other types.

integrity shoppers Undercover agents who test the integrity of retail personnel.

intellectual property rights An umbrella term for various legal entitlements that attach to certain names, written and recorded media, and inventions.

International Association of Security and Investigative Regulators (IASIR) Professional organization involved in security industry regulatory reform, licensing, training, and education.

Internet Crime Complaint Center (IC3) Department of Justice and National White Collar Crime Center reporting mechanism that addresses fraud committed over the Internet and serves as a vehicle to receive, develop, and refer criminal complaints regarding cybercrime.

K

keystroke monitoring system Automated system that records how many and which keystrokes an employee is performing on the computer.

kidnapping The transportation or confinement of a person without authority of law and without his or her consent or the consent of his or her guardian, if a minor.

kidnapping kit A child safety kit whereby vital information (name, age, address, weight, height, etc.) can be stored; usually includes a fingerprint kit and a place to store DNA samples (i.e., hair).

knock-off or copycat goods Counterfeit products.

L

law A system of standards and rules of human conduct that imposes obligations and grants corresponding rights as well as a system of institutional rules on the creation, modification, and enforcement of these standards.

Law Enforcement Management and Administrative Statistics (LEMAS) Statistical reports on law enforcement personnel data issued by the National Institute of Justice.

leapfrog The process of surveillants changing positions during a surveillance to deter observation by the subject.

loose tail The person being followed is not under constant surveillance but the surveillant remains undetected.

loss prevention (LP) The use of methods to reduce the amount of shrinkage in retail stores.

loss prevention investigations Investigative programs to detect and prevent retail theft; can be proprietary or contract.

loss prevention specialist See store detective.

Loss Prevention Research Council (LPRC) A professional organization that evaluates and develops innovative crime and loss control techniques to improve the retail performance of its members.

Loss Prevention Research Team (LPRT) A team of professors, research scientists, practitioners, and graduate students who conduct retail research and provide actionable information to businesses.

M

made When a surveillant is discovered or identified by a subject.

mail drop A method used by undercover agents to leave information for other investigators.

medical fraud Fraud committed by a healthcare provider, patient, or both.

memetic viruses Computerized hoaxes, chain letters, erroneous alerts.

merchant's privilege See shopkeepers privilege.

microprocessor card Smart cards with memory chips that are actually microcontrollers built into them. These cards are similar to the motherboard of a computer.

minimum standards or guidelines Efforts to increase the professionalization of private security employees by requiring them to meet specific standards prior to employment.

minimum training hours Certain required amount of classroom instruction on skills needed for a job.

Miranda **ruling/***Miranda* **warning** Court ruling that police must read this warning that advises the person in custody of his or her rights prior to any interrogation.

mobile security devices (MSDs) Devices placed in vehicles for persons to summon assistance in an emergency.

moonlight When police officers work in private security jobs during their off-duty hours.

moonlighting Term for police officers working in private security jobs during their off-duty hours.

moving surveillance Surveillance that follows a subject on foot or in a vehicle.

multistate criminal records databases Computerized databases used by background investigators to conduct criminal record checks.

mystery shopper Agent who visits a store and observes the performance and operations of store personnel.

N

National Counterterrorism Center (NCTC) The primary organization in the U.S. government for integrating and analyzing all intelligence pertaining to terrorism and counterterrorism and for conducting strategic operational planning by integrating all instruments of national power.

National Cyber Alert System (US-CERT) Federal government early warning system that provides citizens with timely and actionable information to secure their computer systems.

National Industrial Security Program Federal program established in 1952 to oversee, advise, and assist defense-related facilities; formerly known as the National Industrial Defense Program.

National Memorial Institute for the Prevention of Terrorism (MIPT) A nonprofit, nationally recognized think tank creating state-of-the-art knowledge bases and sharing information on terrorism prevention and responder preparedness.

National Retail Federation World's largest retail trade association.

National Retail Security Survey Annual shrinkage report prepared by the University of Florida for loss prevention specialists and executives.

negligence Behavior that inflicts individual harm or injury by mistake or accident.

negligent hiring Hiring an employee without properly confirming that the information on his or her employment application is accurate and factual.

negligent retention Retaining an employee after negative information is discovered after her or his hiring.

night-vision devices High-tech devices used to aid vision in the dark.

O

Occupational Outlook Handbook Published yearly by the U.S. Department of Labor's Bureau of Labor Statistics. Contains extensive information regarding the major industries and occupations in the United States, including nature of the work, working conditions, training, job qualifications, advancement, job outlook, earnings, and related occupations.

online or reverse auctions Process of hiring a contract security force by using the Internet.

Operation Cooperation Comprehensive 2000 government report, *Guidelines for Partnerships between Law Enforcement &*

Private Security Organizations, prepared by the U.S. Department of Justice in collaboration with ASIS International, the IACP, and the National Sheriff's Association and detailing public/private partnerships for security.

overt Conducted openly.

overt security Security using observable methods.

P

panic devices Buttons placed throughout a premise for the use of a person to summon assistance in an emergency.

pedophiles Sexual offenders who receive gratification from sexual contact with children.

peer reporting Programs in which employees monitor and report suspicious, illegal, or unethical behavior by other employees.

personal alarms Alarms carried by persons to summon assistance in an emergency.

personal protection specialist (PPS) Person employed to provide personal protection for a person.

phishing The sending of fraudulent e-mail messages to members of online payment accounts, such as banks, credit-card companies, and online payment services, to update their records; also known as spoofing.

piggybacking When unauthorized persons closely follow authorized employees into restricted areas; also known as tailgating.

Pinkerton National Detective Agency Private detective agency established by Allan Pinkerton in the 1850s.

Pinkerton Protective Patrol Agency established by Allan Pinkerton in 1857 to provide watchman services for businesses and private individuals.

polygraph (lie detector) examination Test using a scientific instrument (polygraph machine, also known as a lie detector) to measure credibility.

Post-9/11 Policing Project Measures to help bring domestic preparedness to the top of the law enforcement agenda.

pre-employment background screening Screening of potential employees.

pretexting Pretending to be someone else to obtain information about that person.

principal Person being protected in an executive protection program or other personal protection program.

private justice system A concept that holds that businesses and corporations might prefer to deal with crime using their own internal systems and controls instead of through the cumbersome and lengthy formal criminal justice system.

private–public partnerships Joint efforts between private security and public agencies to deal with crime.

privatization Government agencies contracting out various services to private agencies.

Private Security Act of 2001 Legislation passed in the United Kingdom to professionalize the private security industry.

private security industry The industry that provides private and corporate security programs to the United States.

Private Security Officer Employment Authorization Act of 2004 Law passed in 2004 giving employers the ability to request criminal background checks from the FBI to process criminal history records checks for candidates for security job positions.

Private Security Officer Selection and Training Guideline ASIS International's suggested criteria for improving selection of and training for security officers.

product liability cases Lawsuits in which a client claims to have been injured by a certain product.

professional certified investigator (PCI) ASIS International board certification accepted as the international standard of competence in security investigations; a positive indicator of state-of-the-art knowledge of investigations applications and best practices.

profiling Use of a person's characteristics to assess the likelihood of criminal activity or wrongdoing.

proprietary security In-house corporate or business security.

proprietary security investigations In-house corporate or business security investigations.

protective vehicles High-tech vehicles designed to protect persons in personal protection situations.

Q

Qualified antiterrorism technologies (QATTs) Designation and certification that protects potential developers of technology that could reduce the risk of terrorism from liability claims. Protected items can include products, software, services, and other forms of intellectual property.

questors Investigative units created in fifth-century Rome.

R

radio frequency identification (RFID) Antishoplifting tags or devices that contain the specific information about the target; if they are taken from the store without being purchased an alarm will sound; also called radio tagging.

Railway Police Acts Laws established in many states in the nineteenth century giving the railroad industry the right to establish a proprietary security force.

retail alert system Program in which businesses in the same area notify each other immediately in the event of a crime; alerts can be done by telephone, voice, video, or data transmission.

risk analysis (or risk assessment) The process of identifying potential areas of security problems and loss and the development and implementation of effective measures or countermeasures to deal with these problems.

risk management The process used to weigh the costs inherent in protecting a business or corporation from possible crime and natural disasters in light of the benefits received; involves the process of risk analysis or risk assessment.

rough tail Surveillant is following someone, but it is not important if she or he is discovered by the subject.

S

Sarbanes-Oxley Act Federal law enacted in 2002 to protect investors by improving the accuracy and reliability of corporate disclosures; also known as the Public Company Accounting Reform and Investor Protector Act.

script kiddies Hackers with little technical knowledge; they follow directions prepared by someone else.

security barriers Standoff barricades used to protect buildings from attack.

security guard A privately and formally employed person who is paid to protect property, and/or assets, and/or people.

Security Industry Authority (SIA) Government agency in the United Kingdom that regulates the private security industry.

Security Research Project University of Florida program that studies various elements of workplace-related crime and deviance with a special emphasis on the retail industry.

security screening points or checkpoints Checkpoints set up in 1973 at all the nation's airports to screen all travelers.

security survey A comprehensive physical examination of a premise and a thorough inspection of all security systems and procedures.

September 11, 2001 (9/11) Date of the historical terrorist attacks of the largest magnitude against the United States by al Qaeda.

sexual harassment Unwanted and uninvited sexual contact or advances.

sexual harassment in the workplace Unwanted and uninvited sexual contact or advances in a workplace.

sexual offender Person convicted of a sexual offense against another person.

shadow A one-person surveillance.

shopkeeper's privilege Common-law doctrine that holds that a merchant or shopkeeper can reasonably detain and question a person if she or he has a justified suspicion that the person is committing an illegal act; also known as the merchant's privilege.

shopping services Services performed by undercover agents posing as customers to test the integrity and efficiency of retail business personnel.

shrinkage The reduction in inventory due to theft or diversion.

smart cards Cards using computer technology for banking applications, identification, and physical access control.

source tagging Antishoplifting tags that are attached to products by manufacturers before they reach stores.

spam Unwanted and uninvited computer messages.

special investigating units (SIUs) Teams used by insurance companies to train claim representatives in dealing with routine fraud cases; they also investigate more-serious fraud cases.

spoofing See phishing.

spyware Bits of computer code that surreptitiously install themselves on the computers of Internet users to track their activities, push them to websites, and barrage them with advertisements.

stalking Repeated harassing, and threatening behavior by one individual against another, which might involve following a person, appearing at a person's home or place of business, making harassing phone calls, leaving written messages or objects, or vandalizing a person's property.

stationary surveillance Surveillance from a fixed location.

store detective A private investigator who investigates retail pilferage and theft.

StoreLab program Academic and industrial program to codevelop and test store and facility layouts, processes, and technologies to maximize productivity, sales, and profit while minimizing losses and crime.

strict liability Civil liability for an action although no intent is present.

subject The person being watched in a surveillance.

surveillance The covert observation of places, persons, and vehicles for the purpose of obtaining information about the identities or activities of subjects.

surveillant The person conducting the surveillance.

Survey of Supermarket Theft A survey to determine the amount of theft that occurs within supermarkets based on the survey's respondents.

sweeping Checking of a premise for electronic surveillance devices.

systems integration (or convergence) The computerized process of bringing together corporate subsystems, such as electronic video surveillance, access control, time and attendance, and intrusion detection, in such a way that data is captured only once and is stored in a central repository accessible to all the subsystems.

T

tailgating Unauthorized persons closely following authorized employees into restricted areas; also known as piggybacking.

telematics The science of two-way communications using global positioning satellite (GPS) technology.

temporary badging Process of identifying visitors, contractors, and others temporarily visiting a building or other facility.

terrorism The unlawful use or threat of force or violence against individuals or property to intimidate or coerce a government, the civilian population, or any segment thereof, in furtherance of political, religious, ideological, or social objectives.

Terrorism Knowledge Base Professional organization dedicated to preventing terrorism on U.S. soil or mitigating its effects; maintains a database of all terrorism incidents, terrorist groups, information sources, and other materials for terrorism researchers.

The 2004 National Policy Summit A joint effort by the International Association of Chiefs of Police (IACP), the Office of Community-Oriented Policing Services (COPS), the U.S. Department of Justice (DOJ), and ASIS International, which addressed the major issues concerning the history and current status of public-private partnerships in an effort to enhance communication and cooperation between the public and private sectors.

thief-takers Individuals who served as a form of private police in sixteenth-, seventeenth-, and eighteenth-century France and England.

threat assessment Common tool in private security to determine who would want to attack a particular company or business and why and how they would do so. Also known as a threat evaluation, facility characterization, or target value assessment.

tight tail A person is under constant surveillance and the surveillant remains undetected; also known as close tail.

torts Personal wrongs, as opposed to criminal wrongs.

Transportation Security Administration (TSA) Federal agency established in the aftermath of the 9/11 terrorist attacks to protect the nation's trans-portations systems and ensure freedom of movement for people and commerce.

Trojan horse Type of computer virus that claims to do something desirable but instead does something destructive.

turnover The process of losing employees when they resign, are involuntarily terminated, or retire; a major problem in the security guard industry.

U

undercover Covert investigation of criminal activity; person who conducts undercover operations.

undercover investigator/operator/agent An investigator who disguises his or her own identity or uses an assumed identity to gain the trust of an individual or organization to learn secret information or to gain the trust of targeted individuals in order to gain information or evidence.

undercover operations Covert activities designed to catch criminals.

unmanned aerial vehicle (UAV) Portable flying device that can be equpped with cameras to transmit live video feeds to surveillants on the ground.

U.S. Department of Homeland Security (DHS) Federal cabinet-level department established in the aftermath of the 9/11 terrorist attacks.

US-VISIT Program A continuum of security measures that begins outside U.S. borders and continues through a visitor's arrival in and departure from the United States.

V

vehicle tracking system Transmitters that enable investigators to track a vehicle during a surveillance; also called transponders, bumper beepers, or homing devices.

verified response Requires burglar alarm companies to confirm break-ins or security breaches before police officers will be deployed to the scene of a ringing alarm.

vetting Another word for pre-employment background investigations.

vicarious liability Responsibility of employers, managers, or supervisors for the legal actions of their employees.

W

web attack Large amount of hostile activity targeted at one particular company.

Wi-Fi Stands for Wireless Fidelity, a brand originally licensed by the Wi-Fi Alliance to describe the embedded technology of wireless local area networks (WLAN).

workplace violence Any criminal misbehavior committed against people in the workplace.

worms Self-replicating computer programs that use a network to send copies of themselves to other nodes (computer terminals on the network), often without any user intervention.

Notes

Chapter 1

1. John Ayto, *Dictionary of Word Origins: The Histories of More Than 8,000 English Language Words* (New York: Little, Brown & Company, 1990), pp. 465–466.

2. National Advisory Commission on Criminal Justice Standards and Goals, *Report of the Task Force on Private Security* (Washington, DC: U.S. Government Printing Office, 1976), p. 4.

3. Milton Lipson, "Private Security: A Retrospective," *The Annals* (July 1988), p. 11.

4. Truett A. Ricks, Bill G. Tillett, and Clifford W. Van Meter, *Principles of Security*, 3rd ed. (Cincinnati, OH: Anderson, 1994), p. 1.

5. Harvey Burstein, *Introduction to Security* (Englewood Cliffs, NJ: Prentice Hall, 1999), p. 1.

6. This history of police and private security in Ancient Rome relies primarily on Philippe Aries and George Dulig, *A History of Private Life from Pagan Rome to Byzantium* (Cambridge, MA: Bellnap Press of Harvard University, 1987); David H. Bayley, "The Development of Modern Police," in Larry K. Gaines and Gary W. Cordner, *Policing Perspectives: An Anthology* (Los Angeles: Roxbury Publishing, 1999), pp. 59–78; Will Durant, *The Story of Civilization, Vol. II: "Christ and Caesar"* (New York: Simon & Schuster, 1944); R. W. Davies, "Police Work in Roman Times," *History Today* (October 1968); Rhys Carpenter, "Ancient Rome Brought to Life," *National Geographic* (November 1946); Moses Hadaz, *A History of Rome* (Garden City, NY: Doubleday & Co., 1956); Martin A. Kelly, "Citizen Survival in Ancient Rome," *Police Studies*, 11(4, Winter 1988), pp. 195–201; Wolfgang Kunkel, *An Introduction to Roman Legal and Constitutional History,* 2nd ed. (Oxford, UK: Clarendon Press, 1973); A. W. Lintott, *Violence in Republican Rome* (Oxford, UK: Clarendon Press, 1968); William Sinnegan, "Roman Secret Service," *Classical Journal* (November 1961); Ramsey MacMullan, *Enemies of the Roman Order* (Cambridge, MA: Harvard University Press, 1966); *Encyclopaedia Britannica*, "Locks"; F. R. Corwell, *The Revolutions of Ancient Rome* (New York: Fred A. Prager, 1963); P. G. W. Glare, *Oxford Latin Dictionary* (Oxford Claridan: Oxford University Press, 1982); D. P. Simpson, *Cassell's Latin Dictionary* (New York: Macmillan, 1978); Olivia Coolidge, *Roman People* (Boston: Houghton Mifflin, 1959); Thomas H. Dyer, *Pompeii* (London: Geo. Bells & Sons, 1889); Mary MacGregor, *Story of Rome* (New York: Frederick A. Stokes, 1914); William Smith, *Dictionary of Greek and Roman Antiquities* (Boston: Charles C. Little & Co., 1854); Eugene Ehrlich, *Amo, Amas, Amat and More* (New York: Harper & Row, 1987); and P. K. Baillie Reynolds, *The Vigiles of Imperial Rome* (London: Oxford University Press, 1926).

7. Durant, *The Story of Civilization, Vol. II*, p. 341.

8. For information about security in Ancient Greece, see Robert J. Bonner and Gertrude Smith, *The Administration of Justice from Homer to Aristotle*, 2 vols. (Chicago: University of Chicago Press, 1928); and Durant, *The Life of Greece: The Story of Civilization II* (New York: Simon & Schuster, 1966).

9. For a brief history of investigations, see Chapter 1 of John S. Dempsey, *Introduction to Investigations*, 2nd ed. (Belmont, CA: Wadsworth, 2003).

10. Kelly, "Citizen Survival in Ancient Rome," p. 195.

11. This section on the English roots of policing is based on the following: S. G. Chapman and T. E. St. Johnston, *The Police Heritage in England and America* (East Lansing: Michigan State University, 1962); T. A. Critchley, *A History of Police in England and Wales*, 2nd ed. rev. (Montclair, NJ: Patterson Smith, 1972); John S. Dempsey, *An Introduction to Public and Private Investigations* (Minneapolis/St.Paul: West, 1996); Dempsey, *An Introduction to Policing*, 2nd ed. (Belmont, CA: West/Wadsworth, 1999); Dempsey, *Introduction to Investigations*; Dempsey and Linda S. Forst, *An Introduction to Policing,* 4th ed. (Belmont, CA: Wadsworth, 2007); Clive Emsley, *Policing and Its Context, 1750–1870* (New York: Schocken, 1984); A. C. Germann, Frank D. Day, and Robert R. J. Gallati, *Introduction to Law Enforcement and Criminal Justice* (Springfield, IL: Charles C. Thomas, 1969); W. E. Hunt, *History of England* (New York: Harper & Brothers, 1938); Luke Owen Pike, *A History of Crime in England* (London: Smith, Elder, 1873–1876); Patrick Pringle, *Highwaymen* (New York: Roy, 1963); Pringle, *Hue and Cry: The Story of Henry and John Fielding and Their Bow Street Runners* (New York: Morrow, 1965); Pringle, *The Thief Takers* (London: Museum Press, 1958); C. Reith, *Blind Eye of History* (Montclair, NJ: Patterson, Smith, 1975); Thomas Reppetto, *The Blue Parade* (New York Free Press, 1978); Albert Rieck, *Justice and Police in England* (London: Butterworth, 1936); Robert Sheehan and Gary W. Cordner, *Introduction to Police Administration*, 2nd ed. (Cincinnati, OH: Anderson Publishing, 1989); Nigel South, "Law, Profit and Private Prisons: Private and Public Policing in English History," in Clifford D. Shearing and Philip C. Stenning, eds., *Private Policing* (Beverly Hills, CA: Sage Publications, 1987), pp. 72–107; and John J. Tobias, *Crime and Police in England, 1700–1900* (New York: St. Martin's Press, 1979).

12. Pringle, *Hue and Cry*, p. 81.

13. Critchley, *A History of Police in England and Wales*, p. 28.

14. "Policing for Profit: Welcome to the New World of Private Security," *The Economist* (April 19, 1997), p. 21.

15. James F. Richardson, *The New York Police: Colonial Times to 1901* (New York: Oxford University Press, 1976), p. 10.

16. This section on U.S. public and private policing is based on the following: Robert Bailey, *Private Heat: An Art Hardin Mystery* (New York: M. Evans & Company, 2001); Carl Bridenbaugh, *Cities in Revolt: Urban Life in America, 1743–1776* (New York: Knopf, 1965); Bridenbaugh, *Cities in the Wilderness: Urban Life in America, 1625–1742* (New York: Capricorn, 1964); Dempsey, *An Introduction to Public and Private Investigations*; Dempsey and Forst, *An Introduction to Policing*, 4th ed.; H. S. Dewhurst, *The Railroad Police* (Springfield, IL: Charles C. Thomas, 1955); Emsley, *Policing and Its Context*; Robert M. Fogelson, *Big City Police* (Cambridge, MA: Harvard University Press, 1977); T. W. Gough, "Railroad Crime: Old West Train Robbers to Modern-Day Cargo Thieves," *FBI Law Enforcement Bulletin* (February 1977), pp. 16–25; Karen M. Hess and Henry M. Wrobleski, *Introduction to Private Security*, 4th ed. (Minneapolis/St. Paul: West, 1996); James D. Horan and Howard Swiggett, *The Pinkerton Story* (New York: Putnam, 1951); James D. Horan, *The Pinkertons: The Detective Dynasty That Made History* (New York: Crown, 1967); Edward Hungerford, *Wells Fargo: Advancing the American Frontier* (New York: Bonanza, 1949); David R.

Johnson, *American Law Enforcement: A History* (St. Louis, MI: Forum Press, 1981); Johnson, *Policing the Urban Underworld* (Philadelphia: Temple University Press,1979); Carolyn Lake, *Undercover for Wells Fargo* (Boston: Houghton Mifflin, 1969); S. A. Lavine, *Allan Pinkerton: America's First Private Eye* (New York: Dodd, Mead, and Company, 1963); Roger Lane, *Policing the City, Boston 1822–1885* (Cambridge, MA: Harvard University Press, 1967); M. Lipson, *On Guard: The Business of Private Security* (New York: Times Books, 1975); Eric Monkkonen, *Police in Urban America: 1860–1920* (Cambridge, MA: Harvard University Press, 1981); A. P. Morris, "Returning Justice to Its Private Roots," *University of Chicago Law Review,* 68(2001), pp. 551–575; Allan Pinkerton, *The Expressman and the Detective* (New York: Arno Press, 1976); Richard Post and Arthur A. Kingsbury, *Security Administration: An Introduction* (Springfield, IL: Charles C. Thomas, 1970); Frank R. Prassel, *The Western Peace Officer: A Legacy of Law and Order* (Norman: University of Oklahoma Press, 1972); Reith, *Blind Eye of History*; Thomas Reppetto, *Blue Parade*; Richardson, *The New York Police*; Richardson, *Urban Police in the United States* (Port Washington, NY: Kennikat Press, 1974); Charles A. Siringo, *A Cowboy Detective: A True Story of Twenty-Two Years with a World-Famous Detective Agency* (Lincoln: University of Nebraska Press, 1988); Bruce Smith, *Police Systems in the United States* (New York: Harper & Row, 1960); Smith, *Rural Crime Control* (New York: Columbia University Institute of Public Administration, 1933); E. Tozer, "Riding with a Million in Cash," *Popular Science* (March 1960), pp. 3–4, 90–91, 246–247; Samuel Walker, *A Critical History of Police Reform: The Emergence of Professionalism* (Lexington, MA: Lexington Books, 1977); Walker, *Popular Justice: History of American Criminal Justice* (New York: Oxford University Press, 1980); Walter Prescott Webb, *The Texas Rangers: A Century of Frontier Defense* (Boston: Houghton Mifflin, 1935).

17 Luc Sante, *Low Life: Lures and Snares of Old New York* (New York: Farrar, Straus & Giroux, 1991), p. 236.

18 Brinks Home Security, "Our History," retrieved August 30, 2004, from http://www.brinkshomesecurity.com.

19 This section on private security in the twentieth century is based on the following: Jay S. Albanese, *Criminal Justice* (Boston: Allyn & Bacon, 1999); Harvey Burstein, *Introduction to Security* (Upper Saddle River, NJ: Prentice Hall, 1999); William C. Cunningham, John J. Strauchs, and Clifford W. Van Meter, *The Hallcrest Report II: Private Security Trends: 1970–2000* (Boston: Butterworth-Heinemann, 1990); Cunningham and Todd H. Taylor, *The Hallcrest Report: Private Security and Police in America* (Portland, OR: Chancellor Press, 1985); Cunningham and Taylor, *Crime and Protection in America: A Study of Private Security and Law Enforcement Resources and Relationships* (Washington, DC: U.S. Government Printing Office, 1985); Mary Alice Davidson, "A Time to Remember," *Security Management* (January 2000), pp. 48–60; Dempsey, *An Introduction to Public and Private Investigations*; Dempsey, *Introduction to Investigations,* 2nd ed.; Dempsey, *An Introduction to Policing,* 2nd ed.; Dempsey and Linda S. Forst, *An Introduction to Policing,* 3rd ed. (Belmont, CA: Thomson/Wadsworth, 2005); Hilary Draper, *Private Police* (Atlantic Highlands, NJ: Humanities Press, 1978); Robert J. Fischer and Gion Green, *Introduction to Security,* 6th ed. (Boston: Butterworth-Heinemann, 1998); Hess and Wrobleski, *Introduction to Private Security* (Minneapolis/St. Paul: West, 1992); Lee Johnston, *The Rebirth of Private Policing* (New York: Routledge, 1992); Johnston, "Regulating Private Security," *International Journal of Sociology of Law,* 20(1992), pp. 1–16; James S. Kakalik and Sorrel Wildhorn, *Private Police in the United States,* 5 vols. (Washington, DC: National Institute of Justice, 1971); Kakalik and Wildhorn, *The Private Police: Security and Danger* (New York: Crane Russak, 1977); Post and Kingsbury, *Security Administration: An Introduction*; Clifford E. Simonsen, *Private Security in America: An Introduction* (Upper Saddle River, NJ: Prentice Hall, 1998); Henry S. Ursic and Leroy E. Pagano, *Security Management Systems* (Springfield, IL: Charles C. Thomas, 1974), p.19; William Walsh, "Private/Public Police Stereotypes: A Different Perspective," *Security Journal,* 1(1989), pp. 21–27.

20 William R. Hunt, *Front-Page Detective: William J. Burns and the Detective Profession, 1880–1930* (Cleveland, OH: Popular Press, 1990).

21 Kakalik and Wildhorn, *Private Police in the United States: Findings and Recommendations* (Santa Monica, CA: The RAND Corporation, 1971).

22 Clifford Van Meter, *Private Security: Report of the Task Force on Private Security* (Washington, DC: National Advisory Committee on Criminal Justice Standards and Goals, 1976).

23 "Policing for Profit," pp. 21–22.

24 The coverage of the Hallcrest Reports is based on Cunningham, Strauchs, and Van Meter, *The Hallcrest Report II: Private Security Trends: 1970–2000*; and Cunningham and Taylor, *The Hallcrest Report: Private Security and Police in America.*

25 Dean J. Champion, *Criminal Justice in the United States,* 2nd ed. (Chicago: Nelson-Hall, 1998), p. 90.

26 Matthew L. Wald, "Most Crimes of Violence and Property Hover at 30-Year Lows," *New York Times* (September 13, 2004), p. A15.

27 Mary Alice Davidson, "Fifty Remarkable Years," *ASIS Dynamics* (September/October 2004), pp. 1, 11.

28 ASIS International, "ASIS International Joins Department of Homeland Security and FBI on Information-Sharing Project," *ASIS International Press Release* (June 23, 2004).

29 ASIS International, "About ASIS," retrieved September 29, 2006, from http://www.asisonline.org/about/index.xml.

30 Mary Alice Davidson, "It IS What You Know," *Security Management* (June 2003), p. 75.

31 ASIS International, "ASIS Dynamics" (September/October 2005), p. 6. For further information, see http://www.asisonline.org or http://www.wharton.upenn.edu/4075.

32 Cunningham, Strauchs, and Van Meter, *The Hallcrest Report II,* p. 2.

33 International Association of Chiefs of Police (IACP), "Private Security Officer Selection, Training, and Licensing Guidelines," retrieved August 26, 2004, from http://www.theiacp.org/documents/index.cfm.

34 International Foundation for Protection Officers (IFPO), "Homepage," retrieved September 29, 2006, from http://www.ifpo.org.

35 Academy of Security Educators and Trainers (ASET), "Homepage," retrieved September 29, 2006, from http://www.asetcse.org.

36 International Association for Healthcare Security and Safety (IAHSS), "Homepage," retrieved September 29, 2006, from http://www.iahss.org.

37 National Association of School Safety and Law Enforcement Officers (NASSLEO), "Homepage," retrieved September 29, 2006, from http://www.nassleo.org.

38 Association of Certified Fraud Examiners (ACFE), "Homepage," retrieved September 29, 2006, from http://www.cfenet.com

39 The Security Industry Association, "Homepage," retrieved September 29, 2006, from http://www.siaonline.org.

40 Robert J. Fischer and Gion Green, *Introduction to Security*, 7th ed. (Burlington, MA: Elsevier/Butterworth-Heinemann, 2005), pp. 90–91.

41 Jack Lichtenstein, "Bush Signs Security Officer Employment Act," *ASIS Dynamics* (March/April 2005), pp. 1, 23–24.

42 ASIS International, "ASIS Guidelines," retrieved September 29, 2006, from http://www.asisonline.org/guidelines/guidelines.htm.

43 *Security Management* (August 2004), p. 12.

44 Ibid.

45 Cunningham, Strauchs, and Van Meter, *Private Security Patterns and Trends* (Washington, DC: U.S. Government Printing Office, 1991), p. 4.

46 "Security's Academic Side," *ASIS Dynamics* (January/February 1999), pp. 2, 16.

47 Davidson, "It IS What You Know," p. 72.

48 Ann Longmore-Etheridge, "Education Discussed at Symposium," *Security Management* (September 1999), pp. 220–221.

49 Davidson, "It IS What You Know," p. 75.

50 Ibid., p. 70.

51 "ASIS Display Promotes Security Careers," *Security Management* (July 1997), pp. 137–138.

52 Claire Hoffman, "As Anxiety Grows, So Does Field of Terror Study," *New York Times* (September 1, 2004), p. C1.

53 Hoffman, "As Anxiety Grows, So Does Field of Terror Study," p. C1; "Universities Do Their Part in Anti-Terror Effort," *Law Enforcement News* (Spring 2004), p. 4.

54 Davidson, "It IS What You Know," p. 69.

55 James N. Gilbert, "Investigative Ethics," in Michael J. Palmiotto, ed., *Critical Issues in Criminal Investigations*, 2nd ed. (Cincinnati, OH: Anderson Publishing, 1988), pp. 7–14.

56 Aristotle, *Nicomachean Ethics*, 1094(a), pp. 1–22.

57 Law Commission of Canada, *In Search of Security: The Roles of Public Police and Private Agencies* (Ottawa, Ontario: Law Commission of Canada, 2002).

58 Jenny Irish, *Policing for Profit: The Future of South Africa's Private Security Industry* (New York: United Nations Development Program, 1999).

59 Samuel Walker, *The Police in America: An Introduction*, 3rd ed. (Boston: McGraw-Hill, 1999), p. 58.

60 Iver Peterson, "Walking the Beat from Macy's to Sears: More Police Departments Assign Officers to a Private Domain, the Mall," *New York Times* (December 23, 1998), pp. B1, B5.

61 Ibid., p. B1.

62 Ibid., p. B5.

63 Marcia Chaiken and Jan Chaiken, *Public Policing—Privately Provided* (Washington, DC: National Institute of Justice, 1987).

64 Walker, *The Police in America: An Introduction*, 3rd ed., p. 58.

65 Rick Sarre, "Accountability and the Private Sector: Putting Accountability of Private Security under the Spotlight," *Security Journal* (March 1998), pp. 97–102.

66 Philip C. Stenning, "Accountability for Private Policing," in Stanley Einstein and Menachem Amir, eds., *Policing, Security and Democracy: Special Aspects of Democratic Policing* (Huntsville, TX: Office of International Criminal Justice, 2001), pp. 201–220.

67 Julia C. Mead, "Cops as Private Guards: To Serve and Protect Whom?," *New York Times* (August 8, 2004), Section 14, pp. 1, 5.

68 Ibid.

69 See Chapter 16 of Dempsey and Forst, *An Introduction to Policing*, 3rd ed.

70 Sherry L. Harowitz, "The New Centurions," *Security Management* (January 2003), pp. 51–58. See also Teresa Anderson, "A Year of Reassessment," *Security Management* (January 2003), pp. 61–65.

71 Harowitz, "The New Centurions," p. 52.

72 E. Meyr, "Tactical Response to Terrorism: The Concept and Its Application," *Law and Order* (March 1999), pp. 44–47.

73 C. Roda, *Executive Safety* (Washington, DC: National Criminal Justice Reference Service, 1997).

74 Richard Perez-Pena, "A Security Blanket, But with No Guarantees," *New York Times* (March 23, 2003), pp. A1, B14, B15.

75 Ibid.

76 "Summit Focuses on Homeland Security," *ASIS Dynamics* (January/February 2003), pp. 1, 12.

Chapter 2

1 "Policing for Profit: Welcome to the New World of Private Security," *The Economist* (April 19, 1997), pp. 20–24.

2 National Advisory Commission on Criminal Justice Standards and Goals, *Report of the Task Force on Private Security* (Washington, DC: U.S. Government Printing Office, 1976), p. 4.

3 Robert J. Fischer and Gion Green, *Introduction to Security*, 7th ed. (Boston: Elsevier/Butterworth-Heinemann, 2005) p. 21.

4 George E. Rush, *The Dictionary of Criminal Justice*, 4th ed. (Guilford, CT: The Dushkin Publishing Group Inc., 1994), p. 274.

5 John S. Dempsey and Linda S. Forst, *An Introduction to Policing*, 3rd ed. (Belmont, CA: Thomson/Wadsworth, 2005), p. 51.

6 William C. Cunningham and Todd H. Taylor, *The Growth of Private Security* (Washington, DC: U.S. Government Printing Office, 1984).

7 ASIS Online, "Professional Development: Security Disciplines," retrieved April 18, 2000, from http://www.asisonline.org/careerdisc.html.

8 ASIS Online, "Professional Development: Security Specialty Areas," retrieved April 18, 2000, from http://www.asisonline.org/careerspecialty.html.

9 William C. Cunningham, John J. Strauchs, and Clifford W. Van Meter, *The Hallcrest Report II: Private Security Trends: 1970–2000* (Boston: Butterworth-Heinemann, 1990), p. 2.

10 "Policing for Profit," p. 23.

11 David H. Bayley and Clifford D. Shearing, *The New Structure of Policing: Description, Conceptualization and Research Agenda* (Washington, DC: National Institute of Justice, 2001).

12 Samuel Walker, *The Police in America: An Introduction*, 3rd ed. (Boston: McGraw-Hill, 1999), p. 57.

13 "Policing for Profit," p. 23.

14 "Welcome to the New World of Private Security," *The Economist* (April 19, 1997); Tucker Carlson, "Safety Inc.," *Policy Review* (Summer 1995), pp. 72–73; William C. Cunningham and Todd H. Taylor, *The Hallcrest Report: Private Security and Police in America* (Portland, OR: Chancellor Press, 1985); Cunningham, Strauchs, and Van Meter, *The Hallcrest Report II*, also published by the National Institute of Justice in summary form for the government as Cunningham, Strauchs, and Van Meter, *Private Security Patterns and Trends* (Washington, DC: U.S. Government Printing Office, 1991); "ASIS Display Promotes Security Careers," *Security Management* (July 1997), pp. 137–138; Security Industry Association, "Homepage," retrieved January 20, 2000, from http://www.siaonline.org; and ASIS Online, "Professional Development: What Is Security?" retrieved August 18, 2000, from http://www.asisonline.org.

15 "George Smiley Joins the Firm," *Newsweek* (May 2, 1988), pp. 46–47.

16 Patricia Leigh Brown, "His Credo: Be Afraid, Be Very Afraid: Security Guru to the Stars, and his Book, Tap an Era's Anxieties," *New York Times* (July 14, 1997), p. C1.

17 Ibid.

18 Ibid.

19 Jay S. Albanese, *Criminal Justice* (Boston: Allyn & Bacon, 1999), p. 175.

20 The Atlanta Committee for the Olympic Games, *Securing the Safest Games Ever* (Atlanta: Author, n.d.).

21 "Olympic Committee to Review Salt Lake Security in Wake of Terror Attacks," *Associated Press* (September 17, 2001).

22 Leslie Wayne, "Security for the Homeland, Made in Alaska," *New York Times* (August 12, 2004), pp. C1, C6.

23 Law Commission of Canada, *In Search of Security: The Roles of Public Police and Private Agencies* (Ottawa, Ontario: Author, 2002).

24 Deborah Ewing, "Protection for the Rich," *Siyaya!* (Winter 1999), pp. 52–57.

25 Security Industry Authority, "Security Legislation," retrieved September 23, 2004, from http://www.the-sia.org.uk.

26 U.S. Department of Labor, Bureau of Labor Statistics, "Occupational Outlook Handbook," retrieved September 28, 2006, from http://www.bls.gov/oco/ocos.htm.

27 Ibid.

28 Ibid.

29 Ibid.

30 Ibid

31 Ibid.

32 Teresa Anderson, "The Key to Earnings," *Security Management* (January 2004), pp. 43–51.

33 Mike Moran, "On the Money," *Security Management* (August 20, 2006), pp. 80–88.

34 David H. Bayley, *Forces of Order: Police Behavior in Japan and the United States* (Berkeley: University of California Press, 1976).

35 Kristen A. Hughes, *Justice Expenditure and Employment in the United States, 2003* (Washington, DC: Bureau of Justice Statistics, U.S. Department of Justice, 2006), p. 1.

36 Ibid., p. 6.

37 Matthew J. Hickman and Brian A. Reaves, *Local Police Departments, 2003* (Washington, DC: Bureau of Justice Statistics, U.S. Department of Justice, 2006), p. 1; Reaves and Hickman, *Census of State and Local Law Enforcement Agencies, 2000* (Washington, DC: Bureau of Justice Statistics, 2002), p. 1; Reaves and Hickman, *Local Police Departments, 2000* (Washington, DC: Bureau of Justice Statistics, 2003), p. v.

38 Hughes, *Justice Expenditure and Employment in the United States, 2003*, p. 3.

39 Federal Bureau of Investigation, *Uniform Crime Reports, 2005* (Washington, DC: Author, 2006). Also see Dempsey and Forst, *An Introduction to Policing*, 3rd ed., Chapters 5 and 13; and Dempsey, *An Introduction to Public and Private Investigations*, 2nd ed., Chapter 2.

40 See Dempsey and Forst, *An Introduction to Policing*, 3rd ed., Chapter 5 for a discussion of the role of the police in society and Chapter 9 for a discussion of police patrol and omnipresence.

41 ASIS Online, "Professional Development: What Is Security?" retrieved April 20, 2000, from http://www.asisonline.org.

42 Robert J. Fischer and Gion Green, *Introduction to Security*, 6th ed. (Boston: Butterworth-Heinemann, 1998), p. 96.

43 National Advisory Commission on Criminal Justice Standards and Goals, *Report of the Task Force on Private Security*.

44 Cunningham and Taylor, *The Growing Role of Private Security* (Washington, DC: U.S. Government Printing Office, 1988).

45 James F. Kakalik and Sorrel Wildhorn, *Private Police in the United States, Vol. 2*, 5 vols. (Washington, DC: National Institute of Justice, 1971), p. 133.

46 Walker, *The Police in America*, p. 58.

47 Harvey N. Morley and Robert S. Fong, "Can We All Get Along? A Study of Why Strained Relations Continue to Exist between Sworn Law Enforcement and Private Security," *Security Journal*, 6(1995), pp. 85–92; and Dennis O'Leary, "Reflection on Police Privatization," *FBI Law Enforcement Bulletin*, 63(1994), pp. 21–26.

48 Cunningham, Strauchs, and Van Meter, *The Hallcrest Report II*, pp. 312–332.

49 Richard Behar, "Thugs in Uniform: Underscreened, Underpaid and Undertrained, Private Security Guards Are Too Often Victimizing Those They Are Hired to Protect," *Time* (March 2, 1992), pp. 44–47.

50 Mathew L. Wald, "U.S. Charges Impropriety in Security at Airport," *New York Times* (April 18, 2000), p. A18.

51 Joseph G. Deegan, "Mandated Training for Private Security," *FBI Law Enforcement Bulletin* (March 1987), pp. 6–8.

52 Bill Zalud, "Law and Order and Security," *Security* (June 1990), p. 55. Also see Fischer and Green, *Introduction to Security*, 6th ed., pp. 42–44.

53 Security Industry Authority, "Security Legislation," retrieved September 23, 2004, from http://www.the-sia.org.uk.

54 U.S. Department of Labor, Bureau of Labor Statistics, "Occupational Outlook Handbook," retrieved September 29, 2006, from http://www.bls.gov/oco/ocos.htm.

55 Ibid.

56 International Association of Security Investigative Regulators, "Licensing," retrieved October 5, 2005, from http://www.iasir.org.

57 U.S. Department of Labor, Bureau of Labor Statistics, "Occupational Outlook Handbook."

58 National Association of Legal Investigators, "Homepage," retrieved September 29, 2006, from http://www.nalionline.org.

59 *New York State General Business Law*, Article 7A.

60 U.S. Department of Labor, Bureau of Labor Statistics, "Occupational Outlook Handbook."

61 The Wackenhut Corporation, "Training Services," retrieved October 1, 2004, from http://www.wackenhut.com.

62 Securitas Online, "Homepage," retrieved October 1, 2004, from http://www.securitasinc.com

63 International Association of Security and Investigative Regulators, "Focus on Public Health and Safety," *IASIR Regulator*, 4(Winter 2004), p. 4.

64 Mike Gambrill, "Armored Car Personnel Training: Task-Specific Security Training Critical to All-Around Safety," *IASIR Regulator* (Winter 2004), pp. 3–4.

65 Ibid.

66 Ibid.

67 Brian Robertson, "Minimum Training Hours: An Outdated Concept?" *IASIR Regulator* (Winter 2004), p. 4.

68 Pamela A. Sexton-Alyea, "Police versus Private Security: Whom Do We Trust?" in Deborah Mitchell Robinson, ed., *Policing and Crime Prevention* (Upper Saddle River, NJ: Prentice Hall, 2002), pp. 31–52.

69 "FBI Checks Urged for Security Officers," *Security Management* (May 2004), p. 16.

70 "A Man the Guard Firms Love to Hate," *Time* (March 2, 1992), p. 47.

71 International Association of Security and Investigative Regulators (IASIR), "Homepage," retrieved September 29, 2006, from http://www.iasir.org.

72 Council on Licensure, Enforcement and Regulation (CLEAR), "Homepage," retrieved September 29, 2006, from http://www.clearhq.org.

73 ASIS International, "Private Security Officer Selection and Training Guideline," retrieved September 29, 2006, from http://www.asisonline.org/guidelines/guidelines.htm.

74 Security Industry Authority, "Security Legislation," retrieved September 23, 2004, from http://www.the-sia.org.uk.

75 Dennis Wagner, "Private Security Guards Play Key Roles," *The Arizona Republic* (January 22, 2006).

76 Ibid.

Chapter 3

1 Yomiuri, "Homeowners Seeking Safety in New Security Devices," *The Daily Yomiuri* (February 24, 2005), p. 8.

2 Wackenhut Consulting and Investigation Services, "Risk Assessments," retrieved March 29, 2005, from http://www.ci-wackenhut.com/risk%20assessments.htm.

3 P. J. Ortmeier, *Security Management,* 2nd ed. (Upper Saddle River, NJ: Pearson/Prentice Hall, 2005).

4 Robert J. Fischer and Gion Green, *Introduction to Security*, 7th ed. (Boston: Elsevier/Butterworth-Heinemann, 2005), p. 130.

5 George E. Curtis and R. Bruce McBride, *Proactive Security Administration* (Upper Saddle River, NJ: Pearson/Prentice Hall, 2005), pp. 43–44.

6 Ibid., pp. 44–45.

7 Clifford E. Simonsen, *Private Security in America: An Introduction* (Upper Saddle River, NJ: Prentice Hall, 1998), pp. 201–203.

8 Pinkerton Consulting and Investigations, "Security Consulting," retrieved March 29, 2005, from http://ci-pinkerton.com/secconsulting.html.

9 "News and Trends," *Security Management* (January 2005), p. 12.

10 Douglas R. Lane, "Surveys Point the Way," *Security Management* (March 1998), pp. 79–86.

11 Fischer and Green, *Introduction to Security*, 7th ed., pp. 131–138.

12 U.S. Department of Labor, Bureau of Labor Statistics, "Occupational Outlook Handbook, 2006."

13 Don Garbera, "Looking for a Few Good Guards," *Access Control & Security Systems Integration* (September 1996).

14 John Giuffo, "More Security in Store for Holidays," *Newsday* (November 27, 1998), p. A47.

15 Paul Herring, "Meeting Management's Expectations," *Security Management* (September 2004), pp. 81–84.

16 Ibid.

17 "George Smiley Joins the Firm," *Newsweek* (May 2, 1988), pp. 46–47.

18 David G. Patterson, "How Smart Is Your Setup?: The Central Station Is the Brains of the Corporate Security Set-up and Must Be Properly Designed for Quick Response," *Security Management* (March 2000), pp. 76–81.

19 Don Garbera, "Looking for a Few Good Guards."

20 Michael A. Gips, "Sporting a New Look: Access Control Trends At New Sports Arenas Show That Security Is Experiencing a Winning Season," *Security Management* (February 2000), pp. 48–56.

21 "Emergency Services," *Security Management* (May 2004), p. 22.

22 Milton Lipson, "Private Security: A Retrospective," *The Annals* (July 1988), pp. 11–22.

23 Ibid.

24 Bill Zalud, "Guarding Diversifies," *Security* (January 2004); "*Security's* Top Guarding Companies," *Security* (January 2004).

25 Timothy M. Wilson and Miles Bielec, "Security's Human Resourcefulness," *Security Management* (March 1999), pp. 97–104.

26 G. R. Haskell, "Security Takes Center Stage," *Security Management* (November 1997), pp. 32–39.

27 Mimi Hall, "Private Security Guards Are Homeland's Weak Link," *USA Today* (January 22, 2003), p. 1, retrieved December 28, 2004, from http:www.usatoday.com/news/nation/2003-01-22-security-cover_x.htm.

28 P. Ohlhausen, "Arms and Guards: Facing the Dangers," *Security Management* (February 1988), pp. 27–32.

29 "Disarmed Guards," *New York Times* (January 6, 1982).

30 National Association of Convenience Stores, "Security Guards," retrieved May 9, 2000, from http://www.cstorecentral.com/register/resource/resource/guards.html.

31 Terry Mann, "Policies That Pay Off: Although Robberies Are Down, They Are Becoming More Costly and Violent," *Security Management* (February 2000), pp. 42–46.

32 Damien Cave and Colin Moynihan, "Union Chief Says Hospital Needs to Arm Its Officers," *New York Times* (September 13, 2004), p. B3.

33 Rick Orlov, "Upgrades Urged for Security Guards," *LA Daily News* (April 7, 2006).

34 Steven W. McNally, "Turn Away Turnover," *Security* (September 2004).

35 Michael A. Gips, "Safe and Secure," *Security Management* (February 2005), pp. 83–90.

36 Louise Arnheim, "A Tour of Guard Patrol Systems: Before Buying an Electronic Guard Tour System, Review the Tips from These Firsthand Tales," *Security Management* (November 1999), p. 48.

37 Don Garbera, "Looking for a Few Good Guards."

38 "Working Wise: GPS Tracks Journey," *Security Management* (February 2005), pp. 22–23. The company that provides the location-based mobile workforce management program for Journey Security Services is the Xora Corporation. It can be accessed at http://www.xora.com. Retrieved March 7, 2005, from http://xora.com/about/about_us.html.

39 "Working Wise: GPS Tracks Journey."

40 Service Employees International Union, "Homepage," retrieved December 28, 2004, from http://www.seiu.org; and Joe Matthews, "Union Hopes to Organize L.A. Security Guards," *Los Angeles Times* (June 26, 2006).

41 National Association of Security Companies, "About NASCO," retrieved December 28, 2004, from http://www.nasco.org.

42 Anthony Ramirez, "Golden Noses; Bomb Sniffers Are in Demand, Earning Far More Than Treats," *New York Times* (August 12, 2004), pp. B1, B6.

43 Ibid.

44 Evan Malakates, "A Cold, Wet Nose for Trouble," *Newsday* (March 31, 2005), p. A47.

45 Ibid.

46 Ramirez, "Golden Noses," pp. B1, B6.

47 Security Industry Association, "Access Control Fact Sheet," retrieved March 8, 2005, from http://www.siaonline.org.

48 Steven P. Pharis, "The Best of All Possible Systems," *Security Management* (January 1999), pp. 65–69.

49 "Looking at Locking," *Security Management* (January 1999), p. 66.

50 Steven P. Pharis, "The Best of All Possible Systems."

51 Marta Roberts, "Laptops Don't Have Legs," *Security Management* (January 2005), pp. 20–23. For further information on guest/visitor badge systems, see "Problems Passé in Passaic Valley," *Security Management* (February 2005), pp. 25–25. The article discusses the Passaic Valley Water Commission in Northeast New Jersey, which has more than fifty visitors and temporary contractors entering its treatment facility on a daily basis.

52 Michael A. Gips, "Sporting a New Look."

53 Mann, "Policies That Pay Off," pp. 42–46.

54 Jay Romano, "The Great Debate: Security vs. Privacy," *New York Times* (March 6, 2005), p. RE11.

55 "Manhattan: Tenants File Suit in ID Plan," *New York Times* (March 29, 2005), p. B6.

56 "Tenants Get Reprieve in Key-Card Fight," *New York Times* (March 30, 2005), p. B5.

57 Keith W. Strandberg, "Present and Future of Biometrics," *Law Enforcement Technology* (August 1999), pp. 74–76.

58 B. Zalud, "Biometrics Bring Human Sense to Electronic Access Control," *Security* (January 1989), pp. 62–64, 66, 68. See also B. Siuru, "Who Are You?" *Corrections Technology and Management* (November/December 1998), pp. 32–35.

59 S. L. Harowitz, "More Than Meets the Eye," *Security Management* (February 1993), pp. 25–28.

60 Brad Stone, "Tired of All Those Passwords? Here Are Some Alternatives," *Newsweek* (November 30, 1998), p. 12.

61 Michael A. Gips, "News and Trends," *Security Management* (March 2005), p. 14.

62 Barnaby J. Feder, "Technology Strains to Find Menace in the Crowd; Face Recognition Attempts to Heal Its Black Eye," *New York Times* (May 31, 2004), pp. C1, C2.

63 "News and Trends," *Security Management*, January 2005, p. 12.

64 "Saudi Biometric Security Move," *AME Info* (March 31, 2005), retrieved April 2, 2005, from http://www.ameinfo.com/cgi-bin/cms/page.cgi?page=print;link=56860.

65 "Emerging Biometric Technologies," retrieved September 17, 2006, from http://www.securityinfowatch.com.

66 Peter Wayner, "Closed-Door Policy: Princeton's Electronic Security System, Designed to Protect Students, Makes Some Feel Safer and Others Uneasy," *New York Times* (November 12, 1998), pp. E1, E8, E9.

67 Christopher Marquis, "Deep Security Flaws Seen at State Dept.: Recent Lapses Are Part of a Pattern of Vulnerability," *New York Times* (May 11, 2000), p. A26.

68 Peter Piazza, "The Smart Cards Are Coming . . . Really," *Security Management* (January 2005), pp. 41–55.

69 Alan Keyes, "One If By Land, Two If By Wireless," *Security Management* (November 1999), pp. 39–46.

70 National Burglar and Fire Alarm Association, "Industry Statistics—Electronic Security Industry," retrieved September 29, 2006, from http://www.alarm.org.

71 "Researchers See $13.5 Billion in Monitoring Demand by 2010," retrieved May 17, 2006, from http://www.securitysales.com.

72 Alan Keyes, "One If By Land, Two If By Wireless."

73 Ibid.

74 Paul J. Steiner Jr., "Abducting the Abductors," *Security Management* (March 2000), pp. 48–56.

75 Tina Kelly, "Umbilical-Cord Alarm Failed to Stop Hospital Kidnapping," *New York Times* (April 9, 2000), p. 35.

76 National Burglar and Fire Alarm Association (NBFAA), "Homepage," retrieved September 29, 2006, from http://www.alarm.org.

77 NBFAA, "NBFAA Education and Training," retrieved September 29, 2006, from http://www.alarm.org.

78 Alarm Industry Research and Educational Foundation, "Homepage," retrieved September 29, 2006, from http://www.airef.org.

79 Security Industry Alarm Coalition, "Homepage," retrieved September 29, 2006, from http://www.siacinc.org.

80 NBFAA, "False Alarms," retrieved March 8, 2005, from http://www.alarm.org/pressreleases/falsealarmqa.html.

81 Chris Paschenko, "False Alarm," *Decatur Daily News* (January 25, 2005).

82 False Alarm Reduction Association (FARA), "Homepage," retrieved September 30, 2006, from http://www.faraonline.org.

83 FARA, "Model Ordinances," retrieved September 30, 2006, from http://www.faraonline.org/html/model_ordinances.asp.

84 California City Puts Alarm Owners on Notice," *Law Enforcement News* (February 2005), p. 5.

85 Central Station Alarm Association (CSAA), "Homepage," retrieved September 30, 2006, from http://www.csaaul.org.

86 CSAA, "CSAA Position Papers: False Alarms," retrieved September 30, 2006, from http://www.csaaul.org/CSAAFalseAlarmsPaper.htm.

87 Deena Kara, Jonathan Kilworth, and Martin Gill, "What Makes CCTV Effective?" *Intersect: The Journal of International Security*, 13(9, September 2003), pp. 293–296.

88 Michael Unger, "For Your Eyes Only: How to Design a Surveillance System That Gets Results," *Campus Safety Journal*, 11(8, September 2003), pp. 12–14.

89 Ronnie Garrett, "Protecting Your Assets: Day and Night," *Law Enforcement Technology*, 29(6, June 2002), pp. 44–52.

90 Don L. Lewis, "Surveillance Video in Law Enforcement," *Journal of Forensic Identification*, 54(5, September/October 2004), pp. 547–559.

91 Tom Chronister, "Digital Video Recorder Revolution," *Law Enforcement Technology*, 29(10, October 2002), pp. 128–134.

92 Pete Conway, "Managing CCTV: The Way to Get More from Your Systems," *Global Security Review* (March/April 2002), pp. 6–8.

93 Ron Lander, "Cheap Trick: Are Fake Video Cameras Inexpensive Solutions or Lawsuits Waiting to Happen?" *Campus Safety Journal*, 10(9, September 2002), pp. 16–17.

94 "Japan Firm to Sell High-Capacity Digital Surveillance Recorder," *Asia Pulse* (March 2, 2005), LexisNexis, retrieved March 2, 2005, from http://www.bnp.com/security-news/new-technology.htm.

95 Lander, "Cheap Trick."

96 Chris A. Williams, "Police Surveillance and the Emergence of CCTV in the 1960s," *Crime Prevention and Community Safety: An International Journal*, 5(3, 2003), pp. 27–37.

97 Anya Sostek, "Here's Looking at You: Electronic Surveillance Systems Make Some Law-Abiding Citizens Feel Safer, They Make Others Very Nervous," *Governing*, 15(11, August 2002), pp. 44–45; Brandon C. Welsh and David P. Farrington, "Surveillance for Crime Prevention in Public Space: Results and Policy Choices in Britain and America," *Criminology and Public Policy*, 3(3, July 2004), pp. 497–525; Welsh and Farrington, "Effects of Closed-Circuit Television on Crime," *The Annals*, 587(May 2003), pp. 110–135; "Anti-Crime Cameras Help in 180 Arrests," *The Gloucester Citizen* (February 25, 2005), LexisNexis, retrieved March 2, 2005, from http://www.bnp.com/security-news/new-technology.htm; Michael R. Chatterton and Samantha J. Frenz, "Closed-Circuit Television: Its Role in Reducing Burglaries and the Fear of Crime in Sheltered Accommodation for the Elderly," *Security Journal*, 5(1994), pp. 133–139; Barry Poyner, "Situational Crime Prevention in Two Parking Facilities," *Security Journal*, 2(1991), pp. 96–101; Nicholas Tilly, *Understanding Car Parks, Crime and CCTV: Evaluation Lessons from Safer Cities: Crime Prevention Unit Paper 42* (London: Home Office, 1993); Ben Brown, *CCTV in Town Centres: Three Case Studies: Crime Detection and Prevention Series Paper 68* (London: Home Office, 1995); Martin Gill and Karryn Loveday, "What Do Offenders Think about CCTV?" *Crime Prevention and Community Safety: An International Journal*, 5(3, 2003), pp. 17–25; Stig Winge and Johannes Knutson, "Evaluation of the CCTV Scheme at Oslo Central Railway Station," *Crime Prevention and Community Safety: An International Journal*, 5(3, 2003), pp. 49–59; and Sam Waples and Martin Gill, "Effectiveness of Redeployable CCTV," *Crime Prevention and Community Safety*, 8(1, February 2006), pp. 1–16.

98 Martin Gill and Angela Spriggs, *Assessing the Impact of CCTV* (London: Great Britain Home Office Research Development and Statistics Directorate, 2005).

99 Tom Levesley and Amanda Martin, *Police Attitudes To and Use of CCTV* (London: Great Britain Home Office Research Development and Statistics Directorate, 2005); and Angela Spriggs, Javier Argomaniz, Martin Gill, and Jane Bryan, *Public Attitudes towards CCTV: Results from the Pre-Intervention Public Attitude Survey Carried Out in Areas Implementing CCTV* (London: Great Britain Home Office Research Development and Statistics Directorate, 2005).

100 John D. Woodward Jr., *Privacy vs. Security: Electronic Surveillance in the Nation's Capital* (Santa Monica, CA: RAND Corporation, 2002).

101 Williams, "Police Surveillance and the Emergence of CCTV in the 1960s."

102 Laura J. Nichols, *Use of CCTV/Video Cameras in Law Enforcement, Executive Brief* (Alexandria, VA: International Association of Chiefs of Police, 2001). For information on police use of video surveillance, see Jerry Ratcliffe, *Video Surveillance of Public Places* (Washington, DC: Office of Community-Oriented Policing Services, 2006).

103 Leonor Vivanco, "More Surveillance Cameras Planned throughout Redlands," *San Bernardino County Sun* (March 24, 2005).

104 Sostek, "Here's Looking at You," pp. 44–45.

105 Suzanne Smalley, "Chelsea to Mount Security Cameras Citywide," *Boston Globe* (June 4, 2005), pp. A1, A16.

106 Jennifer Lee, "Police Seek to Increase Surveillance; Want 400 Cameras for Public Access," *New York Times* (May 31, 2005), p. B3.

107 Grant Fredericks, "CCTV: A Law Enforcement Tool," *Police Chief*, 71(8, August 2004), pp. 68–74.

108 Michael E. Ruane, "Security Camera New Star Witness," *Washington Post* (October 8, 2005), p. B1.

109 Fredericks, "CCTV: A Law Enforcement Tool."

110 Jennifer Lee, "Caught on Tape, Then Just Caught; Private Cameras Transform Police Work," *New York Times* (May 22, 2005), pp. 33, 36.

111 Ibid.

112 Michael E. Ruane, "Security Camera New Star Witness."

113 Jolene Hernon, "CCTV: Constant Cameras Track Violators," *NIJ Journal*, 249(July 2003), pp. 16–23.

114 Katherine E. Finkelstein, "Officials Admit Wrong Man Was Held in Street Attack: Morgenthau Calls Evidence Overwhelming," *New York Times* (July 27, 2000), p. B3; and Joyce Purnick, "The Truth, As Always, Is Stranger," *New York Times* (July 27 2000), p. B1.

115 Jennifer Lee, "Police Seek to Increase Surveillance."

116 Nancy Salem, "Security Firms Have Their Eyes, Cards, Cameras on You," *Script Howard News Service* (February 18, 2005).

117 "News and Trends," *Security Management* (February 2005), p. 16.

118 Sherry L. Harowitz, "Unification Theory: How Advances in Connectivity among Markets, Companies, and Systems Are Reshaping Security Operations," *Security Management* (January 2005), pp. 75–80.

119 Gips, "News and Trends," *Security Management* (March 2005), p. 14.

120 Harowitz, "Unification Theory."

121 Salem, "Security Firms Have Their Eyes, Cards, Cameras on You"; and "The Ultimate Integration—Video Motion Detection," retrieved July 7, 2006, from http://www.securityinfowatch.com.

122 Lee, "Caught on Tape."

123 Ibid.

124 Don Thompson, "Private Security Guards' Training Boosted in Anti-Terror Effort," *San Francisco Gate* (August 2, 2005).

125 Bryan Virasami, "City Launches Security Training Program," *Newsday* (April 27, 2005); and Abeer Allam, "For Security Guards, Some Lessons in Living up to the Name," *New York Times* (July 9, 2005).

Chapter 4

1. Anemona Hartocollis, "Port Authority Found Negligent in 1993 Bombing," *New York Times* (October 27, 2005), p. 1.
2. Audrey J. Aronsohn, "Teaching Criminals the Cost of Crime," *Security Management* (May 1999), pp. 63–68.
3. Mark Lipman and W. R. McGraw, "Employee Theft: A $40 Billion Industry," *The Annals* (July 1988), pp. 51–59.
4. "Inside the Private Justice System," *Security* (August 1987), pp. 44–49.
5. "Policing for Profit: Welcome to the New World of Private Security," *The Economist* (April 19, 1997), pp. 21–24.
6. "Policing for Profit," p. 24.
7. Stephanie McCrummen, "Spotting Shoplifters Takes a Little Stealth," *Newsday* (November 30, 1998), p. A8.
8. *Burdeau v. McDowell*, 256 U.S. 465 (1921).
9. *Burdeau v. McDowell*, 256 U.S. 475 (1921).
10. Alan Kaminsky, "An Arresting Policy," *Security Management* (May 1999), pp. 59–61.
11. Ibid.
12. "Best Practice #1: Detaining Shoplifting Suspects," retrieved April 22, 2005, from http://www.aipsc.org.
13. "Put Procedures in Place," *Security Management* (May 1999), p. 60.
14. Aronsohn, "Teaching Criminals the Cost of Crime."
15. L. W. Klemke, *The Sociology of Shoplifting: Boosters and Snitches Today* (Westport, CT: Praeger, 1992).
16. Richard C. Hollinger and J. L. Davis, *2002 National Retail Security Survey: Final Report* (Gainesville: University of Florida, 2003).
17. *State of West Virginia v. William H. Muegge*, 360 S.E. 216 (1987).
18. Charles Nemeth, *Private Security and the Law*, 3rd ed. (Burlington, MA: Elsevier Butterworth-Heinemann, 2005), p. 170.
19. William C. Cunningham, John J. Strauchs, and Clifford W. Van Meter, *Private Security Trends 1970 to 2000, The Hallcrest Reports II* (Burlington, MA: Butterworth, 1990), pp. 34–35.
20. Nemeth, *Private Security and the Law*, p. 116.
21. Patricia A. Patrick and Shaun L. Gabbidon, "What's True about False Arrests," *Security Management* (October 2004), pp. 49–56.
22. Richard H. de Treville and Ann Longmore-Etheridge, "Time to Check Out Liability Trends," *Security Management* (February 2004), pp. 61–65.
23. Ibid.
24. Ibid.
25. For an excellent discussion of off-duty police officers working for private security concerns and the liability and constitutional issues involved, see David H. Peck, "When Police Walk the Security Beat," *Security Management* (October 1999), pp. 39–45.
26. Peck, "When Police Walk the Security Beat."
27. *Groom v. Safeway, Inc.*, 973 F. Supp. 987, (W.D. Wash. 1997); for further information about Section 1983 suits, see John S. Dempsey and Linda S. Forst, *An Introduction to Policing*, 3rd ed. (Belmont, CA: Thomson/Wadsworth, 2005), pp. 406–407.
28. Section 1983 U.S. Code 42 (1871).
29. *Wilson v. O'Leary*, 895 F.2d 378 (C.A. 7 [Ill.] 1990).
30. Christopher Vail, "Presenting Winning Testimony in Court," *Law and Order* (June 1992), pp. 96–99.
31. Robert L. Donigan, Edward C. Fisher, et al., *The Evidence Handbook*, 4th ed. (Evanston, IL: Traffic Institute, Northwestern University, 1980), pp. 208–214.
32. U.S. Department of Homeland Security, "Homeland Security Act of 2002," retrieved October 27, 2005, from http://www.dhs.gov.
33. Public Law 107-56, USA Patriot Act of 2001.
34. Hartocollis, "Port Authority Found Negligent in 1993 Bombing."
35. Ibid.

Chapter 5

1. Lawrence W. Sherman, et al., *Preventing Crime: What Works, What Doesn't, What's Promising* (Washington, DC: U.S. Department of Justice, 1997), pp. 2–13.
2. George L. Kelling, "On the Accomplishments of the Police," in Maurice Punch, ed., *Control of the Police Organization* (Cambridge, MA: MIT Press, 1983), p. 164.
3. Federal Bureau of Investigation (FBI), *Uniform Crime Reports, 2005* (Washington, DC: Author, 2006).
4. Ibid.
5. Ibid.
6. Department of Justice, *Sourcebook of Criminal Justice Statistics, 2003* (Washington, DC: National Institute of Justice, 2004), Table 82.
7. Blaine Harden, "City Block Puts Its Thumbs to Work as Crime Busters," *New York Times* (September 13, 2000), pp. A1, B3.
8. James Q. Wilson and George Kelling, "'Broken Windows': The Police and Neighborhood Safety," *Atlantic Monthly* (March 1982), pp. 29–38; also see John S. Dempsey and Linda S. Forst, *An Introduction to Policing*, 3rd ed. (Belmont, CA: ITP/Wadsworth, 2005).
9. Wesley G. Skogan, *Disorder and Decline: Crime and the Spiral of Decay in American Neighborhoods* (New York: Free Press, 1990), pp. 21–50; also see Dempsey and Forst, *An Introduction to Policing*, 3rd ed.
10. See Chapter 10 of Dempsey, *An Introduction to Policing*, 2nd ed. (Belmont, CA: West/Wadsworth, 1999), pp. 229–252.
11. Ibid., pp. 53, 217–221.
12. Deborah Lamm Weisel, *Burglary in Single-Family Houses* (Washington, DC: U.S. Department of Justice, Office of Community-Oriented Policing Services, 2002).
13. David Kushner, "Stop, Thief! You've Got Mail: Alarm Systems Are Poised to Be the Command Centers of the Wired Home," *New York Times* (March 9, 2000), p. G1; see also Ellen Mitchell, "Getting Wired," *Newsday* (June 30, 2000), pp. C6, C7.
14. John Gochenouer, "Condo Can Do," *Security Management* (January 2000), pp. 69–70, 115–119.
15. Felicity Barringer and James Dao, "100 Investigators Gather at Subdivision, Seeking Clues to Vast Arson," *New York Times* (December 8, 2004), p. A18; and Barringer, "Arsonists Tried to Burn More Homes, Maryland Officials Say," *New York Times* (December 9, 2004), p. A24.
16. Gary Carson and David A. Armstrong, "The Use of Private Security in Public Housing: A Case Study," *Journal of Security Administration*, 17(1, October 1994), pp. 53–61.
17. Terry Pristin, "A Push for Security Gates That Invite Window Shopping," *New York Times* (August 1, 2000), p. B8.
18. Sherman et al., *Preventing Crime: What Works, What Doesn't, What's Promising*, pp. 7–17.

19 National Association of Convenience Stores (NACS), "Homepage," retrieved December 10, 2004, from, http://www.nacsonline.com.

20 NACS, "Convenience Store Industry Safety Research," retrieved December 10, 2004, from http://www.nacsonline.com/NACS/Resource/Store/Operations/research.htm.

21 Ronald D. Hunter and C. Ray Jeffrey, "Preventing Convenience Store Robbery through Environmental Design," in Ronald V. Clarke (ed.), *Situational Crime Prevention: Successful Case Studies* (Albany, NY: Harrow & Heston, 1972); Nancy G. LaVigne, *Crimes of Convenience: An Analysis of Criminal Decision-Making and Convenience Store Crime in Austin, Texas* (master's thesis, University of Texas at Austin, 1991); NACS, *Convenience Store Security Report and Recommendations: November 1991* (Alexandria, VA: Author, 1991); Wayland Clifton Jr., *Convenience Store Robberies in Gainesville, Florida: An Intervention Strategy by the Gainesville Police Department* (Gainesville, FL: Gainesville Police Department, 1987); Sherman et al., *Preventing Crime: What Works, What Doesn't, What's Promising*, pp. 7–16; Lisa C. Bellamy, "Situational Crime Prevention and Convenience Store Robbery," *Security Journal*, 7(1996), pp. 41–52; Jerry V. Wilson, *Gainesville Convenience Store Ordinance: Findings of Fact, Conclusions and Recommendations* (Crime Control Research Corporation, 1990); NACS, "Convenience Store Industry Safety Research," retrieved December 10, 2004, from, http://www.nacsonline.com/NACS/resource/storeoperations/research,htm.

22 NACS, "Talking Points: Multiple Clerks as a Safety Strategy," retrieved December 10, 2004, from http://www.nacsonline.com/NACS/Resource/StoreOperations/multiple_clerks.htm; NACS, "Talking Points: Concealed Weapons," retrieved December 10, 2004, from http://www.nacsonline.com/NACS/Resource/StoreOperations/weapons.htm; NACS, "Talking Points: Bullet-Resistant Barriers," retrieved December 10, 2004, from http://www.nacsonline.com/NACS/Resource/StoreOperations/barriers.htm; Rosemary J. Erickson, "Two Clerks," *NACS Online*, retrieved December 10, 2004, from http://www.nacsonline.com/NACS/Resource/StoreOperations/store_031100_ir.htm; NACS, "Robbery Awareness/Deterrence: Steps for Safer Stores," retrieved December 10, 2004, from http://www.nacsonline.com/NACS/Resource/StoreOperations/robbery_awareness_072700.htm; NACS, "Talking Points: Security Guards," retrieved December 10, 2004, from http://www.nacsonline.com/NACS/Resource/StoreOperations/store_072500_ir.htm; NACS, "Convenience Store Security at the Millennium," retrieved December 10, 2004, from http://www.nacsonline.com/NACS/Resource/StoreOperations/security_at_millennium.htm; and NACS, "General Liability Insurance: False Arrest, Wrongful Termination, Liquor Liability," retrieved December 10, 2004, from http://www.nacsonline.com/NACS/Resource/StoreOperations/general_insurance_liability.htm.

23 Michael A. Gips, "Talking Turkey," *Security Management* (January 2000), pp. 26, 31.

24 G. Thompson, "Putting Security on the Shopping List," *Security Management* (May 1998), pp. 28, 30–33.

25 A. Beck and A. Willis, "Buying into Security's Retail Value," *Security Management* (May 1998), pp. 35–39.

26 Iver Peterson, "Walking the Beat from Macy's to Sears: More Police Departments Assign Officers to a Private Domain, the Mall," *New York Times* (December 23, 1998), pp. B1, B5.

27 Gang Lee, Richard C. Hollinger, and Dean A. Dabney, "Relationship between Crime and Private Security at U.S. Shopping Centers," *American Journal of Criminal Justice*, 23(2, Spring 1999), pp. 157–177.

28 Peterson, "Walking the Beat," pp. B1, B5.

29 Ibid., p. B5.

30 Ibid.

31 Sana Siwolop, "Rewiring Roosevelt Field for Retailer Alert System," *New York Times* (August 2, 2000), p. B7.

32 Robert Block, "At America's Malls, Grim Preparations for the Unthinkable," *Wall Street Journal* (August 8, 2005), p. A1.

33 Vanessa Drucker, "Office Building Security Is Getting Quite Smart," *National Real Estate Investor* (March 1, 2006).

34 Michael Fickes, "Safeguards on the Rise," *Access Control & Security Systems* (July 8, 2006).

35 Doug Tsuruoka, "Firms Hike Security, Move Staff, Assets in Response to 9/11," *Investor's Business Daily* (September 1, 2006); and David Wighton, "Anxiety Remains on Wall Street Disaster Planning," *Financial Times* (September 8, 2006).

36 Information provided by Temtec Corporation, Branford, CT 06405.

37 Lisa W. Foderaro, "Study Weighs Terror Threat to Kensico Dam," *New York Times* (August 20, 2004), p. B7; Kirk Semple, "Road over Kensico Dam Stays Closed, Executive Says," *New York Times* (September 3, 2004), p. B5.

38 Simon Romero, "If Oil Supplies Were Disrupted, Then . . . ," *New York Times* (May 28, 2004), pp. C1, C6.

39 "Chemical Facilities Remain Vulnerable," *Security Management* (May 2004), p. 20; and "U.S. Wastewater Sites Need More Security Funding—GAO," *Reuters* (May 1, 2006).

40 Andrew C. Revkin, "Few Measures Exist to Avert Truck Bombs, Experts Say," *New York Times* (August 3, 2004), p. A12.

41 Matthew L. Wald, "Review of Nuclear Plant Security Is Faulted," *New York Times* (September 15, 2004), p. A18; L. Wald, "Battle Swirls on Security at A-Plants," *New York Times* (August 6, 2004), p. A15.

42 John F. Kirch, "Following the Drugs: Tough Enforcement of Policies Has Dramatically Cut the Number of Lost or Stolen Narcotics at This Hospital," *Security Management* (January 2000), pp. 24–25.

43 International Association for Healthcare Security and Safety, "Homepage," retrieved December 10, 2004, from http://www.iahss.org/introduce.htm.

44 American Hotel and Lodging Association (AH&LA), "Homepage," retrieved December 10, 2004, from http://www.ahma.com.

45 Ibid.

46 American Hotel & Lodging Educational Institute, "Professional Certification," retrieved December 10, 2004, http://www.ei-ahla.org/certification_clsd.asp; http://www.ei-ahla.org/certification_clss.asp; and http://www.ei-ahla.org/certification_clso.asp.

47 International Hotel and Restaurant Association, "Homepage," retrieved December 10, 2004, from http://www.ih-ra.com/def.html.

48 Federal Protective Service (FPS), "Mission," retrieved December 17, 2004 from http://www.ice.gov/graphics/fps/federalbuildings.htm.

49 Stephen Labaton, "Investigators Identify Security Breaches at Several U.S. Agencies," *New York Times* (May 25, 2000), p. A17; Christopher Marquis, "Lost Laptop Leads Agency to Rethink Its Security," *New York Times* (April 23, 2000), p. 14; and Marquis, "Albright Orders Staff Shake-Up over Security," *New York Times* (April 25, 2000), pp. A1, A21.

50 U.S. Capitol Police, "Homepage," retrieved December 17, 2004, from, http://www.uscapitolpolice.gov/home.html; Michael Janofsky, "As Cost of Capitol Visitors Center Grows, So Does the Criticism," *New York Times* (December 17, 2004), p. A20; and Laurie Kellman, "Capitol Police Chief Requests Independent Probe of Security Breach," *Associated Press* (September 27, 2006).

51 Kellman, "Capitol Police Chief Requests Independent Probe of Security Breach."

52 James Glanz, "Panel Fears Security at Labs Hurts Foreign Hiring," *New York Times* (May 16, 2000), p. A16.

53 James Risen, "Missing Nuclear Data Found behind a Los Alamos Copier," *New York Times* (June 11, 2000), pp. A1, A11; and David Ballingrud, "How Well Are U.S. Secrets Protected?: Successfully, Experts Say, But as the Recent Los Alamos Incident Proves, Electronic Storage Makes It Much More Difficult," *St. Petersburg Times* (June 18, 2000), p. 1A.

54 Leslie Wayne, "Security for the Homeland, Made in Alaska," *New York Times* (August 12, 2004), pp. C1, C6.

55 Sarah Lyall, "Security in Britain Full of Holes, with Another Palace Breached," *New York Times* (September 25, 2004), p. A4.

56 Bernard D. Gollotti, "Studious Attention to Security," *Security Management* (September 2004), pp. 119–125.

57 "Many Colleges Not Seeing Clery," *Security Management* (September 2004), p. 16; and "Performance of the Week," *Time* (September 27, 2004), p. 18.

58 Philip Walzer, "Reports Can Sell Short Crime Rates at Colleges," *Virginia Pilot* (March 31, 2006).

59 Stephen F. Garst, "The School Year in Pictures," *Security Management* (March 2004), pp. 74–79.

60 Michael Cooper, "The Walls Have Ears, and Other High-Tech Crime Gadgets," *New York Times* (April 19, 2000), p. C4

61 Walter Gibbs and Carol Vogel, "Munch's 'Scream' Is Stolen from a Crowded Museum in Oslo," *New York Times* [Electronic version], retrieved August 8, 2004, from http://www.nytimes.com/2004/08/23/international/europe/23scream.html.

62 Gibbs, "Stolen Munch Paintings Are Recovered," *New York Times* (September 1, 2006), p. B3.

63 Lyall, "Stolen Art Can Reappear in Unexpected Ways," *New York Times* (August 26, 2004), pp. E1, E5.

64 Randy Kennedy, "New York Museum Officials Confident Despite Oslo Theft," *New York Times* [Electronic version], retrieved August 24, 2004, from http://www.nytimes.com/2004/08/24/arts/design/24muse.html.

65 Lyall, "Stolen Art Can Reappear in Unexpected Ways."

66 "Interpol's Greatest Hits," *New York Times* (August 29, 2004), p. WK2.

67 Michael Cooper, "The Walls Have Ears."

68 Kennedy, "New York Museum Officials Confident Despite Oslo Theft."

69 Andrew Jacobs, "After Dark, the Stuffed Animals Turn Creepy; Overnight Guards and Scientists Feel Glassy Eyes on Them," *New York Times* (September 29, 2004), pp. B1, B66.

70 Kennedy, "New York Museum Officials Confident Despite Oslo Theft."

71 Association of College and Research Libraries (ACRL), "Guidelines Regarding Thefts in Libraries," retrieved December 18, 2004, from http://www.ala.org/; ACRL, "Guidelines for the Security of Rare Books, Manuscripts, and Other Special Collections," retrieved December 18, 2004, from http://www.ala.org/ala/acrl/acrlstandards/guidelinesecurity.htm; and "Library Security," *Security Management* (February 2000), p. 17.

72 Kim Martineau, "Map Dealer Sentenced to 3½ Years," *Hartford Courant* (September 27, 2006).

73 "From the Grave to the Cradle," *Security Management* (October 1999), p. 16.

74 ASIS International, "2005 Training Offerings for ASIS International," retrieved December 18, 2004, from http://www.asisonline.org/education/programs/training.htm.

75 John Sullivan and Randy Kennedy, "Armed Intruder Exposes Limits of Air Security," *New York Times* (July 29, 2000), pp. A1, B6.

76 Michael L. Wald, "Checking Airport Checkers," *New York Times* (January 17, 1999), p. WR6; "Checkpoint Checkup," *Newsweek* (May 1, 2000); and Teresa Anderson, "Airport Security Fails Test," *Security Management* (February 2000), pp. 73–75.

77 See Chapter 16 of John S. Dempsey and Linda S. Forst, *An Introduction to Policing*, 3rd ed.; and Chapter 13 of Dempsey, *Introduction to Investigations*, 2nd ed. (Belmont, CA: Thomson/Wadsworth, 2003) for a complete description of the events of September 11, 2001, and complete details of the assumption of the duties of airport security by the Department of Homeland Security.

78 Dempsey and Forst, *An Introduction to Policing*, 3rd ed., p. 424; Dempsey, *Introduction to Investigations*, p. 356; and U.S. Department of Homeland Security, "DHS Organization," retrieved March 25, 2003, from http:www.dhs.gov/dhspublic/interapp/editorial/editorial_0086.xml.

79 Dempsey and Forst, "You Are There: Then and Now: Changes at Airports and at Immigration," in *An Introduction to Policing*, 3rd ed., p. 432.

80 Joe Sharkey, "Many Women Say Airport Pat-Downs Are a Humiliation," *New York Times* (November 23, 2004), pp. A1, C11.

81 Del Quentin Wilber, "Newly Banned Items Often Fly Past Airport Screeners," *Washington Post* (September 13, 2006), p. A1.

82 Kathleen McLaughlin, "Airports to Screen Workers," *Herald Tribune* [Electronic version], retrieved October 15, 2006, from http://www.heraldtribune.com.

83 Joe Sharkey, "Recently, Checked Bags Have Become Grab Bags," *New York Times* (August 17, 2004), p. C8; Susan Stellin, "When Screeners Open Your Bags," *New York Times* (May 30, 2004), p. TR2; Wald, "U.S. to Pay Fliers $1.5 Million for Pilfering of Checked Bags," *New York Times* (September 10, 2004), p. A18; "A Feel for Airline Security," *Time* (September 13, 2004), p. 24; Sharkey, "Many Women Say Airport Pat-Downs Are a Humiliation"; Mimi Hall, "Airport Screeners Missed Weapons," *USA Today* [Electronic version], retrieved December 13, 2004, from http://www.usatoday.com/travel/news/2004/09/22-weapons_x.htm; and Thomas Frank, "Crisis Seen in Luggage Screening," *USA Today* (September 19, 2006).

84   John Markoff and Eric Lichtblau, "Gaps Seen in 'Virtual Border' Security System," *New York Times* (May 31, 2004), pp. C1, C3.

85   Sharkey, "A Rising Number of Laptop Computers Are Being Stolen at Airports by Organized Rings of Thieves," *New York Times* (March 29, 2000), p.C10.

86   DHS, "Fact Sheet: Rail and Transit Security Initiatives," retrieved December 13, 2004, from http://www.dhs.gov/dhspublic/interapp/press_release/press_release_0376.xml.

87   DHS, "Travel and Transportation," retrieved December 13, 2004, from http://www.dhs.gov/dhspublic/display?theme=20&content=332.

88   DHS, "Travel and Transportation"; and DHS, "Fact Sheet: Protecting the Nation's Ports," retrieved December 13, 2004, from http://www.dhs.gov/dhspublic/display?content=3380.

89   DHS, *Secure Seas, Open Ports: Keeping Our Waters Safe, Secure, and Open for Business* (Washington, DC: Author, 2004).

90   Eric Lipton, "Audit Faults U.S. for Its Spending on Port Defense," *New York Times,* (February 20, 2005), pp. 1, 22.

91   Toby Eckert, "Cargo Containers Inspected at 'Staggeringly Low' Rate," *Copley News Service* (March 29, 2006).

92   American Trucking Associations, "ATA: Protecting Your Interests, Giving Power to Your Voice," retrieved December 18, 2004, from http://www.truckline.com.

93   ASIS International, "2005 Training Offerings for ASIS International," retrieved December 18, 2004, from http://www.asisonline.org/education/programs/training.htm.

94   Dan M. Bowers, "Assigning a Place for Parking Security," *Security Management* (December 1999), pp. 63–67.

95   Paul Barclay, et al., "Preventing Auto Theft in Suburban Vancouver Commuter Lots: Effects of a Bike Patrol," in Ronald V. Clarke (ed.), *Preventing Mass Transit Crime, Crime Prevention Studies*, Vol. 6 (Monsey, NY: Criminal Justice Press, 1996); Gloria Laycock and Claire Austin, "Crime Prevention in Parking Facilities," *Security Journal,* 3(1992), pp. 154–160; Barry Poyner, "Situational Crime Prevention in Two Parking Facilities," *Security Journal,* 2(1991), pp. 96–101; Poyner, "Lessons from Lisson Green: An Evaluation of Walkway Demolition on a British Housing Estate," in Ronald V. Clarke (ed.), *Crime Prevention Studies*, Vol. 3. (Monsey, NY: Criminal Justice Press, 1994).

96   Gips, "Sporting a New Look: Access Control Trends at New Sports Arenas Show That Security Is Experiencing a Winning Season," *Security Management* (February 2000), pp. 48–56.

97   Mary Schmitt Boyer, "Cavs Try High-Tech Solution to Scalping," *The Cleveland Plain Dealer* (October 8, 2006).

98   Randy Southerland, "First and Goal," *Access Control and Security Systems* 48(5, April 2005), p. 22.

99   "Fires, Looting Mar L.A. Celebration," *St. Petersburg Times* (June 21, 2000), p. C10.

100 Bill Saporito, "Why Fans and Players Are Playing So Rough," *Time* (December 6, 2004), pp. 31–34.

101 "Padres Beef Up Security after Syringe Tossed at Bonds," *ESPN.com News Service* (April 5, 2006).

102 "Nebraska Fans Might Face Metal Detectors," *USA Today* (August 31, 2006), p. C1.

103 Andy Gardiner, "Colleges Boost Stadium Security with Federal Help," *USA Today* (September 8, 2006).

104 Warren Hoge, "As Europe Tenses, England Moves to Leash Soccer Thugs," *New York Times* (June 11, 2000), p. 3.

105 "Festival Stunned by Tragedy," *AP Release* (July 2, 2000); Loraine Ali, "A Horrible Nightmare: Screams Drowned Out the Music at a Pearl Jam Concert in Copenhagen and Eight Fans Died," *Newsweek* (July 10, 2000), p. 32.

106 Saporito, "Out of Control in Europe," *Time* (December 6, 2004), pp. 31–34.

107 Jennifer Smith and Robert Kahn, "Concert Security: Venues Plan Ahead to Thwart Violence," *Newsday* (December 10, 2004), p. 24; and Rick Lyman, "After a Concert Shooting, a Who But Not a Why," *New York Times* (December 10, 2004), p. 22.

108 G. R. Haskell, "Security Takes Center Stage," *Security Management* (November 1997), pp. 32–39.

109 Barbara Stewart, "Beach Patrol in Evening Set to Keep Bathers Out," *New York Times* (June 27, 2000), p. B5.

110 Samuel Hardison, "Crime in the Magic Kingdom," *Crime Beat* (September 1993), pp. 24–31.

111 Anderson, "Cruise Control: The Cruise Ship Industry Is Adapting to Evolving Security Demands," *Security Management* (March 2000), pp. 36–41.

112 ASIS International, "2005 Training Offerings for ASIS International," retrieved December 18, 2004, from http://www.asisonline.org/education/programs/training.htm.

113 Ann Longmore-Etheridge, "Illusions of Grandeur: In Las Vegas, City of Illusions; the New Venetian Casino Has Created the Illusion of a City, But the Security Is No Chimera," *Security Management* (September 1999), pp. 54–60.

114 Longmore-Etheridge, "Digital Detecting," *Security Management* (November 1999), pp. 24–25.

115 Longmore-Etheridge, "No Gambling on Surveillance," *Security Management* (September 2004), pp. 103–107.

116 "Key Control Gets a Hand," *Security Management* (May 2004), p. 28.

117 Longmore-Etheridge, "No Gambling on Surveillance."

118 David W. Dunlap, "Adding Barricades, and Trying to Avoid the Feel of a Fortress," *New York Times* (September 23, 2004), p. B3.

119 Benjamin Weiser and Claudia H. Deutsch, "Offices Hold the Line on Security Spending; Stringent Measures Gather Dust, Experts Say," *New York Times* (August 16, 2004), pp. B1, B4.

Chapter 6

1   Michael J. Scicchitano, Tracy Johns, Read Hayes, and Robert Blackwood, "Peer Reporting to Control Employee Theft," *Security Journal*, 17(2, 2004), pp. 7–19.

2   John McNamara, "Helping Merchants Mind the Store," *Police Chief* (October 1993), pp. 90–92.

3   Dean A. Dabney, Richard C. Hollinger, and Laura Dugan, "Who Actually Steals? A Study of Covertly Observed Shoplifters," *Justice Quarterly*, 21(4, December 2004), pp. 693–725.

4   Richard C. Hollinger and J. L. Davis, *2002 National Retail Security Survey: Final Report* (Gainesville: University of Florida, 2002).

5   Crime Prevention Service, Rutgers University, School of Criminal Justice, "How Much Does Shoplifting Cost Me?" retrieved February 7, 2005, from http://crimeprevention.rutgers.edu/crime/shoplifting/costs.htm.

6   Ibid.

7   Robert L. DiLonardo, "The Financial Impact of Shoplifting," *Retailer News,* retrieved February 7, 2005, from http://retailernews.com/399/unise399.html.

8 Richard Hollinger and L. Langton, *2003 National Retail Security Survey* (Gainesville: University of Florida, 2004), retrieved January 23, 2005, from http://www.soc.ufl.edu/srp.htm; and Centre for Retail Research, "Crime and Fraud," retrieved January 23, 2005, from http://www.chant4.co.uk/retailresearch2003/crime_and_fraud/retail_crime_overseas.phb.

9 Daniel McGinn, "Shoplifting: The Five-Finger Fix?" *Newsweek* (December 20, 2004), p. 13.

10 Dressing Up EAS," *Security Magazine* (October 2004).

11 "The New Face of Shoplifting," *Fashion Monitor Toronto* (August 22, 2005).

12 Jack L. Hayes International, "Sixteenth (16th) Annual Retail Theft Survey," from Centre for Retail Research, *Crime and Fraud*, retrieved January 23, 2005, from http://www.chant4.co.uk/retailresearch2003/crime_and_fraud/retail_crime_overseas.phb.

13 National Retail Federation, "News Release: New ARTS/NRF Initiative Helps Retailers Reduce Shrinkage," retrieved January 16, 2005, from http://www.nrf.com/content/press/release2004/artslprfp0604.htm.

14 Natalie Taylor, *Reporting of Crime against Small Retail Businesses* (Canberra ACT: Australian Institute of Criminology, 2002); and U.S. Department of Justice, Bureau of Justice Statistics, *National Crime Victimization Survey* (Washington, DC: Author, 2006).

15 U.S. Department of Justice, Bureau of Justice Statistics, *National Crime Victimization Survey*.

16 Dabney, Hollinger, and Dugan, "Who Actually Steals? A Study of Covertly Observed Shoplifters"; and Hollinger and Davis, *2002 National Retail Security Survey: Final Report*.

17 D. P. Farrington, "Measuring, Explaining and Preventing Shoplifting: A Review of British Research," *Security Journal*, 12, pp 9–17; and Hollinger and Davis, *2002 National Retail Security Survey: Final Report*.

18 C. W. Osborn, "Restructuring to Reduce Losses," *Security Management* (December 1998), pp. 63–68; Michael C. Budden, *Preventing Shoplifting without Being Sued* (Westport, CT: Quorum Books, 1999); Charles A. Sennewald, *Shoplifters v. Retailers: The Rights of Both* (New York: New Century Press, 2000); and Diana Nelson and Santina Perrone, *Understanding and Controlling Retail Theft* (Woden Act: Australian Institute of Criminology, 2000).

19 Crime Prevention Service, Rutgers University, School of Criminal Justice, "How Much Does Shoplifting Cost Me?"

20 BBC News, "Workplace Theft Hits UK Retailers," *BBC News* (October 5, 2005).

21 John S. Dempsey, *Introduction to Investigations,* 2nd ed. (Belmont, CA: Thomson/Wadsworth, 2003), p. 236.

22 Dabney, Hollinger, and Dugan, "Who Actually Steals? A Study of Covertly Observed Shoplifters."

23 "Baby Formula? The Locked Case at the Front of the Store," *New York Times* (June 5, 2005), p. 33; and Michael Rubinkam, "Baby Formula Going behind Counter to Deter Shoplifters," *The Boston Globe* (June 4, 2005), p. A5.

24 Adrian Beck, Charlotte Bilby, and Paul Chapman, "Tackling Shrinkage in the Fast-Moving Consumer Goods Supply Chain: Developing a Methodology," *Security Journal*, 16(2, 2003), pp. 61–74.

25 "Thieves Can't Hide from Pryin' Eyes," *Security Management* (January 2004), p. 14.

26 Mark Lipman and W. R. McGraw, "Employee Theft: A $40 Billion Industry," *The Annals* (July 1988), pp. 51–59.

27 Troy Williamson, "Solving the Problem of Theft from the University's Workforce," *Campus Law Enforcement Journal*, 31(2, March/April 2001), pp. 21–23.

28 Read Hayes, "Loss Prevention: Senior Management Views on Current Trends and Issues," *Security Management*, 16(2, 2003), pp. 7–20.

29 Dabney, Hollinger, and Dugan, "Who Actually Steals? A Study of Covertly Observed Shoplifters."

30 Crime Prevention Service, Rutgers University, School of Criminal Justice, "Crime Prevention through Environmental Design," retrieved February 2, 2005, from http://crimeprevention.rutgers.edu/case_studies/cpted/cpted_intro.htm.

31 Andrew Lester, *Crime Reduction through Product Design* (Canberra ACT: Australian Institute of Criminology, 2001).

32 Barry Masuda, "Reduction of Employee Theft in a Retail Environment," retrieved February 2, 2005, from http://crimeprevention.rutgers.edu/case_studies/risk/formal_surveillance/formal_surveillance.htm.

33 "Expert: Crooks Are More Creative," *St. Petersburg Times* (October 9, 2005).

34 Andrea Yeutter, "Stopping Shoplifting," *The Daily Telegram* (August 30, 2005).

35 Robert L. DiLonardo, "The Financial Impact of Shoplifting."

36 "Loss Prevention Execs Profiled," *Security Management* (February 2003), retrieved January 20, 2005, from http://www.securitymanagement.com/library/001381.html.

37 U.S. Department of Labor, Bureau of Labor Statistics, "Occupational Outlook Handbook," retrieved October 6, 2006, from http://www.bls.gov.

38 Ibid.

39 Wicklander-Zulawski & Associates, Inc, "Homepage," retrieved October 6, 2006, from http://www.w-z.com.

40 Read Hayes, "U.S. Retail Store Detectives: An Analysis of Their Focus, Selection, and Training," *Security Journal*, 13(1), pp. 7–20.

41 "Watching the Detectives," *Security Management* (December 2003), retrieved January 20, 2005, from http://www.securitymanagement.com/library/001544.html.

42 Alan Kaminsky, "An Arresting Policy," *Security Management* (May 1999), pp. 59–61.

43 Robert Crowe, "Experts Discourage Using Force in Shoplifting Cases," *Houston Chronicle* (August 10, 2005), p. A1.

44 *Van Zante and Jacobson v. Wal-Mart,* Iowa Court of Appeals, No. 3-544, 2003; and "False Imprisonment," *Security Management* (December 2003), retrieved January 20, 2005, from http://www.securitymanagement.com/library/001544.html.

45 Mark B. Rosen, "You Bagged the Shoplifter, Now What?" *Security Management* (April 2004), pp. 59–65.

46 Audrey J. Aronsohn, "Teaching Criminals the Cost of Crime," *Security Management* (May 1999), pp. 63–68.

47 L. W. Klemke, *The Sociology of Shoplifting: Boosters and Snitches Today* (Westport, CT: Praeger, 1992).

48 Hollinger and Davis, *2002 National Retail Security Survey: Final Report*.

49 Dabney, Hollinger, and Dugan, "Who Actually Steals? A Study of Covertly Observed Shoplifters"; Read Hayes, *Shoplifting Control* (Orlando, FL: Prevention Press, 1993); and Hollinger and Davis, *2002 National Retail Security Survey: Final Report*.

50 Scicchitano et al., "Peer Reporting to Control Employee Theft."

51. Pinkerton Consulting Services, "Pinkerton Compliance Services—AlertLine Ethics and Compliance Hotline," retrieved January 15, 2005, from http://www.ci-pinkerton.com/workplace/workplace.html; and Wackenhut Consulting and Investigation Services, "Safe2Say Compliance Hotline," retrieved January 15, 2005 from http://www.ci-wakenhut.com/S2S%20Compliance%20Hotline.htm.

52. Angel Riggs, "Focus: DVS Keeps Eye Out on Security," *Tulsa World* (January 9, 2005), p. E1.

53. Monty Phan, "High-Tech Ways to Catch Shoplifters," *Newsday* (January 16, 2005), p. A47.

54. The Association for Retail Technology Standards, "Homepage," retrieved January 16, 2005, from http://www.nrf-arts.org.

55. Security Industry Association, "What Is Closed-Circuit Television?" retrieved February 3, 2005, from http://www.siaonline.org/response.asp?c=facts_cctv&r=1024.

56. "How Anti-Shoplifting Devices Work," retrieved February 3, 2005, from http://www.howstuffworks.com/anti-shoplifting-device.htm.

57. Monty Phan, "High-Tech Ways to Catch Shoplifters."

58. Security Industry Association, "What Is Closed-Circuit Television?"

59. Crime Prevention Service, Rutgers University, School of Criminal Justice, "Crime Prevention through Environmental Design."

60. Karryn Loveday and Martin Gill, "Impact of Monitored CCTV in a Retail Environment: What CCTV Operators Do and Why," *Crime Prevention and Community Safety: An International Journal*, 6(3, 2004), pp. 43–55.

61. Crime Prevention Service, Rutgers University, School of Criminal Justice, "Crime Prevention through Environmental Design."

62. Ibid.

63. "How Anti-Shoplifting Devices Work."

64. Robert L. DiLonardo, "Defining and Measuring the Economic Benefit of Electronic Article Surveillance," *Security Journal*, 7(1, 1996), pp. 3–9; Ann Longmore-Etheridge, "The Evolution of EAS," *Security Management* (December 1998), pp. 44, 48–50; and Robert L. DiLonardo and R. V. Clarke, "Reducing the Rewards of Shoplifting: An Evaluation of Ink Tags," *Security Journal*, 7(1, 1996), pp. 11–14.

65. "Dressing Up EAS."

66. Daniel McGinn, "Shoplifting: The Five-Finger Fix."

67. David Koenig, "7-Eleven Hoping Computers Help Reduce Excess Inventory; Convenience-Store Chain Tests Hand-Held Devices," *Telegraph Herald* (December 26, 2004), p. B13.

68. "The Future Is Still Smart," *The Economist* (June 2004), p. 63.

69. Tom Belden, "Attention, Shoppers; Tags Monitor Inventory, Deter Theft—Raise Privacy Fears," *Philadelphia Inquirer* (August 15, 2004).

70. Jim Stafford, "In Control: Wal-Mart Is Trying a Bar-Code System That Puts Goods on Shelf," *The Daily Oklahoman* (December 29, 2004), p. B1; and James M. Pethokoukis, "Big Box Meets Big Brother, But Some Suppliers Balk," *U.S. News and World Report* (January 24, 2005).

71. Barnaby J. Feder, "Despite Wal-Mart's Edict, Radio Tags Will Take Time; Big Flaws Slow an Ambitious Schedule," *New York Times* (December 27, 2004), p. C3;

72. "The Future Is Still Smart."

73. John Thorn, "Bracing for Change: A Road Map for the Retail Supply Chain's Transition to EPC/RFID," *Chain Store Age* (April 2004).

74. Hiawatha Bray, "Credit Cards with Radio Tags Speed Purchases But Track Customers, Too," *Boston Globe* (August 14, 2006); and Susan Warren, "Why Some People Put These Credit Cards in the Microwave," *Wall Street Journal* (April 10, 2006), p. 1.

75. Douglas Page, "RFID Tags: Big Brother in a Small Device," *Law Enforcement Technology*, 31(8, August 2004), pp. 128, 130–133; and "How Anti-Shoplifting Devices Work."

76. Jim Stafford, "In Control."

77. Mary Catherine O'Connor, "RFID Security Consortium Receives $1.1 Million NSF Grant," retrieved September 17, 2006, from http://www.rfidjournal.com.

78. "From Genetic Code to Security Code; Tiny DNA Fragments Can Function as Invisible Embedded Security Tags," *The Economist* (June 12, 2004), p. 14.

79. Angel Riggs, "Focus: DVS Keeps Eye Out on Security."

80. National Retail Federation, "Homepage," retrieved January 15, 2005, from http://www.nrf.com.

81. Ibid.

82. National Retail Foundation, "NRF Loss Prevention Conference and Exhibition," retrieved January 16, 2005, from http://lp05.expoexchange.com.

83. Loss Prevention Research Council, "Homepage," retrieved January 21, 2005, from http://www.lpresearch.org.

84. Read Hayes, "Loss Prevention Research Council," retrieved January 23, 2005, from http://www.expertclick.com.

85. Loss Prevention Research Council, "Homepage."

86. Ibid.

87. University of Florida, "Security Research Project," retrieved January 21, 2005, from http://www.soc.ufl.edu/srp.htm.

88. Rutgers University, School of Criminal Justice, "Crime Prevention Service," retrieved September 21, 2005, from http://www.crimeprevention.rutgers.edu.

89. *LossPrevention Magazine,* retrieved January 21, 2005, from http://www.losspreventionmagazine.com.

90. Barnaby J. Feder, "Radio Tags Can Find Stray Bags, But Can Airlines Afford Them?" *New York Times* (March 7, 2005), p. C3.

91. Department of Homeland Security, "US-VISIT: An Overview; and Fact Sheet: Radio Frequency Identification Technology," retrieved October 29, 2005, from http://www.dhs.gov.

92. Department of Homeland Security, "Press Release, August 8, 2005: US-VISIT Begins Testing Radio Frequency Identification Technology to Improve Border Security and Travel," retrieved October 29, 2005, from http://www.dhs.gov.

93. "Baby Formula? The Locked Case at the Front of the Store"; and Rubinkam, "Baby Formula Going behind Counter to Deter Shoplifters."

Chapter 7

1. John Sullivan and Randy Kennedy, "Armed Intruder Exposes Limits of Air Security," *New York Times* (July 29, 2000), p. A1; and Michael Cooper, "Man Charged in Hostage-Taking on Plane," *New York Times* (July 29, 2000), p. B6.

2. Federal Bureau of Investigation (FBI), *Uniform Crime Reports, 2005* (Washington, DC: Author, 2006).

3. Ibid.

4. Ibid.

5 Ann L. Pastore and Kathleen Maguire, eds. *Sourcebook of Criminal Justice Statistics, 2005.* (Washington, DC: U.S. Department of Justice, Bureau of Justice Statistics, 2006), Tables 2.33, 2.35, and 2.37.

6 E. Meyr, "Tactical Response to Terrorism: The Concept and Its Application," *Law and Order* (March 1999), pp. 44–47.

7 E. D. Davis, "Combating Terrorism on the Corporate Level: The Emergence of Executive Protection Specialists in Private Security," *Journal of Contemporary Criminal Justice*, 4(4, November 1988), pp. 241–251. Also see Clyde L. Cronkhite, "Case Study of Executive Security: A Guide for Planning and Implementing a Private Sector Security Program," *Journal of Security Administrations* (June 2003), pp. 39–47; and "Advice to the Traveling American Executive," SecurityInfoWatch, retrieved August 31, 2005, from http://www.securityinfowatch.com.

8 Michelle Martinez, "Global Business, Global Risks," *Crain's Detroit Business* (July 7, 2005).

9 C. Roda, *Executive Safety* (Washington, DC: National Criminal Justice Reference Service, 1997); and Christopher Terzich, "Hundred Years of Preparedness," *Homeland Protection Professional*, 5(5, June 2006).

10 Elmer L. Snow III, "Adapting Technologies to the Task," *Security Management* (June 2000), pp. 60–64; and William M. Besse and Charles T. Whitehead, "New Tools of an Old Trade," *Security Management* (June 2000), pp. 66–72.

11 Dale Carrison and Christopher M. Grande, "In Sickness and In Health," *Security Management* (March 2000), pp. 65–69.

12 Joseph B. Treaster, "A Hedge against Abductions on the Rise: Peace of Mind for Global Executives," *New York Times* (August 21, 1997), p. D1.

13 "A King's Ransom," *The Economist* (August 26, 2006), pp. 58–59.

14 Joseph Autera and Michael Scanlan, "Seeing through Enemy Eyes: Countersurveillance That Seeks Out the Attacker's Perspective Is the Key To Good Corporate Executive Protection," retrieved July 11, 2000, from http://www.securitymanagement.com/library/000663.html.

15 Martinez, "Global Business, Global Risks."

16 Stephen Mueller, "Shoring Up Protection for Overseas Employees," retrieved March 29, 2006, from http://www.rmmag.com.

17 Kirk Semple, "Kidnapped in Iraq: Victim's Tale of Clockwork Death and Ransom," *New York Times* (May 7, 2006).

18 "Kidnapping: How Can EAPs Intervene?" *Business and Management Practices* (May 1, 2005), p. 10.

19 SecurityInfoWatch, "Advice to the Traveling American Executive," retrieved August 31, 2005, from http://www.securityinfowatch.com.

20 "Kidnapping: How Can EAPs Intervene?"

21 Pinkerton Consulting and Investigations Inc., "Global Protection Services," retrieved November 14, 2004, from http://www.ci-pinkerton.com/nes/globalPS.html.

22 Pinkerton Consulting and Investigations Inc., "Executive Travel Security," retrieved November 14, 2004, from http://www.ci-pinkerton.com/nes/globalPS.html.

23 Rose Shyman, "Women at Work," *Security Magazine* (February 2000), pp. 58–62.

24 Marjorie Connelly, "Hotel Rooms of Their Own," *New York Times* (September 18, 2005), p. TR2.

25 Executive Protection Institute, "Homepage," retrieved October 22, 2005, from http://www.personalprotection.com;

"More Than a Bodyguard," *Security Management* (February 1988); "A School for Guards of Rich, Powerful," *Akron Beacon Journal* (April 21, 1986); and Sam Dillon, "Security: A Growth Industry in Mexico: Kidnappers Create New Wealth in Armored Cars and Negotiations," *New York Times* (October 15, 1998), p. C4.

26 B. Figlioa, "Security Must Go On," *Security Management* (December 1997), pp. 52–54, 56–59.

27 See, for example, L. Thompson, *Dead Clients Don't Pay—The Bodyguard's Manual* (Geneva, IL: Paladin House Publishers, 1984); P. Elhanan, *Keep 'em Alive—The Bodyguard's Trade* (Geneva, IL: Paladin House Publishers, 1985); and P. Holder and D. L. Hawley, *Executive Protection Professional's Manual* (Woburn, MA: Butterworth-Heinemann, 1998).

28 International Association of Professional Protection Specialists (IAPPS), "Homepage," retrieved October 22, 2005, from http://www.iapps.org.

29 Kroll Risk Consulting Company, "Security Services: Protective Services and Training," retrieved December 5, 2004, from http://www.krollworldwide.com/services/security/protection.

30 "Doing Business in Dangerous Places," *The Economist* August 14, 2004), p. 11.

31 Ibid.

32 Alina Tugend, "All Stressed Out and Everywhere to Go," *New York Times* (May 25, 2004), p. C8.

33 Joe Sharkey, "In These Days of Insecurity, Stick to Itinerary Is the Rule," *New York Times* (August 10, 2004), p. C7.

34 Ibid.

35 Donald G. McNeil Jr., "The Dicey Game of Travel Risk: Anticipating the Unpredictable," *New York Times* (March 7, 1999), sec. 4, pp. 1, 4.

36 U.S. State Department, "Homepage," retrieved October 22, 2005, from http://www.state.gov/; U.S. State Department, "Current Travel Warnings," retrieved October 22, 2005, from http://travel.state.gov/; and McNeil Jr., "The Dicey Game of Travel Risk."

37 U.S. Department of State, "Current Travel Warnings."

38 U.S. Department of State, Bureau of Consular Affairs, "Top 10 Tips for Traveling Abroad; Travel Tips for Older Americans; Tips for Women Traveling Alone; Travel Tips for Students," retrieved October 22, 2005, from http://travel.state.gov

39 Sharkey, "Tourists Stumble into the Line of Fire," *New York Times* (April 30, 2000), p. WK5.

40 "Travel Security," *Security Management* (February 2004), p. 20.

41 "Crime Takes a Vacation (Yours): Times Correspondents in Eight European Cities Look at the Latest Ways to Victimize Tourists, as well as Some Old Reliables," *New York Times* (July 16, 2000), pp. TR8, TR9, TR19.

42 Wackenhut Consulting and Investigation Services, "Protection Services," retrieved November 13, 2004, from http://www.ci-wackenhut.com/Protection-Services.htm.

43 Ibid.

44 "Police Not Pushing Panic Button," *Security Management* (June 1999), p. 12; Tom Chronister, "Panic over Panic Alarms?" *Law Enforcement Technology*, 28(7, July 2001), pp. 74–76, 78; and David Rich, "Six Strategies for Parking Safety," *Campus Safety Journal*, 11(6, June 2003), pp. 16–19.

45 Safety Now, "Personal Alarms," retrieved November 27, 2004, from http://www.safetynow.com.

46 David Rich, "Six Strategies for Parking Safety."

47 Jayson Blair, "Cellular Phones: The Weapon of Choice for Self-Defense," *New York Times* (May 7, 2000), p. WK5; Blair, "Manhattan: Emergency Cell Phones," *New York Times* (June 29, 2000), p. B7.

48 "Marlboro Prohibits Drivers from Using Cell Phones," *New York Times* (July 14, 2000), p. B5.

49 Darrin Barnett, "Mobiles Not Disaster Answer: Expert," *News.com.au* (October 14, 2005).

50 Ronnie L. Paynter, "Stopping Bullets in Their Tracks: Making Vests That Will Stop a Bullet," *Law Enforcement Technology* (July 1999), pp. 50–53; and Dave Spaulding, "Body Armor Update," *Law and Order*, 49(2, February 2001), pp. 47–49.

51 John Hoffmann, "Body Armor Improvements: Big Advances in the Last Five Years—and More on the Way," *Law and Order* (April 2000), pp. 90–94; and Ronnie L. Garrett, "Quest for Comfortable Armor: Manufacturers Strive to Develop Protection That Will Stop Bullets, Knives, and Ice Picks," *Law Enforcement Technology*, 28(3, March 2001), pp. 70–74.

52 Garrett, "Got Your Back?: Does Today's Body Armor Really Offer the Life-Saving Protection You Need?" *Law Enforcement Technology*, 31(2, February 2004), pp. 30–32, 34–36; National Institute of Standards and Technology, *Surviving a Shooting: Your Guide to Personal Body Armor* (Rockville, MD: National Law Enforcement and Corrections Technology Center, 2004); and National Institute of Standards and Technology, Office of Law Enforcement Standards, "Weapons and Protective Systems," retrieved November 27, 2004, from http://www.eeel.nist.gov/oles/weapons.html.

53 Leanne R. Brecklin, "Self-Defense/Assertiveness Training, Women's Victimization History, and Psychological Characteristics," *Violence against Women*, 10(5, May 2004), pp. 479–497.

54 Jocelyn A. Hollander, "I Can Take Care of Myself: The Impact of Self-Defense Training on Women's Lives," *Violence against Women*, 10(3, March 2004), pp. 205–235.

55 D. M Zima, "This Is Not Your Father's Oldsmobile," *Security Management* (April 1997), pp. 47–50.

56 O'Gara-Hess & Eisenhardt, "Protection Systems for Every Level of Threat," retrieved November 27, 2004, from http://www.ogara-hess.com; and Bill Griffith, "Vehicles for Well-To-Do Take Safety to an Extreme," *Boston Globe* [Electronic version] (February 29, 2004), retrieved December 1, 2004, from http://www.lboston.com/cars/news/march/01_safety.html.

57 Alan Clendenning, "An Extra Measure of Security," *Hartford Courant* (September 23, 2005).

58 Heather Hamilton, "From Bullets to Bombs: RCMP's Armoured Vehicle Protects Dignitaries on the Move," *Gazette*, 64(1, 2002), pp. 12–14; and O'Gara-Hess & Eisenhardt, "Protection Systems for Every Level of Threat."

59 Griffith, "Vehicles for Well-To-Do Take Safety to an Extreme."

60 For information on this subject, see Monique C. Boudreaux, Wayne D. Lord, and Stephen E. Etter, "Child Abduction: An Overview of Current and Historical Perspectives," *Child Maltreatment*, 5(1, February 2000), pp. 63–71; Wayne D. Lord, Monique C. Boudreaux, and Kenneth V. Lanning, "Investigating Potential Child Abduction Cases: A Developmental Perspective," *FBI Law Enforcement Bulletin* (April 2001), pp. 1–10; Linda K. Girdner and Patricia M. Hoff, eds., *Obstacles to the Recovery and Return of Parentally Abducted Children* (Washington, DC: U.S. Department of Justice, 1994); and S. E. Steidel, ed., *Missing and Abducted Children: A Law Enforcement Guide to Case Investigation and Program Management* (Arlington, VA: National Center for Missing and Exploited Children, 1994).

61 Patricia M. Hoff, *Family Abduction: Prevention and Response* (Arlington, VA: National Center for Missing and Exploited Children, 2002). For a copy of this report, go to http://www.missingkids.com/en_US/publications/CN75.pdf.

62 David Finkelhor, Heather Hammer, and Andrea J. Sedlak, *Nonfamily Abducted Children: National Estimates and Characteristics* (Washington, DC: U.S. Department of Justice, Office of Juvenile Justice and Delinquency Prevention, 2002).

63 Joseph B. Treaster, "Kidnapping with Money as the Only Object," *New York Times* (June 30, 2000), pp. A1, A6.

64 Wackenhut Consulting and Investigation Services, "Crisis Management and Response Services: Kidnap and Extortion," retrieved November 14, 2004, from http://www.ci-wackenhut.com/Crisis%20Management.htm.

65 Ibid.

66 Ronnie L. Paynter, "Web of Deceit," *Law Enforcement Technology*, 27(7, July 2000), pp. 92–96; United Nations, *Trafficking in Women and Girls* (New York: United Nations, 2002); U.S. Department of State, *Be Smart, Be Safe . . . Don't Become a Victim of the Trade in People* (Washington, DC: U.S. Department of State, 2005); Suzanne Seltzer, Christa Stewart, Juhu Thukral, and Suzanne Tomatore, *Identification and Legal Advocacy for Trafficking Victims* (New York: NYC Anti-Trafficking Network, 2005); Graeme R. Newman, *Exploitation of Trafficked Women* (Washington, DC: Office of Community-Oriented Policing Services, 2006); Edward J. Schauer and Elizabeth M. Wheaton, "Sex Trafficking into the United States: A Literature Review," *Criminal Justice Review*, (June 2006), pp. 146–169; and U.S. Department of State, *Trafficking in Persons Reports, June 2006* (Washington, DC: Author, 2006.

67 U.S. Department of State, *Trafficking in Persons Reports, June 2006*.

68 Sabrina Feve and Cristina Finzel, "Trafficking of People," *Harvard Journal on Legislation*, 38(1, Winter 2001), pp. 279–290.

69 U.S. Department of Justice, Office for Victims of Crime, *Assessment of U.S. Government Activities to Combat Trafficking in Persons* (Rockville, MD: Author, 2004.)

70 "A Decade Later, GMAC Shooting Still Resonates," *St. Petersburg Times* (June 18, 2000), p. B3.

71 "Three Inspectors Killed at Sausage Factory," *St. Petersburg Times* (June 23, 2000), p. A4.

72 Wackenhut Consulting and Investigation Services, "Protection Services," retrieved November 13, 2004, from http://www.ci-wackenhut.com/Protection-Services.htm; and Frank E. Rudewicz, "The Road to Rage," *Security Management* (February 2004), pp. 41–49.

73 Workplace Violence Research Institute, "Homepage," retrieved November 14, 2004, from http://www.workviolence.com.

74 See, for example, "Safe at Work," *CSO: The Resource for Security Executives* (April 2006); Joseph A. Kinney, *Essentials of Managing Workplace Violence* (Charlotte, NC: National Safe Workplace Institute, 1995); D. W. Myers, "Workplace Violence Prevention Planning Model," *Journal of Security Administration*, 19(2, 1996); and B. S. Michelman, P. Robb, and L. M. Coviello, "A Comprehensive Approach to

Workplace Violence," *Security Management* (July 1998), pp. 28, 30–35.

75 "News and Trends," *Security Management* (October 2004), p. 12.

76 Andrew G. Podolak, "Is Workplace Violence in Need of Refocusing?" *Security Management* (June 2000), pp. 151–152.

77 Dick Grimes, "How to Reduce the Potential of Workplace Violence," *Police Chief* (September 2003), pp. 32–34.

78 Eugene A. Rugala and Arnold R. Isaacs, *Workplace Violence: Issues in Response* (Rockville, MD: VICAP, National Center for the Analysis of Violent Crime, 2003).

79 Pinkerton Consulting and Investigations Services, "Workplace Violence Prevention," retrieved November 14, 2004, from http://www.ci-pinkerton.com/workplace/wkViolence.html.

80 Grimes, "How to Reduce the Potential of Workplace Violence."

81 Handgun-Free America, *Terror Nine to Five: Guns in the American Workplace, 1994–2003* (Arlington, VA: Author, 2004).

82 Ann L. Pastore and Kathleen Maguire, eds, *Sourcebook of Criminal Justice Statistics, 2005* (Washington, DC: U.S. Department of Justice, 2006), Table 3.135.

83 "Homicides More Likely at Workplaces That Allow Guns," *Health Central* (April 27, 2005).

84 Christina Vance, "Some Hurting for Their Paycheck," *Bakersfield Californian* (June 15, 2005).

85 Wackenhut Consulting and Investigation Services, "Protection Services."

86 Pinkerton Consulting and Investigations Services, "Workplace Violence Prevention"; and Pinkerton Consulting and Investigative Services, "Crisis Prevention Planning," retrieved October 18, 2005, from http://www.ci-pinkerton.com/crisis.html.

87 Frank E. Rudewicz, "The Road to Rage," *Security Management* (February 2004), pp. 41–49; also see Karen Karr, "Will Rage Turn to Rampage?" *Security Management* (October 2005), pp. 67–73; and James F. Kenny, "Threats in the Workplace: The Thunder before the Storm," *Security Journal*, 18(3, 2005) p. 45.

88 Karr, "Will Rage Turn to Rampage?"

89 Paul Viollis and Doug Kane, "At-Risk Terminations," *Risk Management* (May 5, 2005), p. 28.

90 Harold Nedd, "Court Upholds Firing for Workplace Violence Joke," *Pacific Business News* (October 16, 2005).

91 "News and Trends," *Security Management* (October 2004), p. 12; and Anne Fisher, "How to Prevent Violence at Work," *Fortune* (February 21, 2005), p. 42.

92 Michael J. Witkowski, "The Gang's All Here," *Security Management* (May 2004), pp. 95–99.

93 MOAB Training International, "Homepage," retrieved October 1, 2006, from http://www.moabtraining.com.

94 U.S. Department of Justice, "Homicide Trends in the United States," in Ann L. Pastore and Kathleen Maguire, eds., *Sourcebook of Criminal Justice Statistics, 2005* (Washington, DC: Author, 2006), Table 3.131.

95 Federal Bureau of Investigation, *Uniform Crime Reports, 2003* (Washington, DC: Author, 2004).

96 Brenda K. Uekert and Denise O. Dancy, *Developing a Domestic Violence Policy for the Workplace* (Williamsburg, VA: National Center for State Courts, 2003).

97 Rebecca Ferrar, "Domestic Violence Costly to State," *Knoxville News-Sentinel* (March 29, 2005).

98 Ibid.

99 T. S. Duncan, "Changing Perception of Domestic Violence," *Law Enforcement News* (October 31, 1991), p. 13. The two books reviewed are Michael Steinman, ed., *Woman Battering: Policy Responses* (Cincinnati, OH: Anderson, 1991), and Douglas J. Besharov, ed., *Family Violence: Research and Public Policy Issues* (Washington, DC: University Press of America, 1990).

100 Pam Paziotopoulos, "Workplace Domestic Violence," *Law and Order* (August 2003), pp. 104–109.

101 Uekert and Dancy, *Developing a Domestic Violence Policy for the Workplace.*

102 National Center for Victims of Crime, *Stalking* (Washington, DC: U.S. Department of Justice, Office of Community-Oriented Policing Services, 2004), p. 1.

103 Karen M. Abrams and Gail Erlick Robinson, "Stalking Part I: An Overview of the Problem," *Canadian Journal of Psychiatry*, 43(5, June 1998), pp. 473–476; P. Tjaden and N. Thoennes, *Stalking in America: Findings from the National Violence against Women Survey* (Washington, DC: National Institute of Justice, 1998); Debra Keenahan and Allen Barlow, "Stalking: A Paradoxical Crime of the Nineties," *International Journal of Risk, Security and Crime Prevention*, 2(4, October 1997), pp. 291–300; and R. M. Emerson, K. O. Ferris, and C. B. Gardner, "On Being Stalked," *Social Problems*, 45(3, August 1998), pp. 289–314.

104 Karl A. Roberts, "Women's Experience of Violence during Stalking by Former Romantic Partners: Factors Predictive of Stalking Violence," *Violence against Women*, (January 2005), pp. 89–114.

105 R. Myers, "Anti-Stalking Statutes," *Crime Victims Report*, 2(5, November/December 1998), pp. 67–69; National Center for Victims of Crime, *Stalking.*

106 National Center for Victims of Crime, *Stalking.*

107 Emily Spence-Diehl, *Stalking: A Handbook for Victims* (Holmes Beach, FL: Learning Publications Inc., 1999); see also Christine Courmarelos and Jacqui Allen, "Predicting Violence against Women: The 1996 Women's Safety Survey," *Crime and Justice Bulletin* (December 1998), pp. 1–22; National Center for Victims of Crime, *Stalking*; P. Tjaden and N. Thoennes, "Stalking in America: Prevalence Characteristics, and Police Response," in C. Brito and E. Gratto (eds.), *Problem-Oriented Policing: Crime-Specific Problems, Critical Issues, and Making POP Work* (Washington, DC: Police Executive Research Forum, 2000); and Tjaden and Thoennes, *Stalking in America: Findings from the National Violence against Women Survey.*

108 See Gavin de Becker, *The Gift of Fear: Survival Signals That Protect Us from Violence* (Boston: Little, Brown, 1997).

109 Lisa Hunter, Gordon MacNeil, and Maurice Elias, "School Violence: Prevalence, Policies, and Prevention," in Albert R. Roberts, ed., *Juvenile Justice Sourcebook: Past, Present and Future* (New York: Oxford University Press, 2004), pp. 101–125.

110 Lynn A. Addington, "Students' Fear after Columbine: Findings from a Randomized Experiment," *Journal of Quantitative Criminology*, 19(4, December 2003), pp. 367–387.

111 Ann L. Pastore and Kathleen Maguire, eds., *Sourcebook of Criminal Justice Statistics, 2003* (Washington, DC: U.S. Department of Justice, Bureau of Justice Statistics, 2004), Table 3.6.

112 David Kocieniewski and Gary Gately, "Man Shoots 11, Killing 4 Girls, in Amish School," *New York Times* (October

3, 2006), pp. A1, A22; "A Quiet Grief," *Time* (October 16, 2006), p. 42; Kirk Johnson, "Student and Gunman Die in Colorado High School Standoff," *New York Times* (September 28, 2006); Johnson, "Shooting Leaves Loss of Life, and Innocence," *New York Times* (September 29, 2006), p. A16; Ian Austen, "Woman Killed by Gunman in Montreal; 19 Are Injured," *New York Times* (September 14, 2006), p. A17; Adam Silverman, "Essex Shootings: Suspect Pleads Guilty," *Burlington Free Press* (August 26, 2006); Susan Snyder and Martha Woodall, "PA Lawmakers to Study Tightening Security at All Schools," *Philadelphia Inquirer* (October 4, 2006); Gail Russell Chaddock and Mark Clayton, "A Pattern in Rural School Shootings: Girls as Targets," *Christian Science Monitor* (October 4, 2006); "Schools Caught Short on Safety," *Philadelphia Inquirer* (October 8, 2006); and Marcus Kabel, "Missouri Teen Fires Assault Rifle in School," *Washington Post* (October 10, 2006), p. A3.

113 Associated Press, "Bush Urges Action Plan for School Safety," retrieved October 15, 2006, from http://www.msnbc.msn.com.

114 Karen S. Peterson, "When School Hurts," *Law Enforcement Trainer*, 16(4, July/August 2001), pp. 16–19; and Kurt Naumann, *Briefing Paper: Bullying* (Little Rock: School Violence Resource Center, University of Arkansas, 2001).

115 Pastore and Maguire, eds., *Sourcebook of Criminal Justice Statistics, 2005*, Table 3.61.

116 Police Association of Higher Education Officers, *Student Survival Guide* (London: Author, 2004).

117 Ashley Fantz and Jeanne Meserve, "Witness Survives by Pretending to Be Dead," *Cnn.com*, retrieved April 17, 2007, from http://www.cnn.com/2007/US/04/16/vtech.shooting/index.html.

118 Michael Pittaro, "School Violence and Weakened Social Bonds: Is There a Relationship?" (working paper, Department of Legal Studies, Lehigh Valley College, 2007).

119 Julie Rawe, "Can We Make Campuses Safer?" *Time.com*, retrieved April 16, 2007, from http://www.time.com/time/nation/article/0,8599,1611164,00.html.

120 Lisa Guernsey, "Where's Johnny? Smart Cards and Satellites Help Keep Track," *New York Times* (August 3, 2005), p. 7.

121 Ann Longmore-Etheridge, "No Child Left Unsafe," *Security Management* (November 2004), pp. 54–59. For further information on the use of security cameras in schools, see Stephen F. Garst, "The School Year in Pictures," *Security Management* (March 2004), pp. 74–79.

122 John C. Lanata, "Behind the Scenes: A Closer Look at the School Shooters," *Sheriff*, 55(2, March/April 2003), pp. 22–26.

123 Martin Dunn, "Assessing Threats Directed at School Facilities," *Law and Order*, 51(9, September 2003), pp. 103–107.

124 Justice Technology Information Network, "School Safety Resources: School Critical Incident Planning: An Internet Resource Directory," retrieved December 5, 2004, from http://www.nlectc.org/assistance/schoolsafety.html.

125 National School Safety and Security Services, "School Security Assessments," retrieved December 6, 2004, from http://schoolsecurity.org/consultants/security-assessments.html.

126 F. S. Haines, "Technology and Taxis: The Challenge of Uncoupling Risk from Reward," *Security Journal*, 10(2, March 1998), pp. 65–78.

127 Christina Vance, "Some Hurting for Their Paycheck."

128 Claire Mayhew, *Violent Assaults on Taxi Drivers: Incidence Patterns and Risk Factors* (Canberra ACT: Australia, Australian Institute of Criminology, 2000).

129 N. Westmarland and J. Anderson, "Safe at the Wheel? Security Issues for Female Taxi Drivers," *Security Journal*, 14(2, 2001), pp. 29–40.

130 iJET Intelligent Risk Systems, "Homepage," retrieved December 30, 2006, from http:www.ijet.com.

131 Sherry L. Harowitz, "Engulfed by Disaster," *Security Management* (November 2005), pp. 60–65.

Chapter 8

1 Privacy Rights Clearinghouse, "Employment Background Checks: A Jobseekers' Guide: Workplace Investigations and Annual File Disclosures," retrieved December 2, 2005, from http://www.privacyrights.org.

2 Peter Cholakis, "How to Implement a Successful Drug-Testing Program," *Risk Management* (November 2005), p. 24.

3 Patricia S. Jacobs, "Who's Minding the Guards?" retrieved November 3, 2006, from http://www.crimewise.com/library/guards.html.

4 Jacobs, "Who's Minding the Guards?"

5 Mark Lipman and W. R. McGraw, "Employee Theft: A $40 Billion Industry," *The Annals* (July 1988), pp. 51–59.

6 Mississippi Office of the Attorney General, *Workplace Violence Prevention Guide* (Jackson, MS: Author, 2004).

7 Defense Personnel Security Research Center (PERSEREC), "History and Mission," retrieved December 10, 2005, from http://www.fas.org/sgp/othergov/perserec.html.

8 Privacy Rights Clearinghouse, "Employment Background Checks: A Jobseekers' Guide."

9 Wackenhut Consulting and Investigation Services, "Homepage," retrieved October 14, 2004, from http://www.ci-wackenhut.com.

10 Corporate Screening Services, "Homepage," retrieved November 23, 2005, from http://www.corporatescreening.com.

11 Privacy Rights Clearinghouse, "Employment Background Checks: A Jobseekers' Guide."

12 Craig Gilbert, "Checking the Checkers," *Security Management* (May 2005), p. 75.

13 Mike Freeman, "NFL Casts a Suspicious Gaze over Prospects," *New York Times* (April 11, 2000), pp. D1, D3.

14 Bob Glauber, "See the Draftee Run; See the Draftee Jump; See the Draftee Investigated by an Ex-FBI Agent," *Newsday* (April 17, 2005), pp. B10–B12.

15 Ibid.

16 Tammy Joyner, "Job Background Checks Surge," *Houston Chronicle* (May 1, 2005).

17 Ibid.

18 Kelly Pate Dwyer, "Sometimes It Feels Like Somebody's Watching Me," *Baltimore Sun* (June 12, 2005).

19 Yvette Armendariz, "Background Checks Widening," *The Arizona Republic* (November 21, 2005).

20 Patricia S. Jacobs, "Who's Minding the Guards?" retrieved April 10, 2007, from http://www.crimewise.com/library/guards.html.

21 "Did You Know That?" *Security Management* (July 2000), p. 16.

22 John F. Kirch, "Screening for Drugs In-House," *Security Management* (June 2000), p. 22.

23 Teresa Anderson, "Legal Reporter," *Security Management* (January 2005), p. 94.

24 Armendariz, "Background Checks Widening."

25 Ibid.

26 Darlene M. Clabault, "Background Checks: What You Need to Know," *Compliance Magazine* (April 2005), p. 18.

27 Privacy Rights Clearinghouse, "Employment Background Checks: A Jobseekers' Guide."

28 Fair Credit Reporting Act, 15 U.S. Code § 1681 *et seq.*

29 Frederick G. Giles, "Checking Credit when It's Due: Applicants Who Feel Discriminated against Because of Their Credit History Can Bring a Lawsuit against a Company," *Security Management* (June 2000), pp. 107–111.

30 Dwyer, "Sometimes It Feels Like Somebody's Watching Me."

31 Ibid.

32 Gary Fields, "Fingerprinting of Job-Seekers Proliferates," *Wall Street Journal* (June 7, 2005), p. B1.

33 Robyn Friedman, "Fingerprinting Made Mandatory for Real Estate Agents in Florida," *Sun-Sentinel* (April 17, 2006).

34 Fields, "Fingerprinting of Job-Seekers Proliferates."

35 John P. Beaudette, "The Truth Is out There: Preemployment Screening," *Security Management* (September 1999), pp. 135–140.

36 Frederick G. Giles, "What Trouble Lurks in Record Searches?" *Security Management* (May 2004), p. 46.

37 Sarah Muench, "Lost Sex Offenders Land Here: Katrina Compounds State's Tracking Woes," *The Arizona Republic* (November 1, 2005).

38 Armendariz, "Background Checks Widening."

39 Frederick G. Giles, "Recent Legal, Financial, and Other Developments Have Made the Task of Completing Background Checks More Challenging," *Security Management* (May 2004).

40 Gerard F. Ramker, *Improving Criminal History Records for Background Checks, 2005.* (Washington, DC: Bureau of Justice Statistics, 2006).

41 Lester S. Rosen, "Criminal Databases and Preemployment Screening," *Security Technology and Design* (July 2005), p. 26.

42 Diane Jennings, "For Victim, Weight of Criminal ID Theft Hard to Bear: Offender's False Use of Name Made Clearing Record Almost Hopeless," *Dallas Morning News* (November 11, 2005).

43 Ibid.

44 "Background Checks," *Security Management* (May 2000), p. 21.

45 Cheryl Dahle, "What's That Felony on Your Resume?" *New York Times* (October 17, 2004), p. B11.

46 N. Alexander Erlam, "You Mean He Works for Us?" *Security Management* (May 2005), pp. 82–88.

47 *Read v .Scott Fetzer C.*, Texas Supreme Court, 1998, as cited in Erlam, "You Mean He Works for Us?"

48 Erlam, "You Mean He Works for Us?"

49 Michael Stewart, "All School Workers Must Pass Background Test," *Pensacola News Journal* (August 22, 2005).

50 Michael Hinman, "Predator Act Fallout Hits Contractors," *Tampa Bay Business Journal* (October 23, 2005).

51 Stewart, "All School Workers Must Pass Background Test."

52 Hinman, "Predator Act Fallout Hits Contractors."

53 National Drug Intelligence Center, *National Drug Threat Assessment 2006* (Washington, DC: Author, 2006); U.S. Department of Health and Human Services, Substance Abuse and Mental Health Services Administration, *2004 National Survey on Drug Use and Health: National Findings* (Washington, DC: Author, 2005); U.S. Department of Labor, *Employer's Guide to Dealing with Substance Abuse* (Washington, DC: Author, 1990); and Eugene F. Ferraro, "Is Drug Testing Good Policy?" *Security Management* (January 2000), p. 166.

54 U.S. Department of Health and Human Services, Substance Abuse and Mental Health Services Administration, *2004 National Survey on Drug Use and Health: National Findings.*

55 U.S. Department of Health and Human Services, Substance Abuse and Mental Health Services Administration, *Emergency Department Trends from the Drug Abuse Warning Network, Final Estimates 1995–2002* (Washington, DC: Author, 2003).

56 Stephanie Armor and Del Jones, "Worker's Positive Drug Tests Decrease," *USA Today* (June 20, 2006).

57 Peter Cholakis, "How to Implement a Successful Drug-Testing Program," *Risk Management* (November 2005), p. 24.

58 Ibid.

59 Ibid.

60 Tom Hughes, "Public Student Drug Testing and the Special Needs Doctrine in *Board of Education v. Earls*: Just Getting Together," *Criminal Justice Policy Review* (March 2005), pp. 3–17; and *Board of Education v. Earls* 536 U.S. 822 (2002).

61 C. J. Dangelo, "Individual Worker and Drug Test: Tort Actions for Defamation, Emotional Distress and Invasion of Privacy," *Duquesne Law Review*, 28(1990), pp. 545–559.

62 Armor and Jones, "Worker's Positive Drug Tests Decrease."

63 U.S. Department of Health and Human Services, Substance Abuse and Mental Health Services Administration, Division of Workplace Programs, "Reasons for Drug Testing," retrieved November 25, 2005, from http://www.dwp.samhsa.gov/index.aspx.

64 U.S. Department of Health and Human Services, Substance Abuse and Mental Health Services Administration, Division of Workplace Programs, "Preventing Employees from Cheating on a Urine Drug Test," retrieved November 25, 2005, from http://www.dwp.samhsa.gov/index.aspx.

65 Deena C. Knight, *Substance Abuse in the Workplace* (Mt. Airy, NC: Office Solutions/Officer Dealer, 2002).

66 Ibid.

67 Cholakis, "How to Implement a Successful Drug-Testing Program."

68 Gary Winn and Thomas McDowell, "Waiting to Exhale: Security Must Understand How Breath Alcohol Detection Technologies Work and Their Relative Advantages and Drawbacks," *Security Management* (November 1999), pp. 129–133.

69 *Board of Education v. Earls* 536 U.S. 822 (2002).

70 "Public Student Drug Testing and the Special Needs Doctrine," and *Board of Education v. Earls* 536 U.S. 822 (2002).

71 Ibid.

72 Stephen L. Mehay and Rosalie L. Pacula, *Effectiveness of Workplace Drug Prevention Policies: Does "Zero Tolerance Work"?* (Cambridge, MA: National Bureau of Economic Research Inc., 1999).

73 Armendariz, "Background Checks Widening."

74 Nancy J. Amick and Richard C. Sorenson, "Factors Influencing Women's Perceptions of a Sexually Hostile Workplace," *Journal of Emotional Abuse* (2004), pp. 49–69.

75. Timothy S. Bland, "Get a Handle on Harassment," *Security Management* (January 2000), pp. 62–67.

76. Sheila Gladstone, "New Era of Sexual Harassment Law," *Perspectives* (Spring 2000), pp. 46–53.

77. Bland, "Get a Handle on Harassment."

78. Sue Carter Collins and Michael S. Vaughn, "Liability for Sexual Harassment in Criminal Justice Agencies," *Journal of Criminal Justice* (November/December 2004), pp. 531–545.

79. Privacy Rights Clearinghouse, "Employee Monitoring: Is There Privacy in the Workplace?" retrieved December 2, 2005, from http://www.privacyrights.org.

80. Rosemary Winters, "E-Mail on the Job Is Risky Biz," retrieved June 12, 2006, from http://www.sltrib.com.

81. John Goemaat, "Here's What Companies Need to Know before Conducting Investigations into Employee Conduct," *Security Management* (May 2004).

82. Privacy Rights Clearinghouse, "Employment Background Checks: A Jobseekers' Guide."

83. Marta Lawrence, "Water Security on Tap," *Security Management* (June 2006), pp. 34–35.

84. ASIS International, "Preemployment Background Screening Guidelines," retrieved December 15, 2006, from http://www.asisonline.org.

Chapter 9

1. K. W. Strandberg, "Cyber Crime Today," *Law Enforcement Technology* (April 1999), pp. 24–29.

2. Adam Liptak, "Laws Involving Contact with Minors Allow Prosecutors a Broad Range of Discretion," *New York Times* (October 2, 2006).

3. Associated Press, "Security Aide Charged in Online Seduction," *New York Times* (April 5, 2006).

4. Molly Moore and Daniel Williams, "France's Youth Battles Also Waged on the Web; Via Internet, Violence Is Incited, Debated, Tracked," *Washington Post* (November 10, 2005), p. A18.

5. Rob Varnon, "Bank Officials Warn against Internet Scams," *Connecticut Post* (October 29, 2005).

6. William Eazel, "One Third of Large Enterprises Admit Being Hacked," *SC Magazine* (November 1, 2005).

7. Timothy L. O'Brien, "Gone in 60 Seconds; Identity Theft Is Epidemic; Can It Be Stopped?" *New York Times* (October 24, 2004), pp. BU1, BU4.

8. Alex Berenson, "On Hair-Trigger Wall Street, a Stock Plunges on Fake News," *New York Times* (August 26, 2000), pp. A1, C4; and Berenson, "Suspect Is Arrested in Fake News Case," *New York Times* (September 1, 2000), pp. B1, B5.

9. Neil MacFaraquhar, "Named a Market Swindler at Fifteen," *New York Times* (September 22, 2000), pp. B1, B5.

10. Tracy Connor, "Cops: Mom Forced Kid into Cyberporn," *New York Post* (August 25, 2000), p. 7.

11. "'Pokey' Virus Infecting PCs," *Newsday* (August 25, 2000), p. A65.

12. Dequendre Neeley, "Protection Progress Report," *Security Management* (May 2000), p. 34.

13. "Home Web Security Falls Short, Survey Shows," *New York Times* (October 25, 2004), p. C4.

14. National Cyber Security Alliance, "Make Cyber Security a Habit," retrieved October 26, 2004, from http://www.staysafeonline.info.

15. "Computer Vulnerability Found at Federal Agency," *New York Times* (August 13, 2000), p. 18.

16. "U.S. Agencies Get Failing Marks for Computer Security Systems," *New York Times* (September 12, 2000), p. A21; and "Systems All Fouled Up," *Security Management* (June 2000), p. 14.

17. W. P. Williams, "National Cybercrime Training Partnership," *Police Chief* (February 1999), pp. 17–27.

18. Seth Schiesel, "Growth of Wireless Internet Opens New Path for Thieves," *New York Times* (March 19, 2005), p. A10

19. Steve Hargreaves, "Stealing Your Neighbor's Net," *CNN/Money* (August 10, 2005).

20. Peter Grabosky, "Global Dimension of Cybercrime," *Global Crime* (February 2004), pp. 146–157; Council of Europe, "Summary of the Organised Crime Situation Report 2004: Focus on the Threat of Cybercrime," *Trends in Organized Crime* (Spring 2005), pp. 41–50; Korean Institute of Criminology and Government of Canada, *Workshop 6: Measures to Combat Computer-Related Crime* (New York: United States Publications, 2005); and Ryan P. Wallace, Adam M. Lusthaus, and Jong Hwan J. Kim, "Computer Crimes," *American Criminal Law Review* (Spring 2005), pp. 223–276.

21. L. E. Quarantiello, *Cyber Crime: How to Protect Yourself from Computer Criminals* (Lake Geneva, WI: LimeLight Books, 1997).

22. Martin L. Forst, *Cybercrime: Appellate Court Interpretations* (San Francisco: Montclair Enterprises, 1999).

23. Business Software Alliance, "Types of Cyber Crime," retrieved October 26, 2004, from http://www.global.bsa.org/cybercrime/cybercrimes

24. Business Software Alliance, "Homepage," retrieved November 1, 2004, from http://www.bsa.org.

25. Chris Hale, "Cybercrime: Facts & Figures Concerning This Global Dilemma," *Crime & Justice International* (September 2002), pp. 5–6, 24–26.

26. Business Software Alliance, "CyberCrime," retrieved October 26, 2004, from http://www.global.bsa.org/cybercrime/cybercrimes.

27. Ramona R. Rantala, *Cybercrime against Businesses* (Washington, DC: U.S. Department of Justice, Office of Justice Programs, Bureau of Justice Statistics, 2004), p. 1.

28. J. Drinkhall, "Internal Fraud," *Journal of Financial Crime* (January 1997), pp. 242–244.

29. Laura Pedersen-Pietersen, "The Hunt for Cybercrime," *New York Times* (December 26, 1999), p. BU8.

30. National White Collar Crime Center, *IC3 2004 Internet Fraud Crime Report, January 1, 2004–December 31, 2004* (Richmond, VA: Author, 2005); Internet Fraud Complaint Center, retrieved September 5, 2004, from http://www.ifccfbi.gov; and "Online Fraud," *Security Management* (August 2000), p. 20.

31. National White Collar Crime Center, *IC3 2004 Internet Fraud Crime Report.*

32. Judith H. Dobrzynski, "FBI Opens Investigation of eBay Bids," *New York Times* (June 7, 2000), pp. C1, C22.

33. O'Brien, "Officials Worried over a Sharp Rise in Identity Theft: Internet's Role Is Cited," *New York Times* (April 3, 2000), pp. A1, A19.

34. Katrina Baum, *Identity Theft, 2004* (Washington, DC: Bureau of Justice Statistics, 2006), p. 1.

35. U.S. Department of Justice, "Identity Theft and Fraud Web Page," retrieved November 10, 2005, from http://www.ncjrs.gov/spotlight/identity_theft/summary.html.

36. 18 USC 1001 to 1028. Public Law 105-318, 112Stat.3007.

37. 18 USC 1001. Public Law 108-275, 118Stat.831.

38 U.S. Federal Trade Commission, "Facts for Consumers: ID Theft: What's It All About?" retrieved November 10, 2005, from http://www.ftc.gov/bcp/conline/pubs/credit/idtheftmini.htm.

39 S. Wexler, "Recovering Stolen Identities," *Law Enforcement Technology*, 26(4, April 1999), pp. 36–39.

40 Matthew L. Lease and Tod W. Burke, "Identity Theft: A Fast-Growing Crime," *FBI Law Enforcement Bulletin* (August 2000), pp. 154–160.

41 Alice Dragoon, "Foiling Phishing," retrieved October 29, 2004, from http://www.csoonline.com/read/100104/phish.html.

42 Candace Heckman, "Phishing Finds Victims Even among Savvy Computer Users," *Seattle Post-Intelligencer* (May 1, 2006).

43 Tony Krone, *Phishing* (Canberra ACT: Australian Institute of Criminology, 2005).

44 Jonathan Jenkins, "ID Theft Ring Hacks Bank Accounts," *Toronto Sun* (October 29, 2005).

45 "Insuring against Identity Theft," *St. Petersburg Times* (June 18, 2000), p. H2.

46 "Victims Describe Identity Theft," *Security Management* (August 2000), p. 16. Also see Tom Zeller Jr., "For Victims, Repairing ID Theft Can Be Grueling," *New York Times* (October 1, 2005).

47 "40 Accused in Internet Identity Theft Ring," *New York Times* (October 29, 2004), p. B7.

48 Steven Martin, "Banks Told to Step Up Security against Identity Theft," *InformationWeek* (October 24, 2005).

49 John Leland, "Some ID Theft Is Not for Profit, But to Get a Job," *New York Times* (September 4, 2006), pp. A1, A13.

50 ASIS International, "Virtual Forum: Identity Theft: Action Items for Detection, Prevention, and Redemption," retrieved November 10, 2005, from http://www.asisonline.org.

51 Mary Henych, Stephen Holmes, and Charles Mesioh, "Cyber Terrorism: An Examination of the Critical Issues," *Journal of Information Warfare*, 2(2, 2003), pp. 1–14.

52 Donna Rogers, "Intercepting the Cybersleuth," *Law Enforcement Technology* (November 2003), pp. 22, 24–27.

53 U.S. General Accounting Office, *Critical Infrastructure Protection: Challenges and Efforts to Secure Control Systems* (Washington, DC: Author, 2004).

54 Louise I. Shelley, *Organized Crime, Terrorism and Cybercrime* (Washington, DC: Transnational Crime and Corruption Center, American University, 2001).

55 Carole Moore, "Protecting Your Backdoor," *Law Enforcement Technology* (June 2005), pp. 80–89.

56 Steven Levy and Brad Stone, "Hunting the Hackers," *Time* (February 21, 2000), pp. 38–49.

57 "Computer Crime Survey," *Security Management* (September 2004), p. 40.

58 Computer Security Institute, "Homepage," retrieved November 1, 2004, from http://www.gocsi.com.

59 M. A. Joyce and S. Barrett, "Evolution of the Computer Hacker's Motives," *Police Chief* (February 1999), pp. 28–35.

60 Neeley, "Hacktivism or Vandalism?" *Security Management* (February 2000), p. 30.

61 Neeley, "Underground Web Sites," *Security Management* (January 2000), p. 34.

62 John M. Deirmenjiian, MD, "Stalking in Cyberspace," *Journal of the American Academy of Psychiatry and the Law*, 27(3, 1999), pp. 407–413.

63 Liptak, "Laws Involving Contact with Minors Allow Prosecutors a Broad Range of Discretion"; and Associated Press, "Security Aide Charged in Online Seduction."

64 National Institute of Justice, *Internet Crimes against Children* (Washington, DC: Author, 2001). Also see Osita Iroegbu, "Who Are Your Kids Talking to Online?" *Richmond Times-Dispatch* (October 21, 2005); and Richard Wortley and Stephen Smallbone, *Child Pornography on the Internet* (Washington, DC: National Institute of Justice, 2006).

65 Ron Stodghill, "Sipowicz Goes Cyber: As Internet Crime Proliferates, Local Cops—Most of Them Young—Pioneer a New Beat on the Web," *Time* (April 10, 2000), p. 50.

66 Krone, *International Police Operations against Online Child Pornography* (Canberra ACT: Australian Institute of Criminology, 2005).

67 Federal Bureau of Investigation, *Parent's Guide to Internet Safety* (Washington, DC: Author, 1999).

68 Osita Iroegbu, "Who Are Your Kids Talking to Online?" *Richmond Times-Dispatch* (October 21, 2005).

69 Chris Gaither and Dawn C. Chmielewski, "Hip Youth Website Gets Grown Up about Safety," *Los Angeles Times* (April 11, 2006).

70 David Harley, "Living with Viruses: A Look at the Latest Virus Threats and Solutions," *Security Management* (August 2000), pp. 88–94.

71 John Markoff, "A Disruptive Virus Invades Computers around the World," *New York Times* (May 5, 2000), pp. Al, C9; see also Brad Stone, "Bitten by Love: How the 'Love Bug' Went on a Worldwide Tear," *Newsweek* (May 15, 2000).

72 Saul Hansell, "When Software Fails to Stop Spam, It's Time to Bring in the Detectives," *New York Times* (May 31, 2004), pp. C1, C7; and Hansell, "Junk E-Mail and Fraud Are Focus of Crackdown," *New York Times* (August 25, 2004), p. C1.

73 Ibid.

74 Ibid.

75 Ibid.

76 America on Line, "The Hottest Celebrity . . . Viruses?" retrieved November 12, 2005, from http://money.cnn.com/2005/06/16/technology/celebrity_viruses/index.htm.

77 Tom Zeller Jr., "FTC Files First Lawsuit against Spyware Concerns," *New York Times* (October 13, 2004), p. C10.

78 Ed Skoudis, "Mission Impossible," *Information Security* (July 2005), p. 36; and Robert L. Mitchell, "Spy stoppers Fight Back," *Computerworld* (October 31, 2005), p. 23.

79 "Software Pirates," *Security Management* (September 2004), p. 40.

80 Greg Sandoval, "Veterans' Data Swiped in Theft," retrieved November 11, 2006, from http://www.news.com.

81 Linda Rosencrance, "Report: Data Loss Widespread at Government Agencies," retrieved October 21, 2006, from http://computerworld.com.

82 Zeller Jr., "The Scramble to Protect Personal Data," *New York Times* (June 9, 2005), p. C1.

83 Randall Stross, "Whoops! We Seem to Have Misplaced Your Identity," *New York Times* (May 8, 2005), p. BU5; and Zeller Jr., "Time Warner Says Data on Employees Is Lost," *New York Times* (May 3, 2005), p. C4.

84 Zeller Jr., "Westlaw to Curtail Access to Personal Data," *New York Times* (March 18, 2005), p. C4.

85 "LexisNexis Restricts Access to Personal Data," *New York Times* (March 19, 2005), p. B4.

86 Eric Dash and Tom Zeller Jr., "MasterCard Says 40 Million Files Are Put at Risk; Scope of Losses Unclear; Many Fraudulent Charges Are Traced to Theft at a Payment Hub," *New York Times* (June 18, 2005), pp. A1, C13.

87 Zeller Jr., "Investigators Argue for Access to Private Data," *New York Times* (March 21, 2005), pp. C1, C5.

88 CIO Homepage, "What Is a CIO?" retrieved October 29, 2004, from http://cio.com/summaries/role/description/indix.html.

89 CSOonline.com, "Who Is the Chief Security Officer?" retrieved October 29, 2004, from http://www.csonline.com/research/security_exec/cso_role.html.

90 Information Systems Security Association (ISSA), "Homepage," retrieved November 1, 2004, from http://www.issa.org.

91 Business Software Alliance (BSA) and ISSA, "BSA–ISSA Information Security Study Online Survey of ISSA Members-December 3, 2003," retrieved October 31, 2004, from http://www.issa.org.

92 Scott Blake, "Protecting the Network Neighborhood," *Security Management* (April 2000), pp. 65–71.

93 John Fontana, "Chevron Has Had It with Passwords," *Network World* (October 31, 2005), p. 1.

94 R. Godson, W. J. Olson, and L. Shelley, "Encryption, Computers, and Law Enforcement," *Trends in Organized Crime*, 3(1, Fall 1997), pp. 82–83.

95 Markoff, "Web Encryption Patent into Public Domain," *New York Times* (September 7, 2000), p. C8.

96 Ed Frauenheim, "Companies Ramping Up E-Mail Monitoring, *CNet* (June 8, 2005).

97 Ibid.

98 Frauenheim, "Companies Ramping Up E-Mail Monitoring"; and Lisa Guernsey, "You've Got Inappropriate Mail: Monitoring of Office E-Mail Is Increasing," *New York Times* (April 5, 2000), pp. C1, C10.

99 Charlotte Faltermayer, "Cyberveillance: Managers Are Increasingly Monitoring Employees' Computer Activity," *Time* (August 14, 2000), pp. B22–B25.

100 Stephanie Armour, "Warning: Your Clever Little Blog Could Get You Fired," *USA Today* (June 14, 2005).

101 Neeley, "You've Been Hacked. Now What?" *Security Management* (February 2000), pp. 65–68.

102 John Markoff, "New IBM Report Will Warn of Computer Security Threats; Early Alerts to Viruses, Worms, and Hacker Activity," *New York Times* (October 25, 2004), p. C4.

103 U.S.-Cert, "National Cyber Alert System," retrieved November 9, 2004, from http://www.us-cert.gov/cas/signup.html.

104 Richard Willing, "Army's New Password: 'Biometrics': To Fight Hacks, Pentagon Turns to Body-Based ID Systems That Can't Be Faked," *New York Times* (June 22, 2000), p. A3.

105 David Griffith, "How to Investigate Cybercrime," *Police* (November 2003), pp. 18–20, 22.

106 Griffith, "How to Investigate Cybercrime"; Angelique C. Grado, "Internet Investigations: The Crime Scene of Cybercrime," *Evidence Technology Magazine* (July/August 2005), pp. 12–15, 38; and Jon Berryhill, "Finding a Qualified Computer Forensic Analyst," *Law Enforcement Technology* (May 2005), pp. 122–127.

107 Patience Wait, "Fighting Cybercrime on a Shoestring Budget," *Government Computer News* (October 24, 2005).

108 R. L. Mendell, *Investigating Computer Crime: A Primer for Security Managers* (Springfield, IL: Charles C. Thomas, 1998).

109 Lois Pilant, "Electronic Evidence Recovery," *Police Chief* (February 1999), pp. 37–48.

110 International Association of Computer Investigative Specialists, "About IACIS," retrieved November 22, 2005, from http://www.iacis.info/iacisv2/pages/about.php.

111 Ibid.

112 National Institute of Justice, *Forensic Examination of Digital Evidence: A Guide for Law Enforcement*, retrieved November 8, 2004, from http://www.ojp.usdoj.gov/nij/pubs-sum/199408.htm.

113 International High Technology Crime Investigation Association, "Homepage," retrieved November 22, 2005, from http://www.htcia.org.

114 Computer Crime Research Center, "Homepage," retrieved November 22, 2005, from http://www.crime-research.org.

115 Sergio D. Kopelev, "Cyber Sex Offenders," *Law Enforcement Technology* (November 1999), pp. 46–50.

116 Janet Reno, "Partners against Crime," *Law Enforcement Technology* (December 1999), pp. 62–66.

117 Federal Bureau of Information, "Homepage," retrieved October 6, 2006, from http://www.fbi.gov.

118 Arshad Mohammed, "New Rules on Internet Wiretapping Challenged," *Washington Post* (October 26, 2005), p. D1. See also Sam Dillon and Stephen Labaton, "Colleges Protest Call to Upgrade Online Systems," *New York Times* (October 23, 2005).

119 Jonathan Krim, "FBI Dealt Setback on Cellular Surveillance," *Washington Post* (October 28, 2005), p. A5.

120 Ibid.

121 Kroll Inc., "Technology Services," retrieved November 1, 2004, from http://www.krollworldwide.com/services/technology/index.

122 Pinkerton Consulting and Investigations, "Monitoring E-Commerce," retrieved November 1, 2004, from http://www.ci-pinkerton.com/brand/comerce.html.

123 Wackenhut Consulting and Investigation Services, "Internet Monitoring," retrieved November 1, 2004, from http://www.ci-wackenhut.com/brand_integrity.htm.

124 Moore and Williams, "France's Youth Battles Also Waged on the Web."

Chapter 10

1 Robert D. McCrie, *Security Letter Source Book* (New York: Security Letter, 1994), p. 6.

2 Pinkerton Consulting and Investigations Services, "Homepage," retrieved October 14, 2004, from http://www.ci-pinkerton.com.

3 Wackenhut Consulting and Investigation Services, "Homepage," retrieved October 14, 2004, from http://www.ci-wackenhut.com.

4 Joseph B. Treaster, "Gumshoes with White Collars: Deal Spotlights New Shrewdness in Detective Business," *New York Times* (August 29, 1997), pp. D1, D4; also see http://www.kroll.com.

5 Sam Brown and Gini Graham Scott, *Private Eyes: The Role of the Private Investigator in American Marriage, Business, and Industry* (New York: Citadel Press, 1991), p. 1.

6 Sandy Granville Sheehy, "The Adventures of Harold Smith, Art Supersleuth," *Town and Country Monthly* (October 1992), p. 118.

7 Dick Adler, "Brian Jenkin's Excellent Adventures," *Inc.* (October 1991), p. 47.

8   Thomas Bancroft, "Growth Business," *Forbes* (September 1992), p. 516.

9   Pamela Marin and Warren Kalbacker, "Love Dicks," *Playboy* (January 1991), p. 102; Steven Edwards, "The Rush to Private Eyes: Wary Lovers Check Up on Partners," *MacLean's* (March 1990), p. 49; and Bill Colligan, "Just Dial 1-900-CHEATER," *Newsweek* (July 29, 1991), p. 58.

10 Peter Wilkinson, "The Big Sleazy," *Gentlemen's Quarterly* (January 1992), p. 112.

11 L. J. Davis, "International Gumshoe," *New York Times Magazine* (August 30, 1992), p. 46.

12 "Checking Out Prospective Mates: Check-a-Mate, a Private Detective Service," *USA Today Magazine* (December 1990), p. 4.

13 Tom Dunkel, "Holy Sleuth Frees Innocent Souls," *Insight* (February 4, 1991), p. 52.

14 Scott Shuger, "Public Eye," *New York Magazine* (September 13, 1992), p. 56.

15 Mary Ivey, "Philip Marlowe? No. Successful? Yes," *Business Week* (October 21, 1991), p. 60.

16 Amanda Gardner, "Corporate Eyes," *Inc.* (November 1991), p. 61.

17 Robert Mortiz, "A Pet Sleuth to the Rescue," *Parade* (July 11, 2004), pp. 8, 9; and "Doggone? Bloodhound Ron Dufault Runs Around in Circles to Help Pet Owners Find Their Missing Pooches," *People Weekly* (September 10, 1990), p. 151.

18 Ronnie Virgets, "Secret Services," *New Orleans Magazine* (March 1992), p. 36.

19 The National Association of Investigative Specialists, "Homepage," retrieved October 15, 2004, from http://www.pimall.com/nais/nais.j.html.

20 International Private Investigators Union, "Homepage," retrieved October 15, 2004, from http://www.ipiu.org.

21 National Investigator Associations, "USA Links," retrieved October 15, 2004, from http://www.pimagazine.com/links_national.htm.

22 *PI Magazine: Journal of Professional Investigators*, "Homepage," retrieved October 15, 2004, from http://www.pi.org.

23 ASIS International, "Professional Certified Investigator," retrieved November 5, 2005, from http://www.asisonline.org; and the International Foundation for Protection Officers, "Crime and Loss Investigation Program," retrieved November 3, 2005, from http://www.ifpo.org.

24 Pamela A. Collins, Truett A. Ricks, and Clifford W. Van Meter, *Principles of Security and Crime Prevention*, 4th ed. (Cincinnati, OH: Anderson, 2000).

25 John S. Dempsey, *Introduction to Investigations*, 2nd ed. (Belmont, CA: Thomson/Wadsworth, 2003).

26 Alex Berenson, "Merck Is Winner in Vioxx Lawsuit on Heart Attack," *New York Times* (November 3, 2005), pp. A1, C2.

27 Keith Naughton, "Throwing the Brakes on Tires That Peel Out: Firestone Issues a Recall as Accidents Pile Up," *Newsweek* (August 21, 2000), p. 60; and John Greenwald, "Firestone's Tire Crisis: Company Recalls 6.5 Million of Its Most Widely Used Tires," *Time* (August 21, 2000), pp. 64–65.

28 For information on information brokers or national computerized databases, see Dempsey, *Introduction to Investigations*, 2nd ed.

29 Traffic Accident Reconstruction Organization, "Homepage," retrieved October 15, 2004, from http:// www.taro.org; and National Association of Professional Accident Reconstruction Specialists, "Homepage," retrieved October 15, 2004, from http://www.napars.org.

30 Dempsey, *Introduction to Investigations*, 2nd ed.

31 Murray Weiss, "Couple's Apt. Cam Bags Thieves," *New York Post* (September 29, 2004), p. 3.

32 Marianne Loschnig-Gspandl, "Corporations, Crime and Restorative Justice," in Elmar G. M. Weitekamp and Hans Jurgen Kerner, eds., *Restorative Justice in Context: International Practice and Dimensions* (Portland, OR: Willan Publishing, 2003), pp. 145–160.

33 "Sarbanes-Oxley Act," *Wikipedia*, retrieved November 4, 2005, from http://en.wikipedia.org/wiki/Sarbanes-Oxley-Act.

34 Robert J. Grossman, "Sox: Are You Clear?" *HR Magazine* (October 2005), p. 54.

35 Greg Winter, "Taking at the Office Reaches New Heights: Employee Larceny Is Bigger and Bolder," *New York Times* (July 12, 2000), pp. C1, C8.

36 American Institute of Certified Public Accountants, "About the AICPA," retrieved November 4, 2005, from http://www.aicpa.org/about/index.htm.

37 Barbara R. Farrell and Joseph R. Franco, "Role of the Auditor in the Prevention and Detection of Business Fraud: SAS No. 82," *Western Criminology Review*, 2(1, 1999), pp. 1–11.

38 C. A. Bradford and C. E. Simonsen, "Need for Cooperative Efforts between Private Security and Public Law Enforcement in the Prevention, Investigation, and Prosecution of Fraud-Related Criminal Activity," *Security Journal*, 10(3, September 1998), pp. 161–168.

39 Winter, "Taking at the Office Reaches New Heights."

40 Ibid.

41 Bob Degen, "Security Profit Potential," *Security Management* (November 1999), p. 28.

42 Winter, "Taking at the Office Reaches New Heights."

43 The Association of Certified Fraud Examiners, "Homepage," retrieved November 4, 2005, from http://www.acfe.com.

44 Joris Evers, "Banks to Blacklist Rogue Workers in Fraud Fight," C/Net News.com (October 26, 2005), retrieved November 8, 2005, from http://news.com.

45 Michael Linnitt, "Credit Card Fraud: Your Card in Their Hands," *Fraud* (May/June 2004), pp. 26, 29–48.

46 Tom Zeller Jr., "To Catch a Thief: How Merchants Are Fighting Back against Credit Card Fraud," *New York Times* (June 25, 2005), pp. C1, C13.

47 The International Association of Financial Crimes Investigators, "Homepage," retrieved October 18, 2004, from http://www.iafci.org.

48 Alfred T. Checkett, "Can We Do More to Fight Counterfeiting?" *Security Management* (February 1999), pp. 129–130. For an informative article on understanding copyright risks and the "fair use defense," see Pamela R. O'Brien, "Understanding Copyright Risks," *Security Management* (April 1999), pp. 68–73.

49 National Insurance Crime Bureau, "About NICB," retrieved October 11, 2004, from http://www.nicb.org.

50 National Society of Professional Insurance Investigators, "About NSPII," retrieved October 11, 2004, from http://www.nspii.com.

51 Phyllis Van Wyhe, "Special Investigative Units (SIUs)," retrieved October 16, 2004, from http://www.insurancece.com; "Special Investigative Unit Success Story—June

2004," retrieved October 16, 2004, from http://www.uticanational.com; and J. D. Decker, "Special Investigative Units Battle Insurance Fraud, 'Crime of the '90s'," retrieved October 16, 2004, from http://www.insurancejournal.com.

52 International Association of Special Investigation Units, "About IASIU," retrieved October 11, 2004, from http://www.iasiu.org.

53 Insurance Information Institute, "About III," retrieved October 11, 2004, from http://www.iii.org.

54 David Howard, "Painful Fall or Profitable Fraud?" *Security Management* (February 2000), pp. 76–82.

55 Jennifer Steinhauer, "Fertility Doctor Loses License during Review," *New York Times* (August 12, 2000), pp. B1, B6.

56 National Health Care Anti-Fraud Association, "Health Care Fraud," retrieved October 16, 2004, from http://www.nhcaa.org.

57 Ibid.

58 Julie Wartell and Nancy G. La Vigne, *Prescription Fraud* (Washington, DC: National Institute of Justice, 2004).

59 Sid Rocke, "Health Care Fraud Prosecution," *Prosecutor*, 38(1, January/February 2004), pp. 30–32.

60 The NHCAA Institute for Health Care Fraud Prevention, "About the Institute," retrieved October 11, 2004, from http://www.nhcaa-institute.org.

61 Carolyn Said, "Spying: Business as Usual. Subterfuge Seen as A Gray Area in World of Corporate Snooping," *San Francisco Chronicle* (September 12, 2006), retrieved September 17, 2006, from http://www.sfgate.com.

62 Randal F. Mueller, "Industrial Espionage: What Is It, Who's Involved and What Harm Can It Cause?" *Polygraph*, 30(1, 2001), pp. 47–55.

63 Peter R. J. Trim, "Counteracting Industrial Espionage through Counterintelligence: The Case for a Corporate Intelligence Unit and Collaboration with Government Agencies," *Security Journal*, 15(4, 2002), pp. 7–24.

64 E. G. Ross, "Corporate Espionage Can't Be This Easy: Industrial Espionage," *Security Management* (September 1999), pp. 75–81.

65 Damon Darlin and Matt Richtel, "Chairwoman Leaves Hewlett in Spying Furor," *New York Times* (September 23, 2006), pp. A1, C4; Matt Richtel, "Hewlett's Hunt for Leak Became a Game of Clue," *New York Times* (September 29, 2006), p. A1; and Damon Darlin and Miguel Helft, "HP before a Skeptical Congress," *New York Times* (September 29, 2006), p. C1.

66 Stephen Labaton, "Data 'Brokers' Battle Critics of Deceptive Practices," *New York Times* (June 14, 1999), pp. 1, 6.

67 "Detective Couple Indicted over Information Leaks," *New York Times* (June 27, 1999), p. 18.

68 See *Federal Trade Commission v. James J. Rapp et al.,* retrieved October 18, 2004, from http://www.ftc.gov/os/2000/06/touchtoneorder.htm.

69 See "The Gramm-Leach-Bliley Act: Pretexting," retrieved October 18, 2004, from http://www.ftc.gov/privacy/privacyinitiatives/pretexting.html.

Chapter 11

1 U.S. Department of Labor, "Occupational Outlook Handbook," retrieved October 24, 2005, from http://www.bls.gov.

2 Sam Brown and Gini Graham Scott, *Private Eyes: The Role of the Private Investigator in American Marriage, Business, and Industry* (New York: Carol Publishing Group, 1991), p. 162.

3 Lois Pilant, "Achieving State-of-the-Art Surveillance," *Police Chief* (June 1993), p. 25.

4 Brown and Scott, *Private Eyes,* p. 144.

5 Pilant, "Achieving State-of-the-Art Surveillance," p. 25.

6 Brown and Scott, *Private Eyes,* p. 168.

7 "Surveillance," *Security Management* (August 2004), p. 20.

8 John T. Nason, "Conducting Surveillance Operations: How to Get the Most Out of Them," *FBI Law Enforcement Bulletin*, 73(5, May 2004), pp. 1–7.

9 For a comprehensive article on advanced surveillance devices, see Lois Pilant, "Achieving State-of-the-Art Surveillance."

10 Aspect Technology and Equipment, "Homepage," retrieved January 13, 2005, from http://www.aspecttechnology.com

11 Pamela Mills-Senn, "Looking Around, Up and Down," *Law Enforcement Technology* (August 2005), pp. 84–93.

12 Jia-Rui Chong, "Probes Appear to Clear Facility; Nurses Had Accused Good Samaritan Hospital of Using Hidden Cameras to Spy On Them," *Los Angeles Times* (January 2, 2005), p. B3.

13 Pilant, "Achieving State-of-the-Art Surveillance."

14 Tom Yates, "Surveillance Vans," *Law and Order* (December 1991), p. 52.

15 Ibid.

16 Ibid., p. 53.

17 Bill Siuru, "Seeing in the Dark and Much More: Thermal Imaging," *Law and Order* (November 1993), pp. 18–20.

18 Ibid.

19 Yates, "'Eyes' in the Night," *Law and Order* (November 1993), pp. 19–24.

20 National Sheriffs' Association, "Law Enforcement Aircraft: A Vital Force Multiplier," *Sheriff*, 52(1, January-February 2000), pp. 32–60.

21 Cyrus Farivar, "A Flying Crime Fighter (Some Assembly Required)," *New York Times* (January 13, 2005), p. G7.

22 Donna Rogers, "GPS: Getting the Proper Positioning," *Law Enforcement Technology*, 27(9, September 2000), pp. 44–50; see also National Institute of Justice, *GPS Applications in Law Enforcement: The SkyTracker Surveillance System, Final Report* (Washington, DC: Author, 1998).

23 Eugene F. Ferraro, "How to Go Undercover," *Security Management* (June 2000), pp. 90–94; and Ferraro, "Ordinary People," *Security Management* (June 2000), pp. 48–50, 99–101.

24 Gary T. Marx, "The New Police Undercover Work," *Urban Life* (January 1980), pp. 399–446.

25 Jennifer Steinhauer, "The Undercover Shoppers: Posing as Customers, Paid Agents Rate the Stores," *New York Times* (February 4, 1998), pp. D1, D23.

26 Wackenhut Consulting and Investigation Services, "Surveillance," retrieved January 15, 2005, from http://www.ci-wackenhut.com.

27 Mystery Shopping Providers Association, "Homepage," retrieved October 24, 2005, from http://www.mystery-shop.org.

28 Pinkerton Investigative Services, "Pinkerton Compliance Services—AlertLine Ethics and Compliance Hotline," retrieved January 15, 2005, from http://www.ci-pinkerton.com.

29 Wackenhut Consulting and Investigation Services, "Safe-2Say Compliance Hotline," retrieved January 15, 2005, from http://www.ci-wackenhut.com.

30 Pinkerton Investigative Services, "Pinkerton Compliance Services—Field Research and Compliance Audits," retrieved January 15, 2005, from http://www.ci-pinkerton.com.

31 Sanford Wexler, "Working Undercover: Holding Onto Your Core Values Is Essential," *Law Enforcement Technology,* 31(11, November 2004), pp. 86, 88–90, 92–93.

32 Wayne W. Bennett and Karen M. Hess, *Criminal Investigation*, 3rd ed. (St. Paul, MN: West, 1991).

33 James N. Gilbert, "Case Study: Donnie Brasco Infiltrates the Mob," in Gilbert, ed., *Criminal Investigation: Essays and Cases* (Columbus, OH: Merrill, 1990), pp. 114–115.

34 James J. Ness and Ellyn K. Ness, "Reflections on Undercover Street Experiences," in Gilbert, ed., *Criminal Investigation,* pp. 110–111.

35 Brown and Scott, *Private Eyes,* p. 181.

36 David Owens, "On Life as an Undercover," in John S. Dempsey, *Introduction to Investigations,* 2nd ed. (Belmont, CA: Thomson/Wadsworth, 2003), pp. 248–249.

37 Doug Hanson, "What's Next—Soft Target Attacks," *Law Enforcement Technology* (August 2005), pp. 18–27.

38 Don Philpott, "Automated Surveillance," *Homeland Defense Journal* (April 2005), pp. 8–11.

Chapter 12

1 "Policing for Profit: Welcome to the New World of Private Security," *The Economist* (April 19, 1997), p. 22.

2 R. H. Moore Jr., "Private Security in the Twenty-First Century: An Opinion," *Journal of Security Administration,* 18(1, June 1995), pp. 3–20.

3 National Institute of Justice, Office of Community-Oriented Policing Services, *The 2004 National Policy Summit: Building Private Security/Public Policing Partnerships to Prevent and Respond to Terrorism and Public Disorder* (Washington, DC: Author, 2004); and Joseph M. Polisar, "President's Message: Cooperation by Private Security and Public Law Enforcement," *Police Chief* (October 2004), p. 10. For a complete list of all members participating in the summit, see Appendix A of the *2004 National Policy Summit;* Appendix B contains the presummit reading list; Appendix C contains the identity of all sponsors; Appendix E lists members of the Summit Advisory Committee; and Appendix F lists the members of the IACP staff participating in the report.

4 Reason Foundation, "About Reason Foundation," retrieved February 19, 2005, from http://www.reason.org.

5 Reason's Privatization Center, "About Privatization.org," retrieved February 19, 2005, from http://www.privatization.org.

6 Reason's Privatization Center, "Policing Services," retrieved February 19, 2005, from http://www.privatization.org.

7 "Policing for Profit," p. 22.

8 Bureau of Justice Assistance, U.S. Department of Justice, *Operation Cooperation* (Washington, DC: Author, 2000); and Edward Connors, William Cunningham, Peter Ohlhausen, Lynn Oliver, and Clifford Van Meter, *Operation Cooperation: Guidelines for Partnerships between Law Enforcement and Private Security Organizations* (Washington, DC: Bureau of Justice Assistance, U.S. Department of Justice, 2000).

9 Ibid.

10 International Association of Chiefs of Police, "IACP's Private Sector Liaison Committee: Partners in Public Safety," retrieved February 18, 2005, from http://www.iacp.org.

11 Community Policing Consortium, *National Business Leadership Strategies: A Guide to Engaging the Private Sector in Community Policing Initiatives* (Washington, DC: U.S. Department of Justice, Office of Community-Oriented Policing Services, 2002).

12 Al Youngs, "Future of Public/Private Partnerships," *FBI Law Enforcement Bulletin,* 73(1, January 2004), pp. 7–11; and "Partnerships," *Security Management* (April 2000), pp. 18–19.

13 Marty L. West, "Get a Piece of the Privatization Pie: Private Security Agencies," *Security Management,* 37(3, March 1993), p. 54.

14 Youngs, "Future of Public/Private Partnerships"; and "Partnerships."

15 Bruce L. Benson, "Privatization in Criminal Justice," *Independent Policy Report, Independent Institute,* retrieved April 30, 2007, from http://www.ncpa.org.

16 Ray Carroll, "Preventing Vehicle Crime in Australia through Partnerships and National Collaboration," *Crime Prevention Studies,* 17(2004), pp. 45–65.

17 Charles Craft, Chris Nelson, and Patti Power, "May the Task Force Be with You: Forging an Alliance to Combat Credit Fraud," *Police Chief,* 68(3, March 2001), pp. 71–73.

18 Daniel Wolfe, "ID-Theft Group Members Say Collaboration Helps," *American Banker* (February 17, 2005).

19 Illinois Motor Vehicle Theft Prevention Council, *Motor Vehicle Theft Prevention Council, 2003 Annual Report* (Chicago, IL: Author, 2003).

20 Downtown Research and Development Center, "Business Improvement Districts," retrieved December 28, 2004, from http://www.downtowndevelopment.com.

21 City of New York, New York City Department of Small Business Services, "Business Improvement Districts," retrieved December 28, 2004, from http://www.nyc.gov.

22 University of Wisconsin-Extension, "Business Improvement Districts," retrieved December 28, 2004, from http://www.uwex.edu.

23 City of Milwaukee, Department of City Development, "Business Improvement Districts," retrieved December 28, 2004, from http://www.mkedcd.org.

24 The City of San Diego, "Business Improvement Districts," retrieved December 28, 2004, from http://www.sannet.gov.

25 City Of Albany, NY, "Business Improvement Districts," retrieved December 28, 2004, from http://www.albanyny.org.

26 Heather MacDonald, *Why Business Improvement Districts Work* (New York: Manhattan Institute for Policy Research, 2004).

27 Jack R. Greene, Thomas M. Seamon, and Paul R. Levy, "Merging Public and Private Security for Collective Benefit: Philadelphia's Center City District," *American Journal of Police,* 14(2, 1995), pp. 3–20; also see Center City District/Central Philadelphia Development Corporation, "Center City District and Central Philadelphia Development Corporation Present: Make It Center City Philadelphia," retrieved November 19, 2006, from http://www.centercityphila.org.

28 Robert Stokes, "Place Management in Commercial Areas: Customer Service Representatives in Philadelphia's Central Business District," *Security Journal,* 15(2, 2002), pp. 7–19.

29 Reason Foundation, "Privatization.org: Policing Services," retrieved February 19, 2005, from http://www.privatization.org.

30 For further information on bail enforcement agents, see B. Burton, *Bail Enforcer: The Advanced Bounty Hunter* (Geneva,

IL: Paladin House Publishers, 1990); for an interesting academic article on bail enforcement agents, see Brian R. Johnson and Greg L. Worchol, "Bail Agents and Bounty Hunters: Adversaries or Allies of the Justice System?" *American Journal of Criminal Justice*, 27(2, Spring 2003), pp. 145–165. In this study, the authors participated in twenty-three successful or attempted apprehensions of bail jumpers in the Michigan area. Also see Ailene Torres, "Bounty Hunters: TV Makes Job Look Flashy, But It's Not," *The Tennessean* (September 13, 2006).

31 *Taylor v. Taintor*, 83 U.S. 366 (1872).

32 *Taylor v. Taintor*, 83 U.S. 366, at 371 (1872).

33 *Lund v. Clyde Police Department*, Nos. 99-3815/3816; 2000 FED App. 0368P (6th Cir) (2000).

34 National Association of Bail Enforcement Agents, "Homepage," retrieved February 18, 2005, from http://www.nabea.org.

35 American Bail Coalition, "Homepage," retrieved February 18, 2005, from http://www.americanbailcoalition.com.

36 American Bail Coalition, "Compendium Laws, Uniform Criminal Extradition Act (UCEA)," retrieved February 18, 2005, from http://www.americanbailcoalition.com.

37 To check a particular state's bail laws, refer to the American Bail Coalition, "Compendium Laws, Uniform Criminal Extradition Act (UCEA)," retrieved February 18, 2005, from, http://www.americanbailcoalition.com; and American Bail Coalition, "Bounty Hunter Laws," retrieved February 18, 2005, from http://www.americanbailcoalition.com.

38 American Bail Coalition, "Compendium Laws, Uniform Criminal Extradition Act (UCEA)."

39 Radford W. Jones, *Critical Incident Protocol—A Public and Private Partnership, 2000* (East Lansing: Michigan State University, School of Criminal Justice, 2000); and Jones, *Critical Incident Protocol—A Public and Private Partnership, 2002* (Washington, DC: U.S. Department of Justice, Office for Domestic Preparedness, 2002).

40 Jones, "Critical Incident Protocol: A Public and Private Partnership," *The Beacon*, 3(6, March 2001), pp. 3–5.

41 Michael A. Gips, "Shared Intelligence Makes Everyone Smarter," *Security Management* (January 2004), pp. 53–63.

42 U.S. Department of Homeland Security, Office for Domestic Preparedness, *Guidelines for Homeland Security: Prevention and Deterrence* (Washington, DC: Author, 2003).

43 "National Strategy for Prevention," *Security Management* (March 2004), p. 92; also see U.S. General Accounting Office, *Critical Infrastructure Protection: Challenges and Efforts to Secure Control Systems* (Washington, DC: Author, 2004).

44 Gips, "Doubts Greet New Info-Sharing Rule," *Security Management* (May 2004), pp. 14–15.

45 National Institute of Justice, Office of Community-Oriented Policing Services, *The 2004 National Policy Summit: Building Private Security/Public Policing Partnerships to Prevent and Respond to Terrorism and Public Disorder* (Washington, DC: Author, 2004); and Joseph M. Polisar, "President's Message: Cooperation by Private Security and Public Law Enforcement," *Police Chief* (October 2004), p. 10. For a complete list of all members participating in the summit, see Appendix A of *The 2004 National Policy Summit*; Appendix B contains the presummit reading list; Appendix C contains the identity of all sponsors; Appendix E lists members of the Summit Advisory Committee; and Appendix F lists the members of the IACP staff participating in the report.

46 Department of Homeland Security, "Working with DHS: Private Sector Office," retrieved December 25, 2004, from http://www.dhs.gov.

47 "ASIS Joins Information-Sharing Network," *Security Management* (October 2004), p. 68.

48 William K. Rashbaum, "Police Tactic against Terror: Let's Network," *New York Times* (August 14, 2004), p. B1.

49 Beth Silver, "Local Security Gets Boost," *Pioneer Press* (February 1, 2005).

50 John F. Kirch, "Keystone to Antiterror Fight," *Security Management* (October 2004), pp. 65–71.

51 For an excellent discussion of off-duty police officers working for private security concerns and the liability and constitutional issues involved, see David H. Peck, "When Police Walk the Security Beat," *Security Management* (October 1999), pp. 39–45.

52 Wackenhut Services Inc., "U.S. Government Services," retrieved February 18, 2005, from http://www.wsihq.com.

53 Ibid.

54 Wackenhut Services Inc., "Homeland Security/WMD," retrieved February 18, 2005, from http://www.wsihq.com.

55 The Wackenhut Corporation, "Wackenhut Nuclear Services," retrieved February 18, 2005, from http://www.wackenhut.com.

56 Pinkerton Government Services Inc., "Introductions to PGS," retrieved October 25, 2005, from http://www.pgs-usa.com.

57 United Government Security Officers of America, "Homepage," retrieved February 19, 2005, from http://www.ugsoa.com.

58 Wesley G. Skogan, *Disorder and Decline: Crime and the Spiral of Decay in American Neighborhoods* (New York: Free Press, 1990), p. 125.

59 "Policing for Profit," p. 22.

60 Rick Bragg, "Killings of Elderly Instill Fear in a Southern City," *New York Times* (December 11, 1998), p. A12.

61 Dennis Jay Kenney, "The Guardian Angels: The Related Social Issues," in Dennis Jay Kenney, ed., *Police and Policing: Contemporary Issues* (New York: Praeger, 1989), pp. 376–400.

62 Susan Pennell et al., "Guardian Angels: A Unique Approach to Crime Prevention," *Crime and Delinquency* (July 1989), pp. 376–400; and "Policing for Profit," p. 22.

63 The Guardian Angels, "Homepage," retrieved March 27, 2004, from http://www.guardianangels.org.

64 Metropolitan Government of Nashville & Davidson County, Tennessee, "Police Home," *Nashville.gov,* retrieved April 10, 2003, from http://www.police.nashville.org.

65 James Garofalo and Maureen McLeod, *Improving the Use and Effectiveness of Neighborhood Watch Programs* (Washington, DC: National Institute of Justice, 1988).

66 Dennis P. Rosenbaum, Arthur J. Lurigio, and Paul J. Lavrakas, *Crime Stoppers: A National Evaluation* (Washington, DC: National Institute of Justice, 1986).

67 Crime Stoppers U.S.A., "Homepage," retrieved November 19, 2006, from http://www.crimestopusa.com.

68 America's Most Wanted, "Homepage," retrieved November 19, 2006, from http://www.americasmostwanted.com.

69 Metropolitan Government of Nashville & Davidson County, Tennessee, "Police Home," *Nashville.gov,* retrieved March 27, 2004, from http://www.police.nashville.org.

70 City of Glendale, CA, "Police Home," retrieved March 27, 2004, from http://www.police.ci.glendale.ca.us.

71 Sanantonio.gov, "Homepage," retrieved March 27, 2004, from http://www.sanantonio.gov.

72 Reason's Privatization Center, "Policing Services," retrieved February 19, 2005, from http://www.privatization.org.

73 U.S. Department of Homeland Security, "Working with DHS: Citizen Corps," retrieved October 25, 2005, from http://www.dhs.gov.

Chapter 13

1 Ann L. Pastore and Kathleen Maguire, *Sourcebook of Criminal Justice Statistics, 2003* (Washington, DC: U.S. Department of Justice, 2004), p. 312.

2 Jonathan R. White, *Terrorism and Homeland Security*, 5th ed. (Belmont, CA: Wadsworth, 2006), p. 354.

3 Office of the President, Office of Homeland Security, *National Strategy for Homeland Security* (Washington, DC: Author, 2002).

4 Ibid., p. vii.

5 White, *Terrorism and Homeland Security*, p. 269.

6 Ibid.

7 Gary Stoller, "Homeland Security Generates Multibillion Dollar Business," September 10, 2006. See the website for the Homeland Security Research Corporation at http://www.homelandsecurityresearch.com, retrieved November 29, 2006.

8 White, *Terrorism and Homeland Security*, p. 6.

9 Ibid., p. 7.

10 National Counterterrorism Center, "NCTC Report on Incidents of Terrorism, 2005," retrieved August 16, 2006, from http://www.nctc.gov.

11 Louis J. Freeh, "Responding to Terrorism," *FBI Law Enforcement Bulletin* (March 1999), pp. 1–2.

12 Terrorism Knowledge Base of the National Memorial Institute for the Prevention of Terrorism, "Homepage," retrieved August 21, 2006, from http://www.tkb.org.

13 Ibid.

14 National Counterterrorism Center, "NCTC Report on Incidents of Terrorism, 2005"; and Karen DeYoung, "Terrorist Attacks Rose Sharply in 2005, State Dept. Says," *Washington Post* (April 29, 2006), p. A1.

15 White, *Terrorism and Homeland Security*, p. 91; and Michael T. Osterholm and John Schwartz, *Living Terrors* (New York: Delta, 2000), pp. 14–23.

16 "Bioterror," *Security Management* (January 2004), p. 18.

17 Department of Homeland Security (DHS), "Remarks by the President at the Signing of S.15-Project BioShield Act of 2004," retrieved September 23, 2006, from http://www.dhs.gov.

18 White, *Terrorism and Homeland Security*, pp. 94, 350–351.

19 See RAND Corporation, *Organizing for Homeland Security* (Santa Monica, CA: Author, 2002); Randall A. Yim, *National Preparedness: Integration of Federal, State, Local and Private Sector Efforts Is Critical to an Effective National Strategy for Homeland Security* (Washington, DC: U.S. General Accounting Office, 2002); David M. Walker, *Homeland Security: Responsibility and Accountability for Achieving National Goals* (Washington, DC: U.S. General Accounting Office, 2002); Michael Barletta, *After 9/11: Preventing Mass-Destruction Terrorism and Weapons Proliferation* (Monterey, CA: Center for Nonproliferation Studies, 2002); and JayEtta Hecker, *Homeland Security: Intergovernmental Coordination and Partnership Will Be Critical to Success* (Washington, DC: U.S. General Accounting Office, 2002). All of these documents are available at NCJRS at http://www.ncjrs.gov. Also see Joe Devanney and Diane Devanney, "Homeland Security and PATRIOT Acts," *Law and Order*, 51(8, August 2003), pp. 10–12.

20 DHS, "Protecting Travelers and Commerce," retrieved August 18, 2006, from http://www.dhs.gov.

21 DHS, "US-VISIT," retrieved December 15, 2005, from http://www.dhs.gov. Also see DHS, "US-Visit Begins Testing Radio Frequency Identification Technology to Improve Border Security and Travel," retrieved December 15, 2005, from http://www.dhs.gov; DHS, "Fact Sheet: Radio Frequency Identification Technology," retrieved December 15, 2005, from http://www.dhs.gov; and Jonathan Krim, "U.S. Passports to Receive Electronic Identification Chips," *Washington Post* (October 26, 2005).

22 Transportation Security Administration, "Federal Air Marshal Service," retrieved August 18, 2006, from http://www.tsa.gov.

23 U.S. Customs and Border Protection, "A Typical Day at U.S. Customs and Border Protection (CBP)," retrieved August 18, 2006, from http://www.cbp.gov.

24 U.S. Immigration and Customs Enforcement, "About Us," retrieved August 18, 2006, from http://www.ice.gov.

25 Cole Maxwell and Tony Blanda, "Terror by Sea: The Unique Challenges of Port Security," *FBI Law Enforcement Bulletin* (September 2005), pp. 22–26.

26 "Where the Money Went," *Newsday* (September 6, 2006), p. A5.

27 Federal Bureau of Investigation, "FBI Priorities," retrieved November 26, 2006, from www.fbi.gov.

28 D. Douglas Bodrero, "Confronting Terrorism on the State and Local Level," *FBI Law Enforcement Bulletin* (March 1999), pp. 11–18.

29 Bodrero, "Law Enforcement's New Challenge to Investigate, Interdict and Prevent Terrorism," *Police Chief* (February 2002), pp. 41–48.

30 Mathew J. Hickman and Brian A. Reaves, "Local Police and Homeland Security: Some Baseline Data," *Police Chief* (October 2002), pp. 83–88.

31 Robert F. Worth, "In a Quiet Office Somewhere, Watching Terrorists," *New York Times* (February 23, 2005), pp. B1, B6; and Erika Martinez, "NYPD's Global Eyes and Ears: Cops Abroad on Terror Beat," *New York Post* (November 28, 2005), p. 20.

32 New York City Police Department, "Operation Nexus," retrieved December 8, 2006, from http:///www.ncy.gov/html/nypd.

33 U.S. Department of Justice, *Assessing and Managing the Terrorism Threat* (Washington, DC: National Institute of Justice, 2005).

34 "National Strategy for Prevention," *Security Management* (March 2004), p. 92.

35 Office of the President, Office of Homeland Security, *National Strategy for Homeland Security* (Washington, DC: Author, 2002), p. viii.

36 Congress of the United States, Congressional Budget Office, *Homeland Security and the Private Sector* (Washington, DC: Author, 2004).

37 Pam Belluck, "States and Cities Must Hunt Terror Plots, Governor Says," *New York Times* (December 15, 2004), p. A22.

38 Ibid.

39 Sherry L. Harowitz, "The New Centurions," *Security Management* (January 2003), pp. 51–58. Also see Teresa Anderson, "A Year of Reassessment," *Security Management* (January 2003), pp. 61–65.

40 Harowitz, "The New Centurions," p. 52.

41 National Commission on Terrorist Attacks upon the United States, *9/11 Commission Report: The Final Report of the National Commission Terrorist Attacks upon the United States* (New York: W.W. Norton & Company, 2004), p. 323.

42 Ibid., pp. 397–398.

43 "ASIS Foundation to Survey Retail Mall Security," *ASIS Dynamics* (July/August 2004), p. 6.

44 "CSO Roundtable Gathers on Capitol Hill," *ASIS Dynamics* (January/February 2005), pp. 1, 23.

45 Lawrence Mark Cohen, "Bombs Away: Bomb Detection Technologies Continue to Improve, and They Are Being Used in Increasingly Effective Ways," *Security Management* (August 2004), pp. 47–54.

46 David W. Dunlap, "Adding Barricades, and Trying to Avoid the Feel of a Fortress," *New York Times* (September 23, 2004), p. B3. Also see Richard Kessinger, "From Jericho to Jersey Barrier," *Security Management* (August 2004), pp. 57–66.

47 "Fear of Flying," *The Economist* (August 19, 2006), p. 20.

48 Judy Keen, "Truckers, Bus Drivers on Lookout for Suspicious Activity on Roads," *USA Today* (August 30, 2006).

49 National Commission on Terrorist Attacks upon the United States, *9/11 Commission Report*, pp. 397–398.

50 Dean C. Alexander, *Business Confronts Terrorism: Risks and Responses* (Madison: University of Wisconsin Press, 2004).

51 Mark Sauter, Ken Holshouser, and Jim Doane, "A Pound of Prevention," *Security Management* (March 2004), pp. 91–102.

52 Michael A. Gips, "Shared Intelligence Makes Everyone Smarter," *Security Management* (January 2004), pp. 53–63.

53 Gips, "The First Link in the Food Chain," *Security Management* (February 2003); and Extension Disaster Education Network, "Plant and Crop Security," retrieved January 8, 2005, from http://www.agctr.osu.edu/eden/issues.

54 Ibid.

55 "Terrorism in the UK," *Security Management* (August 2004), p. 18.

56 Richard Perez-Pena, "A Security Blanket, But with No Guarantees," *New York Times* (March 23, 2003), pp. A1, B14, B15.

57 International Association of Chiefs of Police, *The 2004 National Policy Summit: Building Private Security/Public Policing Partnerships to Prevent and Respond to Terrorism and Public Disorder* (Alexandria: VA: Author, 2004).

58 Christopher Terzich, "Hundred Years of Preparedness," *Homeland Protection Professional* (June 2006), pp. 24–29.

59 "Sessions Focus on Homeland Security," *Security Management* (December 2004), pp. 123–124; "Security's French Connection," *ASIS Dynamics* (July/August 2006), pp. 1, 10; and "Asia-Pacific Security Conference," *ASIS Dynamics* (July/August 2006), p. 7.

60 Leonard A. Hall and Rick Adrian, "When the Front Lines are Local," *Security Management* (February 2004), pp. 70–81.

61 "Protection Goes beyond Prayer," *Security Management* (October 2004), p. 18.

62 Gips, "On the Water Front," *Security Management* (October 2003).

63 Cohen, "Bombs Away."

64 Joe Sharkey, "Tall (and Alert) in the Saddle on Airport Patrol," *New York Times* (March 6, 2005), p. TR6.

65 Derk Boss and Ann Longmore-Etheridge, "Casinos Strengthen Their Security Hand," *Security Management* (September 2006), pp. 78–86.

66 "Building Designs Cope with Threats," *Security Management* (October 2006), p. 34.

67 Grant Woodward, "30-Minute Bomb Patrol by City Centre Workers," *Leeds Today* (September 15, 2005).

68 National Institute of Justice, Office of Community-Oriented Policing Services, *The 2004 National Policy Summit: Building Private Security/Public Policing Partnerships to Prevent and Respond to Terrorism and Public Disorder* (Washington, DC: Author, 2004).

69 James F. Pastor, "Terrorism and Public Safety Policing," *Crime and Justice International* (March/April 2005), pp. 4–8.

70 DHS, "Working with DHS," retrieved December 16, 2005, from http://www.dhs.gov.

71 Gary Stoller, "Homeland Security Generates Multibillion Dollar Business," *USA Today* (September 10, 2006).

72 The SAFTEY Act, Support Anti-Terrorism by Fostering Effective Technologies Act of 2002. PL 107-296; DHS, "Working with DHS: Private Sector Office," retrieved December 25, 2004, from http://www.dhs.gov; and Rob Housman and Tony Anikeeff, "How Companies Can Compete for Contracts," *Law and Order* (January 2004), pp. 64–70.

73 Housman and Anikeeff, "How Companies Can Compete for Contracts."

74 Gips, "So You Want to Sell to the Government," *Security Management* (June 2004), pp. 16–17.

75 Ibid.

76 "ASIS Joins Information Sharing Network," *Security Management* (October 2004), p. 68.

77 Mary Alice Davidson, "DHS's New Schools of Thought," *Security Management* (July 2006), pp. 78–86.

78 Jeffrey Gettleman, "4 from U.S. Killed in Ambush in Iraq; Mob Drags Bodies," *New York Times* (April 1, 2004), pp. A1, A12. For more on these companies, see James Dao, "Private Guards Take Big Risks, for Right Price," *New York Times* (April 2, 2004), pp. A1, A9; David Barstow, "Security Companies: Shadow Soldiers in Iraq," *New York Times* (April 19, 2004), pp. A1, A14; and Eric Schmitt and Thom Shanker, "Big Pay Luring Military's Elite to Private Jobs," *New York Times* (March 30, 2004), pp. A1, A18. See also Daniel Bergner, "The Other Army," *New York Times Sunday Magazine* (August 14, 2005), pp. 29–35, 50–54.

79 David Robertson, "Providing Safe Passage in Hostile Lands," *London Times* (November 16, 2006), p. 68.

80 "Blood and Treasure," *The Economist* (November 4, 2006).

81 "Councils to the Rescue," *Security Management* (December 2004), p. 91.

Bibliography

Books

Albanese, Jay S. *Criminal Justice*. Boston: Allyn & Bacon, 1999.

Albrecht, Kathy. *The Lost Pet Chronicles: Adventures of a K-9 Cop Turned Pet Detective*. New York: Bloomsbury, USA, 2004.

Alexander, Dean C. *Business Confronts Terrorism: Risks and Responses*. Madison: University of Wisconsin Press, 2004.

American Civil Liberties Union. *Workplace Drug Testing Is Ineffective and Unfair: Random Drug Tests Do Not Ensure a Drug-Free Workplace*. New York: Author, 1998.

American Management Association. *American Management Association Survey on Workplace Drug Testing and Drug Abuse Policies, 1996*. New York: Author, 1996.

Aries, Philippe, and George Dulig. *A History of Private Life from Pagan Rome to Byzantium*. Cambridge, MA: Bellnap Press of Harvard University, 1987.

Aristotle. *Nicomachean Ethics*.

ASIS International. *Dynamics*. Alexandria, VA: Author, published yearly.

———. *Security Industry Buyers Guide*. Alexandria, VA: Author, published yearly.

———. *Training Offerings for ASIS International*. Alexandria, VA: Author, published yearly.

Atlanta Committee for the Olympic Games. *Securing the Safest Games Ever*. Atlanta: Author, n.d.

Ayto, John. *Dictionary of Word Origins: The Histories of More Than 8,000 English Language Words*. New York: Little, Brown & Company, 1990.

Bailey, F. Lee, Roger E. Zuckerman, and Kenneth R. Pierce. *The Employee Polygraph Protection Act: A Manual for Polygraph Examiners and Employers*. Severna Park, MD: American Polygraph Association, 1989.

Bailey, Robert. *Private Heat: An Art Hardin Mystery*. New York: M. Evans & Company, 2001.

Barletta, Michael. *After 9/11: Preventing Mass-Destruction Terrorism and Weapons Proliferation*. Monterey, CA: Center for Nonproliferation Studies, 2002.

Bayley, David H. *Forces of Order: Police Behavior in Japan and the United States*. Berkeley: University of California Press, 1976.

Bennett, Wayne W., and Karen M. Hess. *Criminal Investigation*, 3rd ed. St. Paul, MN: West, 1991.

Besharov, Douglas J., ed. *Family Violence: Research and Public Policy Issues*. Washington, DC: University Press of America, 1990.

Bologna, J., and P. Shaw. *Corporate Crime Investigation*. Woburn, MA: Butterworth-Heinemann, 1997.

Bonner, Robert J., and Gertrude Smith. *The Administration of Justice from Homer to Aristotle*. Chicago: University of Chicago Press, 1928.

Bridenbaugh, Carl. *Cities in Revolt: Urban Life in America, 1743–1776*. New York: Knopf, 1965.

———. *Cities in the Wilderness: Urban Life in America, 1625–1742*. New York: Capricorn, 1964.

Brito, C., and E. Gratto, eds. *Problem-Oriented Policing: Crime-Specific Problems, Critical Issues, and Making POP Work*. Washington, DC: Police Executive Research Forum, 2000.

Brown, Sam, and Gini Graham Scott. *Private Eyes: The Role of the Private Investigator in American Marriage, Business, and Industry*. New York: Carol Publishing Group, 1991.

Budden, Michael C. *Preventing Shoplifting without Being Sued*. Westport, CT: Quorum Books, 1999.

Burstein, Harvey. *Introduction to Security*. Upper Saddle River, NJ: Prentice Hall, 1999.

Burton, B. *Bail Enforcer: The Advanced Bounty Hunter*. Geneva, IL: Paladin House Publishers, 1990.

Champion, Dean J. *Criminal Justice in the United States,* 2nd ed. Chicago: Nelson-Hall, 1998.

Chapman, S. G., and T. E. St. Johnston. *The Police Heritage in England and America*. East Lansing: Michigan State University, 1962.

Clarke, Ronald V., ed. *Crime Prevention Studies*, Vol. 3. Monsey, NY: Criminal Justice Press, 1994.

———. *Preventing Mass Transit Crime, Crime Prevention Studies*. Monsey, NY: Criminal Justice Press, 1996.

———. *Situational Crime Prevention: Successful Case Studies*. Albany, NY: Harrow & Heston, 1972.

Clifford, Mary. *Identifying and Exploring Security Essentials*. Upper Saddle River: NJ, 2004.

Collins, Judith, and Sandra K. Hoffman. *Identity Theft: First Responders Manual for Criminal Justice Professionals, Police Officers, Attorneys, and Judges*. Flushing, NY: Looseleaf Law Publications, 2004.

———. *Identity Theft Victim's Assistance Guide*. Flushing, NY: Looseleaf Law Publications, 2004.

Collins, Pamela A., Truett A. Ricks, and Clifford W. Van Meter. *Principles of Security and Crime Prevention*, 4th ed. Cincinnati, OH: Anderson, 2000.

Coolidge, Olivia. *Roman People*. Boston: Houghton Miffin, 1959.

Corwell, F. R. *The Revolutions of Ancient Rome*. New York: Fred A. Prager, 1963.

Critchley, T. A. *A History of Police in England and Wales,* 2nd ed. Montclair, NJ: Patterson Smith, 1967.

———. *A History of Police in England and Wales,* 2nd ed. rev. Montclair, NJ: Patterson Smith, 1972.

Cunningham, William C., John J. Strauchs, and Clifford W. Van Meter. *The Hallcrest Report II: Private Security Trends: 1970–2000*. Boston: Butterworth-Heinemann, 1990.

Cunningham, William C., and Todd H. Taylor. *The Hallcrest Report: Private Security and Police in America*. Portland, OR: Chancellor Press, 1985.

Curtis, George E., and R. Bruce McBride. *Proactive Security Administration*. Upper Saddle River, NJ: Pearson/Prentice Hall, 2005.

Davies, Sandi J., and Ronald R. Minion. *Security Supervision: Theory and Practice of Asset Protection*, 2nd ed. Boston: Butterworth-Heinemann/Elsevier, 1999.

de Becker, Gavin. *The Gift of Fear: Survival Signals That Protect Us from Violence*. Boston: Little, Brown, 1997.

Dempsey, John S. *An Introduction to Public and Private Investigations*. Minneapolis/St.Paul: West, 1996.

———. *Introduction to Investigations*, 2nd ed. Belmont, CA: Wadsworth, 2003.

———. *Policing: An Introduction to Law Enforcement*. Minneapolis/St. Paul: West, 1994.

———. *An Introduction to Policing*, 2nd ed. Belmont, CA: West/Wadsworth, 1999.

Dempsey, John S., and Linda S. Forst. *An Introduction to Policing*, 3rd ed. Belmont, CA: ITP/Wadsworth, 2005.

———. *An Introduction to Policing*, 4th ed. Belmont, CA: Wadsworth, 2007.

Dewhurst, H. S. *The Railroad Police*. Springfield, IL: Charles C. Thomas, 1955.

Donigan, Robert L., Edward C. Fisher, et al. *The Evidence Handbook*, 4th ed. Evanston, IL: Traffic Institute, Northwestern University, 1980.

Draper, Hilary. *Private Police*. Atlantic Highlands, NJ: Humanities Press, 1978.

Durant, Will. *The Life of Greece: The Story of Civilization II*. New York: Simon & Schuster, 1966.

———. *The Story of Civilization, Vol. II: Christ and Caesar*. New York: Simon & Schuster, 1944.

Dyer, Thomas H. *Pompeii*. London: Geo. Bells & Sons, 1889.

Ehrlich, Eugene. *Amo, Amas, Amat and More*. New York: Harper & Row, 1987.

Einstein, Daniel L., and Menachem Amir, eds. *Policing, Security and Democracy: Special Aspects of Democratic Policing*. Huntsville, TX: Office of International Criminal Justice, 2001.

Elhanan, P. *Keep 'em Alive—The Bodyguard's Trade*. Geneva, IL: Paladin House Publishers, 1985.

Emsley, Clive. *Policing and Its Context, 1750–1870*. New York: Schocken, 1984.

Feather, Marni. *Internet and Child Victimization*. Woden Act: Australian Institute of Criminology, 1999.

Figgie International. *The Figgie Report, Part 4: Reducing Crime in America—Successful Community Efforts*. Willowby, OH: Figgie International, 1983.

Fischer, Robert J., and Gion Green. *Introduction to Security*, 6th ed. Boston: Butterworth-Heinemann, 1998.

———. *Introduction to Security*, 7th ed. Boston: Butterworth-Heinemann, 2005.

Fishel, Edwin C. *The Secret War for the Union: The Untold Story of Military Intelligence in the Civil War*. New York: Houghton Mifflin, 1996.

Fogelson, Roger M. *Big City Police*. Cambridge, MA: Harvard University Press, 1977.

Forst, Martin L. *Cybercrime: Appellate Court Interpretations*. San Francisco: Montclair Enterprises, 1999.

Gaines, Larry K., and Gary W. Cordner. *Policing Perspectives: An Anthology*. Los Angeles: Roxbury Publishing Company, 1999.

Gaines, Larry K., and Roger LeRoy Miller. *Criminal Justice in Action*. Belmont, CA: ITP/Wadsworth, 2005.

Germann, A. C., Frank D. Day, and Robert R. J. Gallati. *Introduction to Law Enforcement and Criminal Justice*. Springfield, IL: Charles C. Thomas, 1969.

Gilbert, James N., ed. *Criminal Investigation: Essays and Cases* (Columbus, OH: Merrill, 1990).

Gill, Martin, and Angela Spriggs. *Assessing the Impact of CCTV*. London: Great Britain Home Office Research Development and Statistics Directorate, 2005.

Glare, P. G. W. *Oxford Latin Dictionary*. Oxford Claridan: Oxford University Press, 1982.

Gunaratna, Rohan. *Inside Al Qaeda: Global Network of Terror*. New York: Berkley Books, 2002.

Hadaz, Moses. *A History of Rome*. Garden City, NY: Doubleday & Co., 1956.

Handgun-Free America. *Terror Nine to Five: Guns in the American Workplace, 1994–2003*. Arlington, VA: Author, 2004.

Hayes, Read. *Shoplifting Control*. Orlando, FL: Prevention Press, 1993.

Hess, Karen M., and Henry M. Wrobleski. *Introduction to Private Security*, 4th ed. Minneapolis/St. Paul: West, 1996.

Holder P., and D. L. Hawley. *Executive Protection Professional's Manual*. Woburn, MA: Butterworth-Heinemann, 1998.

Hollinger, Richard C., and J. L. Davis. *2002 National Retail Security Survey: Final Report*. Gainesville: University of Florida, 2003.

Hollinger, Richard C., and L. Langton. *2003 National Retail Security Survey*. Gainesville: University of Florida, 2004.

Horan, James D. *The Pinkertons: The Detective Dynasty That Made History*. New York: Crown, 1967.

Horan, James D., and Howard Swiggett. *The Pinkerton Story*. New York: Putnam, 1951.

Hungerford, Edward. *Wells Fargo: Advancing the American Frontier*. New York: Bonanza, 1949.

Hunt, W. E. *History of England*. New York: Harper & Brothers, 1938.

Hunt, William R. *Front-Page Detective: William J. Burns and the Detective Profession, 1880–1930*. Cleveland, OH: Popular Press, 1990.

International Association of Chiefs of Police. *The 2004 National Policy Summit: Building Private Security/Public Policing Partnerships to Prevent and Respond to Terrorism and Public Disorder*. Alexandria, VA: Author, 2004.

International Foundation for Protection Officers. *Protection Officer Training Manual*, 7th ed. Naples, FL: International Foundation for Protection Officers, 2003.

———. *Security Supervision: Theory and Practice of Asset Protection*, 2nd ed. Boston: Butterworth-Heinemann/Elsevier, 1999.

Johnson, Brian R. *Principles of Security Management*. Upper Saddle River, NJ: Pearson Prentice Hall, 2005.

Johnson, David R. *American Law Enforcement: A History*. St. Louis, MO: Forum Press, 1981.

———. *Policing the Urban Underworld*. Philadelphia: Temple University Press, 1979.

Johnston, Lee. *The Rebirth of Private Policing*. New York: Routledge, 1992.

Jones, Radford W. *Critical Incident Protocol—A Public and Private Partnership, 2000*. East Lansing: Michigan State University, School of Criminal Justice, 2000.

Kakalik, James S., and Sorrel Wildhorn. *The Private Police: Security and Danger*. New York: Crane Russak, 1977.

———. *Private Police in the United States: Findings and Recommendations (RAND Report R-869-DOJ)*. Santa Monica, CA: The RAND Corporation, 1971.

Kenney, Dennis Jay, ed. *Police and Policing: Contemporary Issues*. New York: Praeger, 1989.

Kinney, Joseph A. *Essentials of Managing Workplace Violence*. Charlotte, NC: National Safe Workplace Institute, 1995.

Klemke, L. W. *The Sociology of Shoplifting: Boosters and Snitches Today*. Westport, CT: Praeger, 1992.

Knight, Deena C. *Substance Abuse in the Workplace*. Mt. Airy, NC: Office Solutions/Officer Dealer, 2002.

Korean Institute of Criminology and the Government of Canada. *Workshop 6: Measures to Combat Computer-Related Crime*. New York: United States Publications, 2005.

Koslow, Christopher, and John Sullivan. *Jane's Facility Security Handbook*. Alexandria, VA: Jane's Information Group, 2000.

Krone, Tony. *International Police Operations against Online Child Pornography*. Canberra ACT: Australian Institute of Criminology, 2005.

———. *Phishing*. Canberra ACT: Australian Institute of Criminology, 2005.

Kunkel, Wolfgang. *An Introduction to Roman Legal and Constitutional History*, 2nd ed. Oxford, UK: Clarendon Press, 1973.

Lake, Carolyn. *Undercover for Wells Fargo*. Boston: Houghton Mifflin, 1969.

Lane, Roger. *Policing the City: Boston 1822–1885*. Cambridge, MA: Harvard University Press, 1967.

Lavine, S. A. *Allan Pinkerton: America's First Private Eye*. New York: Dodd, Mead, & Company, 1963.

Lester, Andrew. *Crime Reduction through Product Design*. Canberra ACT: Australian Institute of Criminology, 2001.

Levesley, Tom, and Amanda Martin. *Police Attitudes to and Use of CCTV*. London: Great Britain Home Office Research Development and Statistics Directorate, 2005.

Lintott, W. *Violence in Republican Rome*. Oxford, UK: Clarendon Press, 1968.

Lipson, M. *On Guard: The Business of Private Security*. New York: Times Books, 1975.

Lukas, J. Anthony. *Big Trouble: A Murder in a Small Western Town Sets off a Struggle for the Soul of America*. New York: Simon & Schuster, 1997.

MacDonald, Heather. *Why Business Improvement Districts Work*. New York: Manhattan Institute for Policy Research, 2004.

MacGregor, Mary. *Story of Rome*. New York: Frederick A. Stokes, 1914.

MacMullan, Ramsey. *Enemies of the Roman Order*. Cambridge, MA: Harvard University Press, 1966.

Manley, Anthony D. *The Retail Loss Prevention Officer: The Fundamental Elements of Retail Security and Safety*. Upper Saddle River, NJ: Pearson/Prentice Hall, 2004.

Mariani, Cliff. *Terrorism Prevention and Response*. Flushing, NY: Looseleaf Law Publications, 2003.

Martinez, Liz. *The Retail Manager's Guide to Crime & Loss Prevention: Protecting Your Business from Theft, Fraud and Violence*. Flushing, NY: Looseleaf Law Publications, 2004.

Mayhew, Claire. *Violent Assaults on Taxi Drivers: Incidence Patterns and Risk Factors*. Canberra ACT: Australia, Australian Institute of Criminology, 2000.

McCrie, Robert D. *Security Letter Source Book*. New York: Security Letter, 1994.

Mehay, Stephen L., and Rosalie L. Pacula. *Effectiveness of Workplace Drug Prevention Policies: Does "Zero Tolerance Work"?* Cambridge, MA: National Bureau of Economic Research, 1999.

Mendell, R. L. *Investigating Computer Crime: A Primer for Security Managers*. Springfield, IL: Charles C. Thomas, 1998.

Miller, John, and Michael Stone, with Chris Mitchell. *The Cell: Inside the 9/11 Plot: Why the FBI and CIA Failed to Stop It*. New York: Hyperion, 2002.

Monkkonen, Eric. *Police in Urban America: 1860–1920*. Cambridge, MA: Harvard University Press, 1981.

Moore, Mark A., Carol V. Petrie, Anthony A. Braga, and Brenda L. McLaughlin. *Deadly Lessons: Understanding Lethal School Violence*. Washington, DC: National Academies Press, 2003.

National Association of Convenience Stores. *Convenience Store Security Report and Recommendations: November 1991*. Alexandria VA: Author, 1991.

National Commission on Terrorist Attacks upon the United States. *9/11 Commission Report: Final Report of the National Commission on Terrorist Attacks upon the United States*. New York: W. W. Norton & Company, 2004.

National Counterterrorism Center. *A Chronology of Significant International Terrorism for 2004*. Washington, DC: Author, 2005.

Naumann, Kurt. *Briefing Paper: Bullying*. Little Rock: School Violence Resource Center, University of Arkansas, 2001.

Nelson, Diana, and Santina Perrone. *Understanding and Controlling Retail Theft*. Woden ACT: Australian Institute of Criminology, 2000.

Nemeth, Charles. *Private Security and the Law*, 3rd ed. Burlington, MA: Elsevier Butterworth-Heinemann, 2005.

Nichols, Laura J. *Use of CCTV/Video Cameras in Law Enforcement, Executive Brief*. Alexandria, VA: International Association of Chiefs of Police, 2001.

Ortmeier, P. J. *Security Management: An Introduction*, 2nd ed. Upper Saddle River, NJ: Pearson/Prentice Hall, 2005.

Osterholm, Michael T., and John Schwartz. *Living Terrors*. New York: Delta, 2000.

Palmiotto, Michael, J., ed. *Critical Issues in Criminal Investigations*, 2nd ed. Cincinnati, OH: Anderson Publishing, 1988.

Pike, Luke Owen. *A History of Crime in England*. London: Smith, Elder, 1873–1876.

Pinkerton, Allan. *The Expressman and the Detective*. New York: Arno Press, 1976.

Police Foundation. *Domestic Violence and the Police: Studies in Detroit and Kansas City*. Washington, DC: Police Foundation, 1977.

Post, Richard, and Arthur A. Kingsbury. *Security Administration: An Introduction*. Springfield, IL: Charles C. Thomas, 1970.

Poulin, K. C., and Charles P. Nemeth. *Private Security and Public Safety: A Community-Based Approach*. Upper Saddle River, NJ: Pearson/Prentice Hall, 2005.

Prassel, Frank R. *The Western Peace Officer: A Legacy of Law and Order*. Norman: University of Oklahoma Press, 1972.

Pringle, Patrick. *Highwaymen*. New York: Roy, 1963.

———. *Hue and Cry: The Story of Henry and John Fielding and Their Bow Street Runners*. New York: Morrow, 1965.

———. *The Thief Takers*. London: Museum Press, 1958.

Punch, Maurice, ed. *Control of the Police Organization*. Cambridge, MA: MIT Press, 1983.

Quarantiello, L. E. *Cyber Crime: How to Protect Yourself from Computer Criminals*. Lake Geneva, WI: LimeLight Books, 1997.

RAND Corporation. *Organizing for Homeland Security*. Santa Monica: CA: Author, 2002.

Reith, C. *Blind Eye of History*. Montclair, NJ: Patterson, Smith, 1975.

Reppetto, Thomas. *The Blue Parade*. New York: Free Press, 1978.

Reynolds, P. K. Baillie. *The Vigiles of Imperial Rome*. London: Oxford University Press, 1926.

Richards, James R. *Transnational Criminal Organizations, Cybercrime, and Money Laundering: Handbook for Law Enforcement Officers, Auditors, and Financial Investigators*. Boca Raton, FL: CRC Press, 1999.

Richardson, James F. *The New York Police: Colonial Times to 1901*. New York: Oxford University Press, 1976.

———. *Urban Police in the United States*. Port Washington, NY: Kennikat Press, 1974.

Ricks, Truett A., Bill G. Tillett, and Clifford W. Van Meter. *Principles of Security*, 3rd ed. Cincinnati, OH: Anderson, 1994.

Rieck, Albert. *Justice and Police in England*. London: Butterworth, 1936.

Roberts, Albert R., ed. *Juvenile Justice Sourcebook: Past, Present and Future*. New York: Oxford University Press, 2004.

Robinson, Deborah Mitchell, ed. *Policing and Crime Prevention*. Upper Saddle River, NJ: Prentice Hall Publishing, 2002.

Rush, George E. *The Dictionary of Criminal Justice*, 4th ed. Guilford, CT: The Dushkin Publishing Group, Inc., 1994.

Saferstein, Richard. *Criminalistics: An Introduction to Forensic Science*, 8th ed. Upper Saddle River, NJ: Pearson Prentice Hall, 2005.

Sante, Luc. *Low Life: Lures and Snares of Old New York*. New York: Farrar, Straus & Giroux, 1991.

Savelli, Lou. *Pocket Guide to Identity Theft: Understanding and Investigation*. Flushing, NY: Looseleaf Law Publications, 2004.

———. *A Proactive Law Enforcement Guide for the War on Terror*. Flushing, NY: Looseleaf Law Publications, 2004.

Seltzer, Suzanne, Christa Stewart, Juhu Thukral, and Suzanne Tomatore. *Identification and Legal Advocacy for Trafficking Victims*. New York: NYC Anti-Trafficking Network, 2005.

Sennewald, Charles A. *Effective Security Management,* 4th ed. Boston: Butterworth-Heinemann/Elsevier, 2003.

———. *Shoplifters v. Retailers: The Rights of Both.* New York: New Century Press, 2000.

Shearing, Clifford D., and Philip C. Stenning, eds. *Private Policing.* Beverly Hills, CA: Sage Publications, 1987.

Sheehan, Robert, and Gary W. Cordner. *Introduction to Police Administration,* 2nd ed. Cincinnati, OH: Anderson Publishing Co., 1989.

Shelley, Louise I. *Organized Crime, Terrorism and Cybercrime.* Washington, DC: Transnational Crime and Corruption Center, American University, 2001.

Siegel, Larry J., and Joseph J. Senna. *Introduction to Criminal Justice,* 10th ed. Belmont, CA: ITP/Wadsworth, 2005.

Simonsen, Clifford E. *Private Security in America: An Introduction.* Upper Saddle River, NJ: Prentice Hall, 1998.

Simpson, D. P. *Cassell's Latin Dictionary.* New York: Macmillan, 1978.

Skogan, Wesley G. *Disorder and Decline: Crime and the Spiral of Decay in American Neighborhoods.* New York: Free Press, 1990.

Siringo, Charles A. *A Cowboy Detective: A True Story of Twenty-Two Years with a World-Famous Detective Agency.* Lincoln: University of Nebraska Press, 1988.

Smith, Bruce. *Police Systems in the United States.* New York: Harper & Row, 1960.

———. *Rural Crime Control.* New York: Columbia University Institute of Public Administration, 1933.

Smith, William. *Dictionary of Greek and Roman Antiquities.* Boston: Charles C. Little & Co., 1854.

Spence-Diehl, Emily. *Stalking: A Handbook for Victims.* Holmes Beach, FL: Learning Publications Inc., 1999.

Spriggs, Angela, Javier Argomaniz, Martin Gill, and Jane Bryan. *Public Attitudes towards CCTV: Results from the Pre-Intervention Public Attitude Survey Carried Out in Areas Implementing CCTV.* London: Great Britain Home Office Research Development and Statistics Directorate, 2005.

Steinman, Michael, ed. *Woman Battering: Policy Responses.* Cincinnati, OH: Anderson, 1991.

Stewart, James P. *Blind Eye: The Terrifying Story of a Doctor Who Got Away with Murder.* New York: Simon & Schuster, 1999.

Straus, Murray A., Richard J. Gelles, and Suzanne Steinmetz. *Behind Closed Doors: Violence in the American Family.* Garden City, NY: Anchor Press, 1980.

Sweet, Kathleen M. *Aviation and Airport Security: Terrorism and Safety Concerns.* Upper Saddle River, NJ: Pearson/Prentice Hall, 2004.

Taylor, Natalie. *Reporting of Crime against Small Retail Businesses.* Canberra ACT: Australian Institute of Criminology, 2002.

Thompson, L. *Dead Clients Don't Pay—The Bodyguard's Manual.* Geneva, IL: Paladin House Publishers, 1984.

Tobias, John J. *Crime and Police in England, 1700–1900.* New York: St. Martin's Press, 1979.

Uekert, Brenda K., and Denise O. Dancy. *Developing a Domestic Violence Policy for the Workplace.* Williamsburg, VA: National Center for State Courts, 2003.

Ursic, Henry S., and Leroy E. Pagano. *Security Management Systems.* Springfield, IL: Charles C. Thomas, 1974.

Walker, Samuel. *A Critical History of Police Reform: The Emergence of Professionalism.* Lexington, MA: Lexington Books, 1977.

———. *Popular Justice: History of American Criminal Justice.* New York: Oxford University Press, 1980.

———. *The Police in America: An Introduction,* 3rd ed. Boston: McGraw-Hill, 1999.

Webb, Walter Prescott. *The Texas Rangers: A Century of Frontier Defense.* Boston: Houghton Mifflin, 1935.

Weitekamp, Elmar G. M., and Hans Jurgen Kerner, eds. *Restorative Justice in Context: International Practice and Dimensions.* Portland, OR: Willan Publishing, 2003.

White, Jonathan, R. *Defending The Homeland: Domestic Intelligence, Law Enforcement, and Security.* Belmont, CA: Wadsworth, 2004.

———. *Terrorism and Homeland Security,* 5th ed. Belmont, CA: Wadsworth, 2006.

———. *Terrorism: An Introduction, 2002 Update,* 4th ed. Belmont, CA: Wadsworth, 2004.

Whitman, Michael E., and Herbert J. Mattord. *Principles of Information Security,* 2nd ed. Belmont, CA: Thomson Higher Learning, 2005.

Wilson, Jerry V. *Gainesville Convenience Store Ordinance: Findings of Fact, Conclusions and Recommendations.* Crime Control Research Corporation, 1990.

Woodward, John D. Jr. *Privacy vs. Security: Electronic Surveillance in the Nation's Capital.* Santa Monica, CA: RAND Corporation, 2002.

Zalman, Marvin, and Larry Siegel. *Criminal Procedure: Constitution and Society.* St. Paul: West, 1991.

Government Reports

Baum, Katrina. *Identity Theft, 2004.* Washington, DC: Bureau of Justice Statistics, 2006.

Bayley, David H., and Clifford D. Shearing. *The New Structure of Policing: Description, Conceptualization and Research Agenda.* Washington, DC: National Institute of Justice, 2001.

Blumer, Thomas. *Counterfeit (Copycat) Goods Under International Law and the Laws of Selected Foreign Nations.* Washington, DC: U.S. Library of Congress, 1996.

Brown, Ben. *CCTV in Town Centres: Three Case Studies: Crime Detection and Prevention Series Paper 68.* London: Home Office, 1995.

Bureau of Justice Assistance, U.S. Department of Justice, *Operation Cooperation.* Washington, DC: Author, 2000.

Chaiken, Marcia, and Jan Chaiken. *Public Policing–Privately Provided.* Washington, DC: National Institute of Justice, 1987.

Clifton, Wayland Jr. *Convenience Store Robberies in Gainesville, Florida: An Intervention Strategy by the Gainesville Police Department.* Gainesville, FL: Gainesville Police Department, 1987.

Community Policing Consortium. *National Business Leadership Strategies: A Guide to Engaging the Private Sector in Community Policing Initiatives.* Washington, DC: U.S. Department of Justice, Office of Community-Oriented Policing Services, 2002.

Congress of the United States, Congressional Budget Office. *Homeland Security and the Private Sector.* Washington, DC: Author, 2004.

Connors, Edward, William Cunningham, Peter Ohlhausen, Lynn Oliver, and Clifford Van Meter. *Operation Cooperation: Guidelines for Partnerships between Law Enforcement and Private Security Organizations.* Washington, DC: Bureau of Justice Assistance, U.S. Department of Justice, 2000.

Cunningham, William C., John J. Strauchs, and Clifford W. Van Meter. *Private Security Patterns and Trends.* Washington, DC: U.S. Government Printing Office, 1991.

Cunningham, William C., and Todd H. Taylor. *Crime and Protection in America: A Study of Private Security and Law Enforcement Resources and Relationships.* Washington, DC: U.S. Government Printing Office, 1985.

————. *The Growing Role of Private Security*. Washington, DC: U.S. Government Printing Office, 1988.

————. *The Growth of Private Security*. Washington, DC: U.S. Government Printing Office, 1984.

Federal Bureau of Investigation (FBI). *Parent's Guide to Internet Safety*. Washington, DC: Author, 1999.

————. *Uniform Crime Reports*. Washington, DC: Author, published yearly.

Finkelhor, David, Heather Hammer, and Andrea J. Sedlak. *Nonfamily Abducted Children: National Estimates and Characteristics*. Washington, DC: U.S. Department of Justice, Office of Juvenile Justice and Delinquency Prevention, 2002.

Garofalo, James, and Maureen McLeod. *Improving the Use and Effectiveness of Neighborhood Watch Programs*. Washington, DC: National Institute of Justice, 1988.

Gifford, Sidra Lea. *Justice Expenditures and Employment in the United States, 1999*. Washington, DC: Bureau of Justice Statistics, 2002.

Girdner, Linda R., and Patricia M. Hoff, eds. *Obstacles to the Recovery and Return of Parentally Abducted Children*. Washington, DC: U.S. Department of Justice, 1994.

Gropper, B. A. Jr., and J. A. Reardon Jr. *Developing Drug Testing by Hair Analysis*. Washington, DC: National Institute of Justice, 1993.

Hallcrest Systems Inc. *Combating Workplace Drug Crimes*. Washington, DC: National Institute of Justice, 1993.

Hecker, JayEtta. *Homeland Security: Intergovernmental Coordination and Partnership Will Be Critical to Success*. Washington, DC: U.S. General Accounting Office, 2002.

Hickman, Matthew J., and Brian A. Reaves. *Local Police Departments, 2003*. Washington, DC: Bureau of Justice Statistics, U.S. Department of Justice, 2006.

Hoff, Patricia M. *Family Abduction: Prevention and Response*. Arlington, VA: National Center for Missing and Exploited Children, 2002.

Hoffmann, J. P., C. Larison, and A. Sanderson. *Analysis of Worker Drug Use and Workplace Policies and Programs*. Washington, DC: National Institute of Justice, 1997.

Hughes, Kristen A. *Justice Expenditure and Employment in the United States, 2003*. Washington, DC: Bureau of Justice Statistics, U.S. Department of Justice, 2006.

Idaho State Police. *Elderly Victims of Crime, 2004*. Meridian, ID: Author, 2004.

Illinois Motor Vehicle Theft Prevention Council. *Motor Vehicle Theft Prevention Council, 2003 Annual Report*. Chicago, IL: Author, 2003.

Irish, Jenny. *Policing for Profit: The Future of South Africa's Private Security Industry*. New York: United Nations Development Program, 1999.

Jones, Radford W. *Critical Incident Protocol—A Public and Private Partnership, 2002*. Washington, DC: U.S. Department of Justice, Office for Domestic Preparedness, 2002.

Kakalik, James F., and Sorrel Wildhorn. *Private Police in the United States*. Washington, DC: National Institute of Justice, 1971.

Kaufman, Phillip et al. *Indicators of School Crime and Safety, 2001*. Washington, DC: U.S. Departments of Education and Justice, 2001.

Klaus, Patsy A. *Crime and the Nation's Households, 2002*. Washington, DC: Bureau of Justice Statistics, 2004.

Law Commission of Canada. *In Search of Security: The Roles of Public Police and Private Agencies*. Ottawa, Ontario: Law Commission of Canada, 2002.

Laycock, Gloria. *Property Marking: A Deterrent to Domestic Burglary? Crime Prevention Unit Paper No. 3*. London: Home Office, 1985.

Lewis, L., and E. Farris. *Campus Crime and Security at Postsecondary Education Institutions*. Washington, DC: U.S. Department of Education, 1997.

Mississippi Office of the Attorney General. *Workplace Violence Prevention Guide*. Jackson, MS: Author, 2004.

National Advisory Commission on Criminal Justice Standards and Goals. *Report of the Task Force on Private Security*. Washington, DC: U.S. Government Printing Office, 1976.

National Center for Victims of Crime. *Stalking*. Washington, DC: U.S. Department of Justice, Office of Community-Oriented Policing Services, 2004.

National Commission on Terrorist Attacks upon the United States. *The 9/11 Commission Report: Final Report of the National Commission on Terrorist Attacks upon the United States*. Washington, DC: U.S. Government Printing Office, 2004.

National Counterterrorism Center. *A Chronology of Significant International Terrorism for 2004*. Washington, DC: Author, 2005.

National Crime Prevention Council. *Are We Safe? The 1999 National Crime Prevention Survey*. Washington, DC: National Institute of Justice, 1999.

National Drug Intelligence Center. *National Drug Threat Assessment 2006*. Washington, DC: Author, 2006.

National Institute of Justice. *GPS Applications in Law Enforcement: The SkyTracker Surveillance System, Final Report*. Washington, DC: Author, 1998.

National Institute of Justice. *Internet Crimes against Children*. Washington, DC: Author, 2001.

National Institute of Justice, Office of Community-Oriented Policing Services. *The 2004 National Policy Summit: Building Private Security/Public Policing Partnerships to Prevent and Respond to Terrorism and Public Disorder*. Washington, DC: Author, 2004.

National Institute of Standards and Technology. *Surviving a Shooting: Your Guide to Personal Body Armor*. Rockville, MD: National Law Enforcement and Corrections Technology Center, 2004.

National White Collar Crime Center. *IC3 2004 Internet Fraud Crime Report, January 1, 2004–December 31, 2004*. Richmond, VA: Author, 2005.

Newman, Graeme R. *Exploitation of Trafficked Women*. Washington, DC: Office of Community-Oriented Policing Services, 2006.

Office of the President, Office of Homeland Security. *National Strategy for Homeland Security*. Washington, DC: Author, 2002.

Pastore, Ann L., and Kathleen Maguire, eds. *Sourcebook of Criminal Justice Statistics, 2001*. Washington, DC: U.S. Department of Justice, Bureau of Justice Statistics, 2002.

————. *Sourcebook of Criminal Justice Statistics, 2005*. Washington, DC: U.S. Department of Justice, Bureau of Justice Statistics, 2006.

Police Association of Higher Education Officers. *Student Survival Guide*. London: Author, 2004.

Ramker, Gerard F. *Improving Criminal History Records for Background Checks, 2005*. Washington, DC: Bureau of Justice Statistics, 2006.

Rantala, Ramona R. *Cybercrime against Businesses*. Washington, DC: U.S. Department of Justice, Office of Justice Programs, Bureau of Justice Statistics, 2004.

Ratcliffe, Jerry. *Video Surveillance of Public Places*. Washington, DC: Office of Community-Oriented Policing Services, 2006.

Reaves, Brian A., and Lynn M. Bauer. *Federal Law Enforcement Officers, 2002*. Washington, DC: Bureau of Justice Statistics, 2003.

Reaves, Brian A., and Matthew J. Hickman. *Census of State and Local Law Enforcement Agencies, 2000*. Washington, DC: Bureau of Justice Statistics, 2002.

———. *Local Police Departments, 2000*. Washington, DC: Bureau of Justice Statistics, 2003.

Reiss, Albert. *Private Employment of Public Police*. Washington, DC: National Institute of Justice, 1988.

Rennison, Callie Marie, and Michael R. Rand. *Criminal Victimization, 2002*. Washington, DC: Bureau of Justice Statistics, 2003.

Roda, C. *Executive Safety*. Washington, DC: National Criminal Justice Reference Service, 1997.

Rosenbaum, Dennis P., Arthur J. Lurigio, and Paul J. Lavrakas. *Crime Stoppers: A National Evaluation*. Washington, DC: National Institute of Justice, 1986.

Rugala, Eugene A., and Arnold R. Isaacs. *Workplace Violence: Issues in Response*. Rockville, MD: National Center for the Analysis of Violent Crime, 2003.

Sherman, Lawrence W. et al. *Preventing Crime: What Works, What Doesn't, What's Promising*. Washington, DC: U.S. Department of Justice, 1997.

Steidel, S. E., ed. *Missing and Abducted Children: A Law Enforcement Guide to Case Investigation and Program Management*. Arlington, VA: National Center for Missing and Exploited Children, 1994.

Task Force on Private Security. *Report of the Task Force on Private Security*. Washington, DC: U.S. Government Printing Office, 1976.

Tilly, Nicholas. *Understanding Car Parks, Crime and CCTV: Evaluation Lessons from Safer Cities: Crime Prevention Unit Paper 42*. London: Home Office, 1993.

Tjaden, P. *Stalking in America: Findings From the National Violence against Women Survey*. Washington, DC: National Institute of Justice, 1998.

Tjaden, P., and N. Thoennes. *Stalking in America: Findings from the National Violence against Women Survey*. Washington, DC: U.S. Department of Justice, National Institute of Justice, and Centers for Disease Control and Prevention, 1998.

Uekert, Brenda K., and Denise O. Dancy. *Developing a Domestic Violence Policy for the Workplace*. Williamsburg, VA: National Center for State Courts, 2003.

United Nations. *Trafficking in Women and Girls*. New York: United Nations, 2002.

U.S. Department of Health and Human Services, Substance Abuse and Mental Health Services Administration. *2004 National Survey on Drug Use and Health: National Findings*. Washington, DC: Author, 2005.

U.S. Department of Health and Human Services, Substance Abuse and Mental Health Services Administration. *Emergency Department Trends from the Drug Abuse Warning Network, Final Estimates 1999–2002*. Washington, DC: Author, 2003.

U.S. Department of Health and Human Services, Substance Abuse and Mental Health Services Administration. *Worker Drug Use and Workplace Policies and Programs: Results from 1994 and 1997. NHSDA Press Release*. Washington, DC: Author, n.d.

U.S. Department of Homeland Security. *Secure Seas, Open Ports: Keeping Our Waters Safe, Secure, and Open for Business*. Washington, DC: Author, 2004.

U.S. Department of Homeland Security, Office for Domestic Preparedness. *Guidelines for Homeland Security: Prevention and Deterrence*. Washington, DC: Author, 2003.

U.S. Department of Justice. *Assessing and Managing the Terrorism Threat*. Washington, DC: National Institute of Justice, 2005.

U.S. Department of Justice, Bureau of Justice Assistance. *Census of State and Local Law Enforcement Agencies*. Washington, DC: Author, published periodically.

———. *Crime and the Nation's Households*. Washington, DC: Author, published yearly.

———. *Criminal Victimization in the United States*. Washington, DC: Author, published yearly.

———. *Justice Expenditures and Employment in the United States*. Washington, DC: Author, published periodically.

———. *Law Enforcement Statistics*. Washington, DC: Author, published periodically.

U.S. Department of Justice, Bureau of Justice Statistics. *National Crime Victimization Survey*. Washington, DC: Author, 2006.

———. *Sourcebook of Criminal Justice Statistics*. Washington, DC: U. S. Government Printing Office, published yearly.

U.S. Department of Justice, Office for Victims of Crime. *Assessment of U.S. Government Activities to Combat Trafficking in Persons*. Rockville, MD: Author, 2004.

———. *Reporting School Violence*. Washington, DC: Author, 2002.

U.S. Department of Justice, Office of Community-Policing Services. *National Policy Summit: Building Private Security/Public Policing Partnerships to Prevent and Respond to Terrorism and Public Disorder*. Washington, DC: Author, 2004.

U.S. Department of Labor. *Employer's Guide to Dealing with Substance Abuse*. Washington, DC: Author, 1990.

U.S. Department of Labor, Bureau of Labor Statistics. *Occupational Outlook Handbook*. Washington, DC: Author, published yearly.

U.S. Department of State. *Be Smart, Be Safe . . . Don't Become a Victim of the Trade in People*. Washington, DC: Author, 2005.

———. *Trafficking in Persons Reports, June 2006*. Washington, DC: Author, 2006.

U.S. General Accounting Office. *Critical Infrastructure Protection: Challenges and Efforts to Secure Control Systems*. Washington, DC: Author, 2004.

Van Meter, Clifford. *Private Security: Report of the Task Force on Private Security*. Washington, DC: National Advisory Committee on Criminal Justice Stands and Goals, 1976.

Walker, David M. *Homeland Security: Responsibility and Accountability for Achieving National Goals*. Washington, DC: U.S. General Accounting Office, 2002.

Wartell, Julie, and Nancy G. La Vigne. *Prescription Fraud*. Washington, DC: National Institute of Justice, 2004.

Weisel, Deborah Lamm. *Burglary in Single-Family Houses*. Washington, DC: U.S. Department of Justice, Office of Community-Oriented Policing Services, 2002.

Whitehead, Paula, and Paul Gray. *Pulling the Plug on Computer Theft*. London: Great Britain Home Office, 1998.

Wortley, Richard, and Stephen Smallbone. *Child Pornography on the Internet*. Washington, DC: National Institute of Justice, 2006.

Yim, Randall A. *National Preparedness: Integration of Federal, State, Local, and Private Sector Efforts is Critical to an Effective National Strategy for Homeland Security*. Washington, DC: U.S. General Accounting Office, 2002.

Court Cases

Anheuser-Busch, Inc., 342 NLRB, No. 49 (2004).
Apodaca v. Oregon, 406 U.S. 404 (1972).
Argersinger v. Hamlin, 407 U.S. 25 (1972).
Board of Education v. Earls, 536 U.S. 822 (2002).
Brady v. Maryland, 373 U.S. 83 (1963).
Brown v. Wal-Mart (1998).
Browne v. SCR Medical Transportation Services, Illinois Court of Appeals for the Third Division, No. 96L12925 (2005).
Burdeau v. McDowell, 256 U.S. 465 (1921).
Burlington Industries, Inc. v. Ellerth, 524 U.S. 742 (1998).
Elliott v. Titan Security Service et al., Illinois Court of Appeals, No. 1-01-4226 (2004).
Faragher v. City of Boca Raton, 524 U.S. 775 (1998).
Feinstein v. Beers, Massachusetts Court of Appeals, No. 01-P-1635 (2004).
Fenje v. Feld, U.S. Court of Appeals for the Seventh Circuit, No. 04-1056 (2003).
Franciski v. University of Chicago Hospitals, U.S. Court of Appeals for the Seventh Circuit, No. 02-4358 (2004).
Freeman v. Busch, U.S. Court of Appeals for the Eighth Circuit, No. 02-2650 (2003).
Gamble v. Dollar General Store, Mississippi Supreme Court, No. 2000-CA-01545-SCT (2003).
Gideon v. Wainwright, 372 U.S. 335 (1963).
Gortanez v. Smitty's Super Valu (1984).
Groom v. Safeway, Inc., 973 F. Supp. 987 (W.D. Wash. 1997).
Johnson v. LaRabida Children's Hospital, U.S. Court of Appeals for the Seventh District, No. 03-2339 (2004).
Karraker v. Rent-A-Center, U.S. Court of Appeals for the Seventh Circuit, No. 04-2881 (2005).
Lund v. Clyde Police Department, Nos. 99-3815/3816; 2000 FED App. 0368P (6th Cir) (2000).
Mae Belle Lane v. St. Joseph's Regional Medical Center, Indiana Court of Appeals, No. 71A05-0310-CV-525 (2004).
Maheshwari v. City of New York, New York Court of Appeals, No. 54 (2004).
Mapp v. Ohio, 367 U.S. 643 (1961).
Meritor Savings Bank v. Vinson, 477 U.S. 57 (1986).
Miller v. Department of Corrections, Supreme Court of California, No. S114097 (2005).
Moran v. Murtaugh, Miller, Meyer, & Nelson, 126 Cal. App. 4th 323 (2005).
National Steel Corp. v. NLRB, U.S. Court of Appeals for the Seventh Circuit (2003).
Nina Benjamin v. Jerry Anderson and Joker's Wild Bar and Restaurant, Montana Supreme Court, No. 03-757 (2005).
Oncale v. Sundowner Offshore, 523 U.S. 75 (1998).
Read v. Scott Fetzer C., Texas Supreme Court (1998).
Renner-Wallace v. Cessna Co., U.S. District Court for the District of Kansas (2003).
Robert Relford v. Lexington-Fayette Urban County Government, U.S. Court of Appeals for the Sixth Circuit, No. 03-5600 (2004).
State of West Virginia v. William H. Muegge, 360 S.E. 216 (1987).
Taylor v. Taintor, 83 U.S. 366 (1872).
Thomas J. Tow v. Truck Country of Iowa, Inc., Supreme Court of Iowa, No. 04-0462 (2005).
Weeks v. United States, 232 U.S. 383 (1914).
Williams v. Florida, 399 U.S. 78 (1970).
Wilson v. O'Leary, 895 F.2d 378, (C.A. 7 [Ill.] 1990).
Van Zante and Jacobson v. Wal-Mart, Iowa Court of Appeals, No. 3–544 (2003).

Journals and Trade Publications

Access Control and Security Systems Integration
American Banker
American Criminal Law Review
American Journal of Criminal Justice
American Journal of Police
ASIS Dynamics
Bulletin of the New York Academy of Medicine
Business and Management Practices
Campus Safety Journal
Canadian Journal of Psychiatry
Chain Store Age
Child Maltreatment
Classical Journal
Computer Security Issues and Trends
Corrections Technology and Management
Crime and Delinquency
Crime and Justice Bulletin
Crime and Justice International
Crime Beat
Crime Prevention and Community Safety
Crime Prevention Studies
Crime Victims Report
Criminal Behavior and Mental Health
Criminal Justice Newsletter
Criminal Justice Policy Review
Criminology
Criminology and Public Policy
Duquesne Law Review
European Journal on Criminal Policy and Research
FBI Law Enforcement Bulletin
Fraud
Global Crime
Global Security Review
Governing
Government Computer News
Harvard Journal on Legislation
Health Central
History Today
Homeland Defense Journal
Homeland Protection Professional
HR Magazine
IASIR Regulator
InformationWeek
Insight
International Journal of Comparative and Applied Criminal Justice
International Journal of Risk, Security and Crime Studies
International Journal of Sociology of Law
Intersect: The Journal of International Security
Journal of the American Academy of Psychiatry and the Law
Journal of Contemporary Criminal Justice
Journal of Emotional Abuse
Journal of Financial Crime
Journal of Forensic Identification
Journal of Information Warfare
Journal of Quantitative Criminology
Journal of Security Administration
Justice Quarterly
Law and Order
Law Enforcement News
Law Enforcement Quarterly
Law Enforcement Technology
Law Enforcement Trainer

Minnesota Police Journal
National Real Estate Investor
NCIA Justice Bulletin
NIJ Journal
Pacific Business News
Perspectives
Police
Police Chief
Police Studies
Policing
Policy Review
Polygraph
Prosecutor
Retailer News
Risk Management
Security Journal
Security Magazine
Security Management
Security Technology and Design
Sheriff
Social Problems
The Annals
The Economist
Trends in Organized Crime
University of Chicago Law Review
Urban Life
Violence Against Women
Western Criminology Review
Wired News

Newspapers

Akron Beacon Journal
Bakersfield Californian
BBC News
Beacon
Boston Globe
Boston Herald
Connecticut Post
Crain's Detroit Business
Daily Oklahoman
Daily Yomiuri
Dallas Morning News
Decatur Daily News
Everett Journal
Fashion Monitor Toronto
Financial Times
Gloucester Citizen
Hartford Courant
Houston Chronicle
Investor's Business Daily
Knoxville News-Sentinel
LA Daily News
Leeds Today
Los Angeles Times

New York Post
New York Times
Newsday
Pensacola News Journal
Philadelphia Daily News
Philadelphia Inquirer
Pioneer Press
Richmond Times Dispatch
San Bernardino County Sun
San Francisco Gate
Script Howard News Service
Seattle Post-Intelligencer
Siyaya
St. Petersburg Times
Suffolk Life
Tampa Bay Business Journal
Tampa Tribune
Telegraph Herald
The Arizona Republic
The Cleveland Plain Dealer
The Daily Telegram
Toronto Sun
Tulsa World
USA Today
Virginia Pilot
Washington Post

Magazines

Asia Pulse
Atlantic Monthly
Business Week
Computerworld
Forbes Inc.
Gazette
Gentlemen's Quarterly
Inc.
MacLean's
National Geographic
New Orleans Magazine
Newsweek
Network World
New York Magazine
New York Times Magazine
Parade
People
People Weekly
Popular Science
Playboy
SC Magazine
Time
Town and Country Monthly
USA Today Magazine
U.S. News and World Report
Vanity Fair

Index

TO THE OWNER OF THIS BOOK:

I hope that you have found *Introduction to Private Security* useful. So that this book can be improved in a future edition, would you take the time to complete this sheet and return it? Thank you.

School and address:_____

Department:_____

Instructor's name:_____

1. What I like most about this book is:_____

    _____

    _____

2. What I like least about this book is:

    _____

    _____

3. My general reaction to this book is:

    _____

    _____

4. The name of the course in which I used this book is:

    _____

5. Were all of the chapters of the book assigned for you to read?_____

    If not, which ones weren't?_____

6. In the space below, or on a separate sheet of paper, please write specific suggestions for improving this book and anything else you'd care to share about your experience in using this book.

    _____

    _____

    _____

    _____

BUSINESS REPLY MAIL
FIRST-CLASS MAIL   PERMIT NO. 34   BELMONT CA

POSTAGE WILL BE PAID BY ADDRESSEE

Attn: Carolyn Henderson Meier, Criminal
Justice Editor

Thomson Wadsworth
10 Davis Dr
Belmont CA 94002-9801

OPTIONAL:

Your name:_____ Date: _____

May we quote you, either in promotion for *Introduction to Private Security,* or in future
publishing ventures?

Yes:_____ No: _____

Sincerely yours,

John S. Dempsey